CRAFTING A COMPILER WITH C

Charles N. Fischer

Computer Sciences Department
University of Wisconsin — Madison

Richard J. LeBlanc, Jr.

Information/Computer Science
Georgia Institute of Technology

C Code by
Arnold D. Robbins

The Benjamin/Cummings Publishing Company, Inc.
Redwood City, California • Menlo Park, California
Reading, Massachusetts • New York • Don Mills, Ontario • Wokingham
Amsterdam • Bonn • Sydney • Singapore • Tokyo • Madrid • San Juan

In memory of Fillmore N. Fischer

To Lanie, Christina, and Maria LeBlanc

Sponsoring Editor: Alan R. Apt
Production Assistant: Alyssa Weiner
Cover Designer: Victoria Ann Philp
Copy Editor: Christine Sabooni

Library of Congress Cataloging-in-Publication Data

Fischer, Charles N.
    Crafting a compiler with C / Charles N. Fischer, Richard J.
LeBlanc, Jr.
      p. cm.
    Includes index.
    ISBN 0-8053-2166-7
    1. C (Computer program language) 2. Compilers (Computer programs)
I. LeBlanc, Richard J. (Richard Joseph), 1950- . II. Title.
QA76.73.C15F57   1991
005.4'53--dc20   90-23614
                                    CIP

  2 3 4 5 6 7 8 9 10 MA 9594939291

The Benjamin/Cummings Publishing Company, Inc.
390 Bridge Parkway
Redwood City, CA 94065

PREFACE

This book presents a practical approach to the subject of compiler construction, based on the experience of the authors as compiler implementors and as developers of compiler construction courses. It is intended to provide the reader not only with a good understanding of all of the components of a compiler, but also with a real sense of how they actually fit together to make a working, usable compiler. We believe that this philosophy is a distinguishing feature of the book. Since we are concerned with presenting the most modern compiler construction techniques, we emphasize the use of compiler tools to generate the components, wherever practical. (Source code for the tools described in Appendices B through F is available from the publisher, as described in the Instructor's Guide.)

Crafting a Compiler with C is essentially the same book as *Crafting a Compiler*, with the algorithms and pseudo-code examples written in C syntax rather than Ada syntax. Since the C language is in widespread use in compiler courses, a number of instructors have suggested that such an edition would be valuable. In an attempt to keep all of the pseudo-code as readable as possible even for those readers who are not C experts, we use a few extensions to the standard C syntax (described below) and we do not always make use of common C idioms. Since neither of the authors is accomplished C programmer, we are indebted to Arnold Robbins for doing the translation work and for making numerous other editorial suggestions.

TEXT AND REFERENCE

As a classroom text this book is oriented towards a course organization that we have developed over the last 15 years. The book is very flexible and has been used in courses ranging from a three-credit senior-level course taught in a ten-week quarter, to a six-credit semester-long graduate course. The book is also a valuable professional reference because of its complete coverage of techniques that are of practical importance to compiler writers and designers.

PROJECT APPROACH

The book includes comprehensive coverage of relevant theoretical topics. However, a cohesive implementation project is an important part of our course organization, thus the book has a strong project orientation. Appendix

A contains the definition of a language we call Ada/CS, which is principally a substantial subset of the Ada programming language. For pedagogical reasons, it is not a strict subset. Recommended projects for a course using this book involve implementation of some or all of Ada/CS, depending on the length and level of the course, and on how (un)reasonable the instructor is!

A selection of possible projects is presented in the Instructor's Guide. A recursive descent compiler for a very simple subset of Ada/CS is presented and discussed in Chapter 2. Code for a complete working compiler for this subset is available, on magnetic tape, to instructors, with the tools mentioned above. Making the project an extension of this working compiler enables students to complete a significant project, even in a course as short as one quarter. This extension approach is also valuable when limited time is not a factor. Requiring students to read and extend a substantial program provides them with important experience that is not commonly available in many computer science curricula. It also teaches them a great deal about how the pieces of a compiler fit together—something that is hard to teach in any other way.

The C Programming Language

The examples pseudo-code in this book are written in a syntax based on ANSI C. C is a popular language in many computing environments, from PC to mainframe to super-computer, since it is small yet expressive, efficient, and typically quite portable. C has recently become an American National Standard (ANSI 1989). Compilers supporting the standard dialect of C are already widely available, and will only become more popular. As such, we have chosen to use the ANSI dialect for our examples, over the more widely known dialect described in Kernighan and Ritchie (1978). An excellent reference on ANSI C is the new book by Kernighan and Ritchie (1988).

To allow us to focus on describing algorithms in the most readable way possible (rather than on syntactic details), we have extended C in several ways. First, several places in the text use *anonymous unions*, a feature borrowed from C++ (Stroustrup 1986). An anonymous union looks like this:

```
struct somestruct {
    int elem1;
    union {
        float   f2;
        int     i2;
        double  d2;
        long        l2;
    };
    long    elem3;
} s;
    . . .
s.elem1 = 10;
s.f2 = 10.0
    . . .
```

Note that the **union** member of the structure has no name, and the elements of the union are referred to directly as elements of the structure. In conventional C, the same behavior is usually achieved using the macro preprocessor:

```
struct somestruct {
    int elem1;
    union {
        float   u_f2;
        int     u_i2;
        double u_d2;
        long        u_l2;
    } u;
    long    elem3;
} s;
#define f2 u.u_f2
#define i2 u.u_i2
#define d2 u.u_d2
#define l2 u.u_l2
    .  .  .
s.elem1 = 10;
s.f2 = 10.0
    .  .  .
```

Secondly, starting in Chapter 10, we use *anonymous structures* as members of anonymous unions. In practice, such structures would be implemented using the pre-processor scheme outlined above.

Finally, in a number of the higher-level pseudo-code examples, we will use the following *constructor* mechanism for making a structure expression:

```
struct something {
    int elem1;
    char *elem2;
} v;
    .  .  .
v = (something) {
        .elem1 = 1;
        .elem2 = "string";
    };
```

Although this construct can not be replaced with a macro, its meaning should be obvious.

In general, where we use pseudo-code that is higher-level than regular C, we have attempted to label such figures as "algorithms," as opposed to "programs."

As with *Crafting a Compiler*, it is not necessary that any particular language be used to implement the project in a course based on this book. The pseudocode serves perfectly well as a design description, regardless of the chosen implementation language. In addition, the scanner and parser generation tools we provide produce tables, not programs, so they can be used in any language environment. We do discuss use of Lex and Yacc for those who are implementing a project in C.

THE ROLE OF ADA

We base our recommended project and our discussions of language features on the Ada language because it includes virtually all of the features we wished to discuss in our chapters on semantic analysis. Had we chosen any other language as our basis (Modula-2, for example), we would have had to describe a number of extensions in order to discuss techniques for compiling such things as **exit** statements, exception handling, and operator overloading.

It is certainly not necessary that a student be familiar with Ada to use this book. The presentation of Ada/CS in Appendix A can serve as a tutorial on the features of Ada we discuss in the chapters on semantic analysis. Where appropriate, we also consider the translation features drawn from other languages, including, Modula-2, Pascal, C, ALGOL-60, ALGOL-68, and Simula.

CHAPTER DESCRIPTIONS

For an introductory course, Chapters 1 through 4, 5 or 6, 7, and selected sections from Chapters 8 through 13 and 15 could be used. See the Instructor's Guide for specific chapter section suggestions.

An advanced course could include material from the parsing chapters (5 and 6) and advanced topic sections from Chapters 8 through 13 and 15, plus Chapters 14, 16, and 17.

Chapter 1   Introduction

An overview of the compilation process begins the text. The concept of constructing a compiler from a collection of components is emphasized. The idea of using tools to generate some of these components is introduced.

Chapter 2   A Simple Compiler

A very simple language, Micro, is presented, and each of the components of a compiler is discussed with respect to compiling Micro. Parts of the text of a compiler for Micro (written in Ada) are included in this chapter. The compilation of features of more comprehensive Ada subsets is the motivation for the techniques presented in the following chapters.

Chapter 3   Scanning—Theory and Practice

The basic concepts and techniques for building the lexical analysis component of a compiler are presented. This discussion includes both the development of hand-coded scanners and the use of scanner generation tools for implementation of table-driven scanners.

Chapter 4   Grammars and Parsing

Fundamentals of formal language concepts and grammars are presented in this chapter, including context-free grammars, BNF notation, derivations, and parse trees. Since First and Follow sets are used in the definitions of both top-down and bottom-up parsing techniques, they are defined in this chapter. A discussion of language and grammar relationships is also included.

Chapter 5   LL(1) Grammars and Parsing

Top-down parsing is presented as the initial approach to syntax analysis. Both recursive descent and LL(1) are discussed, with an emphasis on the latter. Use of parser generators is a major focus of this chapter.

Chapter 6   LR Parsing

Bottom-up parsing is presented as an alternative approach to syntax analysis. LR, SLR and LALR parsing concepts are introduced and compared with LL techniques. Again, use of parser generators is a major focus of the chapter.

Chapter 7   Semantic Processing

The fundamentals of semantic processing in conjunction with top-down and bottom-up parsers are presented in this chapter. Topics include a comparison of alternative compiler organizations, addition of action symbols to a grammar (for top-down parsing), rewriting grammars for "semantic hooks" (for bottom-up parsing), definition of semantic records and use of a semantic stack, checking semantic correctness, and producing intermediate code.

Chapter 8   Symbol Tables

This chapter stresses the use of a symbol table as an abstract component, utilized by the rest of the compiler through a precisely defined interface. Possible implementations are presented, followed by discussions of symbol tables for handling nested scopes and language features used to define names accessible from surrounding scopes (such as records and Ada packages).

Chapter 9   Run-time Storage Organization

Basic techniques for run-time storage management is presented, including discussions of static allocation, stack-based allocation and generalized dynamic (heap) allocation.

Chapter 10   Processing Declarations

Basic techniques for processing type, variable, and constant declarations are discussed. The organization of this material is based on semantic routines for handling specific language features.

Chapter 11   Processing Expressions and Data Structure References

Semantic routines for handling variable references and arithmetic and Boolean expressions are outlined. Address computation methods for array elements and record fields are included in the discussion of variables references. In this and the next two chapters, emphasis is placed on techniques for checking semantic correctness and generating intermediate code for use by a target code generator.

Chapter 12   Translating Control Structures

Compilation techniques for features such as **if** statements, **case** statements, and various looping constructs are the focus of this chapter. A point of emphasis is effective use of a semantic stack or syntax tree to simplify the job of handling these constructs, which can be nested and which can extend over arbitrary amounts of program text. Students should gain an understanding of the advantage of this general technique over ad hoc approaches.

Chapter 13   Translating Procedures and Functions

Techniques for processing both declarations and calls of subprograms are presented. Since much of the complexity of this topic involves parameters, considerable material is provided that deals with building parameter descriptions, checking for correctness of actual parameters in subprogram calls, and code-generation techniques required by various parameter modes. The concept of a run-time activation stack is discussed here, and the support routines necessary to implement one are outlined.

Chapter 14   Attribute Grammars and Multipass Translation

Multipass translation is modeled by traversal over an intermediate form. The attribute model of information flow receives particular emphasis.

Chapter 15   Code Generation and Local Code Optimization

The code generator is presented as a separate component that translates from the intermediate code generated by the semantic routines to the final target code of the compiler. Such topics as instruction selection, register management, and use of addressing modes are presented. Use of a code generator-generator is discussed. Discussion of basic block optimizations is included in this chapter.

Chapter 16   Global Optimization

The focus of this chapter is on practical techniques that yield useful improvements from a moderate amount of effort. Thus the main sections of the chapter include global data flow analysis, optimizing subprogram calls, and optimizing loops.

Chapter 17   Parsing in the Real World

This chapter includes material on two major topics necessary for implementing practical compilers: syntax-error handling and table compaction. The error-handling section presents error-recovery and error-repair techniques applicable to recursive descent, LL and LR parsers. The table compaction techniques included are applicable to both LL and LR parser tables, as well as to scanner tables and any other situation requiring efficient storage with fast access to elements of sparse tables.

Acknowledgements

A great many people have contributed to the development of *Crafting a Compiler* and *Crafting a Compiler with C*. First, there are the many students in CS 701/2 at the University of Wisconsin–Madison and ICS 4410 at the Georgia Institute of Technology who have used preliminary versions of the book and, previously, notes that eventually became some sections of the book. Additionally, a number of other instructors on the faculties of our two schools have used our notes in teaching. These people include Raphael Finkel, Marvin Solomon, and K. N. King, who contributed some material to our notes, and also Nancy Lynch, Martin McKendry, Nancy Griffeth, and David Pitts. Arnold Robbins at Georgia Tech provided all the C code that appears in this text. He also contributed some of the chapter exercises, the idea for the cover design, and numerous useful comments on our writing style. G A Venkatesh, Will Winsborough, and Felix Wu provided sample solutions for most of the exercises. Jon Mauney, Gary Sevitsky, Robert Gray, and Felix Wu developed the compiler tools described in the appendices. Kathy Schultz did a fine job in entering final corrections to the manuscript and Sheryl Pomraning, with the help of a friendly gremlin, did an excellent job with the artwork.

We are grateful to C. Wrandel Barth, Jean Gallier, James Harp, Harry Lewis, Eric Roberts, and Henry Shapiro who provided valuable feedback on our initial proposal and sample chapters. We greatly appreciated the valuable suggestions by Steve Allan, Henry Bauer, Roger Eggen, Norman Hutchinson, Sathis Menon, Jim Bitner, Charles Shipley, Donald K. Friesen, Donald Cooley, Susan Graham, Steve Zeigler, and, especially, Paul Hilfinger and Alan Wendt—the reviewers who provided most of the comments that kept us busy for so long producing both this and the earlier version of our book.

Special thanks should also go to Alan Apt, our outstanding editor, for his patience and encouragement and all of the staff at Benjamin/Cummings who have so enthusiastically supported our work; to Todd Proebsting and Chris Sabooni for their careful proofing of the manuscript; to Alyssa Weiner and the rest of the production team for their fine job; and to Jane Rundell and the staff at Impressions.

And finally, thanks to Miriam Robbins for her great patience while Arnold labored to turn innumerable Ada algorithms into clear and concise C.

BRIEF CONTENTS

CONTENTS

Chapter 1 Introduction 1

Chapter 2 A Simple Compiler 23

Chapter 6   LR Parsing   140

Chapter 7   Semantic Processing   216

Chapter 8   Symbol Tables   254

Chapter 9   Run-Time Storage Organization   287

Chapter 10   Processing Declarations   319

Chapter 13 Translating Procedures and Functions 484

Chapter 14 Attribute Grammars and Multipass Translation 510

Chapter 15   Code Generation and Local Code Optimization   546

Chapter 16   Global Optimization   614

Chapter 17   Parsing in the Real World   685

CHAPTER **1**

Introduction

1.1. Overview and History

Compilers are fundamental to modern computing. They act as *translators*, transforming human-oriented *programming languages* into computer-oriented *machine languages*. To most users, a compiler can be viewed as a "black box" that performs the transformation illustrated in Figure 1.1.

A compiler allows virtually all computer users to ignore the machine-dependent details of machine language. Compilers therefore allow programs and programming expertise to be *machine-independent*. This is a particularly valuable asset in an age in which the number and variety of computers continues to grow explosively.

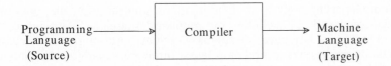

Figure 1.1   A User's View of a Compiler

The term *compiler* was coined in the early 1950s by Grace Murray Hopper. Translation was then viewed as the "compilation" of a sequence of subprograms selected from a library. Indeed, compilation (as we now know it) was then called "automatic programming," and there was almost universal skepticism that it would ever be successful. Today, the automatic translation of programming languages is an accomplished fact, but programming language translators are still termed compilers.

Among the first real compilers in the modern sense were the FORTRAN compilers of the late 1950s. They presented the user with a problem-oriented, largely machine-independent source language and performed some rather ambitious "optimizations" to produce efficient machine code, which was deemed essential to compete successfully against then-dominant assembly languages. These FORTRAN systems proved the viability of *high-level* (that is, less machine-dependent) compiled languages and paved the way for the flood of languages and compilers that was to follow.

The first FORTRAN compiler took 18 person-years to build. Early compilers were ad hoc structures; components and techniques were often devised as a compiler was being built. Building a compiler was a complex and costly undertaking. Today compilation techniques are well understood, and a simple compiler can be built in a few months. Nonetheless, crafting an efficient and reliable compiler is still a challenging task. Our approach will be to master the fundamentals of compilation and then to explore advanced topics and a number of important recent innovations.

We normally think of compilers as translating programming languages into machine-language instructions. Compiler technology, however, is more broadly applicable and has been employed in rather unexpected areas. For example, text-formatting languages have become increasingly sophisticated. Formatters, like *nroff* and *troff* of UNIX®, are really compilers, translating text and formatting commands into very intricate typesetter commands. Like all successful languages, *nroff* and *troff* have been generalized to provide new capabilities. For example, preprocessor packages like *eqn* (to handle equations), *tbl* (to format tables), and *pic* (to draw pictures) are analogous to the preprocessors often used to extend existing programming languages (for example, the Ratfor FORTRAN preprocessor). One of the continuing challenges of language and compiler design is to devise mechanisms that allow existing languages to be *extended* in simple and natural ways.

The creation of VLSI circuits is another task that can be modeled as a translation from a high-level source language to a low-level target language. In this case a so-called *silicon compiler* specifies the layout and composition of a VLSI circuit mask. Just as an ordinary compiler must understand and enforce the rules of a particular machine language, a silicon compiler must understand and enforce the design rules that dictate the feasibility of a given circuit.

Compiler technology is of value in almost any program that presents a nontrivial command set, including the command languages of operating systems and the query languages of database systems. Although our discussion will focus on traditional compilation tasks, innovative readers will undoubtedly find new and unexpected applications for the techniques presented.

1.2. **What Do Compilers Do?**

Figure 1.1 shows a compiler as a translator from the programming language being compiled to some machine language. This description suggests that all compilers do pretty much the same thing, the only difference being in their choice of source and target languages. However, the situation is a bit more complicated than that. The question of the source language accepted is indeed a simple one, but there are many alternatives in describing the output of a compiler that go beyond simply naming a particular computer for which its output is intended.

Compilers may be distinguished according to the kind of target code they generate.

Pure Machine Code – First, compilers may generate code for a particular machine's instruction set, not assuming the existence of any operating system or library routines. Such machine code is often referred to as *pure* code because it includes nothing but instructions that are part of that instruction set. This approach is rare; it is most commonly used in compilers for system implementation languages, which are intended for implementing operating systems and other such low-level software. This form of target code can be executed on bare hardware without dependence on any other software.

Augmented Machine Code – Second, and far more often, compilers generate machine code for a machine architecture *augmented* with operating system routines and language support routines. To execute a program generated by such a compiler, a particular operating system must be present on the target machine and a collection of language-specific support routines (I/O, storage allocation, mathematical functions, and so on) must be loaded with the program. The combination of the target machine's instruction set and these operating system and language support routines can be thought of as defining a *virtual machine*—that is, another machine that exists only as a hardware/software combination.

The degree to which the virtual machine matches the actual hardware can vary greatly. Some common compilers translate almost entirely to hardware instructions (for example, most FORTRAN compilers use software support only for I/O and mathematical functions). Other compilers assume a wide range of virtual instructions. These may include data transfer instructions (for example, to move bit fields), procedure call instructions (to pass parameters, save registers, allocate stack space, and so on) and dynamic storage allocation instructions.

Virtual Machine Code – Finally, the extreme case of virtual machine definition represents the last target machine alternative. The generated code is composed *entirely* of virtual instructions. This approach is particularly attractive as a technique for producing a *transportable* compiler, one that can be run easily on a variety of computers. Transportability can be enhanced, since moving the compiler (if it *bootstraps*—compiles itself—or is written in an available language) entails only writing a simulator for the virtual machine used by the compiler. If this virtual machine is kept simple and clean, the interpreter can be quite easy to write. An outstanding example of this approach is the Pascal P-Compiler, originally written by a group headed by Nicklaus Wirth. This compiler generates code, called *P-code*, for a virtual stack machine. A decent simulator for the P-machine can be written by one programmer in a few weeks. Execution speed is roughly four times slower than compiled code. Alternatively, with more work, a final compilation phase can translate the P-code to equivalent machine code, or the compiler can be modified to generate machine code directly. This approach has made Pascal easily available for almost any machine; thus, this compiler has been an important factor in the development of Pascal's great popularity.

As can be seen from the preceding discussion, virtual instructions serve a variety of purposes. They simplify the job of a compiler by making available primitives suitable for the particular language being translated (such as procedure calls, string manipulation, and so on); they contribute to compiler transportability; and they may allow a significant *decrease* in the size of generated code to be realized. That is, instructions can be designed to closely meet the needs of a particular programming language (for example, P-code for Pascal). Using this approach, a reduction in generated program size of as much as two-thirds has been reported (Tanenbaum 1974).

When an entirely virtual instruction set is used for the target machine language, it is necessary to interpret (simulate) the instruction set in software. A 3:1 to 10:1 speed degradation versus execution of target instructions by hardware is possible with a well-implemented emulator. Compilers that generate code requiring such execution (such as the Berkeley Pascal *pi* processor) are sometimes termed *interpreters*, though we prefer to use that term for language processors that don't distinctly separate translation and execution. Interpreters will be discussed later in this section.

The instruction set of some computers can changed via *microprogramming*. Microprogramming is an ideal mechanism for interpreting a virtual instruction set because of the high execution rate it makes possible. Of course, once microprogramming is used, the virtual instruction set becomes the instruction set of a real machine and thus is no longer virtual!

To summarize, almost all compilers, to a greater or lesser extent, generate code for a virtual machine, some of whose operations must be interpreted in software or firmware. We consider them compilers because they make use of a distinct translation phase that precedes execution.

Another way that compilers differ from one another is in the format of the target machine code they generate. Target machine formats may be categorized as assembly language, relocatable binary, or memory-image.

Assembly Language (Symbolic) Format – The major reason that a compiler writer might choose to generate assembler code is to simplify (and modularize) translation. That is, a number of code generation decisions (jump targets, long versus short address forms, and so on) can be left for the assembler. This approach is common among UNIX compilers. In small computers, for which UNIX was originally designed, this modularity may be mandatory, because a full compiler often cannot fit in available memory. Generating assembler code is also useful for cross-compilation (running a compiler on one computer, with its target language being the machine language of a second computer); a symbolic form is produced that is easily transferred between different computers. This approach also makes it easier to check the correctness of a compiler because we can observe its output.

In spite of these advantages, generation of symbolic code is not common in modern compilers and is not generally recommended. Its chief disadvantage is that the output code must be processed by an assembler after the compiler. Assemblers are typically slow, and having to use one adds another step to the process a programmer must go through to prepare a program for execution. It should be noted that UNIX assemblers are specially designed to process compiler output; therefore they lack many of the features common to most assemblers, and are consequently somewhat faster. Also, the UNIX compiler drivers automatically call the assembler, so its use is transparent to the programmer. However, if a compiler does not generate assembly language, the compiler writer still needs a way to check the correctness of the generated code. In this case, one good approach is to design the compiler so that it optionally produces *pseudo–assembly language,* a listing of what the assembly language would look like if it were produced.

Relocatable Binary Format – As a second alternative, target code may be generated in a binary format in which external references and local instruction and data addresses are not yet bound. Instead, addresses are assigned relative to the beginning of the module or relative to symbolically named locations. (This latter alternative makes it easy to group together code sequences or data areas.) This format is the typical output of an assembler, so this approach simply eliminates one step in the process of preparing a program for execution. A linkage step is required to add any support libraries and other precompiled routines referenced from within a compiled program and to produce an absolute binary program format that is executable.

Both relocatable binary and assembly language formats allow modular compilation (breaking a large program into separately compiled pieces), cross-language references (calls of assembler routines or subprograms in other high-level languages), and support routine libraries (for example, I/O, storage allocation, and math routines).

Memory-Image (Load-and-Go) Format – Alternatively, the compiled output may be loaded into the compiler's address space and immediately executed (instead of being left in a file, as with the first two approaches). This process is usually much faster than going through the fairly slow, and expensive, intermediate step of link/editing. It also allows a program to be prepared and executed in a single step. However, the ability to interface with external, library, and precompiled routines is quite limited, and the program must be recompiled for each execution unless some means is provided for storing the memory-image. Load-and-go compilers are useful for student and debugging use, when frequent changes are the rule and compilation costs far exceed execution costs. It is also useful when we wish *not* to create and save absolutes (for example, to save file space or to guarantee the use of only the most current library and systems routines). An interesting application of load-and-go compilers is the ASAP information retrieval system (Conway 1972). In this system, data is kept in an encrypted format so that it may be accessed only by queries that have been translated by a compiler that inserts a decryption routine into the code. The compiler statically checks the user's access rights, refusing to compile queries that access forbidden data. If the compiled program could be saved, it would be impossible to change or revoke access rights.

These code format alternatives and the target machine alternatives discussed above show that compilers can differ quite substantially from one another while still performing the same sort of translation job. Another kind of language processor, called an *interpreter*, differs from a compiler in that it executes programs without explicitly performing a translation. Figure 1.2 illustrates schematically how interpreters work.

In contrast to compilers, consider the following characteristics of interpreters. To an interpreter, a program is merely data that can be arbitrarily manipulated, just like any other data. The locus of control during execution resides in the interpreter and *not* in the user program (that is, the user program is passive rather than active).

Interpreters allow the following:

- Modification of or addition to user programs as execution proceeds. This facility provides a straightforward interactive debugging capability. Such modification is easiest in non-block-structured languages such as APL or BASIC, because individual statements can be changed without reparsing an entire program.

- Languages in which the type of object that a variable denotes may change dynamically. The user program is continuously reexamined

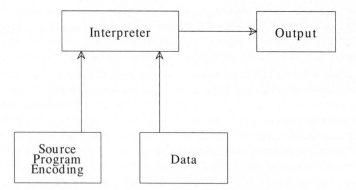

Figure 1.2   An Idealized Interpreter

as execution proceeds, and symbols need not have a fixed meaning (that is, a symbol may denote an integer scalar at one point and a boolean array at a later point). Such *fluid bindings* are obviously much more troublesome for compilers, as dynamic changes in the meaning of a symbol make direct translation into machine code impossible.

- Better diagnostics. Because source text analysis (normally done at compile-time) is intermixed with execution of the program, especially good diagnostics (recreation of source lines in error, use of variable names in error messages, and so on) are produced more easily than they are by compilers.

- A significant degree of machine independence, since no machine code is generated. All operations are performed within the interpreter. Therefore, to move an interpreter, we need only recompile it on a new machine.

However, interpretation can involve large overheads:

- As execution proceeds, program text must be continuously reexamined, with identifier bindings, types, and operations potentially being reconsidered at each reference. For very dynamic languages this can represent a 100:1 (or worse) factor in execution speed. For more static languages (such as BASIC), the speed degradation is closer to 10:1.

- Substantial space overhead may be involved. The interpreter and all support routines must usually be kept available. This program representation is often not as compact as compiled machine code (for example, symbol tables are present, and program text may be stored in a format designed for easy access and modification rather than for space minimization). This size penalty may lead to restrictions in the size of programs, the number of variables or procedures, and so on. Programs beyond these built-in limits cannot be handled by the interpreter.

Finally, some languages (for example, BASIC, LISP, and Pascal) have both interpreters (for debugging and program development) and compilers (for production work). In fact, there is not always a clear-cut dividing line between compilers and interpreters. For example, many BASIC interpreters "translate" the source program into an internal form in which keywords such as **let** and **goto** are represented as one-byte *operation codes*, and identifiers are similarly replaced by internal table references. It is a matter of taste whether or not to call the program that does this compression a compiler and the resulting compressed form a target program. We choose not to because the "translation" done in such cases is completely syntactic. Further, the internal form into which such interpreters transform source programs is in no way visible to programmers using the interpreter, a distinct difference from the visibility of the output of typical compilers.

In summary, all language processing involves interpretation at some level. The processors we have called interpreters directly interpret the source programs they process or syntactically transformed versions of them. They may exploit the availability of a source representation to allow program text to be changed as it is executed and debugged. A compiler has distinct translation and execution phases, but "interpretation" is still involved. The translation phase may generate a virtual machine language that is interpreted by software or a real machine language that is interpreted by a particular computer, either in firmware or hardware.

1.3. The Structure of a Compiler

Any compiler must perform two major tasks: *analysis* of the source program being compiled and *synthesis* of a machine-language program that when executed will correctly perform the activities described by that source program. Almost all modern compilers are *syntax-directed*. That is, the compilation process is driven by the syntactic structure of the source program, as recognized by the *parser*. The parser builds this structure out of *tokens*, the lowest-level symbols used to define a programming language syntax. This recognition of syntactic structure is a major part of the analysis task. The *semantic routines* actually supply the meaning (semantics) of the program, based on the syntactic structure. These routines play a dual role in that they finish the analysis task by performing certain correctness checks (for example, type and scope rules) in addition to beginning or doing all of the synthesis work. The semantic routines may either generate some *intermediate representation* (IR) of the program or directly generate target code. If an IR is generated, it then serves as input to a *code generator* component that actually produces the desired machine-language program. The IR may optionally be transformed by an *optimizer* so that a more efficient machine-language program may be generated. The organization of all these components in a compiler is depicted schematically in Figure 1.3.

The tasks of each component are described in more detail in the rest of this section. A simple compiler is presented in Chapter 2 to provide concrete examples of many of the concepts introduced in this overview.

Scanner – The *scanner* begins the analysis of the source program by reading the input, character by character, and grouping characters into individual words and symbols. These words and symbols are termed *tokens* and represent basic program entities such as identifiers, integers, reserved words, delimiters, and so on. This is the first of several steps that produce successively higher-level interpretations of the input. The tokens are encoded (for example, as integers) and then are fed to the parser for syntactic analysis. Sometimes the actual character string comprising the token (or a pointer into a *string space* that stores the text of all identifiers) is also passed along for subsequent use by the semantic routines.

The scanner does the following:

- Puts the program into a compact and uniform format (tokens).
- Eliminates unneeded information (such as comments).

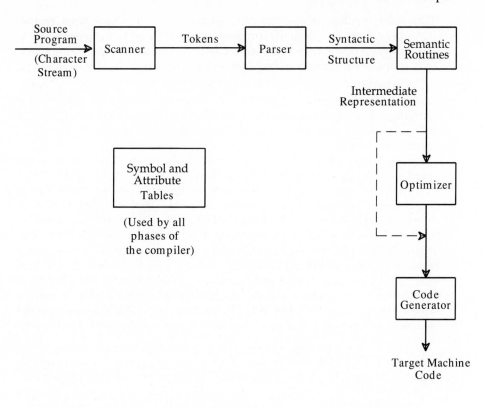

Figure 1.3   The Structure of a Syntax-Directed Compiler

- Processes compiler control directives (turn the listing on or off, include source images from a file, and so on). These directives are often done via *pseudocomments* that have the syntactic form of a comment but include special information intended for processing by the compiler. Another approach is that used in Ada, where a special syntactic structure, the *pragma*, is used for this purpose.

- Enters preliminary information into symbol and attribute tables (for example, to produce a later cross-reference listing).

- Formats and lists the source program.

   The main action of building tokens is often driven by token descriptions. *Regular expression* notation (discussed in Chapter 3) is an effective approach to describing tokens. Regular expressions are a formal notation sufficiently powerful to describe the variety of tokens required by modern programming languages. In addition, they can be used as a specification for the automatic generation of *finite automata* that recognize *regular sets*, that is, the sets that regular expressions define.

This interpretation of regular expressions is the basis of *scanner generators*, programs that actually produce a working scanner, given only a specification of the tokens it is to recognize. Obviously, such a program is a valuable compiler-building tool.

Alternatively, for the sake of simplicity, scanners may be *hand-coded*, that is, built explicitly to recognize the tokens of a particular language. Use of this approach is justified by the fact that the definition of a set of tokens required by a scanner generator can be fairly involved—it may be more work to learn to use such a generator than it is to write the scanner directly. Hand-coding scanners has been the common practice until recently, because conventional wisdom held that the table-driven scanners produced by generators are a bit slower than hand-coded ones. Any extra overhead can be significant because scanning can represent a substantial fraction of the compilation process (because there is so much character-level processing). For example, there are reports of compilers spending 20% of their time just skipping spaces. Recent developments have proven that table-driven scanners can always be faster than hand-coded ones. Furthermore, the advantage of table-driven scanners is that the same driver can be used in a variety of scanners—only the tables need to be changed. Thus scanner creation is much simpler once you know how to use the scanner generator tool.

Parser – Given a formal syntax specification (typically as a *context-free grammar* [CFG]), the parser reads tokens and groups them into units as specified by the *productions* of the CFG being used. (Grammars are discussed in Chapter 4; parsing is discussed in Chapters 5 and 6.) Parsers are typically driven by tables created from the CFG by a *parser generator*.

While parsing, the parser verifies correct syntax, and if a syntax error is found, it issues a suitable diagnostic. Also, it may be able to repair the error (to form a syntactically valid program) or to recover from the error (to allow parsing to be restarted). In many cases syntactic error recovery or repair can be done automatically by consulting *error-repair* tables created by a parser/repair generator.

As syntactic structure is recognized, the parser either calls corresponding semantic routines directly or builds a *syntax tree*, a representation of the structure, which is used to drive semantic processing after the tree is completely constructed.

Semantic Routines – Semantic routines perform two functions. First, they check the *static semantics* of each construct. That is, they verify that the construct is legal and meaningful (that the variables involved are defined, the types are correct, and so on). If the construct is semantically correct, semantic routines also do the actual *translation*. That is, IR code that correctly implements the construct is generated. Semantic routines are usually hand-coded and are associated with individual productions of the CFG or subtrees of the syntax tree.

When a production application is recognized, associated semantic routines are called to check static semantics and do translation operations. Thus for a production E → E+T we might code a semantic routine to first check type compatibility and then to generate IR code to do an addition.

The heart of a compiler, as well as most of its text, lies in its semantic routines, which define the details of how each construct is to be checked and translated. This aspect of compilation can be formalized via *attribute grammars*, which augment ordinary CFGs with values (termed *attributes*) that represent semantic properties such as type, value, or correctness. Attribute grammars and other means of semantic specification are discussed in greater detail later in this chapter.

It is often useful to keep the checking and translation components of a semantic routine distinct. Semantic checking is done first and is governed solely by the semantic rules of the source language. IR generation is influenced by both the source language semantics (the generated IR code must correctly implement language constructs) *and* the target machine (the choice of IR code may reflect the expected capabilities of the target machine). If these two components are cleanly separated, retargeting a compiler to generate code for a different target machine is simplified because only IR generation (to a small extent) and target code generation (to a large extent) are machine-dependent.

Optimizer – The IR code generated by the semantic routines is analyzed and transformed into functionally equivalent but improved IR code by the optimizer. This phase can be *very* complex and slow; it often involves numerous subphases, some of which may need to be applied more than once. Most compilers allow optimizations to be turned off to speed translation. Still others have no optimizer. Rather, semantic routines generate direct calls to the code generator to produce target code.

A less complex (and less expensive) kind of optimization is called *peephole optimization*. This kind of optimization is usually applied to the target code. It considers only a few instructions at a time (in effect, through a "peephole") and attempts to do simple, often machine-dependent, code improvements. For example, common peephole optimizations include eliminating multiplications by 1 or additions of 0, eliminating a load of a value into a register when the previous instruction stored that value from the register to a memory location, and replacing a sequence of instructions by a single instruction with the same effect (for example, an instruction that increments the value of a memory location by 1). A peephole optimizer does not have the potential payoff of a full-scale optimizer, but it can significantly improve code at a very local level and is often useful for "cleaning up" the final code resulting from the application of more-complex optimizations.

Code Generator – The IR code is mapped into target machine code by the code generator. This requires detailed information about the target machine and often involves aspects of machine-specific optimization (such as register allocation, choice of instruction formats, addressing modes). Normally code generators are hand-coded and are quite complex because generation of good target machine code requires consideration of many special cases.

A way to simplify compiler structure, if no optimization is required, is to merge code generation with semantic routines and eliminate the use of an IR. The result is a *one-pass* compiler, a structure frequently used for Pascal compilers (including UW-Pascal [Fischer and LeBlanc 1980]).

In the last few years, the idea of automatic generation of code generators has been widely studied. The idea here is to automatically match a low-level IR to target instruction templates. This localizes the target machine dependencies of a compiler and, at least in principle, makes it possible to *retarget* a compiler to a new target machine. This is an especially desirable goal, as a great deal of work is usually needed to move a compiler to a new machine. The possibility of doing this by simply changing the set of target machine templates and generating (from the templates) a new code generator is therefore very intriguing. It is stimulating a great deal of research.

A practical compiler using techniques based on some of these ideas is GCC, the GNU C compiler (Stallman 1989). GCC is a heavily optimizing compiler with machine description files for more than ten popular computer architectures and at least two language front ends (C and C++).

Symbol and Attribute Tables – A *symbol table* is a mechanism that allows information (*attributes*) to be associated with identifiers. Each time an identifier is used, a symbol table provides access to the information collected about the identifier when its declaration was processed. Thus these tables can be used by any of the compiler components to enter, share, and later retrieve information about variables, procedures, labels, and so on.

Finally, note that in discussing compiler design and construction, we often talk of *compiler writing tools*. These are often packaged as *compiler generators* or *compiler-compilers*. Such packages usually include scanner and parser generators, and some also include symbol table routines and code-generation capabilities. More advanced packages may aid in error repair generation.

These sorts of generators greatly aid in building *pieces* of compilers, but the great bulk of the effort in building a compiler lies in writing and debugging semantic routines. These routines are numerous, often numbering in the hundreds, and do almost all the work of checking static semantics and generation of IR code or, in a one-pass compiler, target machine code.

1.4. The Syntax and Semantics of Programming Languages

A complete definition of a programming language must include specifications of its *syntax* (structure) and its *semantics* (meaning). Given the almost universal use of CFGs as a syntactic specification mechanism for programming languages, syntax is usually divided into *context-free* and *context-sensitive* components. Context-free syntax defines legal sequences of symbols, independent of any notion of what the symbols mean. For example, a context-free syntax might say that A := B + C; is syntactically legal but A := B +; is not. Not all program structure can be described by context-free syntax, however; type compatibility and scoping rules are context-sensitive issues. For example, that A := B + C is illegal if any of the variables is undeclared or if B or C is boolean *cannot* be specified by CFGs; it is a context-sensitive restriction.

Because of the limitations of CFGs, context-sensitive restrictions are handled as semantic concerns. Thus the semantic component of a programming language is typically divided into two classes: *static semantics* and *run-time semantics*. The static semantics of a language defines the context-sensitive restrictions that must be enforced before a program can be considered valid. Typical static semantic rules require that all identifiers be declared, that operators and operands be type-compatible, and that procedures be called with the proper number of parameters. The common thread through all of these restrictions is that they cannot be expressed with a CFG. Static semantics thus *augment* context-free specifications and complete the definition of what valid programs look like. Static semantics can be specified formally or informally. The prose feature descriptions found in most programming language manuals are informal specifications. They tend to be relatively compact and easy to read but usually are imprecise. Formal specifications may be expressed using any of a variety of notations. For example, attribute grammars are a popular method of formally specifying static semantics. They formalize the semantic checks often found in compilers. As an example of attribute grammars, the production $E_1 \rightarrow E_2+T$ might be augmented with a type attribute for E and T and a predicate requiring type compatibility, such as

(E_2.type = numeric) **and** (T.type = numeric)

Attribute grammars are a reasonable blend of formality and readability, but they can still be rather verbose. A number of compiler writing systems employ attribute grammars and provide automatic evaluation of attribute values.

Run-time or execution semantics are used to specify what a program does, that is, what it computes. These semantics are often specified very informally in a language manual or report. Alternately, a more formal *operational* or *interpreter* model can be used. In such a model, a program "state" is defined, and program execution is described in terms of changes to that state. For example, the semantics of the statement A := 1 is that the state component corresponding to A is changed to 1.

The *Vienna definition language* (VDL) (Bjorner and Jones 1978) embodies an operational model in which abstract program trees (a variety of IR) are traversed and decorated with values to model program execution. VDL has been used to define the semantics of PL/I, although the resulting definition is quite large and verbose.

Axiomatic definitions (an excellent reference is Gries [1981]) may be used to model execution at a more abstract level than operational models. These are based on formally specified *relations* or *predicates* that relate program variables. Statements are defined by how they modify these relations.

As an example of axiomatic definitions, the axiom defining var := exp usually states that a predicate involving var is true after statement execution if and only if the predicate obtained by replacing all occurrences of var by exp is true beforehand. For example, for y>3 to be true after execution of the statement y := x+1, the predicate x+1>3 would have to be true before the statement is executed. Similarly y=21 is true after execution of x := 1 if y=21 is true before its execution, which is a roundabout way of saying that changing x doesn't affect y. However, if x is an *alias* (an alternate name) for y, the axiom is invalid. For example, if x is a Pascal **var** parameter bound to y, then x aliases y. In fact, aliasing makes axiomatic definitions much more complex. This is one reason why attempts to limit or ban aliasing are now common in modern language designs. Ada does so by simply declaring programs that use aliasing illegal; others include features and static semantic restrictions that eliminate aliasing.

The axiomatic approach is good for deriving proofs of program correctness because it avoids implementation details and concentrates on how relations among variables are changed by statement execution. Thus in our assignment axiom there is no concept of a location in memory being updated; rather, relations among variables are transformed by the assignment. Although axioms can formalize important properties of the semantics of a programming language, it is difficult to use them to define most programming languages completely. For example, they do not do a good job of modeling implementation considerations like running out of memory.

Denotational models are more mathematical in form than operational models and yet still present notions of memory access and update central to von Neumann languages. Because they rely upon notation and terminology drawn from mathematics, denotational definitions are often fairly compact, especially in comparison with operational definitions.

A denotational definition may be viewed as a syntax-directed definition in that the meaning of a construct is defined in terms of the meaning of its immediate constituents. For example, to define addition, we might use the following rule:

$$E[T1 + T2] = E[T1] \text{ is Integer and } E[T2] \text{ is Integer} \Rightarrow$$
$$\text{range}(E[T1] + E[T2]) \text{ else error}$$

This definition says if both operands (T1 and T2) evaluate to integers (the E operator evaluates the meaning of an expression), then the meaning of T1 + T2 is the sum of operand values, tested to ensure that they are in the range of representable integers. Otherwise, the meaning of the expression is an *error* value.

Denotational techniques have become quite popular, and a definition for most of Ada (excluding concurrency) has been written. This definition has been the basis for a number of early Ada compilers that operate by implementing the denotational representation of a given program. The first Ada system to take this approach was the NYU Ada-Ed system, which unfortunately executes programs very slowly. Its authors claim this slowness is primarily due to inefficient implementation of key denotational functions. A significant amount of effort in compiler research is directed toward finding ways to *automatically* convert denotational representations to equivalent representations that are directly executable (Sethi 1983, Wand 1982, Appel 1985). If this effort is successful, a denotational definition (along with lexical and syntactic definitions) may be sufficient to automatically produce a working interpreter or compiler.

Again, the concern for precise semantic specification is motivated by the fact that writing a complete and accurate compiler for a programming language requires that the language be well defined. This assertion may seem self-evident, but many languages are defined by less-than-precise language reference manuals. Such a manual typically includes a formal syntax specification but otherwise is written in an informal prose style. The resulting definition inevitably is ambiguous or incomplete on certain points. For example, consider the following expression, drawn from Pascal:

(I <> 0) **and** (K **div** I > 10)

Is this expression always well defined (assuming I and K are properly initialized integers)? It depends on whether both operands of the expression must be evaluated (and the order of operand evaluation if both need not be evaluated). If **and** is treated like an ordinary binary operator, both its operands will be evaluated before the **and** is applied. This means the expression will fail (with a zero divide fault) if I = 0. The **and** is special, however, in that both its operands need not always be evaluated to determine its value. In particular, if **and**'s left operand is false, the whole expression must be false. This is *short-circuit* evaluation and is often employed for boolean operators. If short-circuit evaluation is used, the above expression is always well defined.

The original definition of Pascal said nothing about short-circuit evaluation. It simply said that evaluation order was unspecified, and expressions like the one above, which depend on evaluation order, ought to be avoided. As a result, some Pascal compilers use ordinary full evaluation, and others use short-circuit evaluation for boolean operators. Such an incompatibility leads to serious problems in transporting programs among compilers. All languages must allow some details (such as the range of integers and reals) to be implementation-dependent, but obviously each choice left up to an implementor is an opportunity to create an incompatibility among compilers.

A compiler often serves as a de facto language definition. That is, a programming language is, in effect, defined by what a compiler chooses to accept and how it chooses to translate language constructs. In fact, the operational approach to formal semantic definition introduced above takes this view. A standard interpreter is defined for a language, and the meaning of a program is precisely whatever the interpreter says. An early (and very elegant) example of an operational definition is the LISP interpreter originally provided by McCarthy (1965). Assuming only seven primitive functions and notions of argument binding and function call, all of LISP was defined in terms of the actions of a LISP interpreter.

1.5. Compiler Design and Programming Language Design

Our primary interest is the design and implementation of compilers for modern programming languages. An interesting aspect of this study is how programming language design and compiler design influence one another. Obviously, programming language design influences and often dictates compiler design. Many clever and sometimes subtle compiler techniques arise from the need to cope with some programming language construct. An excellent example is the *thunk* mechanism that was invented to handle Algol 60's *call-by-name* parameters. (A thunk is a special kind of function, created by a compiler to be called to obtain the value of a parameter.) The state of the art in compiler design also strongly affects programming language design, if only because a programming language that cannot be compiled effectively will usually remain unused! Most successful programming language designers (such as Niklaus Wirth, designer of Pascal and Modula-2, among others) have extensive compiler design backgrounds. Programming languages that are easy to compile have many advantages:

- They are often easier to learn, read, and understand. If a feature is hard to compile, it may well be hard to understand.

- They will have quality compilers on a wide variety of machines. This fact is often crucial to a language's success. For example, C, Pascal, and FORTRAN are widely available and very popular; PL/I and Algol 68 have limited availability and are far less popular.

- Often, better code will be generated. Poor quality code can be fatal in critical applications.

- Fewer compiler bugs will occur. If a compiler writer does not fully understand a language, how can he or she produce a sound compiler?

- The compiler will be smaller, cheaper, faster, more reliable, and more widely used.

- Compiler diagnostics and program development features will often be better.

Throughout our study of compiler design we will draw ideas, solutions, and shortcomings from many languages. Our primary focus will be on Ada, but we will also consider Pascal, Algol 60, C, and FORTRAN. We concentrate on Ada not because it is easy to compile but rather because it presents a variety of challenges to compiler designers and thus provides us with a unified framework for presenting a wide range of compilation techniques. To a lesser extent, we will reference Simula 67, PL/I, Algol 68, and Euclid. Each of these languages is considered *compilable* (although some are considerably more challenging than others). That is, each can be reasonably translated into machine languages for typical computers. By our earlier discussion, each such language has a clear-cut translation phase.

In contrast, languages such as Snobol and APL are usually considered *noncompilable* because in the most general cases operations specified in these languages cannot be completely translated to machine code using only information available prior to execution. (Compilers for these languages do exist; they attempt to translate as much of a program as possible, leaving the rest to be interpreted by run-time routines.)

What attributes must be found in a programming language to allow compilation? Many considerations apply, but mostly the issue is what can be determined and bound before execution begins and what must be deferred until after execution begins; that is, which aspects are dynamic and which are static? In particular, the following are of concern:

- Can the scope and binding of each identifier reference be determined before execution begins? That is, can the data object, or perhaps a pointer to the data object, denoted by an identifier, be determined at compile-time? If not, it may be necessary to effectively look up an identifier in a run-time symbol table each time it is used.

- Can the type of an object be determined before execution begins? If not, the meaning of each operator may need to be continually reevaluated. For example, A ∗ B may mean something very different if A and B are arrays rather than integers.

  Languages like Snobol and APL that have no type declarations and allow the type of a variable to change dynamically are termed *untyped* or *dynamic-typed*. Note that these are different from *typeless* languages (such as Bliss or BCPL), which have only one type of datum, the cell or word. Many systems implementation languages (SILs) are typeless or nearly so. For example, early versions of C used types more to define object sizes than to specify classes of permissible operations, in contrast to the strong type checking of operands done in languages like Pascal and Ada. C is now much more strongly typed than it was originally.

- Can existing program text be changed or added to during execution? If so, program text will probably need to be kept in some internal representation between source statements and machine code. LISP is the best-known example of a language that allows program text to be created at run-time, but Snobol and APL also have this feature.

In general, compilable languages will be those that have structure, identifier scoping, and type binding fixed at compile-time (that is, before execution). Indeed, knowing that these program components are static is essential to a compiler if it is to be able to completely translate operations to concrete target machine instructions.

The structure of Pascal programs is another example (not really involving language features) of how compilation considerations influence language design. Pascal is designed so that it can be translated by a one-pass compiler. All global declarations must appear at the beginning of the program to ensure their availability to all subprograms that need to reference them. Likewise, the main program appears at the very end of the program text, so that any variables it uses and any subprograms it calls have already been defined. This program structure doesn't particularly enhance program readability, but it does make a positive contribution to compiler efficiency.

1.6. Compiler Classifications

There is a wide variety of compiler variants. *Diagnostic compilers* (such as PL/C [Conway and Wilcox 1973], WATFIV [WATFIV 1981], UW-Pascal) are specially designed to aid in the development and debugging of programs. They provide careful scrutiny of programs and detail programmer errors. They often can automatically *repair* minor errors (for example, a missing comma or parenthesis). Some program errors can be detected only at run-time (that is, while a program is executing). Such errors include invalid subscripts, misuse of pointers, and illegal file manipulations. Diagnostic compilers have the capability to include checking code that can detect run-time errors and abort program execution. Although diagnostic compilers are primarily used in instructional environments, diagnostic techniques are of value in all compilers. In the past, diagnostic compilers were used only in the initial stages of program development. When a program neared completion, a "production compiler," which increased program speed by ignoring diagnostic concerns, was used. This strategy has been likened by Tony Hoare to wearing a life jacket in sailing classes held on dry land, but abandoning the jacket when at sea! Indeed, it is becoming increasingly clear that for almost all programs, correctness rather than speed is the paramount concern.

Optimizing compilers are specially designed to produce efficient machine code at the cost of increased compiler complexity and compilation times. In practice, all production-quality compilers—those whose output will be used in everyday work—make some effort to generate good machine code. For example, no add instruction would normally be generated for the expression $I + 0$.

The term *optimizing compiler* is actually a misnomer, for no compiler, no matter how sophisticated, can produce *optimal* code for all programs. The reason for this is twofold. Theoretical computer science has shown that even so simple a question as whether two programs are equivalent is *undecidable;* that is, it cannot be solved by *any* computer program. Thus, finding the simplest (and most efficient) translation of a program can't always be done. Secondly, many program optimizations require time proportional to an exponential function of the size of the program being compiled. Optimal code, even when theoretically possible, often is in practice infeasible.

Optimizing compilers actually employ a melange of "transforms" that improve the performance of a program. The complexity of an optimizing compiler arises from the need to employ a variety of transforms, some of which interfere with each other. For example, keeping frequently used variables in registers reduces their access time but makes procedure and function calls more expensive, because registers need to be saved across calls. Many optimizing compilers provide a number of levels of optimization, each providing increasingly greater code improvements at increasingly greater costs. The choice of which improvements are most effective (and least expensive) is a matter of judgment and experience. In later chapters, we shall suggest possible optimizations, with the emphasis on those that are both simple and effective. A comprehensive optimizing compiler is beyond the scope of this text, but compilers that produce quality code at reasonable cost are an achievable goal.

Compilers are designed for a particular programming language (the *source language*) and a particular *target computer* (for which it will generate code). Given the wide variety of programming languages and computers that exist, a large number of similar, but not identical, compilers must be written. This situation has decided benefits for those of us in the compiler writing business, but it does make for a lot of duplication of effort and for a wide variance in compiler quality. As a result, a new kind of compiler, the *retargetable compiler,* has become important.

A retargetable compiler is one whose target machine can be changed without rewriting its machine-independent components. A retargetable compiler is more difficult to write than an ordinary compiler because target machine dependencies must be carefully localized. Similarly, it is often difficult for a retargetable compiler to generate code as efficient as that of an ordinary compiler because special cases and machine idiosyncrasies are harder to exploit. Nonetheless, because a retargetable compiler allows development costs to be shared and provides for uniformity across computers, it is an important innovation. While learning the fundamentals of compilation, we shall concentrate on compilers targeted to a single machine. In later chapters, the techniques needed to provide retargetability will be considered.

In practice a compiler is but one tool used in the edit-compile-test cycle. A user first edits a program, then compiles it, and finally tests its performance. Because program bugs must be discovered and corrected, this cycle is repeated many times. A new kind of programming tool, a *program development environment* (PDE), has been designed to integrate this cycle (for example, the Cornell Program Synthesizer [Teitelbaum and Reps 1981], Gandalf [Notkin 1985], Cope [Archer and Conway 1981], Poe [Fischer et al. 1984]). A PDE allows programs to be built incrementally, with program checking and testing fully integrated. A PDE may be viewed as the next stage in the evolution of compilers. The compilation techniques discussed in this text are essential ingredients in the creation of a PDE.

1.7. Influences on Computer Design

In the past, instruction sets of computers have been more oriented to assembler-level programming than high-level programming. As a result, generating high-quality code has been a very difficult goal to attain (Wulf 1981). Problems have been numerous:

- Instruction sets have been notoriously nonuniform. For example, some operations must be done in registers, and others can be done in memory. Often a number of register classes exist, each suitable for some particular class of operations.

- High-level operations have not been well supported. Although most current languages support block structure and dynamic storage allocation, stacks and heap storage are often difficult to implement efficiently. Wulf warns, however, about making general-purpose architectures too closely oriented to a particular language.

- Data and program integrity have been undervalued, and speed has been overemphasized. As a result, programming errors can go undetected because of a fear that extra checking will slow down execution unacceptably.

Because of the wide availability of microprogrammable machines and better communication between engineers and computer scientists, things are improving. By tuning instruction sets to operations most commonly needed, spectacular reductions in program size can be realized (threefold reductions have been reported). Single instructions can support common high-level operations; the VAX, for example, has a single instruction that saves registers, passes parameters, and pushes stack space during a procedure call. Operations deemed prohibitively expensive (such as dynamic storage management) can be made integral parts of a machine design. A good example of this is the MIT LISP machine (Sussman 1981), which contains an integral garbage collector. Radical reorganization of machine design also allows more careful control over the use (and potential misuse) of program and data objects. The Intel iAPX 432, for example, gives direct hardware support to a variety of access control mechanisms.

An alternative school of thought champions the idea that instruction set architectures should be made simpler, not more complex. Machines designed according to such a philosophy are known as *reduced instruction set computers* (RISCs) (Patterson 1985). Curiously enough, these designs can also be considered compiler-oriented, because they typically presume that programs for them will be written in high-level languages and processed by optimizing compilers. The simplicity of their instructions is intended to ease the task of compiler writing by minimizing the number of choices possible for a code generator. It is interesting, however, to note that even some of the RISCs have relatively complex support for subprogram calls.

In summary, the need to efficiently and reliably support modern programming language constructs has begun to have an enormous effect on instruction set design. It is not yet clear which approach of the two we have described is most appropriate. The important point is that both give primary consideration to the execution of programs written in high-level languages, thus significantly easing the burden of compiler writers in making the best use of available hardware resources.

In succeeding chapters, we assume a virtual machine whose instruction set is representative of modern computers. Choosing a particular instruction set makes our discussions concrete. In practice, the reader may well wish to substitute a more familiar architecture. Familiarity with the target machine is vital; the essence of code generation is determining which instruction sequence best implements a given construct. Like so much else in compiler design, experience is the best guide, so we start with the translation of a very simple language, and work our way up to ever-more challenging translation tasks.

Exercises

1. The model of compilation we have introduced is essentially batch-oriented. In particular, it assumes that an entire source program has been written and that the program will be fully compiled before the programmer can execute the program or make any changes. An interesting alternative is an "interactive compiler." An interactive compiler, usually part of a program development environment, allows a programmer to interactively respond to source errors, fixing them as they are detected. It also allows a program to be tested before it is fully written, providing for stepwise implementation and testing.

    Redesign the compiler structure of Figure 1.3 to allow incremental compilation. (The key idea is to allow individual program structures to be changed and compiled without necessarily recompiling everything.)

2. In Section 1.7 we observed that RISC architectures simplify code generation by reducing the number of choices that must be made. In large measure, RISC architectures were inspired by negative reaction to so-called CISC (complex instruction set computer) architectures, which include a large number of operation codes and addressing modes. A well-known CISC architecture is the popular VAX family of computers.

    Assume you are asked to write a compiler targeted for a CISC machine (like the VAX). You have two choices. You can design the compiler to utilize the full range of instructions and address modes, *or* you can select a judicious subset of the available choices and utilize only that subset. Examine the tradeoffs between these two approaches. Under what circumstances would you recommend each approach?

3. To appreciate the differences among *syntax, static semantics,* and *run-time semantics,* look up the definition of Pascal's with statement in your favorite text. For each of the rules defining the with, identify the definitional category to which it belongs.

4. Compilers are often written in the language that they compile. This raises something of a "chicken and egg" problem when one ponders how the primordial compiler came into being. If you need to create the first compiler for language X on system Y, one approach is to create a *cross-compiler.* A cross-compiler runs on one machine but generates code for some different machine. Explain how you might use cross-compilation to create a compiler for language X that runs on systems Y and generates code for system Y. What extra problems arise if system Y is bare—that is, has no operating system or compilers for any language?

5. Cross-compilation assumes that a compiler for language X exists on *some* machine. When the very first compiler for a new language is created, this assumption doesn't hold. In this situation, a *bootstrapping* approach can be taken. First, a subset of language X is chosen that is sufficient to implement a simple compiler. Next, a simple compiler for the X subset is written in any available language. This compiler must be correct, but it ought not to be any more elaborate than is necessary, because it will soon be discarded. The next step is to rewrite the subset compiler for X

in the X subset and then compile it using the subset compiler previously created. Finally, the X subset, and its compiler, can be enhanced until a complete compiler for X, written in X, is available.

Assume you are bootstrapping Pascal (or C). Outline a suitable subset language. What language features *must* be in the language? What other features are desirable?

6. To allow the creation of camera-ready documents, languages like *troff* and TEX have been created. They can be thought of as a variety of programming language, whose output controls laser printers or photo-typesetters. Source language commands control details like spacing, font choice, point size, and special symbols. Using the syntax-directed compiler structure of Figure 1.3, suggest the kind of processing that might occur in each compiler phase if *troff* or TEX input were being translated.

An alternative to "programming" documents is to use a sophisticated editor to interactively enter and edit the document. (Editing operations allow choice of fonts, selection of point size, inclusion of special symbols, and so on.) This approach to document preparation is called "what you see is what you get" because the exact form of the document is always visible.

What are the relative advantages and disadvantages of the two approaches? Do analogues exist for ordinary programming languages?

7. Although compilers are designed to translate a particular language, they often allow calls to subprograms coded in some other language (typically, FORTRAN, C, or assembler). Why are such "foreign calls" allowed? In what ways do they complicate compilation?

A Simple Compiler

To provide an overview of how the compilation process can be organized, we will consider in some detail how a compiler can be built for a very small programming language. Our language is called *Micro*. It is an extremely simple language, lacking even enough features to write a useful program. Micro is designed only to provide a concrete language around which we can discuss a simple example compiler.

We first define Micro informally:

- The only data type is integer.
- All identifiers are implicitly declared and are no longer than 32 characters. Identifiers must begin with a letter and are composed of letters, digits, and underscores.
- Literals are strings of digits.
- Comments begin with −− and end at the end of the current line.

- Statement types are

  Assignment:

    ID := Expression ;

    Expression is an infix expression constructed from identifiers, literals, and the operators + and −; parentheses are also allowed.

  Input/Output:

    read (List of IDs) ;
    write (List of Expressions) ;

- **begin**, **end**, **read**, and **write** are reserved words.
- Each statement is terminated by a semicolon (;). The body of a program is delimited by **begin** and **end**.
- A blank is appended to the right end of each source line; thus tokens may not extend across line boundaries.

2.1. **The Structure of a Micro Compiler**

A simple compiler for Micro is the subject of the rest of this chapter. The structure of this compiler is based on that illustrated in Figure 1.3. In the interest of simplicity, the compiler will be a one-pass type, whose most important feature is that no explicit intermediate representations are used. The interfaces between the components will be as follows:

- The scanner reads a source program from a text file and produces a stream of token representations (these will be defined more precisely in Chapter 3). So that no actual stream need exist at any time, the scanner is actually a function that produces token representations one at a time when called by the parser.
- The parser processes tokens until it recognizes a syntactic structure that requires semantic processing. It then makes a direct call to a semantic routine. Some of these semantic routines use token representation information in their processing.
- The semantic routines produce output in assembly language for a simple three-address virtual machine. Thus the compiler structure includes no optimizer, and code generation is done by direct calls to appropriate support routines from the semantic routines.
- The symbol table is used only by the semantic routines. Its interface is described in Section 2.5.5.

2.2. **A Micro Scanner**

The definition of Micro tokens can be formalized, as we shall see in Chapter 3. For our present purposes an informal definition will suffice. The first step in building a Micro compiler is to construct a Micro scanner. We will define an enumeration type **token** that will represent the set of Micro tokens. Our scanner will be a function of no arguments that returns **token** values.

```
typedef enum token_types {
    BEGIN, END, READ, WRITE, ID, INTLITERAL,
    LPAREN, RPAREN, SEMICOLON, COMMA, ASSIGNOP,
    PLUSOP, MINUSOP, SCANEOF
} token;

extern token scanner(void);
```

The scanner will read characters and group them into tokens. Care is required that we don't sometimes read too much. In particular, we may need to see the beginning of the next token in order to recognize the end of the current token. For Micro, all that is ever needed is one character of lookahead. The extra character can be conveniently "pushed back" onto the input using the standard **ungetc()** function.

For simplicity, we will assume that input is coming from **stdin**; in practice a source file would have to be opened and an explicit **FILE** pointer would be used.

When called, the scanner must find the beginning of some token. To do this, it first inspects the next input character. If the character cannot begin any token, we have a *lexical* or *token* error. An error message is issued, and we then attempt to *recover* from the error. A simple way to do this is to skip the character and restart scanning. This process continues until the beginning of some token is found. Then we match the longest possible character sequence that comprises a legal token.

Figure 2.1 shows code for the main loop of a scanner that can recognize Micro identifiers and literals (integer constants). It also skips white space (blanks, tabs, and end-of-line markers). For simplicity, we assume an "end-of-line" character exists. In C, this is usually called a "newline," and is denoted by the *escape sequence* '\n'. Even if our character set lacks a specific "newline" character, the C I/O library will return '\n' when some sort of end of line marker has been seen.

Operators, comments, and delimiters are easy to add. Figure 2.2 shows code that has been added to the loop in Figure 2.1 for recognizing these tokens.

We have not yet included recognition of reserved words in the Micro scanner. The problem, of course, is that reserved words look the same as identifiers. We might require that reserved words be somehow specially marked (for example, by putting them in quotes or in uppercase), but this

```
#include <stdio.h>
#include <ctype.h>

int in_char, c;

while ((in_char = getchar()) != EOF) {
    if (isspace(in_char))
        continue;      /* do nothing */
    else if (isalpha(in_char)) {
        /*
         * ID ::= LETTER | ID LETTER
         *                | ID DIGIT
         *                | ID UNDERSCORE
         */

        for (c = getchar(); isalnum(c) || c == '_';
                    c = getchar())
            ;
        ungetc(c, stdin);

        return ID;
    } else if (isdigit(in_char)) {
        /*
         * INTLITERAL ::= DIGIT |
         *                INTLITERAL DIGIT
         */
        while (isdigit((c = getchar())))
            ;
        ungetc(c, stdin);

        return INTLITERAL;
    } else
        lexical_error(in_char);
}
```

Figure 2.1   Scanner Loop to Recognize Identifiers and Integer Literals

approach is a nuisance to programmers, so we would rather avoid it. Two other approaches are commonly used to differentiate between identifiers and reserved words. In the first, the scanner has a table of reserved words that is checked whenever an identifier is recognized. If a token is on this list, then it is always interpreted as a reserved word rather than as an identifier. Alternately, reserved words can be entered in the symbol table as part of the initialization of the compiler with a special attribute, *reserved*. After an identifier is recognized by the scanner, it is looked up in the symbol table. If it is found and has this special attribute, it is recognized as a reserved word.

For Micro, either approach is workable. We'll assume the scanner has a routine **check_reserved()** that takes the identifiers as they are recognized and returns the proper token class (either **ID** or some reserved word).

```
#include <stdio.h>
#include <ctype.h>

int in_char, c;

while ((in_char = getchar()) != EOF) {
    if (isspace(in_char))
        /* do nothing */
        continue;
    else if (isalpha(in_char))
        /* code to recognize identifiers goes here */
    else if (isdigit(in_char))
        /* code to recognize int literals goes here */
    else if (in_char == '(')
        return LPAREN;
    else if (in_char == ')')
        return RPAREN;
    else if (in_char == ';')
        return SEMICOLON;
    else if (in_char == ',')
        return COMMA;
    else if (in_char == '+')
        return PLUSOP;
    else if (in_char == ':') {
        /* looking for ":=" */
        c = getchar();
        if (c == '=')
            return ASSIGNOP;
        else {
            ungetc(c, stdin);
            lexical_error(in_char);
        }
    } else if (in_char == '-') {
        /* looking for --, comment start */
        c = getchar();
        if (c == '-') {
            while ((in_char = getchar()) != '\n');
        } else {
            ungetc(c, stdin);
            return MINUSOP;
        }
    } else
        lexical_error(in_char);
}
```

Figure 2.2 Scanner Loop with New Code to Recognize Operators, Comments, and Delimiters

However, the scanner code for identifier recognition in Figure 2.1 is inadequate for discovering reserved words this way. We haven't made any provision for saving the characters of a token as they are scanned. For very simple
tokens, like operators or delimiters, knowing the token class suffices. For others, such as identifiers and literals, we need the actual text of the token. To do
this, we will call a routine **buffer_char()** that adds its argument to a character buffer called **token_buffer**. **clear_buffer()** will reset the buffer
to the empty string. This buffer is visible to any part of the compiler and
always contains the text of the most recently scanned token. In our example
compiler, we will be particularly interested in use of **token_buffer** by
semantic routines. The characters in this buffer also will be used by
check_reserved() to determine whether a token that looks like an
identifier is actually a reserved word.

We also must decide how to handle end of file. The parser must know
when the input is exhausted in order to verify that a complete program has
been parsed, so we have created an end-of-file token called **SCANEOF**. The
token is often denoted by $ in formal descriptions of parsing algorithms and
by parser generators. However, this is not a valid enumeration literal in any
typical programming language, so we use **SCANEOF** instead. Whenever the
scanner is called with **feof(stdin)** true, it will return **SCANEOF**.

Figure 2.3 contains the complete code for the main routine of the
scanner. The auxiliary routines used by this routine (**buffer_char()**, and so
on) are not included.

```
#include <stdio.h>
/* character classification macros */
#include <ctype.h>

extern char token_buffer[];

token scanner(void)
{
    int in_char, c;

    clear_buffer();
    if (feof(stdin))
        return SCANEOF;

    while ((in_char = getchar()) != EOF) {
        if (isspace(in_char))
            continue;       /* do nothing */
        else if (isalpha(in_char)) {
            /*
             * ID ::= LETTER | ID LETTER
             *                | ID DIGIT
             *                | ID UNDERSCORE
             */
            buffer_char(in_char);
            for (c = getchar(); isalnum(c) || c == '_';
                    c = getchar())
                buffer_char(c);
```

```
        ungetc(c, stdin);
        return check_reserved();
    } else if (isdigit(in_char)) {
        /*
         * INTLITERAL ::= DIGIT |
         *                     INTLITERAL DIGIT
         */
        buffer_char(in_char);
        for (c = getchar(); isdigit(c);
                c = getchar())
            buffer_char(c);
        ungetc(c, stdin);
        return INTLITERAL;
    } else if (in_char == '(')
        return LPAREN;
    else if (in_char == ')')
        return RPAREN;
    else if (in_char == ';')
        return SEMICOLON;
    else if (in_char == ',')
        return COMMA;
    else if (in_char == '+')
        return PLUSOP;
    else if (in_char == ':') {
        /* looking for ":=" */
        c = getchar();
        if (c == '=')
            return ASSIGNOP;
        else {
            ungetc(c, stdin);
            lexical_error(in_char);
        }
    } else if (in_char == '-') {
        /* is it --, comment start */
        c = getchar();
        if (c == '-') {
            do
                in_char = getchar();
            while (in_char != '\n');
        } else {
            ungetc(c, stdin);
            return MINUSOP;
        }
    } else
        lexical_error(in_char);
    }
}
```

Figure 2.3   Complete Scanner Function for Micro

2.3. **The Syntax of Micro**

Rather than defining the syntax of Micro informally, we will give a precise definition using a context-free grammar (CFG). A CFG is also sometimes called a BNF (Backus-Naur form) grammar.

Informally, a CFG is simply a set of rewriting rules or *productions*. A production is of the form

A → B C D ··· Z

A is the *left-hand side* (LHS) of the production; B C D ··· Z constitute the *right-hand side* (RHS) of the production. Every production has exactly one symbol on its LHS; it can have any number of symbols (zero or more) on its RHS. A production represents the rule that any occurrence of its LHS symbol can be replaced by the symbols on its RHS. Thus the production

<program> → **begin** <statement list> **end**

states that a program is required to be a statement list delimited by a **begin** and **end**.

Two kinds of symbols may appear in a CFG: *nonterminals* and *terminals*. In this text, nonterminals are often delimited by < and > for ease of recognition. However, nonterminals can also be recognized by the fact that they appear on the left-hand sides of productions. A nonterminal is, in effect, a placeholder. All nonterminals must be replaced, or rewritten, by a production having the appropriate nonterminal on its LHS. In contrast, terminals are never changed or rewritten. Rather, they represent the *tokens* of a language. Thus the overall purpose of a set of productions (a CFG) is to specify what sequences of terminals (tokens) are legal. A CFG does this in a remarkably elegant way: We start with a single nonterminal symbol called the *start* or *goal* symbol. We then apply productions, rewriting nonterminals until only terminals remain. Any sequence of terminals that can be produced by doing this is considered legal. Similarly, if a sequence of terminals *cannot* be produced by any sequence of nonterminal replacements, then that sequence is deemed illegal. To see how this works, let us look at a CFG for Micro. λ will represent the empty or null string. Thus a production A → λ states that A can be replaced by the empty string, effectively erasing it.

Programming language constructs often involve optional items, or lists of items. To cleanly represent such features, an *extended BNF* notation is often utilized. An optional item sequence is enclosed in square brackets, [and]. For example, in

<program> → [ID :] **begin** <statement list> **end**

a program can be optionally labeled. Optional lists are enclosed by braces, { and }. Thus in

<statement list>   →   <statement> {<statement>}

a statement list is defined to be a single statement, optionally followed by *zero or more* additional statements.

An extended BNF has the same definitional capability as ordinary BNFs. In particular, the following transforms can be used to map extended BNFs into standard form. An optional sequence is replaced by a new nonterminal that generates λ or the items in the sequence. Similarly, an optional list is replaced by a new nonterminal that generates λ or the list items *followed by* the nonterminal. Thus our statement list can be transformed into

<statement list>   →   <statement> <statement tail>
<statement tail>   →   λ
<statement tail>   →   <statement> <statement tail>

The advantage of extended BNFs is that they are more compact and readable. We can envision a preprocessor that takes extended BNFs and produces standard BNFs, using these transforms.

Figure 2.4 shows an extended CFG for Micro. An *augmenting* production

<system goal> →   <program> SCANEOF

appears in the grammar to make sure that the string matched by <system goal> includes all the input. It specifies that the end-of-file marker, SCANEOF, *must follow* after the last valid token of a program.

1.	<program>	→ **begin** <statement list> **end**
2.	<statement list>	→ <statement> {<statement>}
3.	<statement>	→ ID := <expression> ;
4.	<statement>	→ **read** (<id list>) ;
5.	<statement>	→ **write** (<expr list>) ;
6.	<id list>	→ ID {, ID}
7.	<expr list>	→ <expression> {, <expression>}
8.	<expression>	→ <primary> {<add op> <primary>}
9.	<primary>	→ (<expression>)
10.	<primary>	→ ID
11.	<primary>	→ INTLITERAL
12.	<add op>	→ PLUSOP
13.	<add op>	→ MINUSOP
14.	<system goal>	→ <program> SCANEOF

Figure 2.4   Extended CFG Defining Micro

To see how this grammar defines legal Micro programs, let's follow the *derivation* of one such program, **begin** ID := ID + (INTLITERAL − ID) ; **end**, starting from the nonterminal <program>.

```
<program>
begin <statement list> end                                              (Apply rule 1)
begin <statement> {<statement>} end                                     (Apply rule 2)
begin <statement> end                                                   (Choose 0 repetitions)
begin ID := <expression> ; end                                          (Apply rule 3)
begin ID := <primary> {<add op> <primary>} ; end                        (Apply rule 8)
begin ID := <primary> <add op> <primary> ; end                          (Choose 1 repetition)
begin ID := <primary> + <primary> ; end                                 (Apply rule 12)
begin ID := ID + <primary> ; end                                        (Apply rule 10)
begin ID := ID + ( <expression> ) ; end                                 (Apply rule 9)
begin ID := ID + ( <primary> {<add op> <primary>} ) ; end               (Apply rule 8)
begin ID := ID + ( <primary> <add op> <primary> ) ; end                 (Choose 1 repetition)
begin ID := ID + ( <primary> – <primary> ) ; end                        (Apply rule 13)
begin ID := ID + ( INTLITERAL – <primary> ) ; end                       (Apply rule 11)
begin ID := ID + ( INTLITERAL – ID ) ; end                              (Apply rule 10)
```

At this point no nonterminals remain, so our derivation of a Micro program is completed.

A CFG defines a *language,* which is a set of sequences of tokens. Any sequence of tokens that can be derived using the grammar is valid; any sequence that cannot be derived is not valid. Actually, to be precise, any token sequence derivable from a CFG is considered syntactically valid. When static semantics are checked by the semantic routines, *semantic errors* in a syntactically valid program may be discovered. For example, in Pascal the statement

A := 'X' + True;

has no syntax errors but it does have a semantic error: the operator + is not defined for adding a character to a boolean value.

Structure as well as syntax can be defined in a CFG. For expressions, this includes *associativity* and *operator precedence.* Associativity is concerned with the order in which consecutive instances of an operator are applied (as in A–B–C). Operator precedence refers to the relative priority of operators. For example, we expect A+B∗C to mean A+(B∗C), since ∗ is usually considered to be a higher precedence operator than +. Micro has only one level of precedence, because it does not include multiplication. If multiplication were included, it would be at a higher level of precedence than addition. The following grammar fragment defines such a precedence relationship.

```
<expression>  →  <factor> {<add op> <factor>}
<factor>      →  <primary> {<mult op> <primary>}
<primary>     →  ( <expression> )
<primary>     →  ID
<primary>     →  INTLITERAL
```

Examining a *derivation tree* for the expression A+B∗C, which is derived from this grammar fragment, illustrates how this definition works. A deriva-

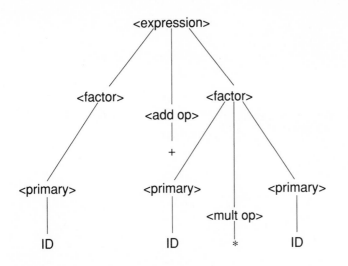

Figure 2.5   Derivation Tree for A+B*C

tion tree is formed by showing nonterminal expansions as subtrees. Figure 2.5 shows the tree for this expression. The tree shows that * has a higher precedence than + because the second and third IDs are grouped together (with *) in a subtree, and *then* this subtree is grouped together with the first ID (using +) in the main derivation tree.

Can a derivation tree with *wrong* precedence ever be formed in this grammar? No—the production rules don't allow it. Try to build ID+ID*ID with + applied first. Since a * can only be generated by a <factor>, ID+ID must appear in a subtree rooted by <primary>. However, <primary> *cannot* generate ID+ID unless the subexpression is enclosed in parentheses. With parentheses, the desired grouping can be forced, as illustrated in Figure 2.6.

2.4. Recursive Descent Parsing

For our Micro parser, we will use a well-known parsing technique called *recursive descent*. Its name is taken from the recursive parsing routines that, in effect, descend through the parse tree it recognizes as it processes a program. Recursive descent is one of the simplest parsing techniques used in practical compilers. The basic idea of recursive descent parsing is that each nonterminal has an associated *parsing procedure* that can recognize any sequence of tokens generated by that nonterminal. Within a parsing procedure, both nonterminals and terminals can be matched. To match a nonterminal A, we call the parsing procedure corresponding to A which, by convention, is named **A**. These calls may be recursive, hence the name recursive descent. To match a terminal symbol **t**, we call a procedure **match(t)**. **match()** calls the scanner to get the next token. If it is **t**, everything is correct and the token is

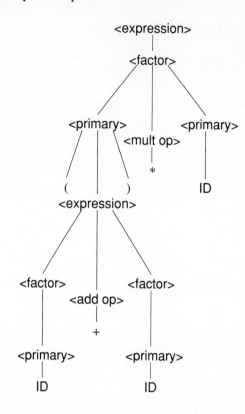

Figure 2.6　Derivation Tree for (A+B)∗C

saved in a global variable named **current_token**. If this token is not **t,** we have found a *syntax error,* and an error message is produced. Some error correction or repair is then done to restart the parser and continue compilation.

　　　To see how this works, consider the parsing routines that would be written to correspond to the productions of the Micro grammar. The parser is started by calling the procedure corresponding to <system goal>:

```
void system_goal(void)
{
    /* <system goal> ::= <program> SCANEOF */
    program();
    match(SCANEOF);
}
```

That is, to correctly parse a Micro program, we must match a token sequence generated by <program> followed by **SCANEOF.** Similarly for <program>, we have the following procedure:

```
void program(void)
{
    /* <program> ::= BEGIN <statement list> END */
    match(BEGIN);
    statement_list();
    match(END);
}
```

For <statement list>, we must decide how to deal with the optional statement sequence. Let **next_token()** be a function that returns the next token
to be matched. If **next_token()** can be generated as the first (that is, leftmost) token from the nonterminal <statement>, we will try to recognize an optional statement. Otherwise, we will conclude that an entire statement list has
been matched. This approach does not work for all CFGs, but it does for LL(1)
grammars, a subset of CFGs that is well suited to recursive descent parsing.
LL(1) grammars and parsing will be discussed in detail in Chapter 5.

How do we decide which tokens can be derived as the first tokens of a
nonterminal? In Chapter 5 we show how to automatically compute these tokens, but for a CFG as small as Micro, this can be done by inspection. Assume
we want the first tokens for a nonterminal A. Denote this token set as First(A).
We select all productions with A as the left-hand side. For each such production, we simply examine the leftmost symbol in its right-hand side. If that
symbol is a terminal, we include it in First(A). If the symbol is a nonterminal,
B, we compute First(B), and include it in First(A). In the case of <statement>,
things are simple because all <statement> productions start with terminals.
The appropriate parsing procedure is as follows:

```
void statement_list(void)
{
    /*
     * <statement list> ::= <statement>
     *                     { <statement> }
     */
    statement();
    while (TRUE)   {
        switch (next_token()) {
        case ID:
        case READ:
        case WRITE:
            statement();
            break;
        default:
            return;
        }
    }
}
```

In defining the parsing procedure corresponding to <statement> we run into the problem that more than one production has <statement> as an LHS; thus we must decide which production to try to match. To do this, we must carefully analyze what each production can generate. We consider the First sets corresponding to each <statement> production. If these sets are unique for each production, we can make a unique choice—we pick the production that contains **next_token()** in its First set. If a production has λ as its RHS, we make it a default and match it whenever no other production is selected (obviously λ generates an empty First set). If **next_token()** appears in *no* First set and we have no λ production, we have a syntax error, because no production can match the next token.

Not all CFGs have the property that productions sharing the same LHS can be distinguished on the basis of their first token sets. However, LL(1) grammars *do* have this property, which is why they are so well suited to recursive descent parsing.

The parsing procedure for <statement> is shown in Figure 2.7, along with the rest of the parsing procedures for Micro, which are constructed using the techniques we have presented in this section.

```
void statement(void)
{
    token tok = next_token();

    switch (tok) {
    case ID:
        /* <statement> ::= ID := <expression> ; */
        match(ID); match(ASSIGNOP);
        expression(); match(SEMICOLON);
        break;

    case READ:
        /* <statement> ::= READ ( <id list> ) ; */
        match(READ); match(LPAREN);
        id_list(); match(RPAREN);
        match(SEMICOLON);
        break;

    case WRITE:
        /* <statement> ::= WRITE ( <expr list> ) ; */
        match(WRITE); match(LPAREN);
        expr_list(); match(RPAREN);
        match(SEMICOLON);
        break;

    default:
        syntax_error(tok);
        break;
    }
}
```

```
void id_list(void)
{
    /* <id list> ::= ID { , ID } */
    match(ID);

    while (next_token() == COMMA) {
        match(COMMA);
        match(ID);
    }
}


void expression(void)
{
    token t;

    /*
     * <expression> ::= <primary>
     *                  { <add op> <primary> }
     */
    primary();
    for (t = next_token(); t == PLUSOP || t == MINUSOP;
                t = next_token()) {
        add_op();
        primary();
    }
}


void expr_list(void)
{
  /* <id list> ::= <expression> { , <expression> } */
    expression();

    while (next_token() == COMMA) {
        match(COMMA);
        expression();
    }
}


void add_op(void)
{
    token tok = next_token();

    /* <addop> ::= PLUSOP | MINUSOP */
    if (tok == PLUSOP || tok == MINUSOP)
        match(tok);
    else
        syntax_error(tok);
}
```

```
void primary(void)
{
    token tok = next_token();

    switch (tok) {
    case LPAREN:
        /* <primary> ::= ( <expression> ) */
        match(LPAREN); expression();
        match(RPAREN);
        break;

    case ID:
        /* <primary> ::= ID */
        match(ID);
        break;

    case INTLITERAL:
        /* <primary> ::= INTLITERAL */
        match(INTLITERAL);
        break;

    default:
        syntax_error(tok);
        break;
    }
}
```

Figure 2.7   Remaining Parsing Procedures for Micro

2.5. **Translating Micro**

2.5.1. **Target Language**

We are now ready to begin work on the actual translation of Micro. First, we must decide what machine we will generate code for and in what form (assembly code, object module, or whatever) the generated code will be produced. For simplicity, we will use assembly code for a three-address machine. Instructions for such a machine have the form

OP A,B,C

in which OP is an op-code (or pseudo-op), A and B designate operands of the specified operation, and C specifies the location where the result of the operation is to be stored. The operands may be variable names or integer literals. For some OPs, A or B or C may not be used (for example, a halt instruction is simply Halt). The format of our output will be character strings. For Micro, all arithmetic operations will be assumed to be done using integer arithmetic.

This target code is for a simple virtual machine; it could be used to drive an interpreter, or the individual instructions could be expanded by a more sophisticated code generator into code for a real machine. In fact, our target code bears a strong resemblance to *quadruples*, a commonly used intermediate representation. This point illustrates an interesting property of virtual instruction sets: They may be viewed as either an intermediate representation or as the output of a compiler, depending on how they are utilized.

2.5.2. Temporaries

During compilation, it is frequently necessary to use temporarily allocated storage locations, known as *temporaries*, to hold intermediate results of a computation. For our Micro compiler we will think of temporaries as *internal variables* that are implicitly declared when needed. This technique works well in Micro because variables are implicitly declared, too. Compilers for more realistic languages allocate temporaries from registers but may also use *storage temporaries* (memory locations, like those used in our Micro compiler) for special purposes—for example, when no registers are available or to save current register values before a procedure call. We will adopt a convention by which the internal variables used as temporaries are of the form Temp&N, where N is the index of the temporary, starting at 1. Since & cannot appear in an ordinary Micro variable, no conflict between variables and temporaries can arise.

2.5.3. Action Symbols

As explained in Chapter 1, the bulk of a translation is done by semantic routines called by the parser. Exactly when a given semantic routine is to be called is up to the compiler writer. *Action symbols* can be added to a grammar to specify when semantic processing should take place. Action symbols, denoted by #name in the examples that follow, can be placed anywhere in the RHS of a production. Corresponding to each action symbol is a semantic routine. Thus action symbol #add corresponds to a semantic routine named **add()**. When parsing procedures are created, calls to semantic routines or in-line code segments to do semantic processing are inserted in the positions designated by action symbols. If a grammar containing action symbols is given as input to a parser generator, the generator must include appropriate information in the tables it produces to trigger calls to semantic routines at corresponding times during the parsing process.

Action symbols have no impact on the language recognized by a parser driven by a CFG. Thus, they are not actually part of the syntax the CFG specifies. In this context, action symbols serve to "comment" a CFG, indicating when semantic actions need to be executed. When a CFG is used as the input to a parser generator, the action symbols are more than a comment. They tell the parser generator when the corresponding semantic routines must be called.

2.5.4. **Semantic Information**

An important issue in the design of semantic routines is the specification of the data on which they operate and the information they produce. Our approach will be to associate a *semantic record* with each kind of grammar symbol (ID, INTLITERAL, <expression>, and so on). Each different symbol will have a distinct record containing information appropriate for that symbol. Each occurrence of the same kind of symbol will have exactly the same kind of data in its semantic record. Thus an ID can be represented by different kinds of data than an INTLITERAL, but all IDs will have the same format for their semantic records. It is possible for a symbol to have a null semantic record if it requires no semantic data. For example, a semicolon requires no semantic record.

The semantic record for a terminal contains the token's **token_buffer** or some value derived from it. For example, the value of an INTLITERAL, represented as an object of type integer, is derived from the text of the token. Such a record is produced by a semantic routine called just after the parser successfully matches a token against an expected terminal symbol.

The semantic record for a nonterminal is created by a semantic routine that has access to information about any of the symbols on the RHS of the production. If some of these symbols are nonterminals, their corresponding semantic records come from semantic routine calls specified within their own productions. To see how this works, consider

<expression> → <primary> + <primary> #add

A semantic record will be generated for each of the <primary>'s in the RHS of the production. These semantic records record data about each of the operands (for example, where it is stored or what its value is). When **add()** is called, it must be given these records as parameters. It uses them to generate the appropriate code, then produces a new semantic record corresponding to <expression> that records necessary information about the expression just processed.

When a recursive descent parser is used, these semantic records may be stored as local variables of the parsing routines. Records containing the semantic information for nonterminal symbols may be returned as result parameters by corresponding parsing routines. When a table-driven parser is used, an explicit *semantic stack* is typically necessary, as described in Chapter 8, to store semantic records between semantic routine calls.

To define the semantic records, we examine each symbol in the CFG and decide what, if any, semantic information needs to be stored for that symbol. Figure 2.8 shows the semantic records **op_rec** and **expr_rec** required to translate Micro. (**expr_rec** is the first use of an anonymous union, which is not part of standard C.)

All other symbols need no associated semantic information and thus have *null* semantic records. For reasons of efficiency, null records are not explicitly defined and stored anywhere. We can, however, add fields to a semantic record if we decide extra data is needed. In deciding on semantic records, we are really deciding what parameters a semantic routine will have.

```
#define MAXIDLEN          33
typedef char string[MAXIDLEN];

typedef struct operator {      /* for operators */
    enum op { PLUS, MINUS } operator;
} op_rec;

/* expression types */
enum expr { IDEXPR, LITERALEXPR, TEMPEXPR };

/* for <primary> and <expression> */
typedef struct expression {
    enum expr kind;
    union {
        string name;       /* for IDEXPR, TEMPEXPR */
        int val;           /* for LITERALEXPR */
    };
} expr_rec;
```

Figure 2.8   Semantic Records for Micro Grammar Symbols

2.5.5. Action Symbols for Micro

Figure 2.9 illustrates a CFG for Micro that includes action symbols. One production has been added from the previous grammar:

<ident> → ID #process_id

This production is useful because ID appeared in several different contexts in the previous grammar, and we need to call **process_id()** immediately after the parser matches any occurrence of an ID (to access the characters in the **token_buffer** and build an appropriate semantic record). Substituting <ident> for ID everywhere in the grammar is a simple way to ensure that **process_id()** is always called.

We will utilize a few auxiliary routines in our compiler: **generate()** will take four string arguments corresponding to the operation code, two operands, and the result field. It will produce a correctly formated instruction in an output file. **extract()** will take a semantic record and return a string corresponding to the semantic information it contains. This string may be an identifier, an op code, a literal, and so on. The extracted information is fed to **generate()** to create a complete instruction.

Our symbol table routines will be simple because Micro is simple. For example, we need not store any type information as an attribute of an identifier because all identifiers represent integer variables. Because we are generating assembly language instructions that will allow the assembler to allocate storage for variables, we need not record any address information as an

```
<program>           → #start begin <statement list> end
<statement list>    → <statement> {<statement>}
<statement>         → <ident> := <expression> #assign ;
<statement>         → read ( <id list> ) ;
<statement>         → write ( <expr list> ) ;
<id list>           → <ident> #read_id {, <ident> #read_id }
<expr list>         → <expression> #write_expr
                         {, <expression> #write_expr}
<expression>        → <primary>
                         {<add op> <primary> #gen_infix}
<primary>           → ( <expression> )
<primary>           → <ident>
<primary>           → INTLITERAL #process_literal
<add op>            → PLUSOP #process_op
<add op>            → MINUSOP #process_op
<ident>             → ID #process_id
<system goal>       → <program> SCANEOF #finish
```

Figure 2.9   Grammar for Micro with Action Symbols

attribute of an identifier. In fact, no explicit attributes will be used. The only information of interest about an identifier is whether it is already in the symbol table, so the compiler will know if it must generate an instruction that will cause space allocation. The specifications of our symbol table routines are

```
/* Is s in the symbol table? */
extern int lookup(string s);

/* Put s unconditionally into symbol table. */
extern void enter(string s);
```

An auxiliary routine used by a number of the semantic routines is **check_id()**:

```
void check_id(string s)
{
    if (! lookup(s)) {
        enter(s);
        generate("Declare", s, "Integer", "");
    }
}
```

lookup() will check whether an entry named **s** is in the symbol table. We will not need to store anything except the name of a symbol in the symbol table. **enter()** will enter string **s** into the symbol table unconditionally. Thus, if necessary, **check_id()** will declare a variable by entering it in the symbol table and then generating an assembler directive to reserve space for it. In our assembly language, Declare is a pseudo-op that declares a name to the assembler and defines its type. It works for simple, nonstructured global variables. The assembler decides how much space is required for the variable and exactly where it will be allocated.

We also need a routine to allocate temporaries. As mentioned earlier, we will allocate temporaries just like variables. The only difference is that temporary names will be generated by the compiler and are not meaningful in a Micro program. They will have the names Temp&1, Temp&2, and so forth. In a more realistic compiler, temporaries are generally treated as virtual registers, with the code generator having the job of mapping them to real registers, as far as possible. The function **get_temp()** allocates temporaries.

```c
char *get_temp(void)
{
    /* max temporary allocated so far */
    static int max_temp = 0;
    static char tempname[MAXIDLEN];

    max_temp++;
    sprintf(tempname, "Temp&%d", max_temp);
    check_id(tempname);
    return tempname;
}
```

We now have the auxiliary routines necessary to define the semantic routines corresponding to Micro's action symbols. They appear in Figure 2.10.

```c
void start(void)
{
    /* Semantic initializations, none needed. */
}


void finish(void)
{
    /* Generate code to finish program. */
    generate("Halt", "", "", "");
}


void assign(expr_rec target, expr_rec source)
{
    /* Generate code for assignment. */
    generate("Store", extract(source),
            target.name, "");
}
```

```c
op_rec process_op(void)
{
    /* Produce operator descriptor. */
    op_rec o;

    if (current_token == PLUSOP)
        o.operator = PLUS;
    else
        o.operator = MINUS;
    return o;
}


expr_rec gen_infix(expr_rec e1, op_rec op,
                    expr_rec e2)
{
    expr_rec e_rec;
    /* An expr_rec with temp variant set. */
    e_rec.kind = TEMPEXPR;

    /*
     * Generate code for infix operation.
     * Get result temp and set up semantic record
     * for result.
     */
    strcpy(erec.name, get_temp());
    generate(extract(op), extract(e1),
            extract(e2), erec.name);
    return erec;
}


void read_id(expr_rec in_var)
{
    /* Generate code for read. */
    generate("Read", in_var.name,
            "Integer", "");
}


expr_rec process_id(void)
{
    expr_rec t;

    /*
     * Declare ID and build a
     * corresponding semantic record.
     */
    check_id(token_buffer);
    t.kind = IDEXPR;
    strcpy(t.name, token_buffer);
    return t;
}
```

```
expr_rec process_literal(void)
{
    expr_rec t;

    /*
     * Convert literal to a numeric representation
     * and build semantic record.
     */
    t.kind = LITERALEXPR;
    (void) sscanf(token_buffer, "%d", & t.val);
    return t;
}


void write_expr(expr_rec out_expr)
{
    generate("Write", extract(out_expr),
            "Integer", "");
}
```

Figure 2.10   Action Routines for Micro

```
void expression(expr_rec *result)
{
    expr_rec left_operand, right_operand;
    op_rec op;

    primary(& left_operand);
    while (next_token() == PLUSOP ||
            next_token() == MINUSOP) {
        add_op(& op);
        primary(& right_operand);
        left_operand = gen_infix(left_operand, op,
                                    right_operand);
    }
    *result = left_operand;
}
```

Figure 2.11   A Parsing Procedure Including Semantic
Processing

Given these semantic routines, we now look again at one of our parsing routines to see how it is altered to handle the inclusion of semantic processing. The procedure **expression()**, shown in Figure 2.11, has been altered to produce an **expr_rec** as an output parameter. Upon return, this **expr_rec** contains the semantic information about the expression recognized by **expression()**. The body of the procedure includes internal variables used to store the semantic records generated by calls to other parsing procedures and used in a call to the code generation routine **gen_infix()**. (Output parameters in C are accomplished by using *pointers* to the semantic records that are to be affected.)

Example of Recursive Descent Parsing and Translation

As an example, consider the compilation of the following simple Micro program:

begin A := BB − 314 + A ; **end** SCANEOF

Following is a trace of the steps taken by the parser while processing this program, along with the input remaining at each step and the code that would be generated during the processing. The parser actions of interest are calling a parsing routine to find a string in the input to match a nonterminal in the grammar, calling **match()** to match a grammar terminal to an input token, and invoking semantic action routines.

Step	Parser Action	Remaining Input	Generated Code
(1)	Call **system_goal()**	**begin** A:=BB–314+A ; **end** SCANEOF	
(2)	Call **program()**	**begin** A:=BB–314+A ; **end** SCANEOF	
(3)	Semantic Action: **start()**	**begin** A:=BB–314+A ; **end** SCANEOF	
(4)	**match(BEGIN)**	**begin** A:=BB–314+A ; **end** SCANEOF	
(5)	Call **statement_list()**	A:=BB–314+A ; **end** SCANEOF	
(6)	Call **statement()**	A:=BB–314+A ; **end** SCANEOF	
(7)	Call **ident()**	A:=BB–314+A ; **end** SCANEOF	
(8)	**match(ID)**	A:=BB–314+A ; **end** SCANEOF	
(9)	Semantic Action: **process_id()**	:=BB–314+A ; **end** SCANEOF	Declare A,Integer
(10)	**match(ASSIGNOP)**	:=BB–314+A ; **end** SCANEOF	
(11)	Call **expression()**	BB–314+A ; **end** SCANEOF	
(12)	Call **primary()**	BB–314+A ; **end** SCANEOF	
(13)	Call **ident()**	BB–314+A ; **end** SCANEOF	
(14)	**match(ID)**	BB–314+A ; **end** SCANEOF	
(15)	Semantic Action: **process_id()**	–314+A ; **end** SCANEOF	Declare BB,Integer
(16)	Call **add_op()**	–314+A ; **end** SCANEOF	
(17)	**match(MINUSOP)**	–314+A ; **end** SCANEOF	
(18)	Semantic Action: **process_op()**	314+A ; **end** SCANEOF	
(19)	Call **primary()**	314+A ; **end** SCANEOF	
(20)	**match(INTLITERAL)**	314+A ; **end** SCANEOF	
(21)	Semantic Action: **process_literal()**	+A ; **end** SCANEOF	
(22)	Semantic Action: **gen_infix()**	+A ; **end** SCANEOF	Declare Temp&1,Integer Sub BB,314,Temp&1
(23)	Call **add_op()**	+A ; **end** SCANEOF	

(24)	`match(PLUSOP)`	+A ; **end** SCANEOF	
(25)	Semantic Action: `process_op()`	A ; **end** SCANEOF	
(26)	Call `primary()`	A ; **end** SCANEOF	
(27)	Call `ident()`	A ; **end** SCANEOF	
(28)	`match(ID)`	A ; **end** SCANEOF	
(29)	Semantic Action: `process_id()`	; **end** SCANEOF	
(30)	Semantic Action: `gen_infix()`	; **end** SCANEOF	Declare Temp&2,Integer Add Temp&1,A,Temp&2 Store Temp&2,A
(31)	Semantic Action: `assign()`	; **end** SCANEOF	
(32)	`match(SEMICOLON)`	; **end** SCANEOF	
(33)	`match(END)`	**end** SCANEOF	
(34)	`match(SCANEOF)`	SCANEOF	
(35)	Semantic Action: `finish()`		Halt

The code generated for

     begin A := BB − 314 + A ; **end** SCANEOF

is summarized below. It is easy to verify that it is correct.

```
Declare  A,Integer
Declare  BB,Integer
Declare Temp&1,Integer
Sub  BB,314,Temp&1
Declare Temp&2,Integer
Add  Temp&1,A,Temp&2
Store  Temp&2,A
Halt
```

Exercises

1. Rewrite the C code in Figure 2.3 using a C **switch** statement instead of the sequence of **if**s and **else**s. Which version do you prefer? Why?

2. Why can't **EOF** be used as an enumeration literal instead of **SCANEOF**?

3. Implement single character input with either lookahead or pushback in a language without such facilities (e.g., Pascal, Modula-2). Keep in mind the need for both an end-of-line marker and an end-of-file marker.

4. Implement the routines necessary for saving token strings, **buffer_char()** and **clear_buffer()**, and identifying reserved words, **check_reserved()**. Keep the nature of C strings in mind as you do so.

5. The addition of the nonterminal <ident> to the grammar for Micro, as shown in Figure 2.9, will require several changes in the recursive descent parsing routines. Rewrite all the routines that would have to be modified to implement this change.

6. Add code for semantic processing to all parsing routines where it is required, using the **expression()** procedure in Figure 2.11 as a model.

7. A practical parser must have some way of responding to syntax errors encountered in the middle of a parse. The parser for Micro uses recursive descent parsing, requiring that each nonterminal in the grammar have a separate procedure written for it. Using this parsing technique potentially requires that error handling be integrated with each of the parsing procedures. From examination of our parsing procedures for Micro, it is apparent that syntax errors can be detected in either of two ways: **match()** may fail to find the correct token in the source program, or a parsing procedure that examines **next_token()** in a **switch** or **if** statement may fail to find an acceptable token. In the latter case, the Micro parsing routines call **syntax_error()**. **match()** and **syntax_error()** must be designed to take some actions that will allow parsing to continue.

    match() could be made into a boolean function in order to indicate whether the required token was found in the input, but such a change would greatly complicate every parsing procedure with any calls to it. A simple alternative would be for **match()** to handle errors by simply pretending that it saw the correct token. In such a case, we must decide if **match()** should consume the incorrect token that it found in the token stream, as it does in the case of a successful match. What are the implications of and the tradeoffs between the two alternative approaches?

    If the second kind of syntax error is encountered, no such simple mechanism is possible, because any of a set of tokens is acceptable to continue the parse. Handling these errors will require explicit reprogramming of some parsing procedures. Suggest a general way that procedures like **statement()** might be changed to handle syntax errors.

8. One optimization that can be implemented even in a compiler as simple as our Micro compiler is *constant folding*, the evaluation of constant expressions at compile-time. If both operands of an expression are constants, there is no need to generate code to evaluate the expression because its value can be determined by the compiler. Identify the semantic action routines that must be changed to implement constant folding, and make the appropriate changes.

9. Suppose you are writing an interpreter for Micro instead of a compiler. The interpreter will execute Micro code as it is being parsed rather than generating assembly language for later execution. How will the semantic action routines and semantic records have to be changed to support interpretation?

10. One useful extension to Micro would be the inclusion of *conditional expressions*, a new form of expression with the following syntax: (E_1 | E_2 |

E_3). When this expression is evaluated, E_2 is returned as the value if E_1 is not zero; otherwise, E_3 is the value of the expression.

(a) Write the appropriate production to add conditional expressions to Micro, including action symbols to specify calls to any required action routines.

(b) Presume the availability of a new assembly language instruction Skip A, which causes the next instruction to be skipped if the operand A evaluates to any value other than 0. Write the action routines necessary to implement conditional expressions.

(c) Don't forget to augment the scanner, too!

CHAPTER 3

Scanning—
Theory and Practice

3.1. Overview

The primary function of a scanner is to group input characters into tokens. A scanner is sometimes called a *lexical analyzer,* and the two terms may be used interchangeably. The Micro scanner we saw in Chapter 2 was quite simple and could easily be coded by any competent programmer. We will now delve into the issues involved in creating scanners for more comprehensive programming languages.

We will introduce *formal notations* for specifying the precise structure of tokens. At first glance this may seem unnecessary, given the simple token structure found in most programming languages. The issue here is that token structure can be more detailed than we might expect. For example, we are all familiar with simple quoted strings in Pascal. The body of a string can be any sequence of characters *except* a quote character (which must be doubled). But is this simple definition really correct? Can a newline character appear in a string? Probably not, as a string split across a line would be difficult to read. "Runaway strings," which lack a closing quote, are much harder to detect if newlines are allowed. C compromises and allows newlines in strings if they have been escaped, whereas Pascal forbids them. Ada goes further still and forbids all unprintable characters (precisely because they are normally unreadable). Similarly, are null strings (of length zero) allowed? Pascal forbids them, because in Pascal a string is a **packed array of** characters, and zero length arrays are disallowed. Ada and C, on the other hand, do allow null strings.

A precise definition of tokens is obviously necessary to ensure that lexical rules are properly enforced. Formal definitions also allow a language designer to anticipate design flaws. For example, virtually all languages allow fixed decimal numbers, such as 0.1 or 10.01. But should .1 or 10. be allowed? In FORTRAN and C they are allowed, but in Pascal and Ada they are not—and for a very interesting reason. Scanners normally seek to make a token as long as possible so that, for example, ABC is scanned as one identifier rather than three. But now consider the character sequence 1..10. In Pascal and Ada, we wish this to be interpreted as a range specifier (1 to 10). If we were careless in our token definitions, we might well scan 1..10 as two real literals, 1. and .10, which would lead to an immediate (and unexpected) syntax error. (The fact that two reals *cannot* be adjacent is reflected in the CFG, which is enforced by the parser, not the scanner.)

Given a formal specification of token and program structure, it is possible to examine a language for design flaws. For example, we could then consider all pairs of tokens that can be adjacent and determine whether the catenation of the two might be incorrectly scanned. If so, a separator might be required (as is the case for adjacent identifiers and reserved words), or the lexical or program syntax might need to be redesigned. The point is that language design is far more involved than we might expect, and formal specifications allow flaws to be discovered before the design is completed.

All scanners, independent of the tokens to be recognized, perform much the same function. Thus writing a scanner from scratch means reimplementing components common to all scanners and is a significant duplication of effort. The goal of a *scanner generator* is to limit the effort in building a scanner to specifying which tokens the scanner is to recognize. Using a formal notation, we tell the scanner generator what tokens we want recognized; it is the generator's responsibility to produce a scanner that meets our specification. Some generators do not produce an entire scanner; rather, they produce tables that can be used with a standard driver program. The combination of generated tables and standard driver yields the desired custom scanner.

Programming a scanner generator is an example of *nonprocedural programming*. That is, unlike ordinary programming, which we call *procedural*, we do not tell a scanner generator *how* to scan but simply *what* we want scanned. This is a higher-level approach and in many ways a more natural one. Much recent research in computer science is directed toward nonprocedural programming styles. (Database query languages and Prolog, a "logic" programming language, are nonprocedural.) Nonprocedural programming is most successful in limited domains, such as scanning, where the range of implementation decisions that must be *automatically* made is limited. Nonetheless, a long-standing (and as yet unrealized) goal of computer scientists is to generate an entire compiler from a specification of the properties of the source language and target computer.

In the following sections, we first introduce a *regular expression* notation that is very well suited to the formal definition of tokens. Next, the correspondence between regular expressions and *finite automata* will be studied. Finite automata are especially useful because they can be "executed" to read characters and group them into tokens. Two scanner generators, *ScanGen* and *Lex*, will be considered in some detail. Each takes token definitions (in the form of regular expressions). ScanGen produces tables that can used with a small scanner driver. Lex produces a complete scanner subprogram, ready to be compiled and used. Our next topic of discussion is the practical considerations needed to build a scanner and integrate it with the rest of the compiler. These considerations include anticipating the tokens and contexts that may complicate scanning, as well as recovering from lexical errors. We conclude the chapter with a section that explains how scanner generators translate regular expressions into finite automata. Readers who wish to view a scanner generator as simply a black box may skip this section. However, the material does serve to reinforce the concepts of regular expressions and finite automata introduced earlier. The section also illustrates how finite automata can be built, merged, simplified, and even optimized.

3.2. **Regular Expressions**

Regular expressions are a convenient means of specifying certain simple (though possibly infinite) sets of strings. They are of practical interest because regular expressions can be used to specify the structure of the tokens used in a programming language. In particular, regular expressions can be used to program a scanner generator.

The sets of strings defined by *regular expressions* are termed *regular sets*. We start with a finite character set, or *vocabulary* (denoted V). This vocabulary is normally the character set used to form tokens. An empty or null string is allowed (denoted λ, "lambda"). Strings are built from characters in V via *catenation* (for example, :=, begin, 123). The null string, when catenated with any string s, yields s. That is, $s\lambda \equiv \lambda s \equiv s$.

Catenation can be extended to sets of strings as follows: Let P and Q be sets of strings. Then string $s \in (P\,Q)$ if and only if s can be broken into two pieces: $s = s_1 s_2$ such that $s_1 \in P$ and $s_2 \in Q$. Small finite sets are conveniently represented by listing their elements, which can be individual characters or strings of characters. Parentheses are used to delimit expressions, and |, the alternation operator, is used to separate alternatives.

The characters (,), ', *, +, and | are *meta-characters* (punctuation and regular expression operators). Meta-characters can be quoted when used as ordinary characters to avoid ambiguity. (Any character or string may be quoted, but unnecessary quotation is avoided to enhance readability.) For example:

Delim = ('(' | ')' | := | ; | , | '+' | − | '*' | / | = | $$$)

Alternation can be extended to sets of strings. Let P and Q be sets of strings. Then string $s \in (P \mid Q)$ if and only if $s \in P$ or $s \in Q$. Large (or infinite) sets are conveniently represented by operations on finite sets of characters and strings. Catenation and alternation may be used. A third operation, *Kleene closure,* is also allowed. The operator * will represent the postfix Kleene closure operator. Let P be a set of strings. String $s \in P^*$ if and only if s can be broken into zero or more pieces: $s = s_1 s_2 s_3 \cdots s_n$ such that each $s_i \in P$. A string in P^* is the catenation of zero or more selections (possibly repeated) from P. (We explicitly allow $n = 0$, so that λ is always in P^*.)

Regular expressions are defined as follows. Each regular expression denotes a set of strings (a *regular set*).

- $\varnothing$ is a regular expression denoting the empty set (the set containing no strings).

- λ is a regular expression denoting the set that contains only the empty string. Note that this set is not the same as the empty set, because it contains one element.

- A string s is a regular expression denoting a set containing only s. If s contains meta-characters, s can be quoted to avoid ambiguity.

- If A and B are regular expressions, then $A \mid B$, $A\,B$, and A^* are also regular expressions, denoting the alternation, catenation, and Kleene closure of the corresponding regular sets.

Any finite set of strings can be represented by a regular expression of the form $(s_1 \mid s_2 \mid \cdots \mid s_k)$.

We often utilize the following operations as a notational convenience. They are not strictly necessary, because their effect can be obtained (albeit somewhat clumsily) using the three standard regular operators (alternation, catenation, Kleene closure):

- P^+ denotes all strings consisting of *one* or more strings in P catenated together: $P^* = (P^+ \mid \lambda)$ and $P^+ = P\,P^*$.

- If A is a set of characters, Not(A) denotes $(V − A)$; that is, all characters in V not included in A. Since Not(A) is finite, it is trivially regular. It is possible to extend Not to strings, rather than just V. That is, if S is a set of strings, we can define Not(S) to be $(V^* − S)$. Although it may be infinite, this set is also regular (see Exercise 20).

- If k is a constant, the set A^k represents all strings formed by catenating k (not necessarily different) strings from A. That is, $A^k = (A\ A\ A\ \cdots)$ (k copies).

We now illustrate how regular expressions can be used to specify tokens. Let

$$D = (0 \mid \cdots \mid 9) \quad L = (A \mid \cdots \mid Z)$$

Then

- A comment that begins with -- and ends with Eol (end of line) can be defined as:

    Comment = -- Not(Eol)* Eol

- A fixed decimal literal can be defined as:

    Lit = D^+ . D^+

- An identifier, composed of letters, digits, and underscores, that begins with a letter, ends with a letter or digit, and contains no consecutive underscores, can be defined as:

    ID = L (L $\mid$ D)* (_ (L $\mid$ D)$^+$)*

- A more complicated example is a comment delimited by ## markers, which allows *single* #'s within the comment body:

    Comment2 = ## ((# $\mid$ λ) Not(#))* ##

All finite sets and many infinite sets, such as those just listed, are regular. But not all infinite sets are regular. For example, consider { [^{i}]^i | i ≥ 1 }, which is the set of balanced brackets of the form [[[[[$\cdots$]]]]]. This is a well-known set that is not regular. The problem is that any regular set either does not get *all* balanced nestings or it includes extra, unwanted strings. (Exercise 16 proves this.)

It is easy to write a CFG that defines balanced brackets precisely. All regular sets can be defined by CFGs; thus, the bracket example shows that CFGs are a more powerful descriptive mechanism than regular expressions. Regular expressions are, however, quite adequate for specifying token-level syntax.

3.3. Finite Automata and Scanners

A *finite automaton* (FA) can be used to recognize the tokens specified by a regular expression. An FA is a simple, idealized computer that recognizes strings belonging to regular sets. It consists of:

- A finite set of *states*
- A set of *transitions* (or *moves*) from one state to another, labeled with characters in V
- A special *start* state
- A set of *final*, or *accepting*, states

Finite automata can be represented graphically using *transition diagrams*:

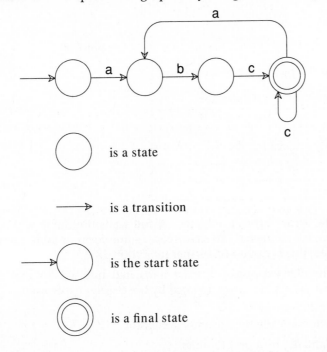

With these diagrams, we start at the start state. If the next input character matches the label on a transition from the current state, we go to the state it points to. If no move is possible, we stop. If we finish in a final state, the sequence of characters read is a *valid* token; otherwise, we do not have a valid token. In the diagram shown, the valid tokens are the strings described by the regular expression (a b (c)$^+$)$^+$.

As an abbreviation, a transition may be labeled with more than one character (for example, Not(c)). The transition may be taken if the current input character matches any of the characters labeling the transition.

If an FA always has a *unique* transition (for a given state and character), the FA is *deterministic* (that is, a deterministic FA, or DFA). Deterministic finite automata are often used to drive a scanner. A DFA is conveniently represented in a computer by a *transition table.* A transition table, T, is indexed by a DFA state and a vocabulary symbol. Table entries are either a DFA state or an error flag. If we are in state s, and read character c, then T[s][c] will be the next state we visit, or it will be an error flag indicating that c cannot be part of the current token. For example, the regular expression

$$-- \, \text{Not(Eol)}^* \, \text{Eol}$$

which defines an Ada comment, might be translated into

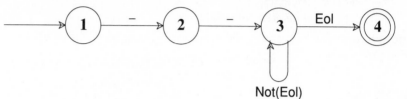

The corresponding transition table is

State	Character				
	–	Eol	a	b	$\cdots$
1	2				
2	3				
3	3	4	3	3	3
4					

In this table, error entries are blank. A full transition table will contain one column for each character. To save space, some form of table compression is often utilized; this is discussed further in Section 3.4.1.

Any regular expression can be translated into a DFA that accepts (as valid tokens) the set of strings denoted by the regular expression. This translation can be done

- Automatically by a scanner generator

- Manually by a programmer

A DFA can be implemented as either a transition table "interpreted" by a driver program or "directly" into the control logic of a program (each statement will correspond to a DFA state). For example, suppose **current_char** is the current input character. Using the DFA for the Ada comments illustrated above, the two approaches would produce the programs illustrated in Figures 3.1 and 3.2.

The first form is commonly used with a scanner generator; it is language-independent. This form is a simple driver that can scan *any* token if the transition table (stored in T) is properly set. The latter form is commonly produced by hand. Here, the token being scanned is "hardwired" into the code.

```
/*
 * Note: current_char is already set to
 * the current input character.
 */
state = initial_state;
while (TRUE) {
    next_state = T[state][current_char];
    if (nextstate == ERROR)
        break;
    state = next_state;
    if (current_char == EOF)
        break;
    current_char = getchar();
}
if (is_final_state(state))
    /* Return or process valid token. */
else
    lexical_error(current_char);
```

Figure 3.1   Scanner Driver Interpreting a Transition Table

```
if (current_char == '-') {
    current_char = getchar();
    if (current_char == '-') {
        do
            current_char = getchar();
        while (current_char != '\n');
    } else {
        ungetc(current_char, stdin);
        lexical_error(current_char);
    }
}
else
    lexical_error(current_char);
/* Return or process valid token. */
```

Figure 3.2   Scanner with Fixed Token Definition

The following are two more examples of regular expressions and their corresponding DFAs:

- A FORTRAN-like real literal (which requires digits on either or both sides of a decimal point, or just a string of digits) can be defined as

$$\text{RealLit} = (D^+ \ (\lambda \ | \ .)) \ | \ (D^* \ . \ D^+)$$

which corresponds to the DFA

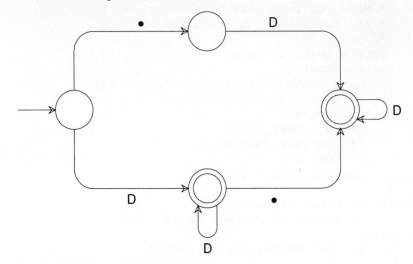

- An identifier consisting of letters, digits, and underscores, with no adjacent or trailing underscores, may be defined as

$$ID = L\,(L\mid D)^*\,(\,\_\,(L\mid D)^+\,)^*$$

which corresponds to the DFA

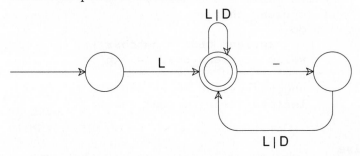

It is possible to add an output facility to an FA; this makes the FA a *transducer*. As characters are read, they can be transformed and catenated to an output string. For our purposes, we shall limit the transformation operations to saving or deleting input characters. After a token is recognized, the transformed input can be passed to other compiler phases for further processing. We use this notation:

$$\xrightarrow{\quad a \quad}$$ means save a in a token buffer

$$\xrightarrow{\quad T(a) \quad}$$ means don't save a (Toss it away)

For example, for comments, we might write

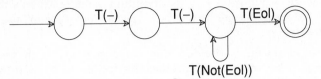

T(Not(Eol))

A more interesting example is given by quoted strings, according to the regular expression

$$(" (Not(") | " ")^* ")$$

A corresponding transducer might be

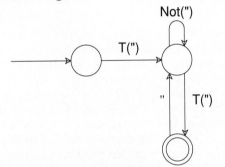

The input """"Hi"""" would produce output "Hi".

3.4. Using a Scanner Generator

In this section, we illustrate the use of two popular scanner generators, ScanGen and Lex. Complete descriptions of ScanGen and Lex can be found in Appendix B and in Lesk and Schmidt (1975). Our purpose here is to show how regular expressions and related information are presented to generators. A good way to learn to use a scanner generator is to start with the simple examples presented here and then gradually generalize them to solve the problem at hand. To inexperienced readers, scanner specifications can appear arcane. It is best to keep in mind that the key is always the specification of tokens as regular expressions; the rest is there simply to increase efficiency and handle various details.

3.4.1. ScanGen

ScanGen is a scanner generator designed to be readily transportable and highly language- and machine-independent. ScanGen produces tables that are used by a driver routine to create a complete scanner. The general structure of a ScanGen driver is discussed in the next section. ScanGen is in use at a number of universities and research laboratories throughout the world.

We will learn how tokens are defined in ScanGen by examining the definition shown in Figure 3.3. This definition extends Micro's token set to include real and string literals as well as a special "error token" used to recognize runaway strings.

Input to ScanGen is divided into three sections, each headed by a reserved word. The first section specifies the options to be used by ScanGen. In our example, a listing of the input is to be made, output tables are to be produced, and a state optimization phase is to be included.

The second section defines *character classes.* In our discussion of finite automata, we assumed that state transitions were labeled by characters drawn from a finite vocabulary. In practice, this vocabulary would be some computer character set, probably ASCII or EBCDIC. Since the size of the transition table that defines an FA is the product of the number of states and the number of characters, the size of the character set is an important issue.

It is easy to see that characters naturally fall into classes, in which all characters in a class are treated identically in a regular expression or FA. In the character class section we define class names in terms of sequences or ranges of characters. A class corresponding to a single character is naturally permitted, and the decimal equivalent of a character can be used for unprintable characters. Any character not mentioned in any character class definition is ignored. If we wish, a class "illegal" can be defined to force a scanner error (and error message). All regular expressions and finite automata are defined in terms of character classes. ScanGen produces a vector, mapping characters to character classes. Use of character classes makes regular expressions more readable and decreases (quite significantly) the size of the transition table.

For a typical programming language, ScanGen produces about 50 states and 30 character classes. Assuming two bytes per entry (one for an **action** flag and one for the **next_state** value), this representation implies a transition table size of about 3000 bytes, using an ordinary array structure. Because the transition table is consulted for every input character, fast access to table entries is important. Thus if the space requirements for an ordinary two-dimensional array can be met, this format may be the best representation for the scanner's transition table.

Nonetheless, compaction of the transition table may be necessary. A number of table compaction techniques are discussed in Chapter 17. These techniques may be used to reduce transition table sizes, but caution is required. In particular, the extra overhead of access to compacted tables may overshadow space savings. It is probably wise to measure the speed and size costs of any compaction scheme before it is adopted.

ScanGen's final section defines tokens in terms of regular expressions, using infix "." (catenation) and "," (alternation), postfix * (Kleene closure) and + (positive closure), and unary **Not**. Catenation is made explicit to enhance readability and simplify translation of regular expressions. **Epsilon** represents a regular expression matching λ. (In some texts, the empty string is represented by ε. We prefer λ.) Regular expressions not directly defining tokens (such as **Letter**) may be defined for use in other regular expressions.

```
Options
    List, tables, optimize

Class
    E            = 'E', 'e';
    OtherLetter  = 'A'..'D','F'..'Z','a'..'d','f'..'z';
    Digit        = '0'..'9';
    Blank        = ' ';
    Dot          = '.';
    Plus         = '+';
    Minus        = '-';
    Equal        = '=';
    Colon        = ':';
    Comma        = ',';
    Semicolon    = ';';
    Lparen       = '(';
    Rparen       = ')';
    Quote        = '"';
    Underscore   = '_';
    Tab          = 9;
    Linefeed     = 10;

Definition
    Token EmptySpace {0} = (Blank, Linefeed, Tab)+;
    Token Comment {0} =
        Minus . Minus . (Not(Linefeed))* . Linefeed;
    Letter = E, OtherLetter;
    Token Identifier {1} = Letter.(Letter,Digit,Underscore)*
        Except
            'Begin' {4},
            'End'   {5},
            'Read'  {6},
            'Write' {7};
    Token IntLit {2,1} = Digit+;
    Token RealLit {2,2} = IntLit.Dot.IntLit.
            (Epsilon, E.(Epsilon, Plus, Minus).IntLit);
    Token StrLit {2,3} = Quote{Toss}.
        (Not(Quote,Linefeed),Quote{Toss}.Quote)* . Quote{Toss};
    Token RunOnStringLit {3} = Quote{Toss}.
        (Not(Quote, Linefeed), Quote{Toss}.Quote)*
            . Linefeed{Toss};
    Token LparenToken {8} = Lparen;
    Token RparenToken {9} = Rparen;
    Token SemicolonToken {10} = Semicolon;
    Token CommaToken {11} = Comma;
    Token AssignOp {12} = Colon . Equal;
    Token PlusOp {13} = Plus;
    Token MinusOp {14} = Minus;
```

Figure 3.3   ScanGen Definition for Extended Micro

A token definition is of the form

```
Token name{major,minor} = regular expression ;
```

All of the instances of a token are considered equivalent by the parser, but sometimes subclasses of the same token are recognized by different regular expressions. In Figure 3.3, three distinct regular expressions are used to recognize integer, real, and string literals. Token subclasses may have different semantic interpretations. For example, different literal classes require different translations into internal form. Hence a useful feature for token description is the ability to label tokens with both a *major token code* and a *minor token code*. The major token code identifies the token to the parser; the minor code may be used by semantic processing routines. In a token definition, major and minor are integer values; the minor code is optional (it defaults to zero).

The same character sequence may be matched by more than one regular expression. In such cases, the regular expression listed earliest in the specification takes precedence; its major and minor codes are not altered.

Some tokens may be "noise tokens" (like comments) that must be deleted (once recognized) rather than returned to the parser. By convention in ScanGen, a major code of zero indicates that the token is to be deleted rather than passed. It is often useful to define a *blank token* (composed of blanks, tabs, and newlines) that consumes the white space between interesting tokens. In Figure 3.3, token **EmptySpace** serves this purpose. Naturally it is marked for deletion.

A token definition may have an *exception clause* (headed by **Except**) that names a list of exceptions. Each exception (defined by a literal with major and minor codes) must match the associated regular expression. ScanGen produces a sorted list of exceptions (suitable for binary search) and a flag indicating that the token definition has exceptions. When a token matching the regular expression is found, the scanner driver must search the exception list to decide what token has been recognized.

Exception lists are well suited for those cases in which a number of distinct tokens have a similar lexical structure. Reserved words, which often overlap lexically with identifiers, are an example of this problem. Handling reserved words as exceptions to identifiers simplifies specification and also can reduce the size of the FA needed by the scanner. This issue is discussed further in Section 3.5.

In regular expressions, character class names or **Not** expressions may be suffixed with **{Toss}**. When a character class name (or complemented class) marked with **{Toss}** is matched in a regular expression, the character matched is tossed away rather than saved. All character class names and **Not** expressions not marked with **{Toss}** are implicitly assumed to save any characters they match.

ScanGen is normally configured for either the ASCII or EBCDIC character sets. It can, however, be compiled to accept pseudocharacters by increasing a character set size parameter. This allows the end-of-file condition to be handled cleanly. In particular, when end of file is signaled, a read character routine can return an Eof pseudocharacter that comprises the definition of an Eof token. (The Eof token was denoted **SCANEOF** in Chapter 2. The C Standard I/O library calls it **EOF**.)

Alternatively, the scanner driver can be modified to test for end of file before consulting the scanner's transition table. If end of file is true when the scanner is called, it immediately returns the Eof token. If end of file becomes true while scanning, the current token is completed and returned; the Eof token will be returned when the scanner is next called.

A ScanGen Driver

In this section we outline driver routines that may be used with ScanGen-generated tables to implement a scanner.

Normally, while scanning, an FA must look ahead. That is, it must examine a character that may not be part of the token in question in order to verify that an entire token has been seen. For example, in scanning an identifier, we must keep reading until we see a character that is *not* part of that identifier (like a blank or ;). We must be careful not to lose this lookahead character, because it may be needed as the head of the next token to be scanned. To control our use of input characters, we will use two routines from the C Standard I/O library.

```
#include <stdio.h>
/* getc() is usually a macro */
extern int getc(FILE *);
extern int ungetc(int, FILE *);
```

`getc()` returns the current input character being processed and advances the position in the file to the next character, thereby "consuming" the current character. `ungetc()` puts a character back on the file being read from, so that the next call to `getc()` will return that character. The position in the file is not changed. One character of "push-back" is guaranteed.

There are times when one character of lookahead and push-back isn't enough. In such cases, the scanner must implement its own buffering mechanism. However, this is generally very straightforward.

In Pascal, the scanner driver would manipulate its input differently, peeking at the current character via input^ and then consuming it via get(input) if the character is valid.

The exact format of ScanGen tables is detailed in Appendix B. The table that controls scanning is the **action** table. **action[state][ch]** can indicate a *move* action (keep scanning) or a *halt* action (a token has been recognized). Because lookahead may need to be consulted and scanned characters may need to be either tossed or retained, the action table contains six different values:

(1) ERROR
     Token error. No valid token can be recognized.

(2)   MOVEAPPEND
Move to the next state. Consume the current character and append it to the token string being built.

(3)   MOVENOAPPEND
Move to the next state. Consume the current character but do not append it to the token string being built.

(4)   HALTAPPEND
Consume the current character and append it to the token string being built. A valid token has been found.

(5)   HALTNOAPPEND
Consume the current character but do not append it to the token string being built. A valid token has been found.

(6)   HALTREUSE
Do not consume the current character. A valid token has been found.

For move actions, the next state to visit is stored in the table **next_state[state][ch]**. Zero indicates no next state.

For halt actions, the major and minor codes are obtained by calling the following procedure:

```
extern void lookup_codes(state current_state,
        char cur_char, codes *major, codes *minor);
```

After looking up the major and minor codes, exceptions are handled by calling

```
extern void check_exceptions(codes *major,
        codes *minor, char *token_text);
```

If **major** and **minor** indicate a token class that has exceptions, then **token_text** is examined to see if it really is an exception. If it is, **major** and **minor** are reset to the codes of the exception. If **token_text** is not an exception, the original codes are returned.

A ScanGen driver program is shown in Figure 3.4.

3.4.2. Lex

Lex is a lexical analyzer generator developed by M.E. Lesk and E. Schmidt of AT&T Bell Laboratories. It is used primarily with programs written in C, running under the UNIX operating system. The original version of Lex also ran under GCOS and OS/370 and could produce scanners coded in Ratfor as well as C. Modern versions produce only C scanners and are only available under UNIX. (The generated scanner, however, is not tied to the UNIX environment.)

Lex produces an entire scanner module that can be compiled and linked with other compiler modules. Lex is broader in its approach than ScanGen is.

```c
#define reset() { ind = 0; \
    token_text[ind] = '\0'; state = STARTSTATE; }
extern enum scan_state next_state[NUMSTATES][NUMCHARS];
extern FILE *srcfile;

void scanner(codes *major, codes *minor,
             char *token_text)
{
    /*
     * major will always be set. minor and
     * token_text may not be, depending on
     * whether a minor code is used, and whether
     * token characters are saved or tossed.
     */
    enum scan_state state;
    int ind;
    int c;

    reset();
    while (TRUE) {
        c = getc(srcfile);
        switch (action[state][c]) {
        case ERROR:
            /*
             * Do lexical error recovery.
             * ungetc(c, srcfile) may or may
             * not be necessary.
             */
            break;

        case MOVEAPPEND:
            state = next_state[state][c];
            token_text[ind++] = c;
            break;

        case MOVENOAPPEND:
            state = next_state[state][c];
            break;

        case HALTAPPEND:
            lookup_codes(state, c, major, minor);
            token_text[ind++] = c;
            token_text[ind] = '\0';
            check_exceptions(major, minor, token_text);
            if (*major == 0) {
                /* Do not return this token. */
                reset();
                continue;
            }
            return;
```

```
      case HALTNOAPPEND:
          lookup_codes(state, c, major, minor);
          token_text[ind] = '\0';
          check_exceptions(major, minor, token_text);
          if (*major == 0) {
              /* Do not return this token. */
              reset();
              continue;
          }
          return;

      case HALTREUSE:
          lookup_codes(state, c, major, minor);
          token_text[ind] = '\0';
          check_exceptions(major, minor, token_text);
          ungetc(c, srcfile);
          if (*major == 0) {
              /* Do not return this token. */
              reset();
              continue;
          }
          return;
    } /* end switch */
  } /* end while */
}
```

Figure 3.4   A ScanGen Driver

In particular, Lex associates regular expressions with arbitrary code fragments. When an expression is matched, the code segment is executed. No
special features like major/minor codes or toss flags are provided because all
these (and more) can be realized in the user-written code segments. Figure 3.5
illustrates a Lex definition of a scanner that is equivalent to that of Figure 3.3.

As was the case in ScanGen, we first define character classes and auxiliary regular expressions. This is done in the first section. (Sections are
separated by %% delimiters.) Character classes are delimited by [and];
individual characters, except for \, ^, and −, are unquoted and catenated
without any separators. Thus [xyz] represents the class that can match an x,
y, or z. Ranges of characters are separated by a −; [x−z] is the same as
[xyz].   \ is the escape character, used to represent unprintables and special
symbols. Following C conventions, \n is the newline (that is, end of line), \t
is the tab character, \\ is the backslash symbol itself, and \10 is the character corresponding to octal 10. The ^ symbol complements a character class
(as **Not** does); [^xy] is the character class that matches all characters except
x and y.

```
E               [Ee]
OtherLetter     [A-DF-Za-df-z]
Digit           [0-9]
Letter          {E} | {OtherLetter}
IntLit          {Digit}+
%%
[ \t\n]+                                 { /* delete */           }
[Bb][Ee][Gg][Ii][Nn]                     { minor=0; return(4);    }
[Ee][Nn][Dd]                             { minor=0; return(5);    }
[Rr][Ee][Aa][Dd]                         { minor=0; return(6);    }
[Ww][Rr][Ii][Tt][Ee]                     { minor=0; return(7);    }
{Letter}({Letter} | {Digit} | _)*        { minor=0; return(1);    }
{IntLit}                                 { minor=1; return(2);    }
({IntLit}[.]{IntLit})({E}[+-]?{IntLit})?{ minor=2; return(2);    }
\"([^\"\n] | \"\")*\"                     { stripquotes();
                                           minor=3; return(2);    }

\"([^\"\n] | \"\")*\n                     { stripquotes();
                                           minor=0; return(3);    }
"("                                      { minor=0; return(8);    }
")"                                      { minor=0; return(9);    }
";"                                      { minor=0; return(10);   }
","                                      { minor=0; return(11);   }
":="                                     { minor=0; return(12);   }
"+"                                      { minor=0; return(13);   }
"-"                                      { minor=0; return(14);   }
%%

/* Strip unwanted quotes from string in yytext; adjust yyleng. */
void stripquotes(void)
{
    int frompos, topos = 0, numquotes = 2;

    for (frompos = 1; frompos < yyleng; frompos++) {
        yytext[topos++] = yytext[frompos];
        if (yytext[frompos] == '"' && yytext[frompos+1] == '"') {
            frompos++;
            numquotes++;
        }
    }
    yyleng -= numquotes;
    yytext[yyleng] = '\0';
}
```

Figure 3.5   A Lex Definition for Extended Micro

Lex provides the standard regular expression operators, as well as some additions. Catenation is specified by the juxtaposition of two expressions; no explicit operator is used. Thus **[ab][cd]** will match any of ad, ac, bc, and bd. When outside of character class brackets, individual letters and numbers match themselves; other characters should be quoted (to avoid misinterpretation as regular expression operators). For example, begin can be matched by the expressions **begin**, **"begin"**, or **[b][e][g][i][n]**.

Case *is* significant. The alternation operator is |, and, as usual, parentheses can be used to control grouping of subexpressions. Therefore in our above definition, to match the reserved word **end**, allowing any mixture of upper- and lowercase, we could have used

(E|e) (N|n) (D|d)

Postfix operators * (Kleene closure) and + (positive closure) are also provided, as is ? (optional inclusion). **Expr?** matches **Expr** zero times or once. It is equivalent to (expr) | λ and obviates the need for an explicit λ symbol.

The **{** and **}** symbols signal the macroexpansion of a symbol defined in the first section. For example, since **Digit** is defined as **[0–9]**, **{Digit}+** expands to **[0–9]+**.

The second section defines a table of regular expressions and corresponding commands. When an expression is matched, its associated command is executed. If an input sequence matches no expression, the sequence is simply copied verbatim to the standard output file. Input that is matched is stored in the string variable **yytext** (whose length is **yyleng**). Commands may alter **yytext** in any way and then write the altered text to the output file.

Lex creates an integer function **yylex()** that may be called from the parser (as is standard in syntax-directed compilation). The value returned is usually the token code of the token scanned by Lex. Tokens like white space can be deleted simply by having their associated command not return anything. Scanning continues until a command with a return in it is executed.

Lex has no special provisions for exception lists as ScanGen does. When an identifier is recognized, it is possible to call a subprogram like the **check_exceptions()** routine of Section 3.4.1 that recognizes exceptions and returns the correct token code.

Alternatively, Lex allows regular expressions to overlap (that is, to match common input sequences). In the case of overlap, two rules apply. First, the longest possible match is performed. Lex automatically performs buffering when necessary. Second, if two expressions match the same string, the earlier expression (in order of definition in the Lex specification) is preferred. Exceptions are therefore handled by placing special expressions (that match only a particular string) *before* the expression that matches the general pattern (typically, an identifier).

No special provision is made for major and minor token numbers. Normally the major token number will be returned as the result of calling the Lex-generated scanner, **yylex()**. A minor code, if needed, can be returned by assigning to a shared variable.

No tossing mechanism is provided. It may therefore be necessary to process the token text (stored in **yytext**) before returning. This is easily done by calling a subroutine (defined in the third section, following the table of expressions and commands) to *reprocess* the token text. The routine **stripquotes()** is an example of this sort of routine.

In Lex, end of file is not handled by regular expressions. The EOF token is signaled by having **yylex()** return the integer value zero. It is up to the parser to recognize the zero return value as signifying the EOF token.

If there are more than one source files to be scanned, this fact is hidden inside the scanner mechanism. **yylex()** uses three user-defined functions to handle character input and output. They are

input()	retrieve a single character, 0 on end of file.
output(c)	write a single character to the output.
unput(c)	put a single character back on the input to be re-read.

When **yylex()** encounters end of file, it calls a user-supplied integer function named **yywrap()**. The purpose of this routine is to "wrap up" input processing. It returns the value one if there is no more input. Otherwise, it returns zero and arranges for **input()** to provide more characters.

The compiler writer may supply the **input()**, **output()**, **unput()**, and **yywrap()** functions (usually as C macros). Lex supplies default versions that read characters from the standard input and write them to the standard output. The default version of **yywrap()** simply returns one, signifying that there is no more input. (The use of **output()** allows Lex to be used as a tool for producing stand-alone data "filters" for transforming a stream of data.)

In summary, Lex is a very flexible generator that can transform input (for example, as a preprocessor) as well as partition, or scan, it. It provides a number of advanced features beyond those discussed here. It does require that code segments be written in C, which makes it less generally usable than a tool like ScanGen, which produces only tables of integers. Lex is representative of the kind of scanner generator tool available to compiler writers.

Lex is widely used in the UNIX community, though not much outside it. It is not efficient enough to be used in production compilers, but more efficient implementations could be written. In fact, recent work by Jacobsen (1987) has shown that Lex can be improved so that it is always faster than a hand-written scanner. Lex has also been re-implemented. Flex (Fast Lex [Paxson 1990]) is a freely distributable Lex clone. It produces scanners that are considerably faster than the ones produced by Lex. Flex also provides options that allow tuning of the scanner size versus its speed, as well as some features that Lex does not have (such as support for eight-bit characters). Flex is widely available, freely distributed, compatible with Lex, and performs better than Lex does; its use is recommended.

An interesting alternative is GLA (Generate Lexical Analyzers [Gray 1988]). GLA takes a description of a scanner based on regular expressions and a library of common lexical idioms (such as "pascal comment") and produces a *directly executable* (that is, not DFA-driven) scanner written in C. GLA was designed with both ease of use and efficiency of the generated scanner in mind.

3.5. **Practical Considerations**

In this section we discuss the practical considerations necessary to build real scanners for real programming languages. As one might expect, the finite automaton model we have developed sometimes falls short and must be supplemented. Further, some provision for error handling must be incorporated into any real-world scanner.

We shall discuss, in turn, a number of potential problem areas. In each case, solutions will be weighed, particularly in conjunction with the scanner generators we have studied.

3.5.1. **Reserved Words**

Virtually all programming languages have symbols (such as **if** and **begin**) that match the lexical syntax of ordinary identifiers. These symbols are termed *key words*. If the language has a rule that key words may not be used as programmer-defined identifiers, then they are termed *reserved words* (that is, they are reserved for special use).

Most programming languages choose to make key words reserved. This simplifies parsing, which drives the compilation process and makes programs more readable. For example, assume that in Pascal begin and end are not reserved, and some devious programmer has declared procedures named begin and end. The following program can be parsed in many ways; hence its meaning is not well defined:

```
begin
  begin;
  end;
  end;
  begin;
end
```

With careful design, outright ambiguities can be avoided. For example, in PL/I key words are not reserved, but procedures are called using an explicit call key word (such as call P). Nonetheless, opportunities for convoluted usage abound because key words may be used as variable names:

```
if if then else = then;
```

The problem with reserved words is that if they are too numerous, they may confuse inexperienced programmers who unknowingly choose an identifier name that clashes with a reserved word. This usually causes a syntax error in a program that "looks right" and in fact *would* be right were the symbol in question not reserved. COBOL is infamous for this problem, having several hundred reserved words. For example, in COBOL, zero is a reserved word. So is zeros. So is zeroes!

The fact that reserved words look just like identifiers significantly complicates the specification of a scanner via regular expressions. In Exercise 20 it is established that any regular expression using **Not** is equivalent to one that does not use **Not**. So we could get a regular expression for nonreserved Ids by getting rid of the **Not**s in the expression

Not (**Not**(Id) | begin | end | $\cdots$)

Alternately, we could just write down the regular expression directly. However, it would be *very* long and complex. Just to get an idea, suppose END was the only reserved word, and the alphabet had only letters. Then we could write

Nonreserved = L | (L L) | ((L L L) L$^+$) | ((L – 'E') L*) |
(L (L – 'N') L*) | (L L (L – 'D') L*)

(That is, anything shorter or longer than three letters, or not starting with E, or without N in position two, and so forth.)

A simpler solution is to treat reserved words as ordinary identifiers (as far as the regular expression is concerned) and use a separate table lookup to detect them. That is, they are treated as exceptions to ordinary identifiers. After what looks like an identifier is scanned, a table of exceptions is consulted to see if a reserved word has been recognized. If case is significant in reserved words, the exception lookup will require an exact match; otherwise, the token should be translated to a standard form (all upper- or lowercase) before the lookup.

An exception table may be organized in a variety of ways. The most common organization is a sorted list of exceptions suitable for a binary search. A hash table may also be used. For example, the length of a token may be used as an index into a list of exceptions of the same length. If exception lengths are well distributed, few comparisons will be needed to determine whether a token is an identifier or a reserved word. It has been shown by Cichelli (1980) that perfect hash functions are possible. That is, each reserved word is mapped to a unique position in the exception table, and no position in the table is unused. A token is either the reserved word selected by the hash function or it is an ordinary identifier.

A third approach to recognizing reserved words is to create distinct regular expressions for each reserved word. This approach is feasible if the scanner generator used allows more than one regular expression to match a character sequence (most scanner generators do allow this). The real problem with this approach is that the underlying finite automaton, and its transition table, will be significantly larger. There are two reasons for this. First, the number of character classes will be greatly increased because all letters will not be mapped to a single class. Depending upon the number and spelling of reserved words, we may have as many as 26 (or even 52) classes just for letters. A second problem is that the number of automaton states will increase significantly, with new states representing partially matched reserved words.

Even in as simple a language as Micro, creating regular expressions for reserved words (all four of them!) causes a very significant increase in table sizes. Using the definition of Section 3.4.1, Figure 3.3 (which treats reserved words as exceptions), 12 states and 17 character classes were created. When the four reserved words were represented by individual regular expressions, 30 states and 26 classes were needed. Assuming a simple array representation for transition tables, this is nearly a fourfold increase. If only nonerror entries are counted, a fivefold increase occurs. And in languages like Ada and Pascal, given their larger numbers of reserved words, many more states and character classes can be expected.

3.5.2. **Compiler Directives and Listing Source Lines**

Compiler directives and pragmas are used to control compiler options (listings, optimizations, profiling, and so on). They may be processed either by the scanner or by semantic routines. If the directive is a simple flag, it can be extracted from a token (perhaps using a toss/save mechanism). The command is then executed, and finally the token is deleted. More elaborate directives, like Ada pragmas, have nontrivial structure and can be parsed and translated like any other statement.

A scanner may also have to handle source inclusion directives, which cause it to read and scan the contents of a file. Languages like C have elaborate macro definition and expansion facilities that are typically handled by a preprocessing phase prior to scanning and parsing.

Some languages (like C and PL/I) include conditional compilation directives that control whether statements are compiled or ignored. Such directives are useful in creating versions of a program from a common source. Usually these directives have the general form of an **if** statement, and hence a conditional expression will be parsed and evaluated. Tokens following the expression will then be passed to the parser or ignored until an **end if** delimiter is reached. If conditional compilation structures can be nested, a skeletal parser for the directives will be needed.

Another possible function of the scanner is to list source lines. Although this seems a trivial function, a bit of care is required. The most obvious way to produce a source listing is to echo characters as they are read, using end-of-line conditions to terminate a line, increment line counters, and so on. This approach has a number of problems, however:

- Error messages may need to be printed, and these should (if possible) be written after the source line, with pointers to the offending symbol.

- A source line may need to be edited before it is written. This may involve inserting or deleting symbols (for example, for error repair), replacing symbols (because of macro preprocessing), and reformatting symbols (to prettyprint a program).

- Source lines that are read in general are not in a one-to-one correspondence with the source listing lines that are written. For example, in UNIX a source program can legally be condensed into a single line (UNIX places no a priori limit on line lengths). A scanner that attempts to buffer entire source lines may well overflow buffer lengths.

In light of these considerations, it is best to build output lines (which normally are bounded by device limits) *incrementally* as tokens are scanned. The token image placed in the output buffer may not be an exact image of the token that was scanned, depending on error repair, prettyprinting, case conversion, or whatever is required. If a token cannot fit on an output line, the line is written and the buffer is cleared. (To simplify editing, line numbers ought to correspond to source lines.) In rare cases a token may need to be broken; this is the case, for example, if a string is so long that its text exceeds the output line length.

As each token is returned by the scanner, its position in the output line buffer should be included. If an error involving the token is noted, this position marker is used to point to the token. Error messages themselves are buffered and normally printed immediately after the corresponding output buffer is written. In some cases, an error may not be detected until long after the line containing the error has been processed. An example of this is a **goto** to an undefined label. If such delayed errors are rare (as they are in Ada and Pascal), a message citing a line number can be produced—for example, "Undefined label in statement 101." In languages that freely allow forward references, however, delayed errors may be numerous. For example, PL/I allows declarations of objects after they are referenced. In this case, a file of error messages keyed with line numbers can be written and later merged with the processed source lines to produce a complete source listing.

The UNIX approach is that compilers should just concentrate on generating code and leave the listing and prettyprinting to other tools. Of course, this considerably simplifies the scanner.

3.5.3. Entry of Identifiers into the Symbol Table

In simple languages with only global variables and declarations, it is common to have the scanner immediately enter an identifier into the symbol table if it is not already there. Whether the identifier is entered or is already in the table, a pointer to the symbol table entry is then returned from the scanner.

In block-structured languages, we usually do not have the scanner enter or look up identifiers in the symbol table because an identifier can be used in many contexts (as a variable, in a declaration, as a field of record, a label, and more). It is not possible, in general, for the scanner to know when an identifier should be entered into the symbol table for the current scope or when it should return a pointer to an instance from an earlier scope. Thus it is wiser to return the character string itself and allow individual semantic routines to resolve the identifier's intended usage. Usually a *string space* is used to represent identifiers (see Chapter 8), so the scanner can enter an identifier into the string space and return a string space pointer rather than the actual text.

In some languages, such as C, case is significant, but in others, such as Ada and Pascal, case is insignificant. If case is significant, identifier text must be returned exactly as it was scanned. Reserved word lookup must distinguish between identifiers and reserved words that differ only in case. However, if case is insignificant, we need to guarantee that case differences in the spelling of an identifier or reserved word do not cause errors. An easy way to do this is to put all tokens scanned as identifiers into a uniform case before they are returned or looked up in the reserved word table.

3.5.4. Scanner Termination

A scanner is designed to read input characters and partition them into tokens. What happens when the end of the input file is reached? It is convenient to create an Eof pseudocharacter when this occurs. This allows the definition of an Eof *token* that can be passed back to the parser. An Eof token is useful in a CFG because it allows the parser to verify that the logical end of a program corresponds to its physical end.

What should happen if a scanner is called after the end of file is reached? Obviously, a fatal error could be registered, but this would destroy our simple model in which the scanner always returns a token. A better approach is to continue to return the Eof token to the parser. This allows the parser to handle termination cleanly, especially when the Eof token is normally syntactically valid *only* after a complete program is parsed. If the Eof token appears too soon or too late, the parser can perform error repair or issue a suitable error message.

3.5.5. Multicharacter Lookahead

We can generalize FAs to look ahead *beyond* the next input character. This feature is important for implementing FORTRAN. For example, the statement DO 10 I = 1,100 is the beginning of a loop, with index I ranging from 1 to 100. The statement DO 10 I = 1.100 is an assignment to the variable DO10I (blanks are not significant in FORTRAN).

A FORTRAN scanner can determine whether the O is the last character of a DO token only after reading as far as the comma (or period). (In fact, the erroneous substitution of a "." for a "," in a FORTRAN DO loop once caused a space launch to fail! Because the substitution resulted in a valid statement, the error was not detected until run-time, which in this case was *after* the rocket had been launched. The rocket deviated from course and had to be destroyed.)

A milder form of this problem occurs in Pascal and Ada: To scan 10..100 we need two-character lookahead after the 10. Suppose we use the FA of Figure 3.6. Given 10..100 we would scan three characters and stop in a nonfinal state. If we stop reading in a nonfinal state, we can back up along accepted characters until a final state is found. Characters we back up over are rescanned to form later tokens. If no final state is reached during backup, we have a lexical error and invoke lexical error recovery.

In Pascal or Ada we know we never have more than two-character lookahead, which simplifies buffering characters to be rescanned. Alternatively,

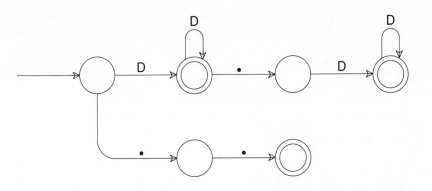

Figure 3.6 An FA That Scans Integer and Real Literals and the Subrange Operator

we can add a new final state to the above automaton, corresponding to a pseudotoken of the form (D⁺ .). If this token is recognized, we strip the trailing "." from the token text and buffer it for later reuse. We then return the token code of an integer literal.

In Ada, the tic character ' is used both as an attribute symbol (arrayname'length) and to delimit character literals ('x'). It is necessary for an Ada scanner to distinguish between the two usages. Consider TypeName'('a','b'). The first tic is an attribute symbol, used to qualify the type of the aggregate expression. The remaining tics delimit the character literals that appear in the aggregate. The solution used by most Ada scanners is to treat the tic character as a special case. When a tic is seen, a flag (set by the parser) is checked to see if an attribute symbol or a character literal may be read next. Depending on the flag, a single tic or a quoted character is scanned.

Multiple character lookahead may also be a consideration in scanning *invalid* programs. For example, 12.3e+q is an invalid token. In this case the scanner could be backed up to produce four tokens. Since this token sequence (12.3, e, +, q) is invalid, the parser will detect a syntax error when it processes the sequence. Whether one chooses to consider this a lexical error or a syntax error (or both) is irrelevant, but some phase of the compiler must detect the error.

It is easy to build a scanner that can perform general backup. As each character is scanned, it is buffered, and a flag is set indicating whether the character sequence scanned so far is a valid token (the flag might be the appropriate token code). If we reach a situation in which we are not in a final state and cannot scan any more characters, backup is invoked. We extract characters from the right end of the buffer and queue them for rescanning. This process continues until we reach a prefix of the scanned characters flagged as a valid token. This token is returned by the scanner. If no prefix is flagged as valid, we have a lexical error. (Lexical errors are discussed in Section 3.5.6.)

As an example of scanning with backup, consider our earlier example of 12.3e+q. The following table illustrates how the buffer is built and flags are set:

Buffered Token	Token Flag
1	Integer Literal
12	Integer Literal
12.	Invalid
12.3	Real Literal
12.3e	Invalid
12.3e+	Invalid

When the q is scanned, backup is invoked. The longest token prefix that is valid is 12.3, so a real literal is returned, and e+ is requeued so that it can be later rescanned.

3.5.6. Lexical Error Recovery

Occasionally a scanner will detect a lexical error. It is unreasonable to stop compilation because of such a minor error, so it is necessary to try some sort of *lexical error recovery*. Two approaches come to mind:

- Delete the characters read so far and restart scanning at the next unread character.

- Delete the first character read by the scanner and resume scanning at the character following it.

Both of these approaches are reasonable. The former is very easy to do. We just reset the scanner and begin scanning anew. The latter is a bit harder but a bit safer (in that less is immediately deleted). It can be implemented using the buffering mechanism described in the previous section for scanner backup.

In most cases, a lexical error is caused by the appearance of some illegal character, which will usually appear as the beginning of a token. In such a case, the above approaches work equally well. The effects of lexical error recovery might well create a syntax error, which will be detected and repaired by the parser. For example, ··· beg#in ··· would probably be repaired into ··· beg in ···, which will almost certainly cause a syntax error. Such occurrences are unavoidable, and a good syntactic error-repair algorithm will make some reasonable repair (although quite possibly *not* the correct one!).

If the parser has a syntactic error-repair mechanism (see Chapter 17), it can be useful to return a special warning token when a lexical error occurs. The semantic value of the warning token is the character string deleted to restart scanning. When the parser sees the warning token, it is warned that the next token is unreliable and that error repair may be required. Furthermore, the text that was deleted may be helpful in choosing the most appropriate repair.

Certain lexical errors require special care. In particular, runaway strings and comments ought to receive special error messages. Consider first runaway strings. Since strings normally are not allowed to cross line boundaries, a runaway string is detected when the end of a line is reached. Ordinary recovery heuristics may be inappropriate for this error. In particular, deleting the first character (the quote character) and restarting scanning will almost certainly lead to a cascade of further errors as the string text is inappropriately scanned as ordinary input.

One way to catch runaway strings is to introduce an *error token* that represents a string terminated by an end of line rather than a quote character. (This was illustrated in the ScanGen and Lex examples.) Thus, for a correct quoted string, we might have

$$\text{" (Not(" | Eol) | "")}^* \text{ "}$$

and for a runaway string we would use

$$\text{" (Not(" | Eol) | "")}^* \text{ Eol}$$

where Eol is the end-of-line character. When a runaway string token is recognized, a special error message should be issued. Further, the string may be repaired into a correct string by returning an ordinary string token with the opening quote and closing Eol stripped (just as ordinary open and close quotes are stripped). Note however that this repair may or may not be "correct." If the close quote is truly missing, the repair will be good; if it is present on a succeeding line, a cascade of inappropriate lexical and syntactic errors will follow.

In languages like Pascal, which allow multiline comments, runaway comments present a similar problem. A runaway comment is not detected until the scanner finds a close comment symbol (possibly belonging to some other comment) or until the end of file is reached. Clearly a special error message is required. To handle comments terminated by Eof, the error token approach can again be used:

$$\{ \text{ Not(})\}^* \} \quad \text{and} \quad \{ \text{ Not(})\}^* \text{ Eof}$$

To handle comments closed by a close comment belonging to another comment (for example, { $\cdots$ missing close comment $\cdots$ { normal comment }), we issue a warning (but not an error message, for this form of comment is lexically legal). In particular, a comment containing an open comment symbol in its body is most probably a symptom of the kind of omission depicted above. We therefore split our legal comment definition into two tokens. The one that accepts an open comment in its body causes a warning message ("Possible unclosed comment") to be printed. We now have

$$\{ \text{ Not(\{ | \})}^* \} \text{ and } \{ \text{ (Not(\{ | \})}^* \{ \text{ Not(\{ | \})}^*)^+ \} \text{ and } \{ \text{ Not(})\}^* \text{ Eof}$$

The first definition matches correct comments that do not contain an open comment in their body. The second definition matches comments that contain at least one open comment in their body. These comments are correct, but cause a warning to be issued. The third definition matches runaway comments closed by an Eof. These tokens cause an error message to be issued.

Of course, Ada's comments, which are always terminated by Eol, do not fall prey to the runaway comment problem. They do, however, require that each line of a multiline comment contain an open comment symbol. Note too that, as we saw above, *nested comments* normally fail because FAs and regular expressions cannot recognize properly balanced open comment/close comment sequences. This failure to recognize such sequences causes problems when we want comments to nest, particularly when we "comment-out" a piece of code (which itself may well contain comments). A common solution to the problem is to have two or more kinds of comment delimiters. For example, UW-Pascal recognizes three classes of comments: (1) those matched by { and }, (2) those matched by (* and *), and (3) those matched by " and ". If one class of comment is used for normal documentation purposes, another may be used *exclusively* to comment-out pieces of code. Unfortunately, the new Pascal standard has decreed that a comment may be opened by one class of opener and closed by another class of closer (for example, (* comment }). This ruling makes nesting of comments impossible.

As we noted earlier, it is often convenient for the scanner to assume an *extended* character set that includes such pseudocharacters as Eol and Eof. These pseudocharacters can be used to define regular expressions. They can also be used to control formatting (using indent, outdent, and newline pseudocharacters). Pseudocharacters can be created by the scanner's read routine (for example, Eol may be returned if the end-of-line predicate is true), or as the result of processing compiler directives—which might signal prettyprinting of the input program.

Fortunately, the C language and standard I/O library do some of this work for us by supplying escape sequences for unprintable characters, such as ' \n' for newline and **EOF** for end of file.

3.6. Translating Regular Expressions into Finite Automata

Regular expressions are equivalent to FAs. In fact, the main job of a scanner generator program is to transform a regular expression definition into an equivalent FA. It does this by first transforming the regular expression into a *nondeterministic finite automaton* (NFA). Upon reading a particular input, an NFA is not required to make a unique (deterministic) choice of which state to visit. For example, as shown in Figure 3.7, an NFA is allowed to have a state that has two transitions (arrows) coming out of it, labeled by the same symbol. As shown in Figure 3.8, an NFA may also have transitions labeled with λ.

Transitions are normally labeled with individual characters (letters) in V, and although λ is a string (the string with no characters in it), it is definitely

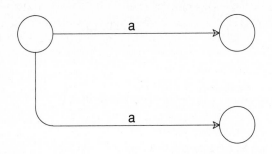

Figure 3.7 An NFA with Two a Transitions

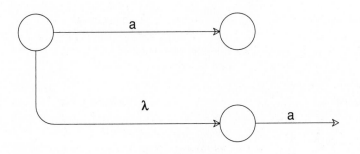

Figure 3.8 An NFA with a λ Transition

not a character. In the last example, when the automaton is in the state at the left and the next input character is a, it may choose to use the transition labeled a or first follow the λ transition (you can always find λ wherever you look for it) and *then* follow an a transition. FAs that contain no λ transitions and that always have unique successor states for any symbol are *deterministic*.

The algorithm to make an FA from a regular expression proceeds in two steps: First, it transforms the regular expression into an NFA, and then it transforms the NFA into a deterministic one. This first step is very easy. In fact, we can transform any regular expression into an NFA with the following properties:

- There is a unique final state.
- The final state has *no* successors.
- Every other state has either one or two successors.

Regular expressions are all built out of the *atomic* regular expressions a (where a is a character in V) and λ by using the three operations A B and A | B and A*. Other operations (like A+) are just abbreviations for combinations of these. As shown in Figure 3.9, NFAs for a and λ are trivial.

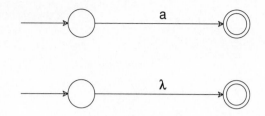

Figure 3.9   NFAs for a and λ

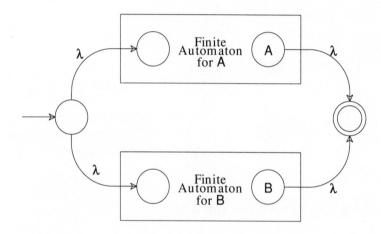

Figure 3.10   An NFA for A | B

Now suppose we have NFAs for A and B and want one for A | B. We construct the NFA shown in Figure 3.10. The states labeled A and B were the final states of the automata for A and B; we create a new final state for the combined automaton.

As shown in Figure 3.11, the construction for A B is even easier. The final state of the combined automaton is the same state that was the final state of B. We could also just merge the final state of A with the initial state of B. We chose not to only because the picture would be more difficult to draw. Finally, the NFA for A^* is shown in Figure 3.12.

3.6.1. Creating Deterministic Automata

The transformation from an NFA N to an equivalent DFA M works by what is sometimes called the *subset construction*. Each state of M corresponds to a *set* of states of N. The idea is that M will be in state {x,y,z} after reading a given

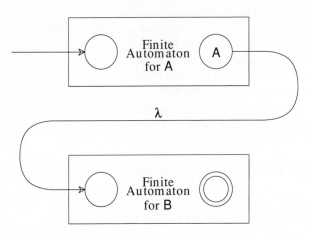

Figure 3.11   An NFA for A B

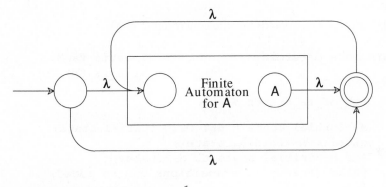

Figure 3.12   An NFA for A*

input string if and only if N could be in *any* of the states x, y, or z, depending on the transitions it chooses. Thus M keeps track of all the possible routes N might take and runs them in parallel. An accepting state of M will be any set containing the accepting state of N, reflecting the convention that N accepts if there is *any* way it could get to its final state by choosing the "right" transition.

The initial state of M is the set of all states that N could be in without reading any input characters—that is, the set of states reachable from the initial state of N following only λ arrows. Algorithm **close()** computes those states that can be reached following only λ transitions. Once the start state of M is built, we begin to create successor states. To do this, we take any state S of M, and any character c, and compute S's successor under c. S is identified with some set of N's states, $\{n_1, n_2, \cdots\}$. We find all the possible successor states to $\{n_1, n_2, \cdots\}$ under c, obtaining a set $\{m_1, m_2, \cdots\}$. Finally, we compute $T = \text{close}(\{m_1, m_2, \cdots\})$. T is included as a state in M, and a transition from S to T labeled with c is added to M. We continue adding states and transitions to M until all possible successors to existing states are added. Because each state corresponds to a (finite) subset of N's states, the process of adding new states to M must eventually terminate.

Complete algorithms for λ-closure and DFA construction follow. (C does not have set operations; we outline them using a macro-like notation.)

```
/*
 * Add to S all states reachable from it
 * using only λ transitions of N
 */
void close(set_of_fa_states *S)
{
    while (there is a state x in S
        and a state y not in S such that
        x→y using a λ transition)
            add y to S
}
```

Using this procedure, we can define the construction of M:

```
void make_deterministic(nondeterministic_fa N,
                        deterministic_fa *M)
{
    set_of_fa_states T;

    M->initial_state = SET_OF(N.initial_state) ;
    close(& M->initial_state);
    Add M->initial_state to M->states;
    while (states or transitions can be added)
    {
        choose S in M->states and c in Alphabet;

        T = SET_OF(y in N.states
            SUCH_THAT x→y for some x in S) ;
        close(& T);
        if (T not in M->states)
            add T to M->states;

        Add the transition to M->transitions: S→T ;
    }
    M->final_states =
        SET_OF(S in M->states SUCH_THAT
                N.final_state in S);
}
```

To see how the subset construction operates, consider the following NFA:

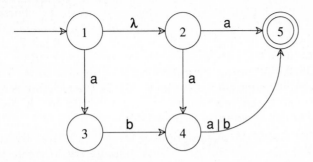

We start with state 1, the start state of N, and add state 2, its λ-successor. Hence M's start state is {1,2}. Neither state 1 nor state 2 has a successor under b. Under a, {1,2}'s successor is {3,4,5}. {3,4,5}'s successors under a and b are {5} and {4,5}. {4,5}'s successor under b is {5}. Final states of M are those state sets that contain N's final state (5). The resulting DFA is:

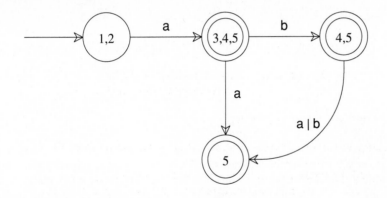

It is not difficult to establish that the DFA constructed by **make_deterministic()** is equivalent to the original NFA (see Exercise 22). What is less obvious is the fact that the DFA that is built can sometimes be *much* larger than the original NFA. States of the DFA are identified with sets of NFA states. If the NFA has n states, there are 2^n distinct sets of NFA states, and hence the DFA may have 2^n states. Exercise 18 discusses an NFA that actually exhibits this exponential blowup in size when it is made deterministic. Fortunately, the NFAs built from the kind of regular expressions used to specify programming language tokens do not exhibit this blowup problem when they are made deterministic. As a rule, DFAs used for scanning are simple and compact.

3.6.2. **Optimizing Finite Automata**

We do not have to stop with the DFA created by **make_deterministic()**. Sometimes this DFA will have more states than necessary. Further, it is known that for every DFA there is a *unique* smallest (in terms of number of states) equivalent DFA. In other words, suppose a DFA (M) has 75 states and there is a DFA M' with 50 states that accepts the same set of strings. Suppose further that no DFA with fewer than 50 states is equivalent to M. Then M' is the *only* DFA with 50 states equivalent to M. Using the techniques discussed below, it is possible to optimize M by replacing it with M'. In fact, this is exactly what the optimize option of ScanGen does.

We begin by trying the most optimistic merger of states. By definition, final and nonfinal states are distinct, so we initially try to create only two states: one representing the merger of all final states and the other representing the merger of all nonfinal states. This merger into only two states is probably too optimistic. In particular, if all the constituents of a merged state do not agree on the same transition for a given character, the state must be split. As an example, assume we start with the following automaton:

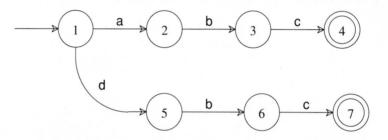

Initially we have a nonfinal state {1,2,3,5,6} and a final state {4,7}. A merger is legal if and only if all constituent states agree on the same successor state. For example, states 3 and 6 would go to a final state given character c; states 1, 2, and 5 would not, so a split must occur. We will add an error state s_E to the original DFA that will be the successor state under any illegal character. (Thus, reaching s_E becomes equivalent to detecting an illegal token.) s_E is not a real state; rather it allows us to assume every state has a successor under every character. s_E is never merged with any real state.

The routine shown in Figure 3.13 will split merged states whose constituents do not agree on a common successor under any given character. When **split()** terminates, we know that the states that remain merged are equivalent in that they always agree on common successors.

Returning to our example, we initially have states {1,2,3,5,6} and {4,7}. Invoking **split()**, we first observe that states 3 and 6 have a common successor under c, and states 1, 2, and 5 have no successor under c (or, equivalently, have the error state s_E). This forces a split, yielding {1,2,5}, {3,6}, {4,7}. Now, for character b, states 2 and 5 would go to the merged state {3,6}, but state 1 would not, so another split occurs. We now have: {1}, {2,5}, {3,6}, {4,7}. At this point we are done, as all constituents of merged states agree on the same successor for each input symbol.

```
void split(set_of_fa_states *ss)
{
    do {
        Let S be any merged state corresponding to
            {s₁ ,..., sₙ} and
            let c be any character;
        Let t₁ ,..., tₙ be the successor states to
            {s₁ ,..., sₙ} under c;
        if (t₁ ,..., tₙ do not all belong to the
            same merged state)
        {
            Split S into new states so that sᵢ and
            sⱼ remain in the same merged state if
            and only if tᵢ and tⱼ are in
            the same merged state;
        }
    } while (more splits are possible);
}
```

Figure 3.13   An Algorithm to Split FA States

Once **split()** is executed, we are essentially done. Transitions between merged states are the same as the transitions between states in the original DFA. That is, if there was a transition between state s_i and s_j under character c, there is now a transition under c from the merged state containing s_i to the merged state containing s_j. The start state is that merged state containing the original start state; final states are those merged states containing final states (recall that final and nonfinal states are never merged).

Returning to our example, the minimum state automaton we obtain is

A proof of the correctness and optimality of this minimization algorithm may be found in Hopcroft and Ullman (1979).

FAs can be viewed as very primitive CPUs designed to match characters rather than to perform more general computations. Regular expressions are the programming language of FAs that are compiled and optimized into executable form. In most cases, we simulate FAs by using simple driver programs like the one presented earlier. It is possible, however, to speculate about *special-purpose* processors (implemented perhaps as VLSI chips) that directly implement FAs. At least one experiment in this direction has been reported, and in any application where scanning is a limiting factor, special-purpose "scanning engines" could prove advantageous.

Exercises

1. Assume the following text is presented to a Pascal scanner:

```
program m(output);
const
     pay=284.00;
var
     bal:real;
     month:0..60;
begin
     month:=0;
     bal:=11163.05;
     while bal>0 do begin
          writeln('Month: ', month:2,
                    ' Balance: ', bal:10:2);
          bal:=bal-(pay-0.015*bal);
          month:=month+1;
     end;
end.
```

   What is the token sequence that is produced? For which tokens must the token text be returned with the token code?

2. How many lexical errors (if any) appear in the following Pascal fragment? How should each error be handled by the scanner?

```
If a = 1. Then b :=1.0else c := 1.0E+N;
Writeln(''',"Hi there!",''');
```

3. Write regular expressions that define the strings recognized by the following FAs:

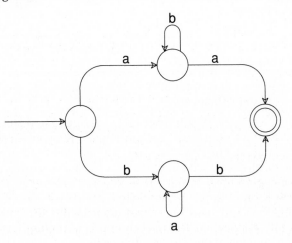

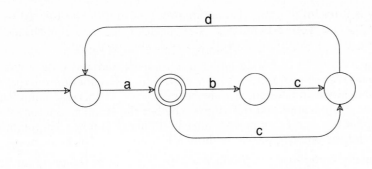

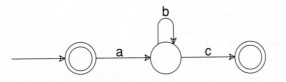

4. Write DFAs that recognize the tokens defined by the following regular expressions:

    (a | (bc)* d)$^+$

    ((0 | 1)* (2 | 3)$^+$) | 0011

    (a Not(a))* aaa

5. Write a regular expression that defines a Pascal-like fixed-decimal literal with no superfluous leading or trailing zeros. That is, 0.0, 123.01, and 123005.0 are legal, but 00.0, 001.000, and 002345.1000 are illegal.

6. Write a regular expression that defines a Pascal-like comment delimited by (* and *). Individual *'s and)'s may appear in the comment body, but the pair *) may not.

7. Take either the ScanGen or Lex definition of extended Micro and extend it further to include definitions for the fixed-decimal literal and Pascal-like comment of Exercises 5 and 6. Run either ScanGen or Lex to verify that your definitions are legal.

8. In Section 3.5.1 we compared two approaches to recognizing reserved words: treating them as exceptions to identifier tokens and creating individual regular expression definitions for them. In the case of Micro, we found that the transition table size increased by roughly a factor of four when individual token definitions were used.

    Repeat the comparison (using either ScanGen or Lex), this time using the reserved words of Ada/CS (as defined in Appendix A). Compare both scanner size *and* scanner speed. Which approach do you recommend?

9. Define a token class AlmostReserved to be those identifiers that are not reserved words but that would be if a single character were changed.

Why is it useful to know that an identifier is "almost" a reserved word? How would you generalize a scanner to recognize AlmostReserved tokens as well as ordinary reserved words and identifiers?

10. When a compiler is first designed and implemented, it is wise to concentrate on correctness and simplicity of design. After the compiler is fully implemented and tested, it may be necessary to increase compilation speed. How would you determine whether the scanner component of a compiler is a significant performance bottleneck? If it is, what might you do to improve performance (without affecting compiler correctness)?

11. Normally compilers can produce a source listing of the program being compiled. This listing is usually just a copy of the source file, perhaps embellished with line numbers and page breaks. Assume we wish to produce a prettyprinted listing (that is, a listing with text properly indented, **begin**–**end** pairs aligned, and so on). How would you modify a ScanGen driver to produce a prettyprinted listing? What would you do in Lex, where a complete scanner module is produced by the Lex processor?

How are compiler diagnostics and line numbering complicated when a prettyprinted listing is produced?

12. For most modern programming languages, scanners require little context information. That is, a token can be recognized by examining its text and perhaps one or two lookahead characters. As discussed in Section 3.5.5, in Ada, additional context is required to distinguish between a single tic (comprising an attribute symbol) and a tic, character, tic sequence (comprising a quoted character).

Assume that a flag **can_parse_char** is set (by the parser) when a quoted character can be parsed. If the next input character is a tic, **can_parse_char** can be used to control how the tic is scanned.

Explain how the **can_parse_char** flag can be *cleanly* integrated into a ScanGen- or Lex-created scanner. The changes you suggest should not unnecessarily complicate or slow the scanning of ordinary tokens.

13. Unlike Pascal and Ada, FORTRAN generally ignores blanks and therefore may need extensive lookahead to determine how to scan an input line. We noted earlier a famous example of this: DO 10 I = 1 , 10 produces seven tokens, whereas DO 10 I = 1 . 10 produces three tokens. How would you design a scanner to handle the extended lookahead that FORTRAN requires?

Lex contains a mechanism for doing lookahead of this sort. How would you match the identifier in this example?

14. Because FORTRAN generally ignores blanks, a character sequence containing n blanks can be scanned as many as 2^n different ways. Are each of these alternatives equally probable? If not, how would you alter the design you proposed in Exercise 13 to examine the most probable alternatives first?

15.   Assume we are designing the ultimate programming language, "Utopia 94." We have already specified the language's tokens (using regular expressions) and the language's syntax (using a CFG). Now we wish to determine those token sequences that require white space to separate them (like **begin** A) and those that require extra lookahead while scanning (like 1..10). Explain how we could use the regular expressions and context-free grammar to *automatically* find all token pairs that need special handling.

16.   Show that the set { [^{i}]^i | i≥1} is not regular. *Hint:* Show that no fixed number of FA states is sufficient to exactly match left and right brackets.

17.   Show the NFA that would be created for the following expression using the techniques of Section 3.6:

$$(a\, b^*\, c) \,|\, (a\, b\, c^*)$$

Using **make_deterministic()**, translate the NFA into a DFA. Using the techniques of Section 3.6.2, optimize the DFA you created into a minimal state equivalent.

18.   Consider the following regular expression:

$$(0\,|\,1)^*\, 0\, (0\,|\,1)\, (0\,|\,1)\, (0\,|\,1) \,\cdots\, (0\,|\,1)$$

Display the NFA corresponding to this expression.

Show that the equivalent DFA is exponentially bigger than the NFA you presented.

19.   Translation of a regular expression into an NFA is fast and simple. Creation of an equivalent DFA is slower and can lead to a much larger automaton. An interesting alternative is to scan using NFAs, thus obviating the need to ever build a DFA. The idea is to mimic the operation of the **close()** and **make_deterministic()** routines (as defined in Section 3.6.1) while scanning. Rather than maintaining a single current state, a set of possible states is maintained. As characters are read, transitions from each state in the current set are followed, creating a new set of states. If any state in the current set is final, the characters read comprise a valid token.

Define a suitable encoding for an NFA (perhaps a generalization of the transition table used for DFAs) and write a scanner driver that can use this encoding, following the set-of-states approach outlined above. This approach to scanning will surely be slower than the standard approach, which uses DFAs. Under what circumstances is scanning using NFAs attractive?

20.   Assume R is any regular expression. **Not**(R) represents the set of all strings not in the regular set defined by R. Show that **Not**(R) is a regular set.

Hint: If R is a regular expression, there is an FA that recognizes the set defined by R. Transform this FA into one that will recognize **Not**(R).

21. Let Rev be the operator that reverses strings. For example, Rev(abc) = cba. Let R be any regular expression. Rev(R) is the set of strings denoted by R, with each string reversed. Is Rev(R) a regular set? Why?

22. Prove that the DFA constructed by **make_deterministic()** in Section 3.6.1 is equivalent to the original NFA. To do so, you must show that an input string can lead to a final state in the NFA if and only if that same string will lead to a final state in the corresponding DFA.

CHAPTER 4

Grammars and Parsing

4.1. Context-Free Grammars: Concepts and Notation

In Chapter 2, we learned the rudiments of context-free grammars. We now formalize our definitions and introduce some useful notation. A context-free grammar (CFG) is defined by the following four components:

(1)   A finite *terminal vocabulary* V_t; this is the token set produced by the scanner.

(2)   A finite set of different, intermediate symbols, called the *nonterminal vocabulary* V_n.

(3)   A *start symbol* $S \in V_n$ that starts all derivations. A start symbol is sometimes called a *goal symbol*.

(4)   P, a finite set of productions (sometimes called rewriting rules) of the form $A \rightarrow X_1 \cdots X_m$, where

$$A \in V_n, X_i \in V_n \cup V_t, 1 \leq i \leq m, m \geq 0$$

Note that $A \rightarrow \lambda$ is a valid production.

These components are often grouped into a "four-tuple" (V_t, V_n, S, P), which is the formal definition of a CFG. The *vocabulary* V of a CFG is the set of terminal and nonterminal symbols (that is, $V_t \cup V_n$).

Starting with S, nonterminals are rewritten using productions until only terminals remain (at which point the derivation is done). The set of strings derivable from S comprises the *context-free language* of grammar G, denoted L(G).

In describing CFGs and their parsers, it is sometimes important to distinguish whether a single symbol is required or whether a string of symbols is possible. Similarly, sometimes only a terminal or nonterminal symbol is appropriate, and at other times any vocabulary symbol may occur. To clarify exactly what sorts of symbols and symbol strings are expected, we will use the following notational conventions:

a,b,c, $\cdots$	denote symbols in V_t
A,B,C, $\cdots$	denote symbols in V_n
U,V,W, $\cdots$	denote symbols in V
$\alpha, \beta, \gamma, \cdots$	denote strings in V^*
u,v,w, $\cdots$	denote strings in V_t^*

Using this notation, a production would be written as $A \rightarrow \alpha$ or $A \rightarrow X_1 \cdots X_m$. This format emphasizes that in a production the left-hand side must be a single nonterminal, but the right-hand side is a string of zero or more vocabulary symbols.

Often more than one production shares the same left-hand side. Rather than repeat the left-hand side, an "or notation" is used:

$$A \rightarrow \alpha \mid \beta \mid \cdots \mid \zeta$$

This is an abbreviation for the sequence of productions:

$$A \rightarrow \alpha$$
$$A \rightarrow \beta$$
$$\cdots$$
$$A \rightarrow \zeta$$

If $A \rightarrow \gamma$ is a production, then $\alpha A \beta \Rightarrow \alpha \gamma \beta$, where $\Rightarrow$ denotes a *one-step derivation* (using production $A \rightarrow \gamma$). We extend $\Rightarrow$ to $\Rightarrow^+$, derived in one or more steps, and $\Rightarrow^*$, derived in zero or more steps. If $S \Rightarrow^* \beta$, then β is said to be a *sentential form* of the CFG. SF(G) is the set of sentential forms of grammar G. Similarly, $L(G) = \{x \in V_t^* | S \Rightarrow^+ x\}$. Note that $L(G) = SF(G) \cap V_t^*$; that is, the language of G is simply those sentential forms of G that are terminal strings.

When deriving a token sequence, if more than one nonterminal is present, we have a choice of which to expand next. To characterize a derivation sequence, we therefore need to specify, at each step, which nonterminal is expanded and what production is applied. We can simplify this characterization if we adopt a convention on what nonterminal must be expanded at each step. One obvious convention is to choose the *leftmost* possible nonterminal at each step. A derivation that follows this convention is termed a *leftmost derivation*. If we know a derivation is leftmost, we need only specify what productions are used; the choice of nonterminal is always fixed. To denote derivations that are leftmost, we use $\Rightarrow_{lm}$, $\Rightarrow_{lm}^{+}$, and $\Rightarrow_{lm}^{*}$. A sentential form produced via a leftmost derivation sequence is called a *left sentential form*. The production sequence discovered by a large class of parsers (the top-down parsers) is a leftmost derivation; hence, these parsers are said to produce a *leftmost parse*.

As an example, consider grammar G_0, which generates simple expressions (V represents variables, F represents functions):

E	$\rightarrow$ Prefix (E)
E	$\rightarrow$ V Tail
Prefix	$\rightarrow$ F
Prefix	$\rightarrow \lambda$
Tail	$\rightarrow$ + E
Tail	$\rightarrow \lambda$

A leftmost derivation of F(V+V) is:

$$
\begin{aligned}
E \Rightarrow_{lm} &\ \text{Prefix (E)} \\
\Rightarrow_{lm} &\ \text{F(E)} \\
\Rightarrow_{lm} &\ \text{F(V Tail)} \\
\Rightarrow_{lm} &\ \text{F(V+E)} \\
\Rightarrow_{lm} &\ \text{F(V+V Tail)} \\
\Rightarrow_{lm} &\ \text{F(V+V)}
\end{aligned}
$$

An alternative to a leftmost derivation is a *rightmost* derivation (sometimes called a *canonical* derivation), in which the rightmost possible nonterminal is always expanded. This derivation sequence may seem less intuitive given our normal left-to-right bias, but it corresponds well to an important class of parsers (the bottom-up parsers). In particular, as a bottom-up parser discovers the productions used to derive a token sequence, it discovers a rightmost derivation, but in *reverse order*. That is, the last production applied in a rightmost derivation is the first that is discovered, whereas the first production used, involving the start symbol, is the last to be discovered. The sequence of productions recognized by a bottom-up parser is termed a *rightmost* or *canonical* parse; as noted, it is the exact reverse of the production sequence that represents a rightmost derivation. For derivations that are rightmost, we use the notation $\Rightarrow_{rm}$, $\Rightarrow_{rm}^{+}$, and $\Rightarrow_{rm}^{*}$. A *right sentential form* is a sentential form produced via a rightmost derivation. A rightmost derivation of F(V+V) in grammar G_0 is:

$$E \Rightarrow_{rm} \text{Prefix (E)}$$
$$\Rightarrow_{rm} \text{Prefix (V Tail)}$$
$$\Rightarrow_{rm} \text{Prefix (V+E)}$$
$$\Rightarrow_{rm} \text{Prefix (V+V Tail)}$$
$$\Rightarrow_{rm} \text{Prefix (V+V)}$$
$$\Rightarrow_{rm} \text{F(V+V)}$$

A derivation is often represented by a *parse tree*. A parse tree is rooted by the start symbol; its leaves are grammar symbols or λ. Interior nodes of a parse tree are nonterminals. The offspring of a nonterminal in a parse tree represent the application of a production. That is, a node A can have offspring $X_1 \cdots X_m$ if and only if there exists a production $A \rightarrow X_1 \cdots X_m$. When a derivation is complete, the leaves of the corresponding parse tree are terminal symbols or λ.

As an example, the parse tree corresponding to F(V+V) in grammar G_0 is shown in Figure 4.1. Both leftmost and rightmost derivations are linear representations of a parse tree.

If we have a sentential form, we know it is derivable from the start symbol. Hence, a parse tree must exist. Given a sentential form and a parse tree for it, a *phrase* of a sentential form is a sequence of symbols descended from a

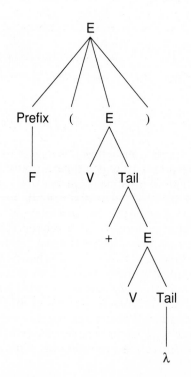

Figure 4.1   The Parse Tree Corresponding to F(V+V)

for it, a *phrase* of a sentential form is a sequence of symbols descended from a single nonterminal in the parse tree. A *simple* or *prime* phrase is a phrase that contains no smaller phrase. That is, a simple phrase is a sequence of symbols directly derived from a nonterminal. The *handle* of a sentential form is the leftmost simple phrase. (Simple phrases cannot overlap, so "leftmost" is unambiguous.) Consider the parse tree in Figure 4.1 and the sentential form F(V Tail). F and V Tail are simple phrases and F is the handle. Handles are important because they represent individual derivation steps, which can be recognized by various parsing techniques.

CFGs that are limited to productions of the form A → a B and C → λ form the class of *regular grammars*. As their name suggests, regular grammars define (exactly) the class of regular sets (see Exercise 6). We observed in Chapter 3 that the language { [^{i}]^i | i≥1} is not regular. This language can be generated by a very simple CFG

    S → [T]
    T → [T] | λ

This grammar establishes that the languages definable by regular grammars (regular sets) are a proper subset of the context-free languages.

Although CFGs are widely used to define the syntax of programming languages, not all syntactic rules are expressible using CFGs. For example, the rule that variables must be declared before they are used cannot be expressed in a CFG—there is no way to transmit the exact set of variables that has been declared to the body of a program. In practice, syntactic details that cannot be represented in a CFG are considered part of the static semantics and are checked by semantic routines (along with scope and type rules).

CFGs can be generalized to create richer definitional mechanisms. *Context-sensitive grammars* require that nonterminals be rewritten only when they appear in a particular context (for example, $\alpha A \beta \rightarrow \alpha \delta \beta$). *Type-0 grammars* are still more general and allow arbitrary patterns to be rewritten (for example, $\alpha \rightarrow \beta$). Although context-sensitive and type-0 grammars are more powerful than CFGs, they are also far less useful. The problem is that efficient parsers for these extended grammar classes do not exist, and without a parser there is no way to use a grammar definition to drive a compiler. Efficient parsers for many classes of CFGs do exist, however; hence, CFGs represent a nice balance between generality and practicality. Throughout this text we will focus on CFGs. Whenever we mention a grammar (without saying which kind), the grammar will be assumed context-free.

4.2. Errors in Context-Free Grammars

CFGs are a definitional mechanism. They may, however, have errors, just as programs may. Some errors are easy to detect and fix; others are far more subtle.

The basic notion of CFGs is that we start with the start symbol and apply productions until a terminal string is produced. Some CFGs are flawed, however, in that they contain "useless" nonterminals. Consider the following grammar (G_1):

$$S \rightarrow A \mid B$$
$$A \rightarrow a$$
$$B \rightarrow B\,b$$
$$C \rightarrow c$$

In G_1, nonterminal C cannot be reached from S (the start symbol), and nonterminal B derives no terminal string. Nonterminals that are unreachable or derive no terminal string are termed *useless*. Useless nonterminals (and productions that involve them) can be safely removed from a grammar without changing the language defined by the grammar. A grammar containing useless nonterminals is said to be *nonreduced*. After useless nonterminals are removed, the grammar is *reduced*. G_1 is nonreduced. After B and C are removed, we obtain an equivalent grammar, G_2, which is reduced:

$$S \rightarrow A$$
$$A \rightarrow a$$

Algorithms that detect useless nonterminals are easy to write (see Exercise 7). Many parser generators check to see if a grammar is reduced. If it is not, the grammar probably contains errors (often caused by mistyping the grammar specification).

A more serious grammar flaw is that sometimes a grammar allows a program to have two or more different parse trees (and thus a nonunique structure). Consider, for example, the following grammar, which generates expressions using just infix –.

$$\text{<expression>} \rightarrow \text{<expression>} - \text{<expression>}$$
$$\text{<expression>} \rightarrow \text{ID}$$

This grammar allows two different parse trees for ID–ID–ID, as illustrated in Figures 4.2 and 4.3.

Grammars that allow different parse trees for the same terminal string are termed *ambiguous*. They are rarely used because a unique structure (that is, parse tree) cannot be guaranteed for all inputs, and hence a unique translation, guided by the parse tree structure, may not be obtained. We normally restrict ourselves to *unambiguous* grammars in order to guarantee unique structure.

Naturally, we would like an algorithm that checks to see if a grammar is ambiguous. However, it is impossible to decide whether a given CFG is ambiguous (Hopcroft and Ullman 1969), so such an algorithm is impossible to create. Fortunately for certain grammar classes, including those for which we can generate parsers, we can prove that constituent grammars are unambiguous.

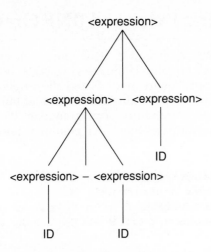

Figure 4.2   A Parse Tree for ID–ID–ID

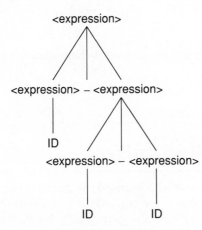

Figure 4.3   An Alternate Parse Tree for ID–ID–ID

serves as the *definition* of a language. Often the correctness of a grammar is tested informally by comparing what one expects to be valid with what a parser for the grammar actually accepts. Although it is rarely done, we might also try to compare for equality the languages defined by a pair of grammars (considering one a standard). For some grammar classes this can be done; for others no comparison algorithm is known. A general comparison algorithm applicable to all CFGs is known to be impossible.

4.3. **Transforming Extended BNF Grammars**

As we noted in Chapter 2, extended BNF grammars are very useful in representing many programming language constructs because they allow options to be specified using square brackets and allow optional list constructs to be defined using braces. In analyzing grammars and building parsers, it is helpful to assume a simpler "standard form" grammar. We can use the algorithm of Figure 4.4 to transform extended BNF grammars into standard form.

```
for (each production P = A → α [X₁ ... Xₙ] β) {
    Create a new nonterminal, N.
    Replace production P with P' = A → α N β
    Add the productions: N → X₁ ... Xₙ and N → λ
}

for (each production Q = B → γ {Y₁ ... Yₘ} δ) {
    Create a new nonterminal, M.
    Replace production Q with Q' = B → γ M δ
    Add the productions: M → Y₁ ... Yₘ M and
                         M → λ
}
```

Figure 4.4   Algorithm to Transform Extended BNF Grammars into Standard Form

4.4. **Parsers and Recognizers**

Assume we somehow know that a grammar is unambiguous. Given an input string as a sequence of tokens, we can ask: Is this input syntactically valid? (That is: Can it be generated from the grammar?) An algorithm that does this boolean-valued test is termed a *recognizer*.

We can also require more of the algorithm and ask: Is this input valid, and, if it is, what is its structure (parse tree)? An algorithm that answers this more general question is termed a *parser*. Since we plan to use language structure to drive compilers, we will be especially interested in parsers.

There are two general approaches to parsing. The first approach, which includes the recursive descent technique we studied in Chapter 2, is termed *top-down*. A parser is considered top-down if it "discovers" the parse tree corresponding to a token sequence by starting at the top of the tree (the start symbol) and then expanding it (via predictions) in a depth-first manner. A top-down parse corresponds to a preorder traversal of the parse tree. Top-down parsing techniques are *predictive* in nature because they always predict the production that is to be matched before matching actually begins.

A wide variety of parsing techniques take a different approach. They belong to the class of *bottom-up* parsers. As the name suggests, bottom-up parsers discover the structure of a parse tree by beginning at its bottom (the leaves of the tree, which are terminal symbols) and determining the productions used to generate the leaves. Then the productions used to generate the immediate parents of the leaves are discovered. The parser continues until it reaches the production used to expand the start symbol. At this point, the entire parse tree has been determined. A bottom-up parse corresponds to a postorder traversal of the parse tree.

To contrast the difference in approach between top-down and bottom-up parsing, consider the following simple grammar, which generates the skeletal block structure of a programming language:

<Program>   → **begin** <Stmts> **end** $
<Stmts>   → <Stmt> ; <Stmts>
<Stmts>   → λ
<Stmt>   → SimpleStmt
<Stmt>   → **begin** <Stmts> **end**

Grammar G_3

A top-down parse of **begin** SimpleStmt ; SimpleStmt ; **end** $ is illustrated in Figure 4.5

A bottom-up parse proceeds by discovering subtrees and linking them into increasingly larger trees. This is shown in Figure 4.6.

The productions predicted by a top-down parser represent a leftmost derivation; hence, as noted earlier, such parsers are said to produce a leftmost parse. The sequence of productions recognized by a bottom-up parser is termed a rightmost parse; and again as noted earlier, it is the exact reverse of the production sequence that represents a rightmost derivation.

When we specify a parsing technique, we must state whether a leftmost or rightmost parse will be produced. The best known and most widely used top-down and bottom-up parsing strategies are called LL and LR. These names seem rather arcane, but they simply encode how the input will be read and the kind of parse that will be produced. In both cases, therefore, the first L states that the token sequence will parse from left to right. The second letter (L or R) states whether a leftmost or rightmost parse will be produced. We may further characterize the parsing technique by including the number of lookahead symbols (that is, symbols beyond the current token) the parser may use to make parsing choices. One-symbol lookahead is most common, so we frequently encounter LL(1) or LR(1) parsers or close variants of these.

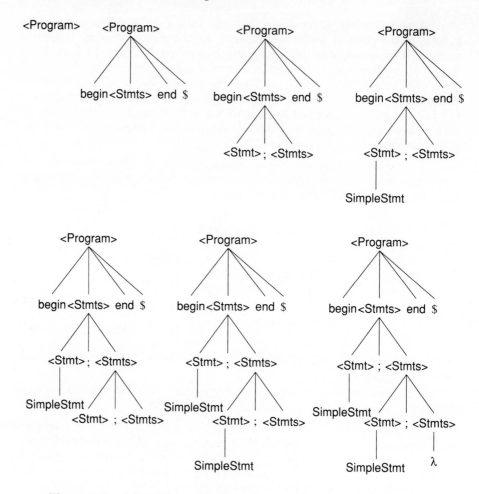

Figure 4.5   A Top-Down Parse

4.5. Grammar Analysis Algorithms

It is often necessary to analyze the properties of a grammar to determine if a grammar is readily parsable and, if so, to build the tables that can be used to drive a parsing algorithm. In this section we discuss a number of important analysis algorithms. Our discussion will serve to reenforce the basic concepts of grammars and derivations. Further, many of the techniques that we discuss are actually needed to build parsers and are found as components of actual parser generators.

To help make our presentation (in this and the following two chapters) more concrete, we will use the following simplified data structure for describing grammars. In particular, we will ignore the details of dynamic allocation

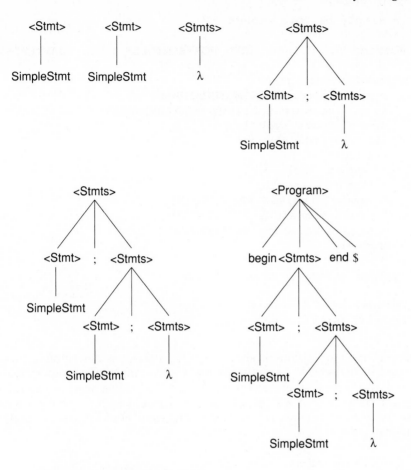

Figure 4.6   A Bottom-Up Parse

that have to be carefully managed in production programs and simply treat each array-valued element as if it was statically allocated.

A grammar, G, is represented by a record (a C **struct**). It has fields named **terminals**, **nonterminals**, **productions**, and **start_symbol**. The **productions** field is an array of **struct**s, each of which has fields **lhs**, **rhs**, and **rhs_length**. In addition, it is sometimes useful to refer to the whole **vocabulary**, which is a combination of the **terminals** and **nonterminals**. (The **vocabulary** information would not actually be duplicated in practice.)

```
typedef int symbol;   /* a symbol in the grammar */
/*
 * The symbolic constants used below, NUM_TERMINALS,
 * NUM_NONTERMINALS, and NUM_PRODUCTIONS are
 * determined by the grammar.  MAX_RHS_LENGTH should
```

```
       * simply be "big enough."
       */
      #define VOCABULARY   (NUM_NONTERMINALS + NUM_TERMINALS)

      typedef struct gram {
         symbol terminals[NUM_TERMINALS];
         symbol nonterminals[NUM_NONTERMINALS];
         symbol start_symbol;
         int num_productions;
         struct prod {
            symbol lhs;
            int rhs_length;
            symbol rhs[MAX_RHS_LENGTH];
         } productions[NUM_PRODUCTIONS];
         symbol vocabulary[VOCABULARY];
      } grammar;

      typedef struct prod production;

      typedef symbol terminal;
      typedef symbol nonterminal;
```

One of the most common grammar computations is determining what nonterminals can derive λ. This information is important because nonterminals that can derive λ may disappear during a parse and hence must be carefully handled. Determining if a nonterminal can derive λ is not entirely trivial because the derivation may take more than one step. For example, we might have the sequence

$$A \Rightarrow BCD \Rightarrow BC \Rightarrow B \Rightarrow \lambda$$

To make this computation, we employ an iterative marking algorithm. First, nonterminals that derive λ trivially (in one step) are marked. Then nonterminals requiring a parse tree height of two are found. We continue with this, finding nonterminals requiring parse trees of ever-increasing height, until no more nonterminals can be marked as deriving λ. The complete algorithm is shown in Figure 4.7.

When constructing parsers, we often analyze a grammar to compute a set Follow(A), where A is any nonterminal. Informally, Follow(A) is the set of terminals that may follow A in some sentential form. If A can appear as the rightmost symbol in a sentential form, λ is included in Follow(A) (signifying that A may have no symbol following it). More precisely, for $A \in V_n$,

$$\text{Follow}(A) = \{a \in V_t \mid S \Rightarrow^+ \cdots Aa \cdots \} \bigcup (\text{if } S \Rightarrow^+ \alpha A \text{ then } \{\lambda\} \text{ else } \varnothing)$$

Follow sets are useful because they define the right context consistent with a given nonterminal. That is, Follow(A) provides the lookaheads that might signal the recognition of a production with A as the left-hand side.

```c
typedef short boolean;
typedef boolean marked_vocabulary[VOCABULARY];

/*
 * Mark those vocabulary symbols found to
 * derive λ (directly or indirectly).
 */
marked_vocabulary mark_lambda(const grammar g)
{
    static marked_vocabulary derives_lambda;
    boolean changes;
                /* any changes during last iteration? */
    boolean rhs_derives_lambda;
                /* does the RHS derive λ? */
    symbol v;       /* a word in the vocabulary */
    production p;   /* a production in the grammar */
    int i, j;       /* loop variables */

    for (v = 0; v < VOCABULARY; v++)
       derives_lambda[v] = FALSE;
       /* initially, nothing is marked */

    do {
       changes = FALSE;
       for (i = 0; i < g.num_productions; i++) {
           p = g.productions[i];
           if (! derives_lambda[p.lhs]) {
               if (p.rhs_length == 0) {
                   /* derives λ directly */
                   changes = derives_lambda[p.lhs] = TRUE;
                   continue;
               }
               /* does each part of RHS derive λ? */
               rhs_derives_lambda = derives_lambda[p.rhs[0]];
               for (j = 1; j < p.rhs_length; j++)
                   rhs_derives_lambda = rhs_derives_lambda
                               && derives_lambda[p.rhs[j]];

               if (rhs_derives_lambda)
                   changes = TRUE;
                   derives_lambda[p.lhs] = TRUE;
           }
       }
    } while (changes);
    return derives_lambda;
}
```

Figure 4.7   Algorithm for Determining If a Nonterminal Can Derive λ

Another set commonly used in building parsers is First(α). First(α) is the set of all the terminal symbols that can begin a sentential form derivable from α. We also include λ if $\alpha \Rightarrow^* \lambda$. Formally,

$$First(\alpha) = \{a \in V_t \mid \alpha \Rightarrow^* a\beta\} \cup (\text{if } \alpha \Rightarrow^* \lambda \text{ then } \{\lambda\} \text{ else } \varnothing)$$

If α is the right-hand side of a production, then First(α) contains terminal symbols that begin strings derivable from α.

We will represent the First set of a grammar by the array `first_set[X]`, in which `X` is any single vocabulary symbol. Elements of `first_set` are terminal symbols and λ. Similarly, our representation of Follow sets will be an array `follow_set[A]`, where `A` is a nonterminal symbol. Again, elements of `follow_set` are terminal symbols and λ.

For an arbitrary string α (of mixed terminals and nonterminals), we can't have the First and Follow sets precomputed, so we use an algorithm `compute_first(`α`)` that returns the set of terminals defined by First(α). If α happens to be exactly one symbol long, `compute_first(`α`)` will simply return `first_set[`α`]`. `compute_first()` and related definitions are shown in Figure 4.8.

```
typedef set_of_terminal_or_lambda termset;
termset follow_set[NUM_NONTERMINAL];
termset first_set[SYMBOL];
marked_vocabulary derives_lambda = mark_lambda(g);
/* mark_lambda(g) as defined above */

termset compute_first(string_of_symbols alpha)
{
 int i, k;
 termset result;

 k = length(alpha);
 if (k == 0)
    result = SET_OF( λ );
 else {
   result = first_set[alpha[0]];
   for (i = 1; i < k && λ ∈ first_set[alpha[i-1]]; i++)
     result = result ∪ (first_set[alpha[i]] − SET_OF( λ ));

   if (i == k && λ ∈ first_set[alpha[k − 1]])
     result = result ∪ SET_OF( λ );
 }
 return result;
}
```

Figure 4.8   Algorithm to Compute First(alpha)

fill_first_set() is defined in Figure 4.9. It initializes **first_set**. The algorithm operates iteratively, first considering single productions, then considering chains of productions.

```
extern grammar g;

void fill_first_set(void)
{
    nonterminal A;
    terminal    a;
    production  p;
    boolean     changes;
    int         i, j;

    for (i = 0; i < NUM_NONTERMINAL; i++) {
      A = g.nonterminals[i];
      if (derives_lambda[A])
         first_set[A] = SET_OF( λ );
      else
         first_set[A] = ∅;
    }
    for (i = 0; i < NUM_TERMINAL; i++) {
      a = g.terminals[i];
      first_set[a] = SET_OF( a );
      for (j = 0; j < NUM_NONTERMINAL; j++) {
        A = g.nonterminals[j];
        if (there exists a production A → aβ)
           first_set[A] = first_set[A] ∪ SET_OF( a );
      }
    }
    do {
      changes = FALSE;
      for (i = 0; i < g.num_productions; i++) {
        p = g.productions[i];
        first_set[p.lhs] = first_set[p.lhs] ∪
           compute_first(p.rhs);
        if ( first_set changed )
           changes = TRUE;
      }
    } while (changes);
}
```

Figure 4.9   Algorithm to Compute First Sets for V

The execution of **fill_first_set()** is illustrated as follows using grammar G_0 (p. 93):

Step	first_set							
	E	Prefix	Tail	(	)	V	F	+
(1) First loop	∅	{λ}	{λ}					
(2) Second (nested) loop	{V}	{F,λ}	{+,λ}	{(}	{)}	{V}	{F}	{+}
(3) Third loop, production 1	{V,F,(}	{F,λ}	{+,λ}	{(}	{)}	{V}	{F}	{+}

fill_follow_set() is defined in Figure 4.10. It initializes **follow_set**. The algorithm locates nonterminal occurrences in a production and then computes First values for the production suffix following the nonterminal. If λ is in the First set, the Follow set of the left-hand side is included.

```
void fill_follow_set(void)
{
   nonterminal A, B;
   int i;
   boolean    changes;

   for (i = 0; i < NUM_NONTERMINAL; i++) {
      A = g.nonterminals[i];
      follow_set[A] = ∅;
   }
   follow_set[g.start_symbol] = SET_OF( λ );

   do {
      changes = FALSE;
      for (each production A → αBβ) {
         /*
          * I.e. for each production and each occurrence
          * of a nonterminal in its right-hand side.
          */
         follow_set[B] = follow_set[B] ∪
               (compute_first(β) - SET_OF( λ ));
         if ( λ ∈ compute_first(β) )
            follow_set[B] = follow_set[B] ∪ follow_set[A];
         if ( follow_set[B] changed )
            changes = TRUE;
      }
   } while (changes);
}
```

Figure 4.10   Algorithm to Compute Follow Sets for All Nonterminals

As an example, we illustrate the execution of `fill_follow_set()` on grammar G_0 (p. 93):

Step	follow_set		
	E	Prefix	Tail
(1) Initialization	{λ}	∅	∅
(2) Process Prefix in production 1	{λ}	{(}	∅
(3) Process E in production 1	{λ,)}	{(}	∅
(4) Process Tail in production 2	{λ,)}	{(}	{λ,)}

First and Follow sets can be generalized to include strings of length k rather than length one. $First_k(\alpha)$ is the set of k-symbol terminal prefixes derivable from α. Similarly, $Follow_k(A)$ is the set of k-symbol terminal strings that can follow A in some sentential form. $First_k$ and $Follow_k$ are used in the definition of parsing techniques that use k-symbol lookaheads (for example, LL(k) and LR(k)). The algorithms that compute $First_1$ and $Follow_1$ can be generalized to compute $First_k$ and $Follow_k$.

More Examples of Computing First and Follow Sets

To further illustrate the operation of the programs that compute First and Follow sets, we present two additional examples. For the following grammar

$$
\begin{aligned}
S &\rightarrow a\,S\,e \\
S &\rightarrow B \\
B &\rightarrow b\,B\,e \\
B &\rightarrow C \\
C &\rightarrow c\,C\,e \\
C &\rightarrow d
\end{aligned}
$$

The execution of `fill_first_set` would proceed as follows:

Step	first_set							
	S	B	C	a	b	c	d	e
(1) First loop	∅	∅	∅					
(2) Second (nested) loop	{a}	{b}	{c,d}	{a}	{b}	{c}	{d}	{e}
(3) Third loop, production 2	{a,b}	{b}	{c,d}	{a}	{b}	{c}	{d}	{e}
(4) Third loop, production 4	{a,b}	{b,c,d}	{c,d}	{a}	{b}	{c}	{d}	{e}
(5) Third loop, production 2	{a,b,c,d}	{b,c,d}	{c,d}	{a}	{b}	{c}	{d}	{e}

The execution of `fill_follow_set` is illustrated by

Step	follow_set		
	S	B	C
(1) Initialization	{λ}	∅	∅
(2) Process S in production 1	{e,λ}	∅	∅
(3) Process B in production 2	{e,λ}	{e,λ}	∅
(4) Process B in production 3	no changes		
(5) Process C in production 4	{e,λ}	{e,λ}	{e,λ}
(6) Process C in production 5	no changes		

For the second example grammar

```
S  → A B c
A  → a
A  → λ
B  → b
B  → λ
```

The execution of `fill_first_set` would proceed as follows:

Step	first_set					
	S	A	B	a	b	c
(1) First loop	∅	{λ}	{λ}			
(2) Second (nested) loop	∅	{a,λ}	{b,λ}	{a}	{b}	{c}
(3) Third loop, production 1	{a,b,c}	{a,λ}	{b,λ}	{a}	{b}	{c}

The execution of `fill_follow_set` is illustrated by

Step	follow_set		
	S	A	B
(1) Initialization	{λ}	∅	∅
(2) Process A in production 1	{λ}	{b,c}	∅
(3) Process B in production 1	{λ}	{b,c}	{c}

Exercises

1.   Take the extended CFG definition of Micro (Figure 2.4 of Chapter 2) and transform it into a standard form CFG using the algorithm of Section 4.3.

2. Take the CFG that defines Micro (in either extended or standard form) and extend it to include an equality operator, =, and an exponentiation operator, **. Equal should have a lower operator precedence than plus and minus, and exponentiation should have a higher precedence. That is, A+B**2=C+D should be equivalent to (A+(B**2))=(C+D). Further, exponentiation should group from the right [so that A**B**C is equivalent to A**(B**C)], and equal should not group at all (A=B=C is illegal). Be sure that your grammar is unambiguous.

3. Use **fill_first_set()** and **fill_follow_set()** to compute **first_set** and **follow_set** for the CFG that defines Micro.

4. A production of the form $A \rightarrow A\alpha$ is said to be *left-recursive*. Similarly, a production of the form $B \rightarrow \beta B$ is said to be *right-recursive*. Show that any grammar that contains both left- and right-recursive productions with the same left-hand side symbol must be ambiguous.

5. Assume we wish to generate a list of options chosen from a set of n choices $\{O_1, \ldots, O_n\}$. The list can contain any subset of options, in any order, but no option may be repeated. Write a CFG that generates lists of the desired form.

    What is the relation between the size of your grammar and n, the number of possible options?

    Is your grammar simplified or made more complicated if we further require that the options appear in a particular order (for example, O_i can appear before O_j only if i<j)?

6. Show that regular grammars and finite automata have equal definitional power by writing algorithms that translate regular grammars into finite automata and vice versa.

7. A CFG is reduced by removing useless nonterminals and productions involving useless nonterminals. We may reduce a grammar by first removing nonterminals not reachable from the start symbol and then removing nonterminals that do not derive any terminal string. Alternatively, we might first remove nonterminals that derive no terminal string and then remove unreachable nonterminals. Are these two alternatives equivalent? If not, which order is preferable?

8. Outline a proof that **fill_first_set()** correctly computes **first_set** values for all vocabulary symbols.

9. Let G be any CFG and assume that $\lambda \notin L(G)$. Show that G can be transformed into an equivalent CFG that uses no λ-productions.

10. A *unit production* is a production of the form $A \rightarrow B$, where B is a single nonterminal. Show that any CFG containing unit productions can be transformed into an equivalent CFG that uses no unit productions.

11. Some CFGs generate languages that have an infinite size; others generate a language of finite size. Write an algorithm that tests whether a given CFG generates an infinite language.

    Hint: Use the results of Exercises 9 and 10 to simplify the analysis.

12.   Let G be an unambiguous CFG without λ-productions. If $x \in L(G)$, show
      that the number of steps needed to derive x is linear in the length of x.

      Does this linearity result hold if λ-productions are included?

      Does this linearity result hold for ambiguous CFGs?

13.   Write a program that takes extended CFGs and transforms them into
      equivalent standard-form CFGs, using the algorithm of Section 4.3.

CHAPTER 5

LL(1) Grammars and Parsers

In Chapter 2, we learned the rudiments of recursive descent parsing. We now study *LL(1) grammars,* which are the class of CFGs suitable for recursive descent parsing. We also define *LL(1) parsers,* which use an *LL(1) parse table* rather than recursive procedures to control parsing.

As we have already seen, CFGs are an extremely useful *definitional mechanism.* They are also frequently used to automatically generate a parser. The idea here is to use a program, a *parser generator,* that takes as input any of a class of grammars and produces as output a parser that will correctly parse the language defined by that grammar. This concept parallels that of a compiler—high-level definitions (source programs or grammars) are translated into executable forms (object programs or parsers). This approach makes building a parser one of the easiest parts of building a compiler—a grammar is written and then fed to an automatic parser generator. Also, changing a parser (for example, because new constructs are added to a language) is equally easy; a new parser is created from an updated grammar.

5.1. **The LL(1) Predict Function**

As we learned in Chapter 2, recursive descent parsers use parsing procedures to match the tokens generated by nonterminals. The main problem in building a parsing procedure is deciding which production to match. This decision can be formalized by defining a **Predict** function that examines the lookahead symbol to deduce the production that must be used to expand each nonterminal.

Consider a production $A \to X_1 \cdots X_m$, $m \geq 0$. We need to compute the set of possible lookahead tokens that might indicate that this production is to be matched. This set is clearly those terminals that can be produced by $X_1 \cdots X_m$. Since a lookahead is only a single token, we want the set of first (that is, leftmost) tokens that can be produced. As we learned in Chapter 4, this set of tokens is $First(X_1 \cdots X_m)$.

We initially consider the leftmost symbol, X_1. If this is a terminal, then $First(X_1 \cdots X_m) = X_1$. If X_1 is a nonterminal, then we compute a First set for each right-hand side corresponding to X_1. What if X_1 can generate λ? Then X_1 can, in effect, be erased, and $First(X_1 \cdots X_m)$ depends on X_2. In particular, if X_2 is a terminal, it is included in $First(X_1 \cdots X_m)$. If it is a nonterminal, we compute First sets for each of its corresponding right-hand sides. Similarly, if both X_1 and X_2 can produce λ, we consider X_3, and so on. What if the entire right-hand side can produce λ? Then the lookahead will be determined by those terminals that can follow the left-hand side (A in our example). We therefore use $Follow(A)$, which is the set of tokens that can follow A in some legal derivation.

We now define the set of lookahead tokens that will cause the prediction of the production $A \to X_1 \cdots X_m$. Call this set **Predict**:

$$
\begin{aligned}
Predict(A \to X_1 \cdots X_m) = \\
&\text{if } \lambda \in First(X_1 \cdots X_m) \\
&\qquad (First(X_1 \cdots X_m) - \lambda) \cup Follow(A) \\
&\text{else} \\
&\qquad First(X_1 \cdots X_m)
\end{aligned}
$$

That is, any token that can be the first symbol produced by the right-hand side of a production will predict that production. Further, if the entire right-hand side can produce λ [$\lambda \in First(X_1 \cdots X_m)$], then tokens that can immediately follow the left-hand side of a production will also predict that production. Because λ is not a terminal symbol, it cannot be a lookahead and hence is not included in any **Predict** set.

We have one final issue that must be dealt with. What if, for two productions, $A \to X_1 \cdots X_m$ and $A \to Y_1 \cdots Y_p$, we have some token t for which $t \in Predict(A \to X_1 \cdots X_m)$ and $t \in Predict(A \to Y_1 \cdots Y_p)$. That is, what if the same token predicts more than one production? This conflict will exclude the grammar from the LL(1) grammar class. LL(1) contains exactly those grammars that have disjoint predict sets for productions that share a common left-hand side. From experience it has been learned that it is usually possible to

1	\<program\>	→ **begin** \<statement list\> **end**
2	\<statement list\>	→ \<statement\> \<statement tail\>
3	\<statement tail\>	→ \<statement\> \<statement tail\>
4	\<statement tail\>	→ λ
5	\<statement\>	→ ID := \<expression\> ;
6	\<statement\>	→ **read** (\<id list\>) ;
7	\<statement\>	→ **write** (\<expr list\>) ;
8	\<id list\>	→ ID \<id tail\>
9	\<id tail\>	→ , ID \<id tail\>
10	\<id tail\>	→ λ
11	\<expr list\>	→ \<expression\> \<expr tail\>
12	\<expr tail\>	→ , \<expression\> \<expr tail\>
13	\<expr tail\>	→ λ
14	\<expression\>	→ \<primary\> \<primary tail\>
15	\<primary tail\>	→ \<add op\> \<primary\> \<primary tail\>
16	\<primary tail\>	→ λ
17	\<primary\>	→ (\<expression\>)
18	\<primary\>	→ ID
19	\<primary\>	→ INTLIT
20	\<add op\>	→ +
21	\<add op\>	→ −
22	\<system goal\>	→ \<program\> $

Figure 5.1   A Micro Grammar in Standard Form

create an LL(1) grammar for a programming language. *Not all* grammars are LL(1), however. Many grammars that are not LL(1) belong to other (more complex) grammar classes for which parsers can be automatically constructed.

To make sure we understand the concepts just introduced, let's see how the **Predict** function is computed for the productions of Micro.

Figure 5.1 shows the Micro grammar of Chapter 2 put into standard form, using the algorithm of Section 4.3 (Figure 4.4). $ is used to denote the end-of-file token.

Figures 5.2 and 5.3 show the First and Follow sets of Micro's nonterminals, computed using the techniques of Section 4.5 (Figures 4.8–4.10). For grammars as small as Micro's, these sets can simply be computed by hand. For larger grammars, it is safer to use an automatic tool. (The LLGen tool of Section 5.8 has an option that causes it to list First and Follow sets.)

Next, **Predict** sets are computed by substituting First and Follow sets and simplifying the expressions. This is illustrated in Figure 5.4.

Nonterminal	First Set
<program>	{**begin**}
<statement list>	{ID, **read**, **write**}
<statement>	{ID, **read**, **write**}
<statement tail>	{ID, **read**, **write**, λ}
<expression>	{ID, INTLIT, (}
<id list>	{ID}
<expr list>	{ID, INTLIT, (}
<id tail>	{COMMA ,λ}
<expr tail>	{COMMA ,λ}
<primary>	{ID, INTLIT, (}
<primary tail>	{+, −, λ}
<add op>	{+, −}
<system goal>	{**begin**}

Figure 5.2   First Sets for Micro

NonTerminal	Follow Set
<program>	{$}
<statement list>	{**end**}
<statement>	{ID, **read**, **write**, **end**}
<statement tail>	{**end**}
<expression>	{COMMA, SEMICOLON,)}
<id list>	{)}
<expr list>	{)}
<id tail>	{)}
<expr tail>	{)}
<primary>	{COMMA, SEMICOLON, +, −,)}
<primary tail>	{COMMA, SEMICOLON,)}
<add op>	{ID, INTLIT, (}
<system goal>	{λ}

Figure 5.3   Follow Sets for Micro

Prod	Predict Set		
1	First(**begin** <statement list> **end**) =	First(**begin**) =	{**begin**}
2	First(<statement> <statement tail>) =	First(<statement>) =	{ID, **read**, **write**}
3	First(<statement> <statement tail>) =	First(<statement>) =	{ID, **read**, **write**}
4	(First(λ)−λ) ∪ Follow(<statement tail>) =	Follow(<statement tail>) =	{**end**}
5	First(ID := <expression> ;) =	First(ID) =	{ID}
6	First(**read** (<id list>) ;) =	First(**read**) =	{**read**}
7	First(**write** (<expr list>) ;) =	First(**write**) =	{**write**}
8	First(ID <id tail>) =	First(ID) =	{ID}
9	First(, ID <id tail>) =	First(,) =	{,}
10	(First(λ)−λ) ∪ Follow(<id tail>) =	Follow(<id tail>) =	{)}
11	First(<expression> <expr tail>) =	First(<expression>) =	{ID, INTLIT, (}
12	First(, <expression> <expr tail>) =	First(,) =	{,}
13	(First(λ)−λ) ∪ Follow(<expr tail>) =	Follow(<expr tail>) =	{)}
14	First(<primary> <primary tail>) =	First(<primary>) =	{ID, INTLIT, (}
15	First(<add op> <primary> <primary tail>) =	First(<add op>) =	{+, −}
16	(First(λ)−λ) ∪ Follow(<primary tail>) =	Follow(<primary tail>) =	{COMMA, ;,)}
17	First((<expression>)) =	First(() =	{(}
18	First(ID) =		{ID}
19	First(INTLIT) =		{INTLIT}
20	First(+) =		{+}
21	First(−) =		{−}
22	First(<program> $) =	First(<program>) =	{**begin**}

Figure 5.4   Calculation of Predict Sets for Micro

5.2. The LL(1) Parse Table

The parsing information contained in the Predict function can be conveniently represented in an *LL(1) parse table*. This table, T, is of the form

$$T : V_n{\times}V_t \rightarrow P \cup \{Error\}$$

where P is the set of all productions. If A is a nonterminal to be matched and t is a lookahead token, T[A][t] tells what production to predict. If no production is appropriate, T[A][t] yields an Error value, indicating a syntax error. T is defined as follows:

$$T[A][t] = A \rightarrow X_1 \cdots X_m \text{ if } t \in Predict(A \rightarrow X_1 \cdots X_m);$$
$$T[A][t] = Error \text{ otherwise}$$

A grammar G is LL(1) if and only if all entries in T contain a unique prediction or an error flag. Stated differently, if G is LL(1), then for any nonterminal A and any lookahead symbol t it cannot be the case that t ∈ Predict(A → α) and t ∈ Predict(A → β), where A → α and A → β are distinct productions.

It is now easy to see why LL(1) grammars are so well suited to top-down parsing. If a grammar is LL(1), we are guaranteed a unique prediction, or an error flag, for any possible combination of nonterminal and lookahead symbol. All predictions are unique, so it is trivial to replace nonterminals with the right-hand side of the correct production. This allows us to build a parse tree for any valid input string, starting at the start symbol and working downward toward the input symbols that are the leaves of the tree.

As an example, we will take the Predict sets we computed for Micro and transform them into the LL(1) parse table of Figure 5.5. This table can then be used to build the parsing procedures that constitute a recursive descent parser for Micro, or the tables can be used directly to drive an LL(1) parser. In the figure, integer entries are production numbers; blanks are error entries.

	ID	INTLIT	:=	,	;	+	−	(	)	begin	end	read	write	$
<program>										1				
<statement list>	2											2	2	
<statement>	5											6	7	
<statement tail>	3										4	3	3	
<expression>	14	14						14						
<id list>	8													
<expr list>	11	11						11						
<id tail>				9					10					
<expr tail>				12					13					
<primary>	18	19						17						
<primary tail>				16	16	15	15		16					
<add op>						20	21							
<system goal>								22						

Figure 5.5   The LL(1) Table for Micro

5.3. Building Recursive Descent Parsers from LL(1) Tables

LL(1) tables are computed from a grammar when a parser is built. The parsing decisions recorded in LL(1) tables can be hardwired into the parsing procedures used by recursive descent parsers. Recall from Chapter 2 that parsing procedures are of the form

```
void non_term(void)
{
    token tok = next_token();
    switch (tok) {
    case TERMINAL_LIST:
        parsing_actions();
        break;
      . . .
    default:
        syntax_error(tok);
        break;
    }
}
```

`non_term()` is the name of the nonterminal the parsing procedure handles.
`next_token()` returns the lookahead symbol.   `TERMINAL_LIST` represents
a list of terminal symbols.   `parsing_actions()` represents a sequence of
parsing actions: calls to parsing procedures to match nonterminals and calls to
`match()` to match terminal symbols.   `syntax_error()` is called if
`next_token()` predicts no valid production.

More tangibly, the parsing procedure of Figure 5.6 matches <statement>
in Micro:

```
void statement(void)
{
    token tok;

    tok = next_token();
    switch (tok) {
    case ID:
        match(ID); match(ASSIGNOP); expression();
        match(SEMICOLON);
        break;

    case READ:
        match(READ); match(LPAREN); id_list();
        match(RPAREN); match(SEMICOLON);
        break;

    case WRITE:
        match(WRITE); match(LPAREN); expr_list();
        match(RPAREN); match(SEMICOLON);
        break;

    default:
        syntax_error(tok);
        break;
    }
}
```

Figure 5.6   Parsing Procedure for <statement>

We shall consider an algorithm that automatically creates parsing procedures like the one in Figure 5.6 from the LL(1) table of a grammar. All procedures will be in this form. The values of **TERMINAL_LIST** and **parsing_actions()** will be instantiated from the LL(1) table.

We now augment the data structure for describing grammars from Chapter 4 with the **names** of the symbols in the grammar. A **grammar** is now

```
typedef int symbol;     /* a symbol in the grammar */

#define VOCABULARY   (NUM_NONTERMINALS + NUM_TERMINALS)

typedef struct gram {
    symbol terminals[NUM_TERMINALS];
    symbol nonterminals[NUM_NONTERMINALS];
    symbol start_symbol;
    int num_productions;
    struct prod {
        symbol lhs;
        int rhs_length;
        symbol rhs[MAX_RHS_LENGTH];
    } productions[NUM_PRODUCTIONS];
    symbol vocabulary[VOCABULARY];
    char *names[VOCABULARY];
} grammar;

typedef struct prod production;

typedef symbol terminal;
typedef symbol nonterminal;
```

Assume we have an array of grammar symbols that we wish to match in a parsing procedure. The routine **gen_actions()** (Figure 5.7) takes the grammar symbols and generates the actions (calls to parsing procedures and **match()**) necessary to match them in a recursive descent parser. **gen_actions()** assumes a function **make_id()** that takes the name of a grammar symbol and transforms it into a valid program identifier. This may involve stripping illegal characters, like < and >, removing embedded blanks, renaming characters, and so on. For example, **make_id("<statement list>")** returns **"statementlist,"** and **make_id(":=")** returns **"COLONEQUAL"**.

make_parsing_proc() is defined in Figure 5.8. This algorithm takes a nonterminal and an LL(1) table and generates a complete parsing procedure for the nonterminal. The routine assumes two functions: **prods()** and **rhs()**. **prods(A)** returns the set of productions with A as the left-hand side. **rhs(P)** returns the string of symbols that is the right-hand side of production P.

```c
extern char *make_id(char *);

void gen_actions(symbol x[], int x_length);
{
    int i;
    char *id;

    /*
     * Generate recursive descent
     * actions needed to match x.
     */
    if (x_length == 0)
        printf ("; /* null */\n");
    else {
        for (i = 0; i < x_length; i++) {
            id = make_id(g.names[x[i]]);
            if (is_terminal(x[i]))
                printf("\t\tmatch(%s);\n", id);
            else
                printf("\t\t%s();\n", id);
        }
    }
}
```

Figure 5.7   Algorithm to Generate Recursive Descent Actions

```c
void make_parsing_proc(const nonterminal A,
                       const lltable T)
{
    /*
     * Generate recursive descent
     * parsing procedure for A.
     */
    extern grammar g;
    production p;
    terminal x;
    int i, j;

    printf("void %s(void)\n{\n", make_id(g.names[A]));
    printf("\ttoken tok = next_token()\n");
    printf("\tswitch (tok) {\n");

    /* for each production where A is the LHS */
    for (i = 0; i < g.num_productions; i++) {
        if (g.productions[i].lhs != A)
            continue;
        p = g.productions[i];
```

```
        /* for each terminal in the grammar */
        for (j = 0; j < NUM_TERMINALS; j++) {
          x = g.terminals[j];
          if (T[A][x] == i)   /* this production */
            printf("\tcase %s:\n", make_id(g.names[x]));
        }
        gen_actions(p.rhs, p.rhs_length);
        printf("\t\tbreak;\n");
      }
      printf("\tdefault:\n");
      printf("\t\tsyntax_error(tok);\n");
      printf("\tbreak;\n\t}\n}\n");
  }
```

Figure 5.8   Algorithm to Generate Parsing Procedures

It is a good exercise to verify that **make_parsing_proc()**, when given <statement> and the LL(1) table shown in Figure 5.5 as arguments, will generate the parsing procedure illustrated in Figure 5.6, with a few identifiers possibly renamed.

make_parsing_proc() can easily be extended to generate more efficient parsing procedures for certain special cases. Most significantly, if a nonterminal can only be expanded one way, there is no need to generate any conditional logic. Rather, the body of the parsing procedure is simply **gen_actions(rhs(p))**, where p is the production to be matched. This optimization was used extensively in the parsing procedures of Chapter 2.

5.4. An LL(1) Parser Driver

Recursive descent parsing procedures are normally augmented with code that performs semantic analysis and code generation. Because of this, parsing procedures, once built and integrated into a compiler, are not easy to change. The grammar that represents the syntax of a programming language often must be updated to accommodate new or modified constructs. It is, therefore, desirable to have a way of updating a parser without unnecessarily affecting other compiler components.

Rather than using the LL(1) table to build parsing procedures, it is possible to use the table in conjunction with a driver program to form an *LL(1) parser*. LL(1) tables are computed only once—when a parser is built. The tables are considered read-only by the LL(1) driver that uses them to control parsing. Because the same driver is used with all LL(1) tables, changing a grammar and building a new parser is easy—new LL(1) tables are computed and substituted for the old tables. Further, since the LL(1) driver uses a stack rather than recursive procedure calls to store symbols yet to be matched, the resulting parser can be expected to be smaller and faster than a corresponding recursive descent parser.

```
void lldriver(void)
{
    /* Push the Start Symbol onto an empty stack. */
    push(s);

    while (! stack_empty() ) {
        /* Let X be the top stack symbol; */
        /* let a be the current input token. */

        if (is_nonterminal(X)
                && T[X][a] == X → Y₁ · · · Yₘ) {
            /* Expand non-terminal */
            pop(1);
            Push Yₘ, Yₘ₋₁, · · · Y₁ onto the stack;
        } else if (X == a) {    /* X in terminals */
            pop(1);                /* Match of X worked */
            scanner(& a);          /* Get next token */
        } else
            /* Process syntax error. */
    }
}
```

Figure 5.9   An LL(1) Parser Driver

The LL(1) driver shown in Figure 5.9 is very simple. It stacks symbols that are to be matched or expanded. Terminal symbols on the stack must match an input symbol; nonterminal symbols are expanded using the LL(1) table.

At this point, we will redo the recursive descent parsing example of Section 2.5.5, this time using the LL(1) parse table and driver. Figure 5.10 illustrates the steps performed by an LL(1) parser given an input of **begin** A := BB – 314 + A; **end** $.

5.5. LL(1) Action Symbols

Recall from Chapter 2 that action symbols of the form #Name are added to a grammar to mark where semantic actions are required. Action symbols are not actually part of a grammar and are ignored when an LL(1) table is computed. During parsing, the appearance of an action symbol in a production will serve to initiate the corresponding semantic action.

In the case of recursive descent parsers, we will extend the **gen_actions()** routine of Section 5.3 (Figure 5.7) to include action symbols as well as grammar symbols. When an action symbol is processed, it will be translated to a call to the corresponding semantic routine. For example, the

Step	Parser Action	Remaining Input	Parse Stack
(1)	Predict 22	**begin** A:=BB–314+A ; **end** $	<system goal>
(2)	Predict 1	**begin** A:=BB–314+A ; **end** $	<program> $
(3)	Match	**begin** A:=BB–314+A ; **end** $	**begin** <statement list> **end** $
(4)	Predict 2	A:=BB–314+A ; **end** $	<statement list> **end** $
(5)	Predict 5	A:=BB–314+A ; **end** $	<statement> <statement tail> **end** $
(6)	Match	A:=BB–314+A ; **end** $	ID := <expression> ; <statement tail> **end** $
(7)	Match	:=BB–314+A ; **end** $	:= <expression> ; <statement tail> **end** $
(8)	Predict 14	BB–314+A ; **end** $	<expression> ; <statement tail> **end** $
(9)	Predict 18	BB–314+A ; **end** $	<primary> <primary tail> ; <statement tail> **end** $
(10)	Match	BB–314+A ; **end** $	ID <primary tail> ; <statement tail> **end** $
(11)	Predict 15	–314+A ; **end** $	<primary tail> ; <statement tail> **end** $
(12)	Predict 21	–314+A ; **end** $	<add op> <primary> <primary tail> ; <statement tail> **end** $
(13)	Match	–314+A ; **end** $	– <primary> <primary tail> ; <statement tail> **end** $
(14)	Predict 19	314+A ; **end** $	<primary> <primary tail> ; <statement tail> **end** $
(15)	Match	314+A ; **end** $	IntLiteral <primary tail> ; <statement tail> **end** $
(16)	Predict 15	+A ; **end** $	<primary tail> ; <statement tail> **end** $
(17)	Predict 20	+A ; **end** $	<add op> <primary> <primary tail> ; <statement tail> **end** $
(18)	Match	+A ; **end** $	+ <primary> <primary tail> ; <statement tail> **end** $
(19)	Predict 18	A ; **end** $	<primary> <primary tail> ; <statement tail> **end** $
(20)	Match	A ; **end** $	ID <primary tail> ; <statement tail> **end** $
(21)	Predict 16	; **end** $	<primary tail> ; <statement tail> **end** $
(22)	Match	; **end** $	; <statement tail> **end** $
(23)	Predict 4	**end** $	<statement tail> **end** $
(24)	Match	**end** $	**end** $
(25)	Match	$	$

Figure 5.10   An LL(1) Parse of **begin** A := BB – 314 + A ; **end** $

call **gen_actions ("ID := <expression> #gen_assign ;")** will generate:

```
match(ID);
match(COLONEQUAL);
expression();
gen_assign();
match(SEMICOLON);
```

The semantic routine calls pass no explicit parameters. Rather, necessary parameters are transmitted through a *semantic stack*. The use of a semantic stack is detailed in Chapter 7. It should be emphasized that the semantic stack is an entirely separate data structure from the parse stack. In recursive descent parsers, the parse stack is "hidden" in the procedure call stack of the running compiler. The semantic stack can be hidden that way as well, by having each parsing routine return a semantic record.

Action symbols make it easy to include semantic actions in recursive descent parsers. Further, since semantic actions are factored from parsing procedures, generating new parsing procedures for an updated grammar is straightforward.

For LL(1) parsers, action symbols that appear in a particular production are pushed onto the parse stack when the production is predicted. When an action symbol appears at the top of the parse stack, it is popped, and the appropriate semantic routine is called. The LL(1) driver of Figure 5.9 is therefore extended as shown in Figure 5.11.

```
void lldriver(void)
{
    /* Push the Start Symbol onto an empty stack */
    push(s);

    while (! stack_empty() ) {
        /* Let X be the top stack symbol; */
        /* let a be the current input token */

        if (is_nonterminal(X)
                && T[X][a] == X → Y₁ · · · Yₘ) {
            /* Expand nonterminal */
            Replace X with Y₁ · · · Yₘ on the stack;
        } else if (is_terminal(X) && X == a) {
            pop(1);            /* Match of X worked */
            scanner(& a);    /* Get next token */
        } else if (is_action_symbol(X)) {
            pop(1);
            Call Semantic Routine corresponding to X;
        } else
            /* Process syntax error */
    }
}
```

Figure 5.11   An LL(1) Driver that Handles Action Symbols

5.6. Making Grammars LL(1)

It is not always easy for inexperienced compiler writers to create LL(1) grammars. The problem is that LL(1) requires a unique prediction for each combination of nonterminal and lookahead symbol, and it is not hard to write productions that violate the unique prediction requirement.

Fortunately, most LL(1) prediction conflicts can be grouped into two categories: *common prefixes* and *left recursion*. Simple grammar transformations that eliminate common prefixes and left recursion are known, and these transformations allow us to rework most grammars into valid LL(1) form.

In the first category of conflicts, two productions with the same left-hand side often have right-hand sides that share a common prefix. For example, we might have

<stmt> → **if** <expr> **then** <stmt list> **end if** ;
<stmt> → **if** <expr> **then** <stmt list> **else** <stmt list> **end if** ;

Productions that share a common prefix cause prediction conflicts since the First sets of each right-hand side will not be disjoint (unless the common prefix generates *only* λ). The solution to prediction conflicts caused by common prefixes is a simple factoring transform, as shown in Figure 5.12.

```
void factor(grammar *G)
{
    while (G has 2 or more productions with the same
            LHS and a common prefix) {
    Let S = {A → αβ , . . . , A → αζ}
            be the set of productions with the same
            left-hand side, A, and a common prefix, α

    Create a new nonterminal, N;

    Replace S with the production set
            SET_OF( A → α N, N → β , . . . , N → ζ )
    }
}
```

Figure 5.12   An Algorithm that Factors Common Prefixes

Using our **if-then-else** example, `factor()` produces

<stmt>   → **if** <expr> **then** <stmt list> <if suffix>
<if suffix>   → **end if** ;
<if suffix>   → **else** <stmt list> **end if** ;

In the second category of conflicts, a production is *left-recursive* if its left-hand side symbol is also the first symbol of its right-hand side. For example, the production E → E+T is left-recursive. A nonterminal is left-recursive if it is the left-hand side of a left-recursive production. Grammars with left-recursive productions can never be LL(1). To see this, assume some lookahead symbol t causes the prediction of some left-recursive production A → Aβ. After the prediction, A will again be the top stack symbol, and hence the same production would be predicted forever.

The algorithm `remove_left_recursion()`, given in Figure 5.13, removes left recursion from a factored grammar.

```
void remove_left_recursion(grammar *G)
{
    while (G contains a left-recursive nonterminal) {
        Let S = {A → Aα, A → β , . . . , A → ζ}
            be the set of productions with the same
            left-hand side, A, where A is
            left-recursive.

        Create two new nonterminals, T and N;

        Replace S with the production set
            SET_OF( A → N T, N → β , . . . , N → ζ,
                T → αT, T → λ )
    }
}
```

Figure 5.13   An Algorithm to Remove Left Recursion

To understand how **remove_left_recursion()** operates, observe that after factoring, at most one of the set of productions sharing the same left-hand side can be left-recursive. Assume it is $A \to A\alpha$. We can apply the left-recursive production any number of times, but eventually one of the other productions must be used, or the nonterminal A will never be erased. The production $A \to N\,T$ generates an N followed by zero or more α's. The N generates any of $\beta, \ldots, \zeta$. For example, consider the following left-recursive expression grammar:

$E \to E + T$
$E \to T$
$T \to T * P$
$T \to P$
$P \to ID$

This grammar contains left recursion and hence is not LL(1). It is in a form that is acceptable to bottom-up parsing techniques and therefore might appear in a programming language grammar. **remove_left_recursion()** can be used to rewrite the two left-recursive productions, obtaining

E	$\to$ E1 Etail
E1	$\to$ T
Etail	$\to$ + T Etail
Etail	$\to$ λ
T	$\to$ T1 Ttail
T1	$\to$ P
Ttail	$\to$ * P Ttail
Ttail	$\to$ λ
P	$\to$ ID

Nonterminals E1 and T1 are the left-hand sides of only one production each, so they can be replaced with their corresponding right-hand side to obtain

```
E      → T Etail
Etail  → + T Etail
Etail  → λ
T      → P Ttail
Ttail  → * P Ttail
Ttail  → λ
P      → ID
```

This grammar is equivalent to the original and is LL(1). In fact, it is very similar to LL(1) grammars ordinarily used for programming languages.

Factoring and left recursion removal are the primary transforms used to make grammars LL(1). It is possible, however, in rare cases, that other transformations may be needed. For example, consider the following grammar fragment that might appear in a language that allows identifiers as labels:

```
<stmt>             → <label> <unlabeled stmt>
<label>            → ID :
<label>            → λ
<unlabeled stmt>   → ID := <expr> ;
```

There are no common prefixes in this fragment, and there is no left recursion, and yet the grammar is not LL(1). The problem is that ID predicts both <label> productions. The solution is to factor ID from the second and fourth productions, obtaining the following equivalent grammar, which is LL(1):

```
<stmt>             → ID <id suffix>
<id suffix>        → : <unlabeled stmt>
<id suffix>        → := <expr> ;
<unlabeled stmt>   → ID := <expr> ;
```

In some cases even more elaborate factoring may be needed. For example, in an Ada array declaration, array bounds can be declared as an explicit range pair or as the name of a discreet type or subtype. That is, we might have A : **array**(I..J, Boolean). In defining an array bound we might write

```
<array bound> → <expr> .. <expr>
<array bound> → ID
```

Because ID can be generated from <expr>, we have a prediction conflict. Factoring ID from <expr> would be very tedious, given the variety of expressions possible in Ada. An alternative, therefore, is to write

```
<array bound>    →  <expr> <bound tail>
<bound tail>     →  .. <expr>
<bound tail>     →  λ
```

If only a single <expr> appears, it must generate an ID. This can be checked during semantic processing, for only an ID can name a type or subtype.

All grammars that include an endmarker can be rewritten into a form in which all right-hand sides begin with a terminal symbol; this form is called *Greibach normal form* (see Exercise 9). Once a grammar is in Greibach normal form, factoring of common prefixes is easy. Surprisingly, though, even this transform does not guarantee that a grammar will be LL(1) (see Exercise 10). In fact, as we shall discuss in the next section, there do exist language constructs that have *no LL(1) grammar*. Fortunately, such constructs are rare in practice and can be handled by modest extensions to the LL(1) parsing technique.

5.7. The If-Then-Else Problem in LL(1) Parsing

Almost all common programming language constructs can be specified by LL(1) grammars. One notable exception, however, is the **if-then-else** construct of Algol 60, Pascal, and C. This construct is subject to what is called the "dangling else" problem because the **else** clause is optional. The problem is that there may be more **then** parts than **else** parts, which means the matching of **then**s to **else**s may not be unique. In effect, we may regard the **if** <expr> **then** <stmt> part as an *open bracket* and the **else** <stmt> part as an *optional close bracket*. Thus we have to parse something structurally equivalent to

$$BL = \{ [^i \;]^j \mid i \geq j \geq 0 \}$$

Unfortunately, this language is not LL(1) and in fact is not LL(k) for any k. We can gain some insight into the problem by considering some grammars that might be used to specify BL (bracket language).

An obvious first try is G_1:

```
S    →  [S CL
S    →  λ
CL   →  ]
CL   →  λ
```

Here CL generates an optional close bracket. G_1, however, has a major problem—it is ambiguous. For example, CL CL can generate] two different ways, depending on which CL generates the] and which generates λ.

To remedy the ambiguity problem, we can create a grammar that follows the Algol 60, Pascal, and C rule of matching each] with the *nearest unmatched* [. This leads to G_2:

$$
\begin{aligned}
S \;&\to\; [\,S \\
S \;&\to\; S1 \\
S1 \;&\to\; [\,S1\,] \\
S1 \;&\to\; \lambda
\end{aligned}
$$

G_2 generates zero or more unmatched ['s followed by zero or more pairs of matched brackets. G_2 is, in fact, parsable using most bottom-up techniques (such as SLR(1), which is discussed in Chapter 6). However, it is not LL(1), nor is it LL(k) for any k. The problem is [$\in$ First([S) and [$\in$ First(S1). Similarly, [[$\in$ First$_2$ ([S) and [[$\in$ First$_2$(S1), and so on. In particular, seeing only open brackets, LL parsers cannot decide whether to predict a matched or unmatched open bracket. This shows where bottom-up parsers have an advantage—they can delay announcing a production until an entire right-hand side is matched. Top-down methods cannot delay—they must predict a production by having seen only the first (or first k) symbols derived from a right-hand side. In this case the ability to delay is crucial.

A technique commonly used to handle the dangling else problem in LL(1) parsers is to use an ambiguous grammar along with some special case rules to resolve any nonunique predictions that arise. This technique is discussed in detail in Section 6.7.3.

Consider G_3:

$$
\begin{aligned}
G \;&\to\; S; \\
S \;&\to\; \textbf{if } S\ E \\
S \;&\to\; \text{Other} \\
E \;&\to\; \textbf{else } S \\
E \;&\to\; \lambda
\end{aligned}
$$

G_3 is ambiguous and leads to the following LL(1) table:

	if	**else**	Other	;
S	Predict 2		Predict 3	
E		Predict 4 Predict 5		Predict 5
G	Predict 1		Predict 1	

The LL(1) table, of course, is not single-valued because G_3 is ambiguous. The auxiliary rule we will enforce here is that an **else** associates with the nearest **if**. That is, in predicting an E, if we see **else** as a lookahead we will match it immediately. Thus we make T[E][**else**] = Predict 4. This can be done by hand or, preferably, by saying that prediction of production 4 has priority over production 5. As described in Section 5.8, the LLGen parser generator allows ambiguous prediction choices to be resolved by using the order in which productions are specified to define their priority.

Finally, let us return briefly to the dangling else issue. In a very real sense, this is not a grammar or parsing issue but rather a *language design issue*. If all **if** statements are terminated with an **end if**, or some equivalent symbol, the problem disappears. We can then use a grammar of the following form:

S → **if** S E
S → Other
E → **else** S **end if**
E → **end if**

This grammar is trivially LL(1). Careful language design can often expand the range of possible parsing options. As always, language design must bear in mind the compiling and parsing problems a construct will induce.

5.8. **The LLGen Parser Generator**

LLGen is an LL(1) parser generator that accepts a CFG specification and produces tables for parsing the specified language. LLGen was written at the University of Wisconsin at Madison by Jon Mauney.

Input to LLGen

The input to LLGen has three main sections: options desired for the run, terminal symbols of the grammar, and production rules of the grammar. The general form of the input is

> *comments*
> ***fmq**
> *options*
> ***define**
> *constant definitions*
> ***terminals**
> *terminal specifications*
> ***productions**
> *production specifications*
> ***end**
> *comments*

A sample specification for Micro is presented in Figure 5.14.

```
This is an LL(1) grammar for the
world famous Micro language
*fmq
bnf vocab
statistics noerrortables parsetables
*terminals
ID
INTLIT
:=
,
;
+
-
(
)
begin
end
read
write
*productions
<program>          ::= begin <statement list> end
<statement list>   ::= <statement> <statement tail>
<statement tail>   ::= <statement> <statement tail>
<statement tail>   ::=
<statement>        ::= ID := <expression> ;
<statement>        ::= read ( <id list> ) ;
<statement>        ::= write ( <expr list> ) ;
<id list>          ::= ID <id tail>
<id tail>          ::= , ID <id tail>
<id tail>          ::=
<expr list>        ::= <expression> <expr tail>
<expr tail>        ::= , <expression> <expr tail>
<expr tail>        ::=
<expression>       ::= <primary> <primary tail>
<primary tail>     ::= <add op> <primary> <primary tail>
<primary tail>     ::=
<primary>          ::= ( <expression> )
<primary>          ::= ID
<primary>          ::= INTLIT
<add op>           ::= +
<add op>           ::= -
*end
```

Figure 5.14   An LLGen Specification of Micro

Symbols

Symbols consist of any sequence of printable characters; they are separated by blanks, tabs, or ends of line. Symbols may not contain blanks or tabs, unless the symbol is surrounded by angle brackets, < and >. If a symbol begins with a <, it must end with a >.

Comments

Anything before *fmq or after *end will be considered a comment and will be ignored. However, comments must not contain any of the above reserved symbols.

Options

Following *fmq is a list of zero or more options, separated by blanks, tabs, or ends of line. Options control the kinds of tables produced and the kind of information that is printed. A complete description of the available options appears in the LLGen User Manual in Appendix C.

Constant Definitions

The constant definition section is optional. If present, it begins with the reserved symbol *define and consists of a list of definitions, each on a separate line. Each definition has the form

    <const name> <integer value>

where <const name> is a symbol, as described above, and <integer value> is an unsigned integer (that is, a symbol containing only digits). This constant can then be used whenever an integer constant is called for: in subsequent constant definitions and for semantic routine numbers. Note that this feature is not as helpful as it seems at first, because the output listing of LLGen will use the numeric value, not the constant name.

Terminals

The reserved symbol *terminals begins the list of terminal symbols. The terminal specification section consists of a list of such specifications, each on a separate line. All terminals must appear in this list. Terminals should be ordered so that the sequence numbers assigned are compatible with any integer codes used by the scanner. That is, if **end** has a major token code of, say, 4, then **end** should appear fourth in the terminal list.

Productions

The symbol *`*productions`* separates the terminals from the productions. The productions are specified by a list of rules, each on a separate line. Specification of one production has the form:

<lhs> ::= <rhs>

The symbol `::=` is a synonym for →, which is not available in most character sets. Either <lhs> or <rhs> may be absent. <lhs> is one symbol representing a nonterminal. If it is absent, the <lhs> of the preceding production is used. <rhs> is a string of symbols, containing the grammar symbols of the production, as well as action symbols indicating semantic routines to be called when the appropriate point in the production is reached. An action symbol consists of a # followed by an unsigned integer or defined constant, without intervening blanks. If <rhs> is absent or contains only action symbols, then <lhs> derives λ, the null string. <rhs> may be continued on subsequent lines by beginning those lines with the reserved symbol ... (only productions may be so continued).

End

The productions are terminated by *`*end`*. After all the productions have been processed, the augmenting production is added. Two symbols, <goal> and $$$, and one production

<goal> ::= <s> $$$

are added to the grammar, where <s> is the left-hand side of the first production specified, <goal> is the start symbol, and $$$ the endmarker. LLGen represents the endmarker as $$$ to allow $ and $$ to be used freely within the language being defined.

Output from LLGen

A detailed description of the format of the parsing tables appears in the LLGen User Manual (Appendix C). The information provided includes

- Size parameters (the number of terminals, the number of productions, and so on)
- The right-hand sides of all productions
- The LL(1) parse table
- A list of symbols that can derive the null string
- Symbolic representations of all symbols in the grammar

If the grammar specified is not LL(1), all conflicts will be reported. If the option `resolve` is enabled, productions will be given precedence in their order of appearance. The first production specified has highest precedence. Thus the dangling else of Pascal and other languages can be parsed by

```
<if stmt>      ::= if <expr> then <stmt> <else part>
<else part>    ::= else <stmt>
               ::=
```

The conflict will be resolved in favor of the first form of the statement, matching the **else** with the most recent **if**.

This resolution mechanism should be used with caution. Conflicts must be carefully examined to ensure that the parse action taken is the action desired. For example, reversing the order of the above <else part> productions would be perfectly acceptable to LLGen, but would have a disastrous effect. When **else** appears in the lookahead, the parse action taken would be always to predict <else part> deriving the null string; the **else** would never be accepted.

The specification of Micro shown in Figure 5.14 illustrates the use of LLGen.

5.9. Properties of LL(1) Parsers

We can establish the following useful properties for LL(1) parsers:

- A correct, leftmost parse is guaranteed.

  This follows from the fact that LL(1) parsers "simulate" a leftmost derivation. For productions that share a common left-hand side, **Predict** sets are always unique. Thus at any given point only one possible prediction that is consonant with the remaining input is possible. This is the prediction that the LL(1) parser chooses.

- All grammars in the LL(1) class are unambiguous.

  If a grammar is ambiguous, then some string has two or more distinct leftmost parses. This means that at some point more than one correct prediction is possible, and this would result in nonunique **Predict** sets for some left-hand sides.

- All LL(1) parsers operate in linear time and, at most, linear space (relative to the length of the input being parsed).

  Each iteration of an LL(1) parser is charged to an input symbol. Moreover, any given input symbol is charged for, at most, a constant number of iterations. A token may induce a sequence of predictions, followed by a match or an error flag. A prediction of A that directly or indirectly derives λ is charged to the input symbol that caused A to be pushed onto the stack. All other predictions are charged to the current input symbol (the lookahead symbol). If the current token induces a prediction of B that does not derive λ, then B cannot appear again until the current token is matched (or an error is discovered). If B did appear again, an infinite loop would result, and this would violate LL(1)'s correctness property (point 1). Thus each input symbol induces a bounded number of iterations, and linearity follows.

The use of more than linear space (on the parse stack) would imply more than linear time, just to push entries on the stack.

5.10. LL(k) Parsing

The single-symbol lookahead used in LL(1) can be extended to k symbols. This yields the *Strong LL(k)* class of grammars. By definition, G is Strong LL(k) if and only if, for productions $A \to \beta$ and $A \to \gamma$ ($\beta \neq \gamma$),

$$\text{First}_k(\beta \ \text{Follow}_k(A)) \cap \text{First}_k(\gamma \ \text{Follow}_k(A)) = \varnothing$$

Recall that First_k and Follow_k are generalizations of First and Follow to k symbols.

Strong LL(k) uses *global lookahead* (via Follow sets) to make parsing decisions. It happens that LL(1) = Strong LL(1), but in general, for k > 1, Strong LL(k) is a proper subset of LL(k).

Intuitively, we can define LL(k) as the most powerful top-down method that uses all of left-context, the nonterminal to be expanded, and k-symbol lookahead to make parsing decisions. This can be formalized as follows: G is LL(k) if and only if the three conditions

(1) $S \Rightarrow^*_{lm} wA\alpha \Rightarrow_{lm} w\beta\alpha \Rightarrow^* wx$

(2) $S \Rightarrow^*_{lm} wA\alpha \Rightarrow_{lm} w\gamma\alpha \Rightarrow^* wy$

(3) $\text{First}_k(x) = \text{First}_k(y)$

imply that $\beta = \gamma$.

This definition simply says that G is LL(k) if and only if knowing all of the left context, w, the symbol to be expanded, A, and the next k input symbols, $\text{First}_k(x) = \text{First}_k(y)$ is always sufficient to uniquely determine the next prediction.

Consider

```
G → S$
S → aAa
S → bAba
A → b
A → λ
```

This grammar is not LL(1) because b predicts both productions with A as the left-hand side. However, it is LL(2). This is because in the context aAa, a lookahead of ba predicts $A \to b$ and a$ predicts $A \to \lambda$. Similarly, in the context bAba, a lookahead of bb predicts $A \to b$, and a lookahead of ba predicts $A \to \lambda$. But this grammar is *not* Strong LL(k) for any $k \geq 1$ because

$First_k(ba\$) \in First_k(bFollow_k(A)) \cap First_k(\lambda\ Follow_k(A))$

The problem is that global lookahead, in which Follow sets are used, is sometimes inexact. That is, if a symbol b can follow A in *some context*, then $b \in Follow(A)$. However, this does not mean b can follow A in *all* contexts. Thus in the above example, ba\$ can follow A in one context but not the other. Strong LL(k) cannot handle this subtlety.

The solution then is to build exact lookahead directly into the LL(k) parsing mechanism. To build an LL(k) parser, we create new nonterminal entries of the form [A,L], where $A \in V_n$ and $L \subseteq V_t^{*k}$. V_t^{*k} is the set of terminal strings no longer than k. L represents an exact set of lookaheads appropriate for A in some context.

We start with $[S,\{\lambda\}]$. Now if we are predicting an entry [A,L], we require that for $x \in L$, $A \to \alpha$, $A \to \beta$ $(\alpha \neq \beta)$ it must always be the case that $First_k(\alpha x) \cap First_k(\beta x) = \varnothing$. That is, we use the local lookaheads stored in L rather than $Follow_k(A)$ to determine how to expand A. Assume that for [A,L] we have decided, as outlined above, to expand A using $A \to \alpha$, where $\alpha = x_0 B_1 x_1 B_2 \cdots B_m x_m$, $m \geq 0$ and $x_i \in V_t^*$, $B_i \in V_n$, $1 \leq i \leq m$. Note that any right-hand side can be written in this form, which isolates the nonterminals in a right-hand side.

We then expand A by placing

$$x_0 [B_1,L_1] x_1 [B_2,L_2] \cdots [B_m,L_m] x_m$$

on the parse stack where for $1 \leq i \leq m$, $L_i = \{x \mid x \in First_k (x_i B_{i+1} \cdots B_m x_m y),$ $y \in L\}$. Naturally we compute these L sets once and then table and use [A,L] pairs as if they were new nonterminals added to an extended CFG.

Reconsider our example grammar

$G \to S\$$
$S \to aAa$
$S \to bAba$
$A \to b$
$A \to \lambda$

and build an LL(2) parser. We start with $[G,\{\lambda\}]$:

Now $[G,\{\lambda\}]$ on lookaheads in {aa,ab,bb} predicts $[S,\{\$\}]$ \$.

$[S,\{\$\}]$ on lookaheads in {aa,ab} predicts a $[A,\{a\$\}]$ a.

$[S,\{\$\}]$ on lookaheads in {bb} predicts b $[A,\{ba\}]$ ba.

$[A,\{a\$\}]$ on lookaheads in {ba} predicts b and on lookaheads in {a\$} predicts λ.

Similarly, $[A,\{ba\}]$ on lookaheads in {bb} predicts b and on lookaheads in {ba} predicts λ.

The key point is that A has been split into *two* nonterminals. This allows [A,{a$}] on a lookahead of ba to predict b, and [A,{ba}] given ba predicts λ. In effect we have created an equivalent, but larger, CFG:

$$
\begin{array}{ll}
[G,\{\lambda\}] & \rightarrow [S,\{\$\}] \; \$ \\
[S,\{\$\}] & \rightarrow a \; [A,\{a\$\}] \; a \\
[S,\{\$\}] & \rightarrow b \; [A,\{ba\}] \; ba \\
[A,\{a\$\}] & \rightarrow b \\
[A,\{a\$\}] & \rightarrow \lambda \\
[A,\{ba\}] & \rightarrow b \\
[A,\{ba\}] & \rightarrow \lambda
\end{array}
$$

Strong LL(k) and LL(k) are primarily of academic interest, as only LL(1) parsers are used in practice. As one might expect, however, interesting grammar containment relations can be established. For example,

- LL(k) $\subset$ LL(k+1)

- Strong LL(k) $\subset$ Strong LL(k+1)

- Strong LL(k) $\subset$ LL(k), k>1

Interestingly, the class of *languages* that can be parsed by LL(k) and Strong LL(k) parsers *increases* as k is increased. The following language can be parsed by LL or Strong LL using k lookahead symbols, but not using fewer:

$$
L_k = \{a^n(b,c,b^k d)^n \mid n \geq 1\}
$$

The idea here is that for each a we must match a b, a c, or a $b^k d$ string. With k-symbol lookahead we can do this: Take a b and if the next k symbols are $b^{k-1}d$, then take them also to form a $b^k d$ string. We cannot do this with a k−1 symbol lookahead because after the first b we see b^{k-1} and cannot tell if this is part of $b^{k-1}d$ or k distinct b's.

We noted earlier that LL(1) = Strong LL(1), although LL(k) $\neq$ Strong LL(k) for k $\geq$ 2. This result is developed in Exercise 12. Although Strong LL(1) and LL(1) represent exactly the same class of grammars, the table sizes required by Strong LL(1) and LL(1) differ, sometimes quite substantially. This is because the LL(1) construction adds new nonterminals and new productions, as we saw above. Therefore the LL(1) parsers used in practice are almost invariably Strong LL(1) parsers, which require smaller tables. Strong LL(1) and LL(1) parsers, however, *do differ* in exactly when syntax errors are discovered. Although this makes no difference while parsing, it can be a problem when syntactic error repair is performed. In Chapter 17, ways of performing LL(1) error repair while using Strong LL(1) parse tables are discussed.

Exercises

1.   Which of the following grammars are LL(1)? Explain why.

    a.   S   → A B c
           A   → a
           A   → λ
           B   → b
           B   → λ

    b.   S   → A b
           A   → a
           A   → B
           A   → λ
           B   → b
           B   → λ

    c.   S   → A B B A
           A   → a
           A   → λ
           B   → b
           B   → λ

    d.   S   → a S e
           S   → B
           B   → b B e
           B   → C
           C   → c C e
           C   → d

2.   Construct the LL(1) table for the following grammar:

Expr	→ − Expr
Expr	→ (Expr)
Expr	→ Var ExprTail
ExprTail	→ − Expr
ExprTail	→ λ
Var	→ ID VarTail
VarTail	→ (Expr)
VarTail	→ λ

3.   Trace the operation of an LL(1) parser for the grammar of Exercise 2 on
       ID– –ID((ID)).

4.   Transform the following grammar into LL(1) form, using the techniques
       of Section 5.6:

DeclList	→ DeclList ; Decl
DeclList	→ Decl
Decl	→ IdList : Type
IdList	→ IdList , ID
IdList	→ ID
Type	→ ScalarType
Type	→ **array** (ScalarTypeList) **of** Type
ScalarType	→ ID
ScalarType	→ Bound .. Bound
Bound	→ Sign INTLIT
Bound	→ ID
Sign	→ +
Sign	→ −
Sign	→ λ
ScalarTypeList	→ ScalarTypeList , ScalarType
ScalarTypeList	→ ScalarType

5.   Run your solution to Exercise 4 through LLGen, or any other LL(1)
       parser generator, to verify that it actually is LL(1). How do you know
       that your solution generates the same language as the original grammar?

6.   Show that every regular set can be defined by an LL(1) grammar.

7.   A grammar is said to have *cycles* if it is the case that $A \Rightarrow^+ A$. Show that
       no grammar that has cycles can be LL(1).

8.   In Section 5.9 it is established that LL(1) parsers operate in linear time.
       That is, when parsing an input, the parser requires *on average* only a
       constant-bounded amount of time per input symbol.

       Is it ever the case that an LL(1) parser requires more than a constant-
       bounded amount of time to accept some particular symbol? Phrased dif-
       ferently, can we bound by a constant the time interval between succes-
       sive calls to the scanner to get the next input token?

9.   A grammar is in *Greibach normal form (GNF)* if all productions are of the
       form $A \rightarrow a\,\alpha$, where a is a terminal and α is an arbitrary string of sym-
       bols. Let G be any grammar that does not generate λ. Give an algorithm
       to transform G into GNF.

10.   If we take a grammar and put it into GNF using the algorithm developed
       in Exercise 9, we know there will be no left recursion. The transformed
       grammar may still have common prefixes and hence may not be LL(1).
       Assume we use `factor()` of Section 5.6 (Figure 5.12) to factor common
       prefixes. The resulting grammar will have neither left recursion nor
       common prefixes and will be "close" to LL(1) in form. Show that the ab-

sence of common prefixes and left recursion in an unambiguous grammar *does not* guarantee that a grammar will be LL(1).

11. Use the techniques of Section 5.10 to create an LL(2) parser for the fol-
     lowing grammar:

$$
\begin{array}{ll}
\text{Stmt} & \rightarrow \text{ID ;} \\
\text{Stmt} & \rightarrow \text{ID (IdList) ;} \\
\text{Stmt} & \rightarrow \text{ID : Stmt} \\
\text{IdList} & \rightarrow \text{ID} \\
\text{IdList} & \rightarrow \text{ID , IdList}
\end{array}
$$

12. Show that every LL(1) grammar is also Strong LL(1).

     Hint: Show that any grammar that fails to satisfy the Strong LL(1)
     definition must also fail to satisfy the LL(1) definition.

13. Show that for every LL(k) grammar there is a Strong LL(k) grammar that
     generates the same language.

     Hint: Consider the expanded grammar formed by creating nonterminals
     of the form [A,L].

14. Using the techniques of Section 5.3, write a program that reads the tables
     generated by LLGen and produces the corresponding recursive descent
     parsing procedures.

CHAPTER 6

LR Parsing Techniques

6.1. **Shift-Reduce Parsers**

The fundamental concern of a top-down parser is deciding which production was used to expand a particular nonterminal. Similarly, the fundamental concern of a bottom-up parser is deciding when what looks like the right-hand side of a production can be replaced by its left-hand side. This is by no means trivial. More than one production may have the same right-hand side. Further, it is possible that what looks like a right-hand side really is not. If the grammar contains λ-productions, identifying right-hand sides is complicated by the fact that λ can be matched in any parsing context.

A *shift-reduce parser* works as follows: A parse stack, initially empty, contains symbols already parsed. The parse stack catenated with the remaining input always represents a right sentential form. Tokens are *shifted* onto the stack until the top of the stack contains the handle of the sentential form. Recall that a handle is a sequence of symbols that match some production's right-hand side and which may be correctly replaced with that production's left-hand side. The handle is *reduced* by replacing it on the parse stack with the nonterminal that is its parent in the parse tree. Success is reported when the input has all been consumed and the stack contains only the goal symbol.

The problem is to know when we have reached the end of the handle, then to determine the length of the handle, and finally, to know what nonterminal to reduce it to in case there are two productions with the same right-hand side.

Let us consider a very simple driver for a shift-reduce parser, as shown in Figure 6.1. The driver utilizes a *parse stack* that contains *parse states,* usually coded as integers. Parse states represent the current state of the parse. Informally, parse states encode the symbol that has been shifted and the handles that are currently being matched. The driver uses two tables, **action** and **go_to**. **action** tells the parser whether to shift, reduce, terminate successfully, or signal a syntax error. The **go_to** table defines successor states after a token or left-hand side is matched and shifted.

Shift-reduce parsers differ depending on how parse states, the **action** table, and the **go_to** table are computed from a context-free grammar. Later sections will describe a number of approaches to this problem, differing in complexity and comprehensiveness.

The following grammar, G_0, generates the block structure of a Pascal-like language:

1. <program> $\rightarrow$ **begin** <stmts> **end** $
2. <stmts> $\rightarrow$ SimpleStmt ; <stmts>
3. <stmts> $\rightarrow$ **begin** <stmts> **end** ; <stmts>
4. <stmts> $\rightarrow \lambda$

```
void shift_reduce_driver(void)
{
    /*
     * Push the Start State, S0,
     * onto an empty parse stack.
     */
    push(S0);

    while (TRUE) {    /* forever */
        /*
         * Let S be the top parse stack state;
         * let T be the current input token.
         */

        switch (action[S][T]) {
        case ERROR:
            announce_syntax_error();
            break;

        case ACCEPT:
            /* The input has been correctly parsed. */
            clean_up_and_finish();
            return;

        case SHIFT:
            push(go_to[S][T]);
            scanner(& T);    /* Get next token. */
            break;

        case Reducei:
            /*
             * Assume i-th production is X → Y1 · · · Ym.
             * Remove states corresponding to
             * the RHS of the production.
             */
            pop(m);
            /* S' is the new stack top. */
            push(go_to[S'][X]);
            break;
        }
    }
}
```

Figure 6.1   A Simple Shift-Reduce Driver

The **action** and **go_to** tables that appear in Figures 6.2 and 6.3 correspond to G_0. We shall detail their construction later; for the present, assume they were created by a suitable shift-reduce parser generator. In the

Symbol	State											
	0	1	2	3	4	5	6	7	8	9	10	11
begin	S	S			S		S			S		
end		R4	S		R4		R4	S		R4	R2	R3
;						S			S			
SimpleStmt		S			S		S			S		
$				A								
<program>												
<stmts>		S			S		S			S		

Figure 6.2   A Shift-Reduce **action** Table for G_0

Symbol	State											
	0	1	2	3	4	5	6	7	8	9	10	11
begin	1	4			4		4			4		
end			3					8				
;						6			9			
SimpleStmt		5			5		5			6		
$												
<program>												
<stmts>		2			7		10			11		

Figure 6.3   A Shift-Reduce **go_to** Table for G_0

action table, S denotes shift, A denotes accept, integers denote reductions, and blanks are error entries. In the **go_to** table, entries are state numbers. The row for the start symbol, <program>, in both tables is empty. This is because parsing terminates as soon as the start symbol is reached. As an optimization, these rows could be removed.

We can now trace the parsing steps performed by our shift-reduce parser on the input **begin** SimpleStmt ; SimpleStmt ; **end** $, as shown in Figure 6.4. The following reduction sequence is produced: production 4, production 2, production 2. This sequence is a rightmost parse; that is, it is the reverse of the corresponding rightmost derivation.

Step	Parse Stack	Remaining Input	Parser Action
(1)	0	**begin** SimpleStmt ; SimpleStmt ; **end** $	Shift
(2)	0,1	SimpleStmt ; SimpleStmt ; **end** $	Shift
(3)	0,1,5	; SimpleStmt ; **end** $	Shift
(4)	0,1,5,6	SimpleStmt ; **end** $	Shift
(5)	0,1,5,6,5	; **end** $	Shift
(6)	0,1,5,6,5,6	**end** $	Reduce 4
(7)	0,1,5,6,5,6,10	**end** $	Reduce 2
(8)	0,1,5,6,10	**end** $	Reduce 2
(9)	0,1,2	**end** $	Shift
(10)	0,1,2,3	$	Accept

Figure 6.4   Example of a Shift-Reduce Parse

6.2. LR Parsers

The concept of LR parsing was introduced by Knuth (1965). Like all parsing techniques, LR parsers are characterized by the number of lookahead symbols that are examined to determine parsing actions. We can make the lookahead parameter explicit and discuss LR(k) parsers, where k is the lookahead size.

Theoretically, LR(k) parsers are of interest in that they are the *most power-ful* class of deterministic bottom-up parsers using at most k lookahead symbols. Deterministic parsers must uniquely determine the correct parsing action at each step; they cannot back up or retry parsing actions. This characterization means that if a grammar, G, can be parsed by any deterministic bottom-up parser using k lookahead symbols, an LR(k) parser can also be built for G. Not surprisingly, the converse does not necessarily hold—some grammars parsable by the LR(k) technique are beyond the capabilities of other bottom-up techniques.

Most of this chapter will be devoted to the problems of constructing parsers for the many variants of LR(k). Before we plunge into implementation details, however, it will be instructive to formalize the definition of LR(k) in terms of the properties an LR(k) grammar must possess.

All shift-reduce parsers operate by shifting symbols and examining look-aheads until the end of the handle is found. Then the handle is reduced to a nonterminal, which replaces it on the stack. For a shift-reduce parser to operate correctly, the parser must decide whether to shift or reduce, knowing only the symbols already shifted and the next k lookahead symbols.

Assume that in some LR(k) grammar there are two sentential forms, $\alpha\beta w$ and $\alpha\beta y$, so similar that they share a common prefix, $\alpha\beta$, and a common k-symbol lookahead, $First_k(y) = First_k(w)$. Assume $\alpha\beta w$ can be reduced to αAw, and $\alpha\beta y$ can be reduced to γBx. Because the two sentential forms are identical in both the prefix already shifted and the lookahead string, the same reduction must be applicable to both. That is, we can reduce $\alpha\beta y$ to γBx *or* to αAy, and we must obtain the *same* result, implying that $\alpha Ay = \gamma Bx$.

LR(k) parsers, by definition, can always determine the correct reduction, knowing all of the left context up to the end of the handle plus k-symbols of lookahead. In formal terms, a grammar, G, is LR(k) if and only if the three conditions

(1) $S \Rightarrow_{rm}^* \alpha Aw \Rightarrow_{rm} \alpha\beta w$, and

(2) $S \Rightarrow_{rm}^* \gamma Bx \Rightarrow_{rm} \alpha\beta y$, and

(3) $First_k(w) = First_k(y)$

imply that $\alpha Ay = \gamma Bx$.

This definition is instructive in that it defines the minimum properties a grammar must possess to be parsable by LR(k) techniques. It does not tell us how to actually *build* an LR(k) parser, and in fact the primary contribution of Knuth's pioneering work was an algorithm for LR(k) construction. We will begin with the simplest possible LR parser: that which uses no lookahead symbols, LR(0). Although LR(0) parsers are too simple to be used to parse real programming languages, they do illustrate many of the principles of general LR(k) parsing. After LR(0) parsers have been discussed, we will then generalize our discussion to LR(1) parsers and their variants.

6.2.1. LR(0) Parsing

LR(0) and all other LR-style parsing methods are based on the idea of a *configuration* or *item* of the form

$$A \rightarrow X_1 \cdots X_i \bullet X_{i+1} \cdots X_j$$

More precisely, configurations of this form are *LR(0) configurations*, because no lookahead information is included.

The dot symbol, $\bullet$, in a configuration may appear anywhere in the right-hand side of a production. It marks how much of the production has already been matched. In general, we will consider a number of possible productions that are applicable, so we will use a *configuration set*. A configuration set contains all the configurations that apply at a given point in a parse.

```
configuration_set closure0 (configuration_set s)
{
    configuration_set s' = s;

    do {
        if (B →δ • Aρ ∈ s' for A∈Vₙ) {
            /*
             * Predict productions with A
             * as the left-hand side.
             */
            Add all configurations of the form
                A → • γ to s'
        }
    } while (more new configurations can be added)

    return s';
}
```

Figure 6.5   An Algorithm to Close LR(0) Configuration Sets

For example, the configuration set

<stmt> → ID • := <expr>
<stmt> → ID • : <stmt>
<stmt> → ID •

represents a situation in which an identifier can be matched as part of any of three different productions. Because we do not yet know which production is applicable, configurations representing all three possibilities are maintained.

We begin parsing with a configuration set {S → • α$}, which predicts the augmenting production. Recall from Chapter 2 that we assume all grammars are augmented so that they have a unique production with S, the start symbol, as the left-hand side. This production always generates $, the end marker, as the last symbol in a derivation.

In general, a configuration with the dot at the extreme left end of the right-hand side of a production is said to *predict* that production. Similarly, a configuration with the dot at the extreme right end of the right-hand side of a production is said to *recognize* that production.

In S → α$, α may begin with a nonterminal, in which case more predictions and configurations will have to be added. This is done by an LR(0) *closure* operation, as defined in Figure 6.5.

As an example, consider G_1:

$$S \rightarrow E\$$$
$$E \rightarrow E + T \mid T$$
$$T \rightarrow ID \mid (E)$$

closure0($\{S \rightarrow \bullet E\$\}$) = { $S \rightarrow \bullet E\$$,
                                $E \rightarrow \bullet E + T$,
                                $E \rightarrow \bullet T$,
                                $T \rightarrow \bullet ID$,
                                $T \rightarrow \bullet (E)$ }

This closure set illustrates the fact that to match the nonterminal E, we must match a production with E as its left-hand side. Because $E \rightarrow T$ may be involved, we may need to match a production with T as its left-hand side. The closure operation guarantees that the configurations necessary to match all legal derivation sequences are included.

To create the initial configuration set, s_0, we predict the augmenting production and close it:

$$s_0 = \text{closure0}(\{S \rightarrow \bullet \alpha\$\})$$

Given a configuration set s, we can compute its *successor*, s', under a symbol X, denoted go_to0(s, X) = s', as shown in Figure 6.6.

```
configuration_set go_to0 (configuration_set s, symbol X)
{
    sb = ∅;
    for (each configuration c ∈ s)
        if (c is of the form A →β • X γ)
            Add A →βX • γ to sb;

    /*
     * That is, we advance the • past the symbol X,
     * if possible.  Configurations not having a
     * dot preceding an X are not included in sb.
     */

    /* Add new predictions to sb via closure0. */
    return closure0 (sb);
}
```

Figure 6.6   An Algorithm to Compute the LR(0) **go_to** Function

It is possible that go_to0(s,X) = ∅, the empty set. This means that no configurations in s have a successor under X, and hence the empty configuration set results. An empty configuration set, reached during parsing, indicates a syntax error.

The number of productions in a context-free grammar is finite, and so too is the number of distinct configurations and configuration sets. Therefore we can build a finite automaton called a characteristic finite state machine (*CFSM*) by identifying configuration sets and successor operations with CFSM states and transitions. An algorithm to build a CFSM is presented in Figure 6.7.

For example, given grammar G_2:

$$S' \rightarrow S\$$$
$$S \rightarrow ID \mid \lambda$$

build_CFSM() would create the CFSM shown in Figure 6.8. For clarity, the error state, corresponding to the empty configuration set, and transitions to it are omitted.

Because the number of possible configuration sets is finite, and **build_CFSM()** processes each set only once, we know the algorithm will always terminate.

```
void build_CFSM(void)
{
    Create the Start State of the CFSM; Label it with s₀
    Create an Error State in the CFSM; Label it with ∅

    S = SET_OF( s₀ );

    while(S is nonempty) {
        Remove a configuration set s from S;
        /* Consider both terminals and nonterminals */
        for (X in Symbols) {
            if (go_to0(s,X) does not label a CFSM state) {
                Create a new CFSM state and label it
                    with go_to0(s,X);
                Put go_to0(s,X) into S;
            }
            Create a transition under X from the state s
                labels to the state go_to0(s,X) labels;
        }
    }
}
```

Figure 6.7   An Algorithm to Compute the CFSM for a Grammar

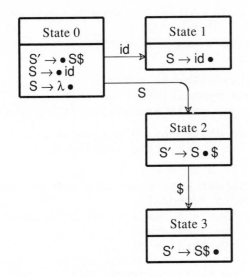

Figure 6.8   CFSM for G_2

In Chapter 3 we learned that finite automata can be represented as transition tables. CFSMs can also be represented in tabular form—in the form of the **go_to** table used by shift-reduce parsers. Figure 6.9 shows an algorithm to build a **go_to** table from a CFSM.

Applying **build_go_to_table()** to the CFSM of Figure 6.8, we obtain the **go_to** table shown in Figure 6.10. Note that state 4, elided in Figure 6.8, is the error state.

In general, we show CFSMs rather than **go_to** tables in our examples. Actual LR(0) parsers use the **go_to** table corresponding to a CFSM, as well as an **action** table, to make parsing decisions.

A *viable prefix* of a right sentential form is any prefix that does not extend beyond the handle. The CFSM, by construction, accepts viable prefixes derivable from the grammar being parsed.

Recall that shift-reduce parsers, including LR-style parsers, are driven by a **go_to** and an **action** table. We have already defined the LR(0) **go_to** table; now we must decide how to compute the **action** table. The role of the **action** table is a simple one—it is used to decide whether the CFSM has reached the end of the handle. If it has, a reduce action or accept action is indicated; otherwise, a shift action is appropriate.

Because LR(0) uses no lookahead, we must extract the **action** function directly from the configuration sets of the CFSM. Let Q ={Shift, Reduce$_1$,Reduce$_2$, $\cdots$} be the set of possible shift and reduce actions. Define a *projection* function, P, that maps a configuration set s into that subset of Q that represents the shift and reduce actions possible in s.

```
int ** build_go_to_table(finite_automaton CFSM)
{
    const int N = num_states(CFSM);
    int **tab;

    Dynamically allocate a table of dimension
        N × num_symbols(CFSM) to represent
        the go_to table and assign it to tab;

    Number the states of CFSM from 0 to N-1,
        with the Start State labeled 0;

    for (S = 0; S <= N - 1; S++) {
        /* Consider both terminals and nonterminals. */
        for (X in Symbols) {
            if (State S has a transition under X
                to some state T)
                tab[S][X] = T;
            else
                tab[S][X] = EMPTY;
        }
    }
    return tab;
}
```

Figure 6.9   An Algorithm to Build the LR(0) `go_to` Table

State	Symbol		
	ID	$	S
0	1	4	2
1	4	4	4
2	4	3	4
3	4	4	4
4			

Figure 6.10   A `go_to` Table for Grammar G_2

Let S_0 be the set of CFSM states, each of which is identified with a particular configuration set. Then $P : S_0 \to 2^Q$. 2^Q is the *power set* of Q; that is, the set of all subsets of Q. P maps each CFSM set into the appropriate subset of Q. P(s) is defined as:

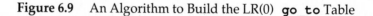

$\{Reduce_i \mid B \to \rho \bullet \in s$ and production i is $B \to \rho\} \cup$

(If $A \to \alpha \bullet a\beta \in s$ for $a \in V_t$ Then {Shift} Else $\varnothing$)

G is LR(0) if and only if $\forall s \in S_0$ $|P(s)| = 1$. ($|P(s)|$ denotes the *size* of the set P(s). Hence $|P(s)| = 1$ means P must be single-valued.)

If G is LR(0), the **action** table is trivially extracted from P:

- $P(s) = \{Shift\} \Rightarrow$ action[s] = Shift
- $P(s) = \{Reduce_j\}$, where production j is the augmenting production, $\Rightarrow$ action[s] = Accept
- $P(s) = \{Reduce_i\}$, $i \neq j \Rightarrow$ action[s] = Reduce$_i$
- $P(s) = \varnothing \Rightarrow$ action[s] = Error; action[$\varnothing$] $\equiv$ Error

Any state $s \in S_0$ for which $|P(s)| > 1$ is said to be *inadequate*. Two kinds of parser conflicts create inadequacies in configuration sets:

- *Shift-reduce conflicts.* Both a shift action and a reduce action are possible in the same configuration set.
- *Reduce-reduce conflicts.* Two or more distinct reduce actions are possible in the same configuration set.

Normally, inadequacies in a CFSM state are resolved by using lookahead in the **action** function.

It is easy to introduce inadequacies in CFSM states. Hence, few real grammars (those used to generate real programming languages) are LR(0). For example, consider λ-productions. Since the right-hand side of a λ-production is empty, it is ready to be reduced as soon as it is predicted. Thus, the only possible configuration involving a λ-production is of the form A → λ • (sometimes written as A → •). However, if A can generate any terminal string other than λ, then a shift action must also be possible (to accept a symbol in First(A)). Therefore a shift-reduce conflict is unavoidable for λ-productions, unless only λ can be generated by the left-hand side of the λ-production.

Similarly, most programming languages have an operator precedence hierarchy. In the absence of explicit parenthesization, some operators take precedence over others. For example, in most programming languages, A := B+C*D; means A := B+(C*D); rather than A := (B+C)*D;.

A compiler using an LR(0) parser will have problems in handling operator precedences properly. If the compiler is translating A := B+C+D;, then it should reduce B+C after shifting C, because addition is left-associative. However, if the compiler is translating A := B+C*D;, then it must not reduce B+C after shifting C, because multiplication takes precedence over addition. Without lookahead (which LR(0) cannot use), the two cases are not easily distinguishable.

The preceding discussion makes it clear that LR(0) grammars are not easy to write for "real" programming languages. A more fundamental question, though, is whether it is ever even *possible* to write LR(0) grammars for interesting languages. Surprisingly, the answer is yes. As we will discuss later in the chapter, if a programming language has an endmarker, which is invariably the case in practice, and can be parsed by any LR-style parsing technique using any amount of lookahead, then an equivalent LR(0) grammar must exist. Of course, this LR(0) grammar may be very large, very hard to read, and not well suited to syntax-directed translation, but it *must* exist.

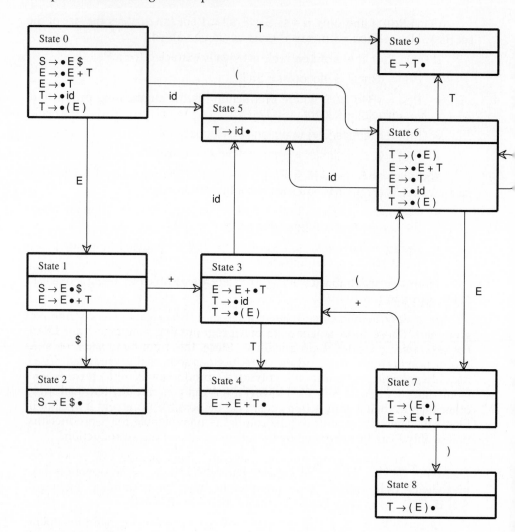

Figure 6.11   CFSM for G_1

As an example of LR(0) parser construction, let us reconsider G_1:

$$S \rightarrow E\$$$
$$E \rightarrow E + T \mid T$$
$$T \rightarrow ID \mid (E)$$

First, we construct the CFSM, as shown in Figure 6.11. CFSM states are marked with the configuration sets they represent and are indexed from zero for ease of reference in the **action** table.

If we inspect the CFSM of Figure 6.11, we see that each state either signals a shift (because the • is to the left of a terminal) or signals a unique reduction (because the • is at the right end of a single configuration). This means there are no shift-reduce or reduce-reduce conflicts; hence, G_1 is LR(0). The `go_to` table can be built using **`build_go_to_table()`**. In the `go_to` table, state 10, elided in the CFSM diagram, is the error state. The **`action`** table is shown in Figure 6.12. S denotes Shift; A denotes Accept; a blank denotes Error; Ri denotes Reduce$_i$.

State:	0	1	2	3	4	5	6	7	8	9	10
Action:	S	S	A	S	R2	R4	S	S	R5	R3	

Figure 6.12   `action` Table for G_1

6.2.2. How Can We Be Sure LR(0) Parsers Work Correctly?

Before we actually use LR(0) parsers, we need to convince ourselves that they will operate properly. This is often done by stating and proving a "correctness theorem." For our purposes, the important part is the insight contained in such a proof. Once the essential ideas are understood, the details of the proof are easy.

The correctness of LR(0) parsers hinges on two insights. First, the CFSM can read only strings that are viable prefixes of the grammar being parsed. This observation is important because it tells us that if an illegal symbol is seen, it will not be accepted by the parser for it cannot be part of a viable prefix.

The second observation is that the parser **`action`** table correctly signals the appropriate move. That is, the **`action`** table signals shift until the end of the handle is seen. Then it signals the reduction necessary to replace the handle with its corresponding left-hand side.

Recall that a viable prefix of a right sentential form is any prefix that does not extend beyond its handle. The handle is the leftmost phrase that may be correctly reduced to a nonterminal. Intuitively, an LR(0) parser, or any other shift-reduce parser, will shift symbols forming a viable prefix until a complete handle is shifted. Then the handle will be reduced to a single nonterminal. The CFSM of an LR(0) parser must be able to read all viable prefixes so that no legal reductions are missed. The CFSM does not need to read all possible prefixes of right sentential forms because handles are reduced as soon as they are shifted and recognized. Similarly, if a sequence of symbols cannot be a prefix of any right sentential form, it cannot be parsed and should not be accepted by the CFSM.

Assume we have a viable prefix, v. How can new viable prefixes be created from it? Any prefix of v is viable, and if v contains only terminals, these prefixes are the only viable prefixes that can be created from it. If v contains at least one nonterminal, B, we can write v as $\alpha B\gamma$. B can be rewritten using some production $B \rightarrow \beta$ to obtain $\alpha\beta\gamma$. Any prefix of $\alpha\beta$ is viable, but no viable prefix can extend beyond β because it is a handle. Thus, as a general rule, we create new viable prefixes by taking a viable prefix ending in a nonterminal B and replacing B with any prefix of β, where $B \rightarrow \beta$.

To establish the correspondence between viable prefixes and strings read by a CFSM, we begin with s_0, the start state of the CFSM. This is reached by reading λ, which is trivially a viable prefix of all right sentential forms. By construction, s_0 contains one basis item: $S \rightarrow \bullet\alpha\$$. s_0 has successors under $\alpha\$$. This is correct, as we know that all prefixes of $\alpha\$$ are viable, because $\alpha\$$ can be reduced to S. Let βC be any prefix of $\alpha\$$ that ends in a nonterminal. After β is read, we will be in a CFSM state s that contains a configuration of the form $D \rightarrow \gamma \bullet C\delta$. A configuration of this form must appear in s because we know C can be read from s. Because C is a nonterminal, the LR(0) closure operation will include configurations of the form $C \rightarrow \bullet\rho$ for each production, with C as its left-hand side. By construction, state s has successors under ρ, meaning that any prefix of $\beta\rho$ can be read from s_0. Repeating the argument, it is easy to see that any viable prefix created from $\beta\rho$ can also be read by the CFSM. Thus, the CFSM, starting in state s_0, can read all possible viable prefixes.

To see that the CFSM reads only viable prefixes, assume that all strings of length n read by the CFSM are viable. This is certainly true for the case of $n = 0$. Let βX be a string of length $n + 1$ that can be read by the CFSM. After reading β, we must be in a state s from which X can be read. This means s contains a configuration of the form $B \rightarrow \gamma \bullet X\delta$. This configuration is either a basis or closure item. If it is a basis item, γ must be at least one symbol long, or the configuration must be the initial configuration, $S \rightarrow \bullet\alpha\$$. We know all prefixes of $\alpha\$$ are viable, so assume $|\gamma| = m \geq 1$. The last m symbols of βX must be γ, because s contains $B \rightarrow \gamma \bullet X\delta$. After reading ω, the first $n-m$ symbols of βX, we will be in a state s' containing $B \rightarrow \bullet\gamma X\delta$. s' must also contain a configuration with the $\bullet$ immediately preceding a B, since $B \rightarrow \bullet\gamma X\delta$ can be created only by prediction. Thus, B can be read from s', and hence ωB can be read from s_0. Since $|\omega B| \leq n$, ωB is viable and hence so is $\omega\gamma X = \beta X$.

If $B \rightarrow \gamma \bullet X\delta$ is a closure item, then γ must be empty. $B \rightarrow \bullet X\delta$ was added, directly or indirectly, by closing a basis item. That is, s must contain a basis item $D \rightarrow \theta \bullet C_1\pi$, where $C_1 \rightarrow C_2\sigma_2, C_2 \rightarrow C_3\sigma_3, , \ldots, C_p \rightarrow B\sigma_{p+1}$. Using the argument of the previous paragraph, we can conclude βC_1 is viable. This means βC_2 is viable, as is $\beta C_3, \ldots$. Using $C_p \rightarrow B\sigma_{p+1}$, we conclude that βB is viable and hence so is βX.

We have shown that the CFSM accepts exactly the set of viable prefixes of the grammar being parsed. All that remains to convince ourselves that LR(0) parsers work correctly is to show that the parser **action** table corresponding to CFSM states always signals the correct parsing action.

Assume we are parsing some valid input string z and have made zero or more correct reductions to obtain the right sentential form γy, where y is the remaining input, and γ has already been shifted onto the parse stack. We reach the next handle by shifting zero or more terminal symbols from y. Assume $S \Rightarrow^*_{rm} \alpha Aw \Rightarrow_{rm} \alpha\beta w$, where $\alpha\beta = \gamma x$, and $xw = y$. That is, the correct parser action is to read x, then signal the reduction of $A \rightarrow \beta$. Can we be sure that this is what our LR(0) parser will do?

Assume we are in state s after shifting γ. We know x can be read from s because $\gamma x = \alpha\beta$ is a viable prefix. Further, the parser will signal no reductions until all of x is shifted. This follows from the fact that each state visited while shifting x must signal a shift action, and hence any reduce action would create a shift-reduce conflict, which is forbidden for LR(0) grammars.

The parser therefore signals no false reductions while x is being read. We know that αA is a viable prefix. The state reached after reading α must contain an item $B \rightarrow v \bullet A\sigma$ and hence also an item $A \rightarrow \bullet \beta$. The successor to this state under β must contain the item $A \rightarrow \beta \bullet$, and this state, reached after shifting x, will signal the expected reduce action.

This argument shows that having reduced the input string z to γy, the parser will correctly perform the next step and reduce $\alpha\beta w$ to $\alpha A w$. By an induction on the number of steps needed to derive z, we conclude that it will eventually be reduced to S, the goal symbol, thus successfully concluding the parse.

As a final point, what if an LR(0) parser is given an incorrect input string? The CFSM can read only viable prefixes, so at some point the input will not be reducible to a viable prefix, and a syntax error will be properly detected.

6.3. LR(1) Parsing

As noted previously, because LR(0) parsers use no lookahead they are incapable of parsing most grammars of interest to compiler writers. LR(1), however, generalizes LR(0) by including a lookahead component in configurations. An LR(1) configuration, or item, is of the form

$$A \rightarrow X_1 \cdots X_i \bullet X_{i+1} \cdots X_j, l \quad \text{where } l \in V_t \cup \{\lambda\}$$

As before, the dotted production represents how much of a right-hand side has been matched. The lookahead component l represents a possible lookahead after the entire right-hand side has been matched. Normally the lookahead component is a terminal symbol. The λ appears as lookahead only for the augmenting production because there is no lookahead after the end-marker.

Often we have a number of LR(1) configurations that differ only in their lookahead components. We use the following notation to represent the *set* of LR(1) configurations that share the same dotted production:

$$A \rightarrow X_1 \cdots X_i \bullet X_{i+1} \cdots X_j, \{l_1 \cdots l_m\}$$

This form is a convenient representation for the set of m configurations with the same dotted production and for lookahead components $l_1, \cdots, l_m$.

The addition of a lookahead component to LR(1) configurations allows us to make parsing decisions beyond the capability of LR(0) parsers. There is, however, a price to be paid. Now there are many more distinct LR(1) configurations than LR(0) configurations (the ratio is equal to $|V_t|$, the size of the token set), and many more LR(1) configuration sets are possible. This can greatly increase the size of the **go_to** and **action** tables, which are are proportional to the number of configuration sets created. In fact, the major difficulty with LR(1) parsers is not their power (recall that LR(1) parsers are the most powerful possible deterministic bottom-up parsers using one-symbol lookahead) but rather finding ways to represent them in storage-efficient ways.

To create an LR(1) parser we repeat the steps used to create LR(0) parsers, but this time we include the lookahead component. Parsing begins with the configuration $S \to \bullet \alpha\$, \{\lambda\}$, which predicts the augmenting production, with the empty string as the sole lookahead. The α may begin with a nonterminal, so closure of the configuration is required. The LR(1) closure operation is defined in Figure 6.13.

As an example, reconsider G_1:

$$S \to E\$$$
$$E \to E + T \mid T$$
$$T \to ID \mid (E)$$

We start with $S \to \bullet E\$, \{\lambda\}$ and predict productions with a left-hand side of E and \$ as a lookahead. This adds $E \to \bullet E{+}T, \{\$\}$ and $E \to \bullet T, \{\$\}$. We again predict productions with E on the left hand, now with + as the lookahead. This adds $E \to \bullet E{+}T, \{+\}$ and $E \to \bullet T, \{+\}$. Now productions with T

```
configuration_set closure1(configuration_set s)
{
    configuration_set s' = s;

    do {
        if (B →δ • Aρ, l ∈ s' for A∈Vₙ) {
            /*
             * Predict productions with A as the
             * left-hand side. Possible lookaheads
             * are First(ρl)
             */
            Add all configurations of the form A →  • γ, u,
                where  u ∈First(ρl), to s'
        }
    } while (more new configurations can be added)
    return s';
}
```

Figure 6.13   An Algorithm to Close LR(1) Configuration Sets

on the left-hand side and with $ and + as lookaheads are predicted: $T \rightarrow \bullet ID, \{+\$\}; T \rightarrow \bullet (E), \{+\$\}$. We therefore have:

$$
\begin{array}{lll}
\text{closure1}(S \rightarrow \bullet E\$,\{\lambda\}) = \{ & S \rightarrow \bullet E\$, & \{\lambda\}; \\
 & E \rightarrow \bullet E + T, & \{\$+\}; \\
 & E \rightarrow \bullet T, & \{\$+\}; \\
 & T \rightarrow \bullet ID, & \{\$+\}; \\
 & T \rightarrow \bullet (E), & \{\$+\} \}
\end{array}
$$

To create the initial LR(1) configuration set, s_0, we predict the augmenting production and close it:

$$
s_0 = \text{closure1}(\{S \rightarrow \bullet \alpha\$\}, \{\lambda\})
$$

Given an LR(1) configuration set s, we compute its *successor*, s', under a symbol X, denoted go_to1(s,X), using the algorithm of Figure 6.14.

The LR(1) **action** function indicates a shift action only if a nonempty successor state exists. This means that the empty configuration set is *unreachable* and can be ignored. The number of distinct LR(1) configurations and configuration sets is finite. We can build a finite automaton that is the analogue of the LR(0) CFSM; we call it the *LR(1) FSM* or, more simply, the *LR(1) machine*. An algorithm to build an LR(1) FSM is presented in Figure 6.15.

The LR(1) machine and the CFSM are closely related. In particular, the CFSM for a grammar can be obtained from the LR(1) machine by "merging" configuration sets that are identical except for the lookahead component. Analogously, if we "split" CFSM configuration sets by adding lookahead information, an LR(1) machine can be created.

```
configuration_set go_to1(configuration_set s, symbol X)
{
    s_b = ∅;
    for (each configuration c ∈ s)
        if (c is of the form A →β • X γ, l)
            Add A →βX • γ, l to s_b;

    /*
     * That is, we advance the • past the symbol X,
     * if possible.  Configurations not having a
     * dot preceding an X are not included in s_b.
     */

    /* Add new predictions to s_b via closure1. */
    return closure1(s_b);
}
```

Figure 6.14   An Algorithm to Compute the LR(1) **go_to** Function

Consider G_3, a simple expression grammar containing both + and *:

$$
\begin{aligned}
S &\rightarrow E\$ \\
E &\rightarrow E + T \mid T \\
T &\rightarrow T * P \mid P \\
P &\rightarrow ID \mid (E)
\end{aligned}
$$

Given grammar G_3, **build_LR1** would create the LR(1) machine shown in Figure 6.16.

The LR(1) machine for G_3 has 23 states, whereas the CFSM for the same grammar has only 13 states. For grammars used for programming languages, the size of an LR(1) machine is usually much larger than that of a corresponding CFSM. For example, early experience with grammars for Algol 60, which are much smaller and simpler than those needed for Ada, showed that *thousands* of LR(1) states were needed.

The **go_to** table used to drive an LR(1) parser is extracted directly from the LR(1) machine using the **build_go_to_table()** routine of Figure 6.9. We can also extract the **action** table directly from the configuration sets of the LR(1) machine, since configurations contain lookahead information. Define a *projection* function, P, that maps a configuration set and a lookahead symbol into the corresponding *set* of possible shift or reduce actions.

```
void build_LR1 (void)
{
  Create the Start State of the FSM; Label it with s0

  Put s0 into an initially empty set, S.

  while (S is nonempty) {
     Remove a configuration set s from S;
     /* Consider both terminals and nonterminals */
     for (X in Symbols) {
        if (go_to1(s,X) != ∅) {
           if (go_to1(s,X) does not label a FSM state) {
              Create a new FSM state and label it
                 with go_to1(s,X);
              Put go_to1(s,X) into S;
           }
           Create a transition under X from the
              state s labels to the state
              go_to1(s,X) labels;
        }
     }
  }
}
```

Figure 6.15   An Algorithm to Build an LR(1) FSM

Let S_1 be the set of LR(1) machine states, each of which is identified with a particular LR(1) configuration set. Then $P : S_1 \times V_t \to 2^Q$, where Q is the set of possible shift and reduce actions. $P(s,a)$ is defined as

$\{Reduce_i | B \to \rho \bullet, a \in s \text{ and production i is } B \to \rho\} \cup$

$(\text{If } A \to \alpha \bullet a\beta, b \in s \text{ Then } \{Shift\} \text{ Else } \varnothing)$

G is LR(1) if and only if $\forall s \in S_1 \ \forall a \in V_t \ |P(s,a)| \leq 1$. That is, P must contain at most one nonerror action for all pairs of states and lookaheads.

If G is LR(1), the action function is easily extracted from P:

- $P(s,\$) = \{Shift\} \Rightarrow action[s][\$] = Accept$
- $P(s,a) = \{Shift\}, a \neq \$ \Rightarrow action[s][a] = Shift$
- $P(s,a) = \{Reduce_i\} \Rightarrow action[s][a] = Reduce_i$
- $P(s,a) = \varnothing \Rightarrow action[s][a] = Error$

An inspection of the configuration sets of Figure 6.16 shows that each possible lookahead symbol induces a unique action. That is, a lookahead l may signal a shift (if a $\bullet$ appears to its left), or it may signal a reduction (given a unique configuration of the form $A \to \alpha \bullet, l$), or the lookahead may signal an error (if it can neither be shifted nor be a lookahead for a reduction). Because no shift-reduce or reduce-reduce conflicts occur, G_3 is LR(1). The **go_to** table can be extracted directly from the LR(1) machine using **build_go_to_table()**. The LR(1) **action** table for G_3 is shown in Figure 6.17.

6.3.1. Correctness of LR(1) Parsing

To prove the correctness of LR(1) parsing, we address the same issues as we did in Section 6.2.2, in which the correctness of LR(0) parsing was established. Like the CFSM, the LR(1) machine reads only viable prefixes. Items in the LR(1) machine contain lookahead components, and it is a simple matter to prove that these lookahead components are correct. That is, a state s contains an LR(1) item $A \to \alpha \bullet, a$ if and only if there exists a rightmost derivation $S \Rightarrow^*_{rm} \beta Aaw \Rightarrow_{rm} \beta \alpha aw$, where state s is reached after shifting $\beta \alpha$.

The proof is very similar to that used to show that the CFSM reads exactly the set of viable prefixes. Again, we start with s_0 and prove that if the lookahead correctness property holds for some state (and it certainly does for s_0), then it also holds for the state's immediate successors.

Once we have proved that LR(1) lookahead components are exact, correctness of the parser immediately follows. Assume we are parsing some valid input string z and have made zero or more correct reductions to obtain the right sentential form γy, where y is the remaining input, and γ has already been shifted onto the parse stack. We reach the next handle by shifting zero or more terminal symbols from y. Assume $S \Rightarrow^*_{rm} \alpha Aw \Rightarrow_{rm} \alpha \beta w$, where $\alpha \beta = \gamma x$ and $xw = y$. That is, the correct parser action is to read x, then signal the reduction of $A \to \beta$.

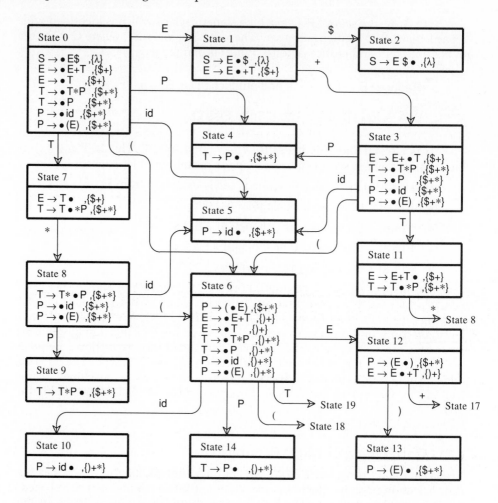

Figure 6.16   LR(1) Machine for G_3

Assume further that we are in state s after shifting γ. We know x can be shifted from s because γx = αβ is a viable prefix. Further, the parser will signal no reductions until all of x is shifted, else a shift-reduce conflict would exist.

Let First(w) = a. Knowing that lookahead symbols in configurations are correct, after reading α, we reach a state s′ containing the item B → v • Aσ, b, where a∈ First(σb). During closure, an item A → •β, a is added. The successor to s′ under β must contain the item A → β •, a, and this state, reached by the parser after shifting x, will signal the expected reduce action.

This argument shows that having reduced the input string z to γy, the parser will correctly perform the next step and reduce αβw to αAw. By an induction on the number of steps needed to derive z, we conclude it will eventually be reduced to S, the goal symbol, successfully concluding the parse.

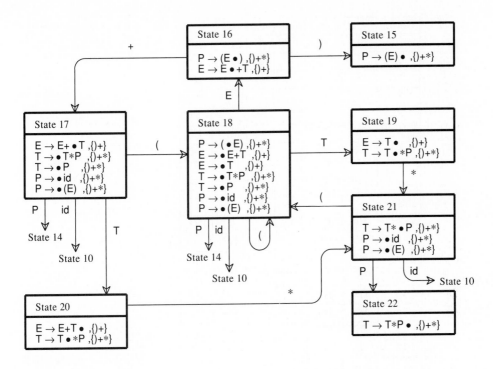

Figure 6.16   (continued)

6.4. **SLR(1) Parsing**

LR(0) parsers yield compact **go_to** and **action** tables but they lack the power to parse grammars used to define real programming languages. LR(1) parsers, however, are the most powerful class of shift-reduce parsers, using a single lookahead. Not surprisingly, LR(1) grammars exist for virtually all programming languages. In fact, language designers usually require that the syntax of a new programming language be specified by a grammar that is LR(1). LR(1)'s problem is that the LR(1) machine contains so many states that the **go_to** and **action** tables become prohibitively large.

In reaction to the space inefficiency of LR(1) tables, computer scientists have devised parsing techniques that are almost as powerful as LR(1) but that require far smaller tables. Two general approaches can be discerned. One is to start with the CFSM, which in general is acceptably small, and then add lookahead *after* the CFSM is built. The best known example of this approach is the SLR(1) technique, which we discuss in this section.

The other approach to reducing LR(1)'s space inefficiencies is to *merge* inessential LR(1) states. If we simply merge all states that correspond to the same CFSM state, we obtain the LALR(1) technique, which is discussed in Sec-

State	Lookahead					
	+	*	ID	(	)	$
0			S	S		
1	S					A
2						
3			S	S		
4	R5	R5				R5
5	R6	R6				R6
6			S	S		
7	R3	S				R3
8			S	S		
9	R4	R4				R4
10	R6	R6			R6	
11	R2	S				R2
12	S				S	
13	R7	R7				R7
14	R5	R5			R5	
15	R7	R7			R7	
16	S				S	
17			S	S		
18			S	S		
19	R3	S			R3	
20	R2	S			R2	
21			S	S		
22	R4	R4			R4	

Figure 6.17   LR(1) **action** Function for G_3

tion 6.5. If we are more careful in how states are merged, it is possible to create parsers as fully powerful as ordinary LR(1) parsers whose space requirements are comparable to SLR(1) and LALR(1). LR(1) optimization techniques are discussed in Section 6.9.

SLR(1) stands for *Simple LR(1)*. The idea was introduced by DeRemer (1969, 1971). SLR(1) uses one-symbol lookahead in conjunction with the LR(0) CFSM. That is, lookaheads are not built directly into configurations but rather are added after the LR(0) configuration sets are built. What results is a parser nearly as powerful as LR(1) but which uses much less space. In fact, until SLR(1) and LALR(1) became widely known (in the early 1970s), LR concepts were viewed as primarily of theoretical rather than practical import. Soon thereafter they displaced the precedence-based techniques then in use (see Section 6.12.2) and are still in wide use today.

Recall that in LR(1) parsers, lookahead components in configurations are used to decide when a reduce action is appropriate. SLR(1) does not extract lookaheads from configurations but instead uses a simpler approach. If we have an LR(0) configuration $B \rightarrow \rho \bullet$, then the minimum requirement on a lookahead symbol that signals a reduce action is that it be compatible with the left-hand side of the production. That is, if lookahead symbol l signals that production $B \rightarrow \rho$ should be reduced, then l must legally be able to follow B, because after the reduction they will be adjacent. Using this logic, an SLR(1) parser will perform a reduce action for configuration $B \rightarrow \rho \bullet$ if the lookahead symbol is in the set Follow(B). This leads to the following definition of the SLR(1) **action** table. The SLR(1) **go_to** table is extracted from the CFSM and is identical to the LR(0) **go_to** table.

Recall that S_0 is the set of CFSM states. The SLR(1) projection function, from CFSM states and lookaheads to possible parser actions, is

$$P : S_0 \times V_t \rightarrow 2^Q \quad \text{where Q is the set of possible shift and reduce actions}$$

P(s,a) is defined as:

{Reduce$_i$ | $B \rightarrow \rho \bullet \in$ s, $a \in$ Follow(B), and production i is $B \rightarrow \rho$} $\cup$

(If $A \rightarrow \alpha \bullet a\beta \in$ s for $a \in V_t$ Then {Shift} Else $\varnothing$)

G is SLR(1) if and only if $\forall s \in S_0$ $\forall a \in V_t$ $|P(s,a)| \leq 1$. That is, P must contain at most one nonerror action for all pairs of states and lookaheads.

If G is SLR(1), the action function is easily extracted from P:

- P(s,$) = {Shift} $\Rightarrow$ action[s][$] = Accept
- P(s,a) = {Shift}, $a \neq$ $ $\Rightarrow$ action[s][a] = Shift
- P(s,a) = {Reduce$_i$} $\Rightarrow$ action[s][a] = Reduce$_i$
- P(s,a) = $\varnothing$ $\Rightarrow$ action[s][a] = Error

Clearly SLR(1) is a proper superset of LR(0).

As an example, reconsider G_3, which we know is LR(1) but not LR(0). Is it SLR(1)? First, we build the CFSM shown in Figure 6.18 using **build_CFSM()**.

States 7 and 11 are inadequate, because each contains a shift-reduce conflict. In both cases, we will reduce if we see a lookahead in Follow(E) = {$,+,)}, and we will shift if we see a *. Since lookaheads resolve the shift-reduce conflicts in both states, G_3 is SLR(1). The complete SLR(1) **action** table is shown in Figure 6.19. Note that lookaheads are used even in those states that are adequate. Using them allows us to detect syntax errors a bit earlier than an LR(0) parser would. However, they can be ignored in adequate states. Doing so allows us to reduce table sizes, which is discussed in detail in Section 6.8.

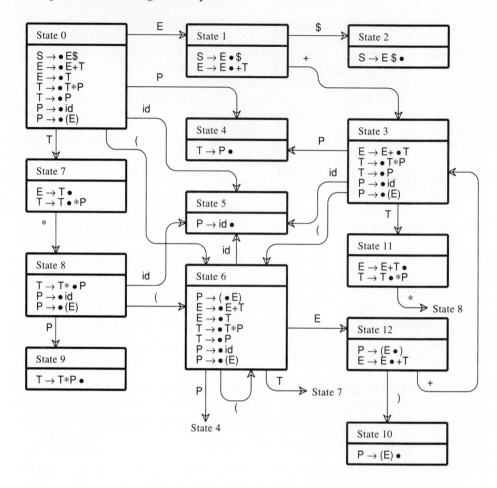

Figure 6.18   CFSM for G_3

6.4.1. Correctness of SLR(1) Parsing

SLR(1) parsing uses a CFSM, as does LR(0) parsing. In fact, the only real difference between the two techniques is that in SLR(1) production p may be reduced only if a lookahead is in the Follow set of p's left-hand side. We really need only to establish that this use of lookaheads leads to correct reductions, and this is easy to do.

While parsing some valid input string z, assume we have made zero or more reductions to obtain the right sentential form $\alpha\beta w$, where $S \Rightarrow^*_{rm} \alpha Aw \Rightarrow_{rm} \alpha\beta w$, and further First(w) = a. The CFSM will shift $\alpha\beta$, reaching a state containing the item $A \rightarrow \beta \bullet$. From the derivation, we know $a \in$ Follow(A), and hence the correct reduction will occur.

State	Lookahead					
	+	*	ID	(	)	$
0			S	S		
1	S					A
2						
3			S	S		
4	R5	R5			R5	R5
5	R6	R6			R6	R6
6			S	S		
7	R3	S			R3	R3
8			S	S		
9	R4	R4			R4	R4
10	R7	R7			R7	R7
11	R2	S			R2	R2
12	S				S	

Figure 6.19   SLR(1) **action** Function for G_3

6.4.2. Limitations of the SLR(1) Technique

G_3 is both SLR(1) and LR(1). In practice, many grammars that are LR(1) are also SLR(1) or can be made SLR(1) with modest effort. As a result, SLR(1) parsers are of practical interest to compiler writers.

The use of Follow sets to estimate the lookaheads that predict reduce actions is less precise than using the exact lookaheads incorporated into LR(1) configurations. It is easy to find grammars that are LR(1) but not SLR(1), and such grammars sometimes come up in practice. For example, consider a grammar that generates lists of two or more elements. Elements can be IDs, or parenthesized IDs or lists. The grammar disallows one-element lists to avoid ambiguity.

The relevant grammar, G_4, is

```
Elem   → (List, Elem)
Elem   → Scalar
List   → List, Elem
List   → Elem
Scalar → ID
Scalar → (Scalar)
```

Part of the corresponding CFSM is shown in Figure 6.20.

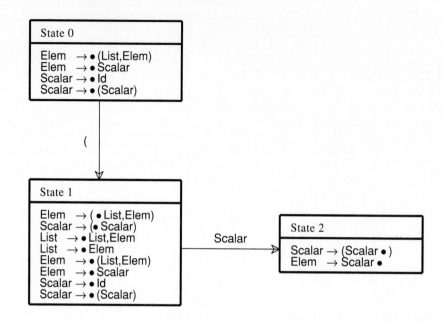

Figure 6.20   Part of the CFSM for G_4

State 2 is inadequate. Since) ∈ Follow(Elem), SLR(1) lookaheads cannot resolve the ambiguity; hence, the grammar cannot be SLR(1). In fact, any number of)'s can follow both Scalar and Elem, so it can be established that this grammar cannot be SLR(k) for any k.

Of course it might be the case that this grammar is simply difficult to parse, but careful analysis will show that this is not the case. Observe that if Elem → Scalar is reduced, it must be that List → Elem is recognized next and then, from state 1, we reach a state where only "," can be read. Thus the LR(1) lookahead is "," and this grammar fragment is LR(1).

This example illustrates that the inexact computation of lookaheads via Follow sets can lead to unnecessary parser conflicts. When such conflicts occur, a compiler writer can either rewrite parts of a grammar to fit the SLR(1) rules or use a more powerful parsing technique. Except for the size of the tables it requires, LR(1) is the obvious choice. In the following section, we discuss LALR(1) parsing. LALR(1) has the space efficiency of SLR(1) parsing but can handle a broader class of grammars (though not all LR(1) grammars). As a result, many compiler writers use LALR(1) parsers rather than SLR(1) parsers, and in fact LALR(1) is the most commonly used bottom-up parsing method.

6.5. LALR(1)

SLR(1) parsers are built by first constructing a CFSM, then determining look-aheads by computing Follow sets. In contrast, LALR(1) parsers can be built by first constructing an LR(1) parser and then merging states. In particular, an LALR(1) parser is an LR(1) parser in which all states that differ *only* in the lookahead components of the configurations are merged. LALR is an acronym for Look Ahead LR. This is a bit of a misnomer in that all shift-reduce parsers except LR(0) use lookahead. The point is that LALR(1) can be viewed as adding lookahead to the underlying CFSM. LALR parsers were first proposed in DeRemer (1969).

Consider any state s in an LR(1) machine. This state can be mapped uniquely to a state $\bar{s}$ of the corresponding CFSM by simply removing the lookahead components of all configurations in s. Thus if s were

$A \rightarrow a \bullet, \{b,c\}$
$B \rightarrow a \bullet, \{d\}$

$\bar{s}$ would be

$A \rightarrow a \bullet$
$B \rightarrow a \bullet$

In general this mapping is *many to one*. We call $\bar{s}$ the *core* of s, and use the notation $\bar{s} = $ Core(s). We can create a *cognate* LR(1) configuration set by joining together configurations in all LR(1) machine states that share the same core. Define this as

Cognate($\bar{s}$) = $\{c | c \in s, \text{Core}(s) = \bar{s}\}$

Using the Cognate function, we create a finite automaton called the *LALR(1) machine* that is identical in structure to the CFSM. That is, the LALR(1) machine and the CFSM will have exactly the same set of states and transitions. The only difference is that CFSM states are LR(0) configuration sets, whereas LALR(1) machine states are LR(1) configuration sets. Because LR(1) configurations contain lookaheads, it is trivial to project LALR(1) states into possible parser actions. The LALR(1) projection function takes a CFSM state and a lookahead symbol. The CFSM state is transformed into its LALR(1) cognate, and possible actions are extracted.

We have $P : S_0 \times V_t \rightarrow 2^Q$ where Q is the set of possible shift and reduce actions. $P(s,a)$ is defined as:

$\{\text{Reduce}_i \mid B \rightarrow \rho \bullet, a \in \text{Cognate}(s), \text{ and production } i \text{ is } B \rightarrow \rho\} \cup$
$\quad (\text{If } A \rightarrow \alpha \bullet a\beta \in s \text{ Then } \{\text{Shift}\} \text{ Else } \varnothing)$

LALR(1) Cognate State	LR(1) States with Common Core
State 0	State 0
State 1	State 1
State 2	State 2
State 3	State 3, State 17
State 4	State 4, State 14
State 5	State 5, State 10
State 6	State 6, State 18
State 7	State 7, State 19
State 8	State 8, State 21
State 9	State 9, State 22
State 10	State 13, State 15
State 11	State 11, State 20
State 12	State 12, State 16

Figure 6.21   Cognate States for G_3

G is LALR(1) if and only if $\forall s \in S_0$ $\forall a \in V_t$ $|P(s,a)| \leq 1$

If G is LALR(1), the action function is trivially extracted from P:

- $P(s,\$) = \{Shift\} \Rightarrow action[s][\$] = Accept$
- $P(s,a) = \{Shift\}, a \neq \$ \Rightarrow action[s][a] = Shift$
- $P(s,a) = \{Reduce_i\} \Rightarrow action[s][a] = Reduce_i$
- $P(s,a) = \varnothing \Rightarrow action[s][a] = Error$

As an example, let us return to G_3. We consider each state of the LR(1) machine (Figure 6.16) and merge into a cognate state those with a common core. The LR(1) states and their LALR(1) cognate state are shown in Figure 6.21; the LALR(1) machine that results after merging cognate states is shown in Figure 6.22.

The LALR(1) **action** table for G_3 is the same as the SLR(1) **action** table. This is not too surprising as the grammar is so simple.

We have already seen an example (G_4) where LALR(1)'s more careful lookahead computation is needed. Another common situation in which LALR(1) is needed is illustrated by grammar G_5:

```
<stmt>  → ID
<stmt>  → <var> := <expr>
<var>   → ID
<var>   → ID [ <expr> ]
<expr>  → <var>
```

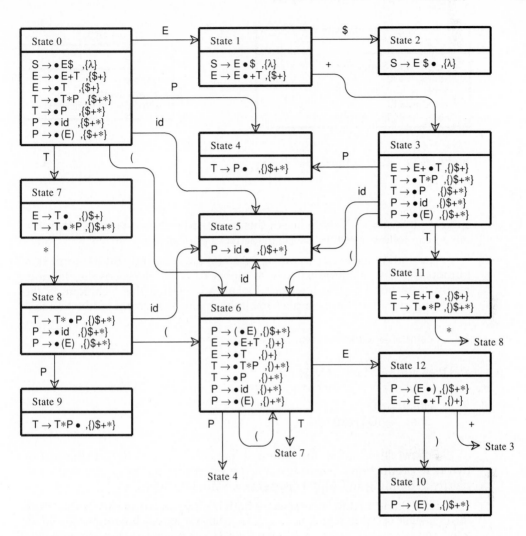

Figure 6.22   LALR(1) Machine for G_3

When we predict a statement using <prog>→<stmt>, we get the CFSM states shown in Figure 6.23.

Assuming statements are separated by ;'s, as is standard, we have

; ∈ Follow(<stmt>) and
; ∈ Follow(<var>), since <expr>→<var>

Because lookaheads derived from **Follow** sets do not resolve the reduce-reduce conflict in state 1, G_5 is not SLR(1). However, once again LALR(1)

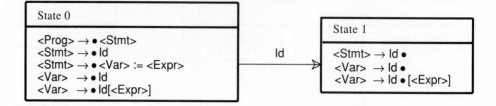

Figure 6.23   Part of the CFSM for G₅

suffices. If <var> → ID is reduced, then := must be shifted next. Neither a :=
nor a [can follow a <stmt>, so the inadequacy is resolved.

A common technique to put an LALR(1) grammar into SLR(1) form is to
introduce a new nonterminal whose global (that is, SLR) lookaheads more
nearly correspond to LALR's exact lookaheads. Using this technique in the
preceding grammar, for example, we might change the second production to

<stmt> → <lhs> := <expr>

and then add two new productions

<lhs> → ID
<lhs> → ID [<expr>]

Follow(<lhs>) = {:=}; the grammar has been made SLR(1), at the cost of
two new productions. These examples suggest that the extra cost and complexity in building an LALR(1) parser is worthwhile in practice.

SLR(1) and LALR(1) parsers are both built upon use of the CFSM. Does
the case ever occur in which *no* **action** table, no matter how carefully calculated and no matter how much lookahead is used, can parse a grammar that
intuitively is "easily" parsable? Yes—at times it is the CFSM itself that is at
fault. Consider G₆:

S   → (Exp1)
S   → [Exp1]
S   → (Exp2]
S   → [Exp2)
Exp1 → ID
Exp2 → ID

G₆ represents a language in which expressions may be delimited with either parentheses or brackets. Mismatched delimiters are allowed; a different

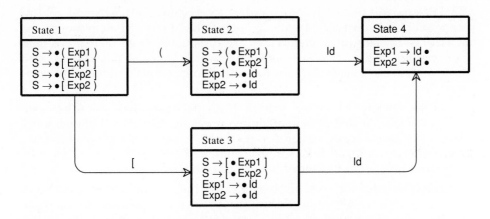

Figure 6.24   Part of the CFSM for Grammar G_6

expression nonterminal is used to allow error or warning diagnostics. Part of the corresponding CFSM is shown in Figure 6.24.

State 4 is inadequate. But no action function can ever resolve it. On input (ID) we must recognize Exp1→ID, and on input [ID] we must recognize Exp2→ID. However, both (ID and [ID lead to state 4, and in both cases) is the lookahead. Extra lookahead cannot help—there is never more than one symbol following the ID in any valid input.

But one-symbol lookahead certainly should suffice, as all valid inputs are only three symbols long and the grammar is unambiguous. That is, with one-symbol lookahead in state 4 we will have seen all of the input string.

If a full LR(1) parser is built, state 4 "splits" into two states that have the same core, and one-symbol lookahead does suffice. This illustrates that LR(1) can handle grammars that LALR(1) cannot. Viewed another way, LALR(1)'s merging of LR(1) states is sometimes too ambitious. We shall discuss other LR(1) state reduction techniques in Section 6.9.

6.5.1. Building LALR(1) Parsers

Our definition of LALR(1) suggested that an LR(1) machine is first built, and then its states are merged to form an automaton identical in structure to the CFSM. In practice this would be quite inefficient because we know an LR(1) machine can have tens of thousands of states for grammars used to define ordinary programming languages. An alternative is to build the CFSM first. Then LALR(1) lookaheads are "propagated" from configuration to configuration. In particular, each configuration is given a *lookahead set*, initially null. By construction when we are done this set will contain the correct lookaheads for that configuration.

We assume that each configuration set contains both basis and closure configurations. (Strictly speaking, only the basis configurations are necessary—the closure configurations are computable from them.) We then *link together* those configurations for which the lookaheads of one configuration can contribute to the lookaheads of another. Call these links *propagate links*.

One obvious situation requiring a propagate link is when one configuration is created from another in a previous state via a shift operation. Thus, if we have a configuration $A \rightarrow \alpha \bullet X\gamma$, L_1, where L_1 is the lookahead set, then we create a propagate link to the configuration $A \rightarrow \alpha X \bullet \gamma$, L_2. This indicates that every symbol included in L_1 must be transmitted to L_2.

Another situation sometimes requiring a link is when a configuration is created as the result of a closure or prediction operation on another configuration. Two subcases arise. Assume $A \rightarrow \bullet \alpha$, L_2 can be added as the result of closing $B \rightarrow \beta \bullet A\gamma$, L_1. L_2 is obtained by computing

$$L_2 = \{x \mid x \in \text{First}(\gamma t) \text{ and } t \in L_1\}$$

This set can be abbreviated as $\text{First}(\gamma L_1)$.

Sometimes symbols in L_2 are *independent* of the value of L_1. This occurs if $\text{First}(\gamma)$ does not contain λ. Such lookahead symbols are termed *spontaneous*, as they are determined solely by γ. They are easy to compute, for the value of L_1 need not be known.

At other times, symbols in $\text{First}(\gamma L_1)$ are dependent on the value of L_1 (when $\gamma \Rightarrow^* \lambda$). Such symbols are termed *propagate* lookaheads because they must be propagated from L_1. We link together $B \rightarrow \beta \bullet A\gamma$, L_1 and $A \rightarrow \bullet \alpha$, L_2 if and only if L_2 can receive propagated lookaheads from L_1. This can occur if and only if $\gamma \Rightarrow^* \lambda$, which is easy to determine.

After the CFSM is built, we can create all the necessary propagate links to transmit lookaheads from one configuration to another. Then spontaneous lookaheads are determined. In a configuration set, this is done by including in L_2, for configuration $A \rightarrow \bullet \alpha$, L_2, all spontaneous lookaheads induced by configurations of the form $B \rightarrow \beta \bullet A\gamma$, L_1. These are simply the non-λ values of $\text{First}(\gamma)$. If more than one configuration can predict $A \rightarrow \bullet \alpha$, L_2, then L_2 may receive spontaneous lookaheads from each possible predictor.

Spontaneous lookaheads are used as initial values in the lookahead calculations. We also initialize the lookahead set of the initial configuration to the empty set.

We then propagate lookaheads via the propagate links. To do this we push items of the form (state, configuration, lookahead symbol) onto a stack or queue. Each such triple is considered in turn, and the lookahead symbol is propagated from the indicated configuration and state.

The stack is initialized with triples for each spontaneous lookahead. We then execute the algorithm shown in Figure 6.25.

```
while (stack is not empty)
{
    pop top item, assign its components to (s,c,L)

    if (configuration c in state s
            has any propagate links) {
        Try, in turn, to add L to the lookahead set of
            each configuration so linked.
        for (each configuration c̄ in state s̄
            to which L is added)
            Push (s̄,c̄,L) onto the stack.
    }
}
```

Figure 6.25   LALR(1) Lookahead Propagation Algorithm

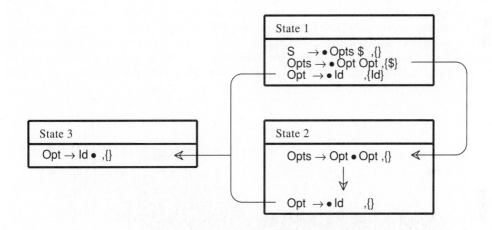

Figure 6.26   Part of CFSM for G₇ with Propagate Links

As an example of how lookaheads are propagated, consider G_7:

```
S    → Opts $
Opts → Opt Opt
Opt  → ID
```

We create the CFSM for G_7, establish propagate links, and initialize lookahead sets with spontaneous lookaheads. This leads to the situation shown in Figure 6.26, with only propagate links shown.

Because there are two spontaneous lookaheads, we push two triples to start the computation. Figure 6.27 shows the steps performed in propagating lookaheads in the CFSM of Figure 6.26.

The final CFSM, with all lookaheads propagated, is shown in Figure 6.28.

To prove that the lookahead propagation algorithm is correct, we must establish that

- It halts.

- It propagates exactly the correct set of lookaheads. That is, a look-ahead x is added to configuration $A \to \alpha \bullet \beta$ in CFSM state s if and only if a configuration $A \to \alpha \bullet \beta, x$ exists in LR(1) state $\bar{s}$, and $\text{Core}(\bar{s}) = s$.

Termination of the algorithm is easy to prove. New stack entries are pushed only when new lookaheads are discovered. The number of states, configurations, and possible lookaheads is finite, so only a finite number of stack entries can occur.

To prove correctness, first observe that spontaneous lookaheads must be correct because they are determined solely by the dotted right-hand side of a configuration and are not influenced by the configuration's lookahead set. Similarly, lookaheads of configurations added by a closure operation are determined solely by the basis configurations. That is, if the lookaheads of basis configurations are correct, then the lookaheads of the whole configuration set will be correct.

Step	Stack	Action
(1)	(s1,c2,$), (s1,c3,ID)	Pop (s1,c2,$) Add $ to c1 in s2 Push (s2,c1,$)
(2)	(s2,c1,$), (s1,c3,ID)	Pop (s2,c1,$) Add $ to c2 in s2 Push (s2,c2,$)
(3)	(s2,c2,$), (s1,c3,ID)	Pop (s2,c2,$) Add $ to c1 in s3 Push (s3,c1,$)
(4)	(s3,c1,$), (s1,c3,ID)	Pop (s3,c1,$) Nothing is added (no links)
(5)	(s1,c3,ID)	Pop (s1,c3,ID) Add ID to c1 in s3 Push (s3,c1,ID)
(6)	(s3,c1,ID)	Pop (s3,c1,ID) Nothing is added (no links)
(7)	Empty	Terminate algorithm

Figure 6.27   Example of Lookahead Propagation

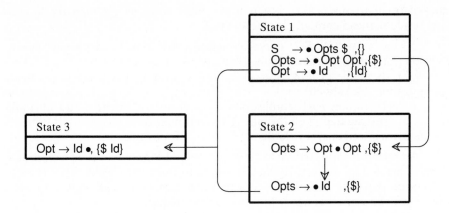

Figure 6.28   Part of CFSM for G_7 with Lookaheads Propagated

Assume that $A \rightarrow \alpha \bullet \beta$, x exists in some LR(1) state $\bar{s}$. The lookahead x was initially created as a spontaneous lookahead in some state s_1 and then propagated through a sequence of states, $s_1, s_2, \ldots, s_n$, where $n \geq 1$ and $s_n = \bar{s}$. As x is created as a spontaneous lookahead in s_1, it will also be created in the CFSM state $\mathsf{Core}(s_1)$. We now observe that propagate links will parallel the original transmission of x, this time from $\mathsf{Core}(s_1)$ to $\mathsf{Core}(s_2)$ and finally to $\mathsf{Core}(s_n)$. This guarantees that there exists a transmission path for x to configuration $A \rightarrow \alpha \bullet \beta$ in CFSM state $\mathsf{Core}(s_n)$. Therefore, the propagation algorithm includes all lookaheads found in LR(1) states.

To see that the propagation algorithm includes only lookaheads found in LR(1) states, again note that initially all lookaheads are spontaneous. These lookaheads must appear in all corresponding LR(1) states. Therefore when we begin, if (s, c, x) is on the stack, then configuration (c, x) exists in LR(1) state $\bar{s}$, where $\mathsf{Core}(\bar{s}) = s$. Propagate links represent the ways LR(1) lookaheads can be transmitted. If we follow a link from (s, c, x) to (s', c') and propagate lookahead x, then we can identify an LR(1) configuration (c', x) in state $\bar{s}'$, where $\mathsf{Core}(\bar{s}') = s'$. Therefore at each iteration, the propagation algorithm transmits a lookahead that corresponds to a valid LR(1) configuration.

Our lookahead propagation algorithm can be expected to be fast in that it only propagates lookaheads known to be new. It may, however, require an excessive amount of space because of the large number of (state, configuration, lookahead) triples.

An alternative is to use pairs of the form (state, configuration) rather than triples. We add to each configuration a flag indicating whether or not that configuration in a particular state is on the stack waiting to be processed. If a symbol is added to the lookahead of a configuration and its flag is false, we push a pair (state, configuration) and set the flag true.

When a pair (s, c) is popped, we set c's flag in state s to false and try to propagate all of c's lookaheads. This saves space, as fewer pairs need to be stacked (in the worse case), but requires more time, as we may try to propagate a lookahead symbol more than once.

A number of LALR(1) parser generators use lookahead propagation to compute the parser **action** table. The LALRGen generator described in Section 6.7.1 uses the propagation algorithm operating on a stack of (state, configuration, lookahead) triples. Yacc does not use a stack (Aho and Ullman 1977, p. 241); rather, each configuration set is visited in turn, and all lookaheads are propagated from the set. This continues until all configuration sets are visited without any new lookaheads being propagated.

An intriguing alternative to propagating LALR lookaheads is to compute them as needed by doing a backward search through the CFSM. That is, rather than propagating lookaheads in a forward direction to all states, we wait until we find a state that needs lookahead information.

Assume we need the lookaheads for the configuration $A \rightarrow \alpha \bullet$ in state s. We know that lookaheads, by definition, are symbols that might be shifted after the reduction in question, $A \rightarrow \alpha$, is performed. To determine possible lookaheads, we can "simulate" this reduction by working backward from s toward states that predicted $A \rightarrow \bullet \alpha$, and then examine their successors under A. For example, consider Figure 6.29. In state 3, we want the lookaheads that signal the reduction of $A \rightarrow ID$. If this reduction were performed, we would pop state 3 from the stack. Either state 1 or 4 would be the new stack top, and after A was shifted, we would be in either state 2 or state 5. Since only) and] can be shifted in these states, these two symbols are the only correct lookaheads for the reduction of $A \rightarrow ID$ in state 3.

We define the *reduction successors* to s under production $A \rightarrow \alpha$, denoted $succ(s, A \rightarrow \alpha)$, to be the set of CFSM states that might be reached if $A \rightarrow \alpha$ is reduced in state s. If a terminal symbol can be shifted from a state in $succ(s, A \rightarrow \alpha)$, then it signals the reduction of $A \rightarrow \alpha$ in state s.

It may occur that in a state s' in $succ(s, A \rightarrow \alpha)$, another reduction is possible. For example, s' may contain the configuration $B \rightarrow \beta A \bullet$. In this case, we examine states in both $succ(s, A \rightarrow \alpha)$ and $succ(s', B \rightarrow \beta A)$ for terminals that can be shifted. In general, whenever a state in a successor set contains a possible reduction, its successors are also considered, representing the situation in which a series of reductions is made before the lookahead is shifted.

The idea of using successor states to determine lookaheads seems straightforward, but there are pitfalls, especially when λ-productions are involved. For example, consider the CFSM state s shown in Figure 6.30.

If we want the lookaheads for $C \rightarrow \lambda \bullet$, we compute $succ(s, C \rightarrow \lambda)$, which is simply go_to[s][C] = s'. Because s' contains $A \rightarrow C \bullet$, we consider $succ(s', A \rightarrow C \bullet)$. This causes problems since $succ(s', A \rightarrow C \bullet)$ may contain states other than go_to[s][A]. The difficulty is that s' may have predecessors other than s, and these are considered when $succ$ is computed. However, we started in s, so other predecessors of s' ought not to be included.

This problem is often not taken into account in LALR implementations that use the backward search approach. As a result, implementations using backward search often do not correctly handle all LALR grammars and have been dubbed *NQLALR* (not quite LALR).

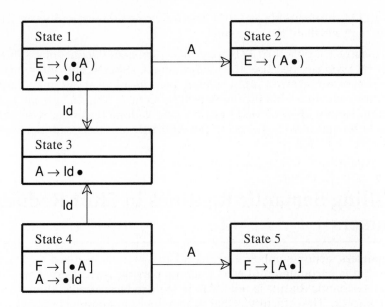

Figure 6.29   A CFSM Analyzed Using Backward Search

$$
\begin{aligned}
B &\to \bullet A \, d \\
A &\to \bullet C \\
C &\to \lambda \bullet
\end{aligned}
$$

Figure 6.30   A CFSM State that May Cause Backward Analysis to Fail

Ways of correctly implementing the backward search approach are discussed by DeRemer and Pennello (1982). Although getting the backward search approach correct is a bit tricky, it does have the advantage of requiring less overall work, which, in turn, leads to significant improvements in parser generator speeds.

6.5.2. Correctness of LALR(1) Parsing

Establishing the correctness of LALR(1) parsing is quite straightforward. Taking the view that LALR(1) is simply a state-merged version of LR(1), how can the two techniques differ? In some cases merging LR(1) states to form an LALR(1) state introduces parser action conflicts. This means that not all LR(1) grammars are LALR(1). If the state merger does not introduce conflicts,

LALR(1) will perform exactly as LR(1) does on correct inputs, and we already know how to prove that LR(1) is correct.

On incorrect inputs, LALR(1) may make erroneous reductions. This is not really a problem because the underlying CFSM accepts only viable prefixes. That is, an incorrect input symbol, used as a lookahead, may induce inappropriate reductions, but it cannot itself be shifted. The slight delay in error detection is only an issue when error repair is done (incorrect reductions may have to be undone). Solutions to this difficulty are discussed in Chapter 17.

6.6. Calling Semantic Routines in Shift-Reduce Parsers

In LL(1) parsers, action symbols correspond to semantic routines. When an action symbol is encountered in a production, parsing is suspended, and the appropriate semantic routine is invoked. In shift-reduce parsers, things are a bit more complex. The difficulty is that shift-reduce parsers are not predictive, so we cannot always be sure what production is being recognized until its entire right-hand side has been matched. For parsing purposes, however, this is an advantage, because it allows a shift-reduce parser to examine more input before making a choice. In fact, shift-reduce parsers can normally handle larger classes of grammars than LL(1) parsers, which is a major reason for their popularity.

As noted, a price that must be paid for the generality afforded by shift-reduce parsers is that semantic routines can be invoked only after a production is recognized and reduced. This corresponds to allowing action symbols only at the extreme right end of a right-hand side. This restriction is not as severe as it first appears, however. In fact, two common tricks are known that allow more flexible placement of semantic routine calls. Consider, for example, a production that generates a conditional statement:

<stmt> → **if** <expr> **then** <stmts> **else** <stmts> **end if**

We need to call semantic routines after the conditional expressions **else** and **end if** are matched. We cannot place action symbols at the necessary positions if a shift-reduce parser is used. To perform the role of action symbols, we can, however, create new nonterminals that generate λ. For example, we might create the following:

\<stmt\>	→ **if** \<expr\> \<test cond\>
	then \<stmts\> \<process then part\>
	else \<stmts\> **end if** ;
\<test cond\>	→ λ
\<process then part\>	→ λ

When either \<test cond\> or \<process then part\> is recognized, the appropriate semantic routine is called, simulating the effect of action symbols.

This substitution of λ-generating nonterminals for action symbols is not as trivial as it appears. It is possible for more than one right-hand side to be under consideration in some parsing context. If the right-hand sides differ in the semantic routines that are to be called, the parser will be unable to correctly determine which routines to invoke. If λ-generating nonterminals are used to invoke semantic routines, this ambiguity will manifest itself as a parsing conflict. For example:

\<stmt\>	→ **if** \<expr\> \<test cond1\>
	then \<stmts\> \<process then part\>
	else \<stmts\> **end if** ;
\<stmt\>	→ **if** \<expr\> \<test cond2\>
	then \<stmts\> \<process then part\>
	end if ;
\<test cond1\>	→ λ
\<test cond2\>	→ λ
\<process then part\>	→ λ

After **if** \<expr\> is parsed, the parser cannot determine whether to recognize \<test cond1\> or \<test cond2\>. This reflects the fact that the contending productions invoke two conflicting semantic routines.

An alternative to the use of λ-generating nonterminals is to break a production into a number of pieces, with the breaks placed where semantic routines are required. For example, our earlier example could be rewritten as:

\<stmt\>	→ \<if head\> \<then part\> \<else part\>
\<if head\>	→ **if** \<expr\>
\<then part\>	→ **then** \<stmts\>
\<else part\>	→ **else** \<stmts\> **end if** ;

This approach can make productions harder to read but has the advantage that no λ-productions are needed. (Early shift-reduce parsers could not handle λ-productions; modern techniques can.)

6.7. **Using a Parser Generator**

In this section we discuss two popular LALR(1) parser generators, LALRGen and Yacc. Complete summaries of LALRGen and Yacc can be found in Appendix D and Johnson (1975), respectively. Our discussion will illustrate how context-free productions, action symbols, and related information are presented to, and utilized by, parser generators. A good way to learn the use of a parser generator is to start with the simple examples presented here and then incrementally generalize them to solve the problem at hand.

6.7.1. **The LALRGen Parser Generator**

LALRGen is an LALR(1) parser generator that accepts a context-free grammar specification and produces tables for parsing the language so specified. LALRGen was written at the University of Wisconsin–Madison by Jon Mauney.

Input to LALRGen

The input to LALRGen has three main sections: options desired for the run, terminal symbols of the grammar, and production rules of the grammar. The general form of the input is

> *comments*
> ***ecp**
> *options*
> ***define**
> *constant definitions*
> ***terminals**
> *terminal specifications*
> ***productions**
> *production specifications*
> ***end**
> *comments*

A sample specification for Micro is presented in Figure 6.31.

```
*ecp
bnf vocab
statistics noerrortables parsetables
*define
start          1
finish         2
push_id        3
assign         4
read_id        5
write_expr     6
gen_infix      7
```

```
copy_expr       8
push_lit        9
push_op        10
*terminals
ID
INTLITERAL
:=
,
;
+
—
(
)
begin
end
read
write
*productions
<program>           ::= begin <start> <statement list> end ## finish
<start>             ::= ## start
<statement list>  ::= <statement list> <statement>
<statement list>  ::= <statement>
<statement>         ::= ID <push id> := <expression> ; ## assign
<statement>         ::= read ( <id list> ) ;
<statement>         ::= write ( <expr list> ) ;
<push id>           ::= ## push_id
<id list>           ::= ID ## read_id
<id list>           ::= <id list> , ID ## read_id
<expr list>         ::= <expression> ## write_expr
<expr list>         ::= <expr list> , <expression> ## write_expr
<expression>        ::= <expression>  <add op> <primary> ## gen_infix
<expression>        ::= <primary> ## copy_expr
<primary>           ::= ( <expression> ) ## copy_expr
<primary>           ::= ID ## push_id
<primary>           ::= INTLITERAL ## push_lit
<add op>            ::= +  ## push_op
<add op>            ::= —  ## push_op
*end
```

Figure 6.31   An LALRGen Specification of Micro

Symbols

Symbols consist of any sequence of printable characters; they are separated by blanks, tabs, or ends of line. Symbols may not contain blanks or tabs, unless the symbol is surrounded by angle brackets, < and >. If a symbol begins with a <, then it must end with a >.

Comments

Anything before *ecp or after *end will be considered a comment and will be ignored. However, comments must not contain any of the above reserved tokens. Comments may also be placed at the end of any line; all text between the token –– and the end of the line will be ignored.

Options

Following *ecp is a list of zero or more options, separated by blanks, tabs, or ends of line. Options control the kind of tables produced and the kind of information that is printed. A complete description of the available options appears in the LALRGen User Manual in Appendix D.

Constant Definitions

The constant definition section is optional. If present, it begins with the reserved token *define and consists of a list of definitions, each on a separate line. Each definition has the form

<const name> <integer value>

where <const name> is a token as described above, and <integer value> is an unsigned integer (a token containing only digits). This constant can then be used whenever an integer constant is called for: in subsequent constant definitions and for semantic routine numbers.

Terminals

The reserved token *terminals begins the list of terminal symbols. The terminal specification section consists of a list of such specifications, each on a separate line. All terminals must appear in this list. Terminals should be ordered so that the sequence numbers assigned are compatible with any integer codes used by the scanner. That is, if end has a token code of 4, then end should appear fourth in the terminal list. It is wise practice to use the option vocab to list the integer codes assigned to terminals. These codes should be compared with those produced by the scanner to be sure the numbering is consistent.

Productions

The token *productions separates the terminals from the productions. The productions are specified by a list of rules, each on a separate line. Specification of one production has the form

<lhs> ::= <rhs> <action symbol>

The symbol ::= is a synonym for →, which is not available in most character sets. Any of <lhs>, <rhs>, and <action symbol> may be absent. The <lhs> is one token representing a nonterminal symbol. If it is absent, the <lhs> of the preceding production is used. The <rhs> is a string of tokens containing the grammar symbols of the production. If <rhs> is absent, then <lhs> derives λ, the null string. The <rhs> may be continued on subsequent lines by beginning those lines with the reserved token "..." (only productions may be so continued). The <action symbol> has the form **## <number>** and specifies the semantic routine to be called when the production is recognized. The <number> is either an unsigned integer or a defined constant. If absent, zero will be used. As discussed in Section 6.6, the effect of action symbols at other than the rightmost end of a production can be obtained by creating new nonterminals and λ-productions that contain the desired action symbol.

End

The productions are terminated by *end. After all the productions have been processed, the augmenting production is added. Two symbols, <goal> and $$$, and one production

<goal> ::= <s> $$$

are added to the grammar, where <s> is the left-hand side of the first production specified, <goal> is the start symbol, and $$$ the endmarker. The augmenting production is given an action symbol with a code of −1.

Output from LALRGen

A detailed description of the format of the parsing tables appears in the LALRGen User Manual. The information provided is

- Size parameters. This includes the number of CFSM states, the number of grammar symbols, and the number of productions.

- The combined **go_to/action** table. Single reduce states are removed (see Section 6.8), so there are three kinds of nonerror entries: go_to states, Reduce actions, and SingleReduce actions. The Accept action is represented as a SingleReduce action for the augmenting production.

- The right-hand side lengths of each production.

- The left-hand side symbols of each production.

- The action symbol number of each production.

- Symbolic representations of all symbols in the grammar.

- The entry symbol of each CFSM state (that is, the symbol shifted to reach the state). This is not actually needed for parsing, but it is useful in error reporting and repair.

6.7.2. Yacc

Yacc is an LALR(1) parser generator developed by S.C. Johnson and others at AT&T Bell Laboratories. Yacc is an acronym for "Yet another compiler-compiler." Strictly speaking, Yacc is not a compiler compiler because it generates an integrated parser, not an entire compiler. However, it does provide for semantic stack manipulation and the specification of semantic routines, so much of the structure of a typical compiler is provided. Also, Yacc generates a file of C subroutines; thus, it is most commonly used on systems running the UNIX operating system. Yacc can use scanners generated by Lex or hand-coded scanners written in C.

Input to Yacc is of the form

> *declarations*
> %%
> *productions*
> %%
> *subroutines*

where %% separates sections of the specification.

The first section includes a variety of declarations, the most important of which is the list of tokens (that is, terminal symbols). Tokens can either be symbol names (beginning with a letter, and possibly including noninitial digits, dots, and underscores) or quoted character literals (for example, '+' or '−'). Named tokens must be declared to distinguish them from nonterminals; quoted literals may optionally be declared. It is a good idea to declare all tokens, both for documentation purposes and to aid in synchronization with the scanner.

A token declaration is of the form

```
%token token1 integer1 token2 integer2 . . .
```

The integer following each token defines the code used for the token by the scanner. The endmarker must have a zero or negative value; all other tokens must have positive codes.

This assignment of token codes is optional; tokens not assigned an explicit code receive either their character code (if they are a single-quoted character) or a value beginning at 257, which is incremented for each unassigned token. A file y.tab.h, containing token code assignments, can optionally be created by Yacc. It is a wise practice to compare the token code assignments assumed by Yacc with those produced by the scanner to be sure the numbering is consistent. This can be automated by having the scanner include y.tab.h and by using the definitions contained there.

Other declarations include C type, variable, and subroutine prototypes; the name of the start symbol; and precedence and associativity declarations (used with ambiguous grammars; see Section 6.7.3).

The productions section defines the grammar that will be parsed. Productions are of the form

```
A : B1  · · ·  BN ;
```

where **A** is the left-hand side of the production, and **B1** ··· **BN** are zero or more terminal or nonterminal symbols. The production may span more than one line; it is terminated by a semicolon. A sequence of productions that share the same left-hand side may be written as

```
A   : B1  · · ·  BN
    | C1  · · ·  CM
        · · ·

    ;
```

The left-hand side of the first production is assumed to be the start symbol unless a directive of the form **%start StartSym** appears in the declaration section. In Yacc, semantic routines, written as C code and delimited by { and }, are intermixed with production rules. Because the underlying parser is LALR(1), semantic routine code normally appears at the end of a production. For example:

```
stmt : STOP ';'     { gen("halt", "", "", ""); } ;
```

Yacc also maintains a parser-controlled semantic stack and provides easy access to values associated with a production. The symbol **$$** represents the semantic stack value of the left-hand side; **$1**, **$2**, ... represent the semantic stack values of the right-hand side, with numbering from left to right. Semantic stack values default to integers, but Yacc creates union types as needed to guarantee type compatibility. For example, the following could be used to generate code for infix addition:

```
Exp : Exp '+' Term
                    { get_temp(n);
                      gen("plus", $1, $3, n);
                      $$ = n; };
```

Semantic routine code may also be inserted in the middle of a right-hand side, as long as it is known that no confusion with other productions can arise. These semantic routines are treated as action symbols and may access and update the semantic stack.

The final section of a Yacc specification contains subprograms needed by the parser; a scanner named **yylex()** must be supplied in this section or as an external subroutine. If a semantic action requires more than a few statements, it is wise practice to encapsulate it as a subroutine and include only the call in the productions section.

As an example, a Yacc definition of a simple Micro compiler appears in Figure 6.32. This definition is adapted directly from the one in Chapter 2. The grammar of Chapter 2 is in LL(1) form; it has been rewritten into typical LALR(1) form. This was not absolutely necessary, as virtually all LL(1) grammars are also LALR(1). However, the revised grammar better illustrates the structures commonly used in bottom-up parsing, especially the frequent use of left-recursive productions, which are forbidden in top-down parsers.

```
%token BEGIN 10    END  11  ID  1  ASG 3    '+'   6
%token ';'    5    READ 12  '('  8  ')'  9  '-' 7
%token WRITE 13    ','   4    INTLITERAL 2
%%
program : BEGIN    { start(); }
            statement_list END    { finish(); }
        ;
statement_list : statement_list statement
               | statement
               ;
statement : ID    { $$ = push_id(); }
        ASG expression ';'    { assign($2, $4); }
      | READ '(' id_list ')' ';'
      | WRITE '(' expr_list ')' ';'
        ;
id_list : ID    { read_id(); }
        | id_list ',' ID    { read_id(); }
        ;
expr_list : expression    { write_expr($1); }
          | expr_list ',' expression
            { write_expr($3); }
          ;
expression : expression add_op primary
             { $$ = gen_infix($1, $2, $3); }
           | primary
           ;
primary : '(' expression ')'    { $$ = $2; }
        | ID    { $$ = push_id(); }
        | INTLITERAL    { $$ = push_lit(); }
        ;
add_op : '+'    { $$ = 1; }
       | '-'    { $$ = 2; }
       ;
%%
/*
 * This section has been elided for brevity. In a
 * complete definition it will contain the definition
 * of action and support routines, from Chapter 2.
 */
```

Figure 6.32   A Yacc Specification for Micro

6.7.3. Uses (and Misuses) of Controlled Ambiguity

Parser generators of all varieties reject ambiguous grammars because they lead to nondeterministic parsing decisions. Research, however, has shown that ambiguity, *if controlled*, can be of value in producing efficient parsers for real programming languages (Aho, Johnson, and Ullman 1975).

In rare cases ambiguity is absolutely essential in parsing a language construct because no unambiguous grammar exists. The best known example of this problem is the dangling else of Algol 60 and Pascal. It is known that LL(1) grammars cannot deterministically generate **if-then** and **if-then-else** statements that match **else** clauses with the nearest unmatched **then** clause, as language semantics require.

LALR(1) grammars that correctly handle the dangling else do exist, but they are not trivial to produce. The obvious productions

> Stmt → **if** Expr **then** Stmt
> Stmt → **if** Expr **then** Stmt **else** Stmt

fail because in, for example, **if** A **then if** B **then** C **else** D, the **else** can be matched with either **then**. The trick is to change the second production to something of the form

> Stmt → **if** Expr **then** RestrictedStmt **else** Stmt

where RestrictedStmt can generate any statement except one that ends with an **if-then** construct.

The simple but ambiguous productions shown here can be used if their ambiguity can somehow be controlled. In LALRGen, if the option `resolve` is enabled, productions are given precedence in order of appearance, with the first production specified given the highest precedence. Thus if the above productions for an **if-then-else** are reordered as

> Stmt → **if** Expr **then** Stmt **else** Stmt
> Stmt → **if** Expr **then** Stmt

the shift-reduce conflict will be resolved in favor of the first production, matching the **else** with the most recent **if**. A conflict between two configurations with the same underlying production will be resolved in favor of reduction. This means the ambiguous grammar

> E → E + E
> E → ID

will correctly parse expressions involving + and ID, enforcing left association because reduction will always be chosen over shifting.

Yacc also allows ambiguous productions (after warning the user), and provides the following resolution of ambiguous parsing choices:

- In a shift-reduce conflict, do the shift.

- In a reduce-reduce conflict, reduce the production listed first in the grammar specification.

In our simple grammar for the **if-then** and **if-then-else** constructs, the first rule is exactly what is needed to provide the appropriate matching. In particular, we want to match an **else** as soon as possible, and shifting rather than reducing does this.

In this case, allowing controlled ambiguity provides for a simpler grammar than an unambiguous LALR(1) parser would accept. There is, however, a price that is paid when ambiguity is allowed. As users of a parser, we do not normally care how it works—any parse it finds is *the correct parse.* But when ambiguity is allowed, we must understand how disambiguation works, and this requires knowledge of the parser and the parser generator that is used. We no longer specify a parser purely in terms of the grammar it parses, but rather we explicitly include auxiliary rules to disambiguate conflicts in the grammar.

The use of controlled ambiguity has its greatest payoff in specifying programming language expressions. A hierarchy of nonterminals and productions is used to encode operator precedence and associativity. This encoding increases significantly the size of grammars and parsing tables. Further, as discussed in Section 6.8, chains of unit reductions can slow parsing speed.

Yacc allows operator precedence and associativity rules to be factored from a grammar and instead can be provided as explicit directives. Expressions can be derived by the *highly ambiguous* productions

Expr → Expr BinaryOp Expr
Expr → UnaryOp Expr

Associativities are specified in the declaration section as `%left`, `%right`, and `%nonassoc`. Most binary operators (like +, −, *, and /) are left-associative (that is, they group from left to right). A few (such as the exponentiation operator) are right-associative, and a few (typically, the relational operators) do not associate at all.

The order in which operators are assigned associativities indicates precedence, with the lowest priorities assigned first and the highest last. In a few cases an operator is used both as a unary and binary operator, but with different precedences. In such cases, a `%prec` directive is used to force the precedence of a particular usage of an operator.

To illustrate the use of the various directives, including `%prec`, we will recast our earlier Micro example into a form utilizing controlled ambiguity for expressions. Micro contains only two binary operators, + and −, which have the same precedence and associativity, so we will define an extended Micro, *MicroPlus,* that has a richer set of operators. MicroPlus's operator set is

Operator	Precedence	Associativity
unary −	highest	
*, /	second highest	left
+, binary −	third highest	left
=	lowest	none

Figure 6.33   MicroPlus Operators

defined in Figure 6.33; the corresponding Yacc definition is shown in Figure 6.34. It is a good exercise to rewrite the definition of Figure 6.34 into a purely context-free form, without the use of explicit precedence and associativity definitions. The subgrammar needed to specify expressions will be significantly larger and more cumbersome.

The precedence values assigned to operators resolve most shift-reduce conflicts of the form

$$\text{Expr} \rightarrow \text{Expr Op}_1 \text{ Expr} \bullet$$
$$\text{Expr} \rightarrow \text{Expr} \bullet \text{Op}_2 \text{ Expr}$$

If Op_1 has a higher precedence than Op_2, we reduce. If Op_2 has the higher precedence, we shift. When Op_1 and Op_2 have the same precedence, we use the associativity definitions. If the two operators are left-associative, we reduce; if the two operators are right-associative, we shift; if the two operators are nonassociative, we signal an error.

The idea of using operator precedence and associativity to guide parsing is derived from the operator precedence parsing technique discussed in Section 6.12.2. Although operator precedence is too limited to handle all the syntax of modern programming languages, it is well suited to the expression structure of most languages.

```
%token  ID     1    INTLITERAL  2    ASG  3    ','  4
%token  ';'    5    '+'         6    '-'  7    '('  8
%token  ')'    9    BEGIN      10    END  11   READ  12
%token  WRITE 13    '*'        14    '/'  15   '='   16
%nonassoc    '='
%left    '+' '-'
%left    '*' '/'
%left unary_minus  /* Placeholder for unary '-'; see below */
%%
program : BEGIN    { start(); }
           statement_list END    { finish(); }
         ;
statement_list : statement_list statement
               | statement
               ;
statement : ID    { $$ = push_id(); }
```

```
                  ASG expression ';'     { assign($1, $3); }
                | READ '(' id_list ')' ';'
                | WRITE '(' expr_list ')' ';'
                ;
       id_list : ID    { read_id(); }
               | id_list ',' ID    { read_id(); }
               ;
       expr_list : expression    { write_expr($1); }
                 | expr_list ',' expression    { write_expr($3); }
                 ;
       expression :
           expression '=' expression    { $$ = gen_infix($1, 0, $3); }
         | expression '+' expression    { $$ = gen_infix($1, 1, $3); }
         | expression '-' expression    { $$ = gen_infix($1, 2, $3); }
         | expression '*' expression    { $$ = gen_infix($1, 3, $3); }
         | expression '/' expression    { $$ = gen_infix($1, 4, $3); }
         | '-' expression    %prec  unary_minus    { $$ = negate($2); }
         | '(' expression ')'    { $$ = $2; }
         | ID    { $$ = push_id(); }
         | INTLITERAL    { $$ = push_lit(); }
         ;
%%
/*
 * The same action and support routines as used in
 * the previous Yacc example, with negate() added.
 */
```

Figure 6.34   Yacc Specification for MicroPlus Using Controlled Ambiguity

6.8. Optimizing Parse Tables

In practice, a number of improvements can be made to decrease the space needs of an LR parser. Rather than having distinct **go_to** and **action** tables, a single merged table can be used. Shift entries in the **action** table are expanded to include the corresponding state entry in the **go_to** table. Nonterminal entries are included in the merged table, which is referred to simply as the parse table.

Returning to G_3, we combine the **go_to** table encoding the CFSM and the SLR(1) or LALR(1) **action** table to obtain the table shown in Figure 6.35.

Parse table entries are usually encoded as integers. A convenient encoding scheme is to represent error entries as zeros, reduce actions as positive integers, shift actions as negative integers, and the accept action as a reduce action for the augmenting production (usually R1, encoded as 1).

Many parser states recognize only a single reduction, given the correct lookahead. Thus state 4 in Figure 6.35 always recognizes production 5 or signals an error. Let us call these states *single reduce states*. As an optimization, we may eliminate all single reduce states. Typically, each production has a

State	Symbol								
	+	*	ID	(	)	$	E	T	P
0			S5	S6			S1	S7	S4
1	S3					A			
2									
3			S5	S6				S11	S4
4	R5	R5			R5	R5			
5	R6	R6			R6	R6			
6			S5	S6			S12	S7	S4
7	R3	S8			R3	R3			
8			S5	S6					S9
9	R4	R4			R4	R4			
10	R7	R7			R7	R7			
11	R2	S8			R2	R2			
12	S3				S10				

Figure 6.35   SLR(1) Parse Table for G_3

corresponding single reduce state, so this optimization can significantly reduce the number of states that must be represented in the parse table.

Parse table entries that refer to a single reduce state will be replaced with a special marker, denoted here by an L-prefix, and the production that is recognized in that state. For example, shifts to state 4 would be replaced by the entry L5. The idea is that if we can make only one possible reduction in a state, we need not ever actually go to that state. Rather, we make the reduction immediately. We also modify the parser driver so that when an L-type reduction is recognized, one fewer state is popped from the parse stack. This is necessary because for L-type entries we reduce immediately rather than shifting to a single reduce state and then reducing.

But what if the lookahead is incorrect? Because we do not examine the lookahead, we do the reduction anyway. Detection of the error is delayed until we try to shift the lookahead token. At this point an error must be detected since we cannot shift a lookahead symbol if it is incorrect. All LR parsing techniques except LR(k) (without compatible state merger) use only approximate lookaheads to determine reduce actions; therefore eliminating single reduce states does not introduce any new complications.

In most cases the slight delay between when an error token is seen and when it is recognized as erroneous makes no difference. If we are doing error repair, we can anticipate the possibility of incorrect lookaheads by *buffering* parser moves. All reductions are saved in a buffer until the lookahead is successfully shifted and thus validated. If it cannot be shifted, the buffer is used to undo reductions before error repair is performed. This will be discussed more fully in Chapter 17, which deals with error repair for LR parsers.

In practice, removing single reduce states significantly reduces parse table sizes (essentially, one state for each production is removed). For G_3 an optimized SLR(1) parse table (with states *not* renumbered) is shown in Figure 6.36. After single reduce states are eliminated, it is a simple matter to renumber the remaining states. Again, parse table entries are readily encoded as integers. Error entries are represented as zeros, reduce actions as positive integers, shift actions as negative integers, and the accept action as a reduce action for the augmenting production. L-entries are encoded as positive integers biased by some integer larger than the number of productions. Thus L7 might be encoded as $1000 + 7 = 1007$.

The removal of single reduce states is a simple and effective optimization. The idea can be carried a bit further by noting that some states are "almost" single reduce states. That is, almost all nonerror entries are a particular reduce action. State 11 in Figure 6.36 illustrates this. There are three R2 actions and one S8 action. We can factor out the R2 action by making it the *default* for the state. That is, we create an auxiliary vector, indexed by states, that contains default reduction actions for each state. Some states will have no default action, in which case the default is error. When a default reduce action is selected, it is entered into the auxiliary table and removed from the parse table. This has the effect of removing a number of identical actions from a row of the parse table and keeping only one copy of the action. The parse table has fewer nonerror entries, so it is easier to compress.

When the parse table indicates an error action, the auxiliary table is consulted. If there is a default reduction, it is performed; otherwise, an error is recognized. As with single action states, this optimization can delay recognition of an error. However, shift actions are never made a default, so no error token can ever be incorrectly accepted. Because LR parse tables are fairly sparse, the compression techniques discussed in Chapter 17 can often significantly reduce storage requirements.

The optimizations just discussed are space optimizations, designed to reduce the size and density of LR parse tables. Speed optimizations are also

State	Symbol									
	+	*	ID	(	)	$	E	T	P
0			L6	S6			S1	S7	L5
1	S3					A			
3			L6	S6				S11	L5
6			L6	S6			S12	S7	L5
7	R3	S8			R3	R3			
8			L6	S6					L4
11	R2	S8			R2	R2			
12	S3				L7				

Figure 6.36   Optimized SLR(1) Parse Table for G_3

possible, however, and one that has received considerable attention is one that eliminates *unit reductions*. Unit reductions replace a right-hand side of length one with a nonterminal (which, of course, is also of length one). Chains of unit reductions often occur, and it is possible to collapse such a chain into a single reduction.

Unit productions, having a right-hand side of length one, are used in expressions to enforce operator precedence. For example, in G_3, we have $E \rightarrow T$, $T \rightarrow P$, and $P \rightarrow ID$. In general, if a programming language has n operator precedence levels, it will have a chain of $n + 1$ unit productions leading from identifiers to expressions. In real languages n can be 10 or greater, and parsing a trivial (and very common) expression consisting of a single identifier or literal can take a significant number of steps.

If none of the intermediate unit productions between ID and the expression contains action symbols, they may safely be skipped. The idea is to examine each legal lookahead and determine how many unit productions will be applied before the lookahead is consumed. As an example, reconsider state 0 of the LALR(1) machine for G_3, as shown in Figure 6.37.

If we shift ID, the possible lookaheads are $, +, and *. If * is the lookahead, ID will be reduced to P, then P to T. If + or $ is the lookahead, ID will be reduced to P, then P to T, and finally T to E. We optimize the unit reduction chain by modifying the parse table entries for state s = go_to[0][ID]. For a * lookahead we recognize the *pseudoproduction* $T \rightarrow ID$ and perform the necessary semantic routines and then push go_to[0][T], skipping the $T \rightarrow P$ reduction. For a + or $ lookahead we recognize $E \rightarrow ID$.

Unit reduction optimization will improve parser speed, but possibly at the cost of new parser states or parse table entries. Researchers have studied ways of optimizing unit productions without unduly increasing parse table size (Soisalon-Soininen 1982, Pager 1977). These techniques are fairly complex and are not always needed in their full generality.

An effective heuristic is to first select those states that predict an expression (for example, states 0 and 6 in the CFSM for G_3, Figure 6.18) and for these states modify only the successor states under symbols that begin a reduction

---

```
┌─────────────────────────────────────┐
│ State 0                             │
├─────────────────────────────────────┤
│ S → • E$    ,{λ}                    │
│ E → • E+T   ,{$+}                   │
│ E → • T     ,{$+}                   │
│ T → • T*P   ,{$+*}                  │
│ T → • P     ,{$+*}                  │
│ P → • ID    ,{$+*}                  │
│ P → • (E)   ,{$+*}                  │
└─────────────────────────────────────┘
```

Figure 6.37   A CFSM State of Grammar G_3

chain (ID or INTLITERAL). The intuition here is that by far the most common expressions are trivial ones comprising a single identifier or literal. Hence, it is most profitable to collapse unit production chains from identifiers or literals to expressions.

The successor states we modify would normally be removed, so there is a modest space penalty. Newly created states can share the same parse table row as long as lookahead symbols agree on the same shift or reduce action (a reduce action can overlay an error action). Thus, in our optimized SLR(1) parse table for G_3, Figure 6.36, the successor to state 0 for ID, with error entries elided, becomes

[$: Reduce E → ID; +: Reduce E → ID; *: Reduce T → ID]

Similarly, the successor to state 6 for ID becomes

[): Reduce E → ID; +: Reduce E → ID; *: Reduce T → ID]

There are no conflicts, so the two rows can be overlaid.

In some states a chain of unit reductions must occur independently of lookaheads. For example, in state 3 of the CFSM for G_3, after ID is reduced to P, P must always be reduced to T. Replacing the L-type reduction of P → ID with the pseudoproduction T → ID optimizes the reduction chain with no space penalty.

6.9. Practical LR(1) Parsers

Conventional wisdom among compiler writers has it that LALR(1) is the most powerful "practical" shift-reduce parser around, and in fact most bottom-up parser generators are LALR(1). Full LR(1) parsers are disregarded because they normally contain far too many states to be of use for real programming languages.

This belief is not entirely justified, however. LALR(1), as we have seen, can be viewed as an optimization of LR(1) parsers in which all states with a common core are merged. LALR(1) is an all or nothing approach; we merge all possible corresponding LR(1) states and then either accept or reject the "optimized" parser.

A more moderate approach would be to merge states when possible, but not if a parsing conflict is introduced. This guarantees that the full class of LR(1) grammars will be accepted and yet still ought to produce significant space savings. If a grammar is LALR(1), then all merges that we attempt must succeed, and we obtain a conventional LALR(1) machine. If a grammar is "almost LALR(1)," then we obtain a parser with only a few more states than the corresponding CFSM.

This idea of merging states when possible is appealing, but it is not as simple as it seems. The main difficulty is that a pair of states may appear to be

$$\boxed{\begin{array}{l} A \to \bullet\, a \,,\, \{a\} \\ B \to \bullet\, a \,,\, \{b\} \end{array}} \qquad\qquad \boxed{\begin{array}{l} A \to \bullet\, a \,,\, \{b\} \\ B \to \bullet\, a \,,\, \{a\} \end{array}}$$

Figure 6.38   Pair of LR(1) States to Be Merged

mergeable when in fact they really are not. When a pair of states is merged, successor states under the same symbol must also be merged, and it is entirely possible that a parsing conflict will appear only when the merger of successor states is performed. Consider the pair of LR(1) states shown in Figure 6.38. Merging these two states is wrong because their successors, when merged, will have an unresolvable reduce-reduce conflict.

Another difficulty is that the order in which states are merged can make a difference in the size of the final "optimized" parser. This means that a minimum state parser cannot be guaranteed in all cases unless all ways of merging states are explored. The practical effect of considering only one merger order is minimal, however, as the deviation from optimality, if any, is likely to be very small.

Let us assume that we have two LR(1) states, s_1 and s_2, that have the same core. We need some way to decide whether merging these states will lead to parsing conflicts. A two-step approach is possible. First, we decide if $s_1 \cup s_2$ has any parsing conflicts not resolved by lookahead. This is easy to do. If the immediate merger is safe, we explore the results of merging successor states—for example, go_to[s_1][X] and go_to[s_2][X]. If merger of any pair of successor states leads to unresolvable conflicts, we *backtrack* and reject the merger of s_1 and s_2.

A real problem with this backtracking approach is that it assumes that the entire LR(1) machine has been built, so that states and their successors can be merged as needed. A better tack is to merge states as they are built, vastly reducing the number of intermediate states that must be manipulated. This approach has been explored by Pager (1977). Rather than merging states and then exploring the effects of merging their successors, which may not even have been built yet, Pager defines criteria that guarantee that a merger is safe.

The simplest criterion is termed *weak compatibility*. Consider two LR(1) states s and $\bar{s}$ that have the same core and hence may possibly be merged. Consider two configurations $A \to \alpha \bullet \beta$, L_1 and $B \to \delta \bullet \gamma$, L_2 from s, where L_1 and L_2 represent the set of lookaheads applicable to the corresponding dotted production. Because $\bar{s}$ and s share a common core, $\bar{s}$ must contain configurations of the form $A \to \alpha \bullet \beta$, $\bar{L}_1$ and $B \to \delta \bullet \gamma$, $\bar{L}_2$. We say s and $\bar{s}$ are weakly compatible if and only if one of the following three conditions holds for all pairs of configurations:

(1) $L_1 \cap \bar{L}_2 = \varnothing$ and $\bar{L}_1 \cap L_2 = \varnothing$.

    (2) $L_1 \cap L_2 \neq \emptyset$

    (3) $\overline{L}_1 \cap \overline{L}_2 \neq \emptyset$

It is not difficult to establish that two states are weakly compatible if and only if their basis sets are weakly compatible. This fact is handy in that it makes checking for weak compatibility easier—only basis configurations need to be checked (pairwise) for conditions 1, 2, and 3.

The importance of weak compatibility is that if two states are weakly compatible, they may be safely merged. To understand why this is the case, first observe that merging two states may introduce reduce-reduce conflicts but not shift-reduce conflicts. That is, if a shift-reduce conflict appears, it must have existed before any states were merged. In particular, the conflict already must exist in the state that contains the symbol to be shifted as a lookahead for a reduce action.

Can a reduce-reduce conflict appear in the merged state? Condition 1 of weak compatibility states that the lookaheads added after a merger cannot conflict because their intersection is empty. Conditions 2 and 3 can hold only if there was a reduce-reduce conflict before the merger, in which case the merger would never be attempted, anyway.

Can a reduce-reduce conflict appear in a successor to the merged state? Consider the immediate successors to s and $\overline{s}$ under some symbol x. Call them s_x and $\overline{s}_x$. $\mathsf{Basis}(s_x)$ and $\mathsf{Basis}(\overline{s}_x)$ are weakly compatible because they are obtained directly from s and $\overline{s}$, which are known to be weakly compatible. As mentioned, we know that if basis sets are weakly compatible, so are the complete configuration sets. This immediately implies that no reduce-reduce conflicts can be introduced if s_x and $\overline{s}_x$ are merged. Repeating this argument, all successor states are weakly compatible and hence may be safely merged.

The notion of weak compatibility leads to a straightforward "on the fly" LR(1) generation algorithm. When an LR(1) state s is created, we examine already created states that have the same core as s. If such a state, $\overline{s}$, which is weakly compatible with s, exists, we merge s and $\overline{s}$. If successors to $\overline{s}$ have already been built, we try to replace them with successors to $s \cup \overline{s}$. This may not always be possible, as successors to $\overline{s}$ may have already been merged with other states. Weak compatibility can be used to verify that the replacement is possible. If it is not, a new successor state is created. If successors to $\overline{s}$ have not yet been created, merging s with $\overline{s}$ will cause the later generation of successors to $s \cup \overline{s}$.

This algorithm always creates a correct LR(1) parser if the underlying grammar actually is LR(1). However, it need not produce a minimum state LR(1) parser. The reason for this is that the weak compatibility rule may preclude the merger of states that actually could be safely merged. For example, assume we had the LR(1) states shown in Figure 6.39.

These two states have the same core but are not weakly compatible. They may, however, be safely merged because in this case no reduce-reduce conflict is possible, and lookaheads are not even needed. The problem is that the lookahead x suggests a future reduce-reduce conflict, when in fact the conflict cannot be reached.

```
┌─────────────────────────┐     ┌─────────────────────────┐
│  A → a • b c, {x}       │     │  A → a • b c, {z}       │
│  B → a • b d, {y}       │     │  B → a • b d, {x}       │
└─────────────────────────┘     └─────────────────────────┘
```

Figure 6.39   A Pair of LR(1) States That Can Be Merged

In practice, this appears to be no problem because in "real" grammars weak compatibility precludes few, if any, feasible merges. Nonetheless, there are ways of guaranteeing that all feasible merges are performed. Pager (1977) defines *strong compatibility* criteria. These criteria improve upon the weak compatibility criteria by requiring that if a merger appears to introduce an eventual reduce-reduce conflict, the conflict must actually be reachable. In the preceding example, the configurations $A \to a \bullet bc$, x and $B \to a \bullet bd$, x cannot lead to an eventual reduce-reduce conflict, so strong compatibility allows the merger. Alternately, once an LR(1) machine has been built using weak compatibility, a backtracking algorithm, similar to that described earlier, can be used to explore states that have not yet been matched. If no conflicts arise, the states that weak compatibility could not handle are merged. Otherwise, we backtrack and consider other possibilities.

A full LR(1) parser generator called *LR* has been built by Wetherell and Shannon (1981). The LR system uses Pager's weak compatibility criteria to merge states as they are built. LR has been used entirely satisfactorily for several commercial developments, and it has generated parsers for Ada and PL/I with no difficulty. LR is written in standard FORTRAN and is readily transportable.

6.10. **Properties of LR Parsing**

All the variants of LR parsing that we have discussed share common properties that are important to know. We have already discussed the most important property: correctness. Each LR-style parser is guaranteed to correctly parse valid inputs and to detect syntax errors when attempts are made to parse invalid inputs. Moreover, because all LR-style parsers accept only viable prefixes, a syntax error is detected as soon as the parser attempts to shift a token that cannot be part of a viable prefix. This allows for prompt and convenient error reporting.

Another important common property is *unambiguity*. That is, if a grammar is known to fit any of the LR-style parsing classes, the grammar will allow no ambiguous derivations. This result is really a side effect of the fact that LR-style parsers are deterministic. In particular, in each state and for each lookahead, a unique parser action is required. Ambiguous grammars allow alternate derivations, which would lead to a shift-reduce or reduce-reduce conflict in some state.

Another important property shared by all LR-style parsers is that they are efficient. If we are parsing a program containing n tokens, then

- The parse stack will never contain more than $c_1 \times n$ states, where c_1 is a constant determined by the grammar being parsed.

- The parser will never make more than $c_2 \times n$ moves, where c_2 is also a grammar-determined constant.

That is, LR parsers are *linear* in operation. This result is actually vital, for programs containing tens of thousands of tokens are routinely parsed by production compilers. Were linearity not guaranteed, the compilation of large programs might well be prohibitively expensive.

To prove linearity we first note that it is known that the parse tree for any string, s, in an unambiguous grammar is linearly proportional in size to s. This result is a generalization of Exercise 12 of Chapter 4. If this fact were not true, then linear parsing using any technique would be impossible because a parser, while operating, "discovers" the corresponding parse tree.

To prove that LR parsers require only linear space, we observe that each symbol occurring in the parse, either terminal or nonterminal, is shifted exactly once. The total number of symbols is proportional to the size of the input and therefore so is the maximum stack depth.

To establish linear time, we first note that each cycle of the parser driver requires a bounded amount of time. Because each cycle consumes a symbol and the total number of symbols is proportional to the input length, so is the total parsing time.

If action symbols are included, the total time required to recognize them and to call semantic routines is again linear. This is because there are only a fixed number of action symbols per production, usually one. The time required to execute a semantic routine *need not* be bounded. Therefore, although parsing must be linear, semantic processing and code generation need not be (although in practice they are, unless extensive optimization is performed).

6.11. LL(1) or LALR(1), That Is the Question

The two dominant parsing techniques in real compilers are LL(1) and LALR(1). Virtually all modern compilers use one of these two techniques or a closely related variant (for example, Recursive Descent or SLR(1)). It is important that compiler writers appreciate the strengths and weaknesses of each so that informed choices can be made.

In the following subsections, LL(1) and LALR(1) will be compared with respect to a number of criteria. As might be expected, each has its own particular strengths. Before a parsing technique is chosen for a particular compiler design, it is probably a good idea to review these criteria and choose the technique that best fits the needs of the design. In many cases, however, nonobjective factors will have a role. As with the hometown ball club, the technique we learn first often becomes our favorite. Such biases aside, neither technique is the universal favorite, and a balanced comparison can be of great value.

Simplicity

Both LL(1) and LALR(1) have very simple drivers. The concepts underlying LL(1) are very easy to visualize and understand. LALR(1) is rather more complicated, given the notions of items, item sets, state merger, and lookahead propagation. Because parser generators are used, internal details of parser construction are normally hidden. Sometimes, however, internal details intrude when a grammar is being debugged (that is, revised to fit a parsing class). In such cases simplicity is a definite plus, so the stronger one here is LL(1).

Generality

All other things being equal, the broader the class of grammars a parsing technique can handle, the better. Neither LL(1) nor LALR(1) can handle all unambiguous grammars. However, all LL(1) grammars are LR(1) and virtually all are also LALR(1). LL(1) parsers are fairly strict about grammar forms, forbidding left recursion and productions that share a common prefix.

It is easier to put a grammar into LALR(1) form, and virtually all modern languages are designed so that an LALR(1) parser can be readily built. In fact, a careful language design effort often includes a "reference grammar" already in LALR(1) form.

In contrast, most reference grammars must be rewritten to put them into LL(1) form. In rare cases, constructs such as Pascal's dangling else have no unambiguous LL(1) formulation. Non-LL(1) language constructs are rare. A good rule of thumb is that LL(1) and LALR(1) grammars can be constructed for any reasonable programming language. However, the LALR(1) grammar will almost certainly be easier to write and may well be easier to read. In summary, therefore, LALR(1) has a definite edge in generality.

Action Symbols

Action symbols are the interface between a parser and semantic routines. LL(1) allows placement of action symbols anywhere in a right-hand side. LALR(1) allows placement of action symbols at the extreme right end of production but may not allow placement elsewhere. Usually, however, an LALR(1) grammar can be rewritten to allow necessary semantic routine calls. In fact, Yacc allows placement of code fragments anywhere in a right-hand side, automatically introducing new anonymous non-terminals in the fashion described at the end of Section 6.6. No parsing conflicts are usually introduced by this, which gives Yacc almost the same flexibility as LL(1) parsers in placement of semantic actions.

In summary, LL(1) allows the most flexibility in action symbol placement. Some LALR(1) generators are almost as flexible, but others are significantly more restrictive in the placement of semantic actions.

Error Repair

Error repair is discussed in detail in Chapter 17. Briefly, LL(1) parse stacks contain symbols that are predicted but not yet matched. This information is clearly of value in determining possible repairs. LALR(1) parse stacks contain information on what has already been seen. Deciding possible continuations, to use as repairs, is not trivial, and therefore LL(1) error repair tends to be somewhat simpler.

Table Sizes

Both LL(1) and LALR(1) require parse tables that can be sizable. If compiler size is an issue, comparing the relative table sizes required is useful.

For LL(1) parsers, the uncompressed parse table size is $|V_n| \times |V_t|$. In addition, a table of right-hand sides and their sizes is needed. This is of size $|G|$, where $|G|$ is the sum of all production lengths.

In contrast, an LALR(1) parser requires an uncompressed parse table size of at most $|\text{States}| \times (|V_n| + |V_t|)$, as well as a table of production lengths and left-hand sides of size $2 \times |P|$. In the worst case (which can be realized; see Exercise 35), the number of states is *exponential* in the size of the grammar. That is, LALR(1) states correspond to configuration sets. The number of different configurations is equal to $|G|$, and thus the number of different configuration sets is $2^{|G|}$.

Because of LALR(1)'s possible exponential blowup in table size, LL(1) appears to have a much safer worst case behavior. A more reasonable comparison, however, is obtained using expected case rather than worst case values. Certainly, no common grammars will result in a exponentially sized parse table. For purposes of comparison the following rules of thumb are frequently used for typical programming language grammars:

- $|V_t| \approx 0.5 \times |V_n|$
- $|P| \approx 2 \times |V_n|$
- $|G| \approx 7 \times |V_n|$ (that is, $3.5 \times |P|$)
- $|\text{States}| \approx |P| \approx 2 \times |V_n|$

Using these rules, a crude estimate of the number of table entries can be computed. Because parse tables are commonly used in compressed form, we consider only nonerror entries. Here an estimate of about 10% nonerror entries is used for LL(1) and 5% for LALR(1).

The number of LL(1) entries is then

$$|\text{LL}(1)| \approx 0.1 \times |V_n| \times |V_t| + |G|$$

$$= 0.1 \times |V_n| \times 0.5 \times |V_n| + 7 \times |V_n|$$

$$= 0.05 \times |V_n|^2 + 7 \times |V_n|$$

Similarly, the number of LALR(1) entries is

$$|LALR(1)| \approx 0.05 \times |P| \times (|V_n| + |V_t|) + 2 \times |P|$$

$$= 0.1 \times |V_n| \times (|V_n| + 0.5 \times |V_n|) + 2 \times 2 \times |V_n|$$

$$= 0.1 \times |V_n| \times (1.5 \times |V_n|) + 4 \times |V_n|$$

$$= 0.15 \times |V_n|^2 + 4 \times |V_n|$$

In general $|LALR(1)|$ will be larger, with a limiting ratio of

$$\lim_{|V_n| \to \infty} \frac{|LALR(1)|}{|LL(1)|} =$$

$$\lim_{|V_n| \to \infty} \frac{0.15 \times |V_n|^2 + 4 \times |V_n|}{0.05 \times |V_n|^2 + 7 \times |V_n|} = 3$$

For typical programming languages, $|V_n| \approx 100$. This gives a ratio of

$$\frac{0.15 \times 100^2 + 4 \times 100}{0.05 \times 100^2 + 7 \times 100} = \frac{1500 + 4 \times 100}{500 + 7 \times 100} \approx 1.58$$

In this range the LL(1) table of right-hand sides takes about as much space as the LL(1) parse table itself. To gauge how reasonable these estimates are, let us consider two actual Pascal grammars, one LL(1) and one LALR(1).

In the LL(1) Pascal grammar $|V_n| = 125$, $|V_t| = 60$, $|P| = 234$. There are 591 nonerror parse table entries and 640 entries for right-hand side information. This gives 1231 entries as compared with a prediction of $0.05 \times 125^2 + 7 \times 125 \approx 1656$.

Similarly, the LALR(1) Pascal grammar has $|V_t| = 60$, $|V_n| = 127$, $|P| = 280$. It has 2798 nonerror parse table entries and 560 entries for production length and left-hand side information, a total of 3358 entries as compared with a prediction of $0.15 \times 127^2 + 4 \times 127 \approx 2927$.

The ratio is then $2927 / 1656 \approx 1.77$. Thus, a good working ratio of about *2 to 1* for LALR(1) versus LL(1) table sizes emerges. LL(1) has a definite advantage in space requirements, and, in cases where space is tight, this difference could be a deciding factor in favor of LL(1).

Because drivers for both LALR(1) and LL(1) examine each terminal and nonterminal in the parse tree, we can expect parsing speeds to be comparable.

Summary of Comparison

LL(1) has the advantage in all areas except generality, where LALR(1) has a decided edge. In all areas, though, both techniques are quite workable. LL(1) is probably the better choice for a first compiler *if* an LL(1) grammar is already available. Knowledgeable compiler writers should be well versed in both techniques. Experience, and the availability of suitable parser generators, can then guide one's choice.

6.12. Other Shift-Reduce Techniques

The LR-based parsing techniques discussed in this chapter are today predominant among shift-reduce parsers. For completeness, in this section a number of other shift-reduce techniques will be discussed. These techniques are primarily of historical or theoretical interest. Nonetheless, a brief overview will demonstrate the range of extensions and alternatives that have been developed over the years.

6.12.1. Extended Lookahead Techniques

The SLR(1), LALR(1), and LR(1) parsing techniques can be generalized to utilize k-symbol lookaheads. The resulting techniques, SLR(k), LALR(k), and LR(k), utilize k-symbol First and Follow sets, denoted $First_k$ and $Follow_k$.

The generalizations are straightforward:

(1) **LR(k)**: When closing a configuration set containing $A \rightarrow \alpha \bullet B\beta$, x, predict $B \rightarrow \bullet \gamma$, y, where $y \in First_k(\beta x)$.
Reduce production $A \rightarrow \alpha$ on lookahead x if the current state contains $A \rightarrow \alpha \bullet$, x.
Shift on lookahead x if the current state contains $A \rightarrow \alpha \bullet a\beta$, y, where $a \in V_t$ and $x \in First_k(a\beta y)$.

(2) **SLR(k)**: Reduce production $A \rightarrow \alpha$ on lookahead x if the current state contains $A \rightarrow \alpha \bullet$, where $x \in Follow_k(A)$.
Shift on lookahead x if the current state contains $A \rightarrow \alpha \bullet a\beta$, where $a \in V_t$ and $x \in First_k(a\beta Follow_k(A))$.

(3) **LALR(k)**: Merge those states and parser actions of the LR(k) machine that share the same core.

As one might expect, these generalizations extend the class of grammars that can be parsed. For example, if LR(k) denotes the set of grammars that is parsable using the LR technique with k-symbol lookahead, then it is easy to show that $LR(0) \subset LR(1) \subset \cdots \subset LR(k) \subset LR(k+1) \cdots$. Similar containment results apply for SLR(k) and LALR(k). Any number of containment questions can be posed, such as: Do there exist grammars that are LR(1) and LALR(2), but not LALR(1), and SLR(3), but not SLR(2)? (The answer is yes.)

In a practical sense, extended lookahead techniques are of little value. Parse table size grows rapidly for extended lookahead techniques. It is questionable whether parse tables one or two orders of magnitude greater in size than conventional tables can be seriously considered. More importantly, extended lookahead techniques do not seem to really be needed. That is, grammars used to define programming languages need only one lookahead symbol. In cases where extra lookaheads appear necessary, simple grammar transformations can reduce the lookahead requirements to a single symbol. Theory supports experience in this observation: All languages deterministically parsable are known to have SLR(1) grammars (and if endmarkers are used, even LR(0) grammars). This suggests that future programming languages will continue to be parsable using conventional one-symbol lookahead techniques.

6.12.2. **Precedence Techniques**

The LR-style parsing techniques we have studied thus far are fairly intricate. It seems unlikely, therefore, that they were the first shift-reduce techniques developed and studied. And, in fact, before LR techniques became dominant, a wide variety of *precedence techniques* were intensively studied and widely used.

Precedence techniques address the fundamental problem of shift-reduce parsing—how to isolate and reduce the handle of a right sentential form. We shall discuss briefly the two best known precedence techniques: *simple precedence* and *operator precedence*.

The version of simple precedence that we shall discuss was formalized by Wirth and Weber (1966). The technique was developed to parse the Algol W language. Simple precedence is quite simple. Three *precedence relations*, $\lessdot$, $\doteq$, and $\gtrdot$, are defined over pairs of grammar symbols. A pair of symbols can appear in at most one of these relations if the grammar is simple precedence. Informally, $\lessdot$ marks the beginning (left end) of a handle, $\doteq$ delimits the interior of a handle, and $\gtrdot$ delimits the (right) end of a handle.

These relations fit nicely into a shift-reduce parser. As symbols are read, they are pushed onto the parse stack as long as $\lessdot$ or $\doteq$ relations apply. When a $\gtrdot$ relation applies between the top stack symbol and the lookahead symbol, the end of the handle has been located. Then stack symbols are popped off until a $\lessdot$ applies between the top stack symbol and the last symbol popped. The symbols popped off form a handle, which is to be reduced. After the reduction, the left-hand side symbol, as usual, replaces the handle on the stack.

Once a handle is isolated there must be no ambiguity as to what production is to be reduced. This is guaranteed by requiring a *unique invertibility* property: No two productions may have the same right-hand side. Given unique invertibility, isolating a handle is equivalent to determining the correct reduction.

As an example, let us consider G_8:

$$S \rightarrow \$E\$$$
$$E \rightarrow F$$
$$F \rightarrow F+T \mid T$$
$$T \rightarrow ID \mid (E)$$

This grammar is a variant of G_1, with nonterminals added to eliminate conflicts in precedence relations. A left endmarker is added to make it easier to isolate the beginning of handles (via the $\lessdot$ relation). The *precedence table* shown in Figure 6.40 can be computed for G_8. (See Aho and Ullman 1972, vol. 1, section 6.2.2 for details on how the precedence relations are computed.)

Figure 6.41 illustrates a simple precedence parse of $\$ID + (ID + ID)\$$. The parser accepts the input if and only if the input is reduced to $\$E\$$. Precedence

	E	F	T	ID	+	(	)	$
E							≐	≐
F					≐		⋗	⋗
T				⋗			⋗	⋗
ID					⋗		⋗	⋗
+			≐	⋖		⋖		
(	≐	⋖	⋖	⋖		⋖		
)					⋗		⋗	⋗
$	≐	⋖	⋖	⋖		⋖		

Figure 6.40   Simple Precedence Parse Table for G_8

relations are shown only for purposes of illustration; they are not actually stacked.

Although simple precedence is conceptually simpler than the LR techniques, it has many drawbacks, primarily the restricted class of grammars it can parse. All simple precedence grammars are SLR(1), but the converse is not true. Although SLR(1) grammars are fairly easy to write, simple precedence grammars are much more difficult to construct. Note that λ-

Step	Parse Stack	Remaining Input
1		$ID+(ID+ID)$
2	$ ⋖	ID+(ID+ID)$
3	$ ⋖ ID ⋗	+(ID+ID)$
4	$ ⋖ T ⋗	+(ID+ID)$
5	$ ⋖ F≐	+(ID+ID)$
6	$ ⋖ F≐+ ⋖	(ID+ID)$
7	$ ⋖ F≐+ ⋖ (⋖	ID+ID)$
8	$ ⋖ F≐+ ⋖ (⋖ ID ⋗	+ID)$
9	$ ⋖ F≐+ ⋖ (⋖ T ⋗	+ID)$
10	$ ⋖ F≐+ ⋖ (⋖ F≐	+id)$
11	$ ⋖ F≐+ ⋖ (⋖ F≐+ ⋖	ID)$
12	$ ⋖ F≐+ ⋖ (⋖ F≐+ ⋖ ID ⋗	)$
13	$ ⋖ F≐+ ⋖ (⋖ F≐+≐T ⋗	)$
14	$ ⋖ F≐+ ⋖ (⋖ F ⋗	)$
15	$ ⋖ F≐+ ⋖ (≐E≐	)$
16	$ ⋖ F≐+ ⋖ (≐E≐) ⋗	$
17	$ ⋖ F≐+≐T ⋗	$
18	$ ⋖ F ⋗	$
19	$≐E≐	$
20	$≐E≐$	

Figure 6.41   Example of a Simple Precedence Parse

productions are not allowed in simple precedence grammars because λ cannot be correctly isolated as a handle using precedence relations. Further, the requirements that productions be uniquely invertible and that precedence relations be disjoint makes grammars larger and more fragile than corresponding LR grammars. They are larger because new nonterminals are often necessary to eliminate precedence conflicts. They are fragile because even modest changes or additions can induce subtle precedence conflicts. In fact, there exist deterministic languages (which can be parsed by all LR techniques) that have no simple precedence grammar.

Given the deficiences of simple precedence, it is not surprising that this technique has been superseded by SLR(1) and LALR(1). Simple precedence is now mostly of historic interest, although it occasionally appears in vintage compilers.

Operator precedence parsing techniques date to the early 1960s, when parsing involved little more than transforming expressions from infix to prefix or postfix form. Indeed, operator precedence is primarily a formalization of the operator precedence levels that appear in programming languages. While parsing an expression, operator precedence parsers seek to isolate simple subexpressions, which are roughly equivalent to handles. Operator precedence relations, defined only on terminals, do this. Basically, an operator Op1 is ⋖ operator Op2 if Op2 has higher precedence. Thus normally + ⋖ * and * ⋗ +. If Op1 and Op2 are on the same level and left-associative, Op1 ⋗ Op2. Parentheses force grouping, so for all operators and identifiers, Op ⋖ (, (⋖ Op, Op ⋗), and) ⋗ Op. For example, parsing $ID + (ID + ID)$ we have

$$\$ \lessdot ID + \lessdot (\lessdot ID + ID \gtrdot) \gtrdot \$$$

where ⋖ and ⋗ isolate subexpressions. Similarly, for $ID*ID + ID*ID$, we have

$$\$ \lessdot ID*ID \gtrdot + \lessdot ID*ID \gtrdot \$$$

which again forces correct grouping.

Because operator precedence focuses on terminals, productions that contain two consecutive nonterminals are forbidden. This is more restrictive than simple precedence, which is more general and inclusive. Historically, simple precedence superseded operator precedence and then in turn gave way to the LR techniques in use today.

6.12.3. General Context-Free Parsers

All the parsing techniques we have described so far are limited to some subset of context-free grammars. Typically, only unambiguous grammars are allowed. If ambiguous grammars are allowed, guarantees of correctness are voided. Further, since lookaheads are fixed, only deterministic languages and grammars can be handled.

Occasionally, a general-purpose context-free parser is needed that can handle any grammar. Probably the best known general context-free parser is *Earley's algorithm,* devised by Jay Earley (1970). Earley's algorithm can be viewed as an *interpretive* version of LR(0) parsing. It is more general than the LR-style techniques we have studied and, not surprisingly, is more expensive. Ordinary parsing techniques, including LL, LR, and precedence methods, always work in linear time and space; Earley's algorithm sometimes requires cubic time and quadratic space, though this nonlinear performance usually occurs while parsing grammars beyond the capability of ordinary parsers. Top-down parsing techniques that can handle any context-free grammar also exist (Graham, Harrison, and Ruzzo 1980).

Unlike LR(k) parsing, Earley's algorithm never needs or uses lookahead. Rather, whenever there is any doubt about when to do a reduction, *all possibilities* are followed, in parallel. Further, we do not compute any states or automata in advance. Rather we compute and manipulate sets of configurations as the parse proceeds, which is why we consider the algorithm interpretive.

In Earley's algorithm, configurations (dotted productions) are augmented with a second component, an integer-valued *prediction pointer.* The prediction pointer represents the configuration set in which the configuration set was predicted. This pointer is needed because ambiguous grammars may predict the same production many times, representing various alternative parses. Configurations are manipulated in much the same way as in ordinary LR-style parsers:

- The initial configuration is $S \to \bullet\alpha$, 0. (We initially predict the augmenting production with a prediction pointer of 0, where 0 is the index of state 0.)

- If state i contains an item $A \to \alpha \bullet B\beta$, j, then we *predict* $B \to \bullet\gamma$, i. The prediction pointer is i because the configuration is predicted in state i.

- If state i contains a configuration $A \to \alpha \bullet X\beta$, j and the next input symbol is X, then add $A \to \alpha X \bullet \beta$, j to state i + 1.

- If state i contains an item $A \to \gamma\bullet$, j, then we know this production was predicted in state j. Go to state j and look for items of the form $B \to \alpha \bullet A\beta$, k. Add corresponding items of the form $B \to \alpha A \bullet \beta$, k to state i. This operation is the cognate of a reduction action in that a right-hand side that has been matched is replaced with its left-hand side, which is then shifted.

- After an input containing n tokens has been parsed, n + 1 configuration sets will have been built. If state n contains the item $S \to \alpha\bullet$, 0, then the input is valid, because the input has allowed the goal symbol to be matched.

As a simple example, we will consider the ambiguous grammar:

$$S \to E$$
$$E \to E + E \mid ID$$

Figure 6.42 illustrates Earley's algorithm, parsing ID + ID + ID. This input has two distinct parses; the algorithm finds both.

Because state 5 contains S → E •, 0, we know the input is valid. In fact, because the input has two distinct parses, this item is added *twice*. Completion of item E → E + E •, 0 causes the augmenting production to be completed. This corresponds to parsing the input as (ID + ID) + ID. Completion of E → E + E •, 2 causes E → ID •, 2 in state 2 to be completed, which in turn completes the augmenting production. This corresponds to a parse of ID + (ID + ID).

In general, to extract a parse, an implementation adds "threads" linking an item to the completed item that added it. If an item is added more than once, distinct threads point to distinct parses.

From our simple example it is easy to see that configuration sets can grow larger as more and more input is parsed. This is because the same dotted production may appear more than once, with different prediction pointers. State i's size can be proportional to i, so the number of configurations in n states can be proportional to n^2. Similarly, because of ambiguity, an item may be added more than once. With care, time proportional to n^3 can be achieved. A faster ($n^{\log_2 7}$), but still more complicated, general context-free parser was created by Valiant (1975).

In the case of LR(0) grammars, Earley's algorithm requires only linear time and space, but with very much larger overhead factors because at each step Earley's algorithm must manipulate and store items, all of which are precomputed for ordinary LR(0) parsers.

Is Earley's algorithm ever actually used? In practice its space and time requirements make it far too costly, but it can be of value in experimental systems. In fact, applications that require ambiguous grammars or unrestricted

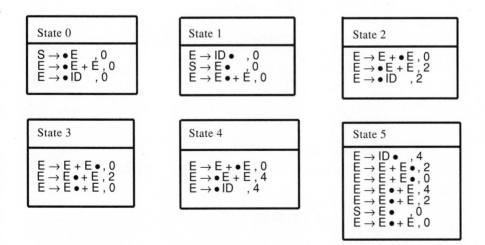

Figure 6.42 An Example of Earley's Algorithm

grammars often experiment with general parsers such as Earley's. Application areas that have such requirements include natural language processing, automatic code generation (Christopher et al. 1984), and user-extensible language development. A variety of approaches that improve upon Earley's algorithm are also known (Graham, Harrison, and Ruzzo 1980), (Aretz 1989).

Exercises

1. Trace the execution of the shift-reduce driver of Figure 6.1 on

    begin begin SimpleStmt ; **end** ; SimpleStmt ; **end** $

    using the **action** and **go_to** tables of Figures 6.2 and 6.3.

2. The following production has been augmented with action symbols to specify the translation of a simple **while** loop:

    <stmt> → **while** #loop_head <expr> #test_expr
        loop <stmts> **end loop** ; #loop_end

    Rewrite this production into a form suitable for shift-reduce parsing.

3. Build the CFSM for the following grammar:

<prog>	→	<block> $
<block>	→	**begin** <stmt list> **end**
<stmt list>	→	<stmt list> ; <stmt>
<stmt list>	→	<stmt>
<stmt>	→	<block>
<stmt>	→	<var> := <expr>
<var>	→	ID
<var>	→	ID [<expr>]
<expr>	→	<expr> + <term>
<expr>	→	<term>
<term>	→	<var>
<term>	→	(<expr>)

    Show the corresponding **go_to** table.

4. Which of the following grammars are not LR(0)? Explain why.

    a. | S | → | StList $ |
        |---|---|---|
        | StList | → | StList ; Stmt |
        | StList | → | Stmt |
        | Stmt | → | **null** |

b. S   → StList $
    StList → Stmt ; StList
    StList → Stmt
    Stmt   → **null**

c. S   → StList $
    StList → StList ; StList
    StList → Stmt
    Stmt   → **null**

d. S   → StList $
    StList → **null** StTail
    StTail → λ
    StTail → ; StList

5. Show that the CFSM corresponding to an LL(1) grammar has the proper-
    ty that each configuration set has exactly one basis item if all nontermi-
    nals derive a string other than λ.

6. Build the LR(1) machine corresponding to the grammar of Exercise 3.

7. Which of the following grammars are LR(1)? Which are LALR(1)?
    Which are SLR(1)? In each case justify your categorization.

    a.   S → ID := E ;
         E → E + P
         E → P
         P → ID
         P → (E)
         P → ID := E

    b.   S → ID := A ;
         A → ID := A
         A → E
         E → E + P
         E → P
         P → ID
         P → (A)

c.   S → ID := A ;
      A → ID := A
      A → E
      E → E + P
      E → P
      E → P +
      P → ID
      P → (A)

d.   S → ID := A ;
      A → Pre E
      Pre→ Pre ID :=
      Pre→ λ
      E → E + P
      E → P
      P → ID
      P → (A)

e.   S → ID := A ;
      A → Pre E
      Pre→ ID := Pre
      Pre→ λ
      E → E + P
      E → P
      P → ID
      P → (A)

f.   S → ID := A ;
      A → ID := A
      A → E
      E → E + P
      E → P
      P → ID
      P → (A ; A)
      P → (V , V)
      P → { A , A }
      P → { V ; V }
      V → ID

g. $S \to ID := A$;
    $A \to ID := A$
    $A \to E$
    $E \to E + P$
    $E \to P$
    $P \to ID$
    $P \to (ID ; ID)$
    $P \to (A)$

8. Show that the lookahead components of LR(1) configurations are exact. That is

    (a) If state s contains an LR(1) configuration $A \to \alpha \bullet$, a then there exists a rightmost derivation $S \Rightarrow_{rm}^{*} \beta Aaw \Rightarrow_{rm} \beta \alpha aw$ where state s is reached after shifting $\beta \alpha$.

    (b) If there exists a rightmost derivation $S \Rightarrow_{rm}^{*} \beta Aaw \Rightarrow_{rm} \beta \alpha aw$, then there exists a state s, reached after shifting $\beta \alpha$, that contains the configuration $A \to \alpha \bullet$, a.

9. Build the SLR(1) **action** table corresponding to the grammar of Exercise 3.

10. Take the LR(1) machine built for Exercise 6 and list the states that share a common core. Merge states that share a common core to create an LALR(1) machine.

11. Starting with the CFSM built in Exercise 3, use the lookahead propagation algorithm of Figure 6.25 to determine LALR(1) lookaheads. Compare the lookaheads that are computed with those computed by state merger in Exercise 10.

12. Modify the lookahead propagation algorithm of Figure 6.25 to stack (state,configuration) pairs rather than (state,configuration,lookahead) triples. Explain why your modified algorithm propagates the same lookahead sets as the original algorithm.

13. When the backward search lookahead propagation algorithm was outlined in Section 6.5.1, it was noted that it was possible for a sequence of reductions to occur before a lookahead was shifted. Write a backward search propagation algorithm that correctly handles reduction sequences. Illustrate your algorithm on the CFSM of Exercise 3.

14. Figure 6.30 illustrates a CFSM state that may cause a backward search propagation algorithm to fail. Modify the algorithm you created in Exercise 13 to correctly handle the problem illustrated in Figure 6.30. Does your modified algorithm compute correct lookaheads for all CFSMs and grammars?

15.   The following grammar is *not* LALR(1):

<prog>	→ <block>
<block>	→ begin <decl list> <stmt list> end
<decl list>	→ <decl> <decl list>
<decl list>	→ λ
<stmt list>	→ <stmt list> <stmt>
<stmt list>	→ <stmt>
<decl>	→ ID : <type> ;
<type>	→ ID
<type>	→ array (<bound>) of <type>
<bound>	→ ID
<bound>	→ <expr>
<stmt>	→ ID := <expr> ;
<stmt>	→ <block> ;
<stmt>	→ ID : <stmt>
<expr>	→ <expr> + <pri>
<expr>	→ <pri>
<pri>	→ (<expr>)
<pri>	→ ID
<pri>	→ ID +

Put this grammar into a form that can be read by either LALRGen or Yacc. Use the parser generator you have selected to identify trouble spots. Then rewrite productions into a valid LALR(1) form. You may change productions as needed, but the language defined by your modified grammar must be the same as that of the original grammar.

16.   Write a context-free grammar for the expression structure of MicroPlus, as defined in Figure 6.33. The grammar you produce must enforce the operator precedence levels and associativities shown in the figure.

17.   Using Yacc-style precedence and associativity definitions, define the expressions structure of Ada/CS as specified in Appendix A. Note that all binary operators except relational operators are left-associative. If you have access to a computer that runs Yacc, test your definition.

18.   In Yacc it is impossible to give precedence and associativity definitions that place left- and right-associative operators at the same precedence level. Is this an oversight, or is there a reason why such definitions are disallowed?

19.   Assume we have a Pascal-like language that has the following control structures:

    if <expr> **then** <stmt>
    if <expr> **then** <stmt> **else** <stmt>
    while <expr> **do** <stmt>

Give an unambiguous LALR(1) grammar that defines these structures
and correctly handles the dangling else problem.

20. Extend the shift-reduce driver of Figure 6.1 to correctly handle the L-type
    entries and default entries created when parse tables are optimized using
    the techniques of Section 6.8.

21. Run the Ada/CS definition through LALRGen using the **parsetable**
    option. LALRGen uses L-type entries to eliminate single reduce states.
    It does not factor default actions. From the listing produced by the
    parsetable option, estimate how much space was saved by eliminat-
    ing single reduce states. How much more space would be saved if de-
    fault actions were factored from the parse table?

22. Modify the SLR(1) **action** table of Figure 6.19 to include optimization
    of unit reductions. That is, the modified table should not signal a chain
    of unit reductions but rather a single reduction that collapses the chain.

23. In Section 6.9 we outlined an LR(1) state merging algorithm that operates
    by merging LR(1) states with a common core as long as parsing action
    conflicts are not introduced. If a merger of two states causes a conflict in
    successor states that are merged, the algorithm backtracks and undoes
    mergers in predecessors that forced the illegal merger.

    Detail an algorithm that implements the approach outlined above. Illus-
    trate the operation of your algorithm on the following grammar:

    $$
    \begin{aligned}
    S &\rightarrow (\text{ Exp1 }) \\
    S &\rightarrow [\text{ Exp1 }] \\
    S &\rightarrow (\text{ Exp2 }] \\
    S &\rightarrow [\text{ Exp2 }) \\
    S &\rightarrow \{ \text{ Exp1 } \} \\
    S &\rightarrow < \text{ Exp1 } > \\
    S &\rightarrow \{ \text{ Exp2 } > \\
    S &\rightarrow < \text{ Exp2 } \} \\
    \text{Exp1} &\rightarrow \# \text{ ID} \\
    \text{Exp2} &\rightarrow \# \text{ ID}
    \end{aligned}
    $$

24. The most common criterion used to merge LR(1) states is weak compati-
    bility, as defined in Section 6.9. Create an LR(1) machine for the gram-
    mar of Exercise 23 and show the states that can be merged using weak
    compatibility.

25. Show that the order in which LR(1) states are merged when optimizing
    LR(1) parsers can make a difference. That is, if states are merged in one
    order, the size of the optimized LR(1) machine may be greater than if
    some other order is chosen.

26. Show that if the basis items of an LR(1) state are weakly compatible, then
    all the items in that state must be weakly compatible.

27. Show that any LL(1) grammar without λ-productions is LR(0).

28. Show that there exist LR(0) grammars, SLR(1) grammars, and LALR(1) grammars that are not LL(1).

29. Normally, an LALR(1) parser produces a canonical or rightmost parse. How could an LALR(1) parser be used to produce a leftmost parse (as LL(1) parsers do)? Would things be simplified if we knew the grammar being parsed was LL(1)?

30. Assume we have a working compiler that uses an LL(1) parser. As a rule of thumb, almost all LL(1) grammars are also LALR(1). Hence, it should be feasible to replace the LL(1) parser with an LALR(1) parser. What must we do to guarantee that the replacement is transparent to the rest of the compiler?

31. Show that all LL(1) grammars are also LR(1).

32. Show that there exist grammars that are SLR(k + 1) and LALR(k + 1) and LR(k + 1), but not SLR(k) or LALR(k) or LR(k).

33. Construct a grammar that has all the following properties:

   - It is SLR(3) but not SLR(2).
   - It is LALR(2) but not LALR(1).
   - It is LR(1).

34. Show that every SLR(1) grammar is also LALR(1) and that every LALR(1) grammar is also LR(1). Do these containment relations hold if we use k-symbol lookahead rather than one-symbol lookahead?

35. Consider the following grammar that has $O(n^2)$ productions:

$$S \rightarrow X_i\, z_i \qquad\qquad 1 \le i \le n$$
$$X_i \rightarrow y_j\, X_i \mid y_j \qquad 1 \le i,j \le n,\ i \ne j$$

Show that the CFSM for this grammar has $O(2^n)$ states. Is the grammar SLR(1)?

36. Trace the execution of a simple precedence parser on $\$((ID + ID) + (ID + ID))\$$ using the parse table of Figure 6.40.

37. Show that all simple precedence grammars are SLR(1). This can be done by showing that a shift-reduce or reduce-reduce conflict not resolvable using SLR(1)-style lookaheads must cause a conflict among the three simple precedence relations or must violate the unique invertibility property of simple precedence grammars.

38. Show the states Earley's algorithm would create while parsing aaa using the following grammar:

$$A \rightarrow AB \mid B$$
$$B \rightarrow BA \mid A$$
$$A \rightarrow a$$
$$B \rightarrow b$$

39. When parsing some grammars, Earley's algorithm will always produce states that are bounded in size by some constant value, independent of the size of the input being parsed. Such grammars are called *bounded state*. It is not difficult to show that Earley's algorithm can parse bounded state grammars in linear time. It is also known that Earley's algorithm can parse all LR(0) grammars in linear time. Is it the case that all LR(0) grammars must be bounded state?

CHAPTER **7**

Semantic Processing

Almost all modern compilers are *syntax-directed.* That is, the compilation process is driven by the syntactic structure of a source program, as recognized by the parser. The semantic routines, the part of the compiler that interprets the meaning (semantics) of a program, perform this interpretation based on its syntactic structure.

These routines actually play a dual role in the processing done by the compiler, as they finish the analysis task of compilation and then begin the synthesis task. Analysis is completed in that the semantic routines associate semantic information from declarations with all uses of identifiers and check that any static semantic restrictions in the language are satisfied by the program. Examples of static semantic checks include making sure that all variables used in the program are declared and that operand types in expressions are compatible with corresponding operators. Synthesis begins with the

216

generation of either an intermediate representation (IR) of the program or actual target code. It is from this synthesis step that the semantic routines get their name, for the output of these routines must reflect the meaning of the syntactic structure recognized by the scanner and the parser. Due to the syntax-directed nature of the translation process, semantic routines are usually associated with individual productions of a context-free grammar or subtrees of a syntax tree.

7.1. Syntax-directed Translation

7.1.1. Using a Syntax Tree Representation of a Parse

We begin our discussion of semantic processing by looking first at the most general approach and proceeding from there to consider specialized implementation alternatives. Because we classify our translation process as syntax-driven, our conceptual approach begins by considering what we do with the syntactic structure recognized by the parser as it examines the tokens that represent a program. In earlier chapters discussing top-down and bottom-up parsing, we saw that the sequence of actions generated by a parser can be interpreted as a sequence of instructions for building a parse tree. Thus the first step in our general approach to semantic processing will be to take the sequence of parse actions and use them to construct a *syntax tree* representation of the input program. Typically, this tree is not the literal parse tree recognized by the parser. For example, it need not include intermediate nodes in expression subtrees for the nonterminals that are usually introduced in our grammars to describe operator precedence and associativity. It does include sufficient structure to drive the semantic processing or even to regenerate the input from which it was produced. Such a tree is usually referred to as an *abstract syntax tree*, indicating its relationship to the actual (*concrete*) syntax and parse tree. Figure 7.1 shows an abstract syntax tree representation of an assignment statement, with an arithmetic expression on the right-hand side.

Given this kind of representation, semantic processing can be accomplished by one or more traversals of the tree. The two semantic processing tasks—static semantic checking and IR or code generation—can be accomplished using semantic *attributes* attached to the nodes of the syntax tree. When semantic processing begins, the only attributes available are those attached to the leaves of the tree representing tokens that have semantic values (identifiers and constants, for example). Such an initial state is illustrated by the tree in Figure 7.2.

A tree traversal that visits nodes using a post-order traversal can, for most languages, propagate semantic attributes throughout the tree and do static semantic checking at the same time. *Propagation* of semantic attributes includes such actions as processing declarations to build a symbol table, looking up identifiers in the symbol table to attach associated attribute information to appropriate nodes of the syntax tree, and examining the types of arguments

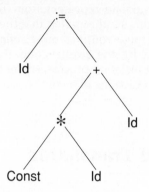

Figure 7.1   Abstract Syntax Tree for Y := 3 ∗ X + I

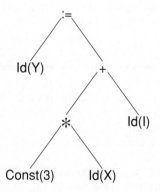

Figure 7.2   Abstract Syntax Tree for Y := 3 ∗ X + I with Initial
Attributes

for operands to determine their result types. Information from declarations
(the symbol table) is propagated top-down through subtrees for statements
and expressions. Expression-type information for semantic checking and code
generation generally propagates bottom-up. After all the attribute propagation
is done, the tree is said to be *decorated*, and it includes sufficient information to
drive a code generation pass.

In the above example, all identifiers must be looked up in the symbol
table to determine such information as their types and storage addresses.
Those items of information (or a reference to a symbol table entry) then
become attributes of the identifier nodes. Once those attributes are available,
we can determine the legality of the operation 3 ∗ X and, if it is legal, determine its result type. Thereafter, the same can be done for the second expression, and, finally, the legality of the assignment operation can be checked.

There are two kinds of static semantic checks (which interact with attribute propagation). Some checks depend entirely on propagated semantic attributes. The check for type compatibility across an assignment is such an example. Others combine structural information from the tree with semantic information. A comparison of the number of actual parameters included in a procedure call (structural information) with the number of formal parameters in its declaration (semantic information propagated from the procedure name) is an example of the latter case.

The translation task of semantic processing is based on another traversal of the syntax tree. The semantic attributes associated with each node are the data used in the translation, which is actually driven by the structure of the syntax tree. The output of the translation can be in any of several forms. Machine code may be generated directly this way; some linearized intermediate representation (such as tuples, like those we saw in Chapter 2) may be produced; or the tree itself with the addition of *code generation attributes* may serve as input to an optimizer or code generator.

This approach of organizing a compiler around syntax tree structure and multiple tree traversals can be described formally using *attribute grammar* notation. Attribute grammars are an extension of context-free grammars, wherein attributes are associated with each grammar symbol in a production, and rules are attached to each production to compute attribute values. Attribute information may flow both up from the leaves of the tree (*synthesized attributes*) and down toward the leaves from higher-level nonterminals (*inherited attributes*). The rules for attribute computation can include all the actions discussed above for attribute computation, static semantic checking, and even code generation. Attribute grammars and their use in constructing multipass compilers are defined and discussed more thoroughly in Chapter 14.

In Chapters 10 through 13, we examine techniques for implementing a wide variety of programming language features. Our organizational framework is to define these techniques in terms of semantic routines that we assume will be called directly by a parser. For the most part, these techniques are generally useful regardless of whether the semantic actions are invoked directly by the parser or by a tree traversal routine.

7.1.2. Compiler Organization Alternatives

As a basis for discussing compiler organization, consider Figure 7.3, the compiler structure diagram that first appeared in Chapter 1. The compiler components shown can be linked together in a variety of different ways, forming the set of compiler organization options to be discussed in this section. In this discussion, *analysis* refers to the analysis task of the compiler performed by the scanner, parser, and static semantic checking components of the semantic routines. Similarly, *synthesis* refers to the synthesis task done by the semantic routine components that generate some program representation, the optimizer, and the code generator. Six organizational options will be considered.

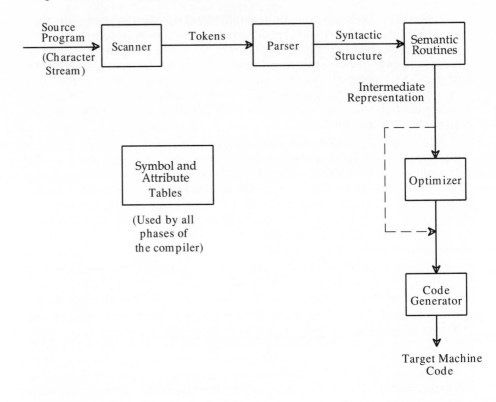

Figure 7.3   The Structure of a Syntax-Directed Compiler

A Single Pass for Analysis and Synthesis

In a common *one-pass compiler*, a single pass is used for both analysis and synthesis. Scanning, parsing, checking, and translation to target machine code are interleaved. No explicit intermediate representation of the source program is generated. This approach is basically the one used in the Micro compiler in Chapter 2, and it strongly resembles the model to be used in the semantic routine chapters. The principal difference is that target machine code rather than tuples must be generated. Such a change can be accomplished fairly transparently by having the **generate()** routine invoked by the semantic routines produce corresponding target machine code rather than tuples. Thus the **generate()** routine defines the interface to the code generator.

Within the code generator, temporaries must be appropriately mapped to registers, and code sequences corresponding to the tuple operators must be chosen. Because the code generator is effectively restricted to looking at only one tuple at a time, few significant optimizations can be performed. Some on-the-fly register management is possible to eliminate redundant loads.

Using the **generate()** routine as a code generator interface keeps the analysis portion of the compiler relatively independent of the target machine. However, a given semantic routine may involve more than one call to **generate()**, and its view of the code to be generated is broader than that of the code generator. For instance, the semantic routine that allocates a temporary typically knows something about how it will eventually be used. If the register set of the target machine is not uniform, such information may be crucial to optimal mapping between temporaries and registers. At the very least, this implies that there should be classes of temporaries corresponding to the register classes of the target machine so that the code generator can take advantage of the information otherwise available only to the semantic routine. This design decision makes the analysis phase of the compiler less independent of the target machine but enables a simple compiler to generate higher-quality code.

One-pass compilers without distinct code generators are also quite common. These compilers include code that makes all code generation decisions directly in the semantic routines. Some support routines that allocate registers and deal with details such as target machine addressing modes and instruction formats are used, but basic tasks such as instruction selection are performed directly in the semantic routines. These compilers might generate slightly better code or execute a bit more efficiently, but their lack of target machine independence makes them very hard to transport or retarget.

One-Pass Compiler Plus Peephole Optimization

An effective means of improving the code quality of a simple one-pass compiler is to add a peephole optimization pass. Peephole optimization is described in more detail in Chapter 15. For purposes of this discussion it is sufficient to know that such optimizers make a pass over the generated machine code, looking at only a few instructions at a time (thus the name), aiming to improve the output code by better instruction selection or more effective register and address mode utilization.

A peephole optimizer may be particularly effective at smoothing out "rough edges" between consecutive segments of code generated by different calls to the code generator. Use of a peephole optimizer allows the code generator to be somewhat simpler, because it can pay less attention to the context in which a code sequence is being generated.

One-Pass Analysis and IR Synthesis Plus a Code Generation Pass

One-pass analysis and IR synthesis plus a code generation pass is the organization assumed in the semantic routine outlines in Chapters 10–13. An explicit intermediate representation is required to serve as the interface to the code generator. The IR is typically a simple linear one, like the tuples we use. The major advantage of this organization over the single-pass approach is flexibility. The code generator may be a simple one that looks at one tuple at a time, as in the single-pass organization with peephole optimization just described. Alternatively, since an explicit intermediate representation exists, it may examine any number of tuples in order to make code generation decisions. More details of these code generation options will be presented in Chapter 15.

One flexibility advantage is the ability to add an IR optimization pass and greater independence of the target machine from the front-end. Addition of an optimizer would, of course, change the compiler to another organization—multipass synthesis. The major point is that the existence of an explicit intermediate representation allows such a change to be made with little or no impact on the existing front-end and code generator.

Keeping a front-end relatively independent of the target machine is advantageous because it makes retargeting a compiler as simple as possible. The target machine independence of the front-end is a function of the target machine independence of its interface with the code generator. A separate code generation pass strictly limits the interface to that provided by the intermediate representation. Thus, the machine independence of the IR defines the difficulty of retargeting a compiler constructed using this organization.

Multipass Analysis

The next two organization alternatives to be discussed are multipass analysis and multipass synthesis. As is obvious from their names, these are not options for organizing complete compilers but rather are for organizing analysis and synthesis components. They may be used together or in conjunction with simpler synthesis and analysis components.

Multipass analysis may be the organization of choice for any of a variety of reasons. Historically, multipass analysis was done in compilers that were required to fit into very constrained address spaces. In such a compiler, the scanner constitutes a pass by itself, producing a file representing a stream of tokens as a result of its analysis of the source program. Identifiers and constants are put into the symbol table by the scanner, so that only a minimal representation for them is required in the token file. The parser is also a separate pass, producing a stream of semantic actions to be invoked or some linearized representation of the parse tree that implicitly conveys the same information. As with the scanner, the output of the parser is saved on secondary storage. Declaration processing and static semantic checking, driven by the parser output, may be implemented in one or two passes, depending upon space constraints and the symbol table processing requirements of the language being compiled. Code or some IR is typically synthesized in the same pass as semantic checking. If an IR is used, simple linear forms like tuples and postfix are the most likely choices.

There are reasons other than space constraints for using some form of multipass analysis. Languages that do not require identifiers to be declared before they are used force such an organization, at least for static semantic checking purposes. The extreme form of multipass analysis described above, with its associated cost of reading and writing intermediate files, is not necessary. However, semantic processing must be partitioned so that a first pass builds the symbol table by processing all declarations, and then a second pass does checking and generates code or an IR. Scanning and parsing can be combined with the first semantic processing pass, in a style much like all of the single-pass analysis options. The interface between this pass and the second semantics pass is quite simple, consisting of the symbol table built by the first pass and a stream of semantic actions to be performed by the second pass, in the order they were generated by the parser. Tokens must also be available for actions that generate semantic records from token values. Thus, if the second pass directly generates code, a two-pass compiler organized along these lines needs to be slightly more complex than a single-pass one.

A final possible motivation for doing multipass analysis is to take advantage of the generality of a tree-structured intermediate representation. All of the analysis organizations described so far have been restricted to using information available during a single pass through a linearization of the parse tree. The availability of an explicit representation of the parse tree allows the use of less restrictive analysis techniques. For example, the specialized techniques for handling operator overloading, presented in Chapter 11, are necessary as a way to get around not having the full expression tree available.

In addition to simply making more information available, use of a tree-structured IR also facilitates use of more formalized semantic processing techniques based on attribute grammars. Using such an organization, scanning and parsing are typically combined into one pass that produces a syntax tree as its output. Semantic information, termed attributes, can be computed using rules associated with each node of the syntax tree. These rules specify not only the semantic values to be computed but also the limitations to be imposed by static semantic checking. One or more passes over the tree may be used to evaluate attributes and check semantic correctness.

The availability of an explicit syntax tree also has the advantage of allowing a complete separation of analysis and synthesis. The process described so far is purely analytic, in contrast to the previously discussed techniques, which mix static semantic checking with the synthesis of some IR or code. This separation is possible because the syntax tree that is the input IR to the semantic analysis phase, with the addition of attributes, also acts as an IR interface between analysis and synthesis.

Multipass Synthesis

As suggested earlier, multipass synthesis can be used with any of the single-pass or multipass analysis schemes just discussed. The only requirement is that some IR be available to drive the synthesis phase. The IR may be either linear or tree-structured.

The simplest multipass synthesis organization is a combination of a code generator and a peephole optimizer. Recall that peephole optimization is a machine-dependent final pass that attempts to improve the code produced by the code generator. This organization is illustrative of the fact that the components used to perform multipass synthesis are much less interdependent than multipass analysis components. In particular, the code generator can be completely unaware of the presence of a peephole optimizer.

A more complex back-end may be created by allowing one or more optimization passes to transform the IR before it is processed by the code generator. Typically, machine-independent optimizations are performed first on the IR. If full global optimization is included, multiple passes are usually required for this phase alone. A separate machine-dependent optimization phase may follow, or such optimizations may be included in the code generation pass. Regardless of what combination is used, however, optimizations are said to *transform* the IR because their output is usually in the same form of IR as their input, in contrast to other compiler phases that typically *translate* from one representation to another. This fact contributes to the typical lack of interdependence among the components of the back-end: Again the code generator need not be aware of the presence or absence of an optimizer.

As we discuss in Chapter 15, the code generator itself may involve one or more passes. Simple code generation algorithms operate quite adequately in a single pass. However, registers can often be allocated more effectively if more than one pass is used to handle the interdependence between register availability and code selection. Further, if a high-level, machine-independent IR is the input to the code generation phase, a pass to translate the IR to a lower-level, more machine-dependent form may be required. Such a step is most likely necessary if one of the machine specification-based code generation techniques (described in Chapter 15) is used.

Multilanguage and Multitargeted Compilers

Use of a standardized organization, usually multipass, in combination with an appropriate intermediate representation allows the construction of a *family* of compilers. A set of compilers for a particular language that use the same analysis and machine-independent optimization components while having distinct code generators targeted for different machines is one example of a family of compilers. This kind of family requires use of a relatively machine-independent IR. Several commercial Ada compilers are constructed this way. They use the Diana intermediate representation, which is a de facto standard IR for Ada and is strongly language-dependent but machine-independent. Construction of multitargeted compiler families is particularly facilitated by using a machine specification-based code generator.

Another kind of compiler family is a multilanguage family. Such a family involves use of a compiler organization based on a language-independent IR (in contrast to Diana). Front-ends for different languages are all constructed to generate the same IR. Common synthesis components are used to generate code for a particular target machine. The IR used by such a family is usually lower level (that is, more machine-oriented) than a language-dependent IR. We say machine-oriented rather than machine-dependent because the IR may be based on some virtual machine, such as a simple stack machine, rather than on any actual hardware. Use of a higher-level IR in a multilanguage family is also possible; however, such an IR can be difficult to define because it must be powerful enough to allow adequate expression of all the constructs of all source languages involved. Just as code generator generation tools facilitate the development of multitargeted families, front-end generation tools support multilanguage families. Such tools include the scanner and parser generators we have previously discussed, as well as more experimental tools, commonly based on attribute grammars, for semantic analysis generation.

The GNU C compiler, GCC (Stallman 1989), uses two intermediate forms. The first is a high-level, tree-oriented intermediate form. The second is called RTL, Register Transfer Language, which is more machine-oriented. GNU compiler front-ends translate a source language into the tree-like intermediate form, a language-independent routine translates the trees into RTL, and then machine-independent passes perform optimizations on the RTL. Finally, the RTL is turned into assembly language, which is optionally peephole optimized.

7.1.3. Parsing, Checking, and Translation in a Single Pass

The Micro compiler of Chapter 2 was structured such that scanning, parsing, and semantic processing (semantic checking and code generation) were interleaved. Such a relationship between these phases is required in any one-pass compiler. Even in a compiler that includes separate optimization and code generation passes, it may still be desirable to generate the intermediate representation used by these latter passes in a single pass. There are two principal advantages of such an approach: (1) The front-end of the compiler is simpler because no tree building or tree traversal code is required and (2) much less storage space is required to process a program if an entire syntax tree is not explicitly built. There are, naturally, some offsetting disadvantages. Not having a complete tree representation limits the amount of information immediately available to each semantic routine. Thus, some special techniques are required to overcome this limitation.

For our examples in the semantic processing chapters (Chapters 10–13), we assume that parsing and semantic processing are interleaved in a single pass. This assumption is motivated by a desire to keep our approach as simple as possible. The techniques we use can be easily generalized to work with an explicit syntax tree representation of a program.

The relationship between the scanner and the parser in a one-pass translator is very simple. The parser wants a stream of tokens from the scanner. Tokens can be produced by the scanner on demand, using its internal data structures and the source program. Thus the parser simply calls the scanner as a subprogram and receives a token as a result of the call. The parser/semantics relationship, as illustrated by the Micro compiler, is more complex. The presence of action symbols within the productions driving the parser causes the parser to call corresponding semantic routines as it parses the source program. Consider the following production describing an **if** statement:

       \<statement\> → **if** \<expression\> #start_if
                  then \<statement list\> **end if** #finish_if

This production specifies that two calls to the semantic routines `start_if()` and `finish_if()` are to occur at appropriate times as the parser processes an **if** statement. Which semantic routines to be called and when they are to be called are explicitly designated for each construct in the language handled by the compiler.

The semantic records produced by calls to semantic routines represent attributes associated with corresponding nodes of the syntax tree. Each different grammar symbol, including both terminals and nonterminals, has a distinct record containing information appropriate for that symbol. However, each occurrence of the same kind of symbol—each ID or <expression>, for example—stores exactly the same set of data in its semantic record. It is also possible for a symbol to have a null semantic record if it has no semantic data to store. For example, a symbol such as ; requires no semantic record.

Even though they never call one another explicitly, semantic routines communicate with one another implicitly through the semantic records they receive as parameters and produce as output. Semantic records for those terminals that do have associated semantic information are constructed by routines like **process_op()** and **process_id()** used in the Micro compiler in Chapter 2. They use the information provided by the scanner about a token to construct an appropriate record. The semantic record corresponding to a nonterminal is typically produced by a semantic routine that is called after the entire right-hand side of a production for the nonterminal is matched. This semantic record is created by a semantic routine that processes records corresponding to symbols in the right-hand side of the production. These records are passed to the semantic routine as parameters. *Processing* these records may include generating code or recording information in the symbol table, as well as constructing a new semantic record. Depending on whether recursive descent or table-driven parsing is used, semantic routines are called either by parsing routines or by a parser driver. In either case, some provision must be made for storing semantic records in between calls to semantic routines, for the routines do not call one another directly. In the Micro compiler in Chapter 2, we saw semantic records stored in local variables of parse routines until they were used as parameters in semantic routine calls. Alternatively, a table-driven parser must depend on an explicit data structure, a stack that we call the *semantic stack*, to hold the semantic records produced by semantic routines until they are used as parameters in successive calls. Figure 7.4 illustrates the effects on a semantic stack of the sequence of semantic routines called by a parser as it parses A := B + 1.

The semantic attribute evaluation that is possible when semantic processing is interleaved with parsing, using either a top-down or bottom-up parser, is restricted to that which is possible during a single post-order traversal of the parse tree. The sequence of parsing actions generated by either kind of parser provides sufficient information to build a parse tree, and it can be thought of as a linearization of the tree. Similarly, the sequence of semantic action calls generated during a parse corresponds to the order in which nodes would be visited and attributes evaluated in a post-order traversal of the tree. These observations point out exactly the disadvantage of interleaving parsing and semantic processing. Constructing an explicit syntax tree while parsing allows use of any information flow desired to support semantic processing. Interleaving the two phases requires that our semantic routines be designed to get their job done using only information available in a single post-order

process_id() produces an **expr_rec** for A

process_id() produces an **expr_rec** for B

process_op() produces an **op_rec** for +

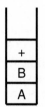

process_lit() produces an **expr_rec** for 1

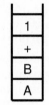

gen_infix() produces code and an **expr_rec** for B+1

gen_assign() produces code to assign B+1 to A and clears the stack

Figure 7.4   Semantic Stack Example   (Processing A := B + 1)

traversal. Whether such a design is even possible depends on the definition of the language being compiled.

7.2. Semantic Processing Techniques

7.2.1. LL Parsers and Action Symbols

The **if** statement production introduced in the previous section illustrates how action symbols may be used with a top-down parser to specify when particular semantic routines are to be called. Action symbols are not necessarily included in every production (some nonterminals have no semantic information associated with them) and thus corresponding productions have no impact on the evaluation of semantic attributes. The production for <statement list> is a good example of such a case. However, some productions, like the **if** statement production, may include more than one action symbol. Multiple action symbols most commonly occur in control structure productions because constructs like **case**, **if**, and **loop** statements require code to be generated at more than one point in the source code.

Specifying semantic routine calls via action symbols works particularly nicely in conjunction with an LL parser, as illustrated by the parsing routine in Figure 5.11. The action symbols are treated just like other grammar symbols and are pushed onto the parse stack when a production is predicted. Only a slight extension of the LL parsing algorithm is required to handle this new grammar symbol type. When an action symbol comes to the top of the stack, the parser simply calls the corresponding semantic routine rather than trying to take some parsing action.

The smooth fit of action symbols with LL parsing is due to the predictive nature of top-down parsing. A production is selected to expand the parse tree *before* the symbols corresponding to its right-hand side are processed by the parser, because an LL(k) parser looks ahead at, but does not consume, the first k symbols of the right-hand side in order to choose a production.

7.2.2. LR Parsers and Action Symbols

In contrast to the LL(k) approach, an LR(k) parser does not decide which production to apply until it has processed its entire right-hand side and looked k symbols beyond that. Because of this uncertainty, action symbols cannot be used to trigger semantic routine calls as right-hand side symbols are accepted by the parser. Two productions whose right-hand sides are identical except for action symbols might be under consideration at the same time. Rather, only after the parser uses the lookahead symbol(s) to choose the appropriate production does it become possible to call the correct semantic routines.

Again, considering the **if** statement production introduced previously,

<statement> → **if** <expression> #start_if
                     then <statement list> **end if** #finish_if

we realize that it is too late to call `start_if()` once we process the entire right-hand side. `start_if()` must generate a conditional jump between the code produced for <expression> and that for <statement list>. Generalizing this realization, it is clear that action symbols can be placed only at the very end of the right-hand side of a production to be used by an LR parser.

The **if** statement production must be rewritten as two separate productions in order to produce semantic routine calls at the right time in the parse. Thus, a new nonterminal must be introduced, corresponding to that part of the right-hand side up to and including the first action symbol. We use the following productions to specify this **if** statement to an LR parser.

<statement>→ <if head> **then** <statement list> **end if** #finish_if
<if head>→ **if** <expression> #start_if

The nonterminal <if head> is sometimes called a *semantic hook* because its presence in the grammar has no effect on the language accepted by the parser. It is used only to enable the parser to call **start_if()** at the right time, before processing the <statement list> that follows **then**.

A similar transformation is required even if there is only one action symbol in the right-hand side of a production if it is not at the end. Consider, for example, the Micro production for <program>, with the same transformation applied to it:

<program>→ #start **begin** <statement list> **end**

must become

<program>   → <program head> **begin** <statement list> **end**
<program head>   → #start

for **start()** to be called before the <statement list> is processed.

Some LR parser generators, most notably Yacc, allow semantic actions to be inserted anywhere within the right-hand side of productions. The transformation just described is then automatically performed by the parser generator whenever necessary.

An important property of this grammar transformation is that it has no impact on semantic routines. They are totally independent of the parsing technique used. The transformation and its inverse make it possible to generate the same sequence of semantic routine calls from either an LL or LR parser. Thus the semantic processing techniques that will be examined in Chapters 10-13 work equally well with either kind of parser. The grammar fragments used to present them can be transformed to accommodate either parsing technique.

Parser generators like Yacc that produce a whole parser rather than just parsing tables can allow arbitrary program code to be inserted in places where we have been showing semantic action symbols. This feature can be particularly useful for small translation jobs, because it allows syntax and semantics to be specified all in one place. For larger translators, like a compiler, this combination can become quite difficult to read unless the inserted semantic actions are limited to subprogram calls. Then the capabilities of the two kinds of generators are about the same, with the table generators being more flexible in that they do not force the use of a particular language for writing semantic actions.

7.2.3. **Semantic Record Representations**

As illustrated by the Micro compiler in Chapter 2, semantic records are parameters to semantic routines. The records accessed by a semantic routine contain the semantic information associated with symbols that have been processed by the parser prior to a call to the semantic routine. Each semantic routine receives some number of records as parameters and, optionally, produces one or more records to represent its results.

The Micro compiler was an example of semantic routine calls occurring within parsing routines. In Sections 7.2.1 and 7.2.2, we discussed how semantic routine calls can be triggered automatically by table-driven parsers. In the example compiler in Chapter 2, two different types of semantic records are used: **op_rec** and **expr_rec**. Local variables of the appropriate types were declared within parsing routines whenever one of these records needed to be temporarily saved for use in a later semantic routine call. When a table-driven parser is used, a semantic stack is required to temporarily save semantic records. Implementations of semantic stacks typically use a single semantic record type. However, the semantic stack entries for the various grammar symbols must include a variety of information.

When using an implementation language that supports strong type checking, the need to put dissimilar information into semantic stack entries can best be handled by using a variant record or type union. These features combine different types into a single type, which is exactly what we need to construct a semantic stack containing different information for the various grammar symbols. A particular advantage of using these features is that the various semantic record versions are explicitly spelled out in declarations, thus enhancing readability and allowing the compiler to perform type checking on the code that uses the records in the semantic stack.

The type declarations in Figure 7.5 illustrate this approach to semantic record definition for Micro. First, the type declarations from Chapter 2 that define the different kinds of semantic records are repeated. Then these are combined with an enumeration variable to make a structure called a **semantic_record** that defines all the alternative entries possible on the semantic stack. (As in Chapter 2, **expr_rec** is an anonymous union, a construct that is not part of standard C but one that we will use heavily in this and the following chapters.)

Error Handling

The semantic record declarations in Figure 7.5 assume that any semantic routine designed to return a semantic record will have something meaningful to put into it. When semantic errors are detected, this assumption is false. In a compiler for a language that requires declarations, for example, a semantic routine that looks up an identifier in the symbol table produces an error message if the identifier is not found or if the definition of the identifier does not fit its use. The semantic routine would normally produce a semantic record containing some information extracted from the symbol table entry. However, when an error is found, no such information is available.

```
#define MAXIDLEN        33
typedef char string[MAXIDLEN];

typedef struct operator {    /* for operators */
   enum op { PLUS, MINUS } operator;
} op_rec;

/* expression types */
enum expr { IDEXPR, LITERALEXPR, TEMPEXPR };

/* for <primary> and <expression> */
typedef struct expression {
   enum expr kind;
   union {
      string name;    /* for IDEXPR and TEMPEXPR */
      int val;        /* for LITERALEXPR */
   };
} expr_rec;

enum semantic_record_kind { OPREC, EXPRREC };

typedef struct sem_rec {
   enum semantic_record_kind record_kind;
   union {
      op_rec   op_record;      /* OPREC */
      expr_rec expr_record;    /* EXPRREC */
   };
} semantic_record;
```

Figure 7.5   `semantic_record` Declaration for Micro

A compiler that attempts to correct program errors might manufacture information for a semantic record to be used by later routines, but that approach runs the risk of causing a long series of meaningless, confusing errors to be reported. There is, however, a simple technique available that guarantees that only one error message will appear for each error the semantic routines detect. The technique requires that we define one additional semantic record kind that we will call **ERROR**. There need be no corresponding variant, for an **ERROR** record only alerts other semantic routines that an error has occurred and that no useful information is present. Thus our definition for **semantic_record** will be changed, as illustrated in Figure 7.6.

Any semantic routine that detects an error must produce an **ERROR** record instead of whatever semantic record it normally produces. Each routine must check the records it receives as parameters before attempting to use them to find whether any are **ERROR** records. If any of its parameters are **ERROR** records, it can skip all of its normal processing and simply return an **ERROR** record, if it normally produces a record. (Some static semantic

```
enum semantic_record_kind { OPREC, EXPRREC, ERROR };

typedef struct sem_rec {
    enum semantic_record_kind record_kind;
    union {
        op_rec   op_record;      /* OPREC */
        expr_rec expr_record;    /* EXPRREC */
        /* empty variant */      /* ERROR */
    };
} semantic_record;
```

Figure 7.6   semantic_record Declaration for Micro with Error Alternative

checking might still be possible if it uses only parameters other than the **ERROR** records, but looking for such possibilities significantly complicates semantic routines.) By this mechanism, all semantic routines consume and produce the same number of semantic records after an error has been detected, and an error indication is propagated until a semantic routine is reached, usually at the <statement> or <declaration> level, which does not produce a semantic record. Compilation of the rest of the program can then proceed normally, and only a single, appropriate error message will have been generated. (Usually, only further *analysis* is done, because generating code for a program with a serious error is probably not worth the trouble.)

7.2.4. **Implementing Action-controlled Semantic Stacks**

An important issue in the design of a stack-based semantic processing phase for a compiler is control of pushing and popping the stack and of passing stack entries as parameters to semantic routines. One approach is to make the stack directly accessible to the semantic action routines. Using this approach, the action routines take their parameters from the top of the stack rather than receiving them explicitly when they are called. Similarly, any semantic record produced by an action routine is pushed onto the semantic stack after the parameters are removed. A stack managed this way is called an *action-controlled* semantic stack.

The semantic stack can be implemented as either an array of records such as the **semantic_record** type defined in Section 7.2.3 or as a linked list of dynamically allocated records. The array approach requires that the maximum amount of space needed by any alternative be allocated for each element in the array. It also puts a fixed bound on the maximum depth to which the stack can grow (unless the implementation language supports dynamic resizing of arrays). However, pushing and popping the stack is quick; all that is required is changing an index variable that defines the top of the stack. The linked list approach, in contrast, allows the stack to grow virtually without bound, and just enough space may be allocated to satisfy the requirements of each individual entry. On the negative side, allocation and deallocation requirements make the push and pop operations much slower than using an array implementation. (The efficiency of these operations can be improved if all of the records are allocated with the maximum size, as in the array implementation, and records are saved for reuse when they are popped, instead of being given back to the dynamic storage manager.) Accessing anything other than the top element of the stack may also be more expensive if an array is not used.

An Example Semantic Stack Implementation

Although semantic routines always take their parameters from and leave their results on top of the semantic stack, within a particular routine the semantic stack is not necessarily treated as an abstract stack. A semantic routine may directly access all of the stack entries that serve as its parameters, because it knows where they are relative to the top of the stack. This approach avoids the copying cost of popping them individually for assignment to variables. Only at the end of the routine are the entries popped and discarded. Similarly, an entry just below those to be popped may be accessed, or even altered, and then left on the stack for further use. As a result of these considerations, an action-controlled semantic stack need not be defined as an abstract data structure. Rather, knowledge of its implementation may used pervasively by the semantic routines.

Figure 7.7 contains the definition of a semantic stack implementation for Micro that allows the stack to be used as described. It uses the **semantic_record** type declaration presented in Figure 7.6 plus the supporting declarations from Figure 7.5. Following these type declarations are the declarations of variables that are actually used to implement the semantic stack, an array and an index variable. Finally come two macros, **push()** and **pop()**, that may be used to manipulate the stack. They are not really necessary because the data structure is completely visible, but they are convenient for altering it. The bodies of the macros are not shown, because the implementation of **push()** and **pop()** is trivial.

```
#define MAXIDLEN        33
typedef char string[MAXIDLEN];

typedef struct operator {    /* for operators */
   enum op { PLUS, MINUS } operator;
} op_rec;

/* expression types */
enum expr { IDEXPR, LITERALEXPR, TEMPEXPR };

/* for <primary> and <expression> */
typedef struct expression {
   enum expr kind;
   union {
      string name;    /* for IDEXPR and TEMPEXPR */
      int val;        /* for LITERALEXPR */
```

```
        };
    } expr_rec;

    enum semantic_record_kind { OPREC, EXPRREC, ERROR };

    typedef struct sem_rec {
        enum semantic_record_kind record_kind;
        union {
            op_rec   op_record;    /* OPREC */
            expr_rec expr_record;  /* EXPRREC */
            /* empty variant */    /* ERROR */
        };
    } semantic_record;

    #define STACKLIMIT    100
    int top = -1;
    semantic_record sem_stack[STACKLIMIT];

    /*
     * Following are two macros that are not strictly
     * necessary since the semantic stack can be freely
     * manipulated by any routine that has access to this
     * header.  However, they do encapsulate some stack
     * manipulation details.
     */

    /*
     * Pushes entry onto the stack; if there is no room
     * generates a "stack full" fatal error.
     */
    #define push(entry)   {  · · ·  }

    /*
     * Removes number entries from the stack by
     * decrementing top. If stack has less than number
     * entries, generates a "stack empty" fatal error.
     */
    #define pop(number)   {  · · ·  }
```

Figure 7.7   An Action-controlled Semantic Stack

Abstract Semantic Stacks

Action-controlled semantic stacks have two disadvantages: (1) Their implementation is completely visible to the action routines, thus making changes in
implementation difficult, and (2) they require that action routines include code
to do semantic stack management. This latter point makes the action routines
more complex than the ones we saw in Chapter 2 (those routines had a very
simple interface to the rest of the compiler through their parameters). This

problem can be solved in two ways. If an appropriate parser generator is available, a *parser-controlled* semantic stack may be used. This technique is described in Section 7.2.5. Alternatively, parameter-driven action routines may be used if they are not called directly by the parser but by intermediate routines that handle the stack manipulation. These intermediate routines are the ones invoked by the parser.

With either approach, it may be appropriate to use an abstract interface to the semantic stack, like the one in Figure 7.8(a). (Figure 7.8(b) contains a corresponding implementation.) This routine differs from the routines of Figure 7.7 in that the implementation of the semantic stack is hidden in actual procedures, which are defined elsewhere. Thus we achieve a cleaner interface between the semantic routines and the semantic stack, but we give up the ability (which we no longer want anyway) to access entries while they are still on the stack. To access an entry, it is necessary to call **pop()**, which will result in the top entry being copied to some variable designated by the calling routine. This copying makes the abstract stack less efficient than using the one we first presented. However, the abstract approach makes it simple to switch from an array to a linked implementation of the stack, a change that would be quite complex using the first version.

```
/* Header file to be included by the action routines.
 */
      .
      .
      .
  /* semantic_record and related type
   * declarations go here.
   */
    .
    .
    .
/*
 * Pushes entry onto the stack; if there is
 * no room, generates a "stack full" fatal error
 */
extern void push(const semantic_record entry);

/*
 * Removes number entries from the stack by
 * decrementing top. If stack has less than number
 * entries, generates a "stack empty" fatal error.
 */
extern semantic_record pop(void);
```

Figure 7.8(a) An Abstract Semantic Stack Interface

```
/* In a separate source file. */

#define STACKLIMIT    100
static int top = -1;
static semantic_record sem_stack[STACKLIMIT];

void push(const semantic_record entry)
{
   if (top >= STACKLIMIT-1)
      fatal_error("semantic stack overflow");
   else
      sem_stack[++top] = entry;
}

semantic_record pop(void)
{
   if (top < 0)
      fatal_error("semantic stack underflow");
   else
      return sem_stack[top--];
}
```

Figure 7.8(b) An Abstract Semantic Stack Implementation

7.2.5. Parser-controlled Semantic Stacks

Action-controlled semantic stacks suffer from the disadvantage that in addition to the rest of their work, each semantic routine must also push and pop appropriate information. The semantic stack grows and shrinks depending on how action routines are programmed, meaning its changes are only loosely related to those of the parse stack. The designer of semantic routines must assume or verify that the appropriate records are on top of the semantic stack as each routine starts and that each routine leaves the semantic stack in the right form. This extra complexity can be removed from the semantic routines by letting the parser control the semantic stack.

LR Parser-controlled Semantic Stacks

At any given point in the process of matching the right-hand side of a production, the parse stack of an LR parser contains one entry for each symbol, terminal or nonterminal, matched so far. For the parser to control the semantic stack, it need only add space in the parse stack entries for semantic records or provide a parallel stack for semantic records. Using this technique the semantic stack will have an entry for *every* matched grammar symbol, including those with null semantic records. They are all popped off the semantic stack when the corresponding right-hand side symbols are popped off the parse stack. Some semantic action must be specified for *every* production; this action must define a semantic record value to be stored corresponding to the left-hand side nonterminal when it is pushed onto the stack.

The Yacc parser generator described in Chapter 6 is a well-known example of a parser generator that provides such a parser-controlled semantic stack mechanism. In the actions that a programmer writes as part of Yacc rules, the semantic records corresponding to right-hand side symbols can be referenced using pseudovariables named **$1**, **$2**, and so on. The semantic value for the left-hand side nonterminal is defined by assigning it the pseudovariable **$$**. If there is no action specified for a production, Yacc automatically generates an assignment of the value of **$1** to **$$**.

LL Parser-controlled Semantic Stacks

An LL parse stack contains predicted symbols rather than symbols already parsed, so it is not possible to use a parallel stack mechanism like the one used by LR parsers to manage the semantic stack. The parser pushes and pops the parse stack as it predicts nonterminals and matches terminals, but the semantic stack must work differently because semantic information about a symbol must, in general, be maintained after the symbol has been matched.

Whenever a production is predicted, not only are symbols (terminals, nonterminals, and action symbols) pushed onto the parse stack, but new entries are also pushed onto the semantic stack for each terminal and nonterminal on the right-hand side of the production. Whenever a production is finished, its right-hand side semantic records are popped. The left-hand side semantic record remains; the left-hand side of the production that just finished is a member of the right-hand side of the production that predicted it. In fact, clever management of the semantic stack allows use of the very same entry for the left-hand side of the current production and the element of the right-hand side of the previous production. Thus, it is not necessary to copy any semantic records as productions terminate.

The parser always maintains several indices into the semantic stack. One, **left_index**, points to the entry that stores the semantic record for the symbol on the left-hand side of the current production. Similarly, **right_index** points to the entry for the first element on the right-hand side. The semantic records for other elements on the right-hand side can be found on the semantic stack at locations **right_index+1**, **right_index+2**, and so on. **current_index** points to the element on the right-hand side that is currently being expanded. Finally, **top_index** points to the first free entry at the top of the semantic stack.

For the parser to tell when a production has been finished, a new kind of parse stack entry is used. Up to now, parse stack entries were terminals, nonterminals, or action symbols. The **lldriver()** routine in Chapter 5 makes this assumption. Our new entry is called *end of production*, **EOP**. Old values of **left_index**, **right_index**, **current_index**, and **top_index** are stored in the **EOP** entry. Actual implementations may use a separate stack for these values, but it is convenient to assume that they are stored in the **EOP** entry. Figure 7.9 shows a version of **lldriver()** that incorporates these extensions for managing a semantic stack.

When the parser is controlling the semantic stack, semantic routines can

```
void lldriver(void)
{
    int left_index = -1, right_index = -1;
    int current_index, top_index;

    /*
     * Push the Start Symbol onto
     * an empty parse stack.
     */
    push(s);

    /* Initialize the semantic stack. */
    current_index = 0;
    top_index = 1;

    while (! stack_empty() ) {
       /* Let a be the current input token. */
       X = pop();

       if (is_nonterminal(X)
           && T[X][a] = X → Y₁ · · · Yₘ) {
          /* Expand nonterminal */
          Push EOP(left_index, right_index,
              current_index, top_index) on the parse stack;
          Push Yₘ · · · Y₁ on the parse stack;
          left_index = current_index;
          right_index = top_index;
          top_index += m;
          /* m is the number of non-action symbols */
          current_index = right_index;
       } else if (is_terminal(X) && X == a) {
          Place token information from scanner
              in sem_stack[current_index];
          current_index++;
          scanner(& a);    /* Get next token */
       } else if (X == EOP) {
          Restore left_index, right_index, current_index,
              top_index from the EOP symbol;
          /* Move to next symbol in RHS */
          /* of previous production */
          current_index++;
       } else if (is_action_symbol(X))
          Call Semantic Routine corresponding to X;
       else
          /* Process syntax error */
    }
}
```

Figure 7.9   `lldriver()` Including Semantic Stack Management

<program>	→ #start **begin** <statement list> **end**
<statement list>	→ <statement> <statement tail>
<statement tail>	→ <statement> <statement tail>
<statement tail>	→ λ
<statement>	→ <ident> := <expression> ; #assign($1,$3)
<statement>	→ **read** (<id list>) ;
<statement>	→ **write** (<expr list>) ;
<id list>	→ <ident> #read_id($1) <id tail>
<id tail>	→ , <ident> #read_id($2) <id tail>
<id tail>	→ λ
<expr list>	→ <expression> #write_expr($1) <expr tail>
<expr tail>	→ , <expression> #write_expr($2) <expr tail>
<expr tail>	→ λ
<expression>	→ <primary> #copy($1,$2) <primary tail> #copy($2,$$)
<primary tail>	→ <add op> <primary> #gen_infix($$,$1,$2,$3)
	<primary tail> #copy($3,$$)
<primary tail>	→ λ
<primary>	→ (<expression>) #copy($2,$$)
<primary>	→ <ident> #copy($1,$$)
<primary>	→ INTLITERAL #process_literal($$)
<add op>	→ PLUSOP #process_op($$)
<add op>	→ MINUSOP #process_op($$)
<ident>	→ ID #process_id($$)
<system goal>	→ <program> $ #finish

Figure 7.10   Micro Grammar with Parameterized Action Symbols

be explicitly parameterized by the semantic records they use for input and output. The semantic routines in Chapter 2 were of such a form, except that their parameters were not of the general **semantic_record** type. We need a notation to tell the parser which semantic stack entries should be passed as parameters to the semantic routines. To provide this information, we enhance our action symbols by allowing them to be suffixed by a list of semantic record references using the same syntax as that used by Yacc. Thus **$$** will designate the semantic stack entry at **left_index**, **$1** will refer to the entry at **right_index**, **$2** will refer to the entry at **right_index+1**, and so forth.

We also need a convention that tells where we store semantic information while we parse a production. Initial information is stored in the semantic record for the left-hand side. Before we parse a nonterminal we transfer any necessary semantic information into the semantic record for that nonterminal so it will be ready when that nonterminal is treated as a left-hand side. After the entire right-hand side of a production has been finished, we store any resulting semantic information in the semantic record for the left-hand side because the semantic stack for the right-hand side is about to disappear.

Figure 7.10 presents the Micro grammar again, with specification of stack entry parameters to action routines, for use with a parser-controlled semantic stack. It is written in standard BNF rather than extended BNF to facilitate positional specification of semantic stack entries as parameters to action routines.

Figure 7.11 illustrates how the semantic stack is built as productions are predicted by an LL(1) parser. The entries in the semantic stack are labeled by the grammar symbols they represent rather than by the semantic record version they contain. Part (a) shows the state of the parse and semantic stacks after the start symbol <system goal> has been pushed onto the parse stack, and the productions <system goal> → <program> $ #finish and <program> → #start **begin** <statement list> **end** have been predicted. Part (b) shows the

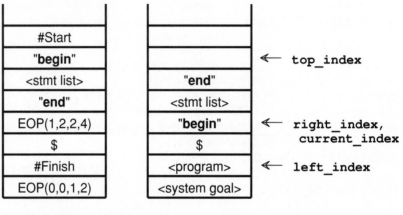

Parse Stack   Semantic Stack

Figure 11(a) Stacks Just After Predicting:
<program> → #start **begin** <statement list> **end**

Parse Stack   Semantic Stack

Figure 7.11(b)   Stacks Just After Predicting:
<statement list> → <statement> <statement tail>

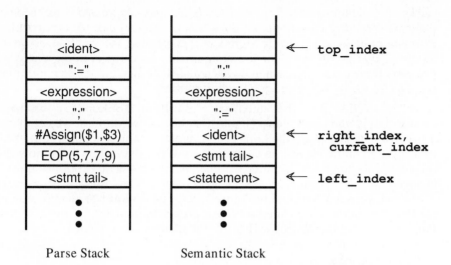

Parse Stack   Semantic Stack

Figure 11(c) Stacks Just After Predicting:
<statement> → <ident> := <expression> ; #assign($1,$3)

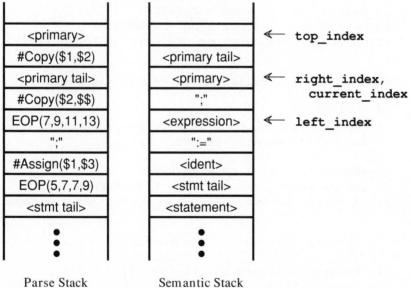

Parse Stack   Semantic Stack

Figure 7.11(d)   Stacks Just After Predicting:
<expression> → <primary> #copy($1,$2) <primary tail> #copy($2,$$)

state of the stacks after **start()** has been called, **begin** has been matched, and <statement list> has been expanded. Part (c) shows the expansion of <statement> as an assignment statement, and part (d) shows the state of the stacks after <ident> and := have been matched and <expression> has been expanded. The entry for <ident> on the semantic stack in part (d) is particularly interesting. It is semantically significant, containing information about the identifier that is the target of the assignment. Its corresponding entry was popped off the parse stack when it was matched earlier, but the semantic entry remains for use by the **assign()** action routine.

The code for the auxiliary routines **lookup()**, **enter()**, **check_id()**, and **get_temp()** and for the action routines **start()** and **finish()** can be exactly the same as in Chapter 2. The semantic routines that produced semantic records in Chapter 2 were written as functions; now they must be procedures with pointer parameters. All the action routines must be changed to take parameters of the generalized type **semantic_record**. These changes are illustrated in Figure 7.12. (The **assert()** macros guarantee that the routines are called with the proper parameters. If the assertions fail, the compiler should exit with an "internal error" diagnostic.)

```
#include <assert.h>

void process_id(semantic_record *id_record)
{
 /* Declare ID & build corresponding semantic record */
 check_id(token_buffer);
 id_record->record_kind = EXPRREC;
 id_record->expr_record.kind = IDEXPR;
 strcpy(id_record->expr_record.name, token_buffer);
}

void process_literal(semantic_record *id_record)
{
 /*
  * Convert literal to a numeric representation
  * and build semantic record.
  */
 id_record->record_kind = EXPRREC;
 id_record->expr_record.kind = LITERALEXPR;
 sscanf(token_buffer, "%d", &id_record->expr_record.val);
}

void process_op(semantic_record *op)
{
  /* Produce operator descriptor. */
  op->record_kind = OPREC;
  if (current_token == PLUSOP)
     op->op_record.operator = PLUS;
  else
     op->op_record.operator = MINUS;
}
```

```c
void gen_infix(const semantic_record e1,
               const semantic_record op,
               const semantic_record e2,
               semantic_record *result)
{
  assert(e1.record_kind == EXPRREC);
  assert(op.record_kind = OPREC);
  assert(e2.record_kind == EXPRREC);

  /* Result is an expr_rec with temp variant set. */
  result->record_kind = EXPRREC;
  result->expr_record.kind = TEMPEXPR;

  /*
   * Generate code for infix operation.
   * Get result temp and semantic record for result.
   */
  strcpy(result->expr_record.name, get_temp());
  generate(extract(op), extract(e1), extract(e2),
           result->expr_record.name);
}

void assign(const semantic_record target,
            const semantic_record source)
{
  assert(target.record_kind == EXPRREC);
  assert(target.expr_record.kind = IDEXPR);
  assert(source.record_kind == EXPRREC);

  /* Generate code for assignment. */
  generate("Store", extract(source),
           target.expr_record.name, "");
}

void read_id(const semantic_record in_var)
{
  assert(in_var.record_kind == EXPRREC);
  assert(in_var.expr_record.kind = IDEXPR);

  /* Generate code for read. */
  generate("Read", in_var.expr_record.name,
           "Integer", "");
}

void write_expr(const semantic_record out_expr)
{
  assert(out_expr.record_kind == EXPRREC);

  generate("Write", extract(out_expr),
           "Integer", "");
}
```

```
/*
 * Copy information from one part of
 * the Semantic Stack to another
 */
void copy(semantic_record *source,
          semantic_record *dest)
{
  *dest = *source;
}
```

Figure 7.12   Modified Action Routines for Micro

These semantic routines make no implicit assumptions about the contents of the semantic stack, nor do they manipulate the stack in any way. The actions embedded in the grammar look more complex than the ones we specified in the Micro grammar in Chapter 2, which could utilize an action-controlled semantic stack. We seem to have more actions, and these actions often just copy semantic records from one location on the stack to another. Actually, all these copies can be performed by pointer manipulations instead of copying if we implement our semantic stack appropriately, so the parser-controlled mechanism is not necessarily less efficient except for the extra procedure calls. The fact that it is easier to program correctly may outweigh the minor inefficiency it introduces.

One apparent drawback to using an LL parser-controlled semantic stack is that the stack may grow very large. For example, if a program has 100 statements, and we use the Micro grammar in Figure 7.10, the semantic stack will require at least 200 entries because of the recursive production for constructing <statement tail>. This stack growth is undesirable because no semantic processing is done with these entries. The problem can be surmounted if our parser generator recognizes nonterminals for which the semantic record is never used. Such nonterminals are easily recognized: Either there are no action symbols in any of their productions or the action symbols in their productions never use **$$** as a parameter. In the grammar in Figure 7.10, <statement list> and <id list> are examples of such nonterminals. Once these nonterminals have been identified, the parser generator will, in effect, insert a new kind of action symbol before the last nonterminal in each of their productions, providing that no action symbols follow that nonterminal. This new symbol, which we will call reuse, tells the parser driver that the semantic information stored with the left-hand side of the current production is not needed, and so the expansion of the following nonterminal may reuse the same portion of the semantic stack. For example, the Micro grammar has the productions:

<statement list> → <statement> <statement tail>
<statement tail> → <statement> <statement tail>
<statement tail> → λ

No semantic information is associated with either <statement tail> or <statement list>. When the parser is matching <statement list>, it can reuse the semantic stack space reserved for the symbols on the right-hand side of the <statement list> production when it expands <statement tail>. The same sort of reuse of previously reserved semantic stack space is appropriate for the recursive expansion of <statement tail>. Thus the reuse symbol would be inserted as shown here:

<statement list> → <statement> #reuse <statement tail>
<statement tail> → <statement> #reuse <statement tail>
<statement tail> → λ

An extra case within the main loop of **lldriver()** to handle reuse is illustrated by the following code:

```
else if (X == reuse) {
    /* Let X be the new top stack symbol. */
    if (T[X][a] == X → Y₁ · · · Yₘ) {
        /* Expand nonterminal */
        Push EOP(left_index, right_index,
            current_index, top_index) on the
            parse stack;
        Push Yₘ · · ·  Y₁ on the parse stack;
        top_index = right_index + m;
        /* m is the number of nonaction symbols */
        current_index = right_index;
    } else
        /* Process syntax error */
}
```

Evaluation

Parser-controlled stacks mesh so well with LR parsing that it is hard to argue against their use with such parsers. The successful integration of these concepts in Yacc demonstrates the simplicity and utility of the combination. The situation is not as clear for LL parsers. The relationship of a parser-controlled semantic stack to the parse stack is more complex for an LL parser than for an LR parser. Thus parser generators that support parser-controlled stacks for LL parsers are rare.

The advantage of parser-controlled stacks in either case is that the semantic routines need not make any implicit assumptions about the contents of the semantic stack, nor must they manipulate the stack in any way. However, more actions must be embedded in the grammar for parser-controlled stacks than in that for action-controlled semantic stacks. The additional actions simply copy semantic records from one location on the stack to another. All of this copying could be performed by pointer manipulations if the semantic stack were implemented appropriately, but this might have other performance implications. The fact that parser-controlled stacks make the semantic routines easier to program correctly must be weighed against the minor inefficiency they introduce.

Finally, use of a parser-controlled semantic stack restricts just how information can be represented in the stack. For example, lists of items corresponding to the single nonterminal, like <identifier list>, can be represented by multiple stack entries using action-controlled stacks. In contrast, each nonterminal is limited to a single stack entry in a parser-controlled stack, requiring use of storage external to the stack itself for the information associated with such nonterminals.

7.3. **Intermediate Representations and Code Generation**

7.3.1. **Intermediate Representations versus Direct Code Generation**

In designing semantic routines and code generators, we must decide whether to generate some intermediate representation (such as quadruples, triples, or trees) or to generate target machine code directly. Both choices have some advantages. The advantages of using intermediate representations include the following

- The target machine is abstracted to some virtual machine. Programming language-oriented primitives like **Open Block** and **Call Procedure** are frequently part of the virtual machine interface. This abstraction helps to separate high-level operations from their possibly low-level, machine-dependent realizations.

- Code generation and, usually, assignment of temporaries to registers are clearly separated from semantic routines, which deal only with the abstraction presented by the intermediate representation. Target-machine dependencies are more carefully isolated to the code generation routines.

- Optimization can be done at the intermediate representation level. This organization helps make optimization largely independent of the target machine, making complex optimization routines more transportable. Because intermediate representations are by design more abstract and uniform, optimization routines can be simpler.

The advantages of generating target code directly include the following

- The overhead of a probable extra pass to translate an internal representation to target code is avoided.

- A conceptually simple one-pass compilation model for suitable programming languages is allowed.

Intermediate representations are of real value if optimization or transportability is an important issue. If these issues are not important, the simplicity of direct generation is preferable.

Extreme care is needed to isolate and parameterize target-machine details. Addressing modes and data sizes, whether or not registers exist, efficiency of operations, and so forth are *all* target machine-dependent. Moreover, if the original design does not ease transport, then later modifications to move a compiler can be extremely difficult and expensive, because all machine dependencies must be found and rooted out.

7.3.2. Forms of Intermediate Representations

A wide variety of intermediate representations have been used for various reasons in the history of compilers. Perhaps the simplest is *postfix notation*, which was well known in mathematics as a parenthesis-free notation for arithmetic expressions long before it was ever used in compilers. As the name implies, postfix notation is a representation in which operators appear *after* the operands to which they apply. The examples in Figure 7.13 illustrate the correspondence between simple programming language expressions and statements and their postfix representations.

The major attractions of postfix notation are the simplicity of the translation process and the conciseness of the representation. These factors make it particularly useful as an intermediate representation for driving an interpreter. In fact, postfix is not particularly effective as input to an optimizer or to a code generator unless the ultimate target machine has a stack architecture.

The next class of IRs we consider is sometimes referred to as *three-address codes*. The IRs in this class are effectively generalized assembly code for a virtual three-address machine. That is, each "instruction" consists of an operator and three addresses, two for operands and one for a result location. The class includes a number of slightly different representations, the most prominent of which are known as *triples* and *quadruples*. The major difference between these notations and postfix is that they include explicit references to results of intermediate computations, whereas with postfix these results are implicitly referenced from a stack. The difference between triples and quadruples is that with triples the intermediate values are referenced by the number of the triple that created them, but quadruples require that they be given explicit names. Using the assignment statement example from Figure 7.13, we get the representation in triples and quadruples shown in Figure 7.14. (A dash, the symbol —, is used in quadruples and triples to denote an unused operand.)

Triples have the obvious advantage of being more concise, but their positional dependency makes optimizations that involve moving or deleting code substantially more complex. Both forms encode the same information as the postfix representation, but triples and quadruples are considerably more convenient for the next translation step, production of target machine code. In the

Infix	Postfix
a + b	a b +
a + b * c	a b c * +
(a + b) * c	a b + c *
a := b * c + b * d	a b c * b d * + :=

Figure 7.13   Postfix Representation Examples

Triples	Quadruples
(1) (*, b, c)	(1) (*, b, c, t1)
(2) (*, b, d)	(2) (*, b, d, t2)
(3) (+, (1), (2))	(3) (+, t1, t2, t3)
(4) (:=, (3), a)	(4) (:=, t3, a, —)

Figure 7.14   Three-Address Representation—Example 1

simplest case, code generation can be pictured as little more than a macro expansion process, with the locations of variables and temporaries acting as parameters to macros for each possible operator.

The triples and quadruples in Figure 7.14 do not actually contain enough information to do code generation by macro expansion. The names that appear as operands presumably stand for symbol table entries, which must be referenced in order to discover the types of the operands, as well as their addresses. The operand types must then be used to determine the actual instructions needed to implement the symbolic operators (+ and *). A slightly more detailed representation might be used if code generator simplicity is the main consideration. In the example in Figure 7.15, presume that a and d are real variables and that b and c are integers. Assume also that this is a Pascal statement, so that this mixture of types is allowed.

The major difference between the three-address examples is that the first is, like postfix, virtually a syntactic *transformation* of the input, whereas the second represents much more of a *translation* based on the semantics of the programming language. In either case, it is assumed that static semantic checking has been done on the input, so that the code generator need not worry about dealing with such problems as undefined variables and type compatibility errors. If such checking is indeed done, then no extra work is necessary to identify specific operators in the IR, as illustrated in Figure 7.15.

a := b * c + b * d

Triples	Quadruples
(1) (MULTI, Addr(b), Addr(c))	(1) (MULTI, Addr(b), Addr(c), t1)
(2) (FLOAT, Addr(b), —)	(2) (FLOAT, Addr(b), t2, —)
(3) (MULTF, (2), Addr(d))	(3) (MULTF, t2, Addr(d), t3)
(4) (FLOAT, (1) —)	(4) (FLOAT, t1, t4, —)
(5) (ADDF, (4), (3))	(5) (ADDF, t4, t3, t5)
(6) (:=, (5), Addr(a))	(6) (:=, t5, Addr(a), —)

Figure 7.15   Three-Address Representation—Example 2

a := b * c + b * d

(1) (MULTI, Addr(b), Addr(c), t1)
(2) (FLOAT, Addr(b), t2)
(3) (MULTF, t2, Addr(d), t3)
(4) (FLOAT, t1, t4)
(5) (ADDF, t4, t3, t5)
(6) (:=, t5, Addr(a))

Figure 7.16   Tuple Representation Example

Triples and quadruples, like postfix notation, are basically expression-oriented. The number of operands they allow is not necessarily ideal for other uses. The assignment operator in the quadruple example, for instance, has one unused operand. An unconditional branch would need only one operand using either notation. Thus, it is useful to generalize the quadruple concept to allow *tuples* with a varying number of operands, depending on the operator. Returning again to our assignment statement example, Figure 7.16 illustrates a corresponding tuple representation.

As suggested at the beginning of this chapter, structures based on parse trees are the most general intermediate representations. Trees were first used to represent expressions within individual statements for code generation purposes. For certain classes of target machines, there are optimal code generation algorithms for expressions based on tree or directed acyclic graph (DAG) representations. (Such algorithms are discussed in Chapter 15.) More recently, this concept of expression trees has been generalized to abstract syntax tree representations of entire programs.

Use of an abstract syntax tree can effectively unify several different aspects of compilation that require some form of intermediate representation. For example, some languages require multipass processing to do static semantic checking because identifier uses might occur textually before corresponding declarations. In such a case, the first pass over the program, including parsing and scanning, can produce a tree and also a symbol table. The second pass, to propagate attributes and do static semantic checking, is then simply a tree traversal. Machine-independent optimizations implemented as tree transformations could be done by another traversal pass. Finally, another tree traversal can generate code directly or produce a different (simpler) representation more appropriate for a particular machine-dependent code generator or optimizer.

Thus we see abstract syntax trees as a multiuse representation, possibly for semantic analysis, optimization, and code generation. In fact, their use can go even further. Many Ada implementations are based on a particular abstract syntax *representation* called Diana. Diana is meant to be used not only within the compiler as described but also as a program library representation of separately compiled units (packages and procedures) and as a common interface to other tools. We called Diana an abstract syntax representation rather than an abstract syntax *tree* representation because it is actually a DAG rather than a true tree. Abstract syntax trees are discussed further in Chapter 14.

7.3.3. A Tuple Language

The semantic routine outlines in Chapters 10-13 will generate tuples as an intermediate representation. Here we define a tuple language for use in those chapters. The tuples for the list of operators in Figure 7.17 include operands and have the standard interpretation defined by

RESULT := ARG1 OP ARG2

The relational and logical operators return 1 for true and 0 for false.

ADDI	ADDF	SUBI	SUBF	MULTI	MULTF	DIVI
DIVF	MOD	REM	EXPI	EXPF	AND	OR
XOR	EQ	NE	GT	GE	LT	LE

Figure 7.17   Standard Three-Address Tuple Operators

The tuples for the operators listed in Figure 7.18 have special interpretations and a varying number of operands, as defined in the figure.

UMINUS	ARG2 := −ARG1
NOT	ARG2 := not ARG1
ASSIGN	ARG3 := ARG1, size is ARG2
FLOAT	ARG2 := FLOAT(ARG1) [ARG1 in an integer]
ADDRESS	ARG2 := the address of ARG1
RANGETEST	abort execution if ARG3 < ARG1 or ARG3 > ARG2
LABEL	ARG1 is used to label the next tuple

JUMP	jump to tuple labeled ARG1
JUMP0	jump to ARG2 if ARG1 = 0
JUMP1	jump to ARG2 if ARG1 = 1
CASEJUMP	ARG1 is case selector expression
CASELABEL	ARG1 is a case statement label
CASERANGE	ARG1 is lower bound of label range,
	ARG2 is upper bound of range
CASEEND	no arguments, end of case statement
PROCENTRY	enter subprogram at nesting level ARG1
PROCEXIT	exit subprogram at nesting level ARG1
STARTCALL	ARG1 is temporary to reference activation record
REFPARAM	ARG1 is actual parameter
	ARG2 is parameter offset
	ARG3 is reference to activation record
COPYIN	ARG1 is actual parameter
	ARG2 is parameter offset
	ARG3 is reference to activation record
COPYOUT	ARG1 is actual parameter
	ARG2 is parameter offset
	ARG3 is reference to activation record
COPYINOUT	ARG1 is actual parameter
	ARG2 is parameter offset
	ARG3 is reference to activation record
PROCJUMP	ARG1 is subprogram start address (a label)
	ARG2 is reference to activation record

Figure 7.18   Special Interpretation Tuple Operators

As an example of how some of these tuples are used, consider the program and corresponding tuples in Figure 7.19. For simplicity, tuple operators for reading and writing integers are assumed in this example.

begin	(READI, A)
read(A,B);	(READI, B)
if A > B **then**	(GT, A, B, t1)
C := A + 5;	(JUMP0, t1, L1)
else	(ADDI, A, 5, C)
C := B + 5;	(JUMP, L2)
end if;	(LABEL, L1)
write(2 $*$ (C - 1));	(ADDI, B, 5, C)
end	(LABEL, L2)
	(SUBI, C, 1, t2)
	(MULTI, 2, t2, t3)
	(WRITEI, t3)

Figure 7.19   Tuple Example

Exercises

1. The discussion of syntax-directed translation in Section 7.1 is based on the assumption that an abstract syntax tree can be constructed from the sequence of parse actions generated by a parser as it parses a program. An abstract syntax tree is not a literal parse tree, but it contains the "semantically useful" details of the corresponding parse tree.

   (a) Give an algorithm for constructing a *parse tree* from the sequence of actions generated by an LL or LR parser.

   (b) Explain how this algorithm would have to be changed to produce an *abstract syntax tree* instead.

2. Examine a programming language you know well in light of the discussion of compiler organization alternatives in Section 7.1.2. Explain how particular features of the language make the alternatives especially appropriate or inappropriate for compiling that language.

3. The discussion of semantic error handling in Section 7.2.3 described standard actions to be taken by every semantic routine to deal with the possibility that one or more of its inputs might be an **ERROR** record. Outline an algorithm for a code preprocessor that would take as input a semantic routine without error handling code and would add the appropriate code to handle **ERROR** records.

4. One distinct disadvantage of implementing a semantic stack as an array is the possibility of stack overflow due to the fixed size of the array. Despite this disadvantage, arrays are used more often than linked lists for semantic stack implementation because of their simplicity and because the **push()** and **pop()** operations are more efficient than using a list of dynamically allocated semantic records. Design an alternative semantic stack implementation that handles stacks of any number of elements but is close to the efficiency of an array as long as the number of records on the stack stays below some fixed number. Analytically or empirically compare the performance of your implementation with that of an array implementation.

5. Add an **if** statement production like the one in Section 7.1.3 to the parser-controlled stack grammar for Micro in Figure 7.10. The following information should be used as a basis for parameterizing the action symbols:

   • The **start_if()** action routine requires the semantic record associated with <expression> as input and leaves information in the semantic record associated with **then**.

   • **finish_if()** uses the output of **start_if()** as input and produces no semantic record.

   Also add an **if** statement production that includes an **else** part. A new action routine will have to be introduced that uses the output of **start_if()** as input and leaves its output for **finish_if()**.

6. Design an algorithm to rewrite productions with internal action symbols to make them usable by an LR parser. (See Section 7.2.2.)

7. Trace the contents of a parser-controlled semantic stack driven by an LL or LR parser using the productions in Figure 7.10 as the following Micro program is compiled:

```
begin
  A := 5;
  B := A - 2;
  C := 1 - (A + B);
end
```

8. Translate the program from Exercise 7 into postfix, triples, and tuples, as in Section 7.3.2.

CHAPTER 8

Symbol Tables

A *symbol table* is a mechanism that associates values, or *attributes*, as we call them, with *names*. Because these attributes are a representation of the meaning (or semantics) of the names with which they are associated, a symbol table is sometimes called a *dictionary*. A symbol table is a necessary component of a compiler because the definition of a name appears in only one place in a program, its declaration, whereas the name may be used in any number of places within the program text. Each time a name is used, the symbol table provides access to the information collected about the name when its declaration was processed. Even in a language like FORTRAN, which does not require explicit declarations, the first occurrence of a name plays the part of a declaration for purposes of building a symbol table entry for the name. Such a first occurrence also results in an immediate use of the symbol entry thus constructed. A symbol table is an integral part of semantic processing, regardless of whether the compiler organization is single pass or multipass.

8.1. A Symbol Table Interface

Two aspects of symbol tables are of interest to us: the operations associated with a symbol table, which are visible to other components of the compiler, and the implementation of those operations. This chapter is mainly concerned with implementation issues, but we first consider an *abstract definition* of a symbol table in order to describe the operations we will be implementing. Our symbol table interface is defined by the definitions and declarations in Figure 8.1. Conventionally, these definitions and declarations would be grouped together in a header file to define the symbol table "package."

```c
typedef char string[MAXSTRING];

typedef struct symtab {
    . . .
} *symbol_table;     /* a pointer */

typedef struct id_entry {
    . . .
} id_entry;

/* Create a new (empty) symbol table. */
extern symbol_table create(void);

/* Remove all entries in table and destroy it. */
extern void destroy(symbol_table table);

/*
 * Enter name in table; return a reference to the
 * entry corresponding to name and a flag to
 * indicate whether the name was already present.
 */
extern void enter(symbol_table table,
                  const string name,
                  id_entry *entry,
                  boolean *present);

/*
 * Search for name in table; return a reference to
 * the entry corresponding to name (if there is one)
 * and a flag to indicate whether the name was present.
 */
extern void find(const symbol_table table,
                 const string name,
                 id_entry *entry,
                 boolean *present);

/* Associate the attrs record with entry. */
extern void set_attributes(id_entry *entry,
                           const attributes *attrs);
```

```
/* Get the attributes record associated with entry. */
extern void get_attributes(const id_entry entry,
                                  attributes *attrs);
```

Figure 8.1   Symbol Table Interface

This interface provides an abstract view of a symbol table in that it doesn't specify how the symbol table is implemented. Even the method for associating attributes with names is left unspecified. In addition, it supports the simultaneous existence of any number of symbol tables. The type **attributes** is defined in Chapter 10.

8.2. Basic Implementation Techniques

The first consideration of symbol table implementation is how **enter()** and **find()** store and search for names. Depending upon the number of names we wish to accommodate and the performance we desire, a wide variety of implementations is possible:

- **Unordered List**
  Use of an unordered list is the simplest possible storage mechanism. The only data structure required is an array, with insertions being performed by adding new names in the next available location. A linked list may be used to avoid the limitations imposed by a fixed array size. Searching is simple using an iterative searching algorithm, but it is impractically slow except for tables containing no more than 20 or so items.

- **Ordered List**
  If a list of names in an array is kept ordered, it may be searched using a binary search, which requires $O(\log(n))$ time for a list of n entries. However, each new entry must be inserted in the array in the appropriate location. Insertion in an ordered array is a relatively expensive operation, in general. Thus, ordered lists are typically used only when the entire set of names in a table is known in advance. They are useful for tables of reserved words or assembler operation codes.

- **Binary Search Trees**
  Binary search trees are designed to combine the size flexibility and insertion efficiency of a linked data structure with the search speed provided by a binary search. On average, entering or searching for a name in a binary search tree built from random inputs requires $O(\log(n))$ time. However, average case performance is by no means guaranteed for a symbol table, because the identifiers used in a program are certainly not random. One advantage of binary search trees is their simple, widely known implementation. This simplicity and the common perception of good average case performance make binary search trees a popular technique for implementing symbol tables. Binary search trees are discussed further in Section 8.2.1.

- **Hash Tables**

  Hash tables are probably the most common means of implementing symbol tables in production compilers and other system software. With a large-enough table, a good hash function, and the appropriate collision-handling technique, searching can be done in *constant time* regardless of the number of entries in the table. Hash tables are discussed in detail in Section 8.2.2.

8.2.1. Binary Search Trees

The algorithm for implementing a simple binary search tree can be found in any data structures book, so it will not be repeated here. Of greater concern is how acceptable performance can be ensured using a binary search tree symbol table implementation. If a binary tree is perfectly balanced, the expected search time is $O(\log(n))$. As mentioned before, a tree built from random inputs also has an expected search time that is proportional to the log of the number of items in the tree, though the average search time will be approximately 38% greater than that for a balanced tree (Knuth 1973). However, the worst-case performance is $O(n)$, and actual occurrence of this worst case is not improbable. For example, entering names in alphabetic order (A, B, C, D, E) results in a "tree" that is really a linear list, and even random-looking sequences of names can produce the same result (A, E, B, D, C, for example).

This problem can be overcome by using an insertion algorithm that keeps the tree approximately balanced (Knuth 1973, p. 451). Doing so affects insertion efficiency only slightly, but it does significantly complicate the implementation. Tree-balancing algorithms are based on the idea of keeping the height of each subtree rooted at a node within one of the height of its sibling subtree. Entire subtrees are moved to different root nodes when an insertion would unbalance a node. The fact that rebalancing can be done by moving subtrees rather than individual nodes keeps the insertion cost at $O(\log(n))$.

One significant advantage of binary trees for implementing symbol tables is that their space overhead, for storing the pointers that define the tree, is directly proportional to the number of nodes in the tree. In contrast, hash tables have a fixed space overhead (storage for the hash table itself) regardless of the number of names that have been entered. One implementation technique discussed in Section 8.3 is to use many symbol tables to represent various program components rather than using one global table. Trees have a clear advantage as the basis of such an implementation.

8.2.2. Hash Tables

Hash Functions

The central idea of a hash table is to map each of a large space of possible names that might be entered into a symbol table to one of a fixed number of positions in a hash table. This mapping is done by a *hash function.*

A hash function is normally assumed to have the following properties:

- h(n) depends solely on n.

- h can be computed quickly.

- h is *uniform* and *randomizing* in mapping names to hash addresses. That is, all hash addresses are mapped with equal probability, and similar names do not cluster to the same hash address.

Some hash functions treat a name as a sequence of *words*, with some number of characters per word. Names longer than one word are folded together into one word, usually by exclusive or operations or by multiplying together two n bit words and keeping the middle n bits of the product. The hash value is then obtained by taking the remainder modulo m, where the hash table has m entries. Note that if m is equal to 2^b, this division simply isolates the rightmost b bits. Thus, such table sizes should be avoided.

An alternative is to compute a hash value character by character, as a token is scanned. Simple hash functions include $(c_1 + c_2 + \cdots + c_n)$ **mod** m or $(c_1 * c_2 * \cdots * c_n)$ **mod** m, where the token is composed of characters $c_1, c_2, \cdots, c_n$, though care must be taken to avoid or handle overflows in doing such computations. The UW-Pascal compiler uses an even simpler hash function: $h(c_1, \cdots, c_n) = (c_1 * c_n)$ **mod** m, with only the first and last characters being used. This very simple hash function seems to work well, although functions that use all characters of a token do a better job of randomizing and are not much more expensive.

Resolving Collisions

Because the number of possible names that can be entered into a symbol table is usually much larger than the number of hash addresses, *collisions* are inevitable. That is, for names n_1 and n_2 ($n_1 \neq n_2$), $h(n_1) = h(n_2)$. When such a collision occurs, a number of collision-handling techniques are possible:

- **Linear Resolution**
  If position h(n) is occupied, try (h(n) + 1) **mod** m, (h(n) + 2) **mod** m, and so on. If any table positions are free, they will be found eventually. The main problem with this technique is that as the table fills, *long chains* tend to form.

- **Add-the-Hash Rehash**
  If h(n) is occupied, try (2∗h(n)) **mod** m, (3∗h(n)) **mod** m, and so on. This helps prevent long chains, but m must be prime if all hash positions are to be eventually tried.

- **Quadratic Rehash**
  If h(n) is occupied, try (h(n) + 1∗∗2) **mod** m, (h(n) + 2∗∗2) **mod** m, and so on.

- **Collision Resolution by Chaining**
  Names are not placed in the hash table at all, but rather records for all names that hash to a given value are chained together on a linked list. Only list headers are stored in the hash table itself. That is, we have the organization illustrated in Figure 8.2.

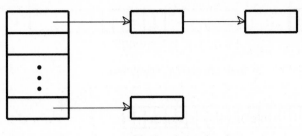

Hash Table   Chained entries for names

Figure 8.2   Hash Table with Chaining for Collision Resolution

Chained collision resolution is attractive for a number of reasons. First, it minimizes the space overhead of the hash table itself, for each entry requires only enough space for one pointer. Second, it does not catastrophically fail, as the other collision resolution techniques do, when all hash table entries are filled, assuming that space is allocated dynamically for name records. In fact, given a uniform hash function, if we have n names and a table size of m, the average (or expected) time to find a name is proportional to $1 + n/2m$, and the time to enter a name is proportional to $2 + n/m$. If a hash table size of between 50 and 100 is used, these search and entry times are essentially constants for all but the largest programs. Even if the number of names greatly exceeds the table size, we still have the efficiency of a linear list with n/m items. It is even possible to improve this performance (on average) by organizing each chain as a binary search tree rather than as a linear list. Finally, chained collision resolution allows us to easily remove individual names, but the other hashing techniques do not. Because of these advantages, collision resolution by chaining is by far the most popular hash table organization.

8.2.3. String Space Arrays

The lengths of strings that can be entered into a symbol table may vary greatly, which could lead to considerable inefficiencies in storing strings. In particular, if each symbol table entry contains a *name field* representing the actual name to which the entry corresponds, we have to allocate enough space in this field to accommodate the longest possible name. If names greater than 8 or 10 characters are allowed, a great deal of space will be wasted, as many names will be relatively short.

One way to reduce this waste is to use a character array, often called a *string space*, to store all names. Using this technique, instead of storing the name itself in a symbol table entry we store the string length and an index into the string space. Thus, if we store a length k and an index i, the name is stored in positions $i, i + 1, \ldots, i + k - 1$ in the string space, as illustrated in Figure 8.3.

Any given string needs to appear in the string space only once. Before a string is entered, we first compute its hash value and check all extant entries on the appropriate hash chain to see if it is already there. Checking entries re-

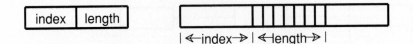

(a) Schematic representation of a string space

string | 1 | 6

space | 7 | 5

example | 12 | 7

(b) Example strings and descriptors

Figure 8.3   One-Level String Space

quires only a comparison of characters for entries that have the same length value. If the string is not found on the hash chain, we then enter it at the left-most free position in the string space.

Because a string should not be entered into the string space unless it is first determined that it is not already there, it is usually the responsibility of the symbol table routines, not the scanner, to maintain the string space. This assignment of responsibility is particularly necessary in block-structured languages in which a name may be used (and defined) in more than one scope. Individual scopes may be represented in different symbol tables and possibly different string spaces, all of which would be managed by the symbol table routines. If scanning, parsing, and semantic analysis are interleaved, it is usually possible to "float" a name on top of a string space from the time it is recognized by the scanner until the appropriate action is resolved. If it is to be entered into the string space, it will stay where it is; otherwise, it will be removed, and the space it occupied will be made available again. Such removal is simple only as long as the name is still at the top of the string space, so semantic processing must be designed to resolve the use of the name before any others are added to the string space.

If a string space is implemented as a fixed-size array, choosing its length is a difficult problem. If we make it too small, we may run out of space to store names. If we make it too long, we will waste space, which is what we sought to avoid in using a string space. However, an effective solution is possible that makes use of dynamic allocation. The string space may be allocated

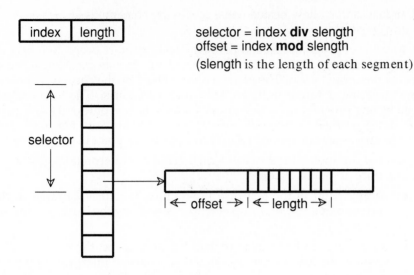

Figure 8.4   Segmented String Space

in *segments* of 500 or 1000 characters and we may treat the string space index as a two-level index. In particular, if each segment is s characters long, an index i represents position (i **mod** s) in segment (i **div** s). (See Figure 8.4 for an illustration.) Naturally, we allocate space for a new segment only when the current segment is filled.

A segmented string space is limited by the size of the segment pointer array. In general, this limit is not a serious problem; for example, something as small as a 50-pointer array used in conjunction with 1000-character segments would provide for 50K characters of string space. Even this limit can be avoided, however, by leaving out the array pointers and using a (segment pointer, offset, length) triple to identify strings. This representation is somewhat larger than the (index, length) representation, and hence is more costly in the average case in which string space requirements are modest. Languages like C that allow character pointers can use a (pointer, length) representation or just a pointer to a dynamically allocated copy of the string if a special terminator character is used to delimit strings. An implementation language that efficiently implements dynamic strings is, of course, an even better solution.

8.3. Block-Structured Symbol Tables

Most programming languages allow *name scopes* to be *nested*, based on concepts introduced by Algol 60. A name scope is usually defined as the program text enclosed by a program unit such as a subprogram, a package, or, originally, a block. In most languages designed since Algol 60, these kinds of program units can be defined within one another, thus allowing name scopes to be nested. Languages that allow nested name scopes are sometimes known as *block-structured languages*.

Any line of program text is contained by one or more program units that define name scopes. The name scope defined by the *innermost* such unit is known as the *current scope*. The name scopes defined by the current scope and by any enclosing program units are known as *open scopes*. The name scopes defined by any program units that do not enclose the line of text are said to be *closed*. Based on these definitions, *current*, *open*, and *closed* are not fixed attributes of scopes; they are defined relative to a particular point in the program.

A set of commonly used *visibility rules* define the interpretation of names in the presence of multiple scopes:

- At any point in the text of a program, only names declared in the current scope and in the open scopes containing the current scope are accessible.

- If a name is declared in more than one open scope, the *innermost* declaration, the one nearest the reference, is used to interpret a reference to that name.

- New declarations can be made only in the current scope.

An obvious implication of these rules is that when a scope is closed, all declarations made within that scope become inaccessible. For example, consider the program fragment in Figure 8.5.

At the position indicated, the declarations of A (as a character), C, H, L, and M are visible. X and Y are not visible because the scope in which they are declared is closed.

The names of the parameters associated with a subprogram are local to the body of the subprogram. However, the name of a subprogram itself is defined in the scope containing the declaration of the subprogram. (If the name of a subprogram was considered local to its own body, it could never be called!)

There are two common approaches to implementing block-structured symbol tables: an individual table for each scope or a single, global table.

An Individual Table for Each Scope

If an individual symbol table is created for each scope, some mechanism must be used to ensure that a search produces the name defined by the nested scope rules. Because name scopes are opened and closed in a last-in, first-out manner, a stack is an appropriate mechanism for organizing such a search. Thus, a *scope stack* of symbol tables is maintained, with one entry in the stack for each open name scope. The innermost scope is at the top of the stack, the next containing scope is second from the top, and so forth. When a new scope is opened, a new symbol table is created and pushed onto the stack; when a scope is closed, the top symbol table is popped. A scope popped from the scope stack can be destroyed in a one-pass compiler, but it must be saved as an attribute of the program unit defining the scope in a multipass compiler so that it can be used to find names during later passes. Thus, for the program

```
declare
    H,A,L : Integer;
begin

    declare
        X,Y : Real;
    begin
        .
        .
        .
    end;

    declare
        A,C,M : Character;
    begin
        .
        .
        -- Current position in program ⇐
        .
        .
    end;

end;
```

Figure 8.5   Nested Scope Example

code in Figure 8.5, we would find a symbol table configuration like that shown in Figure 8.6.

To find a name, we first search for it in the top symbol table, then the second from the top, and so on until it is found or the stack is exhausted. The routines defined in Figure 8.7 could be used along with the symbol table interface from Figure 8.1 to maintain and use a scope stack. **sts_push()** and **sts_pop()** maintain the stack as expected. **sts_pop()** returns the symbol

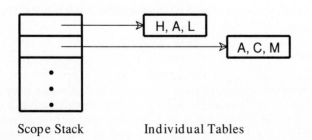

Scope Stack   Individual Tables

Figure 8.6   Individual Table Implementation of Nested Scopes

```
extern void sts_push(const symbol_table table);
extern symbol_table sts_pop(void);
extern symbol_table sts_current_scope(void);

/*
 * Search stack of tables for name; return a
 * reference to the entry corresponding to name
 * (if there is one) and a flag to indicate
 * whether the name was present.
 */
extern void sts_find(const string name,
                     id_entry *entry,
                     boolean *present);
```

Figure 8.7   Scope Stack Routines

table taken from the stack so it can either be saved or destroyed, depending upon the compiler organization. `sts_current_scope()` is used to make a reference to the innermost scope available for calls to `enter()`. `sts_find()` uses `find()` in searching down the stack of scopes for **name**.

One disadvantage of using this scope stack approach is that we may need to search for a name in a number of different symbol tables before it is found. For example, a globally defined name requires a search through all the tables in the stack. The cost of such a search includes referencing each table in the stack, plus referencing the appropriate entry in each table, plus searching each relevant chain. The cost of this stack search varies from one program to another, depending upon the number of nonlocal name references and the depth of nesting of open scopes.

Another problem arises for hash table implementations due to the allocation a block of storage for the hash table for each scope. If each table is large, much storage space may be wasted because many scopes include definitions of only a few names. If the tables are small, searches for identifiers in scopes where many names are defined, like the outermost scope, may be slow due to long hash chains. It is possible (although more complicated) to maintain smaller tables for inner scopes, where large numbers of declarations are unlikely. This problem, of course, does not exist when a binary search tree implementation is used because there is no fixed overhead for each binary tree.

A Single Symbol Table

Using a single-symbol table, all names, for all nested scopes, appear in one single table. Each name scope is given a unique *scope number*. A name may appear in the symbol table more than once, as long as each repetition has a different scope number. Figure 8.8(a) shows one possible structure that might result from building a global symbol table for the program in Figure 8.5 using a single hash table; Figure 8.8(b) shows a corresponding binary search tree.

Using the hash table implementation shown in Figure 8.8(a), new names are added at the front of the chains. Searches are simple; the first occurrence of a target name on its appropriate hash chain is the desired entry. When a scope is closed, all entries with the scope number of the scope being closed are removed from each chain. It is not necessary to examine each chain beyond the first entry with a scope number that does not match.

Figure 8.8(b) illustrates that implementation of multiple scopes in a single binary tree does not work as smoothly as for a hash table. Because insertions in a binary search tree are done at the leaves, a search for a name must continue beyond the first matching entry all the way to the leaves and return the *last* matching entry found. Similarly, deleting entries when a scope is closed requires a traversal of the entire tree and removal of leaves and subtrees with scope numbers matching that of the scope being closed.

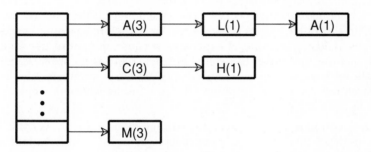

Hash Table   Chained entries for names
                  (with scope numbers)

Figure 8.8(a)   Global Hash Table Implementation of Nested Scopes

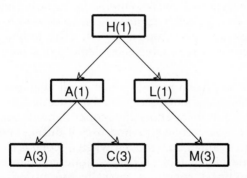

Figure 8.8(b)   Global Binary Tree Implementation of Nested Scopes

the type **`symbol_table`** as a scope number. The **`create()`** operation then simply returns a scope number, and **`destroy()`** removes all the entries labeled by that scope number. The interface to **`find()`** is the only thing that would have to be changed. The **`table`** parameter would be deleted.

Alternatively, we could add **`open_scope()`** and **`close_scope()`** operations to our "package;" these operations would each take a symbol table as a parameter, and the routines would handle scope numbers internally. The advantage of this latter approach is that our interface remains general enough to simultaneously support multiple tables with multiple scopes.

Using a hash table, the global table approach is somewhat more involved to implement than the table per scope approach, but it does provide slightly faster searching because only one table is ever searched. It also tends to use space more efficiently as there is only a single table of list headers rather than one for each scope. However, this space savings is partly counterbalanced by the additional space needed to add a scope number to each entry.

The global approach is less attractive using a binary tree implementation. Searches for names in inner scopes now take longer. The part of the tree corresponding to outer scopes must be traversed before reaching entries for inner scopes. Closing a scope is expensive because the entire tree must be traversed, looking for entries to delete. Further, there is no space savings to compensate for the extra space required to store scope numbers. In short, a binary search tree cannot be recommended for implementing a single global symbol table.

In early compilers (before dynamic storage management was commonly used), a variant of this single table approach was used. In this variant, since all new definitions must be made in the innermost scope, a stack can be used to accommodate symbol table definitions. All definitions made in a scope are adjacent, and the innermost definitions are at the top of this stack. For each scope, a "high water" mark is kept so that the stack can be popped back to that mark when a nested scope is closed.

This variant is usable with a variety of searching techniques, but is less frequently used in modern compilers because of the common use of dynamic data structures (chained collision resolution or binary search trees). One vestige does remain, however. All names entered in the string space for a given scope will be adjacent, so a similar approach can be used to reclaim the string space used by a scope when the scope is closed. (This technique can be used regardless of whether the symbol table is implemented as individual tables or a global table.)

The single table approach is really most applicable to a one-pass compiler, where all information about a scope can be discarded when the compiler reaches the end of the unit that defines the scope. A multipass compiler typically builds a symbol table in one pass and uses it during one or more additional passes. If entries cannot be removed when a scope is closed, the implementation of a single global table becomes quite complex and potentially inefficient. Thus, multipass compilers typically use an individual table for each scope.

8.4. Extensions to Block-Structured Symbol Tables

The block-structured name scoping rules introduced by Algol 60 and described in the previous section form the basis of the scope rules found in most modern programming languages. However, most languages extend the standard scoping rules in a variety of ways, and these extensions can have a significant impact on the design of symbol tables.

In the rest of this chapter, we consider how symbol table structures are affected by language features that control visibility of names, alter search rules, and allow multiple uses of names in one scope. We also consider the impact of features that involve implicit declarations and references to names before they are defined.

Extensions to the standard name scoping rules fall into two categories: those that alter the visibility of individual names or a set of names and those that alter the search rules. We examine techniques to handle features that represent both kinds of extensions. The standard rule of name visibility states that the definition to be associated with a reference to a name is the innermost possible definition found within a scope that contains the reference. However, not all names obey this rule. For example, the names of fields in records are usually visible only if they are *qualified* by a record name. More significantly, modern programming languages often allow the visibility of nonlocal definitions to be explicitly controlled. Such controls can be categorized as either *import rules* or *export rules*. Finally, constructs like the **with** statement in Pascal and the **use** clause in Ada bring new search rules into effect.

For most extensions, either of two implementation approaches can be taken. One approach is to duplicate, usually in the innermost name scope, symbol table entries that are accessible but would not be found in the normal search process. This approach is usually fairly simple to implement and speeds up searching. However, it can incur a significant space overhead, especially if a large number of entries must be copied.

The alternate approach is to try to avoid making copies of entries and to adjust flags and symbol table links so that symbol table nodes are made visible or invisible to the normal search mechanism. This approach is generally more complicated and sometimes slower, but it does tend to reduce the overall space overhead. Graham et al. (1979) provides a good, comprehensive discussion of these alternatives.

8.4.1. Fields and Records

In C, Pascal, or Ada, field names need only be unique within the record in which they are declared, although they are visible in the scope that surrounds the record declaration. They need not be distinct from the names of fields of other records declared in the same scope or from other local and nonlocal names. We must therefore be able to handle declarations like those in the following Pascal example:

```
A,R : record
        A : Integer;
        X : record
                A : Real;
                C : Boolean;
            end;
    end;
```

These rules regarding field names are desirable because they allow programmers to avoid worrying about duplication of field names in different records, thus simplifying a programmer's job and enhancing readability (in contrast to languages that require field names to be unique within a scope). Each field can be given the most appropriate name for its use, even if another record has a field with the same name. For example, the original definition of C required such uniqueness, forcing programmers to adopt naming conventions such as

```
struct rec1 { int r1_contents; struct rec1 *r1_next; };
struct rec2 { char *r2_contents; struct rec2 *r2_next; };
```

The prefixes **r1_** and **r2_** are used in this example solely because both records would not be allowed to have fields named **contents** and **next**. This allows a simple implementation, one symbol table for structure fields and another symbol table for everything else.

Multiple fields with the same name never cause ambiguities in Pascal or Ada because a reference to a record component must always be completely specified—for example, R.A or R.X.A. In PL/I or COBOL, intermediate steps in the reference may be deleted. In these two languages, for example, R.C (meaning R.X.C) is a legal reference, requiring a more elaborate algorithm in order to detect ambiguities and resolve unambiguous abbreviations.

There are two choices for handling field names. The first approach is to allocate a symbol table for each record type. That symbol table does not go on the scope stack but rather is an attribute of the record type. This is done in the Pascal P-compiler, in which every record type has its own binary tree of field names. When the compiler processes a reference like R.A, it first finds R according to the normal search rules and retrieves the reference to the symbol table for the type of R. It then calls **find()** with that symbol table and A as parameters. This approach is easy to implement as it requires no changes in the interface to the symbol table, but it can be expensive in its space requirements if a hash table implementation is used. It fits well, though, with a binary tree implementation, because the number of fields in a record is typically small.

The alternative approach is to treat field names like ordinary identifiers and put them into the regular symbol table along with all the other names in the current scope. Each record is then assigned a unique *record number*. This record number may be generated from a counter, or the address of the symbol table entry for the record might be used. Associating a record number with all field names allows the compiler to determine the record to which a field belongs even if the same field name is used in more than one record. Names other than field names can be thought to have a record number of zero. To interpret a reference like R.A, the compiler first finds R in the symbol table as usual and verifies that it is a record. Say, for example, its record number is k. The compiler then searches the symbol table for a declaration of A that is a field with record number k. This process can be iterated for more-complex expressions like R.X.A. When the compiler is searching the table for an ordinary variable, say A instead of R.A, it uses a record number of zero and thus ignores all entries that are fields.

To use this approach to handle record fields, the interface to the symbol table must be changed by adding a record number parameter to the parameter lists of **enter()** and **find()**:

```
        . . .

extern void enter(symbol_table table,
               const string name,
               const int record_num,
               id_entry *entry,
               boolean *present);

extern void find(const symbol_table table,
               const string name,
               const int record_num,
               id_entry *entry,
               boolean *present);

        . . .
```

8.4.2. Export Rules

Export rules allow a programmer to specify that some names local to a scope are to be made visible outside that scope. This selective visibility is in contrast to the usual block-structured scope rule, which states that names local to a scope are *invisible* outside of it, and to the record field rule, discussed in the previous section, which makes *all* names defined in the record visible with proper qualification. Export rules are typically associated with modularization features, such as Ada packages, Modula-2 modules, and C++ classes, that allow related definitions to be grouped together. Often a module or package will define a data structure, as well as procedures and functions that perform operations on that structure. For example, consider the following Modula-2 module, which defines a stack:

```
MODULE IntegerStack;
   EXPORT Push, Pop;
   CONST StackMax = 100;
   VAR Stack : ARRAY [1..StackMax] OF Integer;
       Top : 1..StackMax;
```

```
PROCEDURE Push(I:Integer);
  BEGIN ··· END;
PROCEDURE Pop : Integer;
  BEGIN ··· END;

BEGIN
  Top := 1
END IntegerStack;
```

Outside the module IntegerStack, the procedures Push and Pop are visible. All other definitions local to the module are hidden. The implementation of the stack, in particular, is not accessible from outside the module. The purpose of export rules is not to simplify compilation but rather to make it easy to group related definitions into a program unit and selectively access those definitions.

To handle export rules correctly, we must make sure that when a scope is ended, exported names remain visible, as if they were declared in the enclosing scope. We can flag exported names and move them to the next outer scope when a scope is closed, also being sure to remove the exported flag. If exported symbols must be listed at the very beginning of a new scope, as is the case in Modula-2, they are easily located when the scope is closed. Using a hash table with chained collision resolution to implement the symbol table, all external symbols will be contiguous and located either at the ends of chains or immediately before symbols belonging to the next outer scope, depending upon whether a single table or multiple tables are being used. If a binary search tree implementation is used with a tree for each scope, all the exported symbols will be found contiguous to the root of the tree.

The most basic change required for our symbol table interface to handle export lists is that an additional parameter, **exported**, must be added to the parameter list for **enter()**. **exported** is a boolean value and indicates whether the **name** being entered is to be visible in the scope that surrounds the current scope. A more complex concern is how symbol table entries are actually exported when a scope is closed. If the symbol table interface includes **open_scope()** and **close_scope()** operations, then scopes are handled internally, and entries can be exported as described previously, without any changes in the interface. If scopes are represented by individual tables and the scope stack is handled externally to the symbol table routines, one new operation must be added to the interface:

```
extern void export(const symbol_table from,
                    symbol_table to);
```

export() must find all the exported entries in the **symbol_table** designated by **from** and move them to the one designated by **to**.

The syntax of Ada packages is oriented toward support of physical segmentation of large programs. Packages are defined in two parts, the first being the *specification part*, which defines the names exported by the package, and the second being the *package body*, in which all declarations are hidden and bodies for procedures declared in the specification part are provided. An Ada version of the Modula-2 stack just defined is

```
package IntegerStack is
  procedure Push(I:Integer);
  function Pop return Integer;
end IntegerStack;

package body IntegerStack is
  StackMax : constant Integer := 100;
  Stack : array (1..StackMax) of Integer;
  Top : Integer range 1..StackMax;

  procedure Push(I:Integer) is
    begin ··· end;
  function Pop return Integer is
    begin ··· end;

begin
  Top := 1;
end IntegerStack;
```

No explicit export list is used; inclusion of a declaration in the specification part of a package makes it externally accessible. Thus, Push and Pop are exported by the Ada package IntegerStack. In Ada, exported objects *are not* automatically imported into other units. Rather, they are accessed by qualifying their names with a package identifier (IntegerStack.Push, for example) or by importing them via a **use** clause.

If the table per scope approach is used, we keep all visible declarations for a package in its symbol table and access it via the package name. For separately compiled packages, a library entry will contain the contents of this table. If the single-symbol table approach is used, we add a special end-of-search marker in each hash chain. This marker terminates the ordinary search down the hash chain. When a package specification is processed, its local declarations are placed *behind* the marker, making them invisible. When a package body is compiled, they are moved in front of the marker and then returned after the body is processed. As we discuss later, the selected access and **use** clause mechanisms search beyond the end of the search marker to find package declarations.

Modula-2 also allows splitting a module into similar parts, as the following example illustrates:

```
DEFINITION MODULE IntegerStack;
  EXPORT QUALIFIED Push, Pop;
  PROCEDURE Push(I:Integer);
  PROCEDURE Pop : Integer;
END IntegerStack.
```

```
IMPLEMENTATION MODULE IntegerStack;
  CONST StackMax = 100;
  VAR Stack : ARRAY [1..StackMax] OF Integer;
    Top : 1..StackMax;

  PROCEDURE Push(I:Integer);
    BEGIN · · · END;
  PROCEDURE Pop : Integer;
    BEGIN · · · END;

BEGIN
  Top := 1
END IntegerStack.
```

Note that the export list in the Modula-2 definition module includes the key-word **QUALIFIED**. This modifier is required when a module is broken into two parts; it is optional otherwise. Qualified exports must be referenced with the module name as a prefix. In this case, we have to use IntegerStack.Push and IntegerStack.Pop to reference the exported procedure names. All Ada identifiers are exported with the requirement that they be *selected* using the package name or imported using Ada's **use** clause. We can use the same techniques to handle qualified exports that we developed for referencing record fields.

Separate Compilation

When package or module declarations are used as individual compilation units, a program may be constructed from separately compiled parts. When a package specification or definition module is compiled, the compiler saves information about the exported declarations in a *library*. (A library in this context is simply a repository that holds information about separately compiled units.) The information saved in the library enables the compiler to build a symbol table for the separately compiled declarations when it compiles the corresponding package body or implementation module and when it compiles other units that import declarations from the separately compiled unit. Thus the library makes it possible to do complete compile-time static semantic checking even when separate compilation is used.

The table per scope symbol table organization is most appropriate for implementing a language that includes separate compilation features, such as those described for Ada and Modula-2. The library can consist of either symbolic (i.e., textual) or memory-image representations of the symbol tables for separately compiled units. When such a unit is referenced during the compilation of another unit, this library entry is used to reconstruct its symbol table, making accessible all the information it contains, just as if it were being compiled along with the other unit.

Languages like C, which do not depend on the concept of a library known to the compiler, require an alternative approach to separate compilation. Descriptions of objects compiled in other modules are included in a compilation unit in source language form using a special compiler directive (for example, **#include** in C). Processing these declarations builds appropriate symbol table entries, but this can be significantly less efficient than loading a previously built symbol table. Further, there is no guarantee that the included declarations match the actual declarations of the imported objects in the module in which they are defined.

Hiding Type Representations

Both Ada and Modula-2 provide features that allow the use of packages and modules to define types, with the actual implementation of the type hidden. Thus, we could export a stack type and then create any number of stacks—in contrast to the examples so far, which allow only a single stack. These stack instances could then only be accessed and manipulated via the provided operations. Such a stack type is called an *abstract data type*. The Ada and Modula-2 features that provide this capability can be seen in the examples in Figures 8.9(a) and 8.9(b). Modula-2 allows only pointer types to be hidden, so the compiler automatically knows the size of any such type. In Ada, the definition of a private type in the *private part* of a package specification provides the necessary size information for any type a programmer defines, without making it visible to the rest of the program.

```
package IntegerStack is
  type Stack is private;
  procedure Initialize (S : in out Stack);
  procedure Push(I:Integer; S : in out Stack);
  procedure Pop(I: out Integer; S : in out Stack);
private
  StackMax : constant Integer := 100;
  type Stack is record
                  Stack : array (1..StackMax) of Integer;
                  Top : Integer range 1..StackMax;
               end record;
end IntegerStack;


package body IntegerStack is

  procedure Initialize (S : in out Stack) is
    begin ··· end;
  procedure Push(I:Integer; S : in out Stack) is
    begin ··· end;
  procedure Pop(I: out Integer; S : in out Stack) is
    begin ··· end;

end IntegerStack;
```

Figure 8.9(a)   IntegerStack as an Abstract Type in Ada

```
DEFINITION MODULE IntegerStack;
  EXPORT QUALIFIED Stack, Initialize, Push, Pop;
  TYPE Stack;
  PROCEDURE Initialize (VAR S:Stack);
  PROCEDURE Push(I:Integer; VAR S:Stack);
  PROCEDURE Pop(VAR S:Stack):Integer;
END IntegerStack.

IMPLEMENTATION MODULE IntegerStack;
  TYPE
    StackEntry = RECORD
                    Value : Integer;
                    Next : Stack
                 END;
    Stack = POINTER TO StackEntry;
  PROCEDURE Initialize (VAR S:Stack);
                 BEGIN · · · END;
  PROCEDURE Push(I:Integer; VAR S:Stack);
                 BEGIN · · · END;
  PROCEDURE Pop(VAR S:Stack):Integer;
                 BEGIN · · · END;
END IntegerStack.
```

Figure 8.9(b)   IntegerStack as an Abstract Type in Modula-2

The interesting features seen in these examples are **type** Stack **is private** in Ada and **TYPE** Stack in Modula-2. Stack is called a private type in Ada and an opaque type in Modula-2. In both cases, only the name Stack is exported; no details of its implementation are made available. Thus, the record field names in the Ada implementation would not be accessible outside of the package body. In both languages, the compiler is given sufficient information to know the size of the hidden type without seeing the body of the package or module. This knowledge is sufficient to compile modules that use such types. The only effect these features have on symbol tables is the restrictions they place on what information is exported. No new techniques are required to handle them.

8.4.3. Import Rules

In languages that impose import rules, scopes are classified as *importing* or *nonimporting*. (The terms *open* and *closed* are sometimes used instead of *importing* and *nonimporting*; we have chosen the latter pair to avoid any confusion with the previous definitions of open and closed scopes in this chapter.) An importing scope automatically receives access to definitions in containing scopes. In Algol 60 and Pascal, all scopes are importing scopes.

In a nonimporting scope, access to some or all nonlocal names must be explicitly requested via an import declaration. Modules in Modula-2 are non-importing scopes. Only standard predefined identifiers are imported automatically and thus need not be listed in an imports list. They are termed *pervasive*.

In some languages, a nonlocal object can be imported with restrictions, such as *read-only*, meaning that it cannot be modified in the importing scope. Objects must be imported level by level between nonimporting scopes, and an object can never be imported with more privileges than those granted to the scope from which it is obtained. That is, once a variable is imported as read-only, it can only be imported to inner scopes as read-only.

C++ has an interesting scope concept, providing three classes of visibility to members of a class: **private**, **protected**, and **public**. Anyone may access the **public** members of a class, typically including most or all of its routines. Subclasses have access to the **public** and **protected** members. Instances of the class itself have access to all three kinds of class members. There is also the notion of a **friend**, which is a function that is not a member of a class but nonetheless has access to all the members of the class, even the **private** ones.

As an example of the use of imports, consider the following module. It is another stack instance, but in this case the type of the stack elements, Thing, is imported from the surrounding scope. Because a Modula-2 module is a nonimporting scope, use of **IMPORT** is required to make the uses of Thing legal.

```
MODULE ThingStack;
  EXPORT Push, Pop;
  IMPORT Thing;
  CONST StackMax = 100;
  VAR Stack : ARRAY [1..StackMax] OF Thing;
     Top : 1..StackMax;

  PROCEDURE Push(I:Thing);
    BEGIN · · · END;
  PROCEDURE Pop : Thing;
    BEGIN · · · END;

BEGIN
  Top := 1
END ThingStack;
```

The purpose of explicit import rules is to control more precisely the interface of major program units such as subprograms and modules. They are intended to increase the readability and reliability of these program units.

To implement import rules, we must first alter the standard search mechanism so that all names or names of certain kinds of objects (variables, typically) cannot be automatically referenced across the boundaries of nonimporting scopes. This is easy to do. We already keep track of the scope to which a definition belongs, so we can make it inaccessible when the scope is nonimporting. We can mark each scope as importing or nonimporting by adding a parameter to the **create()** or **open_scope()** operation of the symbol table, depending on our scope implementation. When a search is done, we check to see if the object found is pervasive (automatically imported). If it is not, and it is found in a scope outer to the innermost nonimporting scope, the result of the search is the same as if the identifier were not present in the table.

To implement an import statement, we simply create entries in the current scope corresponding to imported names. The interface to the symbol table can be extended to support imports by the addition of a single procedure:

```
/*
 * Import name into table; return a reference to
 * the entry corresponding to name and a flag to
 * indicate whether the name was successfully found.
 */

extern void import(symbol_table table,
                   const string name,
                   id_entry *entry,
                   boolean *found);
```

import() will be used instead of **enter()** for imported names. The local entries that it creates contain indirect links to previous entries for names that are imported. Thus, to the search mechanism the name appears to be local and it is found correctly. Further, because there is a local entry for any imported name, if we find a local declaration of a name that conflicts with an imported name, we have discovered a kind of "multiple definition" error.

This approach works well when only nonlocal variables must be imported. In particular, most routines will not access many nonlocal variables, as this is not considered good programming style, so the number of extra entries should be reasonable. Further, implementing read-only imports requires only a simple extension. In the duplicate entry, we either set a flag indicating the restriction or copy the contents of the nonlocal variable's entry, adding an indication that changing the variable is illegal. (Such an indication is also used for **in** parameters in Ada.)

The main difficulty with the extra copies approach appears in languages that require a programmer to import all nonlocal names, not just the names of variables. In this case, the extra space and set-up time could become a significant burden. This is especially true if we have a number of nested nonimporting scopes, because we usually import level by level. The alternative here is to make a special provision to mark when a nonlocal definition is visible. One simple-minded way to do this is to provide with every symbol a list of all the scopes that may see it. Unfortunately, such a list could itself become very long and thus expensive to use. We obviate the need for a list by making an important observation. Nonlocals are imported level by level; therefore, the nested nonimporting scopes that can see a definition must be a contiguous sequence. That is, once a scope doesn't import a symbol, no scope nested within it can import that symbol. Thus we need only label each symbol with a **maximum_depth** field. This field says that the symbol can be seen up to but not beyond this depth. Initially this is set to the nesting depth at which the symbol is defined, with pervasive symbols given a nesting depth of infinity.

If a symbol is not imported into the current scope, the current nesting depth will be greater than the maximum allowed for the symbol, and access to it will be denied. If it is imported, the maximum depth field is incremented, and access will be allowed. Note that when we finish compilation of a scope in which an import was done, the maximum depth field must be reset to its original value. This can be done by looking for all symbols that have a maximum greater than their original nesting level, for the maximum can become greater only as the result of an import.

If read-only imports are allowed, we can use another field that indicates the number of scopes in which read-only reference will be enforced. If this is zero, read-only restrictions are waived. This count too must be updated when a read-only list is processed and decremented when scopes are ended.

A difficulty with this approach is that the entire symbol table must be searched to find entries that were incremented by imports and read-only lists. A number of production compilers actually do this. The overhead can be avoided (with chained resolution hashing), however, by moving imported entries to the head of the hash chain. Now, when a scope is ended, imported entries can be found quickly and restored to their original positions.

8.4.4. Altered Search Rules

with Statements

Pascal's **with** statement is a good example of a feature that alters the order in which scopes are examined in order to interpret the meaning of an identifier. One can write

    with R **do** <statement>

Within <statement>, which can be an arbitrarily large compound statement, all identifiers are interpreted, if possible, as references to a field of record R. That is, the order in which scopes are examined is (1) the record named in the **with** statement (R, in this case), (2) the innermost procedure (or function), (3) the next containing procedure (or function), and (4) the global name scope. **with** statements can be nested, in which case the records they designate are examined from innermost to outermost and *then* the normal nested name scopes are examined.

When a **with** statement is entered, fields that normally are invisible because they require qualification must be made visible to the search process. This is most easily done if each record and each scope has its own symbol table. The symbol table for the record can be pushed onto the scope stack and then popped off at the end of the statement.

If record fields are intermixed with other identifiers in the symbol table, using the record number technique from Section 8.4.1, another approach must be taken to make the field names visible. One way is to open a new scope and copy entries into the scope for all the fields that belong to the designated record. This technique avoids any alteration to the name search process, but the overhead of all the copying may be unacceptable. (This can perhaps be alleviated by just copying pointers instead of copying the entries themselves.) An alternative approach is to keep a stack containing the record numbers designated by all open **with** statements.   `find()` then first searches for a name using the top record number on this stack, then the next, and so on. If no match is found using any record number in the stack, it tries a record number of zero, which causes an ordinary search to occur. With this approach, the search is made slower by the extra scopes that must be tried for each record number in the stack before entries for names that are not fields can be found. Entering the record fields as if they were definitions in a new scope avoids the search penalty but takes extra time at the beginning and end of the statement.

Selected Names

In Ada, objects can be selected by prefixing them with a package, subprogram, block, or loop name. For packages, this mechanism is needed because visible objects are not accessible via ordinary search rules unless a **use** clause is employed. Selection can also be used to make visible objects that otherwise would be hidden by local redefinitions of the object's name. Selection is useful, too, in explicitly choosing a particular definition of an overloaded name (see Section 8.6).

If an identifier names a scope, one of its attributes can be a pointer to the symbol table for that scope or the scope number associated with the scope. Selected access is thus analogous to field access in records. That is, we use the scope name to identify a subset of symbols and then search for the identifier only within this subset.

There can be specialized scoping rules for the scope names themselves to obey. In Ada/CS, packages don't nest, so the names of packages already processed during a compilation, as well as the name of the current package, are treated as global names. In Ada, packages *do* nest and in fact can be declared in blocks and subprograms, as well as in other packages. Package names are therefore treated like the names of other objects. Separately compiled packages are made accessible using a **with** *clause* (which is quite different from Pascal's **with** statement).

Subprogram names also obey the usual scoping rules, but selected access to definitions within a subprogram is allowed *only* within the subprogram. Block and loop names are *local* to the scope of the constructs, making selected access from outside impossible.

Ada's use Clause

Ada has an even more complicated situation. A **use** clause, which is effectively a declaration rather than a statement, can name one or more packages whose visible definitions are to be made directly accessible. When a compiler processes

$$\textsf{use } p_1, p_2, \cdots, p_n;$$

(where $p_1, p_2, \ldots, p_n$ name packages), all the visible definitions of the packages are made accessible, almost as if they had all been locally defined. However, special rules govern name clashes:

- If a name can be found using the usual scoping rules (excluding the names provided by the packages), then that definition applies. That is, names from packages are made directly accessible only if they don't clash with any name declared in any enclosing scope; alternatively, they can be thought of as being declared in a scope that surrounds the program unit being compiled.

- If the same name is provided by more than one package on the **use** list, then *none* of the definitions for that name from the packages are directly visible unless they name entities for which overloading (described in Section 8.6) is allowed. This rule ensures that the order in which packages are named in the **use** list is irrelevant.

Alternatives similar to those discussed for the **with** statement are available for handling Ada's **use** clause. We can try to enter local symbol table entries for all definitions exported from packages that do not clash with any other definitions. This may be costly, because some packages may be large, with hundreds of accessible definitions (for example, a package that provides definitions for I/O or numerical subprograms).

Alternatively, we can use the standard search process, with a new option if this process fails to find a definition for a name. If a definition is found, no packages need be checked. If no definition is found, we must then check *all* packages on the **use** list to verify that exactly one definition is found. This may be slow if names provided by a package are accessed frequently.

An effective compromise is to go through the exhaustive search procedure just discussed only for the first reference to a name. If a definition in a package is found, we then create a local copy of it. We do this because if the name is referenced once, it may be referenced again. Subsequent searches would then be quite fast, and yet entries for unreferenced names in packages would never be made.

8.5. Implicit Declarations

Sometimes the mere occurrence of a symbol serves as an implicit declaration of an object. Thus, in Algol 60 the appearance of a label on a statement serves to declare (and define) it, and the usual scoping rules apply. A more interesting example is **for loop** indices in Ada: A loop index is implicitly declared to be of the same type as the range specifier, *and* a new scope is opened so that a loop index can never clash with an existing variable.

In handling an implicit declaration the crucial consideration is whether the name being implicitly declared obeys normal scoping rules or opens a new scope, making conflict with an existing name impossible. If the name does obey ordinary scope rules and doesn't need its own scope, then we just enter it in the symbol table as for any other declaration. If the symbol doesn't obey the usual scope rules (like labels in Pascal and Ada **for** loop indices), then special handling is necessary.

In Pascal, labels can be stored in the symbol table, but care is needed to mark a label as *inaccessible* once the subprogram or structured statement that immediately contains it is closed. This is done so that it is impossible to jump into a structured statement from outside it. The problem with Pascal labels is that the declaration and access rules don't mesh well. As for other kinds of identifiers, there can be only one declaration of a given label within a name scope (a subprogram or main program), but it is not legal to jump to that label from all points in the scope of that declaration.

A construct like an Ada **for** loop, which opens a new name scope, can be handled by actually opening a whole new symbol table scope that contains only a single declaration. If selected access to names hidden by inner declarations is allowed, as it is in Ada, then creating a new scope is necessary. If selected access isn't allowed, we may, as a minor optimization, try to include the index variable in the current scope. If the name isn't already present, this is easy. If it is, the current entry for the name is "pulled out," and loop index entry replaces it. At the close of the loop, the loop index entry is removed from the current scope, and (if necessary) the previous entry is restored.

8.6. Overloading

Most block-structured languages allow some degree of overloading. That is, the same symbol may, depending on context, mean more than one thing. In Pascal, a simple example of overloading is the fact that the same identifier can denote the name of a function *and* its return value. This overloading can lead to subtle errors. For example, if f := f + 1 occurs in a parameterless function f, the f on the left-hand side denotes the return variable, and the f on the right-hand side specifies a recursive call of the function.

Ada carries overloading much further. The name of a procedure, function, operator, or enumeration literal can be overloaded. That is, more than one distinct definition may be accessible at the same time. For example, we might have

> **function** "+" (X,Y : Complex) **return** Complex **is** . . .

and

function "+" (U,V : Polar) **return** Polar **is** . . .

which overloads the + operator to work for complex and polar values, as well as for integers and reals. All these alternate definitions coexist. Similarly, we might have

type month **is** (Jan, Feb, Mar, Apr, May, Jun, Jul, Aug, Sep, Oct, Nov, Dec);

and

type base **is** (Bin, Oct, Dec);

which overloads Oct and Dec.

The rule for overloading in Ada is that a new definition of a procedure, function, operator, or enumeration literal overloads, rather than hides, an existing definition if context can be used to distinguish among the choices. Thus, if we have

A,B : polar;   then $\cdots$ A + B $\cdots$

is unambiguous because only one of the overloaded definitions of + is legal in this context. Ada has an elaborate algorithm (to be discussed in Chapter 11) that decides which of the possible interpretations of an overloaded symbol is implied by a given context.

C++ also allows overloading of most of its built-in operators, including such operations as array subscripting and function calling.

The symbol table must provide all the possible meanings of a name so that they can be made available to the overloading interpretation algorithm. The key to handling overloaded names properly in the symbol table is to *link together* all possible definitions of an overloaded name. This guarantees that when the name is looked up, access to all possible definitions is immediately provided. A semantic routine that uses an overloaded name then looks at each possible definition and chooses the one that applies by context rules. The algorithm for making such a choice is complex. We discuss it in more detail when we consider semantic routines for translating expressions. To make this approach work, whenever a name that can be overloaded is defined we must first see if the name is already visible. If it is, we enter the name in the current scope if it is not already there and link the new entry to any existing definitions, which otherwise would be rendered invisible. If the name is already found in the current scope, we just add the new definition in the overload chain, if it is a legal overloading. In either case, a check must be performed to ensure that the new meaning of an overloaded name can actually be distinguished from all previously defined meanings by the overloading resolution algorithm.

When a scope is closed, some overloadings may be deleted. This can be done easily as long as the overload chain extends from definitions in the inner scope to definitions in progressively more distant scopes. Closing a scope removes a number of definitions from the head of the chain. For example, a Pascal function definition creates a mild form of overloading involving the return variable and function name. The return variable is inside the scope of the function body, and the function name is external to its body (otherwise a function could not be called from outside its own body). Within the function body, the two overloaded definitions are chained so that reference to the return variable as well as recursive calls to the function are possible. When the function body is closed, the return variable definition disappears, but the name of the function remains. This guarantees that the function can be called from outside, but its return variable is inaccessible there.

8.7. **Forward References**

In languages that allow forward references, there is a danger that a reference to a name may be resolved to an extant, nonlocal definition rather than to a local definition that has yet to be processed. This happens in Pascal with declarations of pointers to types that are to be declared later in the same scope. For example:

```
type T = Integer;
    . . .
procedure PP;
  type
    P = ↑T;
    . . .
    T = Real;
    . . .
end
```

P should be a pointer to Real, although it is easy to (incorrectly) interpret P as a pointer to Integer. Note that forward references are provided to allow mutually referenced and linked types.

A similar problem occurs in languages like Algol 60 that allow **goto**'s to nonlocal labels. Because labels obey scope rules, a **goto** that references a label L can be bound to a nonlocal label L only after all intermediate scopes have been fully processed. This is because an occurrence of L in an intermediate scope would supersede the known occurrence of L, and the only way to verify that no such definition exists is to completely process all such intermediate scopes. In Pascal, things are a bit simpler because labels must be declared before they can be defined. This at least warns us to expect a definition of a label, even if we have not yet found it.

A challenging variant of the forward reference problem occurs when we try to strictly enforce rules *against* forward references. For example, forward references to constants are illegal in Pascal and Ada. But what if the following occurs in Pascal?

```
const C = 10;
    .
    .
    .

procedure PP;
  const D = C;
      .
      .
      .
    C = 20;
end
```

Should D be equal to 10 or 20? Actually, it should be neither because D's definition contains an illegal forward reference. In particular, all references to C in procedure PP must be to the innermost definition of C, but at the point D is defined this is a forward reference.

It is difficult to detect this error because we know that if D is correctly defined, it must be equal to 10. In fact, almost all Pascal compilers would set D to 10 and issue no error message. It is only when the local definition of C is encountered that we have any chance of noting an error, and by that time the processing of D is already completely done. Note, however, that a correct Pascal compiler would have to detect the error. Ada states that the scope of a declaration extends *only* from the point of definition to the end of the containing scope, so this problem doesn't arise.

Handling Forward References

To handle forward references properly, we must avoid resolving a symbol until all its possible definitions have been seen. If unrestricted forward references are allowed, the only way to handle the problem is to make more than one pass over the program text. The first pass finds all definitions and builds the symbol table. Succeeding passes then process declarations and statements, using the already created symbol table to resolve all references to names. It follows that if a one-pass compiler is to be feasible, forward references must be strictly limited.

In Pascal, forward references to type names are allowed in pointer types. These are handled by chaining together all references to a pointer to type T until the end of the type declaration section is reached. All type names can then be looked up and resolved. This process is feasible because type declarations do not generate code, and only internal data structures representing type information need to be updated.

Forward references to labels in **goto**'s are a bit tougher because code is generated for a **goto**, but they are possible even in a one-pass compiler because we know almost exactly the kind of code we will generate—all that is missing is the address to be filled in. More general forward references are usually impossible to handle in one pass. For example, if, as in PL/I, we allowed A := B + C before A, B, or C were defined, simply filling addresses would not suffice because the kind of code (and its size) would depend on the declarations of A, B, and C. Thus a first pass would be needed so that the compiler could determine the types of identifiers *before* trying to generate appropriate code.

Illegal Forward References

To detect illegal forward references in a one-pass compiler, we adopt the techniques used for import lists. The idea here is that if we see a reference to a symbol that can be resolved nonlocally but that has no local definition yet, we treat that symbol as if it had been imported. And in a real sense it has been, for the reference states implicitly that no local definition of that symbol will be provided. If one were to be provided, it would have to precede its first use because of forward reference restrictions. We can mark this implicit import specially, so that if a local definition is found, a clash with the imported symbol is detected, and we can generate a correct diagnostic.

This approach works. The only problem is that we must do a significant amount of work *in all cases* just on the off chance that an illegal local definition may turn up later. This is unavoidable if we want thorough checking, but it is easy to see why many language definitions simply state that until a new definition is found, access to a nonlocal definition will be allowed. This is Ada's scope rule; it is easier (by far) to enforce and in most cases is quite reasonable.

8.8. Summary

Most of this chapter has been devoted to block-structured symbol tables and the impact on symbol tables of various extensions to the basic scope idea. In light of this discussion, the symbol table interface presented in Figure 8.1 is clearly somewhat idealized. The changes that must be made to that interface for use in any particular compiler depend on the set of features in the language being compiled and on the choice of scope representation. The scope representation choice, a single global table or one table per scope, may be essentially dictated by the language, or it may be most strongly influenced by the design of the compiler, particularly if a multipass organization is chosen.

Exercises

1. The two data structures most commonly used to implement symbol tables in production compilers are binary search trees and hash tables. What are the advantages and disadvantages of each of these data structures?

2. If a hash table is being used in a situation where dynamic storage allocation is not practical, external collision resolution may be implemented by

allocating entries on the hash chains from a fixed array. To determine its strengths and weaknesses, compare this approach with internal resolution techniques and with external chaining with dynamic allocation.

3. Describe the two alternative approaches to handling multiple scopes in a symbol table, and list the actions required to open and close a scope for each alternative. Trace the sequence of actions that would be performed for each alternative during compilation of the example in Figure 8.5.

4. Write the four name search algorithms required in order to use binary search trees and hash tables to implement each of the multiple scope alternatives (a single global table and a table for each scope).

5. For what languages is use of a string space representation of identifiers inappropriate? Why?

6. Compare the two approaches to handling the names of record fields. How well does each work with each of the multiple scope alternatives?

7. Describe the handling of names exported by a Modula-2 module (as presented in Section 8.4.2) to a surrounding scope for each of the two multiple scope alternatives.

8. Compare the two approaches to handling imported names. How well does each work with each of the two scope representation alternatives?

9. Analyze your favorite programming language to determine which of its features have an impact on the design of an appropriate symbol table for compiling that language. Describe the impact of each of the relevant features.

    Based on that analysis, give an interface and internal design for the symbol table you would recommend for compiling the language you analyzed.

10. Collect lists of identifiers from several programs that you or other programmers have written. Write a program to store these identifiers in binary search trees and to report on how well balanced the resulting trees are.

11. The concept of perfect hashing was introduced in Section 3.5 as a method for fast recognition of keywords by a scanner. Many of the articles published on this topic have stressed algorithms that create *minimal* perfect hash tables to use as little space as possible. One drawback to such an approach is that most or all of the strings for nonkeyword identifiers produce hash values that collide with keyword hash values, thus requiring a string comparison in order to make the final decision about the token. Because string comparisons are slow on many machines, we would rather avoid them. A larger hash table would allow some hash values to have no associated keyword. If an identifier maps to such a value, no string comparison is required to make the identifier/keyword decision. Study the relationship between hash table size for perfect hash functions and keyword recognition efficiency, either experimentally or analytically.

12. In the discussion of record field names in Section 8.4.1, we mentioned that some languages allow abbreviations of the expressions for naming fields. Using the example in that section, R.X.C and R.C would be equivalent references, as would R.X.A and R.A. Describe necessary data structures and an algorithm for correctly handling such field references.

13. Another way of naming record fields is in the opposite order than that used in Pascal, Ada, and similar languages. That is, C.X.R would be used instead of R.X.C. Describe necessary data structures and an algorithm for correctly handling such field references in a single left-to-right pass.

14. How would the altered search rules described in Exercises 12 and 13 affect the implementation of **with** statements in Pascal?

CHAPTER 9

Run-Time Storage Organization

The evolution of programming language design has led to the creation of increasingly sophisticated methods of run-time storage organization. Originally, all storage allocation was *static*—that is, fixed during the entire execution of a program. Algol 60 and succeeding languages introduced features that required *stack allocation,* in which space is pushed and popped on a run-time stack at particular times during program execution, such as when procedures are called and when they return. LISP and later languages, including Pascal, popularized *heap allocation,* which allows space to be allocated and freed at any time during program execution.

As a way to examine storage allocation requirements of language features, we first consider the concept of a *data area*. A data area is a block of storage for variables and other objects known to the compiler to have uniform storage allocation requirements. That is, when any object in the data area must be allocated, all the objects in it must be allocated. The variables of a Micro program are a simple example of a data area. They are all allocated when execution of a program begins, and they remain allocated until execution terminates. A record allocated dynamically by a call to new in Pascal or Ada also acts as a data area.

9.1. Static Allocation

In many early languages, notably assembly languages and FORTRAN, all storage allocation is static. Space for data objects is allocated in a fixed location for the lifetime of a program. Use of static allocation is possible only when the number and size of all objects to be allocated is known at compile-time. This allocation approach, of course, makes storage allocation trivial, but it can also be quite wasteful of space. As a result, programmers must sometimes *overlay* variables. For example, in FORTRAN the equivalence statement is often used to reduce storage needs. Overlaying can lead to rather subtle programming errors, because assignment to one variable implicitly changes the value of another. Overlaying also reduces program readability.

In modern languages, static allocation is used both for global variables that are fixed in size and accessible throughout program execution and for program literals (that is, constants) that need to be fixed throughout execution. Static allocation can also be used for variables local to a module in Modula-2 or to top-level packages in Ada and for **static** and **extern** variables in C.

Conceptually, we can bind static objects to absolute addresses. It is often preferable to address a static data object as a pair (DataArea, Offset). Offset is fixed at compile-time, but the address of DataArea can be deferred to link- or run-time. In FORTRAN, for example, DataArea can be the start of one of many common blocks, or it can be the start of a block of storage for the variables local to a subroutine. Typically these addresses are bound when the program is linked. Address binding must be deferred until link-time because FORTRAN subroutines may be compiled independently, making it impossible for the compiler to know about all the data areas in a program.

Alternatively, the address of DataArea can be loaded into a register, which allows a static data item to be addressed as (Register, Offset). This addressing form is available on almost every machine. The advantage of addressing a piece of static data this way is that we can defer deciding on where a static object will be loaded until *just before* execution begins. This technique is useful in a load-and-go environment, where no explicit link step is done, because the size of various program components cannot be determined until the whole program is translated. This is exactly the technique used to implement Micro. For example, we cannot decide where to place the literal pool until we know how big the generated program code will be. Thus an absolute address into the literal pool cannot readily be created until we finish compiling statements.

9.2. Stack Allocation

Almost all modern programming languages include recursive procedures, a feature that requires dynamic allocation. Each recursive call requires the allocation of a new copy of a procedure's local variables; thus the number of data objects required during program execution is not known at compile-time. To implement recursion, all the data space required for a procedure or function is treated as a data area that, because of the special way it is handled, is called an *activation record* (AR). An AR is pushed onto a *run-time stack* when the procedure or function is called (activated). When the subprogram returns, the AR is popped from the stack, freeing the routine's local data. To see how stack allocation works, consider the subprogram shown in Figure 9.1.

```
procedure p(a : integer) is
    b : real;
    c : array(1..10) of real;
begin
    b := c(a) * 2.51;
end;
```

Figure 9.1   A Simple Subprogram

In Figure 9.1 the routine requires space for the parameter a as well as the local variables b and c. It also needs space for control information, such as the return address. As the procedure is compiled, the space needs of the procedure are recorded. In particular, the *offset* of each data item relative to the beginning of the AR is stored in the symbol table. The total amount of space needed, and thus the size of the AR, is also recorded. In our example, assume p's control information requires five words (this requirement is usually the same for all routines). Parameter a requires one word, variable b requires two words, and array c requires 20 words. Figure 9.2 shows p's AR.

Within p, each local data object is addressed by its offset relative to the start of the AR. This offset is a fixed constant, determined at compile-time. Because we normally store the start of the AR in a register, each piece of data can be addressed as a (Register, Offset) pair, which is a standard addressing mode in almost all computer architectures. For example, if register R points to the beginning of p's AR, variable b can be addressed as (R,6), with 6 actually being added to the contents of R at run-time, as memory addresses are evaluated.

Normally, the literal 2.51 is not stored in the activation record because the values of local data that are stored in an AR disappear with it at the end of a call. If 2.51 were stored in the AR, its value would have to be initialized

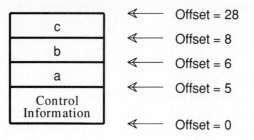

Figure 9.2   Procedure p's Activation Record

before each call. It is easier and more efficient to allocate literals in a static area, often called a *literal pool*.

Many languages, including Ada and Ada/CS, allow *dynamic arrays*. The bounds of dynamic arrays are determined at run-time rather than compile-time, and hence these arrays cannot be allocated within an activation record. Dynamic arrays can be allocated as soon as their associated declarations are *elaborated* (that is, fully evaluated). Declarations precede statements in most languages, so allocating space for dynamic arrays is one of the first things a subprogram does after it is called.

The translation of array declarations is detailed in Chapter 11. For dynamic arrays, a fixed-size descriptor, usually called a *dope vector*, is placed in the activation record of the subprogram containing the array's type declaration. The dope vector contains the size and bounds of the array. This information is obtained when the array declaration is elaborated. Once the array's dope vector is initialized, space for each occurrence of the array can be allocated. It is convenient to allocate this space on the run-time stack, immediately atop the current AR. In effect, the AR is extended to accommodate dynamic arrays.

At compile-time, each dynamic array is assigned a single location in the current AR. At run-time this location will point to the space allocated for the array, somewhere beyond the end of the AR. Dynamic arrays are accessed indirectly: First the run-time address of the array is extracted from the AR, then the array, or elements of it, are accessed.

To see how this works, let us add the declaration

    d, e : **array**(1..N) **of** integer;

to procedure p of Figure 9.1. When p is called, the activation record shown in Figure 9.3 is pushed onto the run-time stack. The array declaration is elaborated immediately after p is called. This causes N to be evaluated, and then the dope vector is initialized. The dope vector contains the size of the array, so space for d and e can be pushed onto the stack, with pointers to the allocations stored in the AR. At this point, we have the AR structure shown in Figure 9.4.

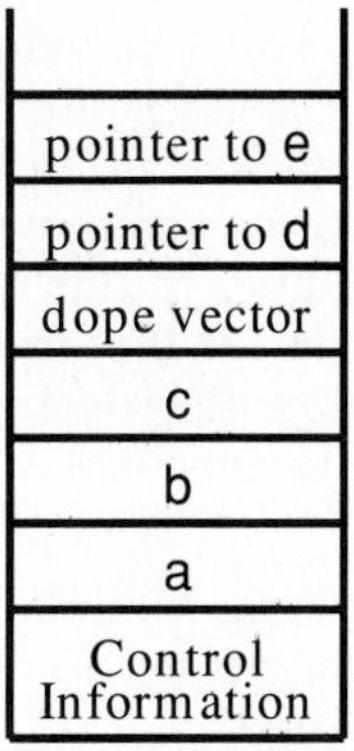

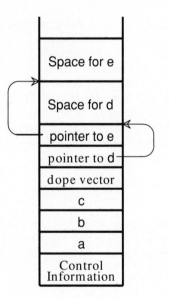

Figure 9.3   Activation Record for New Version of p

Figure 9.4   Activation Record for p after Declaration Elaborization

The size of a dynamic array is fixed once its declaration is elaborated. Further, the lifetime of a dynamic array is the same as any other local variable, so extending an activation record to include space for dynamic arrays is both simple and effective.

Some languages provide for statically allocated variables within a procedure (**static** in C, own in Algol 60). The value of such variables must be preserved across calls. As was the case for literals, static variables are allocated in global locations rather than within an activation record. Algol 60, which allows arrays to be declared own even though their size is not known at compile-time, presents severe difficulties in this regard. As discussed later, it is not hard to find space on the heap for the object, but when it has a larger size during a later call of the procedure that declares it, it has to be copied into a new place that can hold it. Two-dimensional arrays, both of whose bounds are dynamic, are particularly nasty.

In some languages, including Ada, Modula-2, and Simula, a single runtime stack does not suffice. These languages do not follow the Algol model in which subprograms are always exited in last-in, first-out order. Ada and Modula-2 allow control to switch back and forth between processes, each of which is like a procedure in that it has its own referencing environment containing both local and nonlocal variables. In fact, each process must have its own stack. Likewise, Simula allows procedures to be called as coroutines, so all the local variables of a procedure must be retained until it is certain that it has terminated. These languages allocate entire stacks by heap allocation.

Another language feature, found in Ada, Simula, and some LISP implementations, allows two processes to share access to nonlocal variables. It is not enough to copy the shared part of the accessing environment into the run-time stacks of the two processes, because when one process modifies a nonlocal value, the other process should always see the new value. Instead, the stacks are built in segments that may be shared. This method is sometimes called *cactus stacks*, since the organization is reminiscent of the saguaro cactus, which sends out arms from the main trunk and from other arms. It is important that the language be designed so that shared segments are not deallocated until all processes sharing them have terminated.

9.2.1. Displays

An activation record is usually addressed through a register that points to its beginning. However, during execution the number of activation records on the stack may exceed the number of available registers. For example, consider the program shown in Figure 9.5.

```
1    program main is
2
3        procedure p is
4
5            procedure q is
6                . . .
7            end q;
8
9            procedure r is
10               . . .
11           end r;
12       end p;
```

```
13
14          procedure s is
15               . . .
16          end s;
17
18   begin  -- main
19               . . .
20   end main;
```

Figure 9.5   A Program with Nested Procedures

It is possible to have the sequence of calls shown in Figure 9.6.

```
Call main program
Call p
Call s
Call p
Call s
Call p
     . . .
Call p
Call q
Call r
Call q
Call r
     . . .
```

Figure 9.6   A Sequence of Procedure Calls in Program main

How can we handle such involved calling sequences? Fortunately, because of scoping rules, not all activation records need to be accessible at the same time. In particular, the AR for the main program is needed all the time, but it can be allocated statically. All procedures and functions have a *static nesting level* determined by the structure of the program (p and s are at level 1; q and r are at level 2). At any point, only one procedure at any given nesting level can have its variables accessed, following the rules of block structure. We allocate one register for each possible static nesting level. (The maximum static nesting level is often limited as a compiler restriction.) This set of registers is called a *display*, and each register in the display is termed a *display register*. At any given point, the ith display register (denoted $D[i]$) will point to the currently accessible AR, if any, at static nesting level i. In our example above, if we were currently in procedure q, we might have the situation depicted in Figure 9.7.

At any point, many ARs are not addressed by any display register. Their local variables are not, at that point, directly addressable. As procedures return, display registers are updated, and ARs previously inaccessible become addressable through some display register. Therefore, every call must estab-

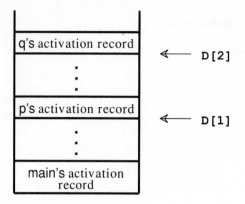

Figure 9.7   A Sequence of Activation Records on a Run-time Stack

lish a proper display for the procedure that is called, and every return must restore the display that was in force before the call.

An extreme policy would be to store the entire display in the AR of each procedure so that when a call returns, the saved display can be used to restore all display registers. The length of the "display area" in the AR would be determined by the lexical level of the procedure. A maximal area could always be set aside long enough to hold the largest-allowed display.

Luckily, it is not necessary to store the entire display. It suffices to store *exactly one* display entry over any call. Calls can be to a lexical level one deeper (we call that "higher"), the same level, or any level shallower (we call that "lower"). In each case, the value of the display register at the level that is being called should be saved in the display area in the AR of the callee. This area can be one word long. When the call returns, this value must be restored. It works just as well to save the display register in the AR of the caller, but then the caller must have different code after calls to procedures at various levels. It is easier to let the callee restore the register; the same register is restored no matter what the level of the caller is.

This mechanism reestablishes the entire display after each call to its original state before the call, even the parts of the display that are not used by the lexical level of the caller. Why is it so important to maintain those higher display registers? Consider the program shown in Figure 9.8.

Let us assume that the following procedures are called in turn:

A B C A′ B′ C′

We use the ′ mark to indicate that a different instantiation of the procedure is called. The display in force at each invocation, as well as the display value that is saved, are shown in Figure 9.9.

```
procedure A is
    procedure B is
        procedure C is
            · · · A; · · ·
        end C;

        · · · C; · · ·
    end B;

    · · · B; · · ·
end A;
```

Figure 9.8 A Program with Nested Procedure Calls

calls	A	B	C	A′	B′	C′
display[3]	??	??	C	C	C	C′
display[2]	?	B	B	B	B′	B′
display[1]	A	A	A	A′	A′	A′
saved	–	?	??	A	B	C

Figure 9.9 An Example of How Displays Are Saved and Restored

When A′ returns to C, the method shown modifies only **display[1]** from A′ to A; the other display registers are already set correctly to B and C. Even though A′ did not itself need those registers, it was essential that calls instituted by A′ preserve their contents so that when A′ returns, only one register needs to be restored to establish the referencing environment of C.

9.2.2. Block-level and Procedure-level Activation Records

Languages such as Algol 60, C, Ada, and Ada/CS allow declaration of local variables within blocks as well as within procedures. A block with local variables can be considered an in-line procedure without parameters, so we can create a new activation record for each block that has local declarations. This approach requires more display registers, because static nesting will be deeper if blocks are included. Further, it makes execution of a block more costly, for an AR needs to be pushed, display registers updated, and so forth. To avoid this overhead, it is possible to use ARs only for true procedures, even if blocks within a procedure can have local declarations. This technique is called *procedure-level* AR allocation, as contrasted with *block-level* AR allocation, which allocates an AR for each block that has local declarations.

The central idea of procedure-level AR allocation is that the relative location of variables in individual blocks within a procedure can be computed and fixed at compile-time. This works because blocks are entered and exited in a strictly textual order. Consider, for example, the procedure of Figure 9.10.

```
procedure A (X,Y : in  real) is
    QQ : integer;
begin
    B1: declare
        D,E: real;
    begin
        . . .
    end B1;

    B2: declare
        G,H,I: integer;
    begin
        B3: declare
            J : real;
        begin
            . . .
        end B3;
    end B2;
end A;
```

Figure 9.10   A Program with Block-level Declarations

Space for the parameters X and Y and the procedure-level variable QQ must always be accessible in A. Space for variables in B1 or B2 may be needed, but space for both need never be allocated at the same time. Similarly, space for B3 needs to be allocated only when we are in B2. We can, therefore, at compile-time create a single AR for procedure A that contains space for all variables declared in A. In particular, space for X, Y, and QQ comes first. Space for D and E can be overlaid with that for G, H, and I, and space for J can be placed just beyond G, H, and I.

The procedure-level activation record shown in Figure 9.11 results.

9.3. **Heap Allocation**

The most flexible and expensive method of storage allocation is *heap allocation*. Data objects can be allocated and freed at any time and in any order. A storage pool, usually called a *heap*, is needed. (Do not confuse our definition of heap as a memory allocation pool with the heap data structure often used for fast retrieval of the minimum element in a set. Unfortunately, both definitions are in wide use.)

Some languages that have explicit commands to allocate heap space (allocate in PL/I, new in Pascal and Ada), but others such as Snobol or LISP implicitly allocate heap space as a result of user statements (for example,

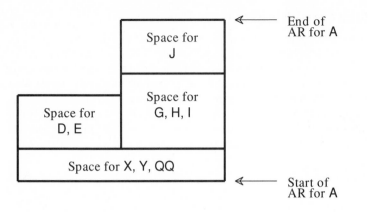

Figure 9.11   A Procedure-level AR for Procedure A

Str = Str 'XYZ' or (CONS A B)). Allocation of heap space is not particularly difficult—we simply keep allocating from the heap until we run out of space. What makes heap allocation complex is the fact that space may be returned to the heap (that is, deallocated) in any order. This situation leads to a number of different deallocation strategies, discussed in further detail below.

A third strategy when designing a language is to have no heap allocation mechanisms at all, either explicit or implicit. C works this way, moving memory allocation into the standard library (with the routines **malloc()** and **free()**). This approach allows the replacement of the general memory allocation mechanisms supplied by the library vendor with one tuned to a particular application. However, it prevents the compiler and run-time system from doing any checking to be sure that the heap is being correctly managed.

The C++ language introduces a compromise. It provides explicit **new** and **delete** operators for allocating and freeing storage; but these operators may be overloaded for any specific class. This means that the programmer can choose to rely on the default memory management mechanisms provided by the C++ compiler and run-time system, or to provide mechanisms tailored to the application.

9.3.1. No Deallocation

We may choose to *ignore* deallocation. When we run out of space, we stop. Some Pascal implementations (for example the Berkeley Pascal interpreter) follow this policy. Such an approach is not that bad if most heap objects, once allocated, stay in use. It may also work for implementations with a large virtual memory; unused data objects do not clutter main store. A programmer who wants to conserve space can still manage deallocation by building a DisposeObject procedure for each object type that links together free objects of that type onto a list. An AllocateObject procedure would first try to return the head of the free list; if the list is empty, it would resort to heap allocation.

9.3.2. **Explicit Deallocation**

If we have explicit allocation commands, we may also have explicit de-allocation commands (unchecked_deallocation in Ada, **free()** in C, and dispose in Pascal). It is the user's responsibility to free unneeded space by executing deallocation commands. The heap manager merely keeps track of freed space and makes it available for reuse when allocation commands are issued. This approach shifts the really hard decision—when space should be freed—to the user and leads to possibly catastrophic *dangling pointer* errors. For example, consider the Pascal program fragment shown in Figure 9.12.

```
var p,q : ↑ real;
     . . .
    new(p);
    q := p;
    dispose(p);
    q↑ := 1.0;
```

Figure 9.12   Creation of a Dangling Pointer in Pascal

After the assignment of p to q, both point to the same object. After p is disposed, q is a dangling pointer. Assignment through q is illegal and, if undetected, can have unpredictable effects. A few implementations, including UW-Pascal, detect use of dangling pointers by checking pointer validity (see Chapter 11), but in most systems this error would go undetected.

9.3.3. **Implicit Deallocation**

With either explicit or implicit allocation we may choose *implicit deallocation*—that is, automatic recovery of unused heap space. This process is often called *garbage collection*. There are a number of different ways to deallocate implicitly.

Single References

One way to deallocate implicitly is to require that there never be more than one reference (that is, pointer) to any heap object. Whenever this reference is changed (for example, when an assignment is done or a scope is closed), we may free the object whose sole reference is being destroyed.

This approach is fairly easy to implement, but it requires that multiple references never exist. It is therefore best for simple data types, such as strings, and not suitable for intricately linked structures (such as graphs, networks, and so on). Nonetheless, Ada/CS string implementations can exploit this method, as we shall discuss later.

Reference Counts

We may also deallocate implicitly by allowing multiple references to a heap object and storing a *reference count* with each heap object, as depicted in Figure 9.13. The reference count indicates how many pointers to the object exist; when this count reaches zero, the object may be freed. We must update this field whenever a reference is created, copied, or destroyed. In some cases (for example, circular lists), a reference count may never go to zero, and some objects may therefore never be freed.

Garbage Collection

Another way to deallocate implicitly is to follow all extant pointers and recursively mark all accessible heap objects. This process is often called *mark-and-sweep garbage collection*. We start with global pointer variables and with pointer variables that appear in ARs (and thus are local to subprograms). Information on where pointer variables are to be found must be kept (perhaps in an auxiliary data structure). Data objects, particularly records, may contain pointers, and these pointers must be followed.

After the marking phase, we know that any object not marked is inaccessible and may be freed. We then sweep through the heap, collecting all unmarked objects and returning them to the free space pool for later reuse. During the sweep phase we also clear all marks from heap objects found to be still in use.

Mark-and-sweep garbage collection is very powerful, but it also is quite complex. It is attractive in that work need be done only when heap space is exhausted and not whenever references are created or destroyed. That is, we pay nothing until we run out of heap space, at which point garbage collection is performed.

In any mark-and-sweep scheme, it is vital that we mark *all* heap objects. If we miss a pointer, we may fail to mark an accessible heap object and later incorrectly free it. Finding all pointers is not too difficult in languages like LISP that have very uniform data structures, but it is fairly tricky in languages like Simula and Ada that have pointers mixed with other objects within data structures, implicit pointers to temporaries, and so forth. Considerable information about data structures and activation records must be available at run-time for this purpose.

A simpler form of garbage collection—one essentially involving only a sweep through the heap—is possible if we know there can be only one pointer

Reference Count	Data Object

Figure 9.13   A Heap Object with a Reference Count

to any heap object. This technique is quite suitable for Ada/CS strings, which are dynamic in length and hence must be allocated from the heap.

Rather than doing a complex marking process, we adopt the following *handshaking convention*. Pointers, of course, point to heap objects. Each heap object has a header field that points back to the single pointer that references it. This process is illustrated in Figure 9.14.

As we sweep through the heap, we follow the pointer in the header field and see if the location it references points back to the header. For all accessible heap objects, this handshake will succeed. If a pointer p has been changed, the heap object previously referenced by p will still point to p, but p will not point back, signaling that the heap object may be freed. Pointers that appear in an activation record are considered inaccessible after the AR is popped from the run-time stack. Any heap object whose header pointer points beyond the current stack top is considered inaccessible and is reused. It may happen that an AR is popped from the stack, and then another AR is pushed, occupying the same space. In this case, the space formerly occupied by a pointer may be overlaid with other data, but the handshake will almost certainly be broken, causing a heap object to be correctly deallocated. There is a slight chance that the new data that overlays the location previously occupied by a pointer will have the same bit pattern that the pointer did. In this unlikely case, a heap object that is inaccessible will not be collected until the data changes value. This is not really a problem—we merely do not collect all inaccessible heap objects.

Many garbage collectors perform a *compaction* phase as inaccessible heap objects are collected. All heap objects still in use are placed together in the heap. This allows inaccessible heap objects to be coalesced into a single free area, making it easier to allocate large objects. If compaction is not performed, it is possible that the heap allocator will have many free areas in the heap, none of which is large enough to satisfy a request. Because of allocation and deallocation, the heap may become *fragmented*; compaction joins small fragments into larger, and more useful, pieces.

When compaction is performed during mark-and-sweep garbage collection, a second pass through all accessible pointers is needed to reset the pointers to the new address of the object they reference. When the handshaking convention is used, things are easier because each object header points to

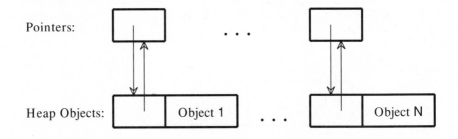

Figure 9.14   A Handshaking Convention for Heap Objects

the pointer that must be reset. There is a danger, though. As noted before, what appears to be a pointer in the run-time stack may actually be a non-pointer that has overlaid the location once held by a valid pointer. If we perform compaction at this point, we may incorrectly change the value of a location that is not a pointer. Hence, it is wise to compact only heap objects referenced from globally allocated pointers—pointers that cannot be overlaid with any other object.

9.3.4. Managing Heap Space

In all storage recovery schemes and in all languages that provide heap allocation, we need to be careful of *uninitialized pointers*. Either we must initialize each pointer with a null value when it is created (Simula does this) or we must check pointer validity before use (UW-Pascal does this). If we do not, we may reference (and change or dispose) through bad pointers almost any area of storage (program text, stack space, literals, and so on).

If both allocation and deallocation are allowed, whether implicit or explicit, the heap manager must be able to allocate variable-sized chunks on demand and accept returned blocks of space. For allocation, several pieces of memory may be currently available for a new chunk. The *best-fit* method picks the free piece that will leave the least amount of waste if we use part of it for the desired chunk. This method is generally very inefficient, however; it leads to a proliferation of tiny and therefore useless free pieces. The *first-fit* method picks the first free piece that is large enough, no matter how much waste there may be. This method is better, but if the algorithm always starts searching from the start of the heap, small pieces tend to cluster near the front. The average search for a suitable chunk of free space, therefore, requires probing about half of all free chunks. The recommended method is *circular first fit*, which is like first fit but starts the search at the point where the previous search left off instead of always starting from the beginning of physical store. Typically only a few probes are needed.

A reasonable data structure for recording the state of the heap is for each free piece to store pointers that link it into a doubly-linked list. Also, each piece, whether free or in use, has the first and last words reserved to indicate its status, free or busy, and its length. When a free chunk is needed, the doubly-linked list is searched from the last stopping point until an adequate piece is found. If necessary, it is split into a new busy piece and a new free piece. If the fit is exact, the entire piece is removed from the doubly-linked free list. When a piece is returned to free space, it is coalesced with the piece before it and after it, if they are free, and then put on the free list. This method is called *boundary tags*.

Although circular first fit is a good general method, programs often require only a small number of different-sized chunks. The compiler knows what many of these sizes are (for example, for records), although perhaps not all (for example, for strings). It is far more efficient to allocate each different space size from a different heap than to use one global heap for all allocation. Then a *bit-map* technique can indicate which chunks in the heap are free. That is, each object in a heap of fixed-size objects is mapped to a bit (in a separate area) that indicates whether it is allocated or free. There is no danger of wasting space with this technique because of small fragments.

9.4. Program Layout in Memory

Now that we have discussed the run-time storage organizations used by compilers, we can consider how a compiled program is laid out in main memory. Many layout schemes are possible; one suitable for Pascal or Ada/CS is shown in Figure 9.15.

Reserved locations are memory locations reserved for special use by the target computer architecture. In some machines, for example, registers or an

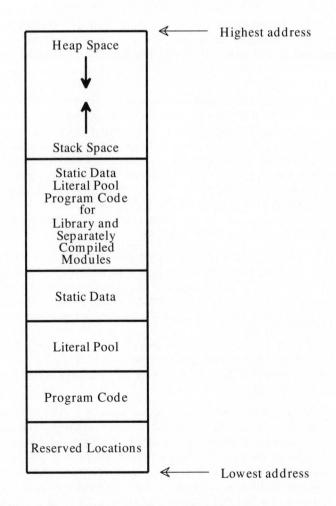

Figure 9.15   A Typical Program Layout in Memory

operand stack are mapped to reserved addresses. The program code generated by the compiler is statically allocated and is normally read-only. The literal pool contains the run-time representation for all literals that appear in the program. This segment is statically allocated and is read-only. The global data segment contains all global and static variables. It is statically allocated and writeable. Next comes library modules used for run-time support (I/O, memory management, profiling and debugging routines, and so on). Separately compiled subprograms and packages may also appear here. Each of these modules normally contains a program code segment, a literal pool, and a static data segment, just as the main program does.

Library modules and separately compiled modules are included by a linker or loader as a result of external references that appear in the main program. The linker or loader must be sure to properly relocate all address references that appear in code segments, including the main program. Cross-module (external) references, too, must be resolved to the correct addresses. The linker or loader also takes responsibility for properly grouping program segments and ordering them in memory. As data and program code are generated, they are assigned offsets relative to a particular relocation unit. These offsets define the internal structure of a relocation unit.

After the statically allocated program segments are assigned memory locations, the remaining memory is partitioned between the two dynamic structures—the stack and the heap. At the beginning of execution, both the stack and the heap are initialized. Often the stack begins just beyond the statically allocated program segments and grows toward higher addresses. The heap begins at the highest addresses and grows toward lower addresses. If the stack and heap ever meet, there will be a conflict in memory use, so each operation that extends the stack or heap must check for a collision. If a collision occurs, it may be possible to invoke garbage collection, with compaction, to separate the two structures.

Some computer architectures, such as the Vax and the Intel 8086, have a segmented memory. That is, available memory spans a number of distinct segments, some for program code and others for data. Code segments are read-only and can be used for program code and the literal pool. Distinct data segments can be used for the stack and heap; thus, the possibility of collisions is eliminated.

Some computers use an operand stack rather than registers to perform arithmetic operations. It is possible to use the top of the run-time AR stack to hold operands, but this can be inconvenient if activation records must be pushed or popped while operands and expressions are being evaluated. It is simpler, therefore, to allocate the operand stack, if one is used, to a separate program segment. This is easy to do if the maximum depth of the operand stack can be determined. Operands are normally not kept on the operand stack across statements, except when a function call appears in an expression. As code for each statement is generated, the stack depth needed for the statement can be determined by examining the order in which pushes and pops are done. The maximum stack needed for any single statement in a function can be computed. This value is used when a function call appears in an expression. Unless function calls are recursive, a bound on the maximum operand stack can be computed and used to allocate space for the operand stack. If recursive function calls occur, it may be necessary to use the activation record stack for operands or to assign an arbitrary bound to the size of the operand stack.

If a compiler is designed for load-and-go operation, as most Ada/CS project compilers are, program layout in memory is changed significantly. Program and data are assigned memory addresses and possibly loaded into memory as they are generated. There are no distinct linking and loading phases, so it is advantageous to minimize the need to relocate addresses and resolve cross-module references. Separate compilation is rarely supported in load-and-go compilers, so we will focus on library modules, which certainly need to be included somehow. Two approaches are attractive. We can make all library routines *self-relocating*, meaning the routines are written so that they operate correctly no matter where they are loaded. (Such code is often termed *position-independent* code.) This is done by making all address references relative to a base register (loaded at run-time with the routine's start address) or to the program counter register (if the machine architecture uses one).

Cross-module references are handled by using a *transfer vector*. Each entry point in a library module that is referenced directly or indirectly from the main program is assigned a position in the transfer vector, which can be allocated in the literal pool. At run-time the transfer vector will contain the addresses assigned to corresponding entry points. All references to library module entry points are made indirectly through the transfer vector. Rather than generating code to branch directly to the OpenFile routine, we assign a fixed position, p, to OpenFile in the transfer vector and generate an indirect branch through location p. When the library module containing OpenFile is loaded, we initialize p with the correct address.

An even simpler approach is possible if the set of library routines is small, as it is in Pascal and Ada/CS—we simply load them all into fixed locations. We assume that the whole run-time support library will always be in fixed locations, probably just past locations reserved by the architecture. Because the library routines are always in the same place, we relocate them in advance and copy into memory an executable, binary image of the routines. Cross-module references are simple, too. Library routines are always loaded into the same locations, and we can maintain, at compile-time, a table of entry point addresses. No indirection is needed. If we want to call OpenFile, we look up the address assigned to it and use it in the code generated for the call.

As a final point, if we load instructions and data into memory as they are generated we cannot put literals and global variables into segments immediately beyond the program segment. The problem is that as literals and global variables are generated, we do not yet know how large the program segment will be, because the entire program is not yet compiled. As an alternative, we can allocate literals and globals to the same program segment and begin filling this segment from the highest memory addresses, growing toward lower addresses. As usual, we fill the program segment from low memory addresses. After the program and data segments are filled, remaining space is split between the stack and heap. This leads to the program layout shown in Figure 9.16.

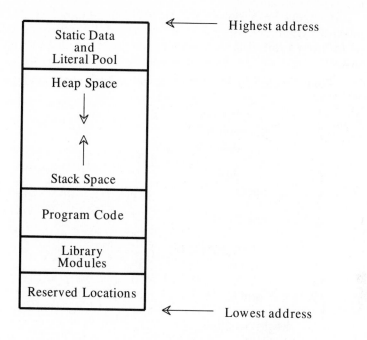

Figure 9.16   A Program Layout for Load-and-Go Compilers

9.5. **Static and Dynamic Chains**

In this section we consider an alternative to the display approach to accessing activation records. Sometimes we are unable or unwilling to allocate a large number of registers as display registers. An alternative, then, is to use a single register, often called an *activation register* or *activation pointer*, that points to the uppermost AR on the run-time stack. All ARs are designed so that they contain (usually at offset 0) a pointer to the AR corresponding to the immediately containing procedure. This pointer is called the *static link* because it reflects the static nesting structure of procedures and functions. Another pointer (again at a fixed offset in the AR), called the *dynamic link*, points to the AR just below the current AR in the run-time stack.

The chain of static links beginning in any AR contains the same information that a display would. In fact, a static chain can be thought of as an alternative implementation of a display. If we are currently in a procedure at level `i`, the activation pointer references the same AR that `D[i]` would. Further, the static link in this AR points to what `D[i-1]` would. By following `j` static links from the uppermost AR, we can get to the AR referenced by `D[i-j]`. When a nonlocal variable must be accessed, the compiler generates code that follows static links the appropriate number of times, which is known at compile-time.

Dynamic links connect the AR of a routine to the AR of the routine that called it. These links are necessary to restore the activation pointer after the return from a call. The sequence of static links is called the *static chain*. Similarly, the sequence of dynamic links is called the *dynamic chain*.

For example, consider the program skeleton shown in Figure 9.17.

```
1     program Main is
2         procedure P is
3             procedure R is
4                   -- Body of R
5             end R;
6         begin  -- P
7             R;
8         end P;
9
10        procedure Q is
11        begin
12            P;
13        end Q;
14
15    begin  -- Main
16        Q;
17    end Main;
```

Figure 9.17   A Program Skeleton

From Main, Q is called. Q calls P, which calls R. When we are in R at line 4, the AR sequence shown in Figure 9.18, which is linked with static and dynamic chains, results. The static link always shows the AR belonging to the procedure in which the current procedure is *statically* nested. The dynamic link always shows the AR that *dynamically* called it.

The use of a static chain rather than a display can make data references slower because the static chain must be followed. Fortunately, this often is not as expensive as it might first appear. In many programs, most data references are to either local data or global data (that is, to the innermost or outermost activation record), and such references are particularly efficient. For example, a study of reference patterns in a wide variety of Simula 67 programs (Magnusson 1982) found that fully 80% of all references were to variables at the outermost level or to local variables. Another 17% of the references were to the block immediately surrounding the local one. Local data is pointed to by the activation pointer; global data is static and does not actually need to be referenced via the static chain. Thus few references will actually require following the static chain, and most of those will require only one level of such indirection. Some machines designed to support Algol-like languages provide hardware support for static chains. In particular, on such machines, a piece of data is addressed by a pair (ChainLength, Offset). Offset is, as usual, relative to the start of an AR. ChainLength is a count of how many static links must be

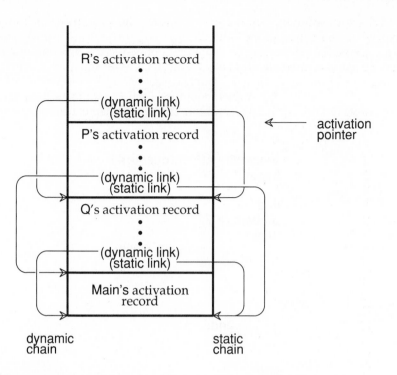

Figure 9.18   An Example of Static and Dynamic Chains

followed to get the appropriate AR (ChainLength = 0 means use the top AR pointed to by the activation pointer). This addressing mode is convenient to use; given reference patterns like those described above and hardware support, it can be almost as efficient as a display mechanism. However, this or any other mechanism that requires memory references rather than register references to obtain pointers to ARs will always be somewhat less efficient.

9.6. Formal Procedures

Formal procedures are subprograms passed as parameters to other subprograms. The details of implementing subprogram calls are discussed in Chapter 13. In this section we concentrate on the impact of formal procedures on AR access through displays or static and dynamic chains.

Formal procedure parameters are tricky to implement because each formal procedure must carry an *environment*. This environment is the set of accessible ARs in which it is to execute. This set of ARs comprising an environment is sometimes called a *closure*. An environment is bound when a subprogram is first *created*, that is, when its declaration is *elaborated*. Elaboration of a declaration occurs when the block or procedure in which it lies is entered during execution. This environment may be very different from that in force when the subprogram is finally invoked through its formal parameter name. Using the referencing environment defined at the time the subprogram was created is termed *static binding;* using the environment from the point of eventual call is termed *dynamic binding.* Algol 60 and its descendants all use static binding. Early LISP implementations used dynamic binding, but many recent descendents, including Common LISP and Scheme, use static binding.

```
1       B0: begin
2               procedure A(F); procedure F;
3               begin
4                       F(1)
5               end;
6               procedure B;
7               begin
8                       procedure G(X); Integer X;
9                       begin
10                              . . .
11                              goto L;
12                              . . .
13                      end;
14                      A(G);
15              L:      ;
16              end;
17              B;
18      end;
```

Figure 9.19   An Example of Formal Procedure Parameters

Consider the Algol 60 fragment shown in Figure 9.19. When the actual procedure G is bound to the formal parameter F at line 14, its environment, bound when G was created at entry to B, is B0 and B. When it is called as the formal F at line 4, the environment in use is B0 and A. Nonetheless, when G executes, it must have access to B's local variables, even though they are not accessible from its calling point (line 4). Thus we must be able to *change environments* upon call of a formal procedure and restore them upon return.

We must even be able to do **goto**s out of a formal procedure, as shown at line 11. The target of the **goto** must be visible in the execution environment for the **goto** to be legal, but there may be several instances of the target's AR on the run-time stack. Only one is in the current environment, though, and this is the one that should continue execution. All other intermediate ARs must be discarded as if their procedures had returned. (As we shall see, reestablishing registers and the display after a nonlocal **goto** can be complicated.)

As it happens, static chains make formal procedures fairly easy; displays are harder. We will consider both.

9.6.1. Static Chains

We have already learned how to build static chains. When a normal (nonformal) procedure is called, the compiler knows the difference in lexical level between the caller and the callee. This difference dictates what the static chain of the callee should point to. If the difference d is −1 (the callee is one level deeper), the static chain points to the caller. Otherwise, the static chain is a copy of the static chain of the caller with d arcs removed.

For formal procedures, the static chain cannot be determined at compile-time. Instead, we require that static chains be passed as part of the formal procedure. Then, when a formal procedure is finally called, its static chain is already available, stored in the caller's activation record as part of the information it knows about this parameter.

The first time a procedure is passed as a formal parameter (say A passes B to C), the actual parameter B is a normal procedure. The compiler can calculate, as before, the difference in lexical level between the caller, A, and B and can generate code to build the static link that would have applied if B were being called directly. The caller, A, passes to C both a pointer to B's code and that static link. C retains both; if it should call B under its formal parameter name, C will give it the stored static link. If C should pass B to yet another routine, C transmits its static link along with it.

Reconsider the example in Figure 9.19. Initially we enter B0, then call B and reach line 14. The run-time stack at that point is shown in Figure 9.20.

G's environment is represented by a pointer to B's AR. A is then called, and we reach line 4. Now the run-time stack is that shown in Figure 9.21.

Here G, called by its formal name F, is to be called. G's static pointer to B's AR is used to set up the static link, as shown in Figure 9.22. Upon normal return, we use the dynamic link, as always, to restore the caller's environment.

The **goto** L from G back into B uses the static link to find the correct instance of B (here there is only one, but in general there may be several). After the **goto**, we have the stack configuration shown in Figure 9.23.

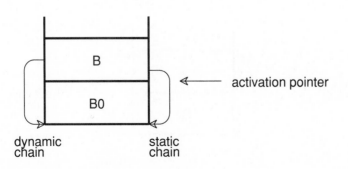

Figure 9.20   Run-time Stack after Calling B

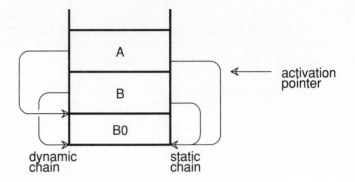
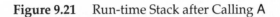

dynamic
chain

static
chain

activation
pointer

Figure 9.21   Run-time Stack after Calling A

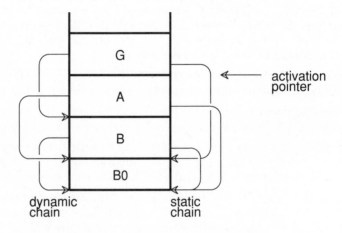

dynamic
chain

static
chain

activation
pointer

Figure 9.22   Run-time Stack after Calling G

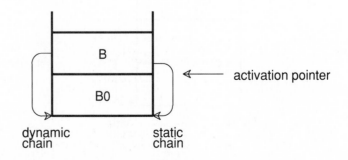

dynamic
chain

static
chain

activation pointer

Figure 9.23   Run-time Stack after **goto** L

This method of implementing formal procedures is quite simple and efficient. It does, however, suffer from the accessing inefficiencies inherent in static chains. Procedure invocation is no more complex than before; it is not much more work to derive and pass a static pointer than to save one display register.

9.6.2. Displays

We can adapt our display mechanism to formal procedures. When a procedure is bound to a formal parameter, we pass the contents of all display registers as well as the address of the procedure. Thus the data passed are as shown in Figure 9.24. The size of this block of data is fixed for a given maximum lexical nesting depth, imposed by the number of display registers. We also make available a global variable or register called **restore_AR**. It is used to restore environments upon return from a formal procedure. Now, just before a formal procedure is called, we

- Save the current value of **restore_AR** in the caller's AR
- Save the current values of display registers (**D[0]** ,..., **D[MAX]**) in the caller's AR
- Set **restore_AR** to point to the current AR
- Replace the display values with those passed as part of the formal procedure's descriptor
- Call the formal procedure via its entry address

Upon return from a formal procedure, we

- Use **restore_AR** to reload the caller's display
- Restore the previous value of **restore_AR**

The overhead of formal procedures (swapping entire displays) is paid only if we use formal procedures. Ordinary procedure calls behave exactly as if formal procedures did not exist.

This method works as long as every formal procedure returns normally. Either we must disallow **goto**s out of subprograms so that a subprogram, when called, does not know (or care) if it is called as a formal procedure or or-

Entry Addresses
Value of **D[1]**
⋮
Value of **D[Max]**

Figure 9.24   Formal Procedure Descriptor, Using a Display

dinary subprogram, or we must extend the technique at some cost to handle **goto**s out of subprograms. This extension can be accomplished with a hybrid method that uses static chains to save and restore displays. This variation unfortunately does have overhead for ordinary calls.

Another way to allow **goto**s out of formal procedures is to simulate a series of procedure returns. The position on the stack of the AR that is to be the local environment after the **goto** is always easy to determine. If the label L is declared at lexical level **i**, then **goto** L should restore, as the local AR, the AR pointed to by **D[i]** at the time the **goto** is executed. Thus, the code for the **goto** repeatedly does all the actions necessary for a procedure return until the activation pointer points to the correct AR. Some of these returns are simple, involving restoring one saved display register. However, those that involve returns from formal procedures involve restoring entire displays. This technique makes **goto**s out of procedures slow, but nonlocal **goto**s must always bear the overhead of restoring register and display values, and this often is not trivial. In any event, nonlocal **goto**s are used by programmers only in exceptional cases, where speed is not necessarily crucial (for example, to abort an operation in the event of an error).

9.6.3. Perspective

The complexity of swapping environments for formal procedures suggests that such procedures are hard to understand in general. For example, what does the Pascal program of Figure 9.25 write as an answer?

F is called by Main and then calls itself recursively 12 times. The twelfth time, it returns a value by calling Arg, which is bound to an occurrence of Local. Local accesses the nonlocal variable Level. The usual static scope rules of Algol-like languages say that the nonlocal reference finds the instance of Level declared in procedure f. But which of the 13 instances of Level should be used? Do not be confused by the difference between static and dynamic scope rules. Static scope rules say that when there is more than one *declaration* of a variable, we find the *closest* rather than *most recent* declaration of the variable. Here, there is only one declaration of Level. Nonetheless, it would be an error to take the most recent occurrence of Level. This mistake is sometimes called the *most-recent* error. The use of Level in an instance of Local is bound to the occurrence of Level in force when the declaration of Local was elaborated—that is, when the block containing the declaration was entered. When the occurrence of Local is picked up and passed as a parameter, it carries its environment, including the binding of Level, with it. The version of Local that eventually gets called has its Level bound to the version whose value is 11. Thus, this program prints 11.

The C language does not allow subprograms to be nested within other subprograms. While this limitation requires that some subprograms be given greater visibility than would be necessary in other languages, it does have the advantage of making formal procedures in C easy to understand and implement. Subprograms passed as parameters need carry no environment because they can access only globals, shared by everyone, and locals created upon subprogram activation. (In fact, formal procedure parameters as such don't really

```
program Main(Output);
    function f(Level : Integer; function Arg : Integer) : Integer;
        function Local : Integer;
        begin {Local}
            Local := Level
        end; {Local}
    begin {f}
        if Level > 10 then
            f := f(Level – 1, Local)
        else if Level > 1 then
            f := f(Level – 1, Arg)
        else
            f := Arg { actually call Arg() }

    end; {f}

    function Dummy : Integer;
    begin {Just a placeholder} end;

begin {Main}
    writeln('The answer is:',f(13,Dummy));
end.
```

Figure 9.25   A Pascal Program That Uses Formal Procedures

exist in C. Instead, the parameters are simply variables of type "pointer to function returning *type*.") Ada is even more restrictive than C and allows no formal procedures. Restricting formal procedures to be subprograms not nested within other subprograms would allow many useful applications of formal procedures and yet would avoid the complexity inherent in maintaining the correct execution environment.

Exercises

1. Programming languages provide constructors for a variety of data objects. Suggest the run-time storage organization most appropriate for each of the classes of data objects described here:

    list of T;

    T is any type name. Lists may be catenated using an **append** operation and decomposed using **head** and **tail** operations.

set of Lower .. Upper;

Lower and Upper are constant values. This is essentially the set constructor provided in Pascal.

set of Lower .. Upper;

Lower and Upper are expressions evaluated at run-time when the set declaration is elaborated.

set of T;

T is any type name.

ExtendedInt;

ExtendedInt is an extended precision integer. There is no MaxInt or MinInt bound; rather, the precision of the representation is extended as needed to accommodate any value.

file of T;

T is any type except a file (or a structure that contains a file). This is the file constructor provided in Pascal.

String(N);

N is a constant value. The string may vary in length from 0 to N.

String(N);

N is an expression evaluated at run-time when the string declaration is elaborated. The string may vary in length from 0 to N. This is essentially the string constructor provided in PL/I.

2.   Show the layout of a procedure-level AR for the following routine:

```
procedure q(a : integer; b: real) is
  c : array(1..N) of real;
  d : string;
begin
  declare
    e : array(1..10) of integer;
  begin
    . . .
  end:
  declare
    f : array(1..M) of integer;
    g : integer;
  begin
```

. . .
    end:
  end q;

Show the corresponding block-level ARs.

3.   Trace the sequence of AR and display manipulations needed to execute the following program:

```
procedure main is

    function m(i : integer) return integer is

        function p(i : integer) return integer is
        begin
            return m(i * 2 + 1);
        end p;

        function q(i : integer) return integer is
        begin
            return m(i + 111);
        end q;

        function r(i : integer) return integer is
        begin
            return i * 3 ;
        end r;

        begin
          case i mod 3 is
            when 0 => return p(i / 3);
            when 1 => return q(i / 3);
            when 2 => return r(i / 3);
          end case;
        end m;

    begin
        write(m(157));
    end main;
```

4.   Show the sequence of ARs on the run-time stack, with static and dynamic links, when function r of Exercise 3 is active.

5.   On some computers it is possible to extend the maximum accessible memory address, thereby increasing the effective size of memory. This memory extension operation could be valuable when a program has exhausted free memory because of the growth of dynamic memory structures. How would you lay out a program in memory to allow for possible expansion?

6.   The handshaking scheme presented in Section 9.3.3 for recognizing accessible heap objects does not safely allow heap compaction. Suggest a generalization of the scheme that does allow compaction. *Hint:* Generalize the two-way handshake into a three-way handshake.

7.   Many compilers allocate a fixed set of registers for use as display registers. In some cases this policy may overallocate registers to the display, wasting them. In other cases the display may be too small, limiting the class of programs that can be successfully compiled.

Outline an algorithm that a compiler might use to determine the exact number of display registers needed for a particular program. What problems arise if this algorithm is used in a one-pass compiler?

8.   Assume we organize a heap so that only one pointer to any heap object is allowed. What operations must be done when a pointer to a heap object is overwritten? What operations must be done when a scope is opened and closed? Can assignment of pointers or heap objects be allowed?

9.   Assume we organize a heap using reference counts. What operations must be done when a pointer to a heap object is assigned? What operations must be done when a scope is opened and closed?

10.   Some languages, including C, contain an operation that creates a pointer to a data object. That is,

```
p =  &x;
```

takes the address of object **x**, whose type is **t**, and assigns it to **p**, whose type is **t**∗.

How is management of the run-time stack complicated if it is possible to create pointers to arbitrary data objects in ARs?

What restrictions on the creation and copying of pointers to data objects suffice to guarantee the integrity of the run-time stack?

11.   Assume that rather than maintaining a single heap we maintain a distinct subheap for each type T that may be dynamically allocated. What are the advantages and disadvantages of maintaining distinct subheaps? How do subheaps simplify reclamation of inaccessible heap objects?

12.   Consider a heap allocation strategy, which we shall term *worst-fit*. Unlike best-fit, which allocates a heap request from the free space chunk that is closest to the requested size, worst-fit allocates a heap request from the largest available free space chunk. What are the advantages and disadvantages of worst-fit as compared with the best-fit, first-fit, and circular first-fit heap allocation strategies?

13.   The performance of complex algorithms is often evaluated by simulating their behavior. Create a program that simulates a random sequence of heap allocations and deallocations. Use it to compare the average number of iterations that the best-fit, first-fit, and circular first-fit heap allocation techniques require to find and allocate space for a heap object.

14. Some programming languages provide the following construct for the concurrent execution of program steps:

cobegin <stmt 1> | <stmt 2> | · · · | <stmt n> **coend**

Each of <stmt 1>, . . . , <stmt n> can be executed concurrently or in any order. Within each statement in the **cobegin** construct, ordinary **begin-end** blocks can be used to force sequential execution.

Does an ordinary run-time stack suffice for a language that contains a **cobegin** construct? If not, how must the stack be generalized to support the concurrent or interleaved execution order allowed by the **cobegin**?

15. Assume display swapping is used to implement formal procedures. Trace the sequence of AR and display manipulations needed to execute the following Pascal program:

```
program prog(output);

procedure q(procedure c(var i:integer));
var z : integer;
begin
    z := 17;
    c(z);
end;

procedure p(procedure a(procedure x(var j:integer));
        procedure b(var k:integer));
begin
    a(b);
end;

procedure r;
var i : integer;
    procedure s(var j:integer);
    begin
        writeln(j + i)
    end;
begin
    i := 10;
    p(q,s);
end;

begin
    r;
end.
```

Now assume that static and dynamic chains are used to implement formal procedures. Again trace the sequence of AR and static/dynamic chain manipulations needed to execute this program.

16. Show that the display-swap approach for implementing formal procedures fails for the following Pascal program:

```
program prog(output);

procedure q;
label 1;
    procedure exec(procedure z);
    begin
        z;
    end;

    procedure r;
    begin
        goto 1;
    end;
begin    exec(r);
1:
end;

procedure p(procedure a);
var v : integer;
begin
    v := 10;
    a;
    writeln(v);
end;

begin
    p(q);
end.
```

Does the static/dynamic chain approach handle this program correctly?

Processing Declarations

There are three major sections to this chapter. The first section presents some basic techniques for processing declarations, including the kinds of structures that represent declarations as well as special ways the semantic stack is used while processing declarations. The second section outlines the semantic routines necessary to process a simple subset of the various kinds of declarations in Ada/CS. This subset includes variable and type name declarations, along with record and static array type definitions. These semantic routine outlines are written in an ANSI C-based pseudocode that should be easily readable to anyone familiar with the basic concepts of ANSI C. (Our extensions to ANSI C are outlined in the Preface.) The third section includes similar semantic routine outlines for the rest of Ada/CS. We continue to use semantic routine outlines in the next three chapters as a mechanism to discuss the compilation of language features. Though this presentation is based on the features of a particular language, the techniques introduced are intended to be general enough for use in compiling a wide variety of languages.

A note on terminology. A "record" is the term used in Algol-derived languages for what C calls a "structure." A "variant record" is what C calls a "union," and a single variant corresponds to an element of a C union. In particular, C **union**s are equivalent to Pascal untagged variants. C does not have anything equivalent to Pascal or Ada's tagged variants; it is up to the programmer to know what is in a union at any particular time.

10.1. Declaration Processing Fundamentals

10.1.1. Attributes in the Symbol Table

In Chapter 8, symbol tables were presented as a means of associating names with some *attribute information*. We did not consider what kind of information was included in the attributes associated with a name or how it was represented. Those topics are considered in this section.

The attributes of a name generally include anything the compiler knows about it. Because a compiler's main source of information about names is declarations, attributes can be thought of as internal representations of declarations. Compilers do generate some attribute information internally, typically from the context in which the declaration of a name appears or, when use is an implicit declaration, from a use of the name. Names are used in many different ways in a modern programming language, including as variables, constants, types, and procedures. Every name, therefore, will not have the same set of attributes associated with it. Rather, it will have a set of attributes corresponding to its usage and thus to its declaration.

The record definition that appears in Figure 10.1 illustrates the style of the name and attribute representation used in the portable Pascal compiler, Pascal P-4, that was the basis of many Pascal implementations. It uses variant records to handle the variety of attributes that must be associated with names, depending on how they are used.

The Name, Llink, and Rlink fields are used to implement the symbol table. As indicated by the comment, the portable Pascal compiler uses a binary tree symbol table representation. Thus the type IdPtr is defined as a pointer to an identifier record. The rest of the fields are used to record the attributes of the identifiers in the symbol table. The first attribute field, IdType, is declared to be a TypePtr, which is a pointer to a TypeDescriptor record. This latter record is another important structure, to be discussed shortly. After IdType comes the variant part of this record, which can store appropriate information for each different kind of identifier. It is not our purpose to study

```
type Identifier =
  record
          Name : Alpha;              (* the identifier represented here *)
          Llink, Rlink : IdPtr;      (* to implement a binary tree symbol table *)
     (* The previous fields implement the symbol table search mechanism; *)
     (* those that follow describe the attributes of Name  *)
          IdType : TypePtr;
          Next : IdPtr;              (* used to construct lists of identifiers *)
          case Class : IdClass of
            Constant: (Value : ValueType);
            Variable : (Vkind : IdKind;
                        Vlevel : LevelRange;
                        Vaddr : AddressRange);
          Field: (FieldOffset : AddressRange);
          Proc, Func: (
             case PFDeclKind : DeclKind of
                 Standard: (  · · ·  );
                 Declared: (  · · ·  ))
  end ;
```

Figure 10.1   Symbol Table Record from the Pascal P-4 Compiler

the portable Pascal compiler, so we will not consider all the details of this
record. However, they should be easily understood after reading about the
compilation techniques presented in this and following chapters for all the
features of Ada/CS. The variant for procedure and function names is worth
noting, as it includes a nested variant to distinguish between standard routines
and those declared as part of the program. Arbitrarily complex structures,
determined by the complexity of the information to be stored, may be used for
attributes.

As we outline the semantic routines for processing Ada/CS declarations,
we define a similar attribute record for the language we are compiling. One
significant difference between our record and the preceding Pascal record is
that we separate the symbol table implementation from the attributes by putting them in different structures. The compiler for any language that allows
multiple definitions for a name in a single scope, such as Ada does with the
overloading feature, must be able to associate more than one set of attributes
with a single name. This requirement is most easily met by putting each set of
attributes in a separate structure and building a list of such structures to
represent overloaded uses of a name.

10.1.2. Type Descriptor Structures

Among the attributes of names illustrated in the record in Figure 10.1 was a
type, included in the attribute record by a pointer to a TypeDescriptor record.
Representing types presents a compiler writer with much the same problem as
representing attributes: There are many different types whose descriptions

require different information. Again our solution will be to use a variant record (in C, a **union**) of the style illustrated in Figure 10.2, which is also based on the structures of Pascal P-4.

The TypeDescriptor record begins with fields giving the size of the type and indicating whether it is packed. This information is universal to all types. The rest of the record is a variant part, depending on the kind of type being described. An important aspect of this record is that almost every field in the variant part is a pointer. For example, an enumeration (scalar) type is described by a list of Identifier records that contain the constants of the type. A record is described by a binary tree used for looking up the fields, just as for other identifiers. An array is represented by pointers to TypeDescriptors for its index and element types. Thus, types are generally described not by just a single record but rather by an extended data structure constructed by using pointers. Such a representation is crucial in handling languages such as C, Modula-2, Pascal, and Ada, which allow types to be constructed using powerful composition rules. Using this technique rather than some kind of fixed tabular representation also makes the compiler much more flexible in what it can allow a programmer to declare. For example, with this technique there is no reason to have an upper bound on the number of dimensions allowed for an array or the number of fields allowed in a record. Such limitations in languages like FORTRAN stem purely from implementation considerations. We generally favor techniques that enable a compiler to avoid rejecting a legal program because of the size of the program or some part of it. Use of dynamic linked structures like those implied by the TypeDescriptor record are an important basis of such techniques.

```
type TypeDescriptor =
  record
        Size : AddressRange;
        PackedFlag : boolean;
        case Form : TypeForm of
          Scalar:       (case ScalarKind : DeclKind of
                            Declared: (FirstConst : IdPtr);
                            Standard: () );
          Subrange:     (RangeBaseType : TypePtr;
                          Min, Max : Value);
          Pointer:      (PtrBaseType : TypePtr);
          SetType:      (SetBaseType : TypePtr);
          ArrayType:    (IndexType, ElementType : TypePtr);
          RecordType:   (FirstField : IdPtr);
          FileType:     (FileBaseType : TypePtr)
      end;
```

Figure 10.2   Type Descriptor from the Pascal P-4 Compiler

10.1.3. Lists in the Semantic Stack

Many constructs in Ada/CS and other programming languages involve lists of things like identifiers, expressions, and so on. Some of these lists, such as a list of declarations, have no semantic significance. Each declaration is processed independently of the others. Other lists, such as the list of actual parameter expressions in a Pascal procedure call, are of semantic significance and may be processed one item at a time as the items are recognized by the parser because sufficient information is available to the compiler from the context in which the list appears. In neither of these cases is it necessary to explicitly collect the list of items on the semantic stack.

Sometimes much of the semantic processing of the items on a list cannot be done until the entire list is collected. The following production from Ada/CS illustrates such a problem:

<object declaration> → <id list> : <object tail>

Semantic information collected during the processing of <object tail> is needed to build attribute records for the identifiers in <id list>. It makes sense to collect these identifiers on the semantic stack until the entire declaration has been parsed. This can be done easily (with an action-controlled semantic stack) if we define a **MARK** semantic stack record kind. A **MARK** record is like an **ERROR** record in that it includes no information. Its presence in a particular place on the semantic stack conveys all the information required. We also need a semantic record alternative for identifiers. In the Micro compiler semantic records discussed in Chapter 7, identifier strings were stored in expression records. In more-complex languages, all identifiers are not interpreted as expressions, so a separate variant of the semantic record is needed.

The production for <id list>, with action symbols included, is

```
<id list>  → #push_mark <id> { , <id> }
<id>       → IDENTIFIER #process_id
```

The semantic routines require only simple actions:

```
push_mark(void)
{
    Push a MARK record onto the semantic stack.
}

process_id(void)
{
    Push an ID record onto the semantic stack, containing
        the token string of the identifier returned by the
        scanner.
}
```

Semantic Stack
Before:

Semantic Stack
After:

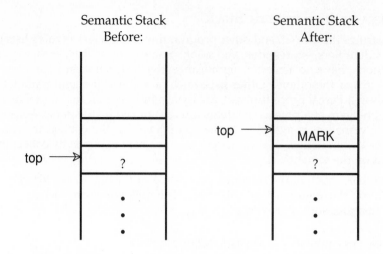

Figure 10.3(a)   Effect of **push_mark()** on the Semantic Stack

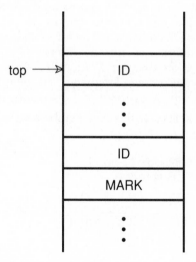

Figure 10.3(b)   Semantic Stack Configuration after Calls to
process_id()

Figure 10.3(a) shows the effect **push_mark()** has on the semantic stack. Figure 10.3(b) shows the semantic stack configuration after some or all of the <id list> has been processed.

The **MARK** record serves as a delimiter for the list. The semantic routine that uses the <id list> may process identifiers by working its way down the stack until it hits the **MARK**. The significant idea of this technique is that an arbitrarily long list may be represented by a sequence of entries in the stack, even though it corresponds to a single nonterminal in the grammar.

The principal advantage of this technique is its simplicity. Its main disadvantage is that a very long list can cause stack overflow if the semantic stack is implemented as an array. Although this problem is unlikely to occur due to a long list of identifiers in a declaration, case statements with a large number of alternatives are common. Thus, we must consider an alternative way of handling lists for such situations. An effective alternative is to represent the list by a single record in the semantic stack, building an explicit linked structure to contain the elements of the list. For an <id list>, after processing some or all of the list, we would have a structure like that shown in Figure 10.4.

In addition to dealing with the overflow problem, this technique is compatible with use of a parser-controlled semantic stack, whereas the list-in-the-stack technique is not. The following, slightly different placement of semantic action symbols is used; the nonterminal <id> is not used in this production for <id list> because the action routine triggered by its production puts an ID record directly on the stack:

<id list> → IDENTIFIER #start_id_list { , IDENTIFIER #next_id }

The corresponding action routines are shown below. We introduce a new notation with this example, so our action routines need not refer explicitly to the semantic stack. The symbols (terminals and nonterminals) whose associated semantic records are used as parameters by an action routine appear in parentheses after the routine name (as if they were parameters). If the action routine produces a semantic record as a result, the symbol with which it is to be associated follows the **=>** symbol. Assignments in action routines are signified by ←. This notation makes our action routine outlines independent of whether an action-controlled or a parser-controlled semantic stack is used. In many cases, particularly when expressions and statements are being considered, they can even be applied as tree attribution routines if an abstract syntax tree representation is used.

```
/*
 * Since identifier lists can be either in the semantic
 * stack or in a list, these two routines are purposely
 * vague about adding new identifiers to the list.
 */

start_id_list (IDENTIFIER)  =>  <id list>
{
    Create an ID record for the token string
        corresponding to IDENTIFIER
```

```
        <id list> ← an IDLIST record containing a
            pointer to that ID record
    }

    next_id(<id list>, IDENTIFIER) => <id list>
    {
        Create an ID record for the token string
            corresponding to IDENTIFIER
        Add this record to the list of such records in the
            IDLIST record
        <id list> ← the updated IDLIST record
    }
```

start_id_list() produces the list header record shown in Figure 10.4 and puts the first identifier on the list. Calls to next_id() add subsequent identifiers to the list.

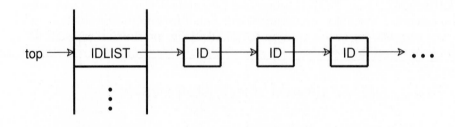

Figure 10.4   Alternative <id list> Representation

10.2. **Action Routines for Simple Declarations**

We now begin to examine the techniques necessary to write an Ada/CS compiler. This section begins with semantic processing techniques for a simple subset of the declarations in Ada/CS.

10.2.1. **Variable Declarations**

To begin our study of declaration processing, we consider variable declarations like those found in such languages as Pascal and Modula-2. Unlike Ada and Ada/CS, these languages have different syntactic forms for variable and constant declarations, and their variable declarations may not include initialization specifications. Thus the syntax for such variable declarations is simply

<variable declaration> → <id list> : <type> #var_decl

The record shown below is used to represent types on the semantic stack. An instance of such a record is left on the stack by the routines called during the parsing of <type>:

```
struct type_ref {
    type_descriptor *object_type;
};
```

Now we present attribute and type descriptor records that suffice to handle the features in our subset. These records resemble the Pascal records discussed earlier but are adapted for handling the features of Ada/CS. Details will be discussed as they are used in processing the various kinds of declarations. The **struct range** used within the array variant is defined in the section on processing array definitions. (This is the first use of *anonymous structures* as elements of anonymous unions.)

Figure 10.6 presents a **semantic_record** structure declaration appropriate for handling the same subset of Ada/CS as the attribute definitions in Figure 10.5.

Bear in mind while reading the semantic routines in this chapter and in Chapters 11–13 that where a terminal or nonterminal name (like <id list>) is used, it represents a **struct semantic_record**.

Only one semantic action symbol appears in the variable declaration production, but the corresponding semantic routine depends on the results of a number of other semantic actions. The parameters of this semantic action include a **TYPEREF** semantic record produced by semantic routines called while <type> is being parsed and an <id list> represented in one of the two ways discussed earlier in this chapter. **var_decl()** enters all the identifiers on the list into the symbol table and builds corresponding attribute records for them. In a one-pass compiler, locations within an activation record are typically allocated for variables at this point. We do this by producing attributes of type **struct address** that include the nesting level of the current procedure, an offset for each particular variable and an indirection flag (which is always **FALSE** for simple variables):

```
var_decl(<id list>, <type>)
{
    for (each identifier in <id list>) {
        Call enter() to put the identifier in the
            current scope of the symbol table
        if (it is already there) {
            generate an appropriate error message
            continue;
        }
        Allocate storage for the variable, recording its
            offset in the local variable offset
        (The size of the block of storage to allocate is
        obtained from <type>.type_ref.object_type.size)
```

The following expression describes the attribute record to be created for the variable:

```
(attributes) {
    .class = VARIABLE;
    .id_type = <type>.type_ref.object_type;
    .id = the id_entry returned by enter();
    .var_address = (struct address) {
        .var_level = current_nesting_level;
        .var_offset = offset;
        .indirect = FALSE;
    }
  }
 }
}
```

```c
#include "symtab.h"    /* see Chapter 8 */
typedef short boolean;
enum id_class { VARIABLE, FIELD, TYPENAME };
enum type_form { INTEGERTYPE, FLOATTYPE, STRINGTYPE,
    ARRAYTYPE, RECORDTYPE, ERRORTYPE };
typedef unsigned long address_range;
struct address {
    short var_level;
    address_range var_offset;
    boolean indirect;
};
typedef struct attributes {
    id_entry id;
    struct type_des *id_type;
    enum id_class class;
    union {
        /* class == VARIABLE */
        struct address var_address;

        /* class == FIELD */
        struct {
            address_range field_offset;
            struct attributes *next_field;
        };
        /* class == TYPENAME --- empty variant */
    };
} attributes;
```

```
typedef struct type_des {
   address_range size;
   enum type_form form;
   union {
      /* form == INTEGERTYPE, FLOATTYPE, STRINGTYPE,
                   ERRORTYPE -- empty variant */

      /* form == ARRAYTYPE */
      struct {
         struct range bounds;
         struct type_des *element_type;
      };
      /* form == RECORDTYPE */
      struct {
         symbol_table fields;
         attributes *field_list;
      };
   };
} type_descriptor;
```

Figure 10.5   Attribute Definitions


```
struct id { string id; };
struct type_ref { type_descriptor *object_type; };
struct record_def {
   type_descriptor *this_type;
   address_range next_offset;
};
struct range { long lower, upper; };
enum semantic_record_kind { ID, TYPEREF, RANGE,
      CONSTOPTION, RECORDDEF, MARK, ERROR };
struct semantic_record {
   enum semantic_record_kind record_kind;
   union {
      struct id id;                 /* ID */
      struct type_ref type_ref;     /* TYPEREF */
      struct range range;           /* RANGE */
      struct const_option const_option; /* CONSTOPTION */
      struct record_def record_def;    /* RECORDDEF */
      /* empty variant */           /* MARK */
      /* empty variant */           /* ERROR */
   };
};
      . . .
```

Figure 10.6   Semantic Record Type Declarations

10.2.2. Type Definitions, Declarations, and References

In the **var_decl()** semantic routine, we assumed that the productions for
<type> would include calls to semantic routines that produce a **TYPEREF** se-
mantic record. We now examine those semantic routines to see the ways in
which a **TYPEREF** record may be produced. The relevant syntax is

<type>	→	<type name>
<type>	→	<type definition>
<type name>	→	<id> #type_reference
<type definition>	→	<record type definition>
<type definition>	→	<array type definition>

A type definition specifies the construction of a new type using one of
the type constructor mechanisms of Ada/CS. The semantic routines in the
type definition productions actually create type descriptors and build
TYPEREF semantic records that reference the descriptors they create. In Sections 10.2.3 and 10.2.4 we study this process for records and arrays.

When the <type name> alternative is used for <type>, the identifier must
be either a predefined type name or a name that previously appeared in a type
declaration. In either case, the corresponding **type_descriptor** reference
will be found in the symbol table by the **type_reference()** semantic routine. Appropriate type descriptors and symbol table entries must be built by a
compiler for predefined type names as part of its initialization phase. For
Ada/CS, Integer, Float, and String are predefined type names. We will see
shortly what their type descriptors look like.

A type declaration is simply a syntactic mechanism for giving a name to
a type. The syntax for a type declaration is

<type declaration> → **type** <id> **is** <type definition> #type_decl

No new semantic record types are required for handling type declarations. Examining the **attributes** record in Figure 10.5, we see a null variant included for a type identifier. A null variant is all that is required because
the only attribute information that needs to be associated with a type name is a
pointer to the descriptor for the associated type. (Unlike Ada, C does not have
explicit **null** variants; their existence is indicated simply by comments.)

As might be expected from examining the <type declaration> production, the semantic routine **type_decl()** operates on an **ID** record and a
TYPEREF record. Because it is a declaration production, it produces no semantic record:

```
type_decl(<id>, <type definition>)
{
    The identifier is entered into the symbol table
    with the following associated attributes record:
```

```
   (attributes) {
      .class = TYPENAME;
      .id_type = <type definition>.type_ref.object_type;
      .id = the id_entry returned by enter(); };
}
```

Declarations of types, like declarations of variables, produce no semantic records to be saved on the semantic stack. Rather, information from a declaration is saved in the symbol table. Because references to declared identifiers can appear at arbitrary places in a program, it should be obvious that a stack is not a useful place for keeping and accessing such information. For the most part, a semantic stack is used to hold information relative to the processing of one declaration, definition, or statement (though these may be nested). The effects of completely processing declarations and statements appear in the symbol table and in the generated code, not in the semantic stack.

Now that we know how a type name is represented in the symbol table, we can define the **type_reference()** semantic routine. As we already have observed, it produces a semantic record containing the appropriate type reference. It gets the type descriptor reference to put into that record from the **attributes** record associated with <id>:

```
type_reference(<id>) => <type name>
{
    Find <id>.id.id in the symbol table
    if (it is there && its attrs.class == TYPENAME)
        <type name> ← (struct type_ref) {
            .object_type = <id>.attrs.id_type };
    else
        <type name>.class = ERROR;
}
```

The semantic routines we have examined so far also have illustrated the generality of our type descriptor technique. We have described the routines for variable and type declaration without any concern for the details of type descriptors other than the use of the size of a type to allocate space for variables. It does not affect these routines if the types involved are scalars or are structured. The only important points are that all the different types are represented by a uniform type descriptor and that semantic records corresponding to types contain pointers to such descriptors. This approach makes it easy to add new types without changing the parts of the compiler that use types.

Handling Type Declaration Errors

In the semantic routine outlines for type definitions, various checks for conformance to static semantic restrictions are specified. In most cases, the semantic routine outlines assume that the checks are successful, presuming that some standard error-handling technique will be used if they are not. In Chapter 7

we introduced the technique of replacing an expected semantic record with an
ERROR record in order to signify that an error has occurred and an error message has been issued. That technique generally applies to all the routines
described in this chapter, with the corresponding expectation that each routine
will check that the semantic records it uses are not erroneous.

When **ERROR** records were introduced, we suggested that these error
flags would be propagated until they reached routines like **var_decl()** and
type_decl(). They would go no further because these routines produce no
semantic records for further propagation. One weakness of this approach is
that identifiers that were to be entered into the symbol table by these declaration routines are ignored. Later uses of these identifiers in the program cause
the generation of more error messages, saying that the identifiers are undeclared. Our goal is to produce the minimum number of error messages per error (preferably one), and we must improve our technique. The principal
source of errors preceding these declaration routines is improper type
definitions, so we will include a special alternative in the **TYPEREF** record,
namely **ERRORTYPE**. When one of these declaration routines finds it has received an **ERROR** record instead of a **TYPEREF** record, it goes ahead and declares the identifier or identifiers it is handling, using an **ERRORTYPE** type
descriptor for its type. When the attributes of any identifier are retrieved from
the symbol table, we always check to see if the associated type is an **ERROR-
TYPE**. If it is, an **ERROR** record is produced instead of the expected record for
the semantic routine processing the identifier. Following our usual protocol
with **ERROR** records, no later semantic routine should generate any error message either.

The `type_descriptor` Record

The next two sections examine the type descriptor structures that must be constructed to handle type definitions for the most common structured types,
records and arrays. To represent these types as well as the predefined numeric types, the type descriptor record must have this organization, as originally
illustrated in Figure 10.5:

```
enum type_form { INTEGERTYPE, FLOATTYPE, STRINGTYPE,
    ARRAYTYPE, RECORDTYPE, ERRORTYPE };

typedef struct type_des {
    address_range size;
    enum type_form form;
    union {
        /* form == INTEGERTYPE, FLOATTYPE, STRINGTYPE,
                    ERRORTYPE -- empty variant */

        /* form == ARRAYTYPE */
        struct {
            struct range bounds;
            struct type_des *element_type;
        };
```

```
    /* form == RECORDTYPE */
    struct {
        symbol_table fields;
        attributes *field_list;
    };
  };
} type_descriptor;
```

Given this type declaration, we can easily construct the type descriptors for the predefined types Integer, Float, and String that would be referenced in the attribute entries for these names in the symbol table. Note that these names must be put into a special scope in the symbol table that contains the outermost scope of the program being compiled. This extra scope is necessary because the names are *not* reserved. They may be redefined, at considerable risk to readability, in any program. The Integer type descriptor is:

```
(type_descriptor) { .form = INTEGERTYPE;
                     .size = INTEGERSIZE;  }
```

The type descriptors for Float and String are quite similar, though they use different constants, **FLOATSIZE** and **STRINGSIZE**, to specify the value for the **size** field. These three constants represent machine dependencies in the front end of a compiler. They obviously are dependent on numeric representation details of the target machine and the implementation chosen for strings. Typical values (in bytes) for **INTEGERSIZE** and **FLOATSIZE** are 2 and 4, respectively. **STRINGSIZE** is discussed in Chapter 11 when string implementations are presented. (The C **sizeof** construct is not necessarily of value here, for these constants represent values for the target machine, which need not be the same as the machine on which the compiler may be running.)

Type Compatibility

One question remains: Just what does it mean for types to be the same or for a constraint to be compatible with a type? Ada, Pascal, and Modula-2 have a strict definition of type equivalence, which says that every type definition defines a new, distinct type that is incompatible with all other types. This definition means that the declarations

```
A, B : array (1..10) of Integer;
C, D : array (1..10) of Integer;
```

are equivalent to

```
type Type1 is array (1..10) of Integer;
A, B : Type1;
type Type2 is array (1..10) of Integer;
C, D : Type2;
```

A and B are of the same type and C and D are of the same type, but the two types are defined by distinct type definitions and thus are incompatible. As a result, assignment of the value of C to A would be illegal. This rule is easily enforced by a compiler. Because every type definition generates a distinct type descriptor, the test for type equivalence requires only a comparison of pointers.

Other languages, most notably Algol 68, use other rules to define type equivalence. The most common alternative is to use *structural* type equivalence. As the name implies, using this rule, two types are equivalent if they have the same definitional structure. Thus Type1 and Type2 from earlier in this section would be considered equivalent. At first glance, this rule seems a more appropriate choice on the grounds that it is more convenient for programmers using the language. However, the designers of more-recent languages have realized that the structural equivalence rule makes it impossible for a programmer to get full benefit from the concept of type checking. That is, even if the programmer wants the compiler to distinguish between Type1 and Type2 for purposes of type checking, the compiler will not do so, for they are obviously structurally equivalent.

Structural equivalence is much harder to implement, too. Type equivalence is not determined by simple pointer comparisons. Instead, a parallel traversal of two type descriptor structures is required. Code for such traversals requires special cases for each of the variants of a type descriptor record. Alternatively, as a type definition is processed by the semantic action routines, the type being defined can be compared against previously defined types so that equivalent types are represented by the same data structure even when they are defined separately. This technique allows the type equivalence test to be implemented by a pointer comparison, but it requires an indexing mechanism that makes it possible to tell during declaration processing whether a newly defined type is equivalent to *any* previously defined type.

Further, the recursion possible with pointer types poses subtle difficulties to the implementation of a structural type equivalence test. Consider the problem of writing a routine that can determine whether the following two Ada types are structurally equivalent:

type A **is access** B;

type B **is access** A;

Even though such a definition is meaningless semantically, it is syntactically legal (presuming there is an incomplete type definition to introduce the name B before the definition of A). Thus a compiler for a language with structural type equivalence rules must be able to make the appropriate determination— that A and B are equivalent. If parallel traversals are used to implement the equivalence test, the traversal routines must "remember" which type descriptors they have visited during the comparison process in order to avoid an infinite loop (see Exercise 1). Suffice it to say that comparing pointers to type descriptors is much simpler.

10.2.3. Record Types

A record definition constructs a new type from a sequence of field declarations. Field declarations look syntactically like variable declarations and are processed similarly. Records are represented by a type descriptor that includes a new symbol table containing the fields.

The syntax for record definitions, with the necessary semantic actions, is

<record type definition>   → **record** #start_record <component list>
                                                    #end_record **end record**
<component list>   → <component declaration>
                                                    { <component declaration> }
<component declaration> → <id list> : <type name> #field_decl ;

Again, one new semantic record type is needed:

```
struct record_def {
    type_descriptor *this_type;
    address_range next_offset;
};
```

In the **TYPEREF** record, we saw the following variant for describing records:

```
struct {   /* form == RECORDTYPE */
    symbol_table fields;
    attributes *field_list;
};
```

This structure represents the fields of a record in two ways: (1) as a separate symbol table, which provides for the fastest searches for field names and (2) as an ordered list, which is useful for processing record aggregates. Records are typically small, so it is reasonable to keep only the list and use that as a special purpose symbol table for locating record field names. We include both to provide the most general capability.

The **attributes** record includes this variant to handle record fields:

```
struct {   /* class == FIELD */
    address_range field_offset;
    struct attributes *next_field;
};
```

field_offset records the offset of the field within the record that contains it; **next_field** is used to build the list of fields for the containing record.

The first action routine called during the processing of a record is **start_record()**. It builds a **RECORDDEF** semantic record that is used by the action routines that process field declarations. The header of the following action routine outline specifies that the semantic record produced by the `start_record()` routine is associated with the symbol **record**. Such an association is useful because this semantic record essentially describes the record declaration in progress and is referenced during the processing of each field declaration:

```
start_record(void) => record
{
    Create a type descriptor, T, as follows:
        (type_descriptor) { .form = RECORDTYPE;
                            .size = 0;
                            .field_list = NULL;
                            .fields = create(); }

    record ← (struct record_def) {
                    .this_type = & T;
                    .next_offset = 0; } ;
}
```

In a compiler using an action-controlled semantic stack, the semantic record produced by `start_record()` is left on the stack and is available for use during calls to `field_decl()`, with the stack in the configuration shown in Figure 10.7 (assuming an in-the-stack representation of identifier lists).

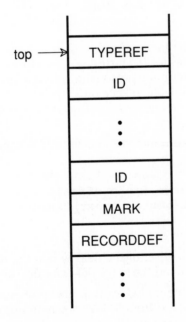

Figure 10.7   Semantic Stack Configuration for `field_decl()`

To illustrate such usage in our semantic routine outline notation, we use *context-sensitive* productions like the following one for <component declaration>:

record <component declaration> → **record** <id list> : <type name> #field_decl ;

The processing done by `field_decl()` is much like that of `var_decl()`, except that everything is done relative to the current record rather than the current procedure scope:

```
field_decl (record, <id list>, <type name>) => record
{
  Let RD name the semantic record associated with record

  for (each identifier in <id list>) {
    Enter the identifier in the symbol table
        referenced by RD.fields
    if (it is already there) {
        generate an appropriate error message
        continue;    /* go on to the next identifier */
    }

    The following expression describes the attribute
    record to be created for the field:

    (attributes) {
        .class = FIELD;
        .id_type = <type name>.type_ref.object_type;
        .id = the id_entry returned by enter();
        .field_offset = RD.next_offset;
        .next_field = NULL; }
    /* Allocate space for the field with the record. */
    RD.next_offset += <type name>.type_ref.object_type.size

    Add this attribute record to the end of the list
        referenced by RD.field_list
  }

    record ← RD ;
}
```

The technique for space allocation used by `field_decl()`, adding the size of each field to `RD.next_offset`, is based on the simplifying assumption that addressing alignment is not necessary. It does not work for architectures that require data objects to start at addresses divisible by 2 or 4, if any field can be smaller than the alignment factor. For such architectures, field sizes must be padded to maintain proper address alignment. We continue to make this same simplifying assumption in other routines that involve space allocation. The extensions necessary to consider alignment are straightforward.

Finally, in the **end_record()** routine, we see a **TYPEREF** semantic record constructed to represent the record type definition just processed:

```
end_record(record) => <record type definition>
{
    type_descriptor *T;

    T ← record.record_def.this_type;
    T.size ← record.record_def.next_offset;
    <record type definition> ← (struct type_ref) {
                .object_type = T; } ;
}
```

Once again, the new type is represented by a **TYPEREF** semantic record. The descriptor of the type consists of a pointer to a list of the **attributes** for the fields of the record in the order of their declaration (useful for processing record aggregates) and a symbol table (of arbitrary structure) that contains one entry for each field of the record. The symbol table entries, of course, also contain references to **attributes** records for each of the fields.

10.2.4. Static Arrays

Arrays declared with a static index range are common enough to merit separate consideration. This is the only form of array-type definition allowed in such prominent languages as C, Pascal, and Modula-2. Because recognition of this special case allows a compiler to significantly reduce the overhead of array implementation, we begin our consideration of arrays with a definition of the data structures and action routines to implement static arrays.

Following is a subset of the Ada/CS syntax for constrained array definitions. (A *constrained* array is one declared with its bounds specified by a particular discrete type.) In particular, this subset is limited to allowing only integer literals in specifications of bounds, thus guaranteeing that all array bounds are static.

```
<array type definition> → array ( <static range> ) of <type> #array_def
<static range>          → INTLITERAL #lower_bound .. INTLITERAL #upper_bound
```

These productions define only one-dimensional arrays. A multidimensional array must be defined as an array of arrays. We need a new semantic record type to represent a <static range>. It is defined by the following declaration:

```
struct range {
    long lower, upper;
};
```

As we have seen, the array alternative in the **TYPEREF** record is

```
struct {    /* form == ARRAYTYPE */
   struct range bounds;
   struct type_des *element_type;
};
```

The semantic routines are defined below. **lower_bound()** and **upper_bound()** build a **RANGE** record. This record is used by **array_def()**, with a **TYPEREF** for the element type of the array, to produce a **TYPEREF** for the array.

```
lower_bound(INTLITERAL) => <static range>
{
   <static range> ← a RANGE record with lower
      set to the value of INTLITERAL
}
```

```
upper_bound(<static range>, INTLITERAL) => <static range>
{
   long u, l;

   <static range>.range.upper ← the value of INTLITERAL

   u = <static range>.range.upper;
   l = <static range>.range.lower;

   if (u >= l)
      <static range> ← the updated RANGE record
   else {
      Produce an appropriate error message
      <static range> ← an ERROR record or a corrected
         version of the RANGE record
   }
}
```

```
array_def(<static range>, <type>) => <array type definition>
{
   long u, l;

   u = <static range>.range.upper;
   l = <static range>.range.lower;

   Create a new type descriptor for an array type:
      T ← (type_descriptor) {
            .form = ARRAYTYPE;
            .element_type = <type>.type_ref.object_type;
            .bounds = <static range>.range;
            .size = .element_type->size * (u - l + 1); }
   <array type definition> ← (struct type_ref) {
            .object_type = T; }
}
```

Thus, for an array definition like

array (1..10) **of array** (1..20) **of** Integer

the **type_descriptor** structure shown in Figure 10.8 is created.

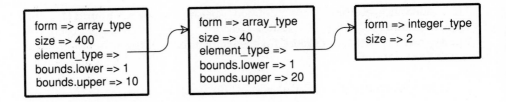

Figure 10.8   Example **type_descriptor**

10.3. **Action Routines for Advanced Features**

10.3.1. **Variable and Constant Declarations**

We now consider the full object declaration syntax of Ada/CS. It includes the following productions, with semantic action tokens included:

<object declaration>	→	<id list> : <object tail>
<object tail>	→	<constant option> <type or subtype>
		<initialization option> #object_decl
<constant option>	→	#not_constant
<constant option>	→	**constant** #is_constant
<type or subtype>	→	<type>
<type or subtype>	→	<subtype definition>
<initialization option>	→	#no_initialization
<initialization option>	→	:= <expression>

One additional semantic record type is required:

```
struct const_option { boolean is_constant; };
```

Two semantic routines are introduced to handle the optional keyword **constant**. They each produce a **CONSTOPTION** semantic record to indicate whether or not the keyword was present:

```
is_constant(void) => <constant option>
{
    <constant option> ← (struct const_option) {
                 .is_constant = TRUE; } ;
}

not_constant(void) => <constant option>
{
    <constant option> ← (struct const_option) {
                 .is_constant = FALSE; } ;
}
```

A constant in Ada and Ada/CS may be a literal constant whose value can be determined at compile-time, or its value may be determined by an expression that cannot be evaluated until run-time. In the case of a literal constant, a new variant in the **attributes** record, labeled by **CONST**, is used:

```
/* class == CONST */
struct value_type value;
```

value_type is defined in Chapter 11, where expressions are discussed.

In the case of a run-time value, the constant acts as a read-only variable because space must be allocated for it just as for other variables, but it may be given a value only by an initialization expression. Thus, this feature requires an extension of the **struct address** type defined in Section 10.2.1:

```
struct address {
    short var_level;
    address_range var_offset;
    boolean indirect, read_only;
};
```

The type of the objects being declared is defined syntactically by the nonterminal <type or subtype>. It is represented by a **TYPEREF** record, just as types were in the simpler subset discussed in Section 10.2. Thus no new semantic routines or semantic record types are required to handle this nonterminal.

An initialization may optionally be present in an object declaration. If it is present, it is represented by the semantic record used for describing expressions (see Chapter 11); if it is not, **no_initialization()** must produce some sort of null record as a placeholder. A **MARK** serves this purpose adequately:

```
no_initialization(void) => <initialization option>
{
    <initialization option> ← a MARK semantic record ;
}
```

object_decl() obviously must be more complex than **var_decl()** because it must handle not only variables but also constants and initialization expressions. Like **var_decl()**, its basic job is to put all the declared identifiers into the symbol table and associate appropriate attribute records with them. However, the **attributes** record associated with an identifier by object_decl() may have its **class** field set to either **VARIABLE** or **CONST**. Likewise, the initialization option figures prominently in the work done by **object_decl()**, an outline of which appears in Figure 10.9.

```
enum init_kind { INITCONST, INITVARIABLE, INITNONE };

object_decl(<id list>,  <constant option>,  <type or subtype>,
            <initialization option>)
{
  enum init_kind initialization;

  if (<initialization option>.kind == DATAOBJECT) {
    Verify the assignability of
        <initialization option>.data_object.object_type
        to <type or subtype>.type_ref.object_type.
    if (the expression has a compile-time value)
        initialization = INITCONST;
    else
        initialization = INITVARIABLE;

  } else {
    /*
     * An initialization expression must be present if
     * so indicated by <const option>.
     */
    if (<constant option>.const_option.is_constant)
        Produce an "Initialization required" error message
    initialization = INITNONE;
  }

  for (each identifier in <id list>) {
    Call enter() to put the identifier in the current
        scope of the symbol table
    if (it is already there)
        generate an appropriate error message
    else if (! <constant option>.const_option.is_constant
        || initialization == INITVARIABLE) {
        Allocate storage for the variable, recording its
        offset in the local variable offset. (The size of
        the block of storage to allocate is obtained from
        <type or subtype>.type_ref.object_type.size)
        The following expression describes the attribute
        record to be created for the variable:
```

```
   (attributes) {
      .class = VARIABLE;
      .id_type = <type or subtype>.type_ref.object_type;
      .id = the id_entry returned by enter();
      .var_address = (struct address) {
         .var_level = current_nesting_level;
         .var_offset = offset;
         .indirect = FALSE;
         .read_only =
            <constant option>.const_option.is_constant; };
   }

   if (initialization != INITNONE)
      Generate assignment code to initialize
      the object
} else   /* the identifier names a literal constant */
   The following expression describes the attribute
   record for the identifier:

   (attributes) {
      .class = CONST,
      .id_type = <type or subtype>.type_ref.object_type;
      .id = the id_entry returned by enter();
      .value = <initialization option>.data_object.value; }
   }
}
```

Figure 10.9   The `object_decl()` Action Routine

The semantic record alternative **DATAOBJECT** is defined in Chapter 11.

10.3.2. Enumeration Types

An enumeration type is defined by a list of distinct identifiers. Each identifier is a constant of the enumeration type. These constants are ordered by their position in the type definition and are represented by integer values. Typically, the value representing the first identifier is zero, and the value for all other identifiers is one more than that for its predecessor in the list. (C **enum**s allow the programmer to optionally specify values for enumeration constants. Furthermore, they are signed integers, not unsigned integers.)

The syntax for <enumeration type definition>, including semantic action tokens, is

```
<enumeration type definition>   → ( <enumeration id list> #finish_enum_type )
<enumeration id list>           → IDENTIFIER #first_enum_id
                                     { , IDENTIFIER #enum_id }
```

A semantic record type is needed for enumeration type declarations:

```
struct enum_def {
    type_descriptor *this_type;
    attributes *last_const;
};
```

The **type_descriptor** record must have a new variant to handle enumerated types:

```
/* form == ENUMTYPE */
attributes *first_const;
```

The **attributes** record also has to be extended to handle enumeration type constants. A new **id_class**, **ENUMCONST**, must be added. Its variant in the **attributes** record is

```
struct {   /* class == ENUMCONST */
    unsigned long enum_value;
    struct attributes *next_const;
};
```

The first field records the value used to represent an enumeration constant, and the second creates a list of all the constants of each enumeration type.

With enumeration type definitions all identifiers need not be collected on the stack before any can be processed. The syntax reveals that an enumeration type definition is present as soon as the parser sees the opening left parenthesis. Thus, the semantic routines that follow handle the enumeration constant identifiers as soon as they are accepted by the parser. **first_enum_id()** allocates a **type_descriptor** for the new type and begins the list of enumeration constants with the IDENTIFIER it receives as a parameter. It also enters it into the symbol table as an **ENUMCONST**. **enum_id()** does the same with its IDENTIFIER parameter, in addition to adding it to the list of constants for the type. **finish_enum_id()** finishes processing at the end of the type definition, producing a **TYPEREF** record, as is typical for type definitions:

```
first_enum_id(IDENTIFIER)  =>  <enumeration id list>
{
    Allocate a type_descriptor for an ENUMTYPE and let
        T point to it.
    Enter the IDENTIFIER into the symbol table.
        There may be more than one use of an identifier
        as enumeration constants of different types
        within a single scope (overloading), but an
        identifier used as an enumeration constant
        cannot have any other uses within a scope.
```

```
    Assuming an error is not reported, the identifier
        just entered into the symbol table has the
        following attributes record, A, associated
        with it:

(attributes) {
    .class = ENUMCONST;
    .id_type = T;
    .id = the id_entry returned by enter();
    .enum_value = 0;
    .next_const = NULL; }

    Set T->size to INTEGERSIZE and T->first_const to point
        to the attribute record just created
    <enumeration id list> ← (struct enum_def) {
                                            .this_type = T;
                                            .last_const = A; };
    /* assuming A references the attributes record */
}

enum_id(<enumeration id list>, IDENTIFIER) => <enumeration id list>
{
    Let ED rename <enumeration id list>.enum_def
    Enter the IDENTIFIER into the symbol table.
        The same error checking must be done as in
        first_enum_id().  In addition, the identifier
        must not already be in the symbol table as a
        constant of the type currently being processed.
    Assuming an error is not found, create an ENUMCONST
        attribute record for the identifier with
        id_type = ED.this_type
        enum_value = ED.last_const.enum_value + 1
        next_const = NULL
    Set ED.last_const.next_const to point to the
        attribute record just created
    Set ED.last_const to ED.last_const.next_const, thus
        adding the new attribute record to the end
        of the list
    <enumeration id list> ← the updated struct enum_def
}

finish_enum_type(<enumeration id list>) => <enumeration type definition>
{
    <enumeration type definition> ← (struct type_ref) {
        .object_type = <enumeration id list>.enum_def.this_type; }
}
```

Ultimately, the enumeration type is represented by a **TYPEREF** record, as all types are. The type descriptor consists of a **type_descriptor** record that points to a list of **attributes**, one for each enumeration constant.

10.3.3. **Subtypes**

A *subtype* declaration gives a name to the application of a *constraint* to a type. (C does not have constrained types.) Because subtypes and types can, for the most part, be used interchangeably, subtypes are also represented by **type_descriptor** records. Describing subtypes requires a new variant in the **type_descriptor** record and a new type, **struct constraint_des**, which is used in the new variant. **type_descriptor** is extended to include

```
struct {   /* form == SUBTYPE */
   struct type_des *base_type;
   struct constraint_des constraint;
};
```

where a constraint is of the following:

```
enum constraint_form { DYNAMICRANGE, STATICRANGE,
      UNCONSTRAINEDINDEX, ARRAYBOUNDS
   };
```

and a **struct constraint_des** looks like this:

```
struct constraint_des {
   enum constraint_form form;
   union {
      /* form == DYNAMICRANGE */
      address_range address;

      /* form == STATICRANGE */
      struct { long lowerbound, upperbound; };

      /* form == UNCONSTRAINEDINDEX - empty */

      /* form == ARRAYBOUNDS */
      struct {
         struct index_list *bounds;
         struct address dope_vector_addr;
      };
   };
};
```

The syntax for subtype definitions and declarations is given by the following productions. Two basic forms are included: range constraints applied to discrete types and index constraints applied to unconstrained array types. The nonterminal <range> also has a number of other uses in other features of the language (in **for loop**s, for example).

<subtype>	→ <type name>
<subtype>	→ <subtype definition>
<subtype declaration>	→ **subtype** <id> **is**
	<subtype definition> #subtype_decl
<subtype definition>	→ <type name> <range constraint> #range_subtype
<subtype definition>	→ <type name> <index constraint> #array_subtype
<range constraint>	→ **range** <range>
<range>	→ <simple expression> .. <simple expression>
	#range_pair
<index constraint>	→ (<discrete range> #start_index_list
	{, <discrete range> #append_index})
<discrete range>	→ <subtype>
<discrete range>	→ <range>

No additional semantic record types are required for processing subtypes. The semantic routines needed for handling range constraints follow. The auxiliary semantic routines `start_index_list()`, `append_index()`, and `array_subtype()` are discussed along with arrays in Section 10.3.4. Thus our interest in this section is subtypes that define range constraints. A range constraint may be applied to any discrete type, which for Ada/CS includes Integer and any user-defined enumeration type. As the name suggests, a subtype does not define a new type. Rather, it describes a constrained range of values of the base type. When a variable is declared to be of a particular subtype, the compiler must guarantee that any value assigned to the variable is within the allowed range. If such a condition cannot be recognized by compile-time analysis, a run-time check is required.

The action routine `range_pair()` builds a **struct constraint_des** from two expressions given as the bounds of the range. `range_subtype()` builds a **type_descriptor** for the subtype. These steps are separated because the <range> nonterminal appears in other contexts in the grammar as well as in subtype definitions.

```
range_pair(<simple expression>₁, <simple expression>₂) => <range>
{
 Check that the two expression entries are of the same
    discrete type.
 If they both denote compile-time constants, then this
    is a static range; otherwise, it is dynamic.

 if (the constraint is static) {
    Create the following compile-time constraint
       descriptor, C:
    (struct constraint_des) {
     .form = STATICRANGE;
     .upperbound = (long) (<simple expression>₂.expr.value);
     .lowerbound = (long) (<simple expression>₁.expr.value); }
```

```
    } else {    /* the constraint is dynamic */
        Allocate space in the data area of the current
        activation record for a run-time descriptor
        (2*INTEGERSIZE words, one for each of
        the bounds).
        Generate code to store the bounds into the
        descriptor.
        Create the following compile-time constraint
        descriptor, C:
                    (struct constraint_des) {
                        .form = DYNAMICRANGE;
                        .address =  · · ·  ; };
                        /* the space just allocated */
    }

    The type descriptor, T, for the range will be:
        (type_descriptor) {
            .form = SUBTYPE;
            .size = <simple expression>₂.expr.expr_type.size;
            .base_type = <simple expression>₂.expr.expr_type;
            .constraint = C; }

    <range> ← (struct type_ref) { .object_type = T; } ;
}


range_subtype(<type name>,
                <range constraint>) => <subtype definition>
{
    <range constraint>.type_ref.object_type.base_type
        must refer to the same type as
        <type name>.type_ref.object_type.
    if (<type name>.type_ref.object_type is constrained)
        The new constraint must not be less restrictive
            than the old one.
    if (no errors)
        <subtype definition> ← <range constraint>
    else
        <subtype definition> ← an ERROR record
}


subtype_decl(<id>, <type definition>)
{
    /* same as type_decl()... */
    type_decl(<id>, <type definition>) ;
}
```

10.3.4. Array Types

Ada and Ada/CS include two forms of array type definitions: constrained and unconstrained. A constrained array type has a fixed number of elements, though the number may be specified by an expression that can be evaluated only at run-time. An unconstrained array type is specified by defining only the index type(s) of the array; the number of elements is left for later specification and may vary from one instance of the type to another. The size of any instance of an unconstrained array type might be determinable at compile-time, or it might depend on a run-time expression, just like for constrained array types.

Implementing Dynamic Arrays

When a variable is of a constrained array type or subtype for which the bounds are computed at run-time rather than at compile-time, it is often referred to as a *dynamic array*. This late binding of the array size is often quite handy when different sizes are needed for different executions of a program. It causes a problem, however, in that space for a dynamic array cannot be allocated within an activation record; its size is not known at compile-time when AR offsets are fixed. Instead, a fixed-size descriptor for the bounds constraint (usually called a *dope vector*) is placed in the AR. This dope vector contains space for the bounds to be stored after they are computed. Each variable of such a type is represented by a word containing the address of its elements and (implicitly) by the dope vector. When a procedure is called, the bounds for its dynamic array types are evaluated, and space for each dynamic array is pushed onto the stack *immediately after* the AR. The address of this space is placed in the designated location for each dynamic array, and all references to array elements are made through this pointer. For example, if we had

```
procedure P (N : Integer) is
A, B : array(1..N) of Integer;
   . . .
end P;
```

the size of the arrays A and B would be determined when P was called. First, the (fixed-size) AR for P would be pushed, then the value of N would be used to fill in the dope vector. Finally, space for A and B would be pushed. This activity would lead to the structure shown in Figure 10.10.

We can handle dynamic arrays declared in blocks as well as those declared in procedures. If block-level allocation is used, the algorithm is simple. We push an AR for the block, then push space for all its dynamic arrays.

But what if procedure-level allocation is used? As before, the AR for all local variables (except dynamic array space) is pushed first. Space for dynamic arrays is pushed whenever a block that has dynamic arrays is opened. We maintain a **stack_top** value for each block (as well as for the procedure). **stack_top** points to the place at which dynamic array space for that block ends. When a block is entered, its **stack_top** value is inherited from the

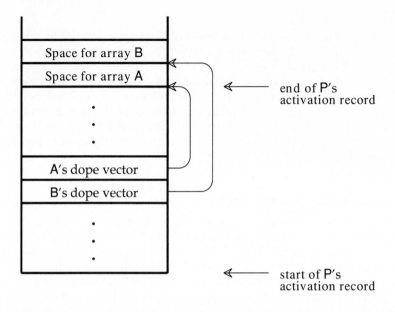

Figure 10.10   Activation Record with Dynamic Arrays

value in the enclosing block (or from the procedure's **stack_top**, if there is no enclosing block). This value dictates where dynamic arrays may be allocated and is incremented as local dynamic array space is pushed. When a block is exited, we revert to using the **stack_top** value of the enclosing block; no work is involved. (This implementation makes **exit**s and **goto**s out of blocks easy to implement.) As an example, reconsider our earlier example, with blocks added:

```
procedure P (N : Integer) is
A : array(1..N) of Integer;
begin
    . . .
    declare
        B : array(1..N) of Integer;
    begin
        . . .
    end;
end P;
```

Figure 10.11 illustrates the structure created using block-level **stack_top** values.

With dynamic arrays the compiler no longer knows the exact amount of space required on the run-time stack for each subprogram call. Decisions must therefore be postponed until run-time, with an associated cost: Space is

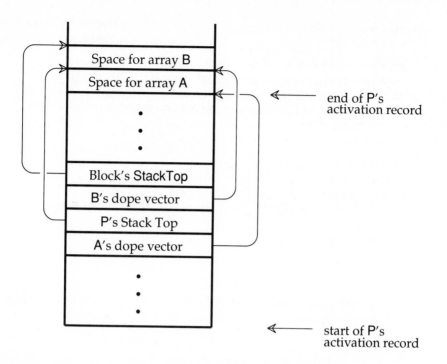

Figure 10.11   Activation Record with Block-level **stack_top** Values

needed in the activation record for the dope vector and for the **stack_top** values. Time is needed on each array reference to access the dope vector and to extract bounds information from it for subscript calculation and bounds checking (discussed in Chapter 11). Time is also needed on block entry for the arrays to be allocated.

The semantic routine **array_def()** acts only slightly different to handle a dynamic array definition. The main difference from handling static arrays is that the amount of space required for the dope vector (rather than for the elements of the array) is used to fill in the **size** field of the **type_descriptor**. The **array_def()** and **object_decl()** routines must generate code to fill in dope vectors and allocate dynamic array space, respectively, when types and variables of dynamic array types are declared.

Semantic Routines for Arrays in Ada

Two slightly different forms of syntax are used to specify the two kinds of arrays available in Ada/CS (constrained and unconstrained). They are shown in the following productions, with action symbols included:

<array type definition>   → <unconstrained array definition>
<array type definition>   → <constrained array definition>

<unconstrained array definition>   →
    array <unconstrained index list> **of** <element type> #array_def
<unconstrained index list>   → (<index subtype def>
    #start_index_list {, <index subtype def> #append_index})
<index subtype def>   →
    <type name> **range** <> #unconstrained_index

<constrained array definition>   →
    array <constrained index list> **of** <element type> #array_def
<constrained index list>   →
    (<discrete range> #start_index_list {, <discrete range> #append_index})
<discrete range>   → <subtype>
<discrete range>   → <range>

<element type>   → <type or subtype>

Because arrays may be defined with lists of index types, handling arrays requires defining a new type to construct these lists:

```
struct index_list {
    type_descriptor *index_type;
    struct index_list *next;
};
```

The **type_descriptor** record requires the following variant—in place of the one shown in Section 10.2.1—for handling Ada/CS array types:

```
struct {    /* form == ARRAYTYPE */
    struct index_list *index_types;
    struct type_des *element_type;
};
```

A new semantic record type is also needed to handle index lists:

```
struct index_list_type {
    struct index_list *list;
    boolean constrained;
};
```

From an examination of the semantic action markers in the preceding array syntax, it should be obvious that the processing done for constrained array definitions is not very different from that required for unconstrained array definitions. To use the same semantic routines for both, we must ensure that the semantic record representation for an unconstrained <index subtype def> be the same as that for <discrete range>. Thus, we need it to be represented by a **TYPEREF** record. **unconstrained_index()** constructs an appropriate descriptor for an unconstrained subtype:

```
unconstrained_index(<type name>) => <index subtype def>
{
    <type name>.type_ref must describe a discrete type.
    <index subtype def> ← (type_descriptor) {
        .form = SUBTYPE;
        .size = <type name>.type_ref.object_type.size;
        .base_type = <type name>.type_ref.object_type;
        .constraint = (struct constraint_des) {
                .form = UNCONSTRAINEDINDEX; } ;
        };
}
```

start_index_list() and **append_index()** are used for processing both unconstrained and constrained index lists. In their parameter lists and their result specifications, <index subtype> stands for either <index subtype def> or <discrete range>, and <index list> stands for either <unconstrained index list> or <constrained index list>. **start_index_list()** processes the first index type of an index list. It constructs an **INDEXLIST** semantic record that includes an entry in the list for the first <index subtype>:

```
start_index_list(<index subtype>) => <index list>
{
    type_descriptor *T;

    T ← <index subtype>.type_ref.object_type
    <index list> ← (struct index_list_type) {
        .constrained =
                (T.constraint.form != UNCONSTRAINEDINDEX);
        .list = (struct index_list_type) {
            .list->index_type = T,
            .list->next = NULL; } ;
        };
}
```

append_index() adds the next index subtype to the list associated with <index list>:

```
append_index(<index list>, <index subtype>) => <index list>
{
    Append the index type referenced in
        <index subtype>.type_ref to the end of the list
        referenced in <index list>.index_list
    <index list> ← the new struct index_list
}
```

array_def() creates a type descriptor corresponding to a type definition. An **ARRAYTYPE** type descriptor is created for an unconstrained array, whereas a **SUBTYPE** type descriptor is created for a constrained array. A **SUBTYPE** type descriptor may be used as the type of a variable, whereas an **ARRAYTYPE** type descriptor may not be. The latter must have an index con-

straint added to create a subtype. The **array_def()** action routine is outlined in Figure 10.12. Figures 10.13(a) and (b) show examples of the type
descriptor structures created for unconstrained and constrained array types.

For a constrained array subtype where all of the index ranges are
compile-time constants, a run-time descriptor is not necessary. As an optimi-

```
array_def(<index list>,  <element type>)  =>  <array type definition>
{
  Create a new type descriptor, T, for the array type:

  if (<index list>.index_list.constrained == FALSE) {
    T ← (type_descriptor) {
      .form = ARRAYTYPE;
      .size = ADDRESSSIZE; /* space for the array adr */
      .element_type = <element type>.type_ref.object_type;
      .index_types = <index list>.index_list.list; };

  } else { /* <index list>.index_list.constrained == TRUE */
    Allocate space in the current activation record
    for a dope vector, 2 integers for each entry on
    <index list>.  Create a struct address describing
    the location of the dope vector and call it
    DV_addr.

    Generate code to copy the static and dynamic
    bounds descriptors on <index list> into the
    appropriate locations in the dope vector.

    T ← (type_descriptor) {
      .form = SUBTYPE;
      .size = ADDRESSSIZE; /* space for the array adr */
      .base_type = (type_descriptor) {
         .form = ARRAYTYPE;
         .size = ARRAYDESCRIPTORSIZE;
         .element_type =
            <element type>.type_ref.object_type,
         .index_types = NULL; };
      .constraint = (struct constraint_des) {
         .form = ARRAYBOUNDS;
         .dope_vector_addr = DV_addr;
         .bounds = <index list>.index_list.list; } ;
    }
  }

        <array type definition> ← (struct type_ref) {
              .object_type = T; } ;
}
```

Figure 10.12   The **array_def()** Action Routine

array (Integer **range** <>, Integer **range** <>) **of** Integer

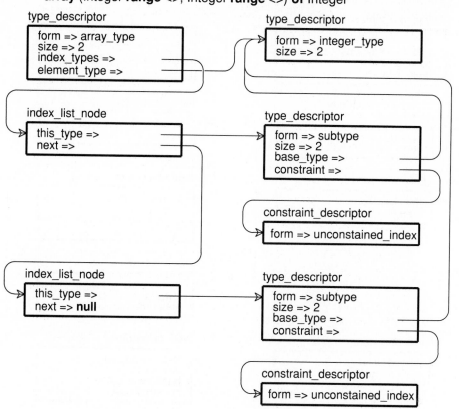

Figure 10.13(a)   `type_descriptor` for an Unconstrained Array Type

zation, the array could be allocated in the current data area at compile-time, with the following size:

```
element_type.size * (product of all index lengths)
```

Using the preceding routines, the definition of a constrained array type results in the creation of two type descriptors: one is a subtype descriptor for the actual bounds of the defined array, and the other is a descriptor for the underlying array type. However, the **index_types** field of the latter record contains a **NULL** pointer rather than a pointer to a list of unconstrained discrete types. Such a list could be constructed from the **base_types** of all the types on the **bounds** list of the subtype descriptor, but there is no point in doing so because it will never be used.

array (1..10, 1..20) **of** Integer

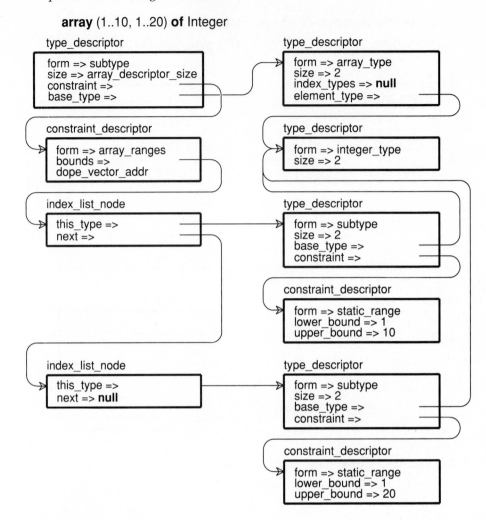

Figure 10.13(b)   `type_descriptor` for a Constrained Array Type

Subtypes Specifying Index Constraints

The relevant syntax for array constraint subtypes is

```
<subtype definition>  →  <type name> <index constraint> #array_subtype
<index constraint>    →  ( <discrete range> #start_index_list
                          {, <discrete range> #append_index} )
```

An index constraint may be applied only to an unconstrained array type. Each <discrete range> in the list supplies a constraint for a positionally corresponding index of the array designated by <type name>. The subtype will be specified by a type descriptor record with a **SUBTYPE** variant that points to a list of constraints, just like previously described constrained array definitions.

The **start_index_list()** and **append_index()** semantic routines have already been described, so we need only to consider one new routine, **array_subtype()**, which builds the **SUBTYPE** type descriptor:

```
array_subtype(<type name>, <index constraint>) => <subtype definition>
{
 <index constraint>.index_list references a list of
     subtype descriptors for discrete ranges.
 <type name>.type_ref represents the unconstrained
     array type.
 Check that this is an unconstrained array type.
 Check that the discrete ranges on the struct index_list
   are valid constraints for the corresponding index
   types of the array.  The number of constraints must
   match the number of index types in the array.
 Allocate space in the current activation record for a
   dope vector, with an entry corresponding to
   each index on <index list>.
 Create a struct address describing the location of
   the dope vector and call it DV_addr.
 Generate code to copy the static and dynamic
   bounds descriptors on the list referenced by
   <index constraint> into the appropriate
   locations in the dope vector.

 Construct a new type descriptor, T:
 (type_descriptor) {
    .form = SUBTYPE;
    .size = ARRAYDESCRIPTORSIZE;
    .base_type = <type name>.type_ref.object_type;
    .constraint = (struct constraint_des) {
        .form = ARRAYBOUNDS;
        .dope_vector_addr = DV_addr;
        .bounds = <index constraint>.index_list.list;
      } ;
  }

 <subtype definition> ← (struct type_ref) {
        .object_type = T; };
}
```

A constrained array subtype defined by applying an index constraint to a previously defined unconstrained array type is represented by a subtype descriptor just like the one created for a constrained array definition. Thus the two definitional approaches produce descriptors that are effectively equivalent. The difference is that the latter approach, discussed previously, results in an underlying array type descriptor with a **NULL** pointer in the **index_list** field. This index list is used only for checking constraint lists in the preceding semantic routine, and it is of no use in an unnamed array type descriptor.

If the unconstrained array type defined in Figure 10.13(a) is named **A**, then the type descriptor structure created by specifying an index constraint for **A** is shown in Figure 10.14.

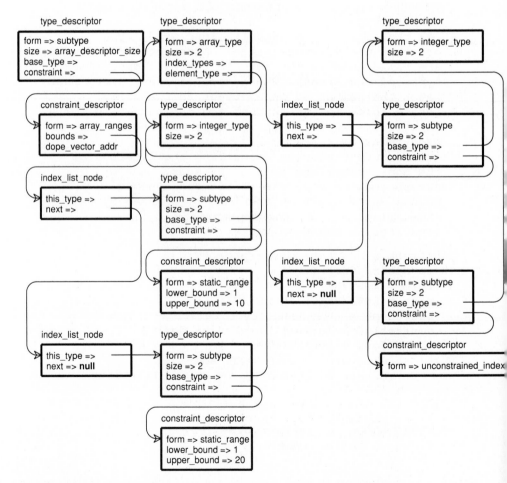

Figure 10.14   type_descriptor for an Index Constraint Applied to an Unconstrained Array Type

10.3.5. Variant Records

Variant records allow the specification of alternative component lists within a single record type. Each variant describes the components of the record corresponding to a specific value (or values) of a discriminant (Ada) or tag field (Pascal and Ada/CS).

To simplify our presentation of the techniques used to compile variant records, the variant record feature of Ada/CS has been defined as somewhat simpler than that of Ada. The syntax for record definitions including variants is

<record type definition>	→ **record** #start_record <component list> #end_record **end record**
<component list>	→ <component declaration> { <component declaration> }
<component list>	→ { <component declaration> } <variant part>
<component list>	→ **null** ;
<component declaration>	→ <id list> : <type name> ; #field_decl
<variant part>	→ **case** <id> : <type name> #tag_field **is** <variant> { <variant> } #end_variant_part **end case** ;
<variant>	→ **when** <choice> #new_variant => <component list>
<choice>	→ <simple expression>

To describe lists of variants, we need a new structure:

```
struct variant_des {
    long choice_value;
    attributes *tag_field, *field_list;
    struct variant_des *inner_variants;
    struct variant_des *next_variant;
};
```

The semantic record type for record definitions must be extended to include a pointer to a variant descriptor for the innermost variant currently being processed:

```
struct record_def {
    type_descriptor *this_type;
    address_range next_offset;
    struct variant_des *current_variant;
};
```

Because variants can be nested, a semantic record type is needed to save the value of **current_variant** when a nested variant part is entered:

```
struct variant_part {
    struct variant_des *outer_variant;
    attributes *tag_field;
};
```

Like the **RECORDDEF** semantic record, the variant in the **type_descriptor** record for describing records also must be extended:

```
struct {    /* form == RECORDTYPE */
    symbol_table fields;
    attributes *field_list;
    struct variant_des *variant_list;
};
```

The list of fields referenced by **field_list** includes only those components declared before the variant part of the record definition. The **variant_list** field points to a list of **struct variant_des** records, each of which includes the list of fields defining a single variant. Thus, for variant records, it is important to have all fields stored in a symbol table as well as on these lists; otherwise, searching for a field name would be complex and relatively inefficient.

The **field** variant of the **attributes** record needs two additional fields to describe record fields when variants are considered:

```
struct {    /* class == FIELD */
    address_range field_offset;
    attributes *next_field;
    struct variant_des *enclosing_variant;
    boolean is_tag;
};
```

enclosing_variant references the **struct variant_des** record for the innermost variant of which the described field is a part. Its value is **NULL** for fields that are not part of a variant. The **is_tag** flag has the obvious meaning and is necessary due to restrictions on how tag fields can be used.

The only change required in **start_record()** is the specification of appropriate initial values for the fields added to **type_descriptor** and **struct record_def** to handle variants:

```
start_record(void) => record
{
    Create a type descriptor, T, as follows:
    (type_descriptor) {
        .form = RECORDTYPE;
        .size = 0;
        .field_list = NULL;
        .variant_list = NULL;
        .fields = create(); };
```

```
      record ← (struct record_def) { .this_type = T;
                     .next_offset = 0;
                     .current_variant = NULL; };
   }
```

field_decl() is similarly changed only to specify **FALSE** as the value for **is_tag** and to give **enclosing_variant** the value of **RD.current_variant** as the **attributes** record for each field is created.

Three new semantic routines are required to process variants: **tag_field()**, **new_variant()**, and **end_variant_part()**. Calls to these action routines occur in the following syntactic contexts:

record { <component declaration> } <variant part> →
    record { <component declaration> } **case** <id> : <type name>
      #tag_field **is** <variant> { <variant> } #end_variant_part **end case** ;
record { <component declaration> } **case** <id> : <type name> **is**
   { <variant> } <variant> →
      record { <component declaration> } **case** <id> : <type name> **is**
        { <variant> } **when** <choice> #new_variant => <component list>

tag_field() processes the declaration of the distinguished field of a variant record, referred to as a tag, whose value during execution determines the interpretation of the variant part of the record. **tag_field()** modifies the semantic record associated with **record**, just as **field_decl()** does in processing ordinary record fields. In addition, **tag_field()** creates a **VARIANTPART** semantic record that is associated with the **case** symbol. The special case of nested variants is handled by saving the value of **record.record_def.current_variant** in the **variant_part** semantic record:

```
tag_field(record, <id>, <type name>) => (record, case)
{
   Let RD name the semantic record associated with record

   Enter <id> in the symbol table referenced by RD.fields
   if (it is already there)
      generate an appropriate error message
   else {
      The following expression describes the attribute
      record, A, to be created for the tag field.  It
      is identical to that for other field except for
      the value of is_tag.
      (attributes) {
         .class = FIELD;
         .id_type = <type name>.type_ref.object_type;
         .id = the id_entry returned by enter();
         .field_offset = RD.next_offset;
         .next_field = NULL;
         .enclosing_variant = RD.current_variant;
         .is_tag = TRUE; }
```

```
        Allocate space for the field within the record by
            adding <type name>.type_ref.object_type.size
            to RD.next_offset
    if (RD.current_variant == NULL)
        Add this attribute record to the end of the
            list referenced by RD.field_list
    else
        Add this attribute record to the end of the
            list referenced by RD.current_variant
    }

        case ← (struct variant_part) {
          .outer_variant = RD.current_variant;
          .tag_field = A; };
    RD.current_variant = NULL;
    record ← the updated RD
}
```

new_variant() is called just after the label of a variant is recognized by the parser. It initializes the **struct variant_des** record for the new variant and links it into the list of variant descriptors for the current record. Figure 10.15 shows the **RECORDDEF** semantic record and the structures it references after a call to **new_variant()**.

```
new_variant(record, case, <choice>) => record
{
  Let RD name the semantic record associated with record

  <choice> must describe a constant value, distinct from
    all other choice_values on the list of
    variant_descriptors referenced by RD.current_variant
  Create a struct variant_des, V, as described by the
    following expression:
  (struct variant_des) {
    .choice_value = (long) <choice>;
    .tag_field = case.variant_part.tag_field;
    .field_list = NULL;
    .inner_variants = NULL;
    .next_variant = RD.current_variant; }

  RD.current_variant ← V
  record ← the updated RD
}
```

end_variant_part(), as its name indicates, is called at the end of the variant part of a component list. The list of **struct variant_des** records for that variant part is accessed by the field reference **record.record_def.current_variant**. After attaching this list to the descriptor for the appropriate containing structure (either the entire record or an outer component list), **end_variant_part()** restores the value of **record.record_def.current_variant** saved by **tag_field()**:

```
end_variant_part(record, case, <choice>) => record
{
  Let RD name the semantic record associated with record

  if (case.variant_record_part.outer_variant == NULL)
      RD.this_type.variant_list ← RD.current_variant;
  else
      case.variant_record_part.outer_variant.inner_variants
          ← RD.current_variant;

  RD.current_variant ←
          case.variant_record_part.outer_variant;
  record ← the updated RD;
}
```

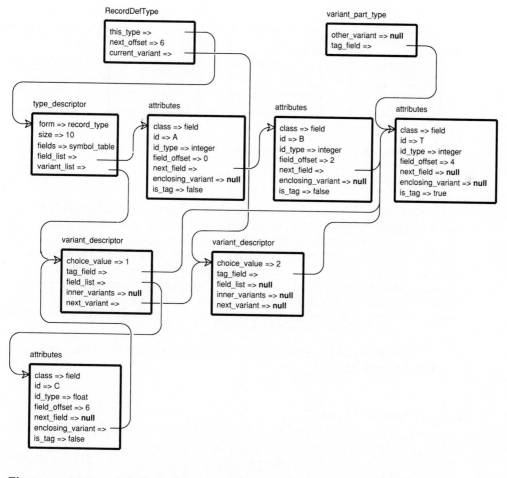

Figure 10.15   **RECORDDEF** Semantic Record during Variant Processing

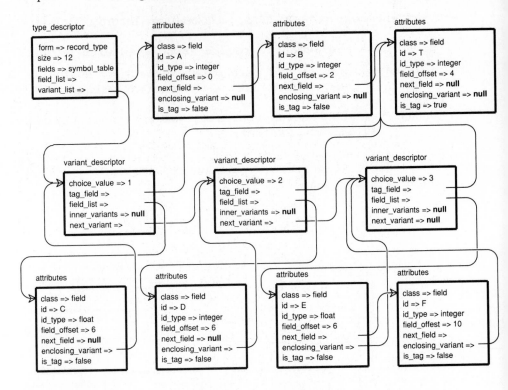

Figure 10.16 `type_descriptor` for a Variant Record

To simplify the preceding discussion and data structures slightly, we have imposed the restriction that each variant have only a single label. In most languages that allow variant records, variants with multiple labels are allowed. Two extensions to the **struct variant_des** record are required to handle multiple labels. The **choice_value** field must be changed from a **long** to a pointer to a list of values, and a **sequence_number** field must be added. Each variant within a list is given a unique sequence number. This number is used instead of the value of the tag field to check variant validity at run-time.

The data structure constructed to describe a variant record has the form shown in Figure 10.16.

10.3.6. Access Types

Dynamically allocated objects in Ada are referenced by *access* types, which are equivalent to pointer or reference types in other languages. Compiling access type declarations is quite simple; providing the run-time support they require is much more complex. The required support includes a heap allocation mechanism, described in Chapter 9.

The syntax of interest is

<type definition> → **access** <subtype> #access_type
<type decl>   → **type** IDENTIFIER #incomplete_type

A new variant will be required in the **type_descriptor** to handle access types:

```
/* form == ACCESSTYPE */
struct type_des *referenced_type;
```

Another will be needed to handle incomplete types:

```
/* form == INCOMPLETETYPE */
struct type_des *dependent_type;
```

Incomplete type declarations are introduced in Ada and Ada/CS to handle forward references in access type declarations—for example, in defining a self-referential type. The following example from the Ada Language Reference Manual illustrates the use of incomplete types:

type Cell; — incomplete type declaration
type Link **is access** Cell; — Cell must already be declared

type Cell **is**
  record
    Value : Integer;
    Succ : Link;
    Pred : Link;
  end record;

Specifications of the required semantic routines follow. **access_type()** and **incomplete_type()** both build **type_descriptor** records. In addition, **incomplete_type()** makes a symbol table entry and **access_type()** checks whether the referenced type is an incomplete type. If it is, the type being declared is saved as a type dependent on the incomplete type.

```
access_type(<subtype>) => <type definition>
{
  Create a new type descriptor, T, for an access type:
  (type_descriptor) {
     .form = ACCESSTYPE;
     .referenced_type = <subtype>.type_ref.object_type;
     .size = ACCESSSIZE; }
     /* ACCESSSIZE is target machine dependent */
```

```
      if (T.referenced_type.form == INCOMPLETETYPE)
         T.referenced_type.dependent_type = T;

   <type definition> ← (struct type_ref) { .object_type = T; };
}
```

```
incomplete_type(IDENTIFIER)
{
   Create a new type descriptor, T, for an
      incomplete type:
   (type_descriptor) {
       .form = INCOMPLETETYPE;
       .dependent_type = NULL;
       .size = 0; }    /* a meaningless value */

   The identifier is entered into the symbol table with
   the following associated attributes record:

   (attributes) { .class = TYPENAME;
       .id_type = T;
       .id = the id_entry returned by enter(); }
}
```

The possibility of incomplete types means that the **type_decl()** routine previously outlined must be extended to check for an incomplete type in case the type name it is trying to declare is already in the symbol table. In such a case, the **dependent_type** field of the incomplete type's **type_descriptor** record is used to update the type descriptor of the access type that was defined using the incomplete type. Then the **INCOMPLETETYPE type_descriptor** is replaced in the attribute record associated with the type name. For completeness, we should also be concerned with handling multiple dependent types for an incomplete type and with checking that all incomplete types are given a complete definition before the end of the scope in which they appear. Exercises 5 and 6 address techniques for handling these concerns.

10.3.7. Packages

Packages allow an arbitrary set of declarations to be grouped together and given a name. Package declarations in Ada consist of two parts: a *specification part* and a *body*. Declarations in the specification part, other than those appearing in the *private part* of the specification, are visible outside the package. Those in the private part or in the body are accessible only inside the package. Ada/CS allows an alternative form, where the two parts are concatenated to form a single declaration (like modules in Modula-2). Compilation of this alternative involves somewhat simpler symbol table handling. The productions that describe package specifications and bodies, as well as the single unit version, are

\<package declaration\>	→ **package** \<package spec or body\> ;
\<package spec or body\>	→ \<id\> #start_package **is** { \<declaration\> } #end_visible_part [\<private part\>] \<body option\> **end** \<id option\> ; #end_package
\<package spec or body\>	→ **body** \<id\> #start_package_body **is** { \<body declaration\> } { \<statement\> } **end** \<id option\> ; #end_package
\<body option\>	→ [**body** { \<body declaration\> } { \<statement\> } #body_present]
\<id option\>	→ [\<id\> #check_package_id]

The principal problems to be dealt with in compiling packages involve visibility of names introduced in the various sections of a package. Names that appear in the specification part (exclusive of those in the private part) play a dual role much like that of procedure parameters. They are visible in the scope surrounding the package, if qualified by the package name, much as record fields are visible in the scope containing a record declaration. They are also directly visible in the body of the package. Further, they can be made directly visible in the surrounding scope if the package name appears in a **use** clause.

One new semantic record type is required:

```
struct package {
    boolean body_seen;
    attributes *old_current_package;
};
```

The **attributes** record must include a variant to handle packages:

```
/* class == PACKAGENAME */
symbol_table scope;
```

The semantic routine outlines appear below. **start_package()** puts the package name in the symbol table and sets a global variable called **current_package** to reference the associated **attributes** record. It also creates a new scope for the package and makes that the new current scope:

```
start_package(<id>) => <package spec or body>
{
    Enter <id> in the symbol table of the current scope.
    Build a PACKAGENAME attribute record for it, creating
      a new symbol table to provide a value for scope.
        <package spec or body> ← (struct package) {
            .body_seen = FALSE;
            .old_current_package = current_package; }
```

```
        Assign a pointer to the new attribute record to
          current_package.
        Call open_scope() to make current_package->scope
          the current scope.
}
```

The identifiers declared in the package before **end_visible_part()** is called make up the set of names exported from the package:

```
end_visible_part(void)
{
    Mark all identifiers declared so far in the current
    scope as exported.  (The scope is referenced by
    current_package->scope)
}
```

end_package() is called at the end of a specification part alone and at the end of the body of a package. It uses information in the semantic record created by **start_package()**, and it refers to the **attributes** record referenced by **current_package**. Lastly, it resets **current_package** to the value it had before **start_package()** was called:

```
end_package(<package spec or body>)
{
    if (<package spec or body>.package.body_seen) {
        Check that all procedures specified in the
            visible part have had a corresponding
            body declaration.
        Delete all but the exported names from the
            current_package->scope
    }
    Exit current symbol table scope, retaining the scope
        as an attribute of current_package;
    current_package ←
        <package spec or body>.package.old_current_package
}
```

start_package_body is called at the beginning of a package body. It expects to find a **PACKAGENAME attributes** record associated with its <id> parameter:

```
start_package_body(<id>) => <package spec or body>
{
    Find <id> in the symbol table and check that it names
        a package
    <package spec or body> ← (struct package) {
                .body_seen = TRUE;
                .old_current_package = current_package; };
    Set current_package to the attribute record found
        in the symbol table
```

```
    Make the scope found in the attribute record the
        current scope
}
```

`check_package_id()` is a simple action routine that ensures that an identifier appearing at the end of a package specification or body matches the name of the package:

```
    check_package_id(<id>)
    {
        Check that <id> names current_package
    }
```

`body_present` is used in the single module package form to note that the body has been processed, differentiating a single module package from a package specification:

```
    body_present(<package spec or body>)  =>  <package spec or body>
    {
        <package spec or body>.package.body_seen = TRUE;
    }
```

Procedure specifications can appear in the visible part of a package specification, with their corresponding bodies to follow in the package body. The syntax is

<declaration> → <subprogram specification> ; #end_proc_spec

`end_proc_spec()` is called at the end of such a specification. Because the processing it does is related to that of other action routines for handling procedures, it is discussed in Chapter 13 rather than here. The principal extension it introduces is requiring the action routine for handling a procedure declaration to accommodate the previous existence of a symbol table entry for the procedure name, with an attribute record describing only a specification. The most complicated part of doing this is checking that lists of parameter descriptors match.

Private Types and the Private Part

One kind of declaration that is legal only in the visible part of a package is

<private type declaration> → **type** <id> **is private** #private_type_decl

It is like an incomplete type declaration in that it enters a type name in the symbol table without specifying the structure of the type it denotes. The complete type declaration of a private type must appear in the private part of the same package specification. Only the type name is visible outside the package; details of the corresponding type declaration are accessible only within the package body.

Thus **private_type_decl()** enters <id> into the symbol table and builds an appropriate type descriptor for it, using the following extension to **type_descriptor**:

```
struct {    /* form == PRIVATETYPE */
   struct type_des *the_type;
   attributes *containing_package;
};
```

```
private_type_decl(<id>)
{
   The identifier is entered into the symbol table with
   the following associated attributes record:

   (attributes) {
      .class = TYPENAME;
      .id_type = (type_descriptor) {
            .form = PRIVATETYPE;
            .the_type = NULL;
            .containing_package = current_package; } ;
      .id = the id_entry returned by enter() ; }
}
```

The private part of a package specification may contain only subtype and type declarations:

<private part>   → **private** <private item> { <private item> }
<private item>   → **subtype** <id> **is** <subtype definition> ;
                     → **type** <id> **is** <non-private type definition> ;

Within the private part, a call to **type_decl()** may occur that finds the identifier already declared as a **PRIVATETYPE**. The type descriptor passed as a parameter to **type_decl()** in this case is used to fill in the value of the field **the_type** of the existing type descriptor. Any time a type descriptor is used, a special case must be made of private types. The field **the_type** may be used to access the details of the type representation only if **containing_package** field of the type descriptor is equal to **current_package**.

10.3.8. The **attributes** and **semantic_record** Structures

Figures 10.17 and 10.18 show the final versions of the **attributes** and **semantic_record** structures, which include all the extensions suggested for handling the various features discussed in this chapter.

```c
#include "symtab.h"    /* see Chapter 8 */

typedef short boolean;

enum id_class { CONST, VARIABLE, ENUMCONST, FIELD,
    TYPENAME, PACKAGENAME };

enum type_form { INTEGERTYPE, FLOATTYPE, STRINGTYPE,
    ENUMTYPE, ARRAYTYPE, RECORDTYPE, SUBTYPE,
    PRIVATETYPE, ACCESSTYPE, INCOMPLETETYPE,
    ERRORTYPE };

typedef unsigned long address_range;

struct address {
    short var_level;
    address_range var_offset;
    boolean indirect, read_only;
};

typedef struct attributes {
    id_entry id;
    struct type_des *id_type;
    enum id_class class;
    union {
        /* class == CONST */
        struct value_type value;

        /* class == VARIABLE */
        struct address var_address;

        /* class == FIELD */
        struct {
            address_range field_offset;
            struct attributes *next_field;
            struct variant_des *enclosing_variant;
            boolean is_tag;
        };

        /* class == TYPENAME --- empty variant */

        /* class == ENUMCONST */
        struct {
            unsigned long enum_value;
            struct attributes *next_const;
        };

        /* class == PACKAGENAME */
        symbol_table scope;
    };
} attributes;
```

```
typedef struct type_des {
    address_range size;
    enum type_form form;
    union {
        /* form == INTEGERTYPE, FLOATTYPE, STRINGTYPE,
               ERRORTYPE -- empty variant */

        /* form == ENUMTYPE */
        attributes *first_const;

        /* form == ARRAYTYPE */
        struct {
            struct index_list *indextypes;
            struct type_des *element_type;
        };

        /* form == RECORDTYPE */
        struct {
            symbol_table fields;
            attributes *field_list;
            struct variant_des *variant_list;
        };

        /* form == SUBTYPE */
        struct {
            struct type_des *base_type;
            struct constraint_des constraint;
        };

        /* form == ACCESSTYPE */
        struct type_des *referenced_type;

        /* form == INCOMPLETETYPE */
        struct type_des *dependent_type;

        /* form == PRIVATETYPE */
        struct {
            struct type_des *the_type;
            attributes *containing_package;
        };
    };
} type_descriptor;

enum constraint_form { DYNAMICRANGE, STATICRANGE,
    UNCONSTRAINEDINDEX, ARRAYBOUNDS };
```

```
struct constraint_des {
   enum constraint_form form;
   union {
      /* form == DYNAMICRANGE */
      address_range address;

      /* form == STATICRANGE */
      struct {
         long lowerbound;
         long upperbound;
      };

      /* form == UNCONSTRAINEDINDEX --- empty variant */

      /* form == ARRAYBOUNDS */
      struct {
         struct index_list *bounds;
         struct address dope_vector_addr;
      };
   };
};

struct index_list {
   type_descriptor *index_type;
   struct index_list *next;
};

struct variant_des {
   long choice_value;
   attributes *tag_field, *field_list;
   struct variant_des *inner_variants;
   struct variant_des *next_variant;
};

extern attributes *current_package;
```

Figure 10.17   Final Version of the **attributes** Structure

```
struct id { string id; };

struct type_ref { type_descriptor *object_type; };

struct record_def {
   type_descriptor *this_type;
   address_range next_offset;
   struct variant_des *current_variant;
};
```

```
struct range { long lower, upper; };

struct const_option { boolean is_constant };

struct enum_def {
   type_descriptor *this_type;
   attributes *last_const;
};

struct index_list_type {
   struct index_list *list;
   boolean constrained;
};

struct variant_part {
   struct variant_des *outer_variant;
   attributes *tag_field;
};

struct package {
   boolean body_seen;
   attributes *old_current_package;
};

enum semantic_record_kind { ID, TYPEREF, RANGE,
      CONSTOPTION, RECORDDEF, ENUMDEF, INDEXLIST,
      VARIANTPART, PACKAGE, MARK, ERROR };

struct semantic_record {
  enum semantic_record_kind record_kind;
  /* initialize to ERROR */
  union {
    struct id id;                    /* ID */
    struct type_ref type_ref;    /* TYPEREF */
    struct range range;              /* RANGE */
    struct const_option const_option;  /* CONSTOPTION */
    struct record_def record_def;       /* RECORDDEF */
    struct enum_def enum_def;            /* ENUMDEF */
    struct index_list_type index_list; /* INDEXLIST */
    struct variant_part variant_part;   /* VARIANTPART */
    struct package package;       /* PACKAGE */
    /* empty variant */          /* MARK */
    /* empty variant */          /* ERROR */
  };
};
```

Figure 10.18   Final Version of the **semantic_record** Structure

Exercises

1. Outline an algorithm for testing the structural type equivalence of two types represented by **type_descriptor** records of the form defined in Figure 10.17.

2. Using the **type_descriptor** record defined in Figure 10.5, show the structures created to describe the following type definitions:

    a. **record**
        I, J : Integer;
        A : **array** (1..10) **of** Float;
        X, Y, Z : Float;
    end record;

    b. **array** (1..10) **of**
        record
            A, B : **array** (2..20) **of** Integer;
            F : Float;
        end record;

    c. **record**
        K : Integer;
        R : **record**
          S, T : Float;
          end record;
        V : Float;
    end record;

3. Construct the **attributes** records based on the declarations in Figure 10.17 that correspond to each of the following declarations:

    A : **constant** Integer := 10;
    B : Integer;
    C : Integer := B+10;

4. Using the **type_descriptor** record defined in Figure 10.17, build the structures that describe the following type and subtype definitions:

    a. (Monday, Tuesday, Wednesday, Thursday, Friday);

    b. Integer **range** 1..10;

   c. **record**
       I, J : Integer;
       A : **array** (1..10) **of** Float;
       X, Y, Z : Float;
   end record;

   d. **record**
       K : Integer;
       case T : Integer **is**
          when 1 => A : Integer;
          when 2 => B : Float;
          when 3 => C : Integer;
                      D : Float;
       end case;
   end record;

5. Describe how **type_descriptor** and the action routines for handling incomplete types (in Section 10.3.6) would have to be changed to handle multiple dependent types for an incomplete type declaration.

6. Describe the data structure and action routine extensions necessary to check that all private types declared in the visible part of a package are completed within the corresponding private part.

7. Explain the error handling that must be done in the semantic routines that handle the following type declaration if T is undefined:

   type A **is array** (1..10) **of array** (1..10) **of** T;

8. Describe the data structure changes and the additional predefined identifiers that are necessary to add boolean to the list of predefined types described in Section 10.2.2.

9. Show the step-by-step construction of the **type_descriptor** for the enumerated type in Exercise 4a. Identify the semantic routine call responsible for each change in the structure.

10. Give examples of type definitions that illustrate the uses of the four variants of the **struct constraint_des** record defined in Figure 10.17.

11. Diagram the **type_descriptor** structure for the type

   type FloatArray **is array** (1..N) **of** Float;

in which N is an Integer variable.

12. Diagram the **type_descriptor** structure for the type

   type ArrayRef **is access** FloatArray;

in which FloatArray is defined in Exercise 11.

13. Extend the variant record in Figure 10.15 to include a variant part nested within a variant. Show the **RECORDDEF** semantic record and associated structures (as in Figure 10.15) after a call to **new_variant()** within the inner variant part.

14. Diagram the entire **type_descriptor** structure (as in Figure 10.16) for the variant record you defined in Exercise 13.

15. Describe in detail the changes necessary to the syntax, data structures, and action routines of Section 10.3.5 to allow variants to have multiple labels.

16. Packages have two features that require special handling by the symbol table implementation: (a) A subset of the identifiers declared in the package are exported, and (b) the package scope, perhaps containing some hidden identifiers, must be saved during the interval between the compilation times of the specification part and the package body. In light of these requirements, how would you design a symbol table implementation to accommodate packages?

17. The implementation of private types presented in Section 10.3.7 is somewhat simplified by the fact that packages may not be nested in Ada/CS. What simplification does this restriction allow? Describe how the presented technique might be extended to support nested packages.

CHAPTER 11

Processing Expressions and Data Structure References

11.1. Introduction

Processing expressions and data structure references includes a variety of tasks that have one principal matter in common: They all produce data objects.

This chapter begins with the definition of a new semantic record to describe data objects. This record is complex, for it is used to describe literal constants, variables, components of composite structures, and expressions. We describe all of these using one type of record because they may be used interchangeably in many different syntactic contexts.

```
enum object_form { OBJECTVALUE, OBJECTADDRESS };

typedef struct data_object {
   type_descriptor *object_type;
   enum object_form form;
   union {
       /* form == OBJECTVALUE */
       struct value_type value;

       /* form == OBJECTADDRESS */
       struct address addr;
   };
} data_object;


enum value_kind { INTKIND, FLOATKIND,
                  STRINGKIND, COMPOSITEKIND };

struct value {
   enum value_kind kind;
   union {
       /* kind == INTKIND */
       long int_value;

       /* kind == FLOATKIND */
       double float_value;

       /* kind == STRINGKIND */
       struct string *string_value;

       /* kind == COMPOSITEKIND */
       struct composite *composite_value;
   };
};
```

The last two variants in the **struct value** record use types that have not yet been defined. They will be discussed in the appropriate sections of this chapter.

The representation for data objects that we have chosen assumes that we want the front end of the compiler to assign addresses for variables. Thus the front end is machine-dependent to the extent that it depends on information such as how much space must be reserved for a data item of any fundamental type. It also depends on the run-time storage model used to implement features such as arrays and procedures. Such dependencies are typical of one-pass compilers or compilers with a simple code-generation pass.

To make our compiler more retargetable, we might want to use a more abstract interface between the front end and code generator. To do so, we would use symbol table attribute references as our representation of data objects. We would do so for values as well as addresses, implying that literal constants as well as identifiers will be represented in the symbol table. The attribute records in the symbol table would not contain any offsets until an address assignment phase in the code generator produced them. Thus the machine dependencies listed in the previous paragraph would be removed from the front end, but the entire symbol table would have to be made available to the code generator.

11.2. Action Routines for Simple Names, Expressions, and Data Structures

11.2.1. Handling Simple Identifiers and Literal Constants

An identifier used as an operand of an expression first appears syntactically in a production for the nonterminal <name>. That production's right-hand side also includes optional occurrences of the nonterminal <name suffix>. In this section we consider the case in which <name suffix> is not used.

```
<name>        → <simple name> { <name suffix> }
<simple name> → <id> #new_name
```

Recall from Chapter 10 that the nonterminal <id> includes a call to **process_id()** that produces an **ID** semantic record. This semantic record contains a string representation of the identifier token. **new_name()** searches the symbol table for this identifier and produces a **DATAOBJECT** semantic record based on its attributes:

```
new_name(<id>) => <simple name>
{
    Find <id>.id.id in the symbol table and acquire its
        attributes.  (For now we will assume that it is
        a variable; other possibilities will be considered
        later.)

    if (there is an entry for <id> in the symbol table)
        <simple name> ← a DATAOBJECT record with
            appropriate information extracted from
            the symbol table attributes.
```

```
    else
        <simple name> ← an ERROR record
}
```

The sequence of productions for expressions in Section 11.2.2, used to encode operator precedence and associativity, begins with two productions for the nonterminal <primary>. One of these introduces yet another nonterminal, <literal>, that includes literal constants within expressions. Named constants are included via <name>.

```
        <primary> → <name> #check_data_object
        <primary> → <literal>

        <literal>    → INTLITERAL #process_literal
        <literal>    → FLOATLITERAL #process_literal
        <literal>    → STRINGLITERAL #process_literal
```

check_data_object() is necessary because some instances of <name>, to be discussed later in this chapter, may be represented by a record other than a **DATAOBJECT**:

```
    check_data_object(<name>) => <primary>
    {
        if (<name>.record_kind == DATAOBJECT)
            <primary> ← <name>
        else {
            Generate an appropriate error message.
            <primary> ← an ERROR record
        }
    }
```

process_literal() is much like **process_id()**; it takes a token value returned by the scanner and creates a semantic record corresponding to it. In this case, the record is a **DATAOBJECT** record, with **form == OBJECTVALUE** and the value recorded appropriately. The **struct value_type** record used in the **object_value** variant contains a compile-time representation of a literal constant. Eventually, a run-time representation must be available to allow a constant to be used in an expression or in another context. At some point in the code-generation process, it will be determined either that a literal can be used as an immediate operand within an instruction or that storage must be allocated for the literal in a constant data area. (Such a data area will be initialized with literal values and be statically allocated.)

The longer that conversion to this run-time representation is delayed, the more target-independent the front end of a compiler is. In addition, keeping source or host machine representations of literal values available enhances the possibility of optimizations, such as computing constant expressions at compile-time. Using a host machine–oriented representation of literals is something of a compromise. For example, our conversion of integer and floating-point literals to host machine representations assumes something about the target architecture, particularly about the allowable ranges of numeric values. As mentioned in our discussion of the **DATAOBJECT** semantic record, the most abstract approach is to put literals in the symbol table as strings and pass them to the code generator as symbol table references.

11.2.2. Processing Expressions

Following is a set of productions that describe expressions in Ada/CS, excluding the productions that define the operator nonterminals:

<expression>	→ <relation> { <logical op> <relation> }
<expression>	→ <relation> { **and then** <relation> }
<expression>	→ <relation> { **or else** <relation> }
<relation>	→ <simple expression>
[<relational op> <simple expression>]
<simple expression>	→ [<unary adding op>] <term> { <adding op> <term> }
<term>	→ <factor> { <multiplying op> <factor> }
<factor>	→ <primary> [** <primary>]
	→ **not** <primary>
	→ **abs** <primary>
<primary>	→ <literal>
	→ <name>
	→ (<expression>)

Several of these productions have similar structures but different components. The semantic processing for productions with similar structures is correspondingly similar, with one exception. The productions for <expression> involving the **and then** and **or else** operators specify *short-circuit* evaluation, which is discussed in Chapter 12. Excluding those productions and adding semantic action symbols, we get the expression grammar shown in Figure 11.1.

We have rewritten one production, that for <simple expression>, by introducing a new nonterminal, <unary term>, to simplify the handling of the optional unary operator.

These productions introduce only three new semantic routines: `process_op()`, `eval_unary()`, and `eval_binary()`. `process_op()` is the simplest of these; it produces a semantic record containing the operator token just returned by the scanner. This operator token is used by one of the other two routines to select the tuple operator appropriate for the token and the types of the operands. A new semantic record type is required for token entries:

```
struct token { token operator; };
```

<expression>	→ <relation> { <logical op> <relation> #eval_binary }
<relation>	→ <simple expression>
	[<relational op> <simple expression> #eval_binary]
<simple expression>	→ <unary term> { <adding op> <term> #eval_binary }
<unary term>	→ <unary adding op> <term> #eval_unary
<unary term>	→ <term>
<term>	→ <factor> { <multiplying op> <factor> #eval_binary }
<factor>	→ <primary> [** #process_op <primary> #eval_binary]
	→ **not** #process_op <primary> #eval_unary
	→ **abs** #process_op <primary> #eval_unary
<primary>	→ <literal>
	→ <name> #check_data_object
	→ (<expression>)
<logical op>	→ **and** #process_op
	→ **or** #process_op
<relational op>	→ = #process_op
	→ /= #process_op
	→ < #process_op
	→ <= #process_op
	→ > #process_op
	→ >= #process_op
<adding op>	→ + #process_op
	→ − #process_op
	→ & #process_op
<unary adding op>	→ + #process_op
	→ − #process_op
<multiplying op>	→ * #process_op
	→ / #process_op
	→ **mod** #process_op

Figure 11.1   Expression Grammar with Action Symbols

The other two routines receive **TOKEN** and **DATAOBJECT** records as parameters and generate the appropriate tuples. Each always produces a **DATAOBJECT** record describing the result of the expression evaluation specified by the operands and the semantics of the operator. This consistent use of **DATAOBJECT** records allows our routines to work with arbitrarily complex expressions. Outlines for the **eval_unary()** and **eval_binary()** action routines are shown in Figures 11.2 and 11.3. The symbol <result> represents an <expression>, <relation>, <simple expression>, <unary term>, or <factor>, as appropriate to the particular productions from which **eval_unary()** and **eval_binary()** are called.

These semantic routines call **select_binary_operator()**, **get_temporary()**, **bi_no_code_needed()**, **un_no_code_needed()**, and **select_unary_operator()**. In addition to selecting tuple operators,

```
eval_unary(<operator>, <operand>) => <result>
{
    tuple_operator tuple_op;
    type_descriptor *result_type;
    struct address T;

    select_unary_operator(<operator>.token,
                        <operand>.data_object,
                        & tuple_op, & result_type);
    if (tuple_op == NONE)
        <result> ← an ERROR record
    else if (un_no_code_needed(tuple_op, & <operand>)) {
        /*
         * un_no_code_needed() checks whether the
         * unary expression can be evaluated at
         * compile-time.  If it can, it does so
         * and updates <operand> to reflect
         * the result.
         */
        <result> ← <operand>
    } else {
        T = get_temporary();
        generate(tuple_op, <operand>.data_object, T, "");
        <result> ← (data_object) {
                .form = OBJECTADDRESS;
                .object_type = /* result type */;
                .addr = T; }
    }
}
```

Figure 11.2   The **eval_unary()** Action Routine

the two operator-selection routines must check to see whether either of the operands are **ERROR** records and ensure that the types of the operands are compatible with the operator token—that is, whether any such operation exists in the language. In the case of a type error, the routine must generate an appropriate error message. If either of the checks fails, the selection routine should return a special operator to indicate this error case. (The operator **NONE** is returned in the code above.) If the language allows implicit type conversions as part of an expression (for example, adding an integer and a real in Pascal), the selection routines generate tuples to affect such conversions.

The **generate()** routine is the simplified interface to a code genrator that we will use in our semantic routine outlines. Rather than denoting a single routine, **generate()** will be used as an overloaded name for a variety of code generation routines distinguished by the number and types of their parameters. The first parameter will always be a tuple operator (as defined in Section 7.3.3). The other parameters will typically be some combination of strings, addresses, and **data_object** structures.

This description of the operator selection routines presumes that there will be no overloading of operators that cannot be resolved by considering the types of the operands. Most programming languages define multiple meanings for symbols like + and *; such symbols are said to be *overloaded*. The particular meaning of an occurrence of one of these symbols is determined by considering the types of the corresponding operands (for example, whether + stands for integer or floating-point addition). Ada and C++ allow user-defined functions to overload the standard operator symbols in such a way that the context of the expression may be required in order to select the appropriate meaning of an operator symbol. In a later section, we consider algorithms to handle this problem.

The **un_no_code_needed()** and **bi_no_code_needed()** routines and their alternatives in the **if** statements are not strictly needed. They can be used to implement certain kinds of simple, machine-independent

```
eval_binary(<operand₁>, <operator>, <operand₂>) => <result>
{
    tuple_operator tuple_op;
    type_descriptor *result_type;
    struct address T;

    select_binary_operator(<operand₁>.data_object
                           <operator>.token,
                           <operand₂>.data_object,
                           & tuple_op, & result_type);
    if (tuple_op == NONE)
        <result> ← an ERROR record
    else if (bi_no_code_needed(& <operand₁>,
                        tuple_op, <operand₂>)) {
        /*
         * bi_no_code_needed() checks whether the binary
         * expression can be evaluated at compile-time.
         * If it can, it does so and updates <operand₁>
         * to reflect the result.
         */
        <result> ← <operand₁>
    } else {
        T = get_temporary();
        generate(tuple_op, <operand₁>.data_object,
                 <operand₂>.data_object, T);
        <result> ← (data_object) {
                     .form = OBJECTADDRESS;
                     .object_type = /* result type */;
                     .addr = T; }
    }
}
```

Figure 11.3   The **eval_binary()** Action Routine

optimizations such as doing compile-time arithmetic if both operands are constants or generating no code for a unary plus operation. Thus the routines can be as simple or as complex as desired, depending on whether certain kinds of optimizations are to be done here at the source language level or later on the intermediate representation.

Temporary Management

As illustrated by the calls to `get_temporary()` in `eval_binary()` and `eval_unary()`, semantic routines for expressions interface with temporary allocation routines. The details of temporary management are discussed in Chapter 15, which deals with code generation. In most cases, registers are used as temporaries, and register management is an integral part of code generation.

The `get_temporary()` routine provides a name or location for the result of an operation. At this level of abstraction, temporaries are thought of as an essentially unlimited supply of virtual registers. The code generator maps temporaries to real registers or memory locations. `get_temporary()`, as illustrated by the calls in `eval_unary()` and `eval_binary()`, returns a `struct address` each time it is called. Some encoding of values in the `var_offset` and `var_level` fields of the `struct address` must be chosen to distinguish temporaries from variables. For instance, negative values might be allowed for `var_level`, designating a temporary, with the `var_offset` field used to hold a unique temporary number. An alternative description is to use a distinct variant for temporaries, but as we shall see later, the `indirect` flag applies to temporaries as well as to other addresses.

A request for a temporary is essentially an anonymous declaration. As might be expected, information characterizing the use of the temporary must be provided. At a minimum, the size of the temporary is needed. Machine-level type information (integer, float, address) simplifies and improves register allocation because many machines provide different register classes.

Often, preferences or hints (such as allocate a register or a storage location) allow semantic routines to aid the code generator during temporary assignment. Thus a *register preference* suggests that a temporary is likely to be referenced often or soon after allocation and thus it might profitably be assigned to a register. Similarly, a *storage preference* suggests that allocation of a temporary to main memory is indicated (if a pointer to the temporary must be created, for example). Frequently, information directly available to a semantic routine is discarded by the time temporary assignment is performed, and hence preferences may be helpful in generating efficient target code.

Once allocated, a temporary must be preserved until it is known that its value is no longer needed. *Dead variables* (and temporaries) are those whose values are no longer needed; they can be discovered by a careful analysis of program flow. However, few nonoptimizing compilers perform the necessary flow analysis, and hence they make worst-case assumptions. For variables, storage is deallocated only when the scope of their declaration is exited. For temporaries, no explicit scope rules are applicable. Thus a temporary manager must either assume that a temporary is no longer needed once it has been referenced or rely upon more-precise advice from semantic routines, which know how a temporary is being used. This advice is usually a call to a **free_temporary()** routine, which indicates that a particular temporary is no longer needed. Calls to **free_temporary()** are not absolutely necessary, but without them unnecessary code (to preserve temporaries thought to be still active) is likely.

Temporary deallocation is easy if the semantic routine that allocated a temporary does not need to pass it on to another semantic routine. However, often a temporary must be allocated in one semantic routine and deallocated in another. For example, a temporary holding the value of a subexpression is used in computing a larger expression. Once the subexpression value has been used, the temporary holding it may be released. The semantic routine using the value must do so explicitly. Some temporaries are longer-lived and require a different technique. For example, a **for loop** index is often assigned to a temporary with a register preference because the index is likely to be accessed frequently. The name of this temporary can be stored in the semantic record corresponding to the loop header so that the semantic routine called at the end of the loop can deallocate the temporary.

A temporary may hold a computed address instead of a value. For example, in compiling a reference to a subscripted variable A(I), we must allocate a temporary (of type **struct address** if the interface to **get_temporary()** allows such a specification) into which the address of A(I) is computed. The **struct address** record for this temporary is used to represent A(I), but the array element is not stored in the temporary; its address is. Thus the **indirect** field in the **struct address** representing the temporary must be set to **TRUE**. The address of A(I) is recognizable to the code generator and temporary manager as a temporary and may be treated as such. However, the value of A(I), accessible via indirection through this address, is not a temporary and must be preserved unless changed by an explicit assignment. Therefore, two distinct uses of temporaries can be recognized, corresponding to the two uses on names in programming languages (*r-values* and *l-values*): An *object* may be stored in a temporary or its *address* may be held in a temporary. It is important to recognize the distinction.

11.2.3. Simple Record and Array References

In this section we discuss the translation of simple record and array references. First, records with fixed-size fields are considered. Thereafter, one-dimensional arrays with constant bounds are studied. Records that contain dynamic-sized fields, multidimensional arrays, and nonconstant bounded arrays are more complex and are discussed later.

Record Field References

The record definition semantic routines of Chapter 10 allocate addresses to fields so that all fields are contiguous. Contiguity simplifies record assignment and field references. Each field in a record, at the time of declaration, is assigned an offset relative to the start of the record. Normally, this is a constant (in Ada/CS it is always a constant). The offset of a field is added (at compile-time, if possible) to the start address of the record to obtain the address of the field. Something else to keep in mind is that machines often have *alignment constraints*. This means that fields of certain types must begin on an even boundary of some sort, e.g., a double precision floating-point number may have to be aligned on an eight-byte boundary.

Consider the following declaration:

>A : **record**
>>B : Integer;
>>C : Float;
>>**end record**;

When processing a reference to, for example, A.C

(1)   We first look up A in the symbol table. We get its address (say [Level = LL, Offset = Loc]) and its type, which must be a record.

(2)   We then look up C in the symbol table contained in the record type descriptor. One of the attributes of C is its offset from the beginning of the record, in this case, 2 (presuming the size of an integer is 2 bytes).

(3)   We can then obtain, at compile-time, the location of A.C = (LL,Loc+2).

The following syntax defines field references and the action symbols used to translate them:

```
<name>              →   <simple name> { <name suffix> }
<simple name>       →   <id> #new_name
<name suffix>       →   . <selected suffix> #field_name
<selected suffix>   →   <id>
```

In the case of A.C, **new_name()** is called to process A, producing a **DATA-OBJECT** record to describe it.   **field_name()** is called to process C. It attempts to interpret the previously constructed **DATAOBJECT** record as a descriptor for a record object, looking up C within the symbol table defined by the containing record. **field_name()** produces a new **DATAOBJECT** record describing the field:

```
field_name(<name>, <selected suffix>) => <name>
{
  struct id suff_id;

  if (<name>.data_object.object_type.form != RECORDTYPE) {
    <name> ← an ERROR record
    return;
  }
```

```
suff_id = <selected suffix>.id.id from the symbol table
    referenced by <name>.data_object.object_type.fields
if (suff_id is not present in that symbol table) {
    <name> ← an ERROR record
    return;
}
Get the attributes record for suff_id from the
record's symbol table.  Add the field_offset
value from the attributes to the address
described in <name>.data_object.  This can
be done at compile-time unless the address is
indirect, in which case a tuple to do so must be
generated.  Adjust the address in data_object to
describe the result.
Set <name>.data_object.object_type to id_type
    from the field name's attributes

    <name> ← the updated DATAOBJECT record
}
```

Referencing Elements of Arrays with Fixed Bounds

One-dimensional arrays have their elements allocated in contiguous order. When array bounds are specified by literal constants, space for the array can be allocated at compile-time within an activation record or a static data area. Consider

> A : **array**(1..10) **of** Integer;

When a reference to A(I) is encountered, we compute the address of the Ith element of the array relative to the starting address of the array. In our example this offset is I–1; in general, the offset is (index–lower_bound)∗element_size. (Arrays in C are simpler; the lower bound is always zero. The offset, therefore, is simply index∗element_size.)

The offset of the Ith element is then added to the starting address of the array to form the desired address. If the array index is nonconstant, the address of the array element is stored in a temporary, a register if possible. The temporary must be marked as holding an address; this is done by setting the **indirect** flag to true in the **DATAOBJECT** record. In a one-pass compiler in which temporaries are known to reside in registers, a simple optimization is possible. If a register contains an address to be accessed indirectly, we can form an equivalent direct address by using the register as an index or base register with an offset value of 0. This transformation exploits the indexed addressing mode available on most computers in order to produce efficient code for accessing array elements.

Returning to our example, A(I), we first allocate a temporary, T, and load it with I. We then subtract the lower bound, 1. If the element size of the array is greater than 1, we must scale (multiply) the value in T by the element size. If subscript checking is enabled, we also check that I is a legal subscript value.

We then add A's starting address to T. Finally, we must produce a **DATA-OBJECT** record describing A(I). The **object_type** field is the element type of the array; its address is T with the **indirect** flag on.

Because subscripted variables are widely used, it is important to make array references efficient. As outlined, to form the address of A(I) we had to load an index value, subtract a lower bound, scale the array offset by the element size, and finally add a starting address. For fixed-size arrays, the lower bound must be constant; to eliminate the subtraction step, we can compute a *virtual origin* for an array—namely, its start_address − lower_bound × element_size. This is the address of A(0), even if 0 is an illegal subscript. Using a virtual origin, we avoid explicitly subtracting the lower array bound. Instead, we load the index value and then add the virtual origin rather than the real array address.

The following productions show how one-dimensional array references are included in the syntax for <name>:

<name>   → <simple name> { <name suffix> }
<name suffix> → (<expression>) #process_index

process_index(), much like **field_name()**, applies a new name suffix, in this case an index expression, to a previously processed name prefix. The name prefix is described by a single **DATAOBJECT** record, regardless of its complexity. The outline for **process_index()** is shown in Figure 11.4.

Handling complex names that include both array and record references requires no additional action routines. For example, given A(3).BB, the array reference is processed first, producing a **DATAOBJECT** record describing A(3). **field_name()** then interprets the **ID** record for BB using that **DATA-OBJECT** record as a record descriptor. The offset of BB is added to the address of A(3), forming the address of A(3).BB.

For languages like Pascal, multidimensional arrays are considered arrays of arrays, and hence a name like A(I,J) can be processed as A(I)(J), using the techniques of this section. Section 11.3 describes more-sophisticated ways of handling multidimensional arrays.

11.2.4. Record and Array Example

Figure 11.5(a) illustrates some Ada/CS record and array declarations, with offsets assigned by the compiler to variables and fields shown to the left of the names. Figure 11.5(b) shows the tuples that would be generated to translate several statements using those variables.

11.2.5. Strings

Strings in many programming languages like Pascal and Ada are of a fixed size and thus may be implemented simply as arrays of characters. Such an implementation is easy and efficient, but it does not support the most useful string operations. Operations that create new strings dynamically, such as

```
process_index(<name>, <expression>) => <name>
{
  if (<name>.data_object.object_type.form != ARRAYTYPE) {
    <name> ← an ERROR record
    return;
  }
  if (<expression>.data_object.object_type does not match
      the index type of the array) {
    <name> ← an ERROR record
    return;
  }
  Allocate a temporary, T.   This temporary should be a
    register if possible.
  Let Index denote the value described by
    <expression>.data_object

  If subscript checking is enabled, generate code to check
    that L <= Index <= U where:
    L == <name>.data_object.object_type.bounds.lower and
    U == <name>.data_object.object_type.bounds.upper

  Let E_type = <name>.data_object.object_type.element_type
  Let E_size = E_type.size
  Generate code to load T with Index × E_size

  Let A_level = <name>.data_object.addr.var_level
  Let A_offset = <name>.data_object.addr.var_offset

  Generate code to add the contents of the A_level
    register to T.
  Generate code to add A_offset − E_size × L
    (a constant value) to T.

  <name> ← (data_object) {
      .object_form = OBJECTADDRESS;
      .object_type = E_type;
      .addr = (struct address) {
         .var_level = T.var_level;
         .var_offset = T.var_offset;
         .indirect = TRUE;
         .read_only = FALSE; } ; };
}
```

Figure 11.4   Action Routine `process_index()`

extracting a substring from a given string or catenating two or more strings, produce new string objects whose size generally can be determined only at run-time.

Declarations	ID Offsets
I,	0
J: Integer;	2
type R **is**	
record	
X,	0
Y: Integer	2
end;	
ARecord: R;	4
A1: **array** (1..10) **of** R;	8
A2: **array** (4..6) **of array** (8..12) **of** Integer;	48

Figure 11.5(a)   Record and Array Declarations

A1(I) := ARecord;
  (SUBI, Addr(A1), 4, t1)   —— 4 = lower(A1)*element_size(A1)
  (RANGETEST, 1, 10, I)
  (MULTI, I, 4, t2)   —— element size is 4
  (ADDI, t1, t2, t3)   —— t3 contains address of A1(I)
  (ASSIGN, ARecord, 4, @t3)   —— @ indicates indirection

ARecord.Y := I;
  (ASSIGN, I, 2, @(Addr(ARecord)+2)) —— offset of Y = 2

A2(I,J) := A1(I).Y;
  (SUBI, Addr(A2), 40, t4)   —— 40 = lower(A2)*element_size(A2)
  (RANGETEST, 4, 6, I)
  (MULTI, I, 10, t5)   —— element size is 10
  (ADDI, t4, t5, t6)   —— t6 contains address of A2(I)
  (SUBI, t6, 16, t7)   —— subtract 8*2
  (RANGETEST, 8, 12, J)   —— no multiplication since
                           —— element size is 1
  (ADDI, t7, J, t8)   —— t8 contains address of A2(I,J)
  (SUBI, Addr(A1), 4, t9)   —— 4 = lower(A1)*element_size(A1)
  (RANGETEST, 1, 10, I)
  (MULTI, I, 4, t10)   —— element size is 4
  (ADDI, t9, t10, t11)   —— t11 contains address of A1(I)
  (ADDI, t11, 2, t12)   —— add offset of Y;
                           —— t12 has address of A1(I).Y

  (ASSIGN, @t12, 2, @t8)

Figure 11.5(b)   Record and Array Statements and Corresponding Tuples

In order to support these more general string operations, Ada/CS includes dynamic strings. As was discussed in Section 10.2.2, String is a predefined type in Ada/CS. A heap-based scheme for managing dynamic objects, suitable for implementing Ada/CS strings, was presented in Section 9.3.3. Using this approach, each string variable or constant is represented by a pointer to a dynamically created string object. Thus the value of **STRING-SIZE**, the constant that describes the amount of space needed in an activation record to represent a string, is 4, allowing four bytes to store a pointer.

Operations on strings can be translated to tuples if appropriate tuple operators are defined. Unlike the tuple operators for arithmetic operations, we do not expect that a string operation tuple will be translated to one or two machine instructions by the code generator. Typically, library routines are invoked to perform string operations, particularly for operations like substring and catenate that create new strings. Some instruction sets do include string manipulation instructions that can be used to implement string operations.

The string operations defined in Ada/CS include lexicographical comparisons using all the typical comparison operators; string catenation, denoted by the operator &; and a predefined substring function, Substr(StringObject, StartPos, Length). In addition, string assignment must have a special implementation, because the string itself is to be copied, not just the pointer that represents it. The tuple operators required to represent these features are

SEQ, SNE, SGT, SGE, SLT, SLE, CATENATE, SUBSTR, SCOPY

All except the substring and copy operators use standard form tuples with three operands. SUBSTR takes four arguments, with the first three being the input parameters to the function and the fourth being the string variable or temporary to which the result is to be assigned. For SCOPY, ARG1 is the source of the copy, and ARG2 is the destination.

Figure 11.6 illustrates the translation of string operations, where S1, S2, and S3 are all strings.

```
if S1 = S2 then             (SEQ, S1, S2, t1)
    S2 := S3;               (JUMP0, t1, L1)
else                        (SCOPY, S3, S2)
    S1 := S2 & Substr(S3,4,3);   (JUMP, L2)
end if;                     (LABEL, L1)
                            (SUBSTR, S3, 4, 3, t2)
                            (CATENATE, S2, t2, t3)
                            (ASSIGN, t3, S1)
                            -- SCOPY not necessary because
                            -- source is a temporary
                            (LABEL, L2)
```

Figure 11.6 Examples of Tuples Generated by String Operators

11.3. **Action Routines for Advanced Features**

11.3.1. **Multidimensional Array Organization and References**

Before outlining the semantic routines for array referencing, we must consider how storage for arrays can be organized. Based on their storage allocation requirements, there are three forms of arrays:

(1)   If all array bounds are constant, the array can be allocated in static, stack, or heap storage. No run-time descriptor is needed, although one may be used for uniformity if more general arrays are allowed.

(2)   If array bounds are evaluated at scope entry, stack or heap storage may be used. A descriptor is needed.

(3)   If array bounds are flexible (that is, changeable *at any time*), then heap storage must be used, and a dope vector, or some sort of descriptor, is needed. Such arrays are treated like strings.

Array organizations differ with respect to how individual elements must be referenced:

- *Contiguous*

All elements are contiguous in storage. The most common orderings are:

(1)   *Row Major*
This ordering corresponds to stepping the *rightmost* subscript most rapidly $[A(1,1), A(1,2), \ldots, A(2,1), A(2,2), \ldots]$. This ordering is used in most modern languages (PL/I, Algol, Pascal, C, Ada, and so on).

(2)   *Column Major*
This ordering corresponds to stepping the *leftmost* subscript most rapidly $[A(1,1), A(2,1), \ldots, A(1,2), A(2,2), \ldots]$. This ordering is used in FORTRAN.

- *By vectors*

A vector has all elements adjacent. An array is a vector of *pointers* to subarrays or vectors.

In the following sections we consider how individual array elements are addressed when various different organizations are used.

Row-Major Order

Consider row-major ordering, which has the attractive property such that an array of the form **array**(1..N, 1..M) **of** T can be treated as equivalent to **array**(1..N) **of array**(1..M) **of** T because subarrays are also contiguous in row-major order.

Assume we have the declaration

A : **array**$(L_1..U_1, \ldots, L_n..U_n)$ **of** T;

Define the number of elements in the jth dimension as:

$$D_j = U_j - L_j + 1$$

The position of $A(i_1, \ldots, i_n)$ relative to the first element, $A(L_1, \ldots, L_n)$, is

$$(i_n - L_n) + (i_{n-1} - L_{n-1})D_n + (i_{n-2} - L_{n-2})D_n D_{n-1} + \cdots + (i_1 - L_1)D_n \cdots D_2$$

This formula can be rewritten as

$$i_1 D_2 \cdots D_n + i_2 D_3 \cdots D_n + \cdots + i_{n-1}D_n + i_n -$$
$$(L_1 D_2 \cdots D_n + L_2 D_3 \cdots D_n + \cdots + L_{n-1}D_n + L_n)$$

The second term is *independent* of the i values (the array subscripts). We call it the **con_part**, since it can be computed in advance when the array bounds (the L, U, and D values) are established.

The preceding expression is then rewritten as

$$((((i_1 D_2 + i_2)D_3 + i_3)D_4 + i_4 \cdots)D_n + i_n - \text{con\_part} = \text{var\_part} - \text{con\_part}$$

The address of an array element is then

$$((\text{var\_part} - \text{con\_part}) \times \text{element\_size}) + \text{array\_start\_adr}$$

We now illustrate how the address of an array element can be computed while a subscript list is parsed and processed by semantic routines. Assume we are processing $A(i_1, \ldots, i_n)$. **var_part** will be stored in a temporary— most probably a register. The following code will be generated as each subscript, and then the closing), is processed:

(1)   Calculate i_1; var_part = i_1
(2)   Calculate i_2; var_part = var_part $\times D_2 + i_2$
. . .   . . .
(n)   Calculate i_n; var_part = var_part $\times D_n + i_n$
(n+1)   element_adr = array_start_adr + (var_part − con_part) × element_size

Often, the array element size is 1, so no multiplication in step (n+1) is needed. Also, if the array bounds are constant, the expression

$$\text{array\_start\_adr} - \text{con\_part} \times \text{element\_size}$$

can be computed at compile-time, saving a subtraction in the final step.

We now outline the semantic routines needed to translate array references. Syntactically, an array reference begins with

<name> → <simple name> { <name suffix> }

Among the possible forms of <name suffix> is

<name suffix> → (<expression> { , <expression> })

We know that the **new_name()** routine called within <simple name> (and the semantic processing done within any other version of <name suffix>) associates a **DATAOBJECT** record with <name>. Three semantic routines, called **start_index()**, **index()**, and **finish_index()**, are required to process array references. These are placed in the <name suffix> production as follows:

<name suffix> → (<expression> #start_index { , <expression> #index })
                #finish_index

A new semantic record associated with the nonterminal <name suffix> is used by the action routines **start_index()** and **index()**:

```
struct index {
   /* How many subscripts have been processed */
   unsigned int count;

   /* Address of var_part of indexed array */
   address_range var_part_adr;
};
```

The **start_index()** action routine begins the computation of **var_part** for the list of index expressions and creates an **INDEX** semantic record to describe the state of the indexing computation:

```
start_index(<name>, <expression>) => <name suffix>
{
   Check that the DATAOBJECT record for <name>
      describes an array
   Check that <expression>.data_object.object_type
      agrees with the type required by array's first
      subscript position
   Allocate a temporary, T, for var_part (a register,
      if possible)
   Generate code for T := <expression>
   If subscript checking is enabled, generate code to
      check that L₁ ≤ <expression> ≤ U₁
      (L₁ and U₁ are obtained from the array's dope vector)
```

<name suffix> ← (struct index) {
        .count = 1;
        .var_part_adr = T; }
```
}
```

The **index()** action routine continues the indexing computation, using the array **DATAOBJECT** record, the **INDEX** record created by **start_index()**, and the **DATAOBJECT** record of the next index expression:

```
index(<name>, <name suffix>, <expression>) => <name suffix>
{
    <name suffix>.index.count += 1;
    /* let Cnt represent this value */
    Check that Cnt does not exceed the number of
        subscripts possessed by the array
        described by <name>.data_object
    Check that <expression>.data_object.object_type
        agrees with the type required by the subscript
        at position Cnt
    Let Vp be the address stored at
            <name suffix>.index.var_part_adr
        Let D_Cnt represent the D value at position Cnt
            of the array's dope vector.
        Generate code for
                Vp *= D_Cnt ;
                Vp += <expression>;
    If subscript checking is enabled, generate code to
        check that L_Cnt ≤ <expression> ≤ U_Cnt
        (L_Cnt and U_Cnt are obtained from the array's
        dope vector.)
    <name suffix> ← the updated INDEX record
}
```

finish_index() completes the index calculation and associates a **DATAOBJECT** record with <name>, describing the array element specified:

```
finish_index(<name>, <name suffix>) => <name>
{
    Check that <name suffix>.index.count equals the dimension
        of the array described by <name>.data_object
    Let Vp be the address stored at
            <name suffix>.index.var_part_adr
        Obtain con_part from the array's dope vector
        element_size is a constant known at compile-time
        Generate code for
                Vp -= con_part;
                Vp *= element_size;
                Vp += <name>.data_object.addr;
    <name> ← a data_object whose type is
        <name>.data_object.object_type.element_type
        and whose address is that of the temporary, Vp,
        with indirect set to TRUE (since the temporary
        contains the address of the element referenced)
}
```

In the case in which all array bounds are compile-time constants, all dope vector information can be obtained from the symbol table. Further, if all array indices are constants, it is possible, as an optimization, to fold all array index calculations so that, for example, A(1,2,3) generates no code. As an example, consider the declaration

A : **array** (1..10, 1..10, 1..20) of Integer;

All the bounds are constant, so **con_part** can be computed by the compiler:

con_part == 2 * 10 * 20 + 2 * 20 + 2 == 442

A reference such as A(I,J,K) would be translated as shown in Figure 11.7.

```
(RANGETEST, 1, 10, I)
(ASSIGN, I, 2, t1)
(RANGETEST, 1, 10, J)
(MULTI, t1, 10, t2)
(ADDI, t2, J, t3)
(RANGETEST, 1, 20, K)
(MULTI, t3, 20, t4)
(ADDI, t4, K, t5)
(ADDI, t5, 442, t6)       –– addition of con_part
(MULTI, t6, 2, t7)        –– multiplication by element size
(ADDI, t7, Addr(A), t8)   –– t8 now contains the address of A(I,J,K)
```

Figure 11.7   Tuples Generated for a Reference to a Multidimensional Array

Pascal (like C) considers multidimensional arrays as arrays of arrays. This means that *partial indexing,* in which not all subscripts are provided, is legal. The result is just a subarray, which is a legitimate data object. To handle this properly, we must be careful not to finish processing subscripts too soon. For example, in Pascal, A[i][j][k] is legal and is equivalent to A[i,j,k]. We must be careful not to misinterpret the first] as the end of subscripting. The key to doing this correctly is to treat a] immediately followed by a [as *exactly equivalent* to a comma. Thus the grammar must be modified to delay a call to **finish_index()** until it is determined that the next token after a] is not a [.

To handle partial subscripting, we have to modify **finish_index()** to recognize the case in which a subarray is selected. **start_index()** and **index()** need not be changed. But what address is appropriate? For row-major order, we exploit the fact that all subarrays are contiguous. Thus the address of a subarray is the address of its first element. That is, for the three-dimensional array just considered, the address A[i] is equivalent to A[i,1,1]. A suitably modified version of **finish_index()** is the following:

```
finish_index(<name>, <name suffix>) => <name>
{
    Let Cnt = <name suffix>.index.count
    Check that Cnt <= n, the dimensionality of the array
        described by <name>.data_object
    If Cnt < n, then use L_Cnt+1, ..., L_n to complete
        calculation of the component address  (Calls to
        index() can be used to help)
    Let Vp be the address stored at
            <name suffix>.index.var_part_adr
        Obtain con_part from the array's dope vector.
        element_size is a constant known at compile-time
        Generate code for
            Vp -= con_part;
            Vp *= element_size;
            Vp += <name>.data_object.addr;
    <name> ← a DATAOBJECT record whose type is
        the type of the selected subarray
        and whose address is that of the temporary, Vp,
        with indirect set to TRUE (since the temporary
        contains the address of the element referenced)
}
```

When partial indexing (to obtain a subarray) is allowed, it is useful to include size information in the dope vector. We derive it from the following:

Let S_1 be the size of an entire array.

Let S_2 be the size of subarray, $A(L_1)$.

Let S_3 be the size of subarray, $A(L_1, L_2)$.

. . .

Let S_n be the size of subarray, $A(L_1, \ldots, L_{n-1})$.

The size of $A(L_1, \ldots, L_n)$ is a compile-time constant, the size of the base type. It is stored in the symbol table rather than the (run-time) dope vector. The dope vector for an array type with n dimensions (subscripts) is thus of the form shown in Figure 11.8.

If all bounds are constant, all this information can be stored in the symbol table. Otherwise, it is computed and used at run-time. If a type declaration such as

type A **is array**(1..N) **of** Float;

is used, all dope vector information, whether in the compile-time symbol table or run-time activation record, is shared by all arrays of type A. Each array is also represented by the start address of its data. If an array generator is used in a variable declaration, such as

A : **array**(1..N) **of** Float;

Figure 11.8   Dope Vector Template for an n-dimensional Array

then the dope vector generated can apply only to A. For example, assume we have a declaration

A : **array**(1..N,10..M) **of** Integer;

At compile-time, we allocate space for A's dope vector and a pointer to its data area in the current activation record. At run-time, just after the scope is opened and necessary activation record manipulation is completed, we execute code to evaluate the array bounds, fill in the dope vector, and allocate space for A. Assume that at the time A is created, N=10 and M=15. We first fill in these bounds to obtain the dope vector in Figure 11.9.

An array allocation library routine is then called with

- The number of dimensions (two in this case).
- The address of the dope vector.
- The address of the data area pointer for A.
- The address of **stack_top** for the current activation record. For this example, we assume that **stack_top** contains a value of 100.
- The array element size (one in this case).

The library routine does the following:

- It computes the D values from the L and U values (which have already been filled in the dope vector): $D_i = U_i - L_i + 1$. In this case, $D_1 = 10$; $D_2 = 6$.
- It then computes **con_part**. In this case, con_part $= L_1 D_2 + L_2 = 16$.
- Then it computes the S values. In this case

$S_2 = D_2 \times \text{element\_size} = 12$
$S_1 = D_1 \times S_2 = 120$

- Finally, it allocates space for A by setting the data area address of A to the current **stack_top** value and then increasing **stack_top** by S_1 words.

Upon return from the library routine, the dope vector and data area pointer are completed as illustrated in Figure 11.10.

To manipulate the entire array A, we use its address (100) and its size ($S_1 = 120$). To manipulate a component such as A(3,12), we compute its address:

$$(i_1 D_2 + i_2 - \text{con\_part}) \times \text{element\_size} + \text{start\_address} = (3 \times 6 + 12 - 16) \times 2 + 100 = 128$$

The element size is a compile-time constant (**INTEGERSIZE == 2**).

To manipulate a subarray A(3), we compute its address, which is the same as A(3,10) = $(3 \times 6 + 10 - 16) \times 2 + 100 = 124$. Its size is $S_2 = 12$.

Row-Major Order with Type Descriptors

Another solution to multidimensional arrays is to treat them uniformly as arrays of arrays (if allowed by the language definition). The symbol table entry for any array type gives the bounds (if known), the index type, and the base type, which itself may be an array. For example, consider

A : **array** (1..10) **of array** (0..5) **of array** (3..4) **of** Integer;

Data area address for A = ?			
ConPart = 16			
D_1=?	L_1=1	U_1=10	S_1=?
D_2=?	L_2=10	U_2=15	S_2=?

(? means not established yet)

Figure 11.9   Dope Vector Initialized with Array Bounds Values

Data area address for A = 100			
ConPart = 16			
$D_1=10$	$L_1=1$	$U_1=10$	$S_1=120$
$D_2=6$	$L_2=10$	$U_2=15$	$S_2=12$

Figure 11.10   Completed Dope Vector

Four different type record entries would be involved for the types. First, the type Integer has a predefined entry that indicates it is a type whose values occupy, say, one word. Next, the type **array** (3..4) **of** Integer has a type record that indicates it is an array type with bounds 3 and 4, with base type Integer. We also indicate that the entire object has size 4. This type is *anonymous*; that is, it has no name, but we still create a type record for it. If the type had a name, say T, then T's symbol table entry would point to this type record. To keep things readable, we will invent a name like Type&1, but this name, of course, will not actually appear in the symbol table. Next, the type **array** (0..5) **of array** (3..4) **of** Integer has a type record (called Type&2) that indicates it is an array type with bounds 0 and 5, with base type Type&1. An object of this type has size $6 \times 4 = 24$. Finally, the type of A would be a third anonymous type, Type&3, also an array, with bounds 1 and 10, base type Type&2, and object size 240. The variable A would have a symbol table entry showing its starting address (as an offset from its activation record) as well as other information, like the lexical scope in which it is declared. (In C, arrays of more than one dimension are, by definition, arrays of arrays, so this technique applies.)

Now consider compiling A(3,4,4). When we see the first index, we check that A is of an array type, and that 3 is a legal index. The address of A(3) is start_address(A) + sizeof(Type&2)$\times$(3–1) = start_address(A)+48. Its type is Type&2. When we see the second index, we check that Type&2 is an array type, and that 4 is a reasonable index. The address of A(3,4) is address(A(3)) + sizeof(Type&1)$\times$(4–0) = start_address(A) + 48 + 4 $\times$ 4 = start_address(A) + 64. Similarly, the address of A(3,4,4) is start_address(A) + 66, and its type is Integer. If we had stopped earlier with, say, A(3,4), we would have the correct address of an object of type Type&1.

We have shown the simplest case in this example: nondynamic arrays with constant subscripts. If the subscripts are arbitrary expressions, then the range checks and address calculations must be delayed until run-time. It is easy for the compiler to generate appropriate code.

In the case of dynamic arrays, the compiler knows only the type, not the bounds. A dope vector is constructed at run-time for each dynamic type, including the anonymous types. These dope vectors need to store the bounds and the object size but do not point to the arrays themselves. We call these dope vectors *type descriptors*. Strictly speaking, all types that are dynamic or have dynamic subtypes need a type descriptor. To achieve uniformity at the expense of efficiency, type descriptors can be built for nondynamic types, too. Type descriptors are stored in activation records just like variables. As a scope is entered, the bounds and the object size in each type descriptor are initialized. For example, assume A is declared like this:

A : **array** (1..10) **of array** (0..n) **of array** (3..4) **of** Integer;

Type&1 requires no type descriptor, for its bounds and the size of its elements are known at compile-time. Type&2 and Type&3, on the other hand, do need run-time type descriptors, for the bounds of Type&2 and the size of Type&3 depend on the run-time value of n. Figure 11.11(a) shows these descriptors as generated by the compiler, before any run-time information has been filled in. Figure 11.11(b) shows the descriptors after they have been initialized at block entry, with all run-time information included, assuming that n = 23.

Variables, such as A in our example, are given positions in the activation record. Actually, all we store there is a pointer to the dynamic region of the run-time stack. When a subscript expression is encountered, the compiler generates code to calculate the address (and check bounds) based on information stored in the type descriptors.

We can implement the array-of-array strategy quite simply. **INDEX** semantic records are unnecessary, as are the routines **start_index()** and **finish_index()**. The following production shows when a modified version of **index()** must be called:

<name> <name suffix> → <name> (<expression> #index
                                    { , <expression> #index })

index() here expects two **DATAOBJECT** semantic records, one representing an array and the other the index expression. A **DATAOBJECT** record describing the selected array element is produced.

| L= 1 | U = 10 | Size = ? | descriptor for Type&3 |
| L = 0 | U = ? | Size = ? | descriptor for Type&2 |

Figure 11.11(a)   Compiler-generated Type Descriptors

| L = 1 | U = 10 | Size = 960 | descriptor for Type&3 |
| L = 0 | U = 23 | Size = 96 | descriptor for Type&2 |

Figure 11.11(b)   Type Descriptors after Scope Entry

```
index(<name>, <expression>) => <name>
{
    Check that <name>.data_object.object_type describes
        an array.
    Check that <expression>.data_object.object_type agrees
        with the index type it requires.

    If subscript checking is enabled, generate code to
        check that L <= <expression> <= U.   L and U are
        obtained from <name>.data_object.object_type.
        The actual values may be in a run-time type
        descriptor for that type, or they may be in the
        symbol table.  If only one of the two bounds is
        known at compile-time, at least that bound might
        be kept in the symbol table, since we can
        usually generate better code with that
        knowledge.  (For machines with a range-check
        instruction, it may be more efficient to put
        even the known bound in the run-time type
        descriptor so that the instruction can be
        applied.)

    Let V be the address of the array described by
        <name>.data_object.  Let D  be the size of the
        element type of the array.  D might be known at
        compile-time or might be stored in a run-time
        type descriptor.  Allocate a temporary T and
        generate code for T = V + (<expression> - L) * D.
        Much of this computation might be done at
        compile-time.  If <expression>, L, and D are all
        known at compile-time, no code needs to be
        generated at all.

    <name> ← a DATAOBJECT record whose type is
        the element type of the array and whose address
        is that of the temporary, T, with indirect set
        to TRUE (since the temporary contains the
        address of the element referenced).
}
```

This array-of-array approach requires a subtraction for each subscript. The virtual origin technique (introduced in Section 11.2.3) for avoiding such subtractions is not applicable, though when **index()** is called after the first expression of an index list, $L \times D$ can be subtracted from the offset of V at compile-time, presuming the address of V is not indirect.

Using the type descriptors in Figure 11.11, a reference such as A(I,J,K) would be translated as follows:

```
(RANGETEST, 1, 10, I)
(SUBI, I, 1, t1)
(MULTI, t1, Type&3.size, t2)
(ADDI, Addr(A), t2, t3)            -- t3 contains the address of A(I)
(RANGETEST, 0, Type&2.upper, J)
(MULTI, J, Type&2.size, t4)
(ADDI, t3, t4, t5)                 -- t5 contains the address of A(I,J)
(RANGETEST, 3, 4, K)
(SUBI, K, 3, t6)
(MULTI, t6, 2, t7)                 -- multiply by Type&1.size
(ADDI, t5, t7, t8)                 -- t8 contains the address of A(I,J,K)
```

In this example, we used components of type descriptors, such as Type&3.size. This was done for simplicity of expression; the notation actually translates to a compile-time computable offset within an activation record just as a variable name like I does.

By-Vector Organization

This organization is sometimes called the *codeword* method (because pointers to subarrays are termed *codewords*).

To find the address of $A(i_1, \ldots, i_n)$, we use subscripts i_1 through i_{n-1} to index vectors of pointers. i_n is then used to index into a vector of elements. For example,

   A : **array**(1..2,1..3,1..4) **of** Integer;

would be stored as shown in Figure 11.12.

This organization has the following properties:

- Vectors *need not* be contiguous, or even memory-resident. This property can be helpful for very large arrays or on machines with limited address ranges or segment sizes.

- No multiplications are needed. This property can be useful if such multiplications are slow. It can also be quite fast if special instructions are available to follow the pointers.

- There is an overhead of storage space for $D_1 + D_1 D_2 + \cdots + D_1 \cdots D_{n-1}$ pointers.

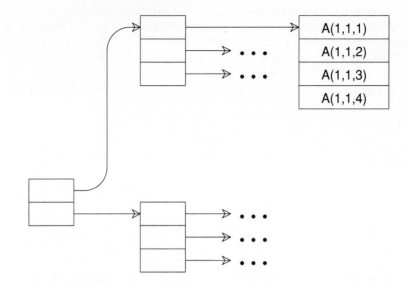

Figure 11.12   By-Vector Array Organization

11.3.2. Records with Dynamic Objects

In this and the following section, we consider the more complex record organizations that may be required by the inclusion of dynamic objects within records. Records containing dynamic objects require more complex processing. We want them to be represented in such a way that record assignment is easy to implement with a single block-transfer instruction (or the equivalent loop). The problem is that dynamic objects are represented by pointers; if we just copy these pointers, dynamic objects in the copied record will be represented by pointers to the very same objects as those in the source record, leading to unwanted aliasing. We must copy the dynamic objects themselves, not the references to them.

Consider first dynamic arrays. For example

```
type A1 is array (1..I) of Integer;
type A2 is array (1..J) of Float;

type R is record
      B : Integer;
      C : Float;
      D : A1;
      E : A2;
      F : Boolean;
   end record;
A : R;
```

The entire record is dynamic in size. We could store it on the run-time stack in the activation record, leaving enough space for pointers for fields D and E. However, these pointers would be copied along with B, C, and F in case of a record assignment, leading to the unwanted aliasing just described. Instead, we can put the entire record on the run-time stack after the fixed-size AR (just like a dynamic array). In the AR itself, we maintain a descriptor of the form shown in Figure 11.13.

Address of Record	Size of Record

Figure 11.13   Dynamic Record Type Descriptor

This descriptor is used to access fields and to do record assignments. The record itself is organized so that the array pointers in the record contain *relative* offsets rather than absolute addresses. Record assignments copy both the normal fields (B, C, and F), the array pointers (D and E), and the dynamic arrays themselves. The copied array pointers point to the new copy of the arrays because the relative distance from the array pointers to the arrays does not change.

As usual, the position of fixed-size objects and array pointers relative to the start of the record is known at compile-time. Elements of dynamic arrays are placed at the end of the record. The layout for record A is thus as shown in Figure 11.14.

To access A.C, for example, we

- Use A's descriptor to get the start address for A
- Add in C's known, constant offset

To access A.E(I) we

- Use A's descriptor to get the start address for A
- Use E's known offset within the record, the dynamic offset stored at that location in the record, and the start address of the record to compute the array start address
- Use the dope vector for E's array type, as usual, to compute (var_part–con_part) × element_size

The only ways in which records containing dynamic arrays differ from ordinary records are the following:

- One level of indirection is needed to reference fields in a dynamic record.
- The array pointers in dynamic records contain the relative offset of array elements, *not* an absolute address. Because the addresses are relative, the pointers can be assigned, as part of a record move, without problems.

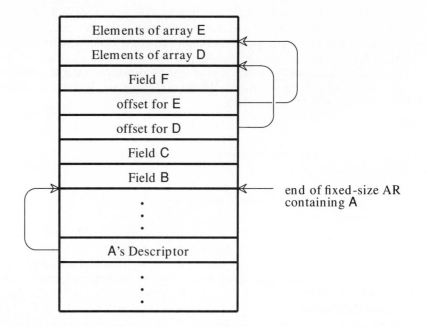

Figure 11.14   Storage Layout for a Dynamic Record

The situation with strings in records is still more troublesome. If incremental reclamation is to be used or if we allow only one reference per string, we need to copy each string individually. Thus we must translate a record move as a series of individual field moves.

As an optimization, we may move adjacent fields that contain no strings as a group. We may even reorder fields so that all nonstring fields are adjacent. (The option to reorder fields depends upon the language being compiled; C requires that fields in structures be placed in memory in the same order as they were declared. However, because C does not have dynamic arrays, this is not an issue, and it is always possible to do a block move when copying structures.)

If we allow *multiple references* to strings and do garbage collection, then no special processing is needed to assign records containing strings. We do, however, still need to be able to go through a record at garbage collection time and mark the strings that it references. Similar considerations apply to arrays of strings, but in this case, individual string descriptors are easier to find and process.

Type Descriptors for Records

Unfortunately, the solution just outlined can become unwieldy for slightly more complex types. Consider, for instance

```
type T1 is array(1..I) of Integer;
type T2 is array(1..J) of Float;
type T3 is record
            B : Integer;
            C : Float;
            D : T1;
            E : T2;
            F : Boolean;
          end record;
type T4 is array(1..10) of T3;
X : T4;
```

If we follow the method of the previous section, we must initialize X by putting a record descriptor in each of its ten entries. Each record in X must also be initialized. If X were a dynamic array, yet another level of complexity would be added. It becomes difficult to understand the general case of arbitrarily nested records and dynamic arrays.

Instead, we consider a general solution that uses the run-time type descriptors that we introduced earlier for multidimensional dynamic arrays. The type descriptors for dynamic arrays work for records as well. The record type descriptor has a single entry for each field, indicating the offset of that field from the start of the record. It also has an entry for the total length of the record. If a field is dynamic, which means it is either a dynamic array or it contains a structure that contains a dynamic array at some level, then the offset for the next field is not known at compile-time, and the length of the entire record is likewise not known at compile-time.

Figure 11.15(a) shows how the run-time descriptors would look for our example before they have been fully filled in at block-entry time. Assuming I is 5 and J is 6 when the block is entered, these descriptors will be modified as shown in Figure 11.15(b).

As before, variables have locations in the activation record. These locations hold absolute pointers to the memory reserved after the fixed-length part of the AR for the objects. The amount of memory to reserve can be found in the **size** field of the type descriptor. Record assignment moves entire blocks of data from one region to another without worrying about embedded pointers: There are none. The length of the block move can be found at run-time in the appropriate **size** field of the appropriate type descriptor at an offset in the AR known at compile-time.

One efficient way to implement the initial picture of the type descriptor is to store a template for it, with as much filled in as possible at compile-time. This template is created by the compiler and placed in the initialized data area of the program. Block entry first copies this template to the AR and then fills in the uninitialized pieces. Alternatively, only the parts that the compiler does

L = 1	U = ?	Size = ?	descriptor for T1
L = 1	U = ?	Size = ?	descriptor for T2
0 (B's offset) 2 (C's offset) 6 (D's offset) ? (E's offset) ? (F's offset) ? (Size)			descriptor for T3
L = 1	U = 10	Size = ?	descriptor for T4

Figure 11.15(a)   Record Type Descriptor before Block Entry

L = 1	U = 5	Size = 10	descriptor for T1
L = 1	U = 6	Size = 24	descriptor for T2
0 (B's offset) 2 (C's offset) 6 (D's offset) 16 (E's offset) 40 (F's offset) 41 (Size)			descriptor for T3
L = 1	U = 10	Size = 410	descriptor for T4

Figure 11.15(b)   Record Type Descriptor after Initialization

not know are actually stored in the AR. This alternative takes some care, because the offsets within the AR are harder to keep track of.

Run-time type descriptors for all dynamic objects simplify storage management. Three run-time areas contain information about any data object, no matter how complex: its type descriptor, its variable space, and the data. The type descriptor has a fixed length, is at a known offset in the AR, and is shared for all variables of that type. The variable space has a fixed length, is at a known offset in the AR, and just points to the data area.

Types that are declared in one scope may be used in nested scopes. The compiler remembers, for each type, the nesting level and the offset of its type descriptor in its AR. Either a static chain or a display may be used to find the type descriptor at run-time for variables declared with nonlocal dynamic types.

11.3.3. Variant Records

Compiling references to fields of variant records is much simpler than processing variant record declarations, as was described in Section 10.3.5. In fact, the **field_name()** action routine outlined in Section 11.2.3 need only be extended slightly in order to handle the possibility that a field being referenced is contained within a variant.

For a reference to a field contained within a variant to be legal, the value of the enclosing tag field must match the label of the variant. Thus a run-time check, much like an array bounds check, must be generated in order to verify the legality of the field reference. The complex **type_descriptor** structures defined for variant records in Chapter 10 are designed to make these checks easy to generate. The **field** variant of the **attributes** record

```
struct {    /* class == FIELD */
   address_range field_offset;
   struct attributes *next_field;
   struct variant_des *enclosing_variant;
   boolean is_tag;
};
```

includes a pointer to a **struct variant_des** in its **enclosing_variant** field. If this pointer is **NULL**, then the field is not within a variant, and no check is required. If the field is within a variant, the **struct variant_des** provides the information needed to generate the check:

```
struct variant_des {
   long choice_value;
   attributes *tag_field;
   attributes *field_list;
   struct variant_des *inner_variants;
   struct variant_des *next_variant;
};
```

The run-time check tests whether the value of the field referenced by **tag_field** equals **choice_value**. If it does not, a run-time error or exception must occur.

Because variants may be nested, the **enclosing_variant** field of the **attributes** record for the tag field must be checked to determine whether the tag field itself is contained within a variant. In such a case, this same process must be repeated using the tag field's enclosing **struct variant_des**.

11.3.4. Access-Type References

In Pascal, pointer references are explicitly designated using the symbol ↑. In Ada and Ada/CS, references to entire objects are expressed using . **all** as a <name suffix> after an access object name. However, references to components of referenced objects require no special syntactic designation. Therefore, A.D may mean a reference to field D of record A, or it may be a reference to field D of the record pointed to by the access object (pointer) A. (In C terms, A.D can mean either **A.D** or **A->D**.)

We first consider the case where the reference is explicit:

<name> → <simple name> { <name suffix> } [. **all** #access_ref]

access_ref() expects to process a **DATAOBJECT** record describing an object of an access type. At first glance, it seems that **access_ref()** has to generate little, if any, code. An access object is just a pointer, so the address of the access object is an indirect address for the object it references. Thus it seems that if the address in the **DATAOBJECT** record is not indirect, we need only change the **indirect** flag to **TRUE**. If it is already indirect, we need to generate a tuple to perform one level of indirection. The type corresponding to the address so computed is that referenced by the access type.

Unfortunately, things are not quite so simple. We have no guarantee that the access object contains a valid reference to a data object. It may contain a null pointer (**null** in Ada, **nil** in Pascal). In languages that do not have syntax for variable initialization and do not require all pointer variables to be initialized (for example, Pascal and Modula-2), the access object may be uninitialized and thus contain a random value. Finally, if explicit deallocation is allowed (Dispose in Pascal, Unchecked_Deallocation in Ada), the access object may point to an area of storage that has been deallocated (using some other reference to the same object). In such a case we have a *dangling pointer.* Thus, pointer references require run-time checking, in much the same spirit as that of the checks that array index expressions are in bounds.

If we wish to check only for null pointers (as many Ada implementations do, because access objects must be initialized, and Unchecked_Deallocations need not be checked), we can choose a special value for **null** such that it will cause an address fault if it is used to address an object. This address fault can then be trapped by the run-time system of the language and transformed into an appropriate error message. Presuming that such an address fault can be generated by the hardware and trapped as necessary, this kind of checking for null pointers is available for free.

To check for uninitialized and dangling pointers (as well as null pointers) requires more explicit checking. An efficient mechanism is implemented in the UW-Pascal compiler (Fischer and LeBlanc 1980). Using this technique, an access object consists of the address referenced *plus* another field called a *key.* An object referenced by an access object has an extra field attached to it called a *lock.* When dynamic objects are allocated, each is given a unique **lock** value (modulo the maximum value expressible in the **lock** field). The pointer created by the allocation routine contains a matching bit string in its **key** field (see Figure 11.16).

Pointer assignments must copy both the **key** and the **address** fields, thus creating a new copy of an access object that can legally access a given dynamic object. For an access to a dynamic object to be legal, the **key** and

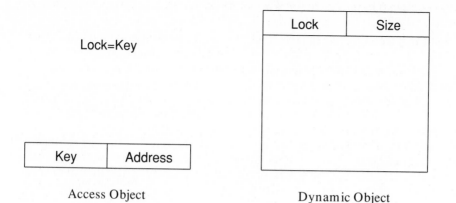

Lock=Key

Access Object   Dynamic Object

Figure 11.16 Storage Layout for a Dynamic Object and Corresponding Pointer

lock fields must match. This check fails for null pointers because any null pointer causes an address fault. Uninitialized pointers may cause an address fault, or the address field may contain a bit string that can be legally interpreted as an address. In the latter case, it is most unlikely that the **key** and **lock** bits will match. To handle dangling pointers, the deallocation routine must modify the lock bits for any objects that it deallocates. Then any remaining pointers to the object will be invalid, due to failure of the **key** and **lock** test.

Given that a pointer reference must involve more than changing an **indirect** flag to **TRUE**, the **access_ref()** semantic routine must generate a tuple to tell the code generator to generate code for a reference to a dynamic object. For example

(AccessRef, <name>.data_object, T)

where T is a new temporary generated for this purpose.

The lack of explicit syntax for a reference to a component of a dynamic object means that the semantic routines **start_index()** and **field_name()** discussed in the previous sections might find an access type object described by one of their input semantic records instead of an array or record. In such a case, each of these routines can make a call to **access_ref()** before proceeding with the rest of the processing specified.

11.3.5. Other Uses of Names in Ada

In Section 11.2.1, we considered the semantic routine **new_name()** in conjunction with the following production for <simple name>:

<simple name> → <id> #new_name

At that time, we assumed that the identifier in question named a constant or a variable; this assumption meant that it was appropriate to represent the identifier by a **DATAOBJECT** record on the semantic stack. However, there are several other possibilities, which are better handled by other semantic stack entries. The identifier might be a type name, a package name, an enclosing subprogram or block name (to be used in a qualified name reference), or a function name (to be used to call the function). If it is a type name, we represent it by a **TYPEREF** record containing a reference to its corresponding **type_descriptor**. For the other cases, we introduce a new semantic stack record type to simply store a reference to the attributes of the identifier until the use of the name is further resolved:

```
struct attributes_type {
    attributes *attribute_ref;
};
```

We can now define the extended version of **new_name()**:

```
new_name(<id>)  =>  <simple name>
{
    Find <id>.id.id in the symbol table
    Let A reference its attributes.

    if (A.class == CONST || A.class == VARIABLE)
        <simple type> ← a DATAOBJECT record with
            appropriate information extracted from the
            symbol table attributes.
    else if (A.class == TYPENAME)
        <simple type> ← (struct type_ref) {
                .object_type = A.id_type; }
    else if (A.class == PACKAGENAME
        || A.class == SUBPROGRAMNAME
        || A.class == BLOCKNAME
        || A.class == LOOPNAME)
        <simple type> ← (struct attributes_type) {
                .attribute_ref = A; }
    else
        <simple type> ← an ERROR record
}
```

After **new_name()**, we must consider the semantic processing possible within the syntax of <name suffix>. First we consider the form previously discussed for handling record field references.

<name>	→ <simple name> { <name suffix> }
<simple name>	→ <id> #new_name
<name suffix>	→ . <selected suffix> #selected_name
<selected suffix>	→ <id>
	→ <operator symbol or string>
<operator symbol or string>	→ STRINGLITERAL

A simplified version of **selected_name()**, called **field_name()**, appeared in the discussion of records in Section 11.2.3. We now consider the other alternatives.

```
selected_name(<name>, <selected suffix>) => <name>
{
    if (<name>.record_kind == DATAOBJECT
        && <selected suffix>.record_kind == ID)
      Process as described for field_name().
    else if (<name>.record_kind == PACKAGENAME) {
      Search the symbol table of the package for the
            identifier or operator symbol designated by
            <selected suffix> and retrieve its
            attributes.
      Process the attributes retrieved above just
            as in new_name().
    } else if (<name>.record_kind == ATTRIBUTES
        && <name>.attributes.attrs names a currently
        open scope) {
      Search for the identifier or operator symbol
            designated by <selected suffix> in
            that symbol table of the scope and
            retrieve its attributes.
      Process the attributes retrieved above just
            as in new_name().
    } else
      <name> ← an ERROR record
}
```

The parenthesized expression list version of <name suffix> presents more-complex problems. Because function calls are syntactically identical to array references in Ada/CS, the semantic processing presented for array references in Sections 11.2.3 and 11.3.1 may not be done as simply as described. **start_index()**, **index()**, and **finish_index()** have parallel semantic routines to be called if the <name> preceding the expression list designates a function rather than an array. The alternatives are to check the semantic record for <name> each time an action routine is triggered and then perform the appropriate action (for an array index or a function parameter) or to collect a list of **DATAOBJECT** semantic records representing the expression list and to process the list at the end based on the semantic record for <name> (again, a function name or an array reference). The latter approach is probably the better choice, because it meshes well with the techniques necessary if the function is overloaded and because the parenthesized expression list is also used in the syntactic form of predefined language attributes. Thus we use the following placement of semantic action symbols:

<name suffix> → (#start_expr_list <expression list>) #name_plus_list

where action routines within the syntax for <expression list> must add the **DATAOBJECT** records to the list initiated by **start_expr_list()**.

name_plus_list() examines the semantic record for <name>. If it is an array reference, the list is processed using one of the techniques described in Section 11.3.1. If it is a function name, the parameters are processed using the techniques to be described in Chapter 13 or the necessary structures for overload resolution are built, as described in Section 11.3.7. Either of these alternatives produces one semantic record, a **DATAOBJECT** record. If <name> is anything else, an **ERROR** record is produced.

One final form of <name suffix> remains:

<name suffix> → ' id #process_attribute

The identifier in this syntax names a predefined language attribute, which acts as a predefined function. Many of the attributes qualify type names, but some also apply to data objects. Some take parameters, in the syntactic form of a parenthesized expression list. Attributes are best handled individually as special cases; most have obvious translations to one or two tuples. Those that take parameters can be set up literally as functions within the compiler to fit into the processing done by **name_plus_list()**, or another alternative can be built into that semantic routine to handle attributes.

Finally, we need to add an action symbol to the <name> production:

<name> → <simple name> { <name suffix> } [. **all** #access_ref] #finish_name

finish_name() does nothing unless it finds the attributes of a parameterless function as its parameter. In this case it triggers the semantic processing necessary to call it.

11.3.6. **Record and Array Aggregates**

An *aggregate* is an operation that combines values into a composite value of a record or array type. The syntax for aggregates in Ada/CS is:

<primary>	→	<aggregate>
<aggregate>	→	<name> ' (<component> { , <component> })
<component>	→	[<choice list> =>] <expression>
<choice list>	→	<choice> {	<choice> }
<choice>	→	<simple name>
	→	<simple expression>
	→	<discrete range>
	→	**others**

The <name> that begins each aggregate must name a record or constrained array type; thus it will be represented by a **TYPEREF** record. The simplest form of aggregate is one in which the components each consist of only an <expression>. It is said to use only positional associations. For example, if A names an array type that has an index range of 1..5 and an element type of Integer, then A'(1,2,3,4,5) is an object of type A, where A(1) = 1, A(2) = 2, and so on. More generally, some or all of the component values could be expressions: A'(I,I+1,I+2,4,5). Now, A(1) = I, A(2) = I+1, and so on, but the first three values are not necessarily available at compile-time.

To compile positional aggregates, we simply collect the component expressions until the end of the list is seen. The semantic routine that processes the aggregate must allocate space for an instance of the type, check that the right number and type(s) of component values are provided (all must be the same type for an array; a variety of types are typically required for a record), and then generate tuples to fill in the aggregate with the component values. The main choice in compiling positional aggregates is to determine where the space for the aggregate should be allocated. The most general way to do this is to allocate space in the current activation record. However, this method has one drawback: If there are any components with constant values, they must be initialized each time an AR for the current scope is created or code must be generated to fill in the constant values. The principal alternative approach is to allocate space for the aggregate in the static data area we have previously called the constant area. Because this data area is allocated statically, constant components need only be initialized at the beginning of program execution. The drawback of this approach is its greater memory requirements; space is statically allocated for every aggregate in the program.

When a <component> of an aggregate is prefixed by a <choice list>, they are said to specify a *named association*. Position within the list is no longer significant. Thus our first example above could be rewritten as

A'(5 => 5, 4 => 4, 3 => 3, 2 => 2, 1 => 1)

From the syntax, we also see that the choice labels may include expressions, ranges, and the keyword **others** (which may only appear last in the list and labels a value to be given to all the rest of the components of the aggregate). These alternatives are only really useful for array aggregates. A combination of positional and named associations is also legal, but all the positional associations must appear first.

The processing for named associations is not materially different, but it is more complex. For example, more information must be collected before processing begins. To avoid ambiguity about where the component list ends, a different delimiter is required for choice lists and the overall component list if lists are collected within a semantic stack. In addition to generating tuples to assign the designated values to the appropriate components of the aggregate, the semantic routine must check that all components are given values and that no component is given more than one value.

Finally, the completed aggregate is represented by a single **DATA-OBJECT** record.

11.3.7. Overload Resolution

To allow user-defined types to extend the language, the standard operator symbols in Ada can be given additional meanings for new types (or for new combinations of existing types). As mentioned in the discussion of **eval_unary()** and **eval_binary()** in Section 11.2.2, this feature is called overloading, and it is simply an extension of a concept commonly found in programming languages. C++ is another prominent language that allows overloading.

In Ada/CS, operators and subprogram names can be overloaded. In Ada, enumeration literals can also be overloaded. Two definitions can share (overload) an operator or subprogram name if they differ in the number or type of their arguments or if they differ in their result type. (An enumeration literal can be viewed as a parameterless function.) For any expression or statement containing overloaded names, we must use context to decide which of the coexisting definitions to use. If a unique choice cannot be made, we have an error. The programmer must then resolve the ambiguity by qualifying an identifier or operator with the block, subprogram, or package in which it is defined [for example, Sqrt.Min(X) rather than Min(X)]. Alternately, a type qualifier [such as Float'(A+B)] can be used to stipulate a result type.

Operators or subprograms that have exactly the same number and type of arguments and the same result type can never coexist. If one definition is in a different scope from the other, normal scoping rules apply, and the inner definition *hides* the other. If both are defined in the same scope, there is a multiple definition error.

In all cases of hiding (including variable, type, and constant names), explicit qualification can be used to reference an otherwise hidden name (which is why blocks are allowed names). Note however that *only* operators, subprograms, and enumeration literals can be overloaded. All other names must have a unique definition determined by scoping rules.

Bottom-Up Resolution

Before the advent of Ada, programming languages that allowed overloading typically required that resolution be made using the number and type of arguments (and not the result type). This is the rule in FORTRAN, Pascal and C++, which allow overloading only for predefined operators and subprograms, as well as for Algol 68, which allows some user-defined overloadings. The chief advantage of this restriction is that overloading does not interfere with the normal bottom-up translation of expressions. That is, we can still compile an expression by translating its operands and operator without regard to the context in which the expression appears.

Unfortunately, bottom-up overload resolution is not sufficient if strong typing is enforced, because type conversion must be implemented using the overloading mechanism. For example, consider A := I + 1;, assuming I is an integer variable. If A is a float, the type of the right-hand side must be a float (to avoid a type error), and this means that the resolution of which definition + represents must be determined by the expression's context as well as its operands. (In C, the conversion rules work differently. The addition is done using integer arithmetic, and then the *result* is converted to a **float** or **double** when the assignment is done. The assignment operator, =, is overloaded, not the addition operator.)

A Top-Down Resolution Algorithm

A compilation model commonly assumed for Ada is one in which a skeletal tree-structured intermediate representation is first built by the parser. This tree is then *decorated* with semantic information by semantic routines and then finally traversed by a code generator to produce object code.

Using this model, the following top-down recursive routine, suggested by Cormack (1981), traverses an expression tree and counts the number of possible consistent interpretations of overloaded symbols. If it returns one, the tree is unambiguous; if it returns zero, no valid interpretations exist; if it returns two or more, the tree is ambiguous.

```
int count(type *target_type, tree_node node)
{
   int solutions = 0, parm_combos;

   if (node is a leaf) {
      if (node.type == target_type)
         return 1;
      else
         return 0;
   }
   /* node is an operator, or subprogram name */
   for (each definition, node.def, associated with node) {
      if (node.def.result_type == target_type &&
          node.def.arg_count ==
           number of subtrees of node) {
         /*
          * This definition is possible;
          * check the args, one by one.
          */
```

```
            parm_combos = 1;
            for (i = 1; i <= node.def.arg_count; i++) {
                parm_combos *=
                    count(node.def.arg[i].type, node.son[i]);
            }
            solutions += parm_combos;
        }
    }
    return solutions;
}
```

This algorithm handles procedures by treating them as functions that return a special type Void. It is a simple matter to augment the routine to label each interior node with the first valid definition it finds. If a count of one is returned, we know the labeling is unique; otherwise, the expression is in error and the labeling can be ignored.

A Bottom-Up Resolution Algorithm

Cormack's algorithm is simple and efficient, but expression trees are built (and often translated) in a bottom-up manner. We would therefore like a bottom-up algorithm that resolves overloading (when possible) using argument information and yet can employ result information when necessary. Such an algorithm has been suggested by Baker (1982). He made two key observations:

(1)   If a subexpression has no legal interpretations, then neither does any expression containing that subexpression.

(2)   If a subexpression has more than one interpretation, then each interpretation must differ in the result type of the subexpression.

These observations lead to a bottom-up algorithm that, if necessary, builds a list of expression trees rather than a single tree. Each tree has a unique type, which limits the number of trees that must be maintained. As the context in which a tree appears becomes known, trees are pruned from the list. Finally, a unique tree is determined, or an error is discovered (no valid interpretations or ambiguous interpretations).

build_tree() (shown in Figure 11.17) is called incrementally to build an expression tree. It takes as arguments the name of a possibly overloaded operator or subprogram and a list of arguments (that will become subtrees). Each argument, however, may be a *list* of subtrees, each with a unique result type. This generalizes the usual sort of tree-building routine in which operands are unique subtrees. **build_tree()** returns a list of trees, each of which has a unique result type. We assume a function **select_tree()** that takes a tree list and a type and that returns a pointer to the (unique) tree on the list that returns the given type, or returns **NULL** if no such tree exists.

Expression trees are built in a bottom-up manner by using **build_tree()** to process each subexpression. When the entire tree is built, **select_tree()** is used to select the unique expression tree that returns the

```
tree_list build_tree(tree_node node,
                     list_of_tree_list arg_list)
{
  tree_list result_trees = { /* empty */ };
  tree_node *P;

  /* node is an operator, or subprogram name */
  for (each definition, node.def, associated with node) {
     if (node.def.arg_count == length(arg_list)) {
        /* This definition is possible;  */
        /* process the args, one by one  */

        /* Create a new tree_node N, as follows: */
        tree_node N;

        N.def = node.def;
        N.type = node.def.result_type;
        N.ambiguous = FALSE;
        /*
         * ambiguous is assigned TRUE if there is
         * more than one overload resolution that
         * returns N.type
         */
        for (i = 1; i <= node.def.arg_count; i++) {
           P = select_tree(arg_list[i],
                              node.def.arg[i].type);
           if (P == NULL) {
              N.type = ERRORTYPE;
              break;    /* loop */
           } else
              N.son[i] = P;
        }
        if (N.type != ERRORTYPE) {
           tree t;

           if (select_tree(result_trees, N.type) == NULL)
              append(result_trees, N);
           else {
              t = select_tree(result_trees, N.type);
              t->ambiguous = TRUE;
           }
        }
     }
  }
  for (i = length(result_trees); i >= 1; i--)
     if (result_trees[i].ambiguous)
        Remove result_trees[i] from result_trees;

  return result_trees;
}
```

Figure 11.17   Algorithm for Building Expression Trees for Overload
Resolution

desired type. Subtrees that appear in **arg_list** but that are not selected by **select_tree()** can be disposed of, for such trees are known to represent invalid interpretations of overloaded symbols. **build_tree()** also works for overloaded enumeration literals, if these are represented as parameterless functions.

To understand how **build_tree()** works, consider the example of building a tree (or list of trees) corresponding to the expression I+J in Ada/CS. The parameter **node** is the operator +, which has the following two definitions associated with it:

((float, float) → float)
((integer, integer) → integer)

If we were compiling a language like Pascal that allows mixed-mode expressions, additional definitions with a combination of float and integer parameters would be included. The parameter **arg_list** is a list of **tree_list**, where each of the elements of that list is a list of possible interpretations of the operands (a **tree_list**). The two operands in this case are simple variables, so each of these **tree_list**s contains a single tree, and that tree is trivial, representing only the type of the variable:

arg_list: ((integer), (integer))

When **build_tree()** compares the definitions associated with **node** to **arg_list**, only the arguments of the second definition match with trees available from **arg_list**. Thus, **build_tree()** will return a **tree_list** containing only a single element, because only one interpretation of I+J is possible.

If, on the other hand, there was another definition associated with +, such as

((integer, integer) → float)

it too would match the trees on **arg_list**, and **build_tree()** would then return a **tree_list** with two alternatives. The two trees would reflect the fact that the language allowed + to be used to add two integers, producing either an integer or a float. One of these two trees would ultimately be selected based on the context in which the expression is used.

Exercises

1.   Discuss the relative advantages and disadvantages of an address-oriented representation for data objects versus representing data objects by symbol table references.

2. Write code to implement the **new_name()** action routine outlined in Section 11.2.1, showing how a **DATAOBJECT** record is created to represent an identifier using information in the symbol table.

3. Outline the routines **select_unary_operator()** and **select_binary_operator()** used by the semantic action routines in Section 11.2.2.

4. In a compiler doing explicit temporary deallocation using a **free_temporary()** routine, what calls to this routine would be added to **eval_unary()** and **eval_binary()** in Section 11.2.2?

5. What tuples would be generated for each of the following Ada/CS statements, given these declarations?

    I, J, K : Integer;
    X, Y, Z : Float;

    (a)   I := −(J + 5);
    (b)   J := I * 2 − J * 3 + K / 4;
    (c)   X := Y * 3.5 + Z / Float(I);

6. Show the offsets assigned to the fields in the following record declaration:

    R : **record**
        X : Float;
        I, J : Integer;
        A : **array** (1..10, 5..9) **of** Float;
        R : **record**
            S : String;
            L : Integer;
            end record;
        S, T : String;
        end record;

7. Give the sequence of action routine calls generated during the processing of each of the statements in Figure 11.5(b), and for each action routine indicate which, if any, of the tuples it produced.

8. Using the declarations from Figure 11.5(a), what tuples would be generated for the following statements?

    (a)   A1(5) := A1(I+J);
    (b)   A2(ARecord.X, ARecord.Y) := J;
    (c)   A1(A1(I).Y).X := J * 3;
    (d)   A2(I,9) := A2(5,J);

9. Outline the run-time routines required to implement string comparison, substring access, and catenation, assuming the dynamic string implementation discussed in Section 11.2.4.

10.   Explain how the tuples generated for access to A(I,J,K) in Figure 11.7 would be changed if all the information about A were accessed from a dope vector like that in Figure 11.8 (rather than being available at compile-time).

11.   If arrays are being implemented using run-time type descriptors like those in Figure 11.11, then

(a)   Show the type descriptors that would be generated for

type T **is array** (1..M) **of array** (2..N) **of** Float;

(b)   If A and B are declared to be of type T within the the same procedure in which T is declared, show an activation record for that procedure illustrating all the data objects related to A, B, and T.

(c)   Show how the type descriptors look after the procedure is entered with M = 5 and N = 8.

(d)   What tuples would be generated for

A(I,J) := B(1,I) + B(J,2);

12.   Show the tuples that would be generated for A(I,J,K) if A is stored using the by-vector organization illustrated in Figure 11.12.

13.   Show the tuples generated for the following expression using the type descriptors defined in Figure 11.15: X(I).C+X(I).E(J).

14.   Given the following declarations and assuming that the offset of I is 5:

```
I : Integer;
R : record
        F1 : Integer;
        case T1 : Integer range 1..2 is
            when 1 => F2 : Integer;
            when 2 => case T2 : Integer range 3..4 is
                          when 3 => F3 : Integer;
                          when 4 => F4 : Integer;
                                    F5 : Integer;
                      end case;
        end case;
    end record;
```

what tuples, including variant checks, would be generated for the following statements?

(a)   I := R.F1;

(b)   R.F1 := R.F2;

(c)   R.F4 := I + R.F5;

15.   The checking technique described in Section 11.3.4 for verifying the validity of pointers to dynamic objects can be defeated by a Pascal

program that declares a variant record that overlays pointers to two different types of objects with different sizes. For example,

```
R : record
    case T1 : boolean of
        True: (P1 : ↑ array [1..10] Integer;);
        False: (P2 : ↑ array [1..100] Integer;);
    end;
```

Because the tag field (T1) can be changed without altering the rest of the information in the record, a dangerous situation exists following a call to new(P1) and an assignment of False to T1. A reference to R.P2↑[50] will pass a variant check, a pointer validity check, and a subscript check, but it will refer to a place in the heap not allocated by the call to new that created the pointer. Explain how the pointer-checking mechanism could be extended to signal an error in such cases.

16. Assume the operator + has the following definitions associated with it:

```
((float, float) → float)
((integer, integer) → integer)
((integer, integer) → float)
```

If I and J are integers and F is a float, explain how the **build_tree()** routine in Figure 11.17 would be used to interpret the expression I+J+F.

CHAPTER 12

Translating
Control Structures

In this chapter, we examine techniques for implementing the features of Ada/CS that specify control flow. These control structures are generally representative of the kinds of control structures found in modern programming languages. The statement types to be considered can be classified into three categories: looping structures, conditional execution structures, and direct transfers of control. The looping structures include a simple **loop** statement, exited at an arbitrary point using an **exit** statement, and special instances of the **loop** statement controlled by **for** and **while** clauses. The conditional structures include a generalized **if-then-else** statement and a **case** statement. Finally, the direct control transfers include the **exit** statement, mentioned above, and exceptions. We also discuss compilation of **goto** statements, which are present in many languages, though not in Ada/CS.

12.1. **if Statements**

Ada/CS includes a generalized **if** statement, with optional **elsif** and **else** parts. These two options combine to produce the following two general forms:

```
if <boolean expr 1> then
   <stmt list 1>
elsif <boolean expr 2> then
   <stmt list 2>
   . . .
elsif <boolean expr N> then
   <stmt list N>
end if;
```

and

```
if <boolean expr 1> then
   <stmt list 1>
elsif <boolean expr 2> then
   <stmt list 2>
   . . .
elsif <boolean expr N> then
   <stmt list N>
else <stmt list N+1>
end if;
```

Without the **elsif**s, these simplify to the basic **if** statement found in most languages, including Pascal. A significant difference from the Pascal **if** statement is the use of the closing keywords **end if**, which improves the readability of **if** statements and allows the use of statement lists rather than single statements within each of the alternatives of the Ada/CS **if** statement.

The form of the tuples produced for **if** statements is shown in Figure 12.1. Two forms are shown, corresponding to **if** statements with and without **else** clauses. Tuples are, as usual, shown as sequences of values enclosed in parentheses. Interspersed with the tuples in this figure are descriptions of potentially longer sequences of tuples. These descriptions are enclosed in braces, { ··· }. Some tuples in this example and in others in the chapter are prefixed with labels. In the intermediate language defined in Chapter 7, tuples are not allowed to have labels; rather, a special label tuple is provided. The prefix labels are used here in our examples for readability, though the semantic routines outlined in the chapter properly generate label tuples in the corresponding places.

For the time being, we follow our usual convention for processing expressions. The semantic routines invoked when <boolean expr> is parsed generate code to calculate the value, either True or False, of the boolean

```
                        {Evaluate <boolean expr 1>}
                        (JUMP0, <boolean expr 1>, Else1)
                          { code for <stmt list 1> }
                        (JUMP, Out)

Else1:                  {Evaluate <boolean expr 2>}
                        (JUMP0, <boolean expr 2>, Else2)
                          { code for <stmt list 2> }
                        (JUMP, Out)


                          . . .


ElseN–1:                {Evaluate <boolean expr N>}
                        (JUMP0, <boolean expr N>, Out)
                          { code for <stmt list N> }
Out:                      . . .
```

Figure 12.1(a)   Tuples for an **if** Statement without an **else** Part

```
                        {Evaluate <boolean expr 1>}
                        (JUMP0, <boolean expr 1>, Else1)
                          { code for <stmt list 1> }
                        (JUMP, Out)

Else1:                  {Evaluate <boolean expr 2>}
                        (JUMP0, <boolean expr 2>, Else2)
                          { code for <stmt list 2> }
                        (JUMP, Out)


                          . . .


ElseN–1:                {Evaluate <boolean expr N>}
                        (JUMP0, <boolean expr N>, ElseN)
                          { code for <stmt list N> }
                        (JUMP, Out)

ElseN:                    { code for <stmt list N+1> }
Out:                      . . .
```

Figure 12.1(b)   Tuples for an **if** Statement with an **else** Part

expression and produce a **DATAOBJECT** semantic record describing the result. In Section 12.7, we look at another way to deal with boolean expressions that generates the appropriate control transfers rather than explicit boolean values.

We need to generate code and do semantic processing in several places:

- After each boolean expression, we need to generate a conditional jump, depending on the value of the expression.

- After a **then** part, we need to generate a jump past the corresponding **else** or **elsif** part, if one is present.

- The appropriate labels for **else** and **elsif** parts and the end of the **if** statement must be generated by the action routines that construct JUMP tuples; corresponding LABEL tuples must be placed at the correct locations within the tuple sequence.

These considerations lead to the following syntax and placement of action symbols:

```
<if statement>     → if #start_if <b expr> #if_test then <stmt list>
                     { elsif #gen_jump #gen_else_label <b expr> #if_test
                     then <stmts> }
                     <else part> end if ; #gen_out_label
<else part>        → else #gen_jump #gen_else_label <stmt list>
<else part>        → #gen_else_label
```

The action routines specified within these above productions all generate JUMP or LABEL tuples. The new semantic record they use to communicate with one another stores labels from the time they are created and used in a JUMP tuple until a corresponding LABEL tuple is produced. We assume the existence of a support routine named **new_label()** that creates a unique label each time it is called. Labels can be represented as strings, so the new semantic record type is

```
struct if_stmt {
    string out_label, next_else_label;
};
```

The **start_if()** action routine builds an **IFSTMT** semantic record and calls **new_label()** to create a label that is to be the target of all jumps out of the **if** statement. (These jumps occur at the end of **then** parts.) This new label is stored in the **out_label** field of the **IFSTMT** record. The **next_else_label** field is initialized to a blank string because all **else** labels are created in the **if_test()** routine, which generates a conditional jump over the following **then** part:

```
start_if(void) => if
{
    if ← (if_stmt) {
            .out_label = new_label();
            .next_else_label = " "; }
}
```

```
if_test(if, <b expr>) => if
{
    Check that <b expr>.data_object.object_type == BOOLEAN
    if.if_stmt.next_else_label = new_label()
    >generate(JUMP0, <b expr>.data_object,
            if.if_stmt.next_else_label, "");
    if ← the updated IFSTMT record
}
```

gen_jump() is the action routine called to generate a jump to the **out_label** if an **else** or **elsif** part follows a **then** part:

```
gen_jump(if)
{
    generate(JUMP, if.if_stmt.out_label, "", "");
}
```

gen_else_label() labels the beginning of an **else** or **elsif** part with the label generated by **if_test()** as the target of the last conditional jump:

```
gen_else_label(if)
{
    generate(LABEL, if.if_stmt.next_else_label, "", "");
}
```

After the entire statement has been processed, **gen_out_label()** generates the LABEL tuple for the **out_label** created by **start_if()**:

```
gen_out_label(if)
{
    generate(LABEL, if.if_stmt.out_label, "", "");
}
```

We suggest that the reader trace through these routines for some example **if** statements, ranging from simple to complex, to verify that the code generated matches the examples at the beginning of this section. It is particularly important to observe how the value of **if.if_stmt.next_else_label** is used in the course of processing an **if** statement.

In this section we examine for the first time a statement that may have other statements nested within it. The semantic routines for **if** statements and those for all other such statements are *completely independent* of the statement lists they contain, so the presence of other control constructs within one of these statement lists causes no problems.

As a final point, we consider **if** statement processing in a one-pass compiler that directly generates binary code. In such a compiler, the techniques just presented do not work because of their dependence on a later pass to resolve references to symbolic labels. The basic problem to be solved is that when the JUMP and JUMP0 tuples are generated in **gen_jump()** and

if_test(), the locations of their targets are unknown. Instead of saving symbolic labels to be generated when those targets are known, some references (such as sequence numbers) to the tuples with the unknown targets must be saved in the **IFSTMT** record. When the appropriate target tuple numbers are discovered, these values can be filled in as operands in the jump tuples. This process is known as *backpatching*.

To implement backpatching within the semantic routine framework presented in this section, the **IFSTMT** record must be changed slightly. In place of the **out_label** field, the record must contain a list of all the JUMP tuples that must be backpatched at the end of the statement. Similarly, the **next_else_label** field is replaced by a **last_else_jump** field that holds the sequence number of the last JUMP0 tuple generated. The **gen_else_label()** action routine must backpatch that tuple to jump to the next available tuple number when it is called. Backpatching is examined in greater detail in Section 12.7.

12.2. **loops**

Translation of **loop** statements is quite simple. We add an action symbol, #gen_loop_label, after the keyword **loop** to generate a LABEL tuple at the beginning of the loop and save it in a semantic record. This label is used by the semantic routine **loop_back()**, at the end of the loop, to generate a jump back to the top of the loop.

The production involved is

<basic loop> → **loop** #gen_loop_label <stmts> **end loop** #loop_back

A new semantic record is needed to save a single loop label:

```
struct label {
    string label;
};
```

The two semantic routines involved are quite simple:

```
gen_loop_label(void) => loop
{
    L = new_label();
    generate(LABEL, L, "", "");
    loop ← (label) { .label = L; }
}


loop_back(loop)
{
    generate(JUMP, loop.label.label, "", "");
}
```

Thus the tuples generated for a simple loop such as

> **loop**
>   <statement list>
> **end loop**;

have the following form:

> (LABEL, LoopStart)
>   { code for <statement list> }
> (JUMP, LoopStart)

12.2.1. **while loops**

The generalized **loop** statement just discussed never terminates. An **exit** statement is necessary to end looping and transfer control to the next statement following the **loop** statement. The **while loop** is an extension to the **loop** statement syntax that handles a particular special case: testing for an exit condition at the beginning of the loop.

The syntactic specification for a **while** statement is

> <while statement>   → **while** #start_while <b expr> #while_test
>   **loop** <stmts> **end loop** #finish_while

One new semantic record is required, which is much like the **IFSTMT** record:

```
struct while_stmt {
    string top_label, out_label;
};
```

start_while() and **while_test()** are much like the **gen_loop_label()** and **if_test()** action routines we have already seen:

```
start_while(void) => while
{
    L = new_label()
    generate(LABEL, L, "", "");
    while ← (while_stmt) {
            .top_label = L;
            .out_label = ""; }
}
```

```
while_test (while,  <b expr>)  => while
{
    Check that <b expr>.data_object.object_type == BOOLEAN
    while.while_stmt.out_label = new_label();
    generate(JUMP0, <b expr>.data_object,
            while.while_stmt.out_label, "");
    while ← the updated struct while_stmt
}
```

`finish_while()` is also familiar, being a combination of the routines called at the end of **if** statements and simple loops:

```
finish_while (while)
{
    generate(JUMP, while.while_stmt.top_label, "", "");
    generate(LABEL, while.while_stmt.out_label, "", "");
}
```

Thus the tuples generated for a **while loop** such as

```
while <boolean expr> loop
    <statement list>
end loop;
```

have this form:

```
(LABEL, LoopStart)
    { code for <boolean expr> }
(JUMP0, <boolean expr>, Out)
    { code for <statement list> }
(JUMP, LoopStart)
(LABEL, Out)
```

12.2.2. for loops

Another specialized extension to the **loop** statement is the **for loop**, used for counter-controlled repetition of a list of statements. Ada and Ada/CS include two forms of **for loop**s:

(1)   The "counting-up" loop, in which the index variable takes on all the values in a range in ascending order:

```
for <identifier> in <range> loop
    <statement list>
end loop;
```

(2)   The "counting-down" loop, in which the index variable takes on all the values in a range in descending order:

for <identifier> **in reverse** <range> **loop**
        <statement list>
end loop;

for loops are complicated to compile because a number of details must be handled correctly. In particular:

- A new scope and data object for the loop index must be created when a **for loop** is opened. The compiler must be concerned with exactly when the loop index is created and when it becomes available. For example, the meaning of the following loop header depends on the details of the language definition:

    for K **in** K .. 10 **loop** · · ·

    It turns out that this interpretation problem is not unique to **for loop**s. A similar problem arises in variable declarations:

    ```
    T : T;                  -- Assume a nonlocal type T exists
    Int : Integer := 2*Int;  -- Assume a nonlocal integer Int exists
    ```

    Ada and Ada/CS solve this problem by dividing a declaration into two steps: A new declaration of an identifier *hides* nonlocal declarations of the same identifier as soon as the identifier is encountered. However, a new declaration is *available* only after the declaration is completed. Therefore, all three of these examples are illegal because the nonlocal identifier is hidden, but the local redeclaration is not yet completed.

- The limit value in an **in** or **in reverse** range must be stored in a temporary so that the value computed at loop entry is used throughout the loop. Thus the following loops ten times:

    ```
    L := 10;
    for LoopVar in 1 .. L loop
       L := 3;
    end loop;
    ```

- A loop may iterate *zero* times; appropriate code to handle this case must be generated.

- The loop index must be protected as a read-only value.

In the following semantic routines for **for loop**s, we put the loop index into a temporary for two reasons. First, this approach requires that space be allocated only for the extent of the loop; there is no need for the action routines to decide to treat the loop index as a variable and allocate a new offset in the current activation record for it. Such a step is a code-generation decision. Second, the temporary allocated is often a register, not only saving activation record space but also probably improving the quality of the code in the loop.

We generate the tuple sequences shown in Figure 12.2 for the two kinds of **for loop**s. These code sequences may appear somewhat convoluted because they each include two different termination tests. However, this code structure is necessary to ensure that a counting-up **for loop** terminates correctly if the upper bound of the iteration is the largest integer that may be represented on a given machine. (A similar problem exists with the lower bound and counting-down loops.) A more obvious code sequence would increment the index variable at the bottom of the loop and then jump back up to the top to test whether the new value is greater than the upper bound. The flaw in this approach is that the increment would cause an overflow before the last test if the upper bound were the largest integer. Our approach has another purpose in languages like Pascal, in which the loop index is a variable that is visible outside the loop. When the index variable is of a subrange type and the iteration range of the loop is that entire subrange, the code sequences in Figure 12.2 ensure that no value outside the range is ever assigned to the variable. Finally, a global optimizer can move loop invariant code (Section 16.3.1) out of a loop body by putting it just before the label Next with a guarantee that this code will never be executed unless the loop is executed at least once.

The productions for **for** statements with action symbols included are

```
<for statement>  →  for <id> #enter_for_id in <reverse option> <discrete range>
                    #init_loop loop <stmts> end loop; #finish_loop
<reverse option> → #set_in
<reverse option> → reverse #set_reverse
```

The action routines specified in these productions require two new semantic records:

```
struct reverse {
    boolean reverse_flag;
};
```

and

```
struct for_stmt {
    data_object id;
    data_object limit_val;
    string next_label, out_label;
    boolean reverse_flag;
};
```

Recall from Chapter 10 that the productions for <discrete range> produce a subtype reference that is implemented as a **TYPEREF** semantic record.

```
              { compute LowerBound }
              { compute UpperBound }
          (GT, LowerBound, UpperBound, t1)
          (JUMP1, t1, Out)
          (ASSIGN, LowerBound, Index)
          (ASSIGN, UpperBound, Limit)
Next:         { code for <statement list> }
          (EQ, Index, Limit, t2)
          (JUMP1, t2, Out)
          (ADDI, Index, 1, Index)
          (JUMP, Next)
Out:      · · ·
```

Figure 12.2(a)   Tuple Sequence for a Counting-up **loop** Statement

```
              { compute LowerBound }
              { compute UpperBound }
          (GT, LowerBound, UpperBound, t1)
          (JUMP1, t1, Out)
          (ASSIGN, LowerBound, Limit)
          (ASSIGN, UpperBound, Index)
Next:         { code for <statement list> }
          (EQ, Index, Limit, t2)
          (JUMP1, t2, Out)
          (SUBI, Index, 1, Index)
          (JUMP, Next)
Out:      · · ·
```

Figure 12.2(b)   Tuple Sequence for a Counting-down **loop** Statement

The first three semantic routines are simple. **enter_for_id()** begins the declaration of the loop index identifier, as discussed earlier, indicating that it is unavailable for use in an expression until the declaration is completed. **set_in()** and **set_reverse()** produce a **REVERSE** record that indicates whether the loop is to count up or down.

```
enter_for_id(<id>)
{
    Open a new name scope
    Enter the identifier in the symbol table in the
        new scope with attributes indicating
        that it is "unavailable"
}
```

```
set_in(void) => <reverse option>
{
    <reverse option> ← (reverse) {
                    .reverse_flag = FALSE; }
}

set_reverse(void) => <reverse option>
{
    <reverse option> ← (reverse) {
                    .reverse_flag = TRUE; }
}
```

init_loop() generates all the tuples in the preceding sequences up to the label Next. It must take care of many of the details listed, including allocating temporaries for the loop index and limit (if necessary). **init_loop()** builds a **FORSTMT** semantic record to provide information needed by **finish_loop()** to generate the necessary code at the end of the loop. As the outlines that follow illustrate, some of the processing done by these two action routines depends on the direction of the loop.

```
init_loop(<id>, <reverse option>, <discrete range>) => for
{
    data_object upper, lower, init, limit;
    struct address T;

    Change the attributes of <id> in the symbol table to
        make it "available"
    Let loop_info be a FORSTMT semantic record
    Allocate a temporary for use as the loop index, and
        create a data_object record, loop_info.id, for it.
    loop_info.id.object_type =
        <discrete range>.type_ref.object_type
    loop_info.id.addr.read_only = TRUE;
    Create data_object records upper and lower describing
        the upper and lower bounds of the index range,
        based on the struct constraint_des:
            <discrete range>.type_ref.object_type.constraint
    T = get_temporary()
    loop_info.out_label = new_label();
    generate(GT, lower, upper, T);
    generate(JUMP1, T, loop_info.out_label, "");
    loop_info.reverse_flag =
        <reverse option>.reverse.reverse_flag
    if (loop_info.reverse_flag) {
        init = upper
        limit = lower
    } else {
        init = lower
        limit = upper
    }
```

```
        generate(ASSIGN, loop_info.id, INTEGERSIZE, init);
        if (limit does not describe a static value) {
            Allocate a temporary to hold the loop limit,
                and create a data_object record,
                loop_info.limit_val, for it
            generate(ASSIGN, loop_info.limit_val, INTEGERSIZE,
                    limit);
        } else
            loop_info.limit_val = limit

        Update the attributes of <id> in the symbol table
            to be consistent with loop_info.id
        loop_info.next_label = new_label()
        generate(LABEL, loop_info.next_label, "", "");
        for ← loop_info
    }
```

The tuples generated by **finish_loop()** include the termination test, the increment of the index variable, and the jump back up to the code for the loop body. This routine must also close the new symbol table scope created for the loop index.

```
finish_loop(for)
{
    struct address T;
    T = get_temporary()
    generate(EQ, for.for_stmt.id, for.for_stmt.limit_val, T);
    generate(JUMP1, T, for.for_stmt.out_label, "");
    if (for.for_stmt.reverse_flag)
        generate(SUBI, for.for_stmt.id, 1, for.for_stmt.id);
    else
        generate(ADDI, for.for_stmt.id, 1, for.for_stmt.id);
    generate(JUMP, for.for_stmt.next_label, "", "");
    generate(LABEL, for.for_stmt.out_label, "", "");
    The temporaries for the loop index and limit value
            can be freed now (if the action routines
            explicitly free such temporaries)
    Terminate the current scope, discarding the symbol
            table entry for the loop index
}
```

for loop Optimizations

for loops can often be optimized without analyzing control flow. For example, loop index variables can be kept in registers, which makes references to these variables—common within loops—quite fast. This technique usually works well, but in certain situations it can make loop execution less efficient or add to the complexity of a compiler.

Because registers that are expected to retain their value across a procedure call must be saved and restored as part of the call, putting an index variable in a register requires such saves and restores for each procedure call within the loop. The value of keeping the index variable in a register for a particular loop thus depends on the number of references to the variable within the loop, the number of procedure calls within the loop, the cost savings for a register reference, and the cost of a register save and restore.

In languages that allow a loop index to be referenced outside the loop body, the situation is even more involved. On exit from a **for loop** (even an abnormal exit), the loop index value must be saved into the memory location corresponding to the index to guarantee that the correct value is available after the exit. The value also must be saved into that location when a procedure is called from within the loop so that the corresponding procedure body, located outside the loop, can reference the current value of the index. In Pascal, for example, the following code is legal:

```
procedure P;
begin
   writeln (I)
end;
   . . .
for I in 1 to 10 do
   P;
```

A compiler can satisfy these visibility requirements by storing the value of the loop index, if held in a register, into the corresponding memory location at the start of each iteration. Despite these complications, the substantial savings available for local references to the loop index and the frequency of such references in a **for loop** make the allocation of registers to loop indices one of the most common optimizations.

In the UW-Pascal compiler, the loop index register is neither saved into nor restored from the corresponding storage location (the location of I in this example) as part of each procedure call. Rather, the register contents are preserved in a storage temporary across a call. This policy has interesting ramifications on the effect of an (illegal) attempt to change the value of the loop variable while the loop is still active. Consider the following illegal Pascal program:

```
program Prog ( Input , Output ) ;
var
   I : Integer ;
procedure P ;
   begin
      I := 0 ;
      Writeln ( I ) ;
   end ; { P }
begin
   for I := 1 to 10 do
   begin
```

```
        P ;
        Writeln ( I ) ;
    end ;
  end .
```

A compiler should give an error message, but it is difficult to detect this sort of error at compile-time. The strategy just outlined causes this program to print: 0 1 0 2 0 3 . . . . The illegal modification to I caused by procedure P is ignored after returning from P because the value of I held in the loop register (and not in I's memory location) is used as the value of the loop index. Although illegal modifications to loop indices are not detected, they are erased upon return to the loop body. This result is a fringe benefit of keeping loop indices in registers.

In Ada, loop indices are treated as named constants (that is, they cannot be modified) that are local to the loop body, so there is no Ada cognate of the preceding program. Hence, assigning loop indices to registers is both simple and effective.

Another optimization is possible because **for loop**s in Pascal, Ada, and Ada/CS are defined so that the range of a loop index is controlled entirely by the initial and final loop bounds appearing in the loop header. If these bounds are constants or statically constrained variables, as they often are, the loop index can be treated as a statically constrained variable within the loop body. This observation allows us to eliminate many subrange or subscript checks associated with the loop index.

For example, given

```
A : array(1..10) of range 1..10;
    . . .
for I in 1 .. 10 loop
    A(I) := I;
end loop;
```

We need no subrange or subscript checks in the loop body. This optimization is easy to implement and can significantly improve the quality of **loop** statement code.

12.3. Compiling **exits**

The **exit** statement is a structured way to jump out of loops. There are two forms that must be handled: unconditional and conditional. The design of the **exit** statement minimizes forward reference problems, because labels referenced in an **exit** are always defined *before* they are used. However, the target of the jump implied by an **exit** is an as yet unknown location. Two problems need to be considered:

- An **exit** can reference an explicit loop name, or it can implicitly reference the innermost containing loop.

- The loop an **exit** references, either implicitly or explicitly, *must* be in the smallest containing package or subprogram that encloses the **exit**.

At any point during compilation, we have a sequence of nested, *open* (that is, not fully translated) loops. To handle the translation problems, we create a compile-time *loop descriptor* for each loop. This descriptor includes a pointer to the descriptor for the immediately containing loop. The innermost loop, which may be referenced implicitly by an **exit** statement that includes no loop name, will be pointed to by a variable called **current_loop**, which is initially **NULL**. Thus **current_loop** and the linked list of loop descriptors define a stack of the records corresponding to all the open loops. This stack can be maintained separately or it can be embedded in a semantic stack. The action routine outlines in this section are general enough to work for either choice.

Loop descriptors have the form shown in Figure 12.3. Within a loop descriptor, **label_entry** points to the symbol table entry for the label of the loop; it is **NULL** for a loop with no label. **exit_label** is a symbolic label used as the target of **exit** jumps. **containing_loop** is the reference to the immediately surrounding loop (if any) that we just discussed. **containing_proc** and **containing_package** are references to the **attributes** descriptors for the immediately containing procedure and package. These are used to check the validity of an **exit**, making sure that it does not specify a jump out of a procedure or package.

The productions that generate **exit** statements, with semantic actions included, are

<exit statement>	→ **exit** <name option> <when option> ;
<name option>	→ <name> #process_name
<name option>	→ #null_name
<when option>	→ **when** <b expr> #exit_cond
<when option>	→ #exit_jump

label_entry
exit_label
containing_loop
containing_proc
containing_package

Figure 12.3   Loop Descriptor Needed for Translating **exit**s

The semantic records required to handle **exit**s are

```
typedef struct loop_des {
    id_entry *label_entry;
    string exit_label;
    struct loop_des *containing_loop;
    attributes *containing_proc, *containing_package;
} loop_descriptor;


struct loop_ref {
    loop_descriptor *descriptor_ref;
};
```

In order to handle **exit** statements, the following addition must be made to the semantic routines executed when a loop is opened. A **LOOPDESCRIPTOR** record must be created and pushed onto a separate **loop_descriptor** stack or onto the semantic stack before any records used by the semantic routines that implement loops. **exit_label** is set to a newly generated label to provide a jump target for any **exit**s within the loop. **containing_loop**, **containing_proc**, and **containing_package** are assigned the values of the variables **current_loop**, **current_proc**, and **current_package**, respectively. **current_loop** is then assigned a pointer to this newly created descriptor. If a labeled loop is being processed, a symbol table entry is created for the label. The **ATTRIBUTES** record corresponding to this label contains a pointer to the corresponding descriptor record. The **label_entry** field of the descriptor record is set to the **id_entry** returned by the call to **enter()** for the label. If the loop is unlabeled, **label_entry** is set to **NULL**.

Because use of a symbolic label as a jump target is impossible in a one-pass compiler, some technique for backpatching jump addresses is needed. Any technique used must handle any number of **exit**s from within a loop, not just a single **exit**. Three approaches may be used to resolve addresses for jump targets:

(1) *Indirect Jump:* When an **exit** is encountered, we allocate a location from the constant area, store its address in the **exit_address** field of the descriptor record (used instead of **exit_label**), and generate a jump to this location. For a conditional **exit** statement, a conditional jump is generated. When the loop is closed, a jump to the now known target address is generated in the location allocated in the constant area. Thus **exit** statements execute an indirect jump (a jump to a jump instruction).

(2) *Chaining References:* Alternatively, we can generate a jump of the form (JUMP, Target?) for each **exit** statement, where the ? indicates an unknown address, and chain them together on a linked list, headed in the second field of the descriptor record that we call **exit_list** in this case. This list contains the addresses of all jump tuples for which Target? is to be filled in. The list is traversed, and Target? is filled in once the target address is known, when the compiler reaches the end of the loop.

(3)   *Direct–indirect:* A variation of the indirect jump method is to generate the jump instruction in the position corresponding to the first **exit** statement encountered (rather than in the constant area). All succeeding **exit**s then jump to this first location. This trick saves a word in the constant area and ensures that the first, and possibly only, **exit** processed is a direct rather than an indirect jump.

The second alternative (chaining references) requires a more elaborate chained data structure, but it generates code that executes slightly faster than the other techniques. This alternative and the third one also require one instruction less than the indirect jump approach (the first alternative). If compiler simplicity were paramount, we would use the direct-indirect approach because the performance of the code it produces matches that of the chained references approach for the most common case, while using a simple data structure. Further, an optimizer that eliminates jump chains would turn the indirect jumps into direct ones. In the following semantic routine outlines, we discuss both symbolic labels and chained references for one-pass target address resolution. An implementation of either of the other one-pass alternatives is simpler and should be easy for the reader to develop.

The **process_name()** and **null_name()** semantic routines find the **LOOPDESCRIPTOR** record for the specified loop (if there is one), check the legality of the **exit** statement, and then produce a **LOOPREF** semantic record to provide direct access to that descriptor record. This **struct loop_ref** is an input parameter to the **exit_jump()** or **exit_cond()** routine that is called to complete the translation of the **exit** statement.

```
process_name(<name>) => <name option>
{
    <name> should be represented by an ATTRIBUTES
        semantic record
    If it is not so represented or if it is not a loop
        name or if it is a loop name with a null
        descriptor pointer, the exit is illegal.
    Otherwise, use the descriptor pointer to access the
        corresponding LOOPDESCRIPTOR record.
    Check that the containing_proc and containing_package
        fields in this record match the values of
        current_proc and current_package
    If either does not match, the exit is illegal,
        because the exit would cause a jump out
        of a subprogram or package.
    If the exit is legal,
        <name option> ← (loop_ref) {
            .descriptor_ref = pointer to the
                descriptor record for the
                loop being exited; }
    If the exit is not legal,
        <name option> ← an ERROR record
}
```

```
null_name(void) => <name option>
{
    Examine the LOOPDESCRIPTOR record referenced by
        current_loop
    If it is NULL or if the containing_proc and
        containing_package fields in this record do not
        match the values of current_proc and
        current_package, then the exit is illegal and
        <name option> ← an ERROR record
    If the exit is legal,
        <name option> ← (loop_ref) {
            .descriptor_ref = current_loop; }
}


exit_jump(<name option>)
{
    If symbolic exit labels are being used,
    Let L be the label found in the LOOPDESCRIPTOR
    record referenced by
    <name option>.loop_ref.descriptor_ref
        generate(JUMP, L, "", "")
    If one-pass target resolution is being used,
        generate(JUMP, Target?, "", "")
        Chain the address of this JUMP tuple onto the
            exit_list of the descriptor record referenced
            by <name option>.loop_ref.descriptor_ref
}


exit_cond(<name option>,  <b expr>)
{
    Generate a JUMP1 tuple to exit the loop if the
        boolean expression is True
    The address of the jump target is handled exactly
        like that in the exit_jump() routine
}
```

When a loop is closed, we find a corresponding **LOOPDESCRIPTOR** record on the **loop_descriptor** stack or on the semantic stack below any other semantic records used to implement the loop. If one-pass target resolution is being used, all the tuple addresses chained through the **exit_list** field in that entry are patched to jump to **next_tuple_number**. If symbolic labels are in use, a LABEL tuple containing the **exit_label** for the loop must be generated at this point. If **label_entry** is not **NULL**, we use it to reference the loop's symbol table entry, and we set the descriptor record pointer to **NULL**. This step is necessary because the scope of a loop name is that of the block, subprogram, or package in which it is contained. An **exit** statement using a loop's name may not appear outside its body, even though its name is visible anywhere within the containing unit. Then the `LOOP-DESCRIPTOR` record is popped from the stack, because the loop is now fully compiled.

12.4. The **case** Statement

Two forms of the **case** statement appear in Ada and Ada/CS:

```
case <expr> is
    when <choice> | · · · | <choice> => <stmts> ;
    . . .
    when <choice> | · · · | <choice> => <stmts> ;
end case;
```

and

```
case <expr> is
    when <choice> | · · · | <choice> => <stmts> ;
    . . .
    when <choice> | · · · | <choice> => <stmts> ;
    when others  => <stmts> ;
end case;
```

They differ only in whether an **others** alternative is included.

Each <choice> is a constant expression, a range pair whose bounds are constant expressions, or a subtype name whose constraints are constant expressions.

Ada and Ada/CS require that all possible values of the **case** index be covered by a choice in some **when** clause. If **others** is the last choice, this is trivially satisfied. If **others** is not used, estimating the range of possible **case** index values may be difficult. For an index that is a simple variable, constraint bounds (if they are constant) may be available from the type information for the variable. Otherwise, the underlying base type is used. For a **case** index that is an expression, it may be difficult to extract bounds, even if the operands of the expression are constrained. In this situation, most compilers assume the full range of values of the base type. Ada and Ada/CS allow an expression to be *qualified*, using the notation TypeOrSubTypeName'(<expr>), in which the bounds of the type or subtype qualify the range of values the expression may assume. (This qualification may result in a run-time check that may, in turn, raise a Constraint_Error exception.) If the **case** index is not qualified, an **others** clause will generally be necessary.

The implementation of a **case** statement typically chooses the appropriate alternative using either a *jump table* or a *search table*. The code we generate uses a jump table, which is probably the most common approach. It has the advantage of executing more efficiently than the search table approach,

```
                {Evaluate <expr>}
                (LT, <expr>, MinChoice, t1)
                (JUMP1, t1, Others)
                (GT, <expr>, MaxChoice, t2)
                (JUMP1, t2, Others)
                (JUMPX, <expr>, Table–MinChoice)
L1:                { code for <statement list 1> }
                (JUMP, Out)
                . . .
LN:                { code for <statement list N> }
                (JUMP, Out)
Others:            { code for <statement list> in others clause }
                (JUMP, Out)
                ––  If no others clause is present, delete the preceding two lines.
Table:          (JUMP, L1) or (JUMP, Others)
                . . .
                (JUMP, LN) or (JUMP, Others)
Out:
```

Figure 12.4   Tuple Sequence for a **case** Statement

although it is not as general a solution as a search table (because it must be of some limited size). More discussion of search tables follows the semantic routine outlined next. The general form of the tuples we generate using a jump table is shown in Figure 12.4.

One new tuple form is introduced in the code skeleton in the figure.

(JUMPX, ARG1, ARG2)   Indexed jump: Add the contents of the location specified by ARG1 to the tuple address specified by ARG2 and jump to that location

In the JUMPX tuple in the code skeleton, the tuple address for ARG2 is specified by a label expression in which a constant known at compile-time (MinChoice) is subtracted from a tuple label (Table).

A grammar for a **case** statement with semantic action tokens inserted is

```
<case statement>    →   case <expr> #start_case is <when list>
                            <others option> end case; #finish_case
<when list>         →   { when <choice list> => <stmts> #finish_choice }
<others option>     →   when others #start_others => <stmts> #finish_choice
<others option>     →   #no_others
<choice list>       →   <choice> { | <choice> }
<choice>            →   <expr> #append_val_or_subtype
<choice>            →   <expr> .. <expr> #append_range
```

Two semantic records required by the action routines are

```
struct case_rec {
    struct type_ref index_type;
    list_of_choice choice_list;
    /* address of the JUMPX tuple */
    tuple_index jump_tuple;
    /* target of branches out */
    string out_label;
    /* label of the code for others clause */
    string others_label;
};
```

and

```
struct choice {
    long lower_bnd, upper_bnd;
    string start_label;
};
```

The **start_case()** semantic routine is called to begin processing of a **case** statement. It generates the tuples displayed in Figure 12.4 through the JUMPX tuple. Several of these tuples depend on values not available at the beginning of a **case** statement, and thus they must be backpatched in a one-pass compiler. The unknown values are marked by use of a ? as a suffix in the following semantic routine outlines. **start_case()** also creates the **CASEREC** semantic record corresponding to the statement.

```
start_case(<expr>) => case
{
    Test that <expr>'s type is an enumeration or
        subtype of Integer
    OthersL = new_label():
    Generate the following tuples:
        (LT, <expr>, MinChoice?, t1)
        (JUMP1, t1, OthersL)
        (GT, <expr>, MaxChoice?, t2)
        (JUMP1, t2, OthersL)
        (JUMPX, <expr>, TableLabel?-MinChoice?)
    Let A = next_tuple_number - 1;
    /* A is address of the JUMPX tuple */
    case ← (case_rec) {
        .index_type = <expr>.data_object.object_type;
        .choice_list = NULL;
        .jump_tuple = A;
        .out_label = new_label();
        .others_label = OthersL; }
}
```

The **append_val_or_subtype()** and **append_range()** routines process constants, ranges, and subtype names that label alternatives of the **case** statement. They each build descriptors for the labels and append them to the **choice_list** in the **CASEREC** record.

```
append_val_or_subtype(case, <expr>) => case
{
  /*
   * <expr> may be an enumeration-valued constant
   * expression or a name that is a subtype with
   * constant constraints.  We assume all constant
   * expressions are folded.
   */

  Check that <expr> is a constant enumeration value or
        the name of an enumeration type or subtype with
        constant constraints
  Create a new struct choice, C

  if (<expr> is a DATAOBJECT record) {
     Check that <expr>.data_object.object_type ==
                  case.case_rec.index_type
     /*
      * A single value in a <choice list> is treated as
      * a range with equal lower and upper bounds
      */
     C.lower_bnd = <expr>.data_object.value.int_value
     C.upper_bnd = <expr>.data_object.value.int_value
  } else {      /* <expr> must be a type or subtype */
     Check that <expr>.type_ref.object_type ==
                  case.case_rec.index_type
     C.lower_bnd =
       <expr>.type_ref.object_type.constraint.lower_bound
     C.upper_bnd =
       <expr>.type_ref.object_type.constraint.upper_bound
  }

  C.start_label = new_label()
  generate(LABEL, C.start_label, "", "");
  Append C onto case.case_rec.choice_list
  case ← the updated struct case_rec
}


append_range(case, <expr1>, <expr2>) => case
{
   Let lower_bound rename <expr1>.data_object
   Let upper_bound rename <expr2>.data_object
```

```
Check that lower_bound and upper_bound are constant
    enumeration values
Check that lower_bound.object_type ==
          case.case_rec.index_type
Check that upper_bound.object_type ==
          case.case_rec.index_type

Create a new struct choice, C
/*  We assume all constant expressions are folded */
C.lower_bnd = lower_bound.value.int_value
C.upper_bnd = upper_bound.value.int_value
if (C.lower_bnd > C.upper_bnd)
    /* We have a null range */
    Issue a warning message
else {
    C.start_label = new_label()
    generate(LABEL, C.start_label, "", "");
    Append C onto case.case_rec.choice_list
    case ← the updated struct case_rec
}
}
```

finish_choice() generates the jump out of the **case** statement that is necessary at the end of each alternative. **start_others()** and **no_others()** are alternative routines, with the one used for processing a particular **case** statement depending on the presence or absence of an alternative labeled by **others**. **no_others()** sets the **others_label** field in the **CASEREC** record to a blank string as a signal to the **finish_case()** routine that no **others** part is included in the statement.

```
finish_choice(case)
{
    generate(JUMP, case.case_rec.out_label, "", "");
}

start_others(case)
{
    generate(LABEL, case.case_rec.others_label, "", "");
}

no_others(case) => case
{
    case ← case.case_rec with others_label
                        set to "" (a null label)
}
```

The action routine **finish_case()**, seen in Figure 12.5, is called at the very end of a **case** statement. It processes **choice_list** to build a jump table and check that all possible values of the index expression select exactly one alternative. It backpatches the necessary fields in the tuples at the beginning of the statement and generates the LABEL tuple for **out_label**, the target of all the exit jumps.

```
finish_case(case)
{
    Let CR rename case.case_rec.

    min_possible = CR.index_type.constraint.lower_bound
    max_possible = CR.index_type.constraint.upper_bound
    choice_list = CR.choice_list

    Sort choice_list into ascending order based on values
        of lower_bnd
    Check that there is no overlap among choices (and
        ranges) by traversing the sorted list, and
        checking that choice_list[i].upper_bnd <
        choice_list[i+1].lower_bnd
    Set min_choice to be choice_list[first].lower_bnd
    Set max_choice to be choice_list[last].upper_bnd
    if (min_choice < min_possible ||
        max_choice > max_possible)
        Issue a warning about unreachable choices
    if (case.case_rec.others_label == "") {
        /* No others clause */
        if (min_choice > min_possible ||
            max_choice < max_possible)
            Issue an error because of index values not
            covered by any when clause
        Check that there is no gap among choices (and
            ranges) by traversing the sorted list, and
            checking that choice_list[i].upper_bnd+1 ==
            choice_list[i+1].lower_bnd
    }

    Let table = next_tuple_number++;
    Let T = CR.jump_tuple
    /*
     * At the beginning of the case statement,
     * we generated these tuples:
     *     (LT, <expr>, min_choice?, t1)
     *     (JUMP1, t1, others_1)
     *     (GT, <expr>, max_choice?, t2)
     *     (JUMP1, t2, others_1)
     *     (JUMPX, <expr>, table_label?-min_choice?)
     * where T is the tuple number of the JUMPX tuple
     */
```

```
if (case.case_rec.others_label == "")
    The first four of these tuples can be deleted
        (since a compile-time range check has been
        performed)
else {
    Backpatch tuple[T].ARG3 with table-min_choice
    Backpatch tuple[T-2].ARG2 with max_choice
    Backpatch tuple[T-4].ARG2 with min_choice
}

for (i = min_choice; i <= max_choice; i++) {
    Let C be the first struct choice on choice_list
    if (C.lower_bnd <= i && i <= C.upper_bnd)
        generate(JUMP, C.start_label, "", "");
    else
        generate(JUMP, case.case_rec.others_label, "", "");
    if (i == C.upper_bnd)
        Remove C from choice_list
}
generate(LABEL, case.case_rec.out_label, "", "");
}
```

Figure 12.5   Outline of the **finish_case()** Action Routine

The jump table approach to translating **case** statements is simple and fast if the range min_choice .. max_choice is densely covered by choice values. If it is not dense enough, the jump table may well waste space, possibly even exceeding storage capacity.

Although some compilers do not worry about this contingency, it is possible to generate some kind of *search table* rather than a jump table. For example, we might generate

```
            (JUMP,Search)
               { code for all the cases }
Table:      (ChoiceValue,Address)
               . . .
            (ChoiceValue,Address)
            (—,OthersAddress)
Search:        { code to search the table and jump to the appropriate address }
```

Table might be searched linearly (for example, with a hardware search instruction), or it might be ordered on ChoiceValue and searched by binary search. It is even possible to use a hashing scheme on ChoiceValue.

The UW-Pascal compiler generates a jump table if (max_choice − min_choice) < 10 or if 50% or more of the possible labels in the range min_choice .. max_choice occur. Otherwise, it generates a search table and performs linear search using a hardware search instruction.

The UNIX C compiler and the Wisconsin UNIX Pascal compiler (both for the VAX) choose among three alternatives. If there are more than three cases and the range is more than three-fourths full, a jump table as described is used. (The VAX has an instruction that combines the range check and the indexed jump.) Otherwise, if there are more than eight cases, it generates code to perform an in-line binary search on the list of cases. Because the set of case values is fixed and known at compile time, the binary search can be coded with no looping. For example, if there are $2n$ cases and val_n is the value of the nth case, the following code would be generated:

$$(GT, expr, val_n, t1)$$
$$(JUMP1, t1, SearchUpper_1)$$
$$(GT, expr, val_{n/2}, t2)$$
$$(JUMP1, t2, SearchUpper_2)$$

```
                         { code to search among cases 1..n/2 }
SearchUpper₂:            { code to search among cases n/2+1..n }
SearchUpper₁:   (GT, expr, val3n/2, t3)
                (JUMP1, t3, SearchUpper₃)
                         { code to search among cases n+1..3n/2 }
SearchUpper₃:   { code to search among cases 3n/2+1..2n }
```

This approach generates two instructions for each case, but only $\log(n)$ of them are actually executed, where n is the number of cases. Finally, if neither of these criteria holds, a straight linear search is performed.

These three approaches could also be combined to create a hybrid approach, as described by the following pseudocode:

```
if (size of choice range < minimum)
    generate a linear search
else if (choices are dense enough)
    generate code for a jump table
else {
    generate code to divide the range in half (as for
    binary search) and then recursively apply this
    algorithm to generate a search of each of the
    halves of the range
}
```

12.5. Compiling **goto** Statements

Even though there is no **goto** statement in Ada/CS, we include a discussion of it because **goto** statements appear in virtually every major language, including Ada. There are similarities between the problems of handling **exit**s and **goto**s, because some **goto**s, like **exit**s, involve forward jumps to as yet undefined labels. If symbolic labels for tuples are included in the IR used by a compiler, the translation of **goto**s is simple, once the appropriate target label for a particular **goto** is determined. If one-pass address resolution is required, again, any of the *indirect jump, chained reference,* or *direct-indirect* techniques can be used.

To translate **goto** statements, we must also handle new problems:

- Labels with the same name may be defined in more than one name scope.

- **goto**s out of a block or procedure may need to restore registers, up-date stack tops, and modify the display.

Label Definitions

Consider first the label-definition problem, using the scoping rules of Algol 60 and Pascal. We may find the following situation in an Algol 60 program, for example:

```
begin
   L: begin
         goto L;
          . . .
         {possible definition of L}
      end
end
```

When we are processing the **goto** statement, we do not know in which scope L will be defined. It is thus necessary to delay resolving a label reference until we are sure which scope contains the label being referenced.

To handle this problem, we must put label identifiers in the symbol table. When encountered, a label identifier is either *resolved,* in which case we have already seen the defining instance of the label and thus we know the target of **goto**s to this label, or it is *unresolved,* in which case we maintain a chain of locations where we have generated jumps to the target that must be back-patched later. This backpatching is necessary even if symbolic labels rather than tuple numbers are used as the targets of JUMP tuples, because an un-resolved label identifier can have no tuple label associated with it.

For compiling **goto**s in Ada and Algol 60, three events are of interest: (1) A **goto** is seen, (2) a label is defined, and (3) a scope is closed. When either of the first two events occur, there may be a resolved entry for the label in the symbol table for the *innermost* scope, there may be an unresolved entry in this symbol table, or there may be no entry present for the label. When a scope is closed, we have to process the resolved and unresolved label entries in its symbol table. Each of the cases is treated differently, as listed in Figure 12.6.

The table entries stand for the following actions. For the **generate** case, a jump to the tuple label contained in the resolved label entry is generated. The **append chain** case requires that a jump to an unknown address be generated

	Resolved	Unresolved	No entry
goto L	generate	append chain	new unresolved entry
<<L>>	error	resolve	new resolved entry
Close scope	flush	propagate	—

Figure 12.6   Processing **goto**s in Ada and Algol 60

and the location of that jump tuple be appended to the chain of such locations in the unresolved label's symbol table entry. The **new unresolved entry** case is just like **append chain** except that a symbol table entry for the label must be created, and the jump tuple location is the first on its chain. The **error** case is obvious; this situation represents a duplicate definition of a label within a scope. For the **resolve** case, the symbol table entry for the label is changed from unresolved to resolved, a LABEL tuple is generated, and all the jump tuples on its chain are backpatched to jump to this new label. The **new resolved entry** case requires only that a LABEL tuple be generated, and that the label and its corresponding tuple address be stored in the symbol table. The **flush** case requires only that the label be removed from the symbol table. Because this normally happens as the scope is closed, nothing explicit is required. The **propagate** case is the only complex one. If the outermost scope of an Algol 60 program, or a procedure, package, or task of an Ada program is being exited, this situation is an error; an undefined label has been targeted. Otherwise, the symbol table may or may not have an entry at the next scope level for this label. If there is no entry, create a new unresolved entry and give it the chain that was on the entry that is disappearing with the exited scope. If there is already a resolved entry, use its value to backpatch all the tuples on the chain of the unresolved entry in the scope being closed. If there is already an unresolved entry, append the current chain to its chain.

Pascal requires that labels be declared at the head of a scope. The label must then be declared in that very scope, not in some enclosed scope. When the label is declared, an unresolved entry is made in the symbol table. When a **goto** is compiled, there must already be an entry in the symbol table for the label it targets, and this entry need not be in the innermost scope. The table of actions in Figure 12.7 is therefore simpler for Pascal, for there is no **propagate** case in that language, and errors are detected sooner.

We create a symbol table entry upon declaration and, as usual, chain references until the label is defined. However, at the close of a scope we need not merge reference chains. Instead, we issue an immediate diagnostic message for any label declared but not defined in a scope.

We can also use a chaining technique to solve other label-scoping problems. Many languages, such as Pascal and Ada, disallow jumping into certain constructs (**for loop**s, **while loop**s, **case** statements). An easy way to enforce this rule is to link together all labels defined in such a construct. Local references to such labels that occur *within* the construct are processed normally.

	Resolved	Unresolved	No entry
Declare L	—	error	new unresolved entry
goto L	generate	append chain	error
L:	error	resolve	error
Close scope	flush	error	—

Figure 12.7   Processing **goto**s in Pascal

However, references from *outside* the construct are blocked by marking such labels *inaccessible*. For example, consider

```
for I := 1 to 10 do
    goto L; { illegal }
    for J := 1 to 20 do
        goto L;  { legal }
        . . .
        L:
    end { for J }
end { for I }
```

Here we link all forward references that occur in each **for loop**. The inner reference is resolved normally when the loop is closed. Then L is marked inaccessible. When the outer loop is closed, its reference to L cannot be legally resolved.

Jumping Out of Blocks or Procedures

We now consider the extra code needed to jump out of a block or procedure. Before jumping, we may need to pop the run-time stack, modify the display, and restore registers.

Popping the stack requires no work, whether we use block- or procedure-level activation records. Each subprogram and block has a local **stack_top**. When we leave a block or a procedure, we revert to a previous **stack_top** value, which has the effect of an implicit pop.

If a static chain is used, there is no display, so no display modifications are required. The correctness of a display, however, depends on a proper sequence of returns. A **goto** referencing a label requires that the label be defined at a visible outer lexical level (labels have the same scope rules as variables). Therefore, the part of the display that is needed after the **goto** is executed is already correct. Unfortunately, as we have seen before, even the *unused* parts of the display must be correct. Let us return to the example we used to discuss displays in Section 9.2.1:

procedure A **is**
  procedure B **is**
    procedure C **is**
      $\cdots$ A; $\cdots$
    end C;

    $\cdots$ C; $\cdots$
  end B;

  $\cdots$ B; $\cdots$
end A;

If the following sequence of procedure calls occurs (where ′ is used to signify a second call of a procedure before the first returns):

A B C A′ B′ C′

then Figure 12.8 shows the display in force during each invocation, as well as the display value that is saved in each case.

If C′ should return directly to A′ by a **goto**, two display registers, B and C, must be restored to levels 2 and 3, respectively. In general, we are required to restore one display register for every activation record on the dynamic chain between the source and the target of the **goto**. Luckily, this extra effort is restricted to the case of a nonlocal **goto**.

Static chains avoid this entire problem; each activation record is formed with the correct referencing environment, and that environment is not modified by further procedure invocations. One can also build hybrid schemes that both retain static chains and build displays. In these schemes, nonlocal **goto**s are expected to recreate the entire display from the static chain, whereas normal returns need to restore only one display register. Now, however, each procedure invocation must pay the slight extra cost of establishing the static chain.

gotos to label variables or label parameters are also far easier to implement with static chains but can be handled with displays as well. The trick is to treat them as formal procedures.

We do not restore registers when we leave a block, so a jump out of a block requires no extra work. We may need to restore registers to jump out of

Calls	A	B	C	A′	B′	C′
`display[2]`	??	??	C	C	C	C′
`display[1]`	?	B	B	B	B′	B′
`display[0]`	A	A	A	A′	A′	A′
Saved	—	?	??	A	B	C

Figure 12.8   Displays Created before a **goto**

a procedure, however (for example, if **for** indices are kept in registers). The way to restore registers depends on how the registers were saved in the first place. Several options are discussed in Chapter 13.

12.6. Exception Handling

Among the control structure features of the Ada programming language, exception handling presents the greatest challenge to compiler writers. Unlike many of the other complex features of Ada, which mostly require greater compile-time complexity, exception handling has significant run-time implications. The exception-handling features of Ada present a number of interesting problems:

- Exceptions can be *implicitly* as well as *explicitly* raised.

- Exception propagation has both static and dynamic properties. Exceptions within blocks and packages are statically propagated to the containing unit if not handled locally, but exceptions in a subprogram are dynamically propagated to the caller (and then reraised).

- Exception names follow ordinary scoping rules, but exception propagation does not. It is therefore possible to propagate an exception into (or through) a scope in which the exception name is unknown.

- Exception propagation rules depend on exactly where an exception is raised. In particular, exceptions raised in declaration parts and exception handlers are propagated differently from those raised in statement parts.

- Exception handlers are optionally declared after the body of a *unit* (block, package, or subprogram). We expect that many units will not provide handlers, and translation of these units should not be impaired by the possibility that a handler will be provided.

- Packages and subprograms can be separately compiled, with an exception declared and raised in one compilation unit and handled in another.

The basic problem presented by exception handling is that when a program raises an exception during execution, the appropriate handler must be located and executed. The most straightforward implementation of exception handling is to keep some run-time data structure representing active exception handlers and to use it to find handlers as required. A disadvantage of this approach is that the data structure has to be modified whenever a scope containing any exception handlers is entered or exited, thus requiring considerable execution time overhead even when no exceptions are raised.

We prefer implementations that do not incur overhead unless the feature they support is used. The approach presented in this section has no run-time cost until an exception is raised. The cost of determining the appropriate handler to process an exception depends only on the number of implicit subprogram returns necessary to reach that handler. This dependency is the minimum possible because calling patterns (and hence active exception handlers) cannot, in general, be predicted in advance. The space requirements of this approach are also modest, being proportional to the number of exception handlers plus the number of subprograms in a program.

We first present a solution that deals only with the static aspects of exception propagation in a single compilation unit. That is, we consider exceptions possibly propagated out of nested blocks and packages but not out of subprograms. In order to correctly handle exceptions, at any point in a block or package, we need to know where the appropriate handler for a given exception can be found. Recall that all exceptions have a default handler if no user-provided handler is found. The characteristics of a default handler are implementation-dependent, but probably the default handler simply prints an error message ("Exception X raised") and then terminates execution.

We assign to each exception—predefined or user-defined—a unique integer, beginning with 1. An exception is represented internally by this integer code, which can be used to index into a transfer vector to exception handlers. At the beginning of the translation of a compilation unit, the exception transfer vector includes only predefined exceptions and has all default entries (which can be the address of a support routine that handles the default case).

For each exception declared, a new element is added to the transfer vector. When an explicit handler is declared, we must compute an updated transfer vector. Let us qualify a transfer vector with the range of addresses it covers. That is, if an exception e is raised at address a, then we look up the transfer vector associated with address a, index into it using e, and jump to the appropriate handler. Each handler, when translated, contains a continuation address, which is the address of the statement or package that follows the unit containing the handler. After the handler (entered through the transfer vector) completes execution, it jumps to the continuation address to continue execution.

In the simplest case, the body of a compilation unit includes no exception handlers. Thus we require only a single address range to cover the entire compilation unit. The associated transfer vector is the initial vector of predefined exceptions and default handlers.

Consider the example in Figure 12.9 of a compilation unit containing exception handlers. The exception handlers in the innermost block apply to the statements in address range 3. The exception handlers at the end of the package body apply to the statements in address ranges 2, 4, and 5; predefined handlers apply to ranges 1 and 6. Exceptions other than Singular and Constraint_Error raised in range 3 propagate to P's exception handlers. Because P has a handler for **others**, no exceptions raised in ranges 2 through 5 can propagate any further.

As illustrated in Figure 12.10, we use three transfer vectors: one applicable to ranges 1 and 6; the second applicable to ranges 2, 4, and 5; and the third applicable to range 3. Because a handler for **others** is provided in package P, we have *factored* its address from the transfer vector. It has been made the *default entry* for the vector. That is, if a position in the vector contains a null entry, the default address is used.

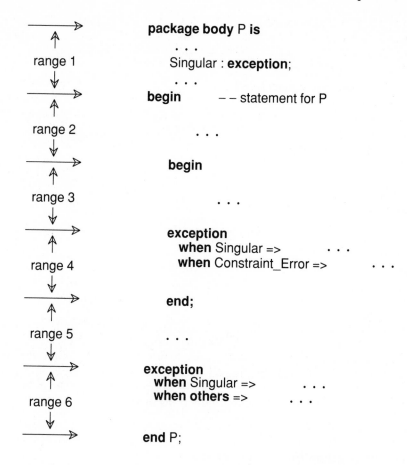

```
                          package body P is

                              . . .
range 1
                              Singular : exception;

                              . . .
                          begin        - - statement for P
range 2
                                  . . .

                              begin
range 3
                                  . . .

                              exception
                                when Singular =>     . . .
                                when Constraint_Error =>        . . .
range 4
                              end;
range 5
                                  . . .

                          exception
                              when Singular =>        . . .
                              when others =>          . . .
range 6
                          end P;
```

Figure 12.9   Compilation Unit with Exception Handlers

If a handler for **others** is not provided, the exception may propagate. This means that if a local handler for an exception is absent, the applicable handler in the containing unit is used. This situation occurs for the innermost block of our example. In terms of implementation, we have copied the transfer vector of the containing unit, package P (with default), and then updated entries for Constraint_Error and Singular to reflect local handler declarations.

When the outermost unit is completed, all the transfer vectors are known. At this point we have a list of address ranges, each with its own transfer vector. The ranges are contiguous and cover the entire program. Adjacent ranges that share the same transfer vector (such as ranges 4 and 5 in our example) can be merged. To save space, we can exploit the fact that the beginning of one range is one address beyond the end of the previous range. This allows us to store one address (say the beginning of the range) and a reference to a transfer vector for each range.

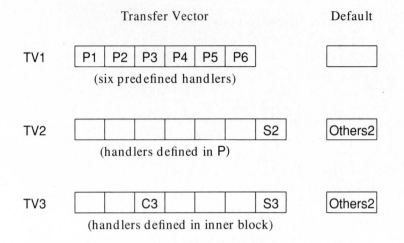

Figure 12.10   Transfer Vectors for Example in Figure 12.9

When an exception is implicitly raised, say by an arithmetic or range fault, we can do a binary search on the range table (Figure 12.11) to quickly find the appropriate transfer vector, through which we then enter the appropriate handler. For explicitly raised exceptions, we generate a jump instruction to the appropriate handler, whose address can be determined at compile-time (using the data encoded in the transfer vectors).

Exception Propagation from Subprograms

When we begin to translate a subprogram, we create a range that covers the entire subprogram, including declarations and locally defined exception handlers. This range has a transfer vector whose default entry references a special **propagate_exception()** routine. This routine performs a normal subprogram return and then immediately upon return reraises the original exception (implicitly). The return address determines the appropriate transfer vector, which determines the handler that is to be entered.

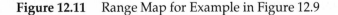

Figure 12.11   Range Map for Example in Figure 12.9

As units within a subprogram are translated, new ranges—with associated transfer vectors—are created if handlers are declared. Exception propagation within a subprogram is static, but if no local handler is provided, the **propagate_exception()** routine reraises the exception at the point of call.

If the called procedure is responsible for restoring registers, the **propagate_exception()** routine is fairly simple. We execute the normal subprogram epilogue routine (to reset the display, restore registers, and so on). However, rather than jumping to the return address, we pass it—together with the exception codes—to the implicit exception handler, exactly as if an implicit exception had been raised. If registers are restored by the caller, we must use the return address to locate register restore code, execute it, and then invoke the implicit exception handler.

Representing Transfer Vectors and Range Maps

The number of ranges can be no more than twice the sum of the number of subprograms and the number of nested units with exception handler declarations. Thus the representation of a range map requires only a few words of storage per subprogram. Units containing handler declarations incur a similar storage overhead.

The number of distinct transfer vectors is essentially the number of units that declare exception handlers. In general, transfer vectors are sparse because they contain nondefault entries only for those exceptions for which explicit handlers have been provided. We can envision a *sparse array* indexed by transfer vector number (stored in the range map) and exception code. A variety of effective compaction algorithms for sparse arrays (such as parse tables) are well known. The most appropriate is double-offset indexing, which provides fast search and near optimal compaction. It is described in detail in Chapter 17.

Separate Compilation

Separate compilation poses one additional problem: exception numbering. Recall that we earlier assigned each exception a unique integer code. We allow each compilation unit to assign codes independently to exceptions declared within it. In much the same way as internally assigned addresses are relocated, exception codes must be *relocated* prior to execution. Thus the exception codes are made unique across compilation units, and the index range of a transfer vector is the total number of exceptions declared in the program.

The compacted transfer vector array is composed of subarrays corresponding to each compilation unit. The complete array must be built and compacted as separately compiled modules are bound together.

In many cases, exceptions declared in one compilation unit are inaccessible in other compilation units. This situation poses no problems and causes virtually no space penalty when compaction is used. Further, the default mechanism we use simply handles the situation in which an exception is propagated through a scope where its name is not known.

Implementation in a One-Pass Compiler

As exception declarations are processed, each exception is assigned a unique integer code, thus extending the transfer vector. When an exception handler is declared, it produces an explicit entry in the transfer vector for the associated statement list. Each handler, when translated, contains a continuation address. This is the address of the statement or package that follows the unit containing the handler. After the handler (entered through the transfer vector) completes execution, it jumps to the continuation address to continue execution. This jump is analogous to the jump to out-address that follows **when** clauses in a **case** statement.

When a **begin** is encountered, we save the start address of the statement list on the semantic stack. At the end of the statement list, we may see **exception** (signaling the start of handler definitions), or an **end**. If we see an **end**, we pop the statement list start address because the statement list uses the transfer vector associated with its immediately containing unit. If **exception** is present, the next available instruction address is recorded as the end of the range that started at **begin**. As the handler declarations that follow are processed, a list is constructed of exception codes handled and their corresponding start addresses. When the **end** is seen, this list and the associated range addresses must be propagated to the semantic stack entry for the enclosing unit, if there is one. Then the stack entry for the current unit is popped.

When the outermost unit is completed, all the transfer vectors can be computed by starting with the default vector and using the range bounds and associated exception handler lists collected as nested units were processed. We then have a list of address ranges, each with an associated transfer vector. (As illustrated in the preceding discussion, ranges may share a transfer vector). If a list of all raise statements in the unit has been kept, the transfer vectors may be used to convert raise exception n library routine calls to direct jumps to handlers in the cases in which exceptions are handled without propagation beyond a procedure boundary. The vectors must also be used to generate a run-time representation for use in handling propagated exceptions, as already described.

A range map, as illustrated in Figure 12.11, is a generally useful technique that can be applied to problems other than the implementation of exception handling. For example, in a language like Pascal, which has no exception-handling features, a program must be terminated if it executes some illegal operation, such as attempting an array indexing operation with an illegal index value. Most compilers generate an error message in such a case that includes the source program line number of the statement that caused the error. A range map that maps code segments to line numbers can be used to derive the line number of the error from the program counter value when the error occurred.

12.7. **Short-circuit Boolean Expressions**

The ordinary boolean **and** and **or** operators are handled like all other infix operators. Both operands are first evaluated; then the operator is applied to compute a result in a temporary. However, the *short-circuit* **and** operator, **and then**, and *short-circuit* **or** operator, **or else**, are more challenging in that both operands are not always evaluated. Rather, the left operand is evaluated first. If that evaluation is sufficient to determine the value of the expression, the right operand is not evaluated. (C's logical operators, **&&** and ‖, are always evaluated using the short-circuit approach.) An example is

```
if I /= 0 and then 10/I > R then
    write (10/I);
else
    write("Undefined");
end if;
```

As *operators*, the short-circuit boolean operators may be combined with any other binary operators, for example, A **and** B **and then** C **and** D.

The code we generate does not produce a value representing a boolean expression unless it is required for assignment to a variable. Rather, the code produces transfers of control to appropriate tuples depending on the value of the expression. In the process of producing such an evaluation, each operand is jumped to and evaluated only if necessary. This form of code is therefore termed *jump code,* to contrast it with the ordinary *expression-oriented code* generated for normal boolean operators.

To contrast the two code forms, consider first A := A **and** B **and** C. Expression-oriented code would be

```
(AND, A, B, t1)
(AND, t1, C, t2)
(ASSIGN, t2, A)
```

On the other hand, for A := A **and then** B **and then** C we might generate the following jump code, which uses a conditional branch tuple that branches to ARG3 if ARG2 is True or to ARG4 if it is False:

```
1 : (BR, A, 2, 6)
2 : (BR, B, 3, 6)
3 : (BR, C, 4, 6)
4 : (ASSIGN, True, t1)
5 : (JUMP, 7)
6 : (ASSIGN, False, t1)
7 : (ASSIGN, t1, A)
```

In this context, the jump code appears terrible, but it is quite well suited for control structures that interrogate a boolean expression, most notably the **if** statement and the **while** loop.

For **if** A **and** B **and** C **then** ... we generate expression-oriented code:

```
(AND, A, B, t1)
(AND, t1, C, t2)
(BR, t2, ThenAdr, ElseAdr)
```

Similarly, for **if** A **and then** B **and then** C **then** ... we generate jump code:

```
1 : (BR, A, 2, ElseAdr)
2 : (BR, B, 3, ElseAdr)
3 : (BR, C, ThenAdr, ElseAdr)
```

Three tuples are generated in each case, but on the average the latter code is substantially faster. For example, assume A, B, and C each have a 50% probability of being true. For the expression-oriented code, we execute three tuples in all cases. However, for the jump code, we execute on the average only 1.75 tuples, a significant improvement.

As we saw earlier, the **DATAOBJECT** record, which contains all the data needed to access a data object at compile-time, provides for three kinds of *addressing modes:*

(1)   Manifest constant

(2)   Address

(3)   Indirect address

That is, we may have the actual value of a data object, its address, or an indirect address that references it.

For boolean values, we add a fourth kind of addressing mode, known as *jump code.* When **form == OBJECTJUMPCODE**, the **data_object** contains two fields, **t_chain** and **f_chain**. We now have

```
enum object_form { OBJECTVALUE, OBJECTADDRESS,
      OBJECTJUMPCODE };

typedef struct data_object {
   type_descriptor *type_ref;
   enum object_form form;
   union {
      /* form == OBJECTVALUE */
      struct value value;

      /* form == OBJECTADDRESS */
      struct address addr;

      /* form == OBJECTJUMPCODE /
      struct {
         patch_node *t_chain, *f_chain;
      };
   };
} data_object;
```

t_chain and **f_chain** head two linked lists of **patch_node** records that are used to backpatch tuples to the location to be jumped to if the boolean expression is true (**t_chain**) or false (**f_chain**).

patch_node is defined as

```
typedef struct patch_node {
    /* Tuple to be backpatched */
    address_range tuple;

    /* Which field to be filled in? (1..4) */
    short field;

    /* next on chain */
    struct patch_node *next;
} patch_node;
```

We need to backpatch through **t_chain** and **f_chain** because we normally do not know where we wish to jump to until after the boolean expression is translated.

Jump code is an unusual method of computing a boolean expression because we never actually store a boolean value in a register or storage location. Rather, the value is always stored *implicitly* in the address where we finally end up. Nevertheless, this address mode can be very useful because boolean expressions are frequently used for flow of control, a task well suited to jump code.

For boolean expressions, we can easily convert from jump code form to direct address form and back again. We define the following conversion routines, **convert_to_jump_code()** and **convert_to_boolean_value()**, which generate the necessary tuples and build a **struct data_object** describing the result of the conversion:

```
convert_to_jump_code(data_object *d)
{
    unsigned br_adr;

    if (d->object_form != OBJECTJUMPCODE) {
        br_adr = next_tuple_number++;
        generate(BR, d, TAdr?, FAdr?);
        d->object_form = OBJECTJUMPCODE;
        d->t_chain = (patch_node) {
                        .tuple = br_adr;
                        .field = 3;
                        .next = NULL; }
        d->f_chain = (patch_node) {
                        .tuple = br_adr;
                        .field = 4;
                        .next = NULL; }
    }
}
```

```
convert_to_boolean_value(data_object *d)
{
    address t;
    unsigned int a;

    if (d->object_form == OBJECTJUMPCODE ) {
        t = get_temporary;
        a = next_tuple_number++;
        generate(ASSIGN, TRUE, t);
        /* backpatch tuple on d.t_chain to address a */
        backpatch(d->t_chain, a);
        generate(JUMP, a+3, "");
        generate(ASSIGN, FALSE, t);
        /* backpatch tuple on d.t_chain to address a + 2 */
        backpatch(d->f_chain, a + 2);
        d->object_form = OBJECTADDRESS;
        d->addr = t;
    }
}
```

Whenever we have a boolean expression in jump code form and need a value (for example, in an assignment statement), we can use **convert_to_boolean_value()**. Similarly, **convert_to_jump_code()** can change a boolean value into a conditional jump (for example, in an **if** statement).

The following productions from the Ada/CS grammar are used to generate boolean expressions. The series of productions from <b primary> to <factor> is necessary because **not** is at a much higher precedence level than the logical operators.

<b expr>	→ <b primary> { <logical op> #start_op <b primary> #finish_op }
<b primary>	→ <a expr> [<relational op> <a expr>]
<a expr>	→ <term 1> { <adding op> <term 1> }
<term 1>	→ <term>
<term>	→ <factor> { <multiplying op> <factor> }
<factor>	→ **not** <primary> #process_not

<b expr>, <b primary>, <a expr>, <term 1>, <term> and <factor> have semantic records of the **DATAOBJECT** form. Further, we shall use the following new semantic record to represent <logical op>:

```
struct bool_op {
    token operator;
    boolean short_circuit;
};
```

The **start_op()** semantic routine is called immediately after a boolean operator is parsed. It begins generation of jump code if the operator is a short-circuit operator.

```
start_op(<b primary>, <logical op>) => <b primary>
{
    if (<logical op>.bool_op.short_circuit) {
        convert_to_jump_code(<b primary>.data_object);
        /* does nothing if <b primary> is already jump code */

        if (<logical op>.bool_op.operator == OR_OP)
            backpatch <b primary>.data_object.f_chain
                to next_tuple_number++
            /* if left operand is false, then right operand
               must be evaluated and tested. */
        else    /* operator is AND_OP */
            backpatch <b primary>.data_object.t_chain
                to next_tuple_number++
            /* if left operand is true, then right operand
               must be evaluated and tested. */
    } else  /* not short circuit */
        convert_to_boolean_value(<b primary>.data_object);
    <b primary> ← the updated DATAOBJECT record
}
```

finish_op() is called after the second operand of a boolean expression has been processed. It need only manipulate chains of patch nodes if jump code is being generated. It calls the standard **eval_binary()** routine if a boolean value is the desired result.

```
finish_op(<b primary₁>, <logical op>, <b primary₂>) => <b expr>
{
    Check that <b primary₁>.data_object.object_type and
        <b primary₂>.data_object.object_type are BOOLEAN
    if (<logical op>.bool_op.short_circuit) {
        convert_to_jump_code(<b primary₂>.data_object);
        if (<logical op>.bool_op.operator == OR_OP) {
            <b expr> ← (data_object) {
                .t_chain =
                    merge(<b primary₁>.data_object.t_chain,
                          <b primary₂>.data_object.t_chain);
                /*
                 * The whole expression is true if the left
                 * operand is true or if the left operand is
                 * false and right operand is true.
                 */
                .f_chain = <b primary₂>.data_object.f_chain; }
```

```
                        /*
                         * The whole expression is false if both the
                         * left and right operands are false.
                         */
              } else {    /* operator == AND_OP */
                 <b expr> ← (data_object) {
                    .f_chain =
                       merge(<b primary₁>.data_object.f_chain,
                             <b primary₂>.data_object.f_chain),
                    /*
                     * The whole expression is false if the left
                     * operand is false or if the left operand is
                     * true and right operand is false.
                     */
                    .t_chain = <b primary₂>.data_object.t_chain; }
                    /*
                     * The whole expression is true if both the
                     * left and right operands are true.
                     */
              }
        } else {    /* ordinary operator */
           convert_to_boolean_value(<b primary₂>.data_object);
           <b expr> ← eval_binary(<b primary₁>,
                                  <logical op>, <b primary₂>)
        }
     }
```

Implementing a **not** operator is straightforward when jump code is being generated. All that is necessary within **process_not()** is an interchange of the **t_chain** and **f_chain** pointers:

```
process_not(<primary>) => <factor>
{
   Check that <primary>.data_object.object_type is BOOLEAN
   if (<primary>.data_object.form == OBJECTJUMPCODE) {
      Interchange <primary>.data_object.t_chain and
         <primary>.data_object.f_chain
      <factor> ← the updated DATAOBJECT record
   } else
      <factor> ← eval_unary(NOT_OP, <primary>)
}
```

As an illustration of how these semantic routines operate, a trace of the translation of

if A **or else not** (B **and then** C) **then** · · ·

is shown in Figure 12.12. Only those steps that generate tuples or modify **t_chain**s and **f_chain**s are included in the trace. The final version of the tuples from Figure 12.12 after all backpatching has been completed is

1 : (BR, A, ThenAdr, 2)
2 : (BR, B, 3, ThenAdr)
3 : (BR, C, ElseAdr, ThenAdr)

This code is easily seen to be correct.

We can freely intermix short-circuit and normal boolean operators in an expression, although intermixing tends to generate poor code due to frequent conversions to and from jump code form. Thus

A := A **and** B **and then** C **and** D;

Actions	Generated Code
(1) start_op(**or else**)	
convert_to_jump_code(A)	1 : (BR,A,?,?)
A.TC = (1,3) A.FC = (1,4)	
Backpatch A.FC to 2	1 : (BR,A,?,2)
A.TC = (1,3) A.FC = **NULL**	
(2) start_op(**and then**)	
convert_to_jump_code(B)	2 : (BR,B,?,?)
B.TC = (2,3) B.FC = (2,4)	
Backpatch B.TC to 3	2 : (BR,B,3,?)
B.TC = **NULL** B.FC = (2,4)	
(3) finish_op(**and then**)	
convert_to_jump_code(C)	3 : (BR,C,?,?)
C.TC = (3,3) C.FC = (3,4)	
Result1.TC = C.TC = (3,3)	
Result1.FC = merge(B.FC,C.FC) =	
((2,4),(3,4))	
(4) process_not()	
Result2.TC = ((2,4),(3,4))	
Result2.FC = (3,3)	
(5) finish_op(**or else**)	
Result3.TC = merge(A.TC,Result2.TC) =	
((1,3),(2,4),(3,4))	
Result3.FC = Result2.FC = (3,3)	
(6) As we process the **if**, we	
Backpatch Result3.TC to the ThenAdr	
and Backpatch Result3.FC to the ElseAdr	

Figure 12.12   Trace of Short-circuit Boolean Expression Translation

generates

```
1 : (AND, A, B, t1)
2 : (BR, t1, 3, 6)
3 : (BR, C, 4, 6)
4 : (ASSIGN, True, t2)
5 : (JUMP, 7)
6 : (ASSIGN, False, t2)
7 : (AND, t2, D, t3)
8 : (ASSIGN, t3, A)
```

Also, short-circuit expressions involving constants are not easily folded. Thus, using the above semantic routines,

A := True **and then** False **and then** True;

generates

```
1 : (BR, True, 2, 6)
2 : (BR, False, 3, 6)
3 : (BR, True, 4, 6)
4 : (ASSIGN, True, t1)
5 : (JUMP, 7)
6 : (ASSIGN, False, t1)
7 : (ASSIGN, t1, A)
```

which is correct but hardly optimal. The problem is that in the context of, for example, False **and then** $\cdots$, we do not know if the right operand is constant or not. If it is, the whole expression can be folded at compile-time. If it is not, code has to be generated for the right operand, so we must generate a BR or JUMP tuple to block its evaluation.

In order to fold short-circuit expressions we can first build an expression tree without generating code for the tree, optimize it (for example, by folding), then generate code from the tree. This approach works well but does not fit easily into a one-pass compiler.

As a final note, some compilers generate jump code for *all* boolean operators (and often claim the boolean expressions are optimized). Short-circuit code is fine if the language definition does not require all operands to be evaluated in all cases (for example, to force possible side effects). Pascal makes this choice *implementation-dependent*. Therefore, some Pascal compilers implement boolean expressions by short-circuit code, and others generate ordinary expression code. In fact, at one time the Berkeley UNIX Pascal interpreter and compiler (*pi* and *pc*) differed on this very point. The UW-Pascal compiler is implemented so that in conditionals (**if**s, **while**s, **repeat**s) short-circuit code is generated, but in assignments, parameter expressions, and so on, ordinary expression code is generated. This compromise improves overall code quality but can lead to surprising results. For example, (I <> 0) **and** (A/I > R) is safe from divide faults in an **if** statement but not in an assignment statement. Thus, in this case, lack of specificity in a language definition has led to inconsistent implementations, which hinders transportability.

In Ada, the operands of **and** and **or** operators (and all non-short-circuit operators) must be evaluated, but the order of evaluation is unspecified. Ordinarily a left-to-right evaluation order can be expected, but evaluation may be reordered as an optimization.

12.7.1. One-address Short-circuit Evaluation

The semantic routines described in the previous section assume that intermediate code, in the form of tuples, is being generated. In most cases, semantic routines do not need to be changed much to generate machine code directly. However, the technique for short-circuit boolean expressions depends heavily on the assumption that the conditional branch instruction specifies *two* addresses: one to branch to if the condition succeeds and another to branch to if it fails.

The following alternative is based on a technique developed by Logothetis and Mishra (1981). This technique postpones generating jumps as long as possible, while remembering what the sense of the jump should be when it finally comes.

We assume that the object language has, in addition to ordinary arithmetic operations, the operations (ASSIGN,loc1,loc2), which copies the contents of loc1 to loc2, and (NOT,loc1,loc2), which assigns the logical negation of the contents of loc1 (a boolean value) to loc2. We also assume a comparison operation (CMP,loc1,loc2), which sets a condition code, and a conditional branch (B,cond,loc), which branches depending on the condition code (cond is one of GT, GE, LT, LE, EQ, NE, or ALWAYS). Note that the CMP operation can be simulated with the tuple operators from Chapter 7 through use of a subtract operation, with the result temporarily being treated as a condition code. In general, we delay generating the conditional branch operation until we know which condition it should use.

The **DATAOBJECT** semantic record must be extended as follows:

```
enum cond { LT, LE, EQ, NE, GT, GE };
enum object_form { OBJECTVALUE, OBJECTADDRESS,
    OBJECTJUMPCODE };

typedef struct data_object {
    type_descriptor *type_ref;
    enum object_form form;
    union {
        /* form == OBJECTVALUE */
        struct value value;

        /* form == OBJECTADDRESS */
        struct {
            struct address addr;
            boolean negated;
        }
```

```
            /* form == OBJECTJUMPCODE /
            struct {
                patch_node *t_chain, *f_chain;
                enum cond condition;
            };
        };
    } data_object;
```

t_chain and **f_chain** are as before: lists of locations where there are branch instructions that want to jump out of the expression when it is determined that the expression is true (**t_chain**) or false (**f_chain**). The field **condition** holds the meaning of the most recent CMP instruction (if any) as follows: Suppose, for example, **condition == GT**. Then the code already generated should be followed by a (B,GT,label) if we want to branch to label when the expression is false and fall through to the next statement when it is true. In other words, **condition** indicates the kind of branch that should follow the code to make it fall through on true. The **negated** field of the **OBJECT-ADDRESS** variant is used to avoid unnecessary code for **not**s.

We assume that we can manipulate chains of **patch_node** records using the functions **append(location, chain2)**, which appends a location onto a chain and returns the updated chain, **merge(chain1, chain2)**, which returns the catenation of the two chains, and the procedure **backpatch(location, chain)**, which causes the address fields of all instructions on the chain to point to the given location. The semantic routine outlines to be defined later use several other subprograms. **to_jump_code()** and **from_jump_code()** are conversion routines much like those in the previous section:

```
to_jump_code(data_object *b)
{
    enum cond c;

    generate(CMP, b, TRUE, "");
    c = b->negated ? EQ : NE;

    b->form = OBJECTJUMPCODE;
    b->t_chain = NULL;
    b->f_chain = NULL;
    b->condition = c;
}


from_jump_code(data_object *b, address t)
{
    /* t is a temporary supplied  */
    /* by the calling routine      */

    fall_through_on_true(b);
    generate(ASSIGN, TRUE, t);
```

```
        generate(b, ALWAYS, next_tuple_number + 2, "");
        backpatch(next_tuple_number++, b->f_chain);
        generate(ASSIGN, FALSE, t, "");

        b->form = OBJECTJUMPCODE;
        b->addr = t;
        b->negated = FALSE;
}
```

fall_through_on_true() and **fall_through_on_false()** generate appropriate branches and manipulate **patch_node** chains to appropriately direct control flow after a single operand has been evaluated:

```
/*
 * Fix up the code for b to fall through to the
 * next statement if b is true
 */

fall_through_on_true(data_object *b)
{
    if (b->form != OBJECTJUMPCODE)
        to_jump_code(b);
    append(next_tuple_number, b->f_chain);
    generate(b, b->condition, ?, "");
    backpatch(next_tuple_number, b->t_chain);
    b->t_chain = NULL;
}


/*
 * Fix up the code for b to fall through to the
 * next statement if b is false
 */

fall_through_on_false(data_object *b)
{
    if (b->form != OBJECTJUMPCODE)
        to_jump_code(b);
    append(next_tuple_number, b->t_chain);
    generate(b, complement(b->condition), ?, "");
    backpatch(next_tuple_number, b->f_chain);
    b->f_chain = NULL;
}
```

negate() is used to implement a **not** without the necessity of any code generation (where possible). It uses **complement()**, which reverses the sense of condition:

```
enum cond complement(enum cond c)
{
    switch (c) {
    case LT:    return GE;
    case LE:    return GT;
    case EQ:    return NE;
    case NE:    return EQ;
    case GT:    return LE;
    case GE:    return LT;
    }
}

negate(data_object *b)
{
    if (b->form == OBJECTVALUE)
        b->value.int_value = - b->value.int_value;
    else if (b->form == OBJECTADDRESS)
        b->negated = ! b->negated;
    else {      /* b->form == OBJECTJUMPCODE */
        exchange b->t_chain and b->f_chain;
        b->condition = complement(b->condition);
    }
}
```

Figure 12.13 gives a grammar for boolean expressions that, for clarity, contains only short-circuit boolean operators. **and then** and **or else** are in the same precedence class, as is the case in the Ada grammar. The productions and semantic routines for arithmetic expressions (<a expr>) and other statements (<other stmt>) are similarly omitted in the interest of simplicity.

The **ftt()** and **ftf()** semantic routines primarily use the **fall_through_on_true()** and **fall_through_on_false()** routines presented earlier:

```
ftt(<b primary>) => <b expr>
{
    fall_through_on_true(<b primary>.data_object)
    <b expr> ← the updated DATAOBJECT record
}


ftf(<b primary>) => <b expr>
{
    fall_through_on_false(<b primary>.data_object)
    <b expr> ← the updated DATAOBJECT record
}
```

<b expr>	→ <b primary> { <b expr tail> }
<b expr tail>	→ #ftt **and then** <b primary> #bool_op
<b expr tail>	→ #ftf **or else** <b primary> #bool_op
<b primary>	→ <a expr> [<relational op> <a expr> #compare]
<a expr>	→ <term 1> { <adding op> <term 1> }
<term 1>	→ <term>
<term>	→ <factor> { <multiplying op> <factor> }
<factor>	→ **not** <primary> #process_not
<stmt>	→ <other stmt> ;
<stmt>	→ <var> := <b expr> #b_assign ;
<stmt>	→ **if** #start_if <b expr> #if_test **then** <stmt list>
	{ **elsif** #gen_jump #patch_else_jumps <b expr> #if_test
	then <stmt list> } <else part> **end if** ; #patch_out_jumps
<else part>	→ **else** #gen_jump #patch_else_jumps <stmt list>
<else part>	→ #patch_else_jumps
<stmt>	→ **while** #start_while <b expr> #while_test
	loop <stmt list> **end loop** #finish_while

Figure 12.13   Boolean Expression Grammar

bool_op() and **process_not()** implement their operations entirely by manipulation of chains of **patch_node** records, except when a conversion to jump code is necessary:

```
bool_op(<b expr>,  <b primary>) => <b expr>
{
    if (<b primary>.data_object.form != OBJECTJUMPCODE)
        to_jump_code(<b primary>.data_object);
    <b expr> ← (data_object) {
               .form = OBJECTJUMPCODE;
               .t_chain = merge(<b expr>.t_chain,
                          <b primary>.t_chain);
               .f_chain = merge(<b expr>.f_chain,
                          <b primary>.f_chain);
               .condition = <b primary>.condition; }
}
```

```
process_not(<primary>) => <factor>
{
    negate(<primary>.data_object)
    <factor> ← the updated DATAOBJECT record
}
```

compare() implements relation operators with a CMP tuple and builds a **DATAOBJECT** record to describe the result in jump code form:

```
compare(<a expr₁>, <relational op>, <a expr₂>) => <b primary>
{
    Check types of <a expr₁> and <a expr₂> for compatibility
    generate(CMP, <a expr₁>.data_object,
                  <a expr₂>.data_object, dummy);
    <b primary> ← (data_object) {
        .form = OBJECTJUMPCODE;
        .t_chain = NULL;
        .f_chain = NULL;
        .condition = complement(<relational op>.op.operator); }
}
```

The **b_assign()** routine is needed to handle the special cases created by the extensions added to the **DATAOBJECT** record for handling short-circuit boolean operators. Because the assignment production shown in Figure 12.13 does not actually allow boolean expressions to be distinguished from other expressions, the processing described for **b_assign()** is simply merged with the standard assignment action routine.

```
b_assign(<var>, <b expr>)
{
    if (<b expr>.data_object.form == OBJECTJUMPCODE)
        from_jump_code(<b expr>.data_object,
                    <var>.data_object.addr);
    else if (<b expr>.data_object.negated)
        generate(NOT, <b expr>.data_object,
                    <var>.data_object, "");
    else
        generate(ASSIGN, <b expr>.data_object,
                    <var>.data_object, "");
}
```

The semantic records required to handle **if** and **while** statements are slightly different from those we saw at the beginning of this chapter, because we are now concerned with lists of **patch_node**s rather than labels.

```
struct if_stmt {
    patch_node *out_list, *else_list;
};

struct while_stmt {
    string top_tuple;
    patch_node *out_list;
};

start_if(void) => if
{
    if ← (if_stmt) {
                    .out_list = NULL;
                    .else_list = NULL; }
}
```

```
if_test(if, <b expr>) => if
{
    Check that <b expr>.data_object.object_type == BOOLEAN
    fall_through_on_true(<b expr>.data_object)
    if.if_stmt.else_list = <b expr>.data_object.f_chain
    if ← the updated IFSTMT record
}
```

gen_jump() is the action routine called to generate a jump over an **else** or **elsif** part following a **then** part:

```
gen_jump(if) => if
{
    Create a new patch_node, P, for next_tuple_number
    if.if_stmt.out_list = append(if.if_stmt.out_list, P)
    generate(B, ALWAYS, ?, "");
    if ← the updated IFSTMT record
}
```

patch_else_jumps() called at the beginning of an **else** or **elsif** part patches all the tuples on the list **else_list** to jump to **next_tuple_number**:

```
patch_else_jumps(if)
{
    backpatch(next_tuple_number, if.if_stmt.else_list);
}
```

After the entire statement has been processed, **patch_out_jumps()** patches all the tuples on the list **out_list** to jump to **next_tuple_number**:

```
patch_out_jumps(if)
{
    backpatch(next_tuple_number, if.if_stmt.out_list);
}
```

```
start_while(void) => while
{
    L = new_label();
    generate(LABEL, L, "", "");
    while ← (while_stmt) {
        .top_tuple = L;
        .out_list = NULL; }
}
```

```
while_test(while, <b expr>) => while
{
    Check that <b expr>.data_object.object_type == BOOLEAN
    fall_through_on_true(<b expr>.data_object);
```

```
        while.while_stmt.out_list = <b expr>.data_object.f_chain
        while ← the updated struct while_stmt
}
```

finish_while() is also familiar, being essentially a combination of the routines called at the end of **if** statements and simple loops:

```
finish_while(while)
{
    generate (B, ALWAYS, while.while_stmt.top_label, "")
    backpatch(next_tuple_number, while.while_stmt.out_list);
}
```

As an illustration of how these semantic routines operate, a trace of the translation of

if A <= B **and then** A >= 0 **or else** A = 100 **then** A := 1; **end if**;

is shown in Figure 12.14. Again, only those steps that generate tuples or modify **t_chain**s and **f_chain**s are included in the trace.

The final version of the tuples from Figure 12.14 after all backpatching has been completed is

```
1: CMP      A,B
2: B        GT,5
3: CMP      A,0
4: B        GE,7
5: CMP      A,100
6: B        NE,8
7: ASSIGN   1,A
```

This code is easily seen to be correct.

	Actions	Generated Code	Semantic Stack (t_chain, f_chain, cond)
(a)	#compare	1: CMP A,B	(null,null,GT)
(b)	#ftt		
	Append 2 to FC		(null,2,GT)
		2: B GT,?	
	Backpatch TC to 3		(null,2,GT)
(c)	#compare	3: CMP A,0	(null,null,LT) (null,2,GT)
(d)	#bool_op		(null,2,LT)

(e)   #ftf
       Append 4 to TC   (4,2,LT)
                              4: B GE,?
       Backpatch FC to 5   2: B GT,5   (4,null,LT)

(f)   #compare   5: CMP A,100   (null,null,NE) (4,null,LT)

(g)   #bool_op   (4,null,NE)

(h)   #ftt
       Append 6 to FC   (4,6,NE)
                              6: B NE,?
       Backpatch TC to 7   4: B GE,7   (null,6,NE)

(i)   #assign   7: ASSIGN 1,A

(j)   #patch_out_jumps
       Backpatch FC to 8   6: B NE,8   (null,null,NE)

Figure 12.14   Trace of Three-address Short-circuit Boolean Expression Translation

Exercises

1.   Trace the sequence of semantic routine calls that occur during the compilation of the following program fragments. Show the tuples that are generated, with an indication of which routine generates each tuple. Assume that I, J, and K are all Integer variables.

   a.   **if** I > J **then**   b.   **if** I > J **then**
            K := I;   K := I;
        elsif J > I **then**   **elsif** J >= I **then**
            K := J;   K := J;
        else   **end if**;
            K := 0;
        end if;

2.   Trace the sequence of semantic routine calls that occur during the compilation of the following program fragment. Show the tuples that are generated, with an indication of which routine generates each tuple. Assume that I, J, Limit, and Sum are Integer variables, and A is a two-dimensional array of Integer.

```
            Sum : = 0;
            I := 0;
OuterLoop: loop
              I := I + 1;
              exit when I > Limit;
              J := 1;
              while J <= Limit loop
                exit OuterLoop when A(I,J) = 0;
                Sum := Sum + A(I,J);
                J := J + 1;
              end loop;
            end loop;
```

3. Trace the sequence of semantic routine calls that occur during the compilation of the following program fragment. Show the tuples that are generated, with an indication of which routine generates each tuple. Assume that I and Limit are Integer variables, and B is a one-dimensional array of Integer.

```
    Sum := 0;
    for I in 1..Limit loop
        Sum := Sum + B(I);
    end loop;
```

4. Write a **case** statement with at least six labeled alternatives plus an **others** alternative. The labels should include ranges as well as single values. Trace the sequence of semantic routine calls that would occur during the compilation of your **case** statement. Show the tuples that are generated by all action routines other than `finish_case()` and diagram the data structures created to describe the labels of the alternatives.

5. Show the tuples that would be generated by `finish_case()` for your **case** statement from Exercise 4 using the jump table approach.

6. Show the tuples that would be generated by `finish_case()` for your **case** statement from Exercise 4 using the in-line binary search approach.

7. Rewrite the semantic routine outlines and semantic record declarations for compiling basic **loop**s and **while loop**s to use backpatching rather than symbolic labels to handle jump address resolution. (*Hint:* See the discussion of backpatching at the end of Section 12.1.)

8. Rewrite the semantic routine outlines and semantic record declarations for compiling **if** statements to use backpatching rather than symbolic labels to handle jump address resolution.

9. Illustrate the sequence of changes to the `loop_descriptor` stack (described in Section 12.3) that occurs during the compilation of the nested loops in Exercise 2. Explain which semantic routine makes each change.

10. Explain the processing done by a compiler for the labels and **goto**s in the following Ada program fragment, according to the technique summarized in Figure 12.6:

```
declare
   . . .
begin
  <<L>>
  declare
     . . .
  begin
     . . .
    goto L;
     . . .
    goto M;
     . . .
    <<M>>
     . . .
  end;
   . . .
end;
```

11. Using the techniques of Section 12.6, illustrate the significant address ranges, the exception transfer vectors, and the range map for the following program. Explain how the **raise** statement within procedure Q is handled and how the occurrence of a Constraint_Error exception within Q is handled.

```
procedure P is
   . . .
  Fault : exception;

  procedure Q is
  begin
     . . .
    raise Fault;
     . . .
  exception
    when Fault => · · · ;
  end Q;

begin
   . . .
  Q;
   . . .
exception
  when Constraint_Error => · · · ;
end P;
```

12. Using the techniques of Section 12.6, illustrate the significant address ranges, the exception transfer vectors, and the range map for the following program. Explain how the **raise** statement within procedure R is handled when it is called from Q and when it is called from P.

```
procedure P is
    . . .
  Fault : exception;

  procedure R is
  begin
      . . .
    raise Fault;
      . . .
  end R;

  procedure Q is
  begin
      . . .
    R;
      . . .
  exception
    when Fault => · · · ;
  end Q;

begin
    . . .
  Q;
    . . .
  R;
    . . .
exception
  when Fault => · · · ;
end P;
```

13. There are interesting interactions between exception-handling features and an interactive debugger. Normally, such a debugger is invoked when a run-time error occurs. However, in a language with exception-handling features, such errors are manifested as predefined exceptions. Thus the debugger is invoked only when no handler is supplied for an exception (predefined or defined in the program). Explain how the exception-handling implementation techniques of Section 12.6 would have to be changed to interact with a debugger, given that the debugger should be given control with a view of the program state in which the unhandled exception was raised.

14. Using the technique presented in Section 12.7, do a trace like that in Figure 12.12 of the translation of

if A and B and then C or else not D then · · ·

15. Using the technique presented in Section 12.7.1, do a trace like that in Figure 12.14 of the translation of

   if A >= C **or else not** (C <> A **and then** B < 77) **then** A := B; **end if**;

CHAPTER 13

Translating Procedures and Functions

There are two essential parts to translating procedures and functions (hereafter referred to collectively as *subprograms*): processing declarations and processing calls. First, the compiler encounters the declaration of a subprogram. As is the case with any other declaration, the declaration of a subprogram results in the construction of a symbol table entry and an associated attribute record. After a declaration, references to a subprogram will occur and must be appropriately translated using the attribute information built from the declaration. In the case of subprograms, these references are known as *calls*. Because of the transfer-of-control implications of a subprogram call, coupled with the possibility of parameters, handling references to subprogram names is much more complex than handling references to other declared names.

13.1. Simple Subprograms

13.1.1. Declaring Subprograms without Parameters

Several forms of subprogram declarations must be handled. Ada and Ada/CS include distinct syntactic forms for procedures and functions, and they allow either kind of subprogram to be declared with the specification of its body deferred. Thus in the productions below, we find four versions of subprogram declarations: procedures with and without bodies and functions with and without bodies.

<declaration>   → <subprogram spec> <subprogram tail>

<subprogram spec>   → **procedure** <id> #start_proc [<formal part>]
                     → **function** <designator> #start_proc [<formal part>]
                        return <type name> #return_type

<subprogram tail>   → ; #end_proc_spec
                     → **is** #start_proc_body <decl pt>
                        begin <stmts> <exception part> **end**
                        [<designator> #check_proc_id] ;
                        #end_proc_body

   The semantic routines in these productions use one new semantic record type, **SUBPROGRAM**. An instance of this record type is created by **start_proc** and is available to all the routines that process a subprogram declaration.

```
typedef struct subprogram {
    attributes *old_current_proc;
    id_entry st_entry;
    string end_label;
} subprogram;
```

The **attributes** type must be extended to include the following variant:

```
/* class == SUBPROGRAMNAME */
struct {
    level_range nesting_level;
    string start_label;
    address_range activation_rec_size;
    symbol_table local_decls;
    attributes *parameters;
    struct type_des *return_type;
        /* -- NULL except for functions */
    boolean body_declared;
};
```

We first consider the semantic routines necessary to handle procedures and functions with no parameters. We use a globally visible variable named **current_proc** to contain a pointer to the attribute record for the innermost subprogram currently being processed.

```
start_proc(<id>) => procedure
{
    Enter the identifier represented by <id> into the
        symbol table for the current scope.
    Due to the possibility of overloading, it may already
        be present in this scope.
    Save the id_entry returned by enter() in subprog_entry.
    Let A = (attributes) {
        .class = SUBPROGRAMNAME;
        .id = subprog_entry;
        .id_type = NULL;
        .nesting_level = current_proc.nesting_level + 1;
        .start_label = "";
        .activation_rec_size = CONTROLSIZE;
        .local_decls = create();
        .parameters = NULL;
        .return_type = NULL;
        .body_declared = FALSE; }

    procedure ← (subprogram) {
        .old_current_proc = current_proc;
        .st_entry = subprog_entry;
        .end_label = ""; }
    current_proc ← A;
}
```

In the **attributes** structure created to describe a new subprogram, the **activation_rec_size** field is initialized to the value of a constant called **CONTROLSIZE**. Its value is implementation-dependent, denoting the amount of space required at the beginning of each activation record for control information (see Section 9.1.2). This field is used by the **var_decl()** semantic routine (described in Section 10.2.1) to assign offsets while processing variable declarations. As each variable is declared, the **activation_rec_size** field of the **current_proc** structure is used to obtain a value for the **var_offset** field of its **address** in its **attributes** record. To allocate space for the variable, the size of objects of its type is then added to **current_proc.activation_rec_size**.

```
return_type(<type or subtype>)
{
    /*
     * Set the return_type field of the function currently
     * being compiled using the TYPEREF record
     * representing <type or subtype>
     */
```

```
    current_proc.return_type ←
        <type or subtype>.type_ref.object_type
}


end_proc_spec(procedure)
{
    /*
     * Called only for subprogram specifications
     * that appear without a body
     */
    string start
    start = new_label()
    /*
     * A corresponding label tuple will be generated
     * when the body is encountered
     */
    Record the label start as current_proc.start_label
    Call the symbol table routine set_attributes() to
        associate current_proc with
        procedure.subprogram.st_entry.
    Generate an error message if this call fails because
        st_entry already has associated attributes that
        current_proc may not overload.
    current_proc ← procedure.subprogram.old_current_proc
}


start_proc_body(procedure) => procedure
{
    Take the appropriate actions to make
        current_proc.local_decls the current scope.
    /*
     * This may require no action if creating a scope
     * automatically does this.  Such an implementation
     * is common for languages without packages or a
     * similar feature.
     */
    procedure.subprogram.end_label = new_label()
    generate(JUMP, procedure.subprogram.end_label, "", "");
    /*
     * Execution of enclosing scope will jump
     * over this procedure body
     */
    if (current_proc.start_label == "")
        current_proc.start_label = new_label();
    generate(LABEL, current_proc.start_label, "", "");
    generate(STARTSUBPROG, current_proc.nesting_level,
            "", "");
    procedure ← the updated SUBPROGRAM record
}
```

We must generate the STARTSUBPROG tuple before processing the declaration list because declarations in Ada/CS can cause code to be generated. For example, variable initialization expressions and dynamically sized arrays produce code that must be executed at the beginning of a subprogram body. If we were compiling a language like Pascal, in which the declarations generate no code, we would not want to generate this tuple until the beginning of the statement list. The reason that such a delay is preferable is to avoid the nesting of STARTSUBPROG-ENDSUBPROG pairs for nested procedures. Our code generator either has to move tuples to undo the nesting and make subprogram bodies contiguous or insert jumps to cause execution of a subprogram body to skip over any nested subprograms.

```
check_proc_id(<id>)
{
    Check that the identifier on top of the semantic
    stack is the name of current_proc
}
```

```
end_proc_body(procedure)
{
    Take the appropriate actions to remove
        current_proc.local_decls as the current scope.
    Call destroy(current_proc.local_decls), since any
        names declared within the subprogram must no
        longer be accessible.
    generate(ENDSUBPROG, current_proc.activation_rec_size,
            "", "");
    generate(LABEL, procedure.subprogram.end_label, "", "");
    current_proc = procedure.subprogram.old_current_proc
}
```

13.1.2. Calling Parameterless Procedures

A call to a parameterless procedure consists of the procedure identifier used as a statement, as indicated by the following production:

<statement> → <id> #simple_proc_stmt

The semantic routine **simple_proc_stmt()** must first verify that the <id> does name a procedure. It then generates two tuples using other information from the identifier's **attributes** record. STARTCALL must eventually be translated to code that allocates an activation record for the procedure to be called, whereas PROCJUMP specifies the actual transfer of control to the procedure. In Section 13.3, where calling subprograms with parameters is discussed, these two tuples are generated by different semantic routines, with tuples for handling parameters generated between them.

```
simple_proc_stmt(<id>)
{
    Search for <id> in the symbol table and obtain
        a reference to its Attributes, A
    Check that A.class == SUBPROGRAMNAME &&
                A.return_type == NULL
    T = get_temporary()
    generate(STARTCALL, T, A.activation_rec_size, "");
    generate(PROCJUMP, A.start_label, T, "");
}
```

13.2. Passing Parameters to Subprograms

Typically, locations are allocated in a subprogram's activation record to hold information about parameters. Usually the caller places some information, a value, an address, or a dope vector, in a parameter location that the called procedure uses to access the actual parameter. Exactly what should be passed depends on the *type* of the actual parameter and the parameter-passing *mode*.

The parameter-passing modes in the following list are grouped according to the similarity of implementation techniques they require.

- *value (copy)*, *result*, and *value-result*.
  The value of the actual parameter is copied into the formal parameter, or a copy of the final value of the formal parameter is copied back to the actual parameter.

- *reference* (**var**), *read-only* (**in**).
  Reference parameters represent the address of an actual parameter. Changes to a reference mode formal parameter immediately change the actual parameter. Read-only parameters can be read but not changed. They are often implemented like reference parameters by passing an address (alternatively, they can be implemented by passing a copy).

- *name, formal procedures, label parameters*
  Name parameters are, if necessary, reevaluated each time they are referenced. Formal procedures are subprograms that are passed as parameters to other routines. Label parameters allow, in effect, indirect **goto**s.

Ada's parameter passing modes, **in**, **out**, and **in out**, correspond roughly to read-only, result, and value-result. An **in** parameter acts as a local constant, with its value supplied by the corresponding actual parameter. An **out** parameter acts as an uninitialized local variable whose value is transmitted to the corresponding actual parameter when the subprogram returns. An **in out** parameter behaves substantially like an **out** parameter except that it is initialized with the value of the actual parameter at the time the subprogram is invoked. The definition of Ada mandates that for scalars these three modes be implemented by value, result and value-result, respectively. For nonscalars, these modes may be implemented by actually copying parameters or by passing an address and implementing them as reference parameters. However, **in** parameters must be treated as read-only, no matter how formal/actual correspondence is implemented. Any Ada program that depends on how nonscalar parameter modes are implemented is erroneous.

For types, we consider the classes found in Ada/CS:

- *scalar types* (integer, real, and so forth)
- *arrays* (possibly with dynamic bounds)
- *strings*
- *records*

In implementing data objects (constants, variables, parameters), we must distinguish at compile-time how a value is referenced. It may be

- A value—for example, a manifest constant
- The address of a value (ordinary variables)
- The address of the location containing the address of a value (reference parameters)

We must also record how a value may be accessed; that is, if it may be changed or if only read access is allowed.

We call the reference and access patterns together the *access data*. Keeping careful track of access data in our semantic record data object descriptors is important in generating correct code. It also makes compiling easier as, for example, we can treat constants as read-only variables if no folding is to be done (say, for string constants).

Access data also reminds us to be careful when data objects are manipulated. For example, a reference parameter passed by reference to a second procedure requires different code at the call site than an ordinary variable (or value parameter) passed by reference. We want to use only one level of indirection, even when a reference parameter is passed as a reference parameter, because the subprogram invoked by the second call cannot, in general, know whether any of its actual parameters require extra levels of indirection.

13.2.1. Value, Result, and Value-Result Parameters

In value mode, we copy the value of the actual parameter and treat it as a local variable. Any expression or value of the correct type can be passed.

In result mode, a local, uninitialized variable is created. Upon return, its value is assigned to the actual parameter. Only names (that is, expressions that can be used as the target of an assignment, sometimes called *l-values*) can be passed as result parameters so that the assignment is legal.

In value-result mode, we copy the actual parameter into a local copy, then, upon return, copy it back into the actual parameter. Again a name is required as the corresponding actual parameter so that the assignment is legal.

One approach to implementing parameter modes that require copying is to locate the code to copy each value in the called procedure. The caller passes an address, as in reference mode, and code at the beginning or end of the procedure actually does the copying. In result and value-result modes, we need two distinct local data objects: the address of the actual parameter and the local copy of the parameter's value. For value mode, we can get by with one object; the copied value can overwrite the passed address. It is also possible to have the calling procedure do the copying. For result or value-result modes, the activation record has to be arranged so that the caller—and not the callee—removes the actual parameters from the stack.

We can consider the various type classes in turn:

- For scalars, we generally pass the address of the actual parameter and copy a value into or out of the local copy, although for value mode we usually simply pass the actual parameter value itself because doing so is no more costly than passing just the address. In the two cases involving a copy out when the called procedure returns, we must also be concerned with the possibility that the actual parameter type is a constrained subtype of the formal parameter type. In such a case, we must additionally ensure that the value copied out to the actual parameter is a legal value for its subtype. This can either involve range information being passed with its address for a check within the called procedure or a check at the call site immediately after the return.

- For arrays, we can pass a (fixed-size) dope vector as the actual parameter. Usually, this descriptor can be just a pointer to the data of the array; the type is described by a type descriptor that is either completely known at compile-time (constant bounds) or whose location (static level and offset in that activation record) is known at compile-time (dynamic bounds). In the case of *unconstrained* or *conformant* arrays—that is, formal array parameters that are incompletely specified (typically, the dimension, base, and index types are specified, but not the bounds)—a pointer to the type descriptor containing the bounds of the actual parameter must be passed, as well as a pointer to its data space. A procedure, when called, allocates space for the local copy of this array parameter using the associated bounds information; the procedure then copies it, if necessary, and initializes its own local dope vector. When the procedure returns, the array can be copied back to the actual parameter, if necessary, using the two dope vectors. However, for value mode, only a single dope vector is necessary; it can be overwritten with the dope vector for the local copy.

- Strings, which are dynamic in size, require a descriptor. In Ada/CS, the descriptor is just the address of the string, for the size of the string is stored as part of the string itself. This simple approach is possible because of the restricted nature of Ada/CS strings. To support more-general string features, such as allowing substrings to be result parameters, a descriptor must contain the string length as well as its address, as illustrated in Figure 13.1.

  For value mode, we can pass the descriptor itself. For result and value-result modes, we need to pass the address of the descriptor,

Address	String length

Figure 13.1   A Descriptor for a String Parameter

because assignment to the string can change the contents of the descriptor. Using this descriptor, we copy into and out of the local string copy, just as in previous cases.

As an optimization, we can copy the local descriptor (rather than the string itself) to the actual parameter upon return. The local copy of the string normally disappears upon return. (We cannot use this optimization for arrays because all space for a local array is popped upon return because it is allocated in the activation record.)

- Records are handled as scalars because they are fixed in size, although it is usually better to pass the address of a record passed in value mode and let the callee copy the record. This technique makes the call more compact, especially if the machine does not have a multiword move instruction. Even dynamic records (those with fields of a dynamic type) do not need explicit type descriptors passed; the run-time type descriptor, if any, is visible to the callee at a place known at compile-time.

13.2.2. Reference and Read-only Parameters

We usually pass the address of a reference or read-only parameter.

- For scalar values, we handle reference mode by passing the address of the actual parameter in the parameter slot. In read-only mode, we could pass an address, but sometimes this action is inconvenient if the actual parameter is a temporary [for example, in F(A+B)]. Furthermore, it is no more expensive to copy a scalar than to pass its address, and direct access is faster than indirect access. Implementing read-only scalar parameters as read-only locals is probably best. In fact, Ada mandates that scalar **in** parameters, which are read-only, be implemented by doing an actual copy.

- For arrays, we pass the address of the dope vector or, more simply, the dope vector itself. If an array has no dope vector, we create one. (As an optimization, we might omit passing a dope vector for all but unconstrained arrays.)

- We handle strings by passing the address of the string's descriptor.

- We pass the address of records. Again, even dynamic records do not need explicit type descriptors.

13.2.3. Semantic Routines for Parameter Declarations

Ada/CS, like Ada, allows parameters to be passed using any of three modes: **in**, **in out**, and **out**, which were defined in Section 13.2. Within the body of a procedure, parameters are accessed in the same way as variables; hence, they must be entered into the symbol table. The symbol table entry for a parameter must give its mode so that the proper code can be generated to access it. We must also link all the parameter attribute records together, in the order in which they are declared, so they can be used in processing subprogram calls. Thus, the attributes for a parameter name are as follows:

```
/* class == PARAMNAME */
struct {
    level_range param_level;
    address_range param_offset;
    enum parameter_mode mode;
    attributes *next_param;
};
```

where

```
enum parameter_mode { INMODE, OUTMODE, INOUTMODE };
```

The productions for the declaration of parameters are

<formal part>   → (
                                  { ; <parameter declaration> })
→ <id list> : <mode> <type or subtype> #param_decl
<mode>   → [**in**] #set_in
                             → **out** #set_out
                             → **in out** #set_in_out

We need a new semantic record option to hold the mode of the parameters currently being processed:

```
struct mode {
    enum parameter_mode mode_kind;
};
```

The semantic routines for processing the mode specifications are quite simple:

```
set_in(void) => <mode>
{
    <mode> ← (mode) { .mode_kind = INMODE; }
}
```

```
set_out(void) => <mode>
{
    <mode> ← (mode) { .mode_kind = OUTMODE; }
}

set_in_out(void) => <mode>
{
    <mode> ← (mode) { .mode_kind = INOUTMODE; }
}


param_decl(<id list>, <mode>, <type or subtype>)
{
    for (each identifier in <id list>) {
        Call enter() to put the identifier in the symbol
            table referenced by current_proc.local_decls.
        if (it is already there) {
            generate an appropriate error message
            continue;  /* go on to next identifier */
        }
        Allocate storage for the parameter, recording
        its offset in the local variable offset.  (The
        size of the block of storage to allocate is
        calculated according to how parameters of
        <type or subtype>.type_ref.object_type and <mode>
        are implemented.)

        The following expression describes the attribute
        record to be created for the parameter:
        (attributes) {
            .class = PARAMNAME;
            .id_type = <type or subtype>.type_ref.object_type;
            .id = the id_entry returned by enter();
            .param_level = current_proc.nesting_level;
            .param_offset = offset;
            .mode = <mode>.mode.mode_kind;
            .next_param = NULL; }

        In addition to associating this attribute record
        with the identifier just entered into the symbol
        table, also add it to the end of the list
        referenced by current_proc.parameters
        (constructed using next_param fields).
    }
}
```

The semantic routine **new_name()** requires modification to allow parameters to be interpreted as variables. **PARAMNAME** is added as another alternative that it must handle, producing a **DATAOBJECT** record in this case.

The **var_level** and **var_offset** fields of the **address** record **addr** get their values from **param_level** and **param_offset**. The **indirect** and **read_only** flags are set according to the appropriate values for the chosen implementation for the type of the parameter and its mode. For example, **PARAMNAME** always sets the **read_only** flag to **TRUE** if the mode of the parameter is **INMODE**. The value of the **indirect** flag depends on whether the actual parameter is represented by an address or a copy.

Because the parameter list for a subprogram is represented by a linked list of attribute records for each of the parameters, special care must be taken when the symbol table for the procedure is deallocated when **end_subprog_body()** is called. These attribute records must not be deallocated at this point, for the information they contain must be available so that calls to the procedure can be handled correctly. They must be copied, removed from the symbol table, or protected in some other way before the symbol table routine **destroy()** is called.

13.3. Processing Subprogram Calls and Parameter Lists

As we discussed in Chapter 11, the syntax for specifying subprogram calls in Ada and Ada/CS is identical to that for array references. These two distinct features must be distinguished by the semantic routine **name_plus_list()**. However, this section treats the semantic routines necessary to handle subprogram calls as if they could be triggered directly by the syntax, as is the case in Pascal. We also simplify the syntax of subprogram names, allowing—for purposes of this discussion—only simple identifiers. We present the semantic routines as they apply to procedures rather than functions; the extension to functions should be obvious.

The productions for a procedure call are

```
<statement>     →  <proc id> [ <parameters> ] #gen_proc_jump
<proc id>       →  <id> #start_proc_stmt
<parameters>    →  ( <expression> #process_param
                    { , <expression> #process_param } )
```

One new semantic stack record is required to hold information about the subprogram being called while the parameters, if any, are being processed:

```
struct proc_call {
    string start_label;
    attributes *parameters;
    address AR_ref;
};
```

start_proc_stmt() is called to process an **ID** record, interpreting it as a procedure name and producing a corresponding **PROCCALL** record. The **AR_ref** field holds a reference to the activation record for the subprogram being called. It is used to fill in parameter information as the call is being processed.

```
start_proc_stmt (<id>) => <proc id>
{
    Search for <id> in the symbol table and obtain
        a reference to its attributes, A
    Check that A.class == SUBPROGRAMNAME
    T = get_temporary()
    <proc id> ← (proc_call) {
        .start_label = A.start_label;
        .parameters = A.parameters;
        .AR_ref = T; }
    generate(STARTCALL, T, A.activation_rec_size, "");
}
```

STARTCALL delimits the beginning of a subprogram calling sequence, and so it allows a function call to appear as all or part of an actual parameter expression. **process_param()** generates an appropriate tuple for each parameter to be passed to the subprogram, after it checks that the type of the parameter is compatible with the corresponding formal parameter:

```
process_param(<proc id>, <expression>) => <proc id>
{
    Verify that the <expression>.data_object.object_type
        matches the type of the first parameter on the list
        <proc id>.proc_call.parameters (Generate a
        "Too many actual parameters" error message if this
        parameter list pointer is NULL.)
    If the parameter mode requires an L-value actual
        parameter (OUTMODE or INOUTMODE), verify that the
        actual parameter describes a legal L-value
        (constants, expressions, and read-only variables
        not allowed)
    Set op to REFPARAM, COPYIN, COPYOUT or COPYINOUT,
        depending on how the parameter is to be transmitted.
    generate(op, <expression>.data_object,
                <proc id>.proc_call.parameters.param_offset,
                <proc id>.proc_call.AR_ref);
    <proc id>.proc_call.parameters =
                <proc id>.proc_call.parameters.next_param
    <proc id> ← the updated struct proc_call
}
```

`gen_proc_jump()` checks that enough parameters have been supplied, and then it generates the PROCJUMP tuple, which specifies the transfer of control to the called subprogram:

```
gen_proc_jump(<proc id>)
{
    if (<proc id>.proc_call.parameters != NULL)
        Generate a "Too few actual parameters" error message.

    generate(PROCJUMP, <proc id>.proc_call.start_label,
                        <proc id>.proc_call.AR_ref, "");
}
```

Example: Calling Procedures with Parameters

Assume that an Ada/CS program contains the following declarations:

```
I, J, K: Integer;
procedure P (X : in Integer; Y : in out Integer) is
  begin
    Y := X * J;
  end P;
```

Suppose that the nesting level of P is 2 and that **CONTROLSIZE** is 3, so that the offset of X is 3, the offset of Y is 4, and **activation_rec_size** for P is 5. The following tuples would be generated for the procedure declaration (the names of the semantic routines that cause the code to be generated are also shown):

```
start_proc_body():    (STARTSUBPROG, 2)
eval_binary():        (MULTI, X, J, t1)
assign():             (ASSIGN, t1, INTEGERSIZE, Y)
end_subprog_body():   (ENDSUBPROG, 5)
                       -- 5 is activation_rec_size for P
```

The tuples generated by the procedure call

```
P(I+J,K);
```

would look like

```
start_proc_stmt():    (STARTCALL, t2, P.activation_rec_size)
eval_binary():        (ADDI, I, J, t3)
process_param():      (COPYIN, t3, 4, t2)
                       -- 4 is the offset of the first parameter
process_param():      (COPYINOUT, K, 5, t2)
                       -- 5 is the offset of the second parameter
gen_proc_jump():      (PROCJUMP, P.start_label, t2)
```

13.4. **Subprogram Invocation**

In this section, we look at some additional implementation-specific details about subprogram invocation that are necessary to generate code from tuples like STARTSUBPROG and ENDSUBPROG.

13.4.1. **Saving and Restoring Registers**

Registers in use by a subprogram must be preserved across calls it makes because the called subprogram may use the same registers, thus overwriting any values they contain. The method chosen to preserve registers influences the costs in space and time for normal procedure call and return and for non-local **goto** or exception handling. Some RISC architectures save registers automatically as part of a procedure call instruction, but most architectures require explicit save and restore instructions. One dimension of choice is whether the registers that are saved are the ones that the caller is currently using (typically only a few), the ones that the callee might modify (often a substantial number), or all the registers. The other dimension of choice is whether the caller or the callee does the saving and restoring. Assuming that procedures are called from more than one place, it is more code-space efficient to let the callee perform these operations.

We discuss six methods, as enumerated in Figure 13.2. Other issues being equal, we prefer items in the left-hand columns (they save fewer registers) and in the first row (the code need not be replicated for every call). However, other issues are not equal. We must implement whatever method we choose so that procedure call and return are fast (they happen so often that efficiency is important) and to implement it in a way that supports nonlocal **goto**s or propagated exceptions (if necessary).

(1)   For the callee to save the caller's registers, the call instruction must include a description of which registers are being used (perhaps a bit vector, also known as a *bit map*, or the address of a byte vector). The compiler can create either one at the point where a call is processed. Because of the complexity of testing each bit in a bit vector, such an approach is useful only if there is a hardware save/restore register instruction that takes the bit vector and the address of a register-save area and performs all the work. Such instructions exist on some current machines. A byte vector can be accessed somewhat more efficiently, but it may still be faster just to save all the registers (method 5).

	caller's registers	callee's registers	all registers
callee saves	1	3	5
caller saves	2	4	6

Figure 13.2   Register Save Alternatives

(2)   It is a simple matter for the caller to save its own registers and to restore them when the procedure returns. However, procedures that return to locations other than the code following the call (for example, through a **goto** or by propagating an exception) have to restore registers by finding the restoration code (perhaps through the return address) and executing it out of line.

(3)   The compiler knows what registers the callee is using for nonvolatile temporaries—but only when the procedure has been completely translated and code has been generated. Because registers must be saved at the start of the procedure, the procedure prologue might have a backpatched jump to the end, where the procedure-save code is placed, followed by a jump to the start of the actual procedure code. On the VAX, the compiler just backpatches the first word of the procedure to contain a bit map of the registers the procedure uses. The procedure-call instruction uses that map to save the appropriate registers. A copy of the map is placed in the activation record. The procedure-return instruction uses the map again to restore the registers.

(4)   The only way the caller could know which registers the callee plans to use is by a bit-map technique, such as the one the VAX uses. Bit maps are efficient only with hardware support. The VAX method could be considered to fit either as method 3 or method 4. A pure method 4 technique would be to use the save/restore-register instruction mentioned under method 1. Saving only the registers needed by the callee complicates exception propagation and nonlocal **goto**s; every activation record in the dynamic chain must be inspected, and the register values saved in that record must be restored. The AR must therefore indicate not only the old values but also which registers were saved. Many FORTRAN implementations use method 3. In these implementations, nonlocal **goto**s present no particular problem because the language does not allow them. Instead, label parameters are available, but only one level of return is allowed using a label parameter. That is, you can pass only a label constant, not a label parameter.

(5)   It is easy for the callee to save all registers, particularly if there are only a few of them, as on the PDP-11. The original C compiler for the PDP-11 generates a procedure prologue and epilogue that saves the three nonvolatile general-purpose registers. Although this code could use a loop if registers are addressable, an unrolled version is far more efficient. (Actually, C generates a call to a short utility routine that performs the actual saves and restores; this technique saves code space at a minor time cost.)

(6)   The caller can also save all registers quite easily. Here it is most likely preferable to use a utility routine to save code space, for calls are fairly common in most programs. When all registers are saved, nonlocal **goto**s and propagated exceptions need only restore the original set of registers.

13.4.2. Subprogram Entry and Exit

We now consider subprogram-call and subprogram-return mechanisms. If block-level activation records are used, these routines are also applicable to block entry and block exit. We first present a method 5 algorithm. The activation record must contain several slots for procedure-call information. Its general form is that shown in Figure 13.3.

Assume we are calling a procedure declared at lexical level **i**. Before the procedure is called, the caller

- Pushes space to store: the return value (if a function is being called), the procedure's **stack_top** value, the return address, the display-swap location, and the register-save area.

- Evaluates each of the actual parameters and pushes them onto the stack.

- Resets the caller's local **stack_top** to point just below the new activation record being set up. (The function-return value is therefore visualized as *below* the AR of the routine being called. However, if an operating system interrupt can occur while this activity proceeds, it is important to leave no important information beyond the end of the stack as defined by the hardware stack register. Otherwise, an interrupt could destroy that information.)

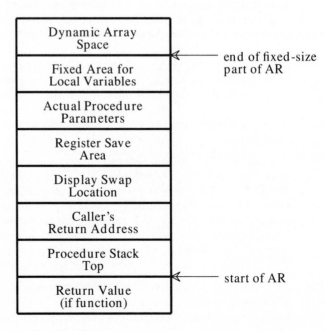

Figure 13.3   Sample Activation Record Layout

- Places this updated **stack_top** value in some known, global communications location, **S**.
- Sets the return address and calls the procedure.

After being called, the procedure (that is, the *callee*)

- Saves current register values in the register-save area (excluding display registers, which are saved in the display-swap location)
- Computes its local **stack_top** from the global **S** (which points to the beginning of this activation record) and the known, fixed size of its activation record
- Saves the current value of **display[i]** in the display-swap area, where **i** is its lexical level
- Sets **display[i]** to point to the start of its activation record (stored in **S**)
- If necessary, copies by-value arrays and records using dope vectors and addresses passed as actual parameters
- If necessary, allocates dynamic arrays, using the local **stack_top**

When the procedure is about to exit, it

- Restores previous values of registers from the register-save area
- Restores the previous value of **display[i]** from the display-swap area
- Jumps to the return address of caller

The return value of a function is at the top of the caller's stack. If block-level allocation is used, each block entry and exit needs to push and pop activation records and update and restore display registers as in the procedure call/return case.

More commonly, procedure-level allocation is used even when local blocks are present. In such a case, the following actions are necessary at block entry and exit:

Block Entry

- Copy the value of **stack_top** from the enclosing block or procedure into this block's local **stack_top**.

    For each dynamic array allocated in the block

    (a) Compute the array bounds and space needed
    (b) Push needed space on the stack and update the local **stack_top**
    (c) Update the dope vector of the array

Block Exit

- Nothing (!)

Block exit requires no work because the local **stack_top** of the enclosing block becomes active after a block exit. This scheme also makes it easy to leave many blocks at once (by a **goto** or **exit** statement).

The procedure-call model used in this section assumes that the callee saves, and later restores, all registers. The choice of whether the caller or callee saves and restores registers and which registers are saved is influenced by size and speed concerns, as well as complexity issues. The preceding model can be readily adapted to any save/restore mechanism that is chosen.

Using this model, the caller must allocate much of the record, because the actual parameters are computed by the caller. An alternative organization puts the actual parameters below the AR in the part of the stack that belongs to the caller. This approach is common in machines that provide hardware (or microcode) support for procedure calls and the associated AR stack manipulation. For example, the VAX instruction set includes a powerful procedure-call instruction that does most of the work of procedure entry and exit. It provides an extra pointer into the AR so that the callee need not know how much space is occupied by saved registers. Its AR layout is shown in Figure 13.4.

The stack top, frame pointer, and argument pointer are special hardware registers. *Frame* is another name for activation record. The caller pushes the actual parameters (or *arguments*) onto the stack and issues the command **calls   argcount,procedure** (the **s** in **calls** stands for stack). At the entry point to the procedure is a bit map indicating which registers are used by the procedure. The **calls** instruction pushes the **argcount** and return address and then saves the registers indicated by the bit map as well as the argument pointer and frame pointer. Then it pushes the stack mark, a record of which registers were saved as well as other information, such as condition codes. Finally, it sets the argument pointer and frame pointer and begins subprogram execution by jumping to the word following the bit map. The procedure can access local variables using the frame pointer and arguments using the argument pointer.

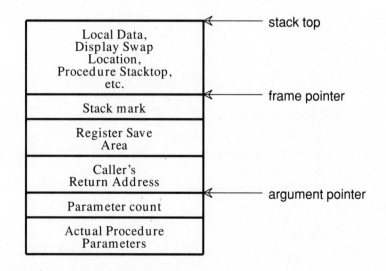

Figure 13.4   VAX Activation Record Layout

The procedure returns by executing the zero-operand instruction **ret**. This instruction restores registers and condition codes as indicated in the stack mark, restores the frame and argument pointers to their original values, and sets the **stack_top** to just below the actual parameters (as indicated by the argument pointer and the argument count), thus popping the arguments off the stack.

Unfortunately, the mechanism does not directly support return values or block structure (nested name scopes). Return values can be passed in registers or by result parameters. The register approach is frequently used for scalar values, with R0 and R1 commonly used for this purpose in VAX programs. When result parameters are used, the return parameter should be first (lowest) on the stack and should not be included in the argument count, so it is not popped on return. Block structure can be handled by either displays or static chains, but each AR pointer must be represented by a *pair* of values: the argument pointer and the frame pointer.

This scheme needs to be extended a bit if procedures can be passed as parameters, as in Algol 60 or Pascal. Ada and Ada/CS do not have this concern. Such procedures, termed *formal procedures*, were discussed in Section 9.6.

The scheme supported by the VAX differs substantially from the model introduced in this section in the way it handles the **stack_top** pointer. The VAX scheme supports a global pointer, whereas the scheme introduced here had a local pointer for each procedure-level activation record and for any local blocks. Either approach can be made to work, however, regardless of hardware support. The main difference is that the global pointer approach requires that the old pointer value be restored at block or procedure exit. No corresponding operation is necessary using a local pointer; rather, the appropriate local pointer implicitly becomes the active **stack_top** when an exit occurs.

13.5. Label Parameters

Some languages (FORTRAN and Algol 60, for example) allow statement labels to be passed as parameters. A **goto** to a label parameter can be used to implement an alternative return from a procedure in a language that does not include exceptions, as Ada does. Surprisingly, label parameters are not particularly difficult to implement. When an actual label L is bound as a label parameter, we create a small formal procedure (whose body is **goto** L) and, as usual, bind the current environment to it (as we do for all formal procedures). Now we just use the formal procedure mechanism. When a formal label parameter is jumped to, we execute the procedure, which reinstates the correct environment and does the actual jump.

If static chains are used, label parameters can be passed as two pointers: (1) the location in code defined by the label (effectively, the body of the small formal procedure whose body is **goto** L) and (2) the static pointer for the lexical level of the label. Executing a **goto** means resetting the current activation record to where that static pointer suggests and jumping to the location specified. We must also make sure that registers are restored, and this can make things more complex.

The proper handling of procedure and label parameters using static chains is illustrated by the somewhat complicated program shown in Figure 13.5 (adapted slightly from an example by Pratt [1975, p. 225]). We have modified it to use an Ada-style syntax, in which a statement label L is denoted <<L>>. The line numbers are referenced in the discussion to follow.

Figure 13.6 shows the essential contents of each activation record in the run-time stack after the initial chain of calls, just before line 24 is executed. All formal labels and formal procedures are specified by two data items: (1) the address (depicted in the figure by actual procedure name or label) and (2) the static link (an activation record). The most recent call, represented by AR5, is at the top of the stack. For the variable N in AR1, the figure includes a history

```
1    procedure B is
2       N : Integer;
3
4       procedure P(X : procedure; C : Integer) is
5          procedure R(label T) is
6          begin
7             N := N + C;
8             X(K);
9             goto T;
10         end  R;
11      begin  --  P
12         <<J>> if C > N then
13            X(J);
14         else
15            P(R,C+1);
16         end if;
17         <<K>> N := N + C;
18         goto L;
19      end  P;
20
21      procedure Q(label T) is
22      begin
23         N := N + 1;
24         goto T;
25      end Q;
26
27   begin  -- B
28      N := 2;
29      P(Q,2);
30      <<L>>    write(N);
31   end B;
```

Figure 13.5   Label Parameter Example

AR5 (Q):

static link	AR1
T	K, AR2
return	AR4, line 9

AR4 (R):

static link	AR2
T	J, AR3
return	AR3, line 17

AR3 (P):

static link	AR1
X	R, AR2
C	3
return	AR2, line 17

AR2 (P):

static link	AR1
X	Q, AR1
C	2
return	AR1, line 30

AR1 (B):

static link	none
N	5 (AR5) 4 (AR4) 2 (AR1)
return	none

Figure 13.6   Activation Records Just before First **goto**

of all its values and which activation record was at the top of the run-time stack when it acquired each value.

Once the state depicted in Figure 13.6 is reached, procedure Q executes **goto** T at line 24. T is bound to K in AR2, so activation records AR5, AR4, and AR3 are popped, leaving the run-time stack in the state shown in Figure 13.7 after the statement labeled by K is executed.

Next the statement **goto** L is executed. L is one-level global, so AR2 is popped, and we print the value of N, namely 7, before exiting block B.

AR2 (P):

static link	AR1
X	Q, AR1
C	2
return	AR1, line 30

AR1 (B):

static link	none
N	7 (AR2) 5 (AR5) 4 (AR4) 2 (AR1)
return	none

Figure 13.7   Activation Records Just after First **goto**

13.6. **Name Parameters**

Call by name was introduced by Algol 60 to model parameter passing as the systematic substitution of actual parameters for formal parameters in each call. That is, at each call we pretend that the body of the called procedure is macroexpanded, with actuals replacing formals. This seems conceptually simple, but it is complicated by the fact that actuals must be evaluated in the environment of the caller rather than the environment of the callee (we compile a procedure body only once). Moreover, actual by-name parameters must be reevaluated each time they are referenced (in the caller's environment, not the callee's environment).

Because of the complexity of implementing by-name parameters, they are today regarded as something of an aberration. However, this mode is worth studying as an exercise in understanding the issues of parameter passing.

For arguments that require no code to evaluate (for example, simple variables or constants), we may pass just an address. However, if any code at all is needed to evaluate an actual parameter, the compiler needs to encapsulate this code into an internally generated procedure (usually called a *thunk*). This procedure, with its environment, is then passed as the actual parameter, using the same methods as formal procedures. The thunk may be requested to evaluate to either an address (*l-value*) or value (*r-value*), depending on the context in which the formal parameter is accessed. To guarantee that expressions are not assigned to, a thunk for a by-name actual expression must generate a run-time error if asked to produce an l-value. Although not common in practice, read-only name mode can be implemented in a similar fashion.

To see some of the unusual effects of name mode, consider

```
declare
    I : Integer;
    A : array(1..2) of Integer;
    procedure P (J : name Integer) is
    begin
        Read (J);
        I := I+1;
        Read (J);
    end P;

begin
    I := 1;
    P(A(I));
end;
```

This program reads values into A(1) and A(2), whereas other parameter modes would bind J permanently to A(1).

A practical use of name mode, called *Jensen's device,* is illustrated in

```
function Sum(Expr : name Real; Index : name Integer;  Max : Integer)
return  Integer is
    Answer : Real := 0;
begin
    for i in 1 .. Max loop
        Index := i;
        Answer := Answer + Expr;
    end loop;
    return Answer;
end Sum;

write(Sum(i,i,5));        -- Sum of first five integers
writeln(Sum(j*j,j,10));        -- Sum of first 10 squares
writeln(Sum(log(sin(x/pi)),x,100));    -- integration?
```

The modification of Index by the **for loop** has the side effect of giving Expr a different value each time. The function Sum thus sums Expr as it changes, stepping Index from 1 to Max and reevaluating Expr at each step.

An instructive exercise is to program a Swap routine that interchanges two integer values, using only name mode parameters. The obvious solution fails, because one of the two parameters (say, the first one) is assigned a new value first, and that change can influence the meaning of the other parameter. For example, if i=1 and a(1)=3, the call Swap(i,a(i)) would end up setting i correctly (to 3) but changing a(3) instead of a(1). If we assign the second parameter its new value first, then Swap(a(i),i) fails. We need to grab and retain l-values for both arguments and then modify their r-values. The trick is to use a subordinate procedure, as illustrated in the following example. (However, even this solution fails for Swap(A,B[f(i)]), where f(i) returns a different value for each call. Because each actual parameter must be evaluated twice—to fetch its original value and store its new value—a fully general call-by-name solution seems to be impossible. See [Fleck 1976].)

```
function GiveSecond(x, y : name  Integer) return Integer is
-- Returns original r-value of y, gives y a new r-value from x.
   tmp : Integer;
begin
   tmp := y;
   y := a;
   return tmp;
end GiveSecond;


procedure Swap(a, b :name Integer);
begin
   a := GiveSecond(a,b);
end Swap;
```

Exercises

1. Explain how the **simple_proc_stmt()** action routine of Section 13.1.2 and **gen_proc_jump()** of Section 13.3 would have to be changed to handle functions as well as procedures.

2. A call to a function with no parameters looks exactly like a reference to a variable. Determine which of the action routines presented in Chapter 11 would have to be modified to handle parameterless functions, and describe the necessary modifications.

3. For a language of your choice other than Ada, list the parameter-passing mode(s) defined in the language. Describe how any other modes can be simulated using the defined parameter modes plus other features of the language.

4. Pascal compilers are required by the Pascal Standard to implement **var** parameters by reference. Write a Pascal program that would produce a different result if **var** parameters were implemented by value-result. Compile and execute it using any Pascal compiler to which you have access to verify that the compiler correctly implements **var** parameters.

5. Write an Ada program that can detect the implementation of **in out** parameters for an array type. Use it to discover the implementation used by any Ada compiler to which you have access.

6. Show the **attributes** record that describes the procedure P declared in the example in Section 13.3, including the list of **attributes** records for its parameters.

7. Show the **attributes** record, including parameter list, for the following procedure declaration:

```
type A is array (1..20) of Integer;
procedure P (X : in Integer; InArray : in A; InOutArray : in out A);
begin
   for I in 1..20 loop
      InOutArray(I) := X * InArray(I);
   end loop;
end P;
```

8. Assuming that the array parameters are implemented by value or value-result, show the tuples generated for the procedure in Exercise 7. Use (level, offset) pairs, rather than symbolic names, to specify variables and parameters in the tuples. Assume that P is declared at nesting level 2.

9. Assuming that the array parameters are implemented by reference, show the tuples generated for the procedure in Exercise 7. Use (level, offset) pairs, rather than symbolic names, to specify variables and parameters in the tuples. Assume that P is declared at nesting level 2.

10. Given the following declarations at the same level as P in Exercise 7

```
A1, A2 : A;
J, K: Integer;
```

and that the offset of A1 is 5, show the tuples that would be generated for the call

```
P(J*K, A1, A2);
```

for each of the parameter implementations assumed in Exercises 8 and 9.

11. The subprogram call and return steps listed at the beginning of Section 13.4.2 assumed that it was the responsibility of the called subprogram to save all registers. Rewrite these call and return sequences for each of the other register-save alternatives discussed in Section 13.4.1.

12. The example illustrating label parameters in Section 13.5 assumes that static chains are being used for referencing nonlocal environments. Thus only a static link is necessary to describe an environment. Explain what is necessary to describe an environment if displays are being used instead of static chains. Redo the example, assuming use of displays.

13. Explain in detail what computation is done to implement each reference to the call-by-name parameter J of procedure P in the first example in Section 13.6.

CHAPTER 14

Attribute Grammars and Multipass Translation

In Chapters 10–13, we examined techniques for implementing a wide variety of programming language features. Our organizational framework has been to define these techniques in terms of semantic routines that we have assumed would be called directly by a parser. The semantic routines form the most crucial part of a compiler because they finish the analysis task of compilation and then begin the synthesis task. Analysis is completed in that the semantic routines associate semantic information (from declarations) with all uses of identifiers and check that any static semantic restrictions in the language are satisfied by the program. Synthesis begins with the generation of either an intermediate representation of the program or actual target code. It is from this synthesis step that the semantic routines get their name, for the output of these routines must reflect the "meaning" of the syntactic structure recognized by the scanner and the parser.

The techniques described in the semantic routine chapters are generally useful regardless of whether the compiler is organized so that semantic actions are invoked directly by the parser. The first section of this chapter is a detailed presentation of *attribute grammars*, which were introduced briefly in Section

7.1.1. Attribute grammars provide a practical formalism for describing semantic processing, in contrast to the informal pseudocode descriptions we used in Chapters 10–13. Attribute grammars may be used to describe semantic processing in any of the compiler organization alternatives presented in Section 7.1.2; however, the full power of their descriptiveness can be best utilized in a compiler organized around a tree-structured intermediate representation. Thus the second major section of this chapter examines tree-structured intermediate representations and tools that support their utilization.

14.1. **Attribute Grammars**

Attribute grammars were proposed by Knuth (1968) as a means of including semantics with the context-free syntax of a language. Each grammar symbol (terminal or nonterminal) may have a fixed number of associated values, termed *attributes*. These attributes represent information associated with the symbol, such as its type, value, code sequence, symbol table, and so on. Attributes may be evaluated as an input is parsed, or they may be evaluated after a syntax tree is constructed by the parser. The resulting syntax tree, augmented with attributes, represents the semantics of the input.

The attributes associated with a given symbol can be divided into two classes: *synthetic* and *inherited*. Briefly, synthetic attributes are used to pass information up a syntax tree, and inherited attributes are used to pass information down a syntax tree. In particular

- Terminals may have only synthetic attributes. These are supplied with the terminal by the scanner.

- Nonterminals may have both synthetic and inherited attributes. All inherited attributes of the *start symbol* are supplied as initial values (in effect, parameters) before evaluation begins.

Each context-free production has a set of associated attribute evaluation rules. A rule must be supplied for each inherited attribute appearing on the right-hand side of a production as well as for each synthetic attribute on the left-hand side. Attribute rules may use only attributes associated with symbols of the corresponding production to compute values. This helps to "package" attribute dependencies within a given production. Inherited attributes of the left-hand side and synthetic attributes of the right-hand side, however, are not computed by attribute evaluation rules of the given production. Rather, they are computed in other productions and act as input parameters to the attribute evaluation rules.

The traditional notation for describing attribute evaluation rules is based on Algol and Pascal; we use a notation that also borrows from Ada. In particular, := is used for assignment, = for equivalence, & for string concatenation, and −− to start comments.

As an example of attribute evaluation rules, consider nonterminal symbols A, B, and C, in which A has an inherited attribute a and a synthetic attribute b, B has a synthetic attribute c, and C has an inherited attribute d. The production A → B C might have rules

```
C.d := B.c + 1;
A.b := A.a + B.c;
```

Note that A.a (attribute a of A) and B.c are computed elsewhere.

As a more concrete example, consider the context-free grammar (CFG) in Figure 14.1, which generates integer constant expressions using the operators + and *. Each expression and subexpression is labeled with an attribute denoting its value.

In Figure 14.1, superscripts are used on some nonterminals to distinguish multiple occurrences on the same nonterminal within a production. This distinction is necessary to disambiguate references to these nonterminals in the attribute rules for the first and third productions of G1. These and all other attribute rules of this grammar use only synthetic attributes because information flow is strictly bottom-up along the syntax tree.

An input of 12+3*6 generates the attributed syntax tree shown in Figure 14.2 (symbols are suffixed with the value of their val attribute).

As suggested before, attribute rules and information flow are often straightforward. However, attribute grammars are basically a very powerful formalism. *Nothing* is assumed about attribute rules. They may be very complex and expensive to evaluate, for example, and the evaluation process may not even terminate in all cases. An attribute grammar using such rules might thus specify translations that are very costly or sometimes even undefined.

Attribute rules may also have side effects (such as generating code) or they may not be strict functions of their input arguments (such as a rule that gives the next available data address). The use of rules like these can lead to ambiguous results unless the order of attribute evaluation is fixed in advance (for example, left to right).

G1: V_n = {E,T,P} Each of these symbols has a single synthetic attribute, val.

V_t = {C} This symbol also has a synthetic attribute, val.

Productions		Attribute Rules
E^1	→ E^2 + T	E^1.val := E^2.val + T.val
E	→ T	E.val := T.val
T^1	→ T^2 * P	T^1.val := T^2.val * P.val
T	→ P	T.val := P.val
P	→ C	P.val := C.val
P	→ (E)	P.val := E.val

Figure 14.1   An Attribute Grammar for Integer Constant Expressions

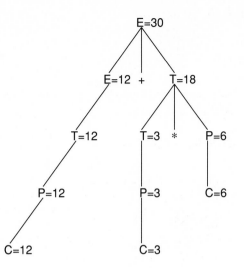

Figure 14.2   Attributed Parse Tree for 12+3*6

Thus attribute rules give a user a great deal of power, but they require care in their definition and use. Also, the way in which information flows in a syntax tree is determined by the functional dependencies of attribute rules. Often this is simply top-down or bottom-up. But sometimes attribute rules can lead to very complex flow patterns. For example, consider grammar G2 in Figure 14.3.

The sole syntax tree derivable from G2 is shown in Figure 14.4, with the order of attribute evaluation denoted by numbers in parentheses next to each node. The order of evaluation is thus S.A (supplied as an initial value), Z.H, Z.G, X.C, X.D, S.B, Y.E, Y.F.

This sort of attribute flow can drive an attribute evaluator crazy. Not surprisingly, therefore, many attribute evaluators limit the kinds of attribute flow they will allow (such as left to right). However, even worse sorts of attribute flow are possible. If, in G2, the rule Z.H := S.A is replaced with Z.H := S.B, then we have a situation in which S.B is defined indirectly in terms of itself (S.B defines Z.H, which defines Z.G, then X.C, then X.D, then S.B). In such situations, a *circularity* of definition exists, and no legitimate order of attribute evaluation is defined.

Attribute grammars with such definitions are termed *circular* and are considered pathologic. An algorithm that tests for circularity is known (Jazayeri, Ogden, and Rounds 1975), but its run-time may be exponential in the size of the grammar tested. Fortunately, most evaluation methods limit themselves to noncircular subsets of attribute grammars (just as parsing techniques limit themselves to unambiguous subsets of CFGs).

$G2 : V_n = \{S,X,Y,Z\}$ $V_t = \{x,y,z\}$

Attributes:
S: A{inh}, B{syn}
X: C{inh}, D{syn}
Y: E{inh}, F{syn}
Z: H{inh}, G{syn}

Productions	*Attribute Rules*	
$S \rightarrow XYZ$	Z.H := S.A	{inh←inh}
	X.C := Z.G	{inh←syn}
	S.B := X.D–2	{syn←syn}
	Y.E := S.B	{inh←syn}
$X \rightarrow x$	X.D := 2*X.C	{syn←inh}
$Y \rightarrow y$	Y.F := Y.E*3	{syn←inh}
$Z \rightarrow z$	Z.G := Z.H+1	{syn←inh}

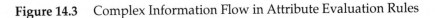

Figure 14.3   Complex Information Flow in Attribute Evaluation Rules

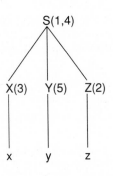

Figure 14.4   Syntax Tree for Grammar G2

14.1.1. Simple Assignment Form and Action Symbols

It is very common for an attribute evaluation rule to be simply the assignment of an attribute value or a constant to another attribute. Such rules are termed *copy rules*. Because such copy rules can be handled automatically by an attribute evaluator, a special form of attribute grammar, termed *simple assignment form*, is often used. In this form, *action symbols* are used to realize all nontrivial attribute rules (that is, all rules other than copy rules). Input values to the action symbol are its inherited attributes, and output values (those computed by it) are its synthetic attributes.

Thus, given a production $E^1 \rightarrow E^2 + T$ and an attribute rule $E^1.val := E^2.val + T.val$ (which is not in simple assignment form), we could instead use $E^1 \rightarrow E^2 + T$ <add>, where <add> is an action symbol with inherited attributes v1 and v2 and a synthetic attribute sum. The copy rules used would then be

$$<add>.v1 := E^2.val$$
$$<add>.v2 := T.val$$
$$E^1.val := <add>.sum$$

Using copy rules, all nontrivial attribute evaluations are replaced by action symbols that can be realized as subprogram (or semantic routine) calls. The copying of attribute values is easily automated.

Further, action symbols can be used to enforce context-sensitive restrictions. We allow an action symbol to signal a semantic error if its input values (that is, its inherited attributes) are incorrect. This signal is the semantic cognate of a parser error. If input values are correct, the action symbol computes its results (its synthetic attributes) and signals no error.

Thus action symbols can be used to both check and compute attribute values. As such, they are very convenient abstractions of semantic routines. We shall see later that attribute evaluators can automate everything but action symbols that are (presumably) coded by hand (from the definition of the action symbol that may or may not be in the form of a program).

Consider a modification of G1 that uses an inherited attribute Max. Max is the largest value of a constant or constant expression allowed. An attempt to use a larger value is treated as a semantic error in the attribute grammar. This modified grammar G3 is shown in Figure 14.5.

The entire definition of G3 in Figure 14.5 could be automatically translated into a parser and attributes evaluator/checker for constant expressions using techniques developed by, for example, Farrow (1982) and Ganzinger et al. (1982).

As an example, consider processing 30*30+125, where Max = 1000. (This is a semantically *illegal expression*.) The corresponding syntax tree appears in Figure 14.6. An undefined value (=?) is associated with the expression because the value it computes is illegal (because it is greater than Max).

14.1.2. Tree-Walk Attribute Evaluators

This section and the next examine the effectiveness and constraints of various algorithms for evaluating attributes. Attribute evaluation algorithms can be divided into two classes: (1) tree traversal algorithms, which generally use more than one traversal to evaluate all attributes (thus requiring the existence of a syntax tree) and (2) "on-the-fly" evaluation algorithms, which compute attribute values as a program is being parsed. Tree traversal approaches are treated in this section, and on-the-fly evaluators are examined in Section 14.1.3.

G3: $V_n = \{E,T,P\}$ $V_t = \{C\}$,   Action Symbols = {<add>,<mult>,<check>}

E, T, and P have an inherited attribute Max and a synthetic attribute Val.

<add> and <mult> have inherited attributes v1, v2, and Max. They each have a synthetic attribute Result.

<check> has inherited attributes Val and Max and a synthetic attribute Result.

Productions	*Copy Rules*
$E^1 \rightarrow E^2 + T$ <add>	<add>.v1 := E^2.Val
	<add>.v2 := T.Val
	<add>.Max := E^1.Max
	E^1.Val := <add>.Result
	E^2.Max := E^1.Max
	T.Max := E^1.Max
$E \rightarrow T$	E.Val := T.Val
	T.Max := E.Max
$T^1 \rightarrow T^2 * P$ <mult>	<mult>.v1 := T^2.Val
	<mult>.v2 := P.Val
	<mult>.Max := T^1.Max
	T^1.Val := <mult>.Result
	T^2.Max := T^1.Max
	P.Max := T^1.Max
$T \rightarrow P$	P.Max := T.Max
	T.Val := P.Val
$P \rightarrow C$ <check>	<check>.Max := P.Max
	<check>.Val := C.Val
	P.Val := <check>.Result
$P \rightarrow (E)$	E.Max := P.Max
	P.Val := E.Val

Definition of Action Symbols

<add> : if (v1 + v2 > Max) ERROR else Result := v1 + v2

<mult> : if (v1 * v2 > Max) ERROR else Result := v1 * v2

<check>: if (Val > Max) ERROR else Result := Val

Figure 14.5   A Single Assignment Form Attribute Grammar

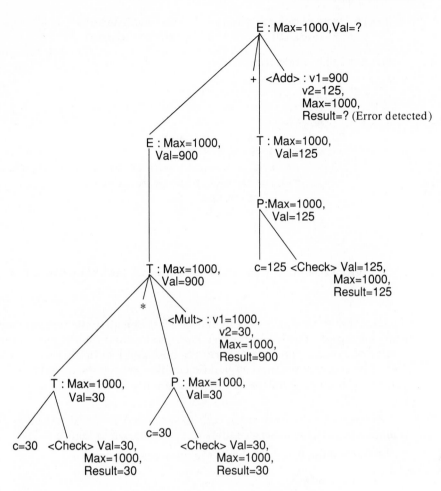

Figure 14.6   Attributed Syntax Tree for 30*30+125

Left-to-Right Traversal Methods

We now consider ways in which attribute values can be determined. A number of attribute evaluation methods are termed *tree-walk* evaluators. These methods assume that a syntax tree has been created and labeled with the inherited attributes of the start symbol and synthetic attributes of all terminals. These methods then traverse the syntax tree, in some order, until all attributes are evaluated. A particularly common traversal order is a depth-first, left-to-right traversal. If necessary, more than one traversal (or "pass") is used.

The following method can evaluate *any noncircular* attribute grammar:

```
while (attributes remain to be evaluated)
   visit_node(S);    /* S is Start symbol */

void visit_node(node N)
{
   if (N is a nonterminal) {
      /* Assume it roots production
         N →X₁ · · · Xₘ */
      for (i = 1; i <= m; i++) {
         if (! Xᵢ ∈ Vₜ) {
            /* i.e., a nonterminal or action symbol */
            Evaluate all possible inherited
                attributes of Xᵢ.
            visit_node(Xᵢ)
         }
      }
   }
   Evaluate all possible synthetic attributes of N
}
```

As long as the grammar is noncircular, at least one attribute will be evaluated during each pass. Further, if the tree has n nodes (and thus at most $O(n)$ attributes), a worst-case time of $O(n^2)$ results (independent of attribute evaluation time). This algorithm can even handle circular grammars, as long as we verify, after each pass, that at least one attribute has been evaluated during that pass.

As an example, reconsider G2. Assume S.A is initialized to 0. Before evaluation begins, the abstract syntax tree is as shown in Figure 14.7(a).

A trace of the first pass shows the following actions:

```
visit_node(S)
   X.C can't be evaluated
   visit_node(X)
         X.D  can't be evaluated
   Y.E  can't be evaluated
   visit_node(Y)
         Y.F  can't be evaluated
   Z.H := 0
   visit_node(Z)
         Z.G := 1
   S.B  can't be evaluated
```

After one pass, the state of the tree is as illustrated in Figure 14.7(b). A second call to **visit_node(S)** results in the computation of X.C, X.D, and S.B (in that order), leaving the tree in the state illustrated in Figure 14.7(c). Finally, the third evaluation pass computes the two attributes of Y. The final state of the tree is shown in Figure 14.7(d).

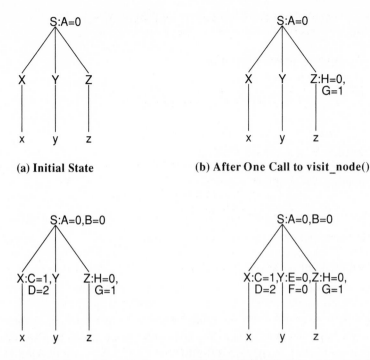

(a) Initial State

(b) After One Call to visit_node()

(c) After Second Call to visit_node()

(d) After Third Call to visit_node()

Figure 14.7   Attribute Evaluation Steps for Abstract Syntax Tree for Grammar G2

This algorithm is very general; it is also very crude and often inefficient (we repeatedly visit nodes already evaluated). An evaluation algorithm is more attractive when we can show that some fixed number **N** of passes will always suffice (independent of the actual tree to be evaluated).

A particularly interesting case is the one in which one pass suffices. Attribute grammars for which one left-to-right pass always allows *all* attributes to be evaluated are termed *L-attributed*. Note that if the underlying CFG is LL(1), we can evaluate attributes on the fly as a parse proceeds. An attribute grammar is L-attributed if and only if

- Each inherited attribute of a right-hand-side symbol depends only on inherited attributes of the left-hand side and arbitrary attributes of symbols to the *left* of the given right-hand-side symbol.

- Each synthetic attribute of the left-hand side depends only on inherited attributes of that symbol and arbitrary attributes of right-hand-side symbols.

- Each synthetic attribute of an action symbol depends only on its inherited attributes.

These limitations on attribute flow, in effect, assume the following order of attribute evaluation in a production $X \rightarrow Y_1 \cdots Y_n$:

Evaluate X's inherited attributes.
Evaluate Y_1's inherited attributes.
Call **visit_node**(Y_1) to get Y_1's synthetic attributes.

.
.
.

Evaluate Y_n's inherited attributes.
Call **visit_node**(Y_n) to get Y_n's synthetic attributes.
Evaluate X's synthetic attributes.

Note that attribute grammars G1 and G3 (but not G2) are L-attributed.

The more general question of when N passes suffice was analyzed by Bochmann (1976). An algorithm is presented that determines when some fixed number, N, of passes, will always suffice.

For some noncircular attribute grammars, no number N can be fixed in advance for all syntax trees. Consider the attribute grammar in Figure 14.8, which generates a list of a's and counts them (in a slightly tricky manner).

An attributed syntax tree for the string aaa is shown in Figure 14.9. Note that information flow is right to left and that O(n) passes are needed to evaluate a tree with n a's [which implies that $O(n^2)$ time is needed].

The observation that sometimes right-to-left depth-first tree traversals are superior (trees of G4 can be evaluated in one right-to-left pass) led to the idea of using alternating left-to-right and right-to-left passes (Jazayeri and Walter 1975). Unfortunately, not all noncircular attribute grammars can be evaluated in a fixed number of alternating passes.

G4: V_t = {a} V_n = {L,A}

L has a synthetic attribute C (for count) that is a count of a's in its subtree.

A has an inherited attribute RC (for right count) that is a count of the number of a's to its right.

Productions	Attribute Rules
$L^1 \rightarrow A L^2$	$A.RC := L^2.C$
	$L^1.C := A.RC + 1$
$L \rightarrow A$	$A.RC := 0$
	$L.C := 1$
$A \rightarrow a$	

Figure 14.8   Attribution Rules with Right-to-Left Information Flow

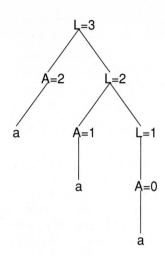

Figure 14.9   An Attributed Syntax Tree for Grammar G4

G5: V_t = {a} V_n = {L,L2,A}.

> L and L2 have synthetic attributes named C (for count) that are counts of the number of a's in the subtrees they root.

> A has an inherited attribute BC (for brother's count) that is a count of the a's in the subtree that is a sibling of A.

Productions   *Attribute Rules*

L	→ A L2	A.BC := L2.C
		L.C := A.BC+1
L	→ A	A.BC := 0
		L.C := 1
L2	→ L A	A.BC := L.C
		L2.C := A.BC+1
L2	→ A	A.BC := 0
		L2.C := 1
A	→ a	

Figure 14.10   Attribution Rules with Alternating Information Flow

Consider the grammar **G5** in Figure 14.10, a generalization of **G4** that again counts the number of **a**'s generated. Here, alternating passes aren't really useful in that the flow of information zigzags across the tree, as illustrated by the arrows in Figure 14.11.

On each pass, information flows up only one level, so $O(n)$ passes are needed for a tree with n A's [and again $O(n^2)$ time is needed].

In summary, depth-first traversals (left-to-right or right-to-left) are very general, but except in the L-attributed case, they are quite inefficient in that nodes are repeatedly visited that either can't be evaluated *or* that already have been entirely evaluated.

Alternate Traversal Methods

As we have seen, left-to-right and right-to-left traversal methods are deficient in that nodes are often visited when there is no need to do so. We now consider a scheme that is more purposeful in its visits. The key idea comes from the following observation: Every nonterminal and action symbol needs to be visited at least once, but once visited, a symbol *need not be visited again* until at least one more attribute for that symbol is made available (that is, is evaluated).

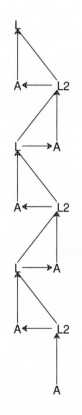

Figure 14.11   Information Flow in an Attributed Tree Based on Grammar G5

This simply says that all information flow *into* a subtree is through its root, and thus a subtree evaluation is keyed by evaluating the root's attributes. Using this idea, we can substantially improve the **visit_node()** routine defined earlier. Assume we label each node of a syntax tree with a value State. For a node A, State(A) is the *set of attributes* of A evaluated when A was last visited; NV is used if A has never been visited. All nonterminals and action symbols have an initial state value of NV. All terminal symbols have an initial state equal to the set of all of the terminal's synthetic attributes (because all these values are supplied by the scanner). Further, we make use of a function Atr. Atr(A) gives all the attributes currently evaluated for A. Note that State(A) $\subseteq$ Atr(A) except when State(A) = NV.

We can now use this state information to *intelligently* guide an evaluator:

```
void visit_node2 (node N)
{
    if (N is an Action Symbol)
        Evaluate all possible attributes in N
    else {          /* N  is a nonterminal */
        while (TRUE) {
            Evaluate all possible attributes in the
                production rooted by N;
            if (there exists an offspring, X_i, of N
                    such that State(X_i) != Atr(X_i))
                visit_node2 (X_i);
            else
                break;
        }
    }
    State[N] = Atr[N];
}
```

Note that nodes are visited only if they have not yet been visited *or* if a new attribute has been evaluated since its last visit. This means that each node is visited a bounded number of times, and linearity results. Also, only noncircular attribute grammars can be evaluated.

As an example, again reconsider G2. We start with the tree in Figure 14.12. (Actual attribute values are not shown; nonterminals have not been visited; terminals have no attributes.)

We start with Atr(S) = {A} and call **visit_node2** (S):

(1)   We immediately evaluate Z.H so Atr(S) = {A}, Atr(Z) = {H}.

(2)   Now Atr(X) = $\varnothing$ $\neq$ State(X) = {NV}, so X is visited.

(3)   **visit_node2** (X).
       No attributes can be evaluated, so we set State(X) = $\varnothing$ and return.

(4)   Now State(X) = Atr(X) = $\varnothing$, so we visit Y. (Again Atr(Y) = $\varnothing$ $\neq$ State(Y) = NV.)

(5)   **visit_node2(Y).**
No attributes can be evaluated, so we set State(Y) = ∅ and return.

(6)   Now we have State(Y) = Atr(Y) = ∅, so we visit Z (Atr(Z) = {H} ≠ State(Z) = NV).

(7)   **visit_node2(Z).**
We evaluate Z.G, and State(Z) becomes {G,H}.

(8)   Now X.C can be evaluated. Because Atr(X) = C ≠ State(X) = ∅, we visit X.

(9)   **visit_node2(X).**
We evaluate X.D, and State(X) becomes {C,D}.

(10)   Now S.B and Y.E can be evaluated. Since Atr(Y) = E ≠ State(Y) = ∅, we visit Y.

(11)   **visit_node2(Y).**
We evaluate Y.F, and State(Y) becomes {E,F}.

(12)   No more attributes can be evaluated, and no more nodes need to be visited (Atr(X) = State(X), Atr(Y) = State(Y), · · ·). We are done.

Note that evaluation using this technique is much more directed and deliberate than was the case using the original **visit_node()** procedure.

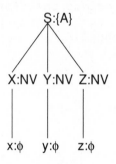

Figure 14.12   Attributed Tree for G2 before Application of **visit_node2()**

14.1.3. On-the-Fly Attribute Evaluators

Unlike tree-walk evaluators, on-the-fly evaluators evaluate attributes in conjunction with a parse rather than after it. As such, they are good models of one-pass syntax-directed compilers. These kinds of evaluators discard attribute values when they are no longer needed in order to evaluate other attributes. Thus translations are usually realized via side effects (for example, code or IR generation) or by building the translation into a synthetic attribute of the goal symbol. However, if necessary, attribute values can clearly be written into a file rather than discarded. We can therefore produce a fully attributed syntax tree if we really need it.

On-the-fly methods operate in conjunction with a parser, and so such methods are characterized by two factors: (1) the parser to be used and (2) the kind of attribute flow to be accommodated. Normally, for a given parsing method we try to allow the most general possible attribute flow. However, all these schemes assume, at the very least, a left-to-right attribute flow. Thus forward references are a problem (as they are for one-pass compilers).

LL(1) L-Attributed Evaluators

The LL(1) L-attributed class of evaluators is quite well known and rather powerful (Lewis, Rosenkrantz, and Stearns 1976). We assume that the attribute grammar is L-attributed (as defined earlier), that the underlying CFG is LL(1), and that the grammer is in *simple assignment form*. Recall that any attribute grammar can easily be put into simple assignment form.

L-attributed attribute flow is ideally suited for LL(1)-based evaluation. Recall that L-attributed rules say, in effect, that in evaluating the attributes of a production we should first evaluate inherited attributes of the left-hand side, then attributes of the right-hand side (from left to right), and then finally the synthetic attributes of the left-hand side. This meshes well with an LL(1) parser that first predicts the left-hand side of a production and then predicts and matches symbols on the right-hand side of that production.

We shall assume that our evaluator uses an attribute stack (which is really just a semantic stack). When a nonterminal is predicted, its inherited attributes are pushed onto the stack. As the right-hand side of a production is recognized, inherited and then synthetic attributes of each symbol are pushed. Finally, when the entire right-hand side is recognized, all attributes of the right-hand side are popped, and the synthetic attributes of the left-hand side are pushed.

Thus, if $X \to YZ$ is predicted and recognized, the attribute stack is manipulated as follows:

(1) Push inherited attributes of X:
     Stack = $\cdots$ Inh(X)

(2) Push inherited attributes of Y:
     Stack = $\cdots$ Inh(X) Inh(Y)

(3) Push synthetic attributes of Y (after parsing Y):
     Stack = $\cdots$ Inh(X) Inh(Y) Syn(Y)

(4) Push inherited attributes of Z:
     Stack = $\cdots$ Inh(X) Inh(Y) Syn(Y) Inh(Z)

(5) Push synthetic attributes of Z (after parsing Z):
     Stack = $\cdots$ Inh(X) Inh(Y) Syn(Y) Inh(Z) Syn(Z)

(6) Pop off attributes of right-hand side and push synthetic attributes of X:
     Stack = $\cdots$ Inh(X) Syn(X)

Because of the L-attributed restrictions, all attribute values, when needed, are on the stack *and* are at a known location (relative to the stacktop).

To complete our evaluator, we need only provide a means of manipulating the attribute stack. To do this, we introduce *copy symbols*. These are essentially action symbols that move attributes rather than compute them. These copy symbols are *automatically* generated from copy rules and appear when inherited or synthetic attributes are manipulated.

A simple example will make the use of copy symbols obvious. Figure 14.13 presents a new version of G1 (call it G1A) that uses only the operator +. It is LL(1), L-attributed, and in simple assignment form. Replacing copy rules in grammar G1A with copy symbols, denoted as #1, #2, $\cdots$, produces the grammar shown in Figure 14.14.

Figure 14.15 shows a trace of parsing and evaluation of 10 + 11 $ using this transformed version of G1A. The parse is completed, with the synthetic attribute of E (E.val) remaining on the stack.

Note that many optimizations of stack manipulation routines are possible. For example, in

E → T #1 T-List $ #2

the copy implied by #1 could be eliminated by allowing T.val and T-List.LeftVal to share the same stack location. As we shall see later, for LR-based evaluators this optimization can be crucial. So too, the sequence #4 <add> #1 could be collapsed into one routine. Such optimizations are straightforward to implement and would certainly be used in practice.

G1A: V_n = {E,T,T-List} V_t = {C,$,+} Action symbols = <add>

Attributes:
Syn(E) = Syn(T) = Syn(T-List) = Syn(C) = {Val}
Inh(T-List) = {LeftVal}
Inh(<add>) = {V1,V2}   Syn(<add>) = {Result}

Productions		*Attribute Rules*
E	→ T T-List $	E.Val := T-List.Val
		T-List.LeftVal := T.Val
T	→ C	T.Val := C.Val
T–List^1	→ + T <add> T–List^2	<add>.v1 := T–List^1.LeftVal
		<add>.v2 := T.Val
		T–List^2.LeftVal := <add>.Result
		T–List^1.Val := T–List^2.Val
T-List	→ λ	T-List.Val := T-List.LeftVal

Figure 14.13   An L-Attributed Grammar Using Only Copy Rules

```
E        → T #1 T-List $ #2
T        → C #3
T-List   → + T #4 <add> #1 T-List #5
T-List   → #1
```

#1 : Push copy of Top Element
#2 : Temp := Top Element; Pop 3; Push Temp
#3 : None -- Equivalent to Temp := Top; Pop 1; Push Temp
#4 : Push copy of Top–1; Push copy of Top–1.
#5 : Temp := Top; Pop 6; Push Temp

Figure 14.14   Transformation of Grammar G1A Using Copy Symbols

Attribute Stack	Parse Stack	Input
Empty	E	C:10+C:11 $
Empty	T #1 T-List $ #2	C:10+C:11 $
Empty	C:10 #3 #1 T-List $ #2	C:10+C:11 $
10	#3 #1 T-List $ #2	+C:11 $
10	#1 T-List $ #2	+C:11 $
10 10	T-List $ #2	+C:11 $
10 10	+T $ #2	+C:11 $
10 10	+T #4 <add> #2 T-List #5 $ #2	+C:11 $
10 10	T #4 <add> #1 T-List #5 $ #2	C:11 $
10 10	C:11 #3 #4 <add> #1 T-List #5 $ #2	C:11 $
10 10 11	#3 #4 <add> #1 T-List #5 $ #2	$
10 10 11	#4 <add> #1 T-List #5 $ #2	$
10 10 11 10 11	<add> #1 T-List #5 $ #2	$
10 10 11 10 11 21	#1 T-List #5 $ #2	$
10 10 11 10 11 21	#1 T-List #5 $ #2	$
10 10 11 10 11 21 21	T-List #5 $ #2	$
10 10 11 10 11 21 21 21	#5 $ #2	$
10 10 21	$ #2	$
10 10 21	#2	Empty
21	Empty	Empty

Figure 14.15   Trace of Evaluation Using G1A

LR S-Attributed Evaluators

The advantage LR-type parsers have over LL parsers is their ability to delay production recognition until after the entire right-hand side has been recognized. However, when attribute evaluation is considered, this "advantage" limits the attribute flow that can be accommodated. In particular, because an LR parser generally does not know what production it is recognizing, it cannot provide inherited attributes to symbols. Thus LR techniques are commonly limited to S-attributed grammars, which allow only synthetic attributes for nonterminals. In particular, an attribute grammar is *S-attributed* if and only if

- It is L-attributed.
- Nonterminals have only synthetic attributes.
- All action symbols (and copy symbols) occur to the right of all terminals and nonterminals in a right-hand side.

Consider G1B, an S-attributed, LR(0), simple assignment form version of G1 that uses only the operator +, shown in Figure 14.16. Again using a copy symbols transformation, we get the grammar in Figure 14.17.

Observe that the clusters of copy symbols and action symbols comprise the standard semantic routines of bottom-up compilers and are invoked when a reduction is signaled by the parser.

LR LC-Attributed Evaluators

The S-attributed class is unattractive in that no inherited attributes are allowed. In practice, inherited attributes are used and should be allowed, if possible. Note that in general, productions need not be recognized at their extreme left (as in LL) or their extreme right (as in LR) but rather can be recognized somewhere in the middle of a right-hand side. In fact, in a production

G1B: V_n = {E} V_t = {C,+}   Action Symbols = {<add>}
Attributes:
  Syn(E) = Syn(C) = {Val}
  Syn(<add>) = {Result}   Inh(<add>) = {v1,v2}

Productions	*Attribute Rules*
$E^1 \to E^2$ + C <add>	<add>.v1 := E^2.val
	<add>.v2 := C.val
	E^1.val := <add>.Result
E → C	E.val := C.val

Figure 14.16   An S-Attributed Grammar Using Copy Rules

E → E + C #1 <add> #2
E → C #3

#1: Push copy of Top-1; Push copy of Top-1
#2: Temp := Top; Pop 5; Push Temp
#3: No action -- In effect Temp := Top; Pop 1; Push Temp

Figure 14.17   Transformation of Grammar G1B Using Copy Symbols

A → αβ, the right-hand side can be divided into two pieces: the *left corner* (α) and the *trailing part* (β). By definition, any production can be correctly recognized right after the left corner is processed. In LL(1), the left corner is always empty; in LR(1), the left corner can sometimes comprise the entire right-hand side (although in many LR grammars left corners are quite small). This division of the right-hand side suggests that β (the trailing part) can be allowed inherited attributes. Thus the following hybrid of S-attributed and L-attributed flow results. An attribute grammar is *LC-attributed* if and only if

- It is L-attributed.

- No nonterminal that occurs in a left corner has any inherited attributes.

- No action symbols occur in a left corner.

Note that in effect, left corners are allowed S-attributed flow, but trailing parts are allowed L-attributed flow.

LC-attributed grammars are certainly an improvement over S-attributed grammars. Equally important, we can parse them with any LR-type parser. The idea is that conceptually we create a CFG with special *recognition symbols* delimiting left corners. If the attribute grammar is LC-attributed, action symbols and copy symbols occur only in trailing parts but not necessarily at the extreme right. Thus we might have

A → X Y & <A1> Z <A2>

(The & is the recognition symbol; it is not seen by the LR parser—it is present only to delimit the left corner.) Action symbols and copy symbols at the extreme right, such as <A2>, are handled, as usual, when the production is recognized. To handle <A1>, we introduce a new nonterminal and production (say, <call A1> → λ). Because this new nonterminal (which always generates λ) *must be* in the trailing part, we can always be sure it will be parsed correctly. In fact, one way to define the trailing part is as that section of a right-hand side in which we can place, without destroying parsability, a new nonterminal that generates only λ.

We then associate the copy symbols and action symbols with the λ-production just created. The preceding is therefore transformed into

A → XY<call A1>Z<A2>
<call A1> → <A1>

These productions can be parsed using ordinary LR-type techniques. The LC-attributed class was originally defined by Rowland (1977).

The Limited Use of Inherited Attributes in Left Corners

The use of LC-attributed grammars is not entirely satisfactory because at times it is necessary to provide inherited attributes for left-corner symbols. Consider G3A, a version of G3 using only the operator + with minimal left corners, shown in Figure 14.18.

G3A *is not* LC-attributed because E, a left-corner symbol, has an inherited attribute. However, copy symbols needed for inherited attributes in left corners can often be *optimized away* (Watt 1977). In this case, a copy of E^1.Max to E^2.Max can be obviated by letting them share the same stack location. In fact, copies of the top i (i ≥ 1) stack locations can be optimized away by sharing (the attributes are in effect read-only). Removing this copy in the left corner yields

> E → E & + C #1 <add> #2
> E → & C #3 <check> #4
>
> #1: Push Top–1; Push Top–1; Push Top–4;
> #2: Temp := Top; Pop 6; Push Temp
> #3: Push Top; Push Top–2
> #4: Temp := Top; Pop 4; Push Temp

This grammar can be handled by the methods of the previous section. This copy optimization doesn't allow arbitrary inherited attributes in left corners (or any action symbols in left corners), but Watt claims it is enough to handle, for example, a Pascal attribute grammar (using an LR-type parser).

> G3A: V_n = {E} V_t = {+,C} Action Symbols = {<add>,<check>}
>
> Attributes:
>   Inh(E) = {Max}   Syn(E) = {Val}
>   Syn(C) = {Val}
>   Inh(<add>) = {v1,v2,Max}   Syn(<add>) = {Result}
>   Inh(<check>) = {Val,Max}   Syn(<check>) = {Result}

Productions	*Attribute Rules*
E^1 → E^2 & + C <add>	E^2.Max := E^1.Max
	<add>.v1 := E^2.Val
	<add>.v2 := C.Val
	<add>.Max := E^1.Max
	E^1.Val := <add>.Result
E → & C <check>	<check>.Val := C.Val
	<check>.Max := E.Max
	E.Val := <check>.Result

Figure 14.18   An Illustration of the Need for Inherited Attributes in Left Corners

14.1.4. An Attribute Grammar Example

In Figure 14.19, we present an example attribute grammar for a grammar fragment that includes **if** statements and **while** loops. The example serves two purposes: (1) to show a more realistic attribute grammar than the mostly abstract preceding examples have and (2) to illustrate how a semantic processing algorithm can be simplified if one-pass processing is not required. The example is based on one developed by Tomasz Kowaltowski. It is somewhat simpler than the algorithms presented in Chapter 12 for short-circuit evaluation of boolean expressions due to the use of right-to-left attribute flows in evaluating such expressions.

In this grammar, statements (designated by nonterminal S) have an inherited attribute next, which is the label of the statement to be executed after the statement under consideration, and a synthesized attribute code, which is a string containing the code generated by the statement. (The attribute rules presume that the tuple generation routine **generate()** returns a tuple as a string.) Each expression, designated by nonterminal E, has two inherited attributes: label, a symbolic label, and case (true or false). These attributes are interpreted as follows: The code for the expression should result in a jump to label if the expression evaluates to case; otherwise, the code should "fall through" to the next instruction.

This approach is simpler than the two algorithms seen in Chapter 12, which require the maintenance of chains of tuples to be backpatched for both true and false results of expressions. Here, only *one* label is associated with each expression (or one chain if a backpatching formulation is used). The key to the simplification is found in the attribute evaluation rules for the production $E \rightarrow E^1$ BoolOp E^2. The attribute operator of BoolOp is used to compute E^1.label (a right-to-left attribute flow), making it possible to produce an appropriate jump during the processing of E^1 to handle the case when it alone determines the result of the expression.

–– The symbol "&" represents string concatenation

S → **if** E **then** L **end if**
   E.case:=FALSE
   E.label:=S.next
   L.next:=S.next
   S.code:=E.code & L.code &
     generate(LABEL,S.next,"","")

S → **if** E **then** L^1 **else** L^2 **end if**
   E.case:=FALSE
   E.label:=new_label()
   L^1.next:=S.next
   L^2.next:=S.next
   S.code:=E.code & L^1.code &
     generate(JUMP,S.next,"","") &
     generate(LABEL,E.label,"","") &
     L^2.code &
     generate(LABEL,S.next,"","")

S → **while** E **loop** L **end loop**;
   E.case:=FALSE
   E.label:=S.next

	S.begin:=new_label()
	L.next:=S.begin
	S.code:=generate(LABEL,S.begin,"","") &
	       E.code & L.code &
	       generate(JUMP,S.begin,"","") &
	       generate(LABEL,S.next,"","")

$S \rightarrow$ OtherS	S.code:=OtherS.code
$L \rightarrow S$	S.next:=L.next L.code:=S.code
$L \rightarrow L^1 S$	L^1.next:=new_label() S.next:=L.next L.code:=L^1.code & S.code

$E \rightarrow E^1$ BoolOp E^2	E^2.label:=E.label
	E^2.case:=E.case
	if BoolOp.operator = OrElseOp **then**
	  E^1.case := TRUE
	  if E.case **then**
	    E^1.label:=E.label
	    E.code:= E^1.code & E^2.code
	  else
	    E^1.label:=new_label()
	    E.code:= E^1.code & E^2.code &
	       generate(LABEL,E^1.label,"","")
	  end if;
	else -- BoolOp.operator = AndThenOp
	  E^1.case := FALSE
	  if E.case **then**
	    E^1.label:=new_label()
	    E.code:= E^1.code & E^2.code &
	       generate(LABEL,E^1.label,"","")
	  else
	    E^1.label:=E.label
	    E.code:= E^1.code & E^2.code
	  end if;

$E \rightarrow$ **not** E^1	E^1.label:=E.label E^1.case:=**not** E.case E.code:=E^1.code
$E \rightarrow (E^1)$	E^1.label:=E.label E^1.case:=E.case E.code:=E^1.code

$E \rightarrow$ id^1 RelOp id^2	E.code:= **if** E.case **then**
	    generate(BR,RelOp.operator,
	        id^1.loc,id^2.loc,E.label)
	  else
	    generate(BR,
	      complement(RelOp.operator),
	      id^1.loc,id^2.loc,E.label)
	  end if

$E \rightarrow$ true	E.code:=**if** E.case **then**
	generate(JUMP,E.label,"","")
	else
	empty
	end if
$E \rightarrow$ false	E.code:=**if** E.case **then**
	empty
	else
	generate(JUMP,E.label,"","")
	end if

Figure 14.19   Attribute Grammar for Short-circuit Evaluation

Consider the following **if** statement as an example of code generation using this grammar:

if A > B **or else** C < D **then**
    OtherS^1
else
    OtherS^2
end if

Attribute evaluation for this example is illustrated in Figure 14.20, beginning at the tree node for the production

$S \rightarrow$ **if** E **then** L^1 **else** L^2 **end if**

We assume that the inherited attribute S.next = L1. Only visits to nodes corresponding to symbols with attribute evaluation rules are included.

```
visit_node(S):
    E.case := FALSE
    E.label := L2   /* a new label */
    L¹.next := L1
    L².next := L1

    visit_node(E):  /* E → E¹ BoolOP E² */
        E².label := L2
        E².case := FALSE
        /* The next two attributes depend on right-to-left information flow, */
        /* since the rules to generate them consider the operator BoolOp */
        E¹.case := TRUE
        E¹.label := L3   /* a new label */

    visit_node(E¹)
        E¹.code := (BR,>,A.loc,B.loc,L3)

    visit_node(E²)
        E².code := (BR,>=,C.loc,D.loc,L2)
```

E.code := (BR,>,A.loc,B.loc,L3)
           (BR,>=,C.loc,D.loc,L2)
           (LABEL,L3)

visit_node(L^1): /* $L^1 \rightarrow$ S */
  S.next := L1

    visit_node(S): /* S $\rightarrow$ OtherS */
      S.code := {code for OtherS}

  L^1.code := {code for OtherS}

visit_node(L^2): /* $L^2 \rightarrow$ S */
  S.next := L1

    visit_node(S): /* S $\rightarrow$ OtherS */
      S.code := {code for OtherS}

  L^2.code := {code for OtherS}

S.code := (BR,>,A.loc,B.loc,L3)
         (BR,>=,C.loc,D.loc,L2)
         (LABEL,L3)
         {code for OtherS}
         (JUMP,L1)
         (LABEL,L2)
         {code for OtherS}
         (LABEL,L1)

Figure 14.20   Trace of Attribute Evaluation Using the Grammar in Figure 14.19

14.2. Tree-structured Intermediate Representations

The discussion of intermediate representations in Chapter 8 introduced the idea of a tree-structured IR for an entire program as a generalization of expression trees. Such IRs were said to be based on *abstract syntax trees*. An abstract syntax tree is derived from a parse tree by eliminating the explicit representation of syntactic elements that have no semantic significance. Abstract syntax trees can easily be used as an IR to store attributes for use by a multipass attribute evaluator.

Consider, for example, the simplest **if** statement production from Figure 14.19:

S → **if** E **then** L **end if**

The parse tree for this production has the form shown in Figure 14.21(a). To contrast this, an equivalent abstract syntax tree representation is shown in Figure 14.21(b).

Two fundamental differences are illustrated here. The first is the replacement of the generic statement node S by the explicit IfThenStmt. This replacement makes it possible for the node name to convey information about the structure expected below. Particularly, it makes the second difference possible: All the keywords have been removed from among the descendants of the IfThenStmt node. Their presence in the source program is implied by the name of the node. Because they convey no semantic information beyond the fact of their presence, an explicit representation of them in the tree is unnecessary.

The subtrees for the E and L nodes are similarly transformed in a complete abstract syntax tree definition. The change is particularly profound for the statement list subtree rooted at L. In the parse tree, this subtree represents a list produced by the productions L→L S and L→S. Thus a subordinate L node is created if the list is more than one statement long, and the same construction is applied recursively. In an abstract syntax tree, a StmtList node is used that points to the head of an explicit list of the subordinate statement nodes.

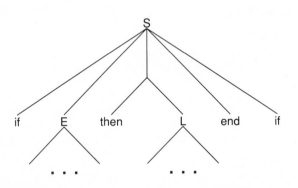

Figure 14.21(a)   Parse Tree for a Simple **if** Statement

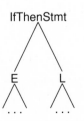

Figure 14.21(b)   Abstract Syntax Tree for a Simple **if** Statement

Abstract syntax trees as described thus far are essentially just more concise descriptions than parse trees of the syntax of source programs. Such a tree could serve as the interface between the parser and semantic analysis phases of a compiler with a multipass analysis organization. To facilitate semantic analysis, more information must be added. The concept of attributes serves this purpose well. We can think of the pointers to the expressions and statement list subtrees from the IfThenStmt tree node as *structural attributes*. In a complete attribute grammar formulation, the statement has an inherited attribute environment that represents the name space (symbol table) in which any identifiers encountered within the statement are to be interpreted. environment is an example of a *semantic attribute*. Later examples use one additional kind of attribute, *code generation attributes*.

Attributes beyond those required to convey structural information can be added to tree nodes as required to provide necessary information for any phase of a compiler. For example, expression subtrees synthesize a semantic attribute that describes the type of the expression. Such attributes can be used in rules that check type compatibility to enforce static semantic restrictions or, more generally, to resolve overloaded operators. Semantic and code-generation attributes are typically computed during separate tree traversals, because the former are machine-independent and the latter are obviously target-dependent.

14.2.1. Interfaces to Abstract Syntax Trees

Abstract syntax trees are typically implemented by using structures to represent nodes and pointers to link them together. The major design choice is whether to define a distinct type for each kind of tree node or to make all the tree nodes a single type. In the latter case, a *node name* field is used to distinguish among the possible node types, and variants based on the node name contain the appropriate attributes. Use of a single node type is the most common choice, principally because it makes the code necessary to perform a tree traversal far simpler. Tree traversal is, of course, the most fundamental operation done on an abstract syntax tree.

Consider the following simple expression grammar:

```
<Exp>      → <T> { <addop> <T> }
<T>        → <P> { <multop> <P> }
<P>        → ID
<add op>   → PLUS | MINUS
<mult op>  → TIMES | DIVIDE
```

The nonterminals <Exp>, <T>, and <P> are distinguished syntactically only for the purpose of specifying precedence of operators. They have no semantic differences other than whether they represent a simple identifier or a tree involving an operator. These two cases can be represented by two kinds of abstract syntax tree nodes called tree and leaf. The four operators have dif-

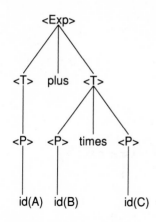

Figure 14.22(a) Parse Tree for A+B∗C

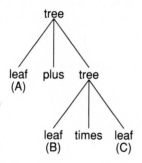

Figure 14.22(b) Abstract Syntax Tree for A+B∗C

ferent semantic meanings, and four different node types are appropriate to represent them. The names of the operator tokens are appropriate for tree node names. Thus the expression A+B∗C has the parse tree shown in Figure 14.22(a) and can be represented by the abstract syntax tree in Figure 14.22(b).

The abstract syntax tree shown in this figure can be built according to the single record type approach using the following declarations:

```
enum node_type { TREE, LEAF, PLUS, MINUS, TIMES, DIVIDE };

typedef struct tn {
   enum node_type node_name;
   union {
      /* node_name == TREE */
      struct {
         struct tn *op, *left, *right;
      };
```

```
      /* node_name == LEAF */
      string id;

      /* anything else, empty */
   }
} tree_node;
```

14.2.2. Abstract Interfaces to Syntax Trees

If an abstract interface to the syntax tree is used, the preceding design decision need have no impact on the rest of the compiler. By use of an *abstract interface*, we mean that the fields of tree node records are not directly accessed by semantic routines and the code generator. Rather, attributes are accessible outside a syntax tree "package" only through procedures, which can set their values, and functions, which can retrieve these values; the definition of the tree node type is not exported. This abstract approach hides not only the fundamental structural design decision but also decisions about how individual attributes are represented (for example, as an explicit value or as information that allows computation of the value). In C, the procedural interface can actually be a set of macros. This allows for efficient access to the attributes while still providing data hiding through the interface.

Diana (Goos and Wulf 1981) is a *de facto* standard IR for Ada programs. It is a tree-structured IR defined by an abstract interface such as that just described. The interface to Diana is, in fact, defined in a special notation for describing abstract data structures: the interface description language (IDL) (Nestor, Wulf, and Lamb 1981). Because Diana is too complex for us to provide a concise example by using it, we instead present an IDL description of the expression abstract syntax tree from Figure 14.22 and the corresponding C declarations for the interface it defines. A more complex IDL example is presented at the end of the chapter. These examples illustrate the notion of abstract interfaces to abstract syntax trees that is fundamental to Diana.

A Simple IDL Example

This first IDL example, in Figure 14.23, is adapted from the *IDL Reference Manual*. It is the definition of an abstract data type for representing simple arithmetic expressions as defined for Figure 14.22.

EXP and OPERATOR are examples of class names. They are used to define the structure of the tree but do not actually appear as nodes in the tree. Six node names are defined: tree, leaf, plus, minus, times, and divide. Each of these may appear as a node in a tree. Of these, only tree and leaf nodes have attributes, with the names and types of the attributes given by the two lines of attribute definitions. The type of the name attribute of a leaf node, String, is a built-in type of IDL. The fact that the root of a tree must be an EXP (further defined later as a tree or a leaf) is specified by the header line.

The C declarations corresponding to the IDL description in Figure 14.23 are shown in Figure 14.24.

mode AST **root** EXP **is**

    −− first we define the notion of an expression, EXP

    EXP ::= leaf | tree ;

    −− next we define the nodes and their attributes

    tree => op : OPERATOR, left : EXP, right : EXP ;
    leaf => name : String ;

    −− finally we define the notion of an OPERATOR as the union of
    −− a collection of nodes; note these particular nodes have no
    −− attributes and hence have no further definitions

    OPERATOR ::= plus | minus | times | divide ;

end

Figure 14.23   IDL Description of Abstract Syntax Trees for Expressions

Given these declarations (Figure 14.24), the sequence of calls in Figure 14.25 constructs the tree corresponding to A+B∗C, assuming that variables T1, T2, T3, T4, and T5 are of type **(tree_node *)**. This code principally illustrates the use of tree construction and attribute-setting procedures and functions.

The procedure **postfix()** in Figure 14.26 uses the same routines from Figure 14.24 to do a traversal of an expression tree and to write out the expression in postfix notation. The emphasis in this example is on the functions that access the attributes of the tree nodes.

IDL Definitions for the Short-circuit Evaluation Example

Figure 14.27 contains an IDL definition for the abstract syntax required for the short-circuit evaluation attribute grammar in Figure 14.19. An important feature of this definition is the division of the attribute definitions into two sections: one for attributes that define the tree structure and one for those used to drive the code-generation process. Diana, the IR for Ada, is defined using the same sort of definition as this, although the Diana definition distinguishes four kinds of attributes: structural, lexical (information to allow precise recreation of the source program), semantic, and code generation.

One new IDL feature appears in this example. The attribute list of the StmtList node is defined using a sequence type (Seq). As a consequence of this feature, the C declarations corresponding to an IDL definition that includes sequence types must include functions for manipulating sequences.

```
/* specification of AST */

typedef struct tn {
          . . .
                              /* contents are "private" */
} tree_node;

typedef enum {
    TREE, LEAF, PLUS, MINUS, TIMES, DIVIDE
} node_name;

/*
 * Tree constructors. Pointers are used both for
 * efficiency and due to C's call-by-value semantics.
 */

tree_node *make(node_name n);
void destroy(tree_node *t);
node_name kind(tree_node *t);

/*
 * The following procedure/function pairs are used to
 * set and access attributes of nodes.
 */

void       set_op(tree_node *node, tree_node *value);
tree_node *get_op(tree_node *node);
void       set_left(tree_node *node, tree_node *value);
tree_node *get_left(tree_node *node);
void       set_right(tree_node *node, tree_node *value);
tree_node *get_right(tree_node *node);
void       set_name(tree_node *node, string value);
string    *get_name(tree_node *node);
```

Figure 14.24   C Declarations Corresponding to Figure 14.23

The declarations in Figure 14.28 are a C interface that corresponds to the IDL definition in Figure 14.27. They are based on a standard template that includes the types and subprograms necessary for creating and manipulating trees and sequences. The declarations of the type **node_name** and the subprograms for setting and accessing attributes are, of course, based on this particular IDL definition.

```
T1 = make(LEAF);
set_name(T1, "A");
T2 = make(LEAF);
set_name(T2, "B");
T3 = make(LEAF);
set_name(T3, "C");
T4 = make(TREE);
set_left(T4, T2);
set_right(T4, T3);
set_op(T4, make(TIMES));   /* T4 is the tree for B*C */
T5 = make(TREE);
set_op(T5, make(PLUS));
set_left(T5, T1);
set_right(T5, T4);         /* T5 is the tree for A+B*C */
```

Figure 14.25   Abstract Syntax Tree Construction Using the **AST** routines

```
void postfix(tree_node *t)
{
    switch (kind(t)) {
    case LEAF:    printf(" %s", name(t)); break;
    case PLUS:    printf(" +"); break;
    case MINUS:   printf(" -"); break;
    case TIMES:   printf(" *"); break;
    case DIVIDE:  printf(" /"); break;
    case TREE:    postfix(get_left(t));
                  postfix(get_right(t));
                  postfix(get_op(t));
                  break;
    }
}
```

Figure 14.26   Postfix Printing of Expressions Represented by **AST**

mode SyntaxTree **root** STMT **is**

 STMT ::= IfThenStmt | IfThenElseStmt | WhileStmt | OtherStmt ;
 LIST ::= StmtList ;
 EXP ::= BoolExp | Negation | Parens | RelExp | TrueExp | FalseExp ;

 -- The following attributes define the structure of the abstract syntax tree
 -- for statements

 IfThenStmt => condition : EXP, thenpart : LIST ;

IfThenElseStmt => condition : EXP, thenpart : LIST, elsepart : LIST ;
WhileStmt => condition : EXP, loopbody : LIST ;
StmtList => list : Seq of STMT ;

BoolExp => left : EXP, operator : BOOLOP, right : EXP ;
RelExp => left : EXP, operator : RELOP, right : EXP ;
Negation => expression : EXP ;
Parens => expression : EXP ;

-- the following declarations are of the attributes used by the
-- code-generation process encoded in the attribute grammar

IfThenStmt => next : String, code : String ;
IfThenElseStmt => next : String, code : String ;
WhileStmt => next : String, begin : String, code : String ;
OtherStmt => code : String ;

BoolExp => case : Boolean, label : String, code : String ;
Negation => case : Boolean, label : String, code : String ;
Parens => case : Boolean, label : String, code : String ;
RelExp => case : Boolean, label : String, code : String ;
TrueExp => case : Boolean, label : String, code : String ;
FalseExp => case : Boolean, label : String, code : String ;

end

Figure 14.27   An IDL Definition for Representing the Grammar in Figure
14.19

```
/* specification of SyntaxTree */

typedef struct tn {
    · · ·               /* contents are "private" */
} tree_node;

typedef  · · ·  seq_type;   /* also private */

typedef enum {
    IFTHENSTMT, IFTHENELSESTMT, WHILESTMT, OTHERSTMT,
    STMTLIST, BOOLEXP, NEGATION, PARENS, RELEXP, TRUEEXP,
    FALSEEXP) ;
} node_name;

/*
 * Tree constructors. Pointers are used both for
 * efficiency and due to C's call-by-value semantics.
 */

tree_node *make(node_name n);
```

```
void destroy(tree_node *t);
node_name kind(tree_node *t);

/* handling of list constructs (for STMTLIST) */

tree_node *head(seq_type *l);
seq_type  *tail(seq_type *l);
seq_type  *seq_make(void);   /* returns an empty list */
boolean    is_empty(seq_type *l);
/* inserts t at start of l */
seq_type  *insert(seq_type *l, tree_node *t);
/* inserts t at end of l */
seq_type  *append(seq_type *l, tree_node *t);

/*
 * The following procedure/function pairs are used to set
 * and access attributes of nodes.  The first group deals
 * with the attributes that define the structure of the
 * abstract syntax tree.
 */

void    set_condition(tree_node *node, tree_node *value);
void    set_thenpart(tree_node *node, tree_node *value);
tree_node *get_condition(tree_node *node);
tree_node *get_thenpart(tree_node *node);
        .
        . /* similar subprograms for elsepart, loopbody */
        . /* list, left, right, operation and expression */
        .

/*
 * This second group of procedures and functions handles
 * the attributes that drive the code-generation algorithm.
 * Different nodes that have attributes with the same name
 * may share a pair of these routines, since all nodes are
 * tree_nodes.
 */

void    set_next(tree_node *node, string value);
string get_next(tree_node *node);
void    set_code(tree_node *node, string value);
string get_code(tree_node *node);
        .
/* similar subprograms for begin, label and case */
        .
        .
```

Figure 14.28   C Declarations Corresponding to Figure 14.27

14.2.3. Implementing Trees

Tree-structured intermediate representations are commonly thought of as requiring large amounts of storage. This characterization is not necessarily accurate. If the most obvious compiler organization is used, that of the front-end producing a tree for an entire program (with each node represented by a dynamically allocated variant record), then considerable storage space will be required for even modestly sized programs. However, other organizations are certainly possible if storage requirements are a significant issue.

If only limited optimization (or none at all) is required, a compiler can be organized so that its components run as coroutines (as in a one-pass compiler). Part of the program (often a procedure or function) is processed by each of the components, and then its tree is discarded. This process is repeated until the whole program has been compiled.

As an alternative to saving space by storing only a partial tree at any given time, a variety of approaches is available to storing whole trees more compactly. Trees can be linearized (as with postfix representations), for example, in order to save the space that would be required by pointers, for in such a representation subnodes are positioned implicitly with respect to a node. Linearizations simplify certain kinds of tree traversals (usually left to right) at the expense of making generalized traversals more expensive. Linearized representations are also useful as external representations of trees, because they eliminate the memory address dependency inherent in typical pointer implementations.

Another space-saving technique is to turn the tree into a directed acyclic graph (dag) by sharing identical subtrees. The most obvious nodes to share are the leaf nodes that represent literal values and, especially, identifiers. However, more substantial subtrees may be shared if they are recognized.

Finally, certain trivial nodes need not be represented as nodes at all. For example, the nodes of the OPERATOR class from the AST example have no attributes. Their only significance is the various operators they denote. References to such nodes from tree nodes can be optimized away, replaced by a value of a simple enumerated type implemented as a small integer stored in the tree node instead of a pointer to a real node.

Exercises

1. Based on the examples of Section 14.2, informally state a general algorithm for deriving an appropriate abstract syntax tree representation, given a grammar describing the concrete syntax of a language. Would it be feasible to automate this derivation?

2. The attribute evaluation rules for all the example grammars in Section 14.1 are written to compute attributes for the nodes of complete parse trees. How would the algorithm you proposed in Exercise 1 have to be extended to handle the transformation of evaluation rules to apply to the derived abstract syntax tree? Apply your algorithm to grammars G1 and G3 to verify its correctness.

3. Using the grammar in Figure 14.19, trace the evaluation of attributes for the following program (using the format of Figure 14.20):

```
while not (A = B) and then C < D loop
   OtherS;
   if A /= B then
     if C = D then
        OtherS;
     end if;
   else
     OtherS;
   end if;
   OtherS;
end loop;
```

4. The procedures in Figures 14.25 and 14.26 illustrate the use of an abstract interface to a syntax tree. Write procedures that perform equivalent functions using the direct interface defined by the type **tree_node** in Section 14.2.1.

5. Analytically or empirically determine the magnitude of the space savings available through use of the syntax tree implementation optimizations discussed in Section 14.2.3, such as subtree sharing and trivial node removal.

CHAPTER 15

Code Generation and Local Code Optimization

15.1. **An Overview**

In the compiler model we have developed, the synthesis component is subdivided into distinct translation and code-generation phases. There are many advantages to this approach. Most importantly, the translation phase, incorporated into a compiler's semantic routines, is overwhelmingly source language–dependent, whereas the code-generation phase is target machine–dependent. Maintaining a clean separation is vital if retargetability (to alternate target machines) is to be achieved. And even if retargetability is not an initial concern, after a compiler proves successful a demand often arises to move it to new machines or to new versions of existing machines. Hence a design that provides a clean separation between source language and target machine concerns anticipates future needs.

The simplest code generator is *no* code generator at all! This may seem facetious, but there are circumstances in which it is desirable to have a compiler produce intermediate representation (IR) code rather than actual target code.

A simple compiler might produce a tree-structured IR that can be interpreted by an execution phase. Such a compiler could be designed for use in an educational environment in which programs are frequently modified and recompiled. Execution speed is not important because programs are tested on fairly simple data and need to execute (successfully) only a few times. However, because recompilation is frequent, compiler speed is important, and dispensing with the code-generation phase, and later linking and loading, is a big plus. The tradeoff is faster compilation at the cost of slower execution, and in an educational or debugging environment the net gain can be quite substantial.

Another good example of a compiler that produces IR code rather than target code is the Pascal *P-Compiler*. The P-Compiler is designed to be highly transportable, and it achieved this goal by generating *P-code* for a hypothetical stack machine termed the *virtual stack machine* (VSM). P-code was designed to be simple and compact. The P-Compiler is distributed in both source form (Pascal) and object form (P-code).

To transport the P-Compiler to a new machine, a P-code interpreter is first written. (This is estimated to take about a month.) Once a P-code interpreter is available, the object form of the P-compiler can be executed, and hence Pascal programs can be compiled and executed. Furthermore, because the P-Compiler source is also available, the compiler itself can be modified and recompiled. Often, the next step is implementation of a code generator for P-code, producing a true Pascal compiler for the new machine. An estimated 50 to 75% of all current Pascal compilers are lineal descendants of the original P-Compiler.

The simplest way to translate IR code into target code is to macroexpand each IR tuple or subtree into an equivalent sequence of target machine instructions. The case analysis and selection inherent in choosing target code sequences can be organized in many ways. As illustrated in Section 15.3, a distinct code generator can be written for each tuple or subtree. Other approaches include using a set of mutually recursive template routines written in a special *coding language* (Wilcox 1971) and a table of templates with a template-matching routine (Johnson 1978).

The main liability of a macroexpansion approach is that poor quality code may be produced if each IR instruction is expanded independently. For example, given the tuples (+,A,B,C), (*,C,D,E), a naive code generator would store a value into C and then immediately refetch it in the expansion of the next tuple. To improve code quality, some context information or *state* must be maintained as IR code is expanded, allowing unnecessary or inferior code sequences to be suppressed.

Another problem with viewing code generation as macroexpansion of IR code is that sometimes more than one IR instruction can be replaced by a single target machine instruction. This may occur if a target machine has a rich set of addressing modes, or *exotic* instructions that bundle many operations in a single instruction (for example, a single loop control instruction that increments a register, tests it, and conditionally jumps).

Consider the Pascal statement A := P↑;, which might well be translated into a single instruction if indirect addressing is available. Not all machines support indirect addressing, and so a compiler might generate, at the IR level, an indirect fetch followed by a store. It becomes the responsibility of the code generator to determine if the effect of the two IR instructions can be achieved by a single target machine instruction.

IR code such as tuples or P-code is usually more compact than equivalent target machine code because it is specifically designed to represent compiled source code. Compact code is an asset, but if it must be interpreted, execution can be unacceptably slow. An interesting balance between compact code and fast execution is possible if a *threaded code* approach (Bell 1973) is employed. In threaded code, each IR instruction is replaced with a subroutine call to a support routine that implements the IR instruction (parameters, if any, follow the call). After executing the instruction, an implementation routine uses the return address to select the next IR instruction, which is another subroutine call to an implementation routine. Control is threaded through a sequence of calls to implementation routines that realize the generated IR code. Only one implementation of each IR instruction is needed, and program size is much less than if a macroexpansion approach had been taken. Also, execution is much faster than if the IR code had been interpreted because the only overhead is a call and return (two instructions) for each IR instruction. In fact, threaded code is the basis for Forth (Brodie 1981), an innovative language that has received much attention.

15.2. **Register and Temporary Management**

In Chapter 11, we presented a very abstract approach to temporary allocation. With this approach, temporary allocation involves only assigning a unique index for the temporary and storing elementary size and type information. All the hard work of temporary management is left to the code generator, which has to map temporaries to registers and generate code that uses registers effectively.

Compiler temporaries are locations assigned for a limited time to hold data relevant to the current computation. Temporaries are usually registers, though *storage temporaries,* which reside in memory, may also be necessary. A compiler must carefully manage temporaries to avoid conflict in their use.

Usually the registers available on a particular machine are partitioned into a number of classes: *allocatable registers, reserved registers,* and *volatile registers.*

Allocatable registers are explicitly allocated and freed by compile-time calls to register management routines. While allocated, registers are protected from use by any but the "owner" of the register. Thus it is possible to guarantee that a register containing a data item will not be incorrectly changed by another use of the same register.

Requests for allocatable registers are usually *generic;* that is, requests are for any member of a register class, not for a particular register in that class. Usually any member of a register class will do. Further, generic requests eliminate the problem that arises if a particular requested register is already in use but many other registers in the same class are available.

A register, once allocated, must be freed when its assignment to a particular temporary is completed. A register is usually freed in response to a **free_temp()** directive issued by a semantic routine. A **free_temp()** directive also allows us to mark the last use of a register as *dead.* As we will see, this is valuable information because better code may be possible if the contents of a register need not be preserved.

Reserved and volatile registers, on the other hand, are never explicitly allocated or freed. Reserved registers are assigned a fixed function throughout a program. Examples include display registers, stacktop registers, and registers used to pass information to subroutines.

Volatile registers may be used at any time by any routine. Volatile registers may safely be used only in local code sequences, over which the code generator has complete control. That is, if we were generating code to do an indexing operation on an array [say, $A(I + J)$], it would be wrong to use a volatile register to hold the address of the array element because computation of the subscript might change the volatile register. An allocatable register would, of course, be protected.

Volatile temporaries are useful in several circumstances:

- Sometimes we need a work location for a very brief time. (For example, in compiling $A := B$; we load B into a register and then store the register into A.) Using a volatile temporary saves the overhead of allocating and then immediately freeing a temporary.

- Sometimes registers are built into an instruction. For example, many computers use designated registers to hold pointers and byte counts during multiple-word instructions such as block transfer. These values must be placed in programmer-accessible registers (as opposed to internal "microengine" registers, invisible to the programmer), because such instructions may be interrupted during execution. However, instruction formats may not have enough fields to allow the programmer to specify the registers explicitly. Many computer architects solve this potential problem by reserving certain registers for this purpose. For example, on the VAX, one multiword move instruction modifies registers 0 to 4. If the total number of registers available is small, a compiler may choose to avoid using such instructions in order to keep more registers allocatable, or it may use them only in certain special contexts, perhaps saving and restoring the relevant registers around each use.

A significant aspect of compiler design is deciding how to allocate available registers. Some are reserved for use in the display, to hold the top of the run-time stack or to hold information during calls. Other registers are made allocatable, and others volatile. The decision of how to partition registers is primarily based on the number of available registers (their kind also, if more than one variety exists) and on system conventions. In production compilers, this choice is important and should be made with care.

15.2.1. Classes of Temporaries

As we have seen, temporaries can be grouped into several classes. *Storage temporaries are useful for saving registers or holding large* data objects. Registers may comprise one or more classes, depending on hardware design. (For example, the Univac 1100 has three distinct classes, two of which partially overlap.) We therefore expect a request to a temporary allocation routine to specify the *number* and *kind* of temporary needed.

We must also deal with the possibility that no temporary of a particular class is available. If this situation occurs, we may, as one alternative, simply terminate compilation or code generation as a simple but extreme response. This response may be fine if the probability of exhausting a temporary class is very small. A more robust allocation routine, however, may substitute a temporary of another class rather than signal failure. Most often this occurs when a storage temporary is returned in response to a request for a register. Such a temporary can be used as a *pseudoregister.* A code generator, seeing a reference to a pseudoregister, loads it into a volatile register, generates the instruction using the volatile register, and then saves the volatile register back into the pseudoregister. The quality of code generated for pseudoregisters may be poor, but this alternative is much better than just giving up.

Reassigning a temporary from a real register to a pseudoregister is called *spilling.* Determining which temporary to spill is a difficult problem that will be discussed in Section 15.4.3. Intuitively, we wish to spill the least important temporary, and often a least recently referenced criterion is used. Calls to **free_temp()** at the semantic routine level greatly simplify the problem of register spilling, as unneeded temporaries are explicitly identified. Without such identification, inactive temporaries will eventually be spilled, at the cost of transferring their values (unnecessarily) to pseudoregisters.

In practice, storage temporaries are effectively unlimited in number, but careful allocation is required. In particular

- Storage temporaries must be allocated in the local activation record and not in a global area. Otherwise recursive procedures may fail.

- When needed, space is created in the local activation record by extending, at compile-time, the size of the activation record. In effect, implicit declarations are generated for storage temporaries.

15.2.2. Allocating and Freeing Temporaries

To allocate temporaries, we usually keep a pool or set of available temporaries. Available registers can be maintained in a set (in C, a bitmap); storage temporaries can be kept in a list that indicates their size and their offset in the activation record. Temporary allocation and deallocation often follows a first-allocated, last-freed (LIFO or stack) discipline. In other words, R_i is allocated only when $R_1, R_2, \ldots, R_{i-1}$ are in use. However, this stack-like discipline may be violated in some cases, particularly if optimization is done. Because a more general allocation technique in which a set of temporaries is used is quite easy to program, this is the recommended technique.

During code generation, a register temporary may be in one of three states: *unallocated, live,* or *dead.* An unallocated register temporary is one that has not yet been assigned to an actual register. Register assignment is often delayed until code involving the temporary must be generated. This delay allows the context in which the register is referenced to influence assignment. (For example, an index register or odd-numbered register may be needed to generate a particular instruction.)

A live register temporary is one that has already been allocated to a register and whose value must be protected. Similarly, a dead register temporary is one that has been allocated but whose value is no longer needed.

15.3. A Simple Code Generator

We now consider the design of a simple code generator, using tuples as the IR. A code generator for each tuple is provided, modularizing the overall code-generation task. Each tuple generator is responsible for generating the best possible target code for its associated IR tuple. In doing so, it must perform three subtasks:

- Instruction selection

- Address-mode selection

- Register allocation

These three tasks are tightly intertwined. Target machine instructions often allow only a subset of the available addressing modes. For example, many machines allow register-to-register or memory-to-register adds, but not memory-to-memory adds. This limitation means that the address mode used to access an operand affects the choice of instructions that may be selected to implement a tuple. Similarly, many instructions require a register; sometimes a particular class is stipulated (for example, an index register or an odd-even pair). How registers are assigned to temporaries strongly influences the kind of instructions that can be generated.

Tuple generators are organized as follows. Addressing modes are those associated with operands in the semantic records for data objects (literal, indexed, indirect, temporary). Each tuple operand includes this information, which we map to hardware addressing modes. In effect, the generator implements a decision table, indexed by the combination of addressing modes associated with tuple operands. The tuple generator interacts with the register allocator, binding temporaries to actual registers.

To illustrate the complexities that can arise, assume we have a machine with register, indexed, and immediate addressing modes. A register operand is represented as r. An indexed address is represented as d(r), in which d is an unsigned offset and r is an index register. An immediate address is represented as #s, in which s is a signed value. We outline a tuple-based generator for +, assuming we have register-to-register, storage-to-register, and literal-to-register addition. That is, the contents of a register or a storage location or a literal value (the *source*) can be added to a register (the *destination*), with the sum stored in the destination (always a register). Register load and store instructions are also assumed.

The generator for + takes three operand descriptors and produces the appropriate code sequence. The two addends can be in any of five address modes (literal, indexed, indirect, live register, dead register), and the result can be in any of four modes (indexed, indirect, live register, unassigned register). This means that 100 different combinations can be expected, and almost all require different code sequences if high-quality code is to be produced.

Exhaustive enumeration of all cases is tedious, error prone, and certainly would not be space-efficient. Figure 15.1 illustrates a more common approach that builds an appropriate code sequence, depending on the states of the operands. This approach illustrates how instruction selection, register allocation, and address mode selection are interrelated, even when generating code for something as simple as an add tuple.

Generate code for integer add: (+,A,B,C)

Possible operand modes for A and B are:
  (1) Literal (stored in value field)
  (2) Indexed (stored in adr field as (Reg,Displacement) pair)
  (3) Indirect (stored in adr field as (Reg,Displacement) pair)
  (4) Live register (stored in Reg field)
  (5) Dead register (stored in Reg field)

Possible operand modes for C are:
  (1) Indexed (stored in adr field as (Reg,Displacement) pair)
  (2) Indirect (stored in adr field as (Reg,Displacement) pair)
  (3) Live register (stored in Reg field)
  (4) Unassigned register (stored in Reg field, when assigned)

(a) Swap operands (knowing addition is commutative)

```
if (B.mode == DEAD_REGISTER || A.mode == LITERAL)
     Swap A and B;   /* This may save a load or store
                         since addition overwrites the
                         first operand. */
```

(b) "Target" the result of the addition directly into C (if possible).

```
switch (C.mode) {
case LIVE_REGISTER: Target = C.reg; break;

case UNASSIGNED_REGISTER:
     if (A.mode == DEAD_REGISTER)
          C.reg = A.reg; /* Compute into A's reg,
                             then assign it to C. */
     else
          Assign a register to C.reg;
     C.mode = LIVE_REGISTER;
     Target = C.reg;
     break;

case INDIRECT:
case INDEXED:
     if (A.mode == DEAD_REGISTER)
          Target = A.reg;
     else
          Target = v2;
          /* vi is the i-th volatile register. */
     break;
}
```

(c) Map operand B to right operand of add instruction (the "Source")

```
if (B.mode == INDIRECT) {
     /* Use indexing to simulate indirection. */
     generate(LOAD,B.adr,v1,"");
     /* v1 is a volatile register. */
     B.mode = INDEXED;
     B.adr = (address) { .reg = v1;
                         .displacement = 0; };
}
Source = B;
```

(d) Now generate the add instruction

```
if (A.mode == LITERAL && B.mode == LITERAL)
     /* "Fold" the addition. */
     generate(LOAD,#(A.val+B.val),Target,"");
```

```
        else {
           address t;
           /* Load operand A (if necessary). */
           switch (A.mode) {
           case LITERAL:   generate(LOAD,#A.val,Target,"");
                           break;
           case INDEXED:   generate(LOAD,A.adr,Target,"");
                           break;
           case LIVE_REGISTER:
                           generate(LOAD,A.reg,Target,"");
                           break;
           case INDIRECT:  generate(LOAD,A.adr,v2,"");
                           t.reg = v2; t.displacement = 0;
                           generate(LOAD,t,Target,"");
                           break;
           case DEAD_REGISTER:
                           if (Target != A.reg)
                               generate(LOAD,A.reg,Target,"");
                           break;
           }
           generate(ADD,Source,Target,"");
        }
```

(e) Store result into C (if necessary)

```
    if (C.mode == INDEXED)
        generate(STORE,C.adr,Target,"");
    else if (C.mode == INDIRECT) {
        generate(LOAD,C.adr,v3,"");
        t.reg = v3; t.displacement = 0;
        generate(STORE,t,Target,"");
    }
```

Figure 15.1   A Code Generator for the + Tuple

This routine examines operand modes carefully, and generates high-quality code. For example, given (+,T1,10,G), in which T1 is a dead temporary assigned to register r1, and G is an ordinary variable addressed as (base,offset), we would obtain

    Add #10,r1
    Store offset(base),r1

Even though our code generator is rather thorough in examining cases, still more cases might be included. For example, the case that A or B (or both) are the literal 0 isn't specially handled, nor is the case that the same operand appears more than once in a tuple. These extensions could easily be included (see Exercise 3 at the end of the chapter) at the expense of a still more detailed case analysis. To prevent unpleasant surprises, it is wise to drive a tuple generator through all possible cases, examining the code produced for correctness and optimality.

The biggest advantage of organizing code generation as a number of tuple generators is the modularization that is obtained. It is easy to isolate the routine responsible for any tuple, and hence debugging or code improvement is straightforward though often tedious. A significant drawback is that code-generation decisions and the description of machine properties are intermixed. For example, a tuple generator for subtraction should be similar to that used for addition, but it will not be identical because subtraction is not commutative. A cleaner separation of machine properties from code-generation details is desirable.

Another problem with generating code on a tuple-by-tuple basis is that no *state* is retained across tuples. Thus expressions may be needlessly recomputed, redundant register loads and stores may occur, and addressing modes may not be fully exploited. We shall therefore next examine ways of *tracking* information as code is generated. This approach is called *interpretive* because we interpret tuples, sometimes generating code and sometimes just remembering what the code *would have done,* hoping to find more-efficient ways of producing the desired computations.

15.4. Interpretive Code Generation

Interpretive code generators view an IR as code for a virtual machine that is to be expanded into real target code. If the IR is standardized, it is possible to create compilers for P programming languages on M target machines by using P front ends and M code generators. This approach was introduced in *UNCOL* (Universal Compiler-oriented Language), a proposed universal IR (Steel 1961). UNCOL was perhaps ahead of its time and proved unsuccessful. More recently, P-code and U-code (Perkins and Sites 1979) have been suggested as IRs suitable for interpretive code generation.

Code generation is typically macro-like, although some notion of state, as found in an interpreter, is needed to produce good code quality. *U-code* represents a significant improvement upon P-code (which is usually macroexpanded) because it supports an interpretive code-generation model.

When a U-code interpreter reads a U-code instruction, it updates its state, like an ordinary CPU, and as a side effect may generate target code. To retarget a U-code compiler to a new machine, we redefine the target code sequences associated with changes in the U-code interpreter's internal state. Target code is associated not with U-code instructions but rather with changes to the U-code interpreter's internal state, which means that significant improvements in target code quality can be realized.

The code we generate must be correct over any execution path, so we limit our code generator's analysis to simple straight-line flow paths through tuples. That is, we limit our attention to *basic blocks*, which are linear sequences of tuples that contain no branches except at the very end. A basic block begins execution at its top, executes all instructions in sequence, then ends with a conditional or unconditional branch. No branches into the middle of a basic block are allowed. Every program can be represented as a series of basic blocks, linked together by branch instructions.

Optimizations within a basic block are called *local optimizations* because they are determined by the local properties of a basic block and not by other basic blocks or flow-of-control considerations. Within a basic block, we seek to recognize and eliminate redundant computations and to optimize address computations. Redundant computations may involve recomputation of an expression already computed or may involve use of registers to hold active values so that loads and stores can be reduced.

15.4.1. Optimizing Address Calculation

Address calculations are common in generated code and, if handled naively, are often inefficiently computed. It is necessary to recognize calculations that build addresses and to map them to any special address modes and instructions provided by the target machine. The basic idea is to anticipate common hardware address modes and to delay generating code to build an address until absolutely necessary. For example, we know that an indexed address mode (register plus offset) is normally available, so we represent addresses as a (variable plus constant) pair.

We may anticipate other address modes, such as indirect (or deferred) addressing, and we can often delay generating address code by converting one address mode to another. Expressions involving pointers or reference parameters often can be translated by simply transforming a direct address into an indirect address. For example, given the Pascal statement A := P↑ + 1 we might generate

```
(Fetch Indirect,P,T)
(Add,T,1,A)
```

Anticipating an indirect addressing mode, this pair of tuples could be improved by delaying explicit calculation of T, representing it rather as the address mode (P,indirect). (If indirect addressing isn't available, the indirection can be simulated, as it was in the example of Section 15.3.)

As we saw in Chapter 11, array references are translated very carefully to eliminate unnecessary calculations. Thus a reference to A(I) may well require no more than the addition of I to A's constant part (which is A's start address biased by the array's lower bound). Often, however, a reference to A(I−1) generates more code than a reference to A(I) does. This is clearly suboptimal, as the subtraction of 1 can be folded into A's constant part. The problem is that the routine that translates the subscript expression may not know that it is part of an address calculation rather than an ordinary calculation. It is therefore necessary to provide context information to semantic routines for expressions, indicating whether an address or ordinary value is being computed. Addresses can be represented as the familiar (variable,constant) pair, for we know that eventually hardware addressing modes will provide a "free" addition of the pair. Thus in translating A(I−1), we represent I−1 as the pair (I,−1) and A as the pair (base_reg,constant_part). This representation reduces the code needed to that for the addition of I and the base register, possibly with I scaled to reflect the size of the array component. That is, to compute the address of A(I−1) we would generate

```
Load    I,reg1
Mult    #element_size,reg1    −− Omit if element_size = 1
Add     base_reg,reg1         −− Usually a Display register
```

The address of A(I−1) is (reg1,constant_part−1×element_size).

Machines such as the IBM 360/370 series allow array references to be optimized further by providing an address mode that forms an address by adding a constant offset to the sum of two registers, one a *base* register for the array and the other an *index* register for the subscript. To exploit this address mode, addresses must be represented as a triple (Base,Index,Offset), with addition of the three components delayed until addresses are formed. [This double register mode isn't available in all instructions, so sometimes an explicit addition to form an ordinary (Base,Offset) pair is required.]

The VAX architecture provides an even more elaborate address mode termed *indexed displacement,* in which the type (byte, word, or long) of the accessed object is included. Addresses are again a triple (Base,Index,Offset), but here the index is automatically multiplied by an object size of 1, 2, or 4 before the scaled index is added to the base and offset components. Now two additions *and* a multiplication can be hidden in address calculation if the code generator defers premature address calculation. In fact, a general pattern emerges. Hardware address modes are nonuniform and often elaborate, so it is useful to defer, or buffer, *all* address calculations. When an object must finally be accessed, an "address expert" is called that is specially designed to exploit available address modes. The expert determines what address modes are feasible and how to best establish an access path to the desired object. It works hard to optimize data access, knowing that many special cases can be fruitfully exploited.

On some machines (such as the MC 68000) address and operand registers are distinct. For such machines, the result of an address calculation must be *targeted* to an address register. That is, although calculations may utilize operand registers, the final step of an address calculation should leave its result in an address register where it can be immediately utilized.

Instruction selection is complicated by the fact that address modes are not provided uniformly in instructions. For example, many machines require that at least one operand of an instruction be a register. If neither operand is currently in a register, a load will probably be required. Before an instruction is generated, the *cost* of matching operands to available address modes can be computed. If an operation is commutative, as addition is, a careful code generator will consider both operand orders, often finding that one leads to distinctly better code.

Instruction selection for the VAX is complicated by the fact that both two- and three-operand forms are available. The inclusion of three-operand instructions often improves code quality, obviating the need for extra loads and stores. Unfortunately, however, not all instructions provide both two- and three-operand forms, and this can lead to difficult choices. For example, multiplication by powers of 2 is often implemented by shift instructions. Multiplication comes in both two- and three-operand forms, but arithmetic shift has only a three-operand form. It may therefore become necessary to choose between a smaller, but slower, multiplication and a larger, but faster, shift instruction.

Architectures sometimes include autoincrement and autodecrement address modes, which allow an index to be stepped up or down while it is being used to address an operand. Autoincrement and autodecrement are often difficult to exploit in generated code unless they are directly represented in the source language (as they are in C). One problem is that they are not symmetric—autoincrement increases the index *after* it is used, whereas autodecrement decreases the index *before* it is used. Normally, source code steps through an array in increasing order, which means that the tuple to increase an index appears after the index is used to access an array element. It is therefore necessary to search forward in a basic block, looking for an addition that can be precomputed as an autoincrement. A further problem is that autoincrements and autodecrements are often performed in units of 2 or 4, reflecting the fact that a word is two or four bytes long. Unless we employ an optimization called *strength reduction* (see Chapter 16), which replaces multiplication with repeated addition, the fact that an index is incremented by 1, then multiplied by a word size of 2 or 4, will probably mask the possibility of exploiting autoincrement at all.

Autoincrement and autodecrement are useful in accessing stacks, and we often increment the stacktop and then store a value, or we copy a value and then decrement the stacktop. To allow stacktop manipulation to be performed via autoincrements and autodecrements, it is necessary to organize a stack so that it appears to grow backward. That is, the stack must start at a high address and grow toward lower addresses. This allows a push to be implemented using autodecrement and a pop to be implemented using autoincrement.

A final problem in address mode selection involves the branch instructions that link basic blocks. Architectures such as the PDP-11 and VAX provide both *long* and *short* form branches. Short form branches store a signed *relative offset* in a byte or word, but a long form builds an absolute (nonrelative) address. Naturally a short form branch is preferred, as it requires less space. The optimal choice of short or long form branches has been studied (Szymanski 1978) and found to be surprisingly difficult. The problem is that the choice of a long or short form for one branch can affect the span of other branches. To obtain optimal code, an indefinite number of passes over the generated code (setting long or short form branches) may be needed.

Usually, however, heuristics that provide *near optimal* branch form selection are used. Assume that basic blocks are not reordered by the code generator (though they may be by a separate optimization phase). We first generate code for the basic blocks, leaving the form of branch instructions unresolved. This allows us to estimate the distance between a branch and its target, assuming all branches are long form. We then use this estimate to make an initial determination of long or short form and update our estimates of spans between branches and their targets. As an alternative, we can reprocess any long branches that can be converted to short form, using our updated span information. (This process of reconsideration could be repeated, but normally at most one fix-up pass is needed.)

15.4.2. Avoiding Redundant Computations

Within basic blocks it is often possible to determine that a particular computation is redundant. A value that need not be recomputed is termed a *common subexpression* (CSE).

To recognize CSEs in a basic block, we must be able to determine whether a particular expression has already been computed, and, if it has, whether its value has been *killed*. A value is considered killed if recomputing it would yield a different value. Assignment to operands of an expression kills previously computed values of that expression.

Whenever our code generator is asked to compute an expression, we look for a previous computation of the value, in the same basic block, that is still alive. If we find one, we suppress code generation and instead reuse the already computed value.

Assume we use tuples as our IR. Normally, as an expression is computed at the IR level, it is assigned a new and unique temporary. We now require that temporary names be chosen to correspond uniquely with a particular operator–operand combination. That is, given the tuples (OP1,A1,B1,T1) and (OP2,A2,B2,T2) if (OP1=OP2) and (A1=A2) and (B1=B2), then T1 = T2.

This convention makes finding possible CSEs easy because they must have the same result temporary. It also guarantees that all CSEs discovered will share a common temporary. A simple hashing scheme can determine the appropriate result temporary as tuples are generated.

Redundant computations are those for which the value of a temporary T just before its recalculation is, of necessity, the same as after the calculation. How do we decide that this is the case? Our approach is based on the idea of *value numbering*, which was first proposed by Cocke and Schwartz (1970). Consider first the case in which aliasing through array elements, reference parameters, pointers, and so forth is ignored. (Complications induced by aliasing are discussed later in the section.)

For each distinct program variable and temporary in a basic block, keep an integer value **last_def** that points to the most recent tuple in the basic block that assigned a value to the variable or temporary. Initially, **last_def** values are set to 0. In the case where T contains an address, we maintain two values: one for the address and one for the object referenced by the address. Naturally, changing the address stored in a temporary also changes the value referenced through the address.

We assume, as we process a basic block, that all tuples generated and all CSEs optimized are correct. Thus—*ignoring aliasing*—if the condition

```
last_def[A] < last_def[T] && last_def[B] < last_def[T]
```

holds, then a calculation of (OP,A,B,T) must be redundant, as neither A nor B has been changed since the last calculation of T. In this case, (OP,A,B,T) is a CSE and can be eliminated; the value in T is still correct. Of course, if either A or B has had anything assigned to it since T was last calculated, the computation of T is not redundant.

After CSE values are recognized, we must make sure that temporaries holding such values are marked dead only after they are used for the final time in a basic block. This precaution guarantees that needed values will be preserved, usually in a register temporary.

Consider the following example, in which T↑ denotes the value referenced indirectly through an address stored in T. We will remove CSEs from the tuples generated for the statements shown in Figure 15.2.

$$
\begin{aligned}
A(I,J) \quad &:= A(I,J) + B + C; \\
A(I,J+1) &:= A(I,J) + B + D; \\
A(I,J) \quad &:= A(I,J) + B;
\end{aligned}
$$

Figure 15.2   A Simple Basic Block

Figure 15.3 shows the tuples generated for the statements of Figure 15.2. A suffix of R denotes a redundant tuple that may be deleted. Note that the table shows values of **last_def** that *change* at a given tuple. The notation Ti_a denotes an address stored in Ti, and Ti_v denotes the value referenced through the address stored in Ti. Entries marked with a † show changes if aliasing through array A is considered.

Aliasing

The processing just described is fairly easy to do as tuples are generated for a basic block. However, we must keep in mind that aliasing is a problem. Consider first aliasing of array elements. Assignment to one subscripted variable may mean a change to another subscripted variable if both reference the same array component [for example, A(I) can alias A(J) if I = J].

How can we deal with this? One simple way is to keep a list of all temporaries that address an element of a given array (for example, T1, T2, and T6 for array A in the example). Now an assignment to an array component through any such temporary changes (that is, assigns to) the value part of **last_def** for all such temporaries. Thus, in the preceding examples, assignments to elements accessed through T1, T2, or T6 update all three value parts, as denoted by the † suffix. As a result, when this more careful algorithm is employed, tuple 20 no longer appears redundant. This change occurs because

			I	J	B	C	D	$T1_a$	$T1_v$	$T2_a$	$T2_v$	T3	T4	T5	$T6_a$	$T6_v$	T7
(1)	(Index,A,I,T1)		0	0	0	0	0	1	1	0	0	0	0	0	0	0	0
(2)	(Index,T1,J,T2)									2	2						
(3)	(Index,A,I,T1)	R															
(4)	(Index,T1,J,T2)	R															
(5)	(+,T2↑,B,T3)											5					
(6)	(+,T3,C,T4)												6				
(7)	(:=,T4,T2↑)								7†		7					7†	
(8)	(Index,A,I,T1)	R															
(9)	(+,J,1,T5)													9			
(10)	(Index,T1,T5,T6)														10	10	
(11)	(Index,A,I,T1)	R															
(12)	(Index,T1,J,T2)	R															
(13)	(+,T2↑,B,T3)											13					
(14)	(+,T3,D,T7)																14
(15)	(:=,T7,T6↑)								15†		15†					15	
(16)	(Index,A,I,T1)	R															
(17)	(Index,T1,J,T2)	R															
(18)	(Index,A,I,T1)	R															
(19)	(Index,T1,J,T2)	R															
(20)	(+,T2↑,B,T3)	R†										13					
(21)	(:=,T3,T2↑)								21†		21					21†	

Figure 15.3   Tuples and Value Numberings Generated for Statements of Figure 15.2

the assignment of a value through T6 (in tuple 15) to A(I,J+1) kills the value referenced through T2 (A(I,J)). Of course, in the strictest sense this action is not really needed because A(I,J) and A(I,J+1) cannot reference the same location. However, the extra complexity needed to recognize this fairly deep law (J ≠ J+1 for any value of J) is far beyond the sort of analysis used here.

Aliasing problems also arise if we assign a value to a formal reference parameter or to an object referenced through a pointer. We must somehow kill all CSEs that are potentially invalidated. The most accurate thing to do is to kill only those CSEs involving a formal parameter *or* variables that might actually be bound to that formal parameter. Similarly for pointers we might kill only those CSEs involving the pointer in question *or* other pointers that might reference the same object. Care is required to ensure that all access paths to the object in question are accounted for.

The problem of determining the set of variables that can be aliased by a formal parameter is discussed in Section 16.2.3. A similar technique can be used to determine the set of pointers that can access the same heap object. In a one-pass compiler, exact determination of potential aliases is impractical. To simplify, all CSEs involving variables or pointers to heap objects of the appropriate type are killed. This is much simpler than the analyses just mentioned and does guarantee that CSE optimizations are safe, although of course some optimizations will be missed.

Procedure and function calls are allowed within a basic block and are treated as a single composite operation, as if their bodies had been expanded at the point of call. Of course, we must account for the side effects of a call. Normally we simply assume that all CSEs are killed. In an optimizing compiler, we can do an *interprocedural* analysis to see what variables might be changed and hence what CSEs might be killed. This analysis is discussed in detail in Section 16.2.3.

15.4.3. Register Tracking

The code generators we have described so far have not used registers very effectively. In particular, little information regarding the contents of registers is maintained. As a result, values may be unnecessarily loaded into registers or stored into memory. Further, we have assumed that our register allocator simply binds a register to a temporary until that temporary is freed. This approach proves too simplistic when registers must be spilled (that is, when the demand for registers exceeds their supply).

We shall improve upon the simple code generator of Section 15.3 by utilizing a simple local register allocation scheme in which we track the contents of allocatable registers within basic blocks. This scheme allows us to allocate registers to frequently accessed variables and temporaries, an approach that has the effect of reducing the number of register loads and stores needed. It also tends to replace storage-to-register–type instructions with register-to-register–type instructions, which are smaller and faster. Both size and speed improvements are realized.

The scheme is designed to be easy and efficient to use. It is *not optimal*, although more expensive algorithms for basic blocks that yield optimal solutions are known (Horwitz et al. 1966). As in the last section, we initially ignore the effects of aliasing and subprogram calls.

We generate code from tuples for assignment and binary operators, either commutative or noncommutative. Our machine, the BB1 (bare-bones 1), has $n \geq 2$ registers available for allocation. It includes the following kinds of machine instructions:

(a)	Load Storage,Reg	-- Cost = 2
(b)	Store Storage,Reg	-- Cost = 2
(c)	OP Storage,Reg	-- Reg := Reg OP Storage; Cost = 2
(d)	OP Reg1,Reg2	-- Reg2 := Reg2 OP Reg1; Cost = 1

Forms (a) to (c) are storage-to-register and cost 2 units each to generate. Form (d) is register-to-register and costs 1 unit to generate. Storage addresses may be direct or indexed (register plus offset).

For each operand register, we maintain a list of the variables and temporaries it contains, if any. Call this the *register association list*. Each variable or temporary associated with a register has two status flags:

(1)   L (live) or D (dead)

(2)   S (to be saved) or NS (not to be saved)

A variable or temporary that is live will be referenced again in this basic block *before* its value is changed (that is, it is valuable to keep the value of a live variable or temporary in a register). A variable should always be saved at the end of a basic block if it is not already stored in memory (that is, it is saved if it has a flag of S). Temporaries normally *are not* saved after they become dead.

Live status is normally determined by a *backward* pass through a basic block. (That is, we must buffer the block, do the backward pass, then do a forward pass to allocate registers and generate code.) Further, if the next reference to a variable or temporary is the assignment of a new value, then its status is (D,NS) because it won't be used before redefinition, and there is no need ever to save this value in memory for a new value will be computed. With each register we associate a *cost* of freeing it (that is, a cost of losing its current contents). This cost is defined as the sum of the individual costs of freeing all variables and temporaries associated with the register. The cost of freeing an individual variable or temporary from a given register is defined as

0   If its status is (D,NS) or (D,S)
    [For a status of (D,S), the variable or temporary won't be used again, and it must be saved, so there is no disadvantage or cost in freeing the register and doing the save immediately.]

2   If its status is (L,NS)
    (A load is needed to restore the variable or temporary to a register.)

4   If its status is (L,S)
    (A store is needed to save the value, then a load is needed to restore the value to a register.)

A register that has no associations costs zero to allocate. To allocate a register, we call a routine **get_reg()** defined in Figure 15.4, which allocates the *cheapest* available register. The return type **machine_reg** is simply a small integer between zero and the number of machine registers minus one.

get_reg() chooses the cheapest possible register, with the added proviso that if more than one register with the same nonzero cost exists, it chooses that register whose associated variables and temporaries have the *most distant* next reference. The idea here is that the closer the next use of a value in a register is, the more reasonable it is to retain that register. Conversely, if the next use of the value in a register is distant, then that register can

```
machine_reg get_reg(void)
{
  /*
   * Any register already allocated to the current tuple
   * is NOT AVAILABLE for allocation during this call.
   */

  if (there exists some register R with cost(R) == 0)
      Choose R
  else {
     C = 2;
     while (TRUE) {
        if (there exists at least one register
            with cost == C) {
            Choose that register, R, with cost C that
                has the most distant next reference to an
                associated variable or temporary
            break;
        }
        C += 2;
     }

     Save the value of R for any associated variables or
        temporaries with a status == (L,S) or (D,S)
  }
  return R;
}
```

Figure 15.4   A Cost-based Register Allocator

be freed without immediate impact (keeping the value in that register is a "long shot"). Note also that next-use information can be determined during the same backward pass used to determine live or dead status.

Let **get_reg_cost()** be a function that determines the minimum cost of getting a register (that is, the cost of freeing the register that **get_reg()**, if called, would choose). Once **get_reg()** allocates a register, we generate code to load it with the desired variable or temporary. The register then has its past associations cleared, and its current status is set to (L,NS) or (D,NS), depending on whether the variable or temporary is live *after* the current tuple is processed.

We use the code-generation routines that are defined in Figures 15.5 and 15.6.

Assignment (:=,X,Y):

```
if (X is not already in a register)
    Call get_reg() and generate a load of X

if (Y, after this tuple, has a status of (D,S) )
    generate(STORE,Y,Reg,"")
else
    Append Y to Reg's association list with a status
        of (L,S)
    /* The generation of the STORE instruction
       has been postponed */
```

(OP,U,V,W) where OP is noncommutative:

```
if (U is not in some register, R1)
    Call get_reg() and generate code to load U
else  /* R1's current value will be destroyed */
    Generate any necessary saves of R1's value
    as indicated by the S/NS flag on R1's
    association list

if (V is in a register, R2)
    /* including the possibility that U == V */
    generate(OP,R2,R1,"")
else if (get_reg_cost() > 0 || V is dead after this tuple)
    generate(OP,V,R1,"")
else {
    /*
     * Invest 1 unit of cost so that V is
     * in a register for later use
     */
    R2 = get_reg()
    generate(Load,V,R2,"")
    generate(OP,R2,R1,"")
}
```

Update R1's association list to include W *only*.

Figure 15.5   Code Generators for Assignment and Noncommutative Binary Operators

We can compute the *cost* of the code generated for (OP,U,V,W) if the algorithm of Figure 15.5 is used. It is

```
cost = (U is in a register ? 0
          : get_reg_cost() + 2) /* Cost to load U into R1 */
       + cost(R1)                /* Cost of losing U */
       + (V is in a register || U == V
          ? 1 : 2)        /* Cost of register-to-register */
                          /* vs. storage-to-register */
```

We can use this cost measure to decide which order to use for commutative operators, as shown in Figure 15.6.

As an example, consider the basic block shown in Figure 15.7. The corresponding tuples are shown in Figure 15.8.

```
(OP,U,V,W) where OP is commutative:

if (cost((OP,U,V,W)) <= cost((OP,V,U,W)))
        generate(OP,U,V,W);
        /* using noncommutative code generator */
else
        generate(OP,V,U,W);
        /* using noncommutative code generator */
```

Figure 15.6   Code Generator for Commutative Binary Operators

```
A    := B * C + D * E;
D    := C + (D − B);
F    := E + A + C;
A    := D + E;
```

Figure 15.7   A Simple Basic Block

(1)	(∗,B,C,T1)	(8)	(+,E,A,T6)
(2)	(∗,D,E,T2)	(9)	(+,T6,C,T7)
(3)	(+,T1,T2,T3)	(10)	(:=,T7,F)
(4)	(:=,T3,A)		
		(11)	(+,D,E,T8)
(5)	(−,D,B,T4)	(12)	(:=,T8,A)
(6)	(+,C,T4,T5)		
(7)	(:=,T5,D)		

Figure 15.8   Tuples Corresponding to Basic Block of Figure 15.7

Assuming four registers and a straightforward code generator that doesn't monitor register contents, we might generate the code shown in Figure 15.9 for the tuples of Figure 15.8.

This code sequence takes six loads, four stores, six storage-to-register operations, and two register-to-register operations. The total cost of the sequence generated is 34.

Code generation using register tracking is illustrated in Figure 15.10. (The symbol ⇐ marks the operand sequence chosen for commutative operators.) The register-tracking approach generates five loads, three stores, one storage-to-register operation, and seven register-to-register operations. The total cost of the sequence generated is 25 rather than 34—a significant improvement.

Effects of Aliasing and Subprogram Calls

When tracking the contents of registers in a basic block, it is necessary to include the effects of aliasing and subprogram calls.

First consider aliasing effects. Let N be a name that can alias data objects. It may be a formal reference parameter, a pointer, or an indexed variable with a nonconstant subscript. For N we compute a set O of data objects that it may alias. O may be computed very carefully using the techniques of Section 16.2.3, or it may simply be the set of all variables, heap objects, or array elements that might ever correspond to N (for example, all variables of the correct type, or all elements in a given array).

Whenever a reference to the value of N is made, we must examine the register association list. If any data object o ∈ O appears in the register association list with a status of S, the corresponding register must be saved into o. This procedure guarantees that N will reference the proper value, should N actually alias o.

(1)	(Load	B,R1)	(12)	(Load	E,R1)
(2)	(*	C,R1)	(13)	(+	A,R1)
(3)	(Load	D,R2)	(14)	(+	C,R1)
(4)	(*	E,R2)	(15)	(Store	F,R1)
(5)	(+	R2,R1)			
(6)	(Store	A,R1)	(16)	(Load	D,R1)
			(17)	(+	E,R1)
(7)	(Load	D,R1)	(18)	(Store	A,R1)
(8)	(–	B,R1)			
(9)	(Load	C,R2)			
(10)	(+	R1,R2)			
(11)	(Store	D,R2)			

Figure 15.9   Code Generated without Register Tracking

Tuple/Code generated	Register Associations			
	R1	R2	R3	R4

(∗,B,C,T1)
    Cost(∗,B,C,T1) = 2+2+2 ⇐
    Cost(∗,C,B,T1) = 2+2+2
 	
(Load B,R1)
(Load C,R2)
(∗ R2,R1)
	
	B(L,NS)
	B(L,NS)
	T1(L,S)
		
		C(L,NS)
		C(L,NS)		

(∗,D,E,T2)
    Cost(∗,D,E,T2) = 2+2+2 ⇐
    Cost(∗,E,D,T2) = 2+2+2
 	
(Load D,R3)
(Load E,R4)
(∗ R4,R3)
	
	T1(L,S)
	T1(L,S)
	T1(L,S)
		
		C(L,NS)
		C(L,NS)
		C(L,NS)
			
			D(L,NS)
			D(L,NS)
			T2(L,S)
				
				E(L,NS)
				E(L,NS)

(+,T1,T2,T3)
    Cost(+,T1,T2,T3) = 0+0+1 ⇐
    Cost(+,T2,T1,T3) = 0+0+1
 	
(+ R3,R1)
–– (D,NS) associations
–– can be immediately removed
	
	T3(L,S)
		
		C(L,NS)
			
			T2(D,NS)
				
				E(L,NS)

(:=,T3,A) –– The store is deferred	A(L,S)	C(L,NS)		E(L,NS)
(–,D,B,T4) (Load D,R3) (– B,R3) –– B is not live after this tuple	 A(L,S) A(L,S)	 C(L,NS) C(L,NS)	 D(D,NS) T4(L,S)	 E(L,NS) E(L,NS)

(+,C,T4,T5)
    Cost(+,C,T4,T5) = 0+2+1
    Cost(+,T4,C,T5) = 0+0+1 ⇐
 	
(+ R2,R3)
	
	A(L,S)
		
		C(L,NS)
			
			T5(L,S)
				
				E(L,NS)

(:=,T5,D) –– Store is deferred	A(L,S)	C(L,NS)	D(L,S)	E(L,NS)

(+,E,A,T6)
    Cost(+,E,A,T6) = 0+2+1
    Cost(+,A,E,T6) = 0+0+1 ⇐
    –– A is dead after this
 	
(+ R4,R1)
	
	T6(L,S)
		
		C(L,NS)
			
			D(L,S)
				
				E(L,NS)

Tuple/Code generated	Register Associations			
	R1	R2	R3	R4

(+,T6,C,T7)
  Cost(+,T6,C,T7) = 0+0+1 ⇐
  Cost(+,C,T6,T7) = 0+0+1
 	
(+ R2,R1)
	T7(L,S)	C(D,NS)	D(L,S)	E(L,NS)

(:=,T7,F)
(Store F,R1)
  -- Do store since F is not
  -- live in this block
	T7(D,NS)		D(L,S)	E(L,NS)

(+,D,E,T8)
  Cost(+,D,E,T8) = 0+0+1 ⇐
  Cost(+,E,D,T8) = 0+0+1
 	
(Store D,R3)
  -- Store is unavoidable
(+ R4,R3)
			D(L,NS)
			
			T8(L,S)
				E(L,NS)
				
				E(D,NS)

(:=,T8,A) (Store A,R3) -- Store is unavoidable				

Figure 15.10   Code Generated with Register Tracking

Similarly, should an assignment to N be made, we must again examine the register association list. If any data object o ∈ O appears in the register association list, it must be removed. This removal reflects the fact that the assignment to N may have changed the value of o, invalidating the value currently held in the register associated with o.

As discussed in Chapter 13, allocatable registers are normally saved and restored across subprogram calls, either by the caller or callee. (Ways of avoiding unnecessary register saves are discussed in Section 16.2.2.)

If the caller does the saving and restoring, it is profitable to clear all register associations before the call. That is, registers with a status of S are saved, and all registers are freed. Upon return, those register values that are needed can be incrementally reloaded. At worst, we save a register and later reload it. We may, however, do better because registers with a status of NS need not be saved, and registers are reloaded only when actually needed.

If the callee saves and restores registers, we examine two sets, Def and Use, when a subprogram is called. Def and Use reflect the set of variables that may be defined (that is, updated) and used (that is, read from) during the subprogram call. Def and Use may be computed using the techniques of Section 16.2.3, or they may simply be assumed to be the set of all variables accessible to the subprogram. Before the call, we save all data objects o ∈ Use that appear in the register association list with a status of S. Similarly, we remove from the register association list all data objects o ∈ Def. That is, we save values that may be referenced during the call and remove associations that may have been invalidated by assignments during the call.

In the simplest case, in which we assume all variables may be read or updated during a call, this approach amounts to saving all registers with an S status before the call and then completely clearing the association list after the call. Fortunately, if a call is made to a nonlocal subprogram, it may be possible to trivially establish that local variables are unaffected by the call. Thus we can be sure that library subprograms (I/O, storage management, math functions, and so on) do not affect program variables except through explicit reference parameters.

Other Register-Tracking Issues

The register-tracking scheme presented above is representative of a whole range of local register allocation routines. Many variations and extensions are possible:

- An algorithm has been proposed that spills the register whose next reference is most distant (Kim 1978). Also, an algorithm has been studied that considers the *next two* references to a register (Hsu 1987). This approach produces better code than approaches that consider only the next use of a register.

  Register allocation may also be performed using a *coloring algorithm* (Chaitin 1982). A *conflict graph* is created, with a graph node assigned to each variable or temporary that is to be assigned a register. An arc is built between two nodes if the objects they represent (variables or temporaries) must coexist. That is, two nodes that are linked cannot be allocated to the same register. Register allocation becomes a problem in coloring the nodes of the graph: Each color is a register, and no two nodes that are linked can have the same color. If a conflict graph requires more colors than there are registers, registers must be spilled. Various heuristics to do so, by breaking the conflict graph into subgraphs, have been proposed.

- We can use different costs for various operations, based on instruction size or timing.

- We can include additional address modes (immediate, indirect, index+base, and so on).

- We can allow for different register classes and for the allocation of pairs of adjacent registers.

- We can allow register-to-register moves to protect register contents. For example, given (C−A) + (C+B) we could generate

```
(Load    C,R1)
(–       A,R1)
(Load    C,R2)
(+       B,R2)
(+       R2,R1)
```

at a cost of 9. Better code, using a register move, is

```
(Load    C,R1)
(Move    R1,R2)
(–       A,R1)
(+       B,R2)
(+       R2,R1)
```

which costs only 8.

- We can allow for the fact that a register containing a variable or temporary with status (L,NS) may really cost only 1 to free if its value can be referenced from storage in a storage-to-register instruction (that is, we may be able to avoid reloading the value). Similarly, a variable with status (L,S) may cost only 3 to free (rather than 4) if we do a save and later reference the value in a storage-to-register instruction.

- If we do *peephole optimization* (using logical adjacency; see Section 15.5), we can replace an instruction pair (Load V,Rj), (OP Rj,Ri) with (OP V,Ri) if V's value is not referenced from Rj by a subsequent instruction. This combination of instructions may occur if we load V into Rj because V is live but are later forced to release Rj for other use before the reference to V is encountered.

The most important point in this discussion is that we can establish a formal model of register allocation, based on costs, that leads to very significant code improvements, even if the model is fairly simple in scope and detail. If we have available registers, *it pays to use them.*

What should be done at the global level for register allocation? Usually we assume no register values are preserved between basic blocks (that is, we do only local register optimization). However, we can provide for limited register use between basic blocks:

- Special operands such as loop indices or procedure arguments can be allocated to fixed registers within the loop or procedure.

- We can carry register status information forward to basic blocks whose predecessors are unique. Blocks with unique predecessors occur frequently in **if** and **case** statements, in which each of the conditionally executed alternatives has a unique predecessor. However, it is not always a good idea to delay saves across block boundaries, for we might do saves in each of several successor blocks rather than in a single predecessor block (this wastes space; time is unaffected).

An optimizing compiler might do full global register allocation. This is a very difficult optimization to do well because

- We must agree in all blocks to keep a given data object in the same register or do extra moves.

- We must decide which of possibly thousands of variables and temporaries to keep in a much smaller set of available registers. This decision involves flow-of-control analysis, complicated by some mechanism to estimate *frequency* of reference to given variables and temporaries. Solutions often have the flavor of integer programming problems (Johnsson 1975).

15.5. Peephole Optimization

To produce high-quality code, it is necessary to recognize a multitude of special cases. For example, it is clear we would like to avoid generating code for an addition of zero to an operand. But where should we check for this special case? In each semantic routine that might generate an add tuple? In each code-generation routine that might emit an addition?

Rather than distribute knowledge of special cases throughout semantic routines or code-generation routines, it is often preferable to utilize a distinct *peephole optimization* phase that looks for special cases and replaces them with improved code. Peephole optimization may be performed on tuples (Tanenbaum et al. 1982) or generated code (McKeeman 1965). As the term *peephole* suggests, a small window of two or three instructions or tuples is examined. If the instructions in the peephole match a particular pattern, they are replaced with a *replacement sequence*. After replacement, the new instructions are reconsidered for further optimization.

In general, we represent the collection of special cases that define a peephole optimizer as a list of pattern-replacement pairs. Thus, pattern ⇒ replacement means that if a code or tuple sequence matching the pattern is seen, it is replaced with the replacement sequence. If no pattern applies, the code sequence is unchanged. Clearly the number of special cases that might be included is unlimited, and we illustrate here only a few of the most useful *classes* of replacement rules. Rules applicable to any machine architecture are shown at the tuple level; rules that exploit a particular instruction or addressing mode are shown at the machine-code level.

- Constant folding (evaluate constant expressions in advance)

(+,Lit1,Lit2,Result)	⇒ (:=,Lit1+Lit2,Result)
(:=,Lit1,Result1), (+,Lit2,Result1,Result2)	⇒ (:=,Lit1,Result1),
	(:=,Lit1+Lit2,Result2)

- Strength reduction (replace slow operations with faster equivalents)

    (∗,Operand,2,Result)   ⇒ (ShiftLeft,Operand,1,Result)
    (∗,Operand,4,Result)   ⇒ (ShiftLeft,Operand,2,Result)

- Null sequences (delete useless operations)

    (+,Operand,0,Result)   ⇒ (:=,Operand,Result)
    (∗,Operand,1,Result)   ⇒ (:=,Operand,Result)

- Combine operations (replace several operations with one equivalent)

    Load A,R_i; Load A+1,R_{i+1} ⇒ DoubleLoad A,R_i
    BranchZero L1,R1; Branch L2; L1:   ⇒ BranchNotZero L2,R1
    Subtract #1,R1; BranchZero L1,R1   ⇒ SubtractOneBranch L1,R1

- Algebraic laws (use algebraic laws to simplify or reorder instructions)

    (+,Lit,Operand,Result)   ⇒ (+,Operand,Lit,Result)
    (−,0,Operand,Result)   ⇒ (Negate,Operand,Result)

- Special case instructions (use instructions designed for special operand cases)

    Subtract #1,R1   ⇒ Decrement R1
    Add #1,R1   ⇒ Increment R1
    Load #0,R1; Store A,R1   ⇒ Clear A

- Address mode operations (use address modes to simplify code)

    Load A,R1; Add 0(R1),R2   ⇒ Add @A,R2
                                -- @A denotes indirect addressing
    Subtract #2,R1; Clear 0(R1)   ⇒ Clear −(R1)
                                -- "−(Ri)" denotes autodecrement

To reduce the number of replacement rules, *pattern variables* that can match any operator or operand are often employed. For example, if % prefixes pattern variables, we can specify a single pattern that recognizes possible applications of indirect addressing:

    Load %IndirAdr,%VolatileReg; %OpCode 0(%VolatileReg),%ResultReg ⇒
        %OpCode @%IndirAdr,%ResultReg

To make pattern matching fast, operator–operand types of combinations are hashed to applicable patterns. Also, the size of a peephole window is normally limited to two or three instructions. Using a careful hashed implementation, speeds of several thousand instructions per second have been achieved (Davidson and Fraser 1984).

The concept of analyzing physically adjacent instructions has been generalized to logically adjacent instructions (Davidson and Fraser 1982). Two instructions are *logically adjacent* if they are linked by flow of control or if they are unaffected by intervening instructions. By analyzing logically adjacent instructions it is possible to remove jump chains (jumps to jump instructions) and redundant computations (for example, unnecessarily setting a condition code). Detecting logical adjacency can be costly, so care is required to keep peephole optimization fast.

15.6. **Generating Code from Trees**

We have concentrated on generating code from IR tuples. When processing an expression, a translation to tuples represents a linearization of the expression's tree structure. An expression tree may be traversed and translated in many different orders; normally, a depth-first, left-to-right traversal is used to generate tuples. A depth-first, left-to-right traversal always produces a *valid* translation; however, alternate traversals may lead to better code. Consider (A–B) + ((C+D)+(E∗F)). The normal depth-first traversal first translates A–B, leaving its result in a register. Then (C+D)+(E∗F) is translated, requiring two registers (one for each subexpression). Thus a total of three registers is used. However, if the right subexpression, ((C+D)+(E∗F)), is evaluated first, only two registers are needed, because once this subexpression is computed its value can be held in one register, while the other is used to compute A+B.

A node in a tree has the following structure:

```
typedef struct expr_tr {
    struct expr_tr *left_subtree;
    struct expr_tr *right_subtree;
    int reg_count;
    boolean is_right;
    enum { ID, BINARY_OPERATOR,
           COMMUTATIVE_OPERATOR } kind;
} expression_tree;
```

We now consider an algorithm that determines the minimum number of registers needed to evaluate any expression or subexpression. We ignore for the moment common subexpressions and special properties of operators, like commutativity. The algorithm labels each node in a tree with the minimum number of registers needed to evaluate the subexpression rooted by that node. This labeling is called *Sethi-Ullman numbering* (Sethi and Ullman 1970). Once the minimum number of registers needed for each expression and subexpres-

```
void register_needs(expression_tree *T)
{
    /*
     * Mark each node in T with a field "reg_count".
     * Node.reg_count is the minimum number of registers
     * needed to evaluate the subexpression rooted by
     * Node in T.
     */
    if (T->kind == ID) {
        if (is_a_right_subtree(T))
            T->reg_count = 0;
        else
            T->reg_count = 1;
    } else {        /* T must be a binary operator. */
        register_needs(T->left_subtree);
        register_needs(T->right_subtree);
        if (T->left_subtree.reg_count ==
            T->right_subtree.reg_count)
            T->reg_count = T->right_subtree.reg_count + 1;
        else
            T->reg_count = max(T->left_subtree.reg_count,
                               T->right_subtree.reg_count);
    }
}
```

Figure 15.11   An Algorithm to Label Expression Trees with Register Needs

sion is known, we traverse the tree in a manner that generates optimal code (that is, code that minimizes register use and hence register spilling).

As we did in previous sections, we assume a machine model that provides register-to-register and storage-to-register operand modes, with the first operand and result always residing in a register.

The algorithm works in a bottom-up direction, first labeling leaves of the tree. If a leaf is a left operand, it is labeled with 1 because it must be loaded into a register. A leaf that is a right operand is labeled with 0 because it may be accessed directly from memory. For interior nodes, which are assumed to be binary operators, the register requirements for each operand are considered. If both operands require r registers, the operator requires $r+1$ registers because an operand, once computed, will be held in a register. If the two operands require a different number of registers, the whole expression requires the same number of registers as the more complex of the two operands. (Evaluate the more complex operand first and save it in a register. The simpler operand needs fewer registers, and hence the registers used for the previous, more complex operand can be reused.) This analysis leads to the algorithm of Figure 15.11.

As an example of this algorithm, **register_needs()** would label the expression tree for (A–B)+((C+D)+(E∗F)) as shown in Figure 15.12 (**reg_count** for each operator node is shown in parentheses).

We can use the **reg_count()** labeling to drive a simple, but optimal, code generator, **tree_code()**, defined in Figure 15.13.   **tree_code()** takes a labeled expression tree and a list of registers it may use. It generates code to evaluate the tree, and leaves the result of the expression in the first register on the list. If **tree_code()** is given too few registers, it will spill registers, when necessary, into storage temporaries. (We assume some straightforward list manipulation functions, which are not shown here for brevity.)

As an example of the **tree_code()** program, if we call **tree_code()** with the labeled tree of Figure 15.12 and a list of two registers, (R1,R2), we obtain the following code sequence:

```
(1)    Load    C,R2
(2)    Add     D,R2
(3)    Load    E,R1
(4)    Mult    F,R1
(5)    Add     R1,R2
(6)    Load    A,R1
(7)    Sub     B,R1
(8)    Add     R2,R1
```

tree_code() illustrates well the principle of *register targeting*. That is, code is generated in such a way that the final result appears in the targeted register, without any unnecessary moves.

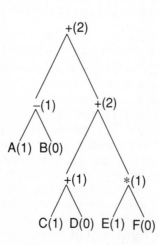

Figure 15.12   Expression Tree for (A–B)+((C+D)+(E∗F)) Labeled with Register Needs

```
void tree_code(expression_tree *T, register_list reglist)
{
    /*
     * Generate code to evaluate T using registers in
     * reglist (at least two registers are assumed).
     */
    extern register_list listcat(register_list,...);
    expression_tree *left_t, *right_t;
    machine_reg R1, R2;
    register_list remaining_regs;
    address temp;

    R1 = head(reglist);
    if (T->kind == ID)
        /* Must be a left subtree or trivial expression. */
        generate(LOAD,T,R1,"");
    else {   /* T->kind must be a binary operator. */
        left_t = T->left_subtree;
        right_t = T->right_subtree;
        if (right_t->reg_count == 0) { /* right_t is an ID. */
            tree_code(left_t,reglist);
            generate(T->op,right_t,R1,"");
        } else if (left_t->reg_count >= length(reglist) &&
                right_t->reg_count >= length(reglist)) {
            /* Must spill a register */
            tree_code(right_t,reglist);
            get_storage_temp(& temp);
            generate(STORE,temp,R1,"");
            tree_code(left_t,reglist);
            generate(T->op,temp,R1,"");
        } else {
            /* One or both subtrees don't need all registers */
            R2 = head(tail(reglist));
            if (left_t->reg_count >= right_t->reg_count) {
                tree_code(left_t,reglist);
                tree_code(right_t,tail(reglist));
                generate(T->op,R2,R1,"");
            } else {
                remaining_regs = tail(tail(reglist));
                tree_code(right_t,listcat(R2,R1,remaining_regs));
                /* Leave result in R2. */
                tree_code(left_t,listcat(R1,remaining_regs));
                /* Leave result in R1. */
                generate(T->op,R2,R1,"");
            }
        }
    }
}
```

Figure 15.13   An Algorithm to Generate Code from Expression Trees

The quality of code produced by the **tree_code()** routine can be improved if commutativity is exploited where possible. Consider the case of a commutative operator, with subtrees T1 and T2. If T1 and T2 are both identifiers, commuting operands clearly has no effect. Similarly, if T1 and T2 are both nontrivial expressions, commuting operands again has no effect, because the more expensive subtree is always evaluated first, and both subtrees leave their results in registers. However, if the left subtree, T1, is an identifier, and the right subtree is a nontrivial expression, then commuting operands is advantageous. This is because in the original form the left operand would have to be loaded into a register, whereas in the commuted form the operand (necessarily an identifier) can be accessed from memory.

Using this analysis, we can define a routine, **commute()**, in Figure 15.14 that recursively traverses an expression tree, commuting operands whenever it is advantageous to do so. After execution of the **commute()** routine, **register_needs()** and **tree_code()** can be used as usual.

Code quality can be further improved if associativity can be assumed (see Exercise 15). Note, however, that because of overflow issues and rounding when computing real values, computer arithmetic is usually *not* associative.

15.7. Generating Code from Dags

In Section 15.6 we concentrated on the problem of generating optimal code for single expressions. In this section we consider the more challenging problem of generating code for entire basic blocks. In doing so, we need to deal with common subexpressions and assignments. We therefore generalize expression trees to *computation dags*. A *dag* is a directed acyclic graph—that is, a tree structure generalized so that a node may have more than one parent. Multiple parents are allowed so that an expression may be used more than once. No

```
void commute(expression_tree *T)
{
    /* Commute subtrees in T, where advantageous. */

    if (T->kind == BINARY_OPERATOR) {
        commute(T->left_subtree);
        commute(T->right_subtree);
        if (T->left_subtree.kind == ID
            && T->right_subtree.kind == BINARY_OPERATOR
            && commutative(T->op))
                swap(T->left_subtree, T->right_subtree);
    }
}
```

Figure 15.14   Algorithm That Generates Code for Commutative Operators

cycles are allowed, however, as this would lead to an infinite loop when the expression was evaluated. Any node that has no parents is a root; in general, a dag may have many roots.

The dag shown in Figure 15.15 corresponds to (A+B)+(A+B). It illustrates how dags represent *sharing* of common subexpressions. To represent assignment, we will allow an operator node to be labeled with the name of a variable. Such a labeling indicates that the value of the expression rooted by the operator has been assigned to the variable. For example, we will represent I:=I+1 as shown in Figure 15.16 and note that I appears more than once in that dag. (Every tree is a trivial dag.) To mark the current value of a variable, we highlight it in boldface. Hence the dag of Figure 15.16 becomes the dag shown in Figure 15.17.

In a dag for an entire basic block, a variable name may appear more than once: The initial value is always a leaf, and the final value, which must be

Figure 15.15   A Dag Corresponding to (A+B)+(A+B)

Figure 15.16   A Dag Corresponding to I:=I+1

Figure 15.17   A Dag Corresponding to I:=I+1, with Updated Variables Highlighted

```
dag_node *look_up(tree_node *T)
{
  if (T is a literal) {
    if (a dag node labeled with T exists)
      Return a pointer to the node
    else
      Create a new dag node, label it with T
          and return a pointer to it
  } else {       /* T is a variable */
    if (no dag node labeled with T exists)
      Create a new dag node, label it with T
          and return a pointer to it
    else if (a highlighted node labeled with T exists)
      Return a pointer to the node
    else
      Return a pointer to the nonhighlighted
          node labeled with T
  }
}
```

Figure 15.18　Algorithm That Maps Tree Nodes to Dag Nodes

saved, is in boldface. If a variable is not assigned to, it appears once (as a leaf) and is not highlighted because its value need not be saved. **set_label(node,label)** assigns **label** (in highlighted form) to **node**, removing other highlighted occurrences of **label** in the dag.

We now present an algorithm that takes a list of assignment statements comprising a basic block and produces the block's computation dag. We assume that each assignment statement is of the form ID := Expr, where Expr is a subtree representing the statement's right-hand side.

First, we define in Figure 15.18 a function **look_up()**, which takes a tree node (which can be a literal or variable) and returns a corresponding dag node. Using **look_up()**, we can determine (or create) the dag nodes corresponding to variables and the literals. If assignments have occurred, the value of the most recent assignment is highlighted and returned by **look_up()**.

tree_to_dag(), as defined in Figure 15.19, takes a tree and merges it into an existing dag structure. In doing so, the function provides for the sharing of common subexpressions and the effects of assignments. A pointer to the dag node that corresponds to the value of tree is returned.

As an example, consider the basic block shown in Figure 15.20. The corresponding expression trees are shown in Figure 15.21. We merge each tree in the figure, in turn, using **tree_to_dag()** to form the three computation dags shown in Figure 15.22.

```
dag_node *tree_to_dag(tree_node *N)
{
  dag_node *RHS, *l_opnd, *r_opnd, *p;

  if (N is a leaf)    /* must be a literal or variable */
      return look_up(N);
  else if (N is a ":=" operator) {
      RHS = tree_to_dag(r_sub_tree(N));
      set_label(RHS, l_sub_tree(N));
      return RHS;
  } else {
      /* N is a binary operator
         (the unary case is analogous). */
      l_opnd = tree_to_dag(l_sub_tree(N));
      r_opnd = tree_to_dag(r_sub_tree(N));
      if (there exists a dag node, P, that is the
          same operator as N and has l_opnd and
          r_opnd as left and right descendants)
            return P;
      else {
            Create a new dag node, P, that is an
               N-type operator and has l_opnd and
               r_opnd as left and right descendants
            return P;
      }
  }
}
```

Figure 15.19   Algorithm That Merges Trees into a Dag Structure

```
G    := C*(A+B)+(A+B);
C    := A+B;
A    :=(C*D)+(E−F);
```

Figure 15.20   A Simple Basic Block

Operators that have highlighted labels must have their value saved at the end of the basic block. Values that can be shared, like A+B, have more than one parent in the dag that uses the value.

Clearly, generating code from a dag is more complicated than generating code from a tree. One obvious problem is that if a value is to be shared, it must be held in a register until code for all its uses has been generated. Thus, minimizing register use is a problem. Surprisingly, this is not the only problem. In fact, it is shown by Aho, Johnson, and Ullman (1977) that even if an

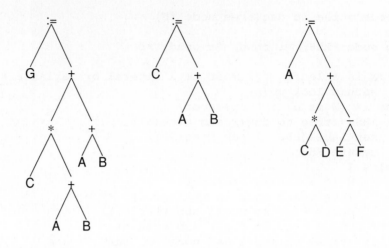

Figure 15.21   Expression Trees for the Basic Block of Figure 15.20

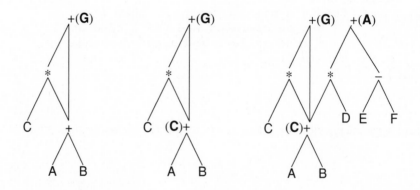

Figure 15.22   Computation Dags for the Basic Block of Figure 15.20

infinite number of registers is assumed, generating optimal code is still very complicated (the best algorithms currently known take time exponential in the size of the dag). The problem is that values used as left operands are normally destroyed. If a value is to be shared, this may force a value to be copied before it is used as a left operand. An optimal code generator therefore has to order dag evaluation to minimize register copies.

We shall present a heuristic algorithm that generally produces an efficient translation of a dag. The insight is simple. We try to order dag evaluation so that the *last time* an operand is used it is used as a left operand. This procedure is obviously preferable to copying an operand, using it as a left operand, and *then* using the copied value as a right operand.

We define a dag traversal algorithm called **schedule()** that schedules the operators in a dag for evaluation. **schedule()** operates in a top-down manner; the first operator scheduled will be the *last* to be evaluated (all operands must be fully evaluated before an operator can be evaluated).

Because a dag may have more than one root we start at the rightmost root and work leftward, scheduling each subdag in turn. (Nodes are added to a dag from left to right, so the rightmost root was the last one created and added to the dag.) We schedule from right to left because the first subdag scheduled will be the last to be evaluated, and normally the rightmost subdag is that corresponding to the last statement in a basic block. We want the code we generate to roughly parallel the statements the code is generated from.

Within a subdag, we schedule an operator if all its parents have already been scheduled. This guarantees that all operands will be evaluated before they are used. We schedule left operands before right operands because we want left operands evaluated last, and scheduling represents the exact reverse of evaluation order. Therefore, we have the algorithm shown in Figure 15.23, which schedules recursively, beginning at the root of a subdag.

We depict a scheduling by numbering operator nodes in the order in which they are scheduled. For the dag of Figure 15.22, we have the scheduled dag shown in Figure 15.24.

Recall that roots are scheduled from right to left; the evaluation order for the dag is the reverse of the chosen scheduling. Before code is generated, we must allocate registers. We do this in two steps. First, virtual registers are allocated; then these are mapped to actual registers.

Our register allocator, **allocate_v_regs()** shown in Figure 15.25, seeks to map an operator and its left operand to the same register. This procedure allows the left operand to be used (and destroyed) without copying its value.

allocate_v_regs() tries iteratively to assign the same virtual register to an operator and all its left operands, as long as the operator is the last use of the operand (that is, as long as it has the lowest schedule number). Returning

```
void schedule(dag_node D)
{
    if (D is an operator all of whose parents
        have been scheduled) {
        /* if D is a root, then we assume it
           is immediately schedulable. */
        Mark D as the next node scheduled
        schedule(left_operand(D));
        schedule(right_operand(D));
    }
}
```

Figure 15.23   Algorithm That Schedules Dag Nodes for Evaluation

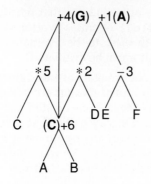

Figure 15.24   Dag with Operators Scheduled for Evaluation

```
void allocate_v_regs(void)
{
    /* Allocate virtual registers. */
    int v_reg = 1;      /* Current virtual register */
    dag_node N;
    operator left_op;

    while (all operator nodes have not been
            allocated a virtual register) {
        Choose N, the operator node with the lowest
            schedule number still unallocated
        while (TRUE) {
            Allocate v_reg to N;
            left_op = left_operand(N);
            if (left_op is an operator not yet allocated
                    a virtual register and left_op's lowest
                    schedule-numbered parent is N)
                N = left_op;
            else
                break;
        }
        v_reg++;
    }
}
```

Figure 15.25   Algorithm That Allocates Virtual Registers

to the dag of Figure 15.24, we allocate virtual registers to set the dag shown in Figure 15.26, with virtual registers denoted as V1, V2, ...

Mapping virtual registers to real registers is easy. We define the *span* of a virtual register to be the range of schedule numbers of the operators that assign to or use the virtual register. For the example of Figure 15.26, we have the mapping shown in Figure 15.27.

Two virtual registers may be mapped to the same hardware register if and only if their spans do not overlap. Hence, in our example, V1 may be mapped to R1, and V2 and V3 mapped to R2.

Given an evaluation order and a register assignment, code generation is almost done. What remains is to generate code to store values into variables that have been updated in the basic block. We have labeled, in highlighted form, those variables that must receive a final value. If a node N is labeled with a highlighted variable V, we must store the register allocated to N into V. There is a danger, however! If we store the value too soon, we may destroy the variable's initial value before all operators that need it have been evaluated. For example, the updated value of C is computed at the node labeled 6, but C's initial value is needed until node 5 is evaluated. Therefore, we delay stores until a register value is about to be lost. If a value is computed at node N, it is preserved until the node's lowest numbered parent, P_{min}, is evaluated. If all operators that use a variable's initial value have a greater schedule number than P_{min}, then the updated value is stored just before P_{min} is evaluated. Otherwise, the value is stored in another register or storage temporary and copied into the variable at the end of the code that evaluates the dag.

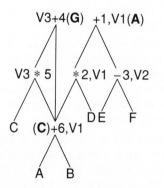

Figure 15.26   Dag with Virtual Registers Allocated

Register	Span
V1	1-6
V2	1-3
V3	4-5

Figure 15.27   Span of Virtual Registers

```
(1)    Load    A,R1
(2)    Add     B,R1
(3)    Load    C,R2
(4)    Mult    R1,R2
(5)    Add     R1,R2
(6)    Store   G,R2
(7)    Load    E,R2
(8)    Sub     F,R2
(9)    Store   C,R1
(10)   Mult    D,R1
(11)   Add     R2,R1
(12)   Store   A,R1
```

Figure 15.28   Code Generated for Dag of Figure 15.26

In our example, the new value of C, computed at node 6 into register R1, is preserved until node 2 is evaluated. Because the last reference to C's original value is at node 5, we may store R1 directly into C before node 2 is evaluated.

The code produced for the example uses the scheduling, register allocation, and variable updating just discussed and is shown in Figure 15.28.

Our heuristic scheduling algorithm is sometimes suboptimal because of the sharing that occurs among operands. Consider, for example, the two "diamond dags," with scheduling, shown in Figure 15.29.

The scheduling on the left dag is suboptimal because node 4 is used as a left operand before it is used as a right operand, thus necessitating a register copy. On the other hand, the right dag gets the same scheduling, but here it *is* optimal, for node 4 is used as a right operand and then as a left operand. Unless our scheduler examines the suboperands of an expression and how they are shared, it cannot always produce the best execution order.

Our heuristic dag evaluation scheduler can be improved in many ways. For example, an operand subexpression is often a tree rather than a dag and can be processed using the techniques of Section 15.6. For commutative operators, operands may be commuted. In cases in which an operand is used as a left operand by more than one operator (forcing a register copy), commuting operands may change a left operand into a right operand, thus improving code quality. Other heuristics are discussed in Aho, Johnson, and Ullman (1977).

15.7.1. Aliasing

When the effect of aliasing is included in dags, code generation becomes much more complicated. For example, an assignment to one array element, say A(I), may affect the value of a seemingly different array element, A(J). Dags must be generated so that such aliasing is anticipated.

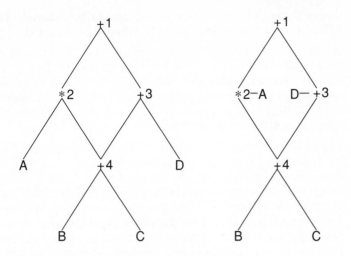

Figure 15.29   Two Dags, with Scheduling

Figure 15.30   Dag Corresponding to A(I)

To handle arrays and pointers, we allow expressions that yield addresses. In particular, A(I) is represented as shown in Figure 15.30, where **Ind** is the index operator.

The **Ind** operator yields an address. To access the value referenced by an address expression, we will use ↑ as a dereferencing operator, as in Pascal. For example, J := A(I) would be represented by the dag shown in Figure 15.31. The values referenced by pointers and reference parameters are also accessed using the ↑ operator.

We will uniquely label all address expressions with *internal names* of the form %1,%2, ... We do this so that we can allow address expressions on the left-hand sides of assignments. After an assignment, dereferenced address expressions may label a node. For example, A(I) := J is represented by the dags shown in Figure 15.32.

If aliasing were not an issue, arrays and pointers would be fairly easy to handle, with address expressions shared as other common subexpressions are. However, aliasing must be accounted for, and the following three requirements must be satisfied:

(1)   Stores through address expressions cannot be delayed. That is, A(I) := J must force a store into A(I) when it is evaluated.

(2)   An assignment to an array element or heap object or reference parameter must kill all labeled subexpressions that might be aliased. For example, after A(I) := J, variable J is labeled as representing the current value of A(I), which is represented as %1↑. If A(L) := K is processed next, the label on J must be removed, as A(I)'s value will have been changed if I = L.

(3)   The order of writes to, and reads from, aliased data objects must be preserved. Assume we translate A(I) := J; K := A(L); to the dags shown in Figure 15.33. These dags indicate that the two statements are independent, which they would be if A(I) and A(L) were simple variables. To enforce proper ordering, we introduce *dependency arcs*, which force proper evaluation order by making one dag appear to be dependent on another. Using dependency arcs, we rewrite the dags into the form shown in Figure 15.34. Now the assignment to A(I) is forced to precede the use of A(L).

With these modifications, the scheduling and register allocation techniques of the previous section can be extended to handle references to array elements, heap objects, and reference parameters.

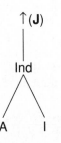

Figure 15.31   Dag Corresponding to J := A(I)

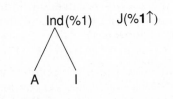

Figure 15.32   Dags Corresponding to A(I) := J

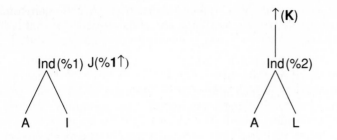

Figure 15.33   Dags Corresponding to A(I) := J; K := A(L);

Figure 15.34   Dags with Dependency Arcs

15.8. Code Generator Generators

In recent years, use of code generator generators has become increasingly common. A code generator driver routine selects target code by following a set of rules that define when a particular target instruction may be used. If the rules are changed, new instructions or architectures can be accommodated.

As one might expect, producing a code generator generator is quite a challenge. The following are some of the problems that must be addressed:

- Machine architectures are notoriously nonuniform. A code generator generator must be able to adapt to the quirks of a particular machine without even knowing exactly what the quirks might be!

- Although target code need not be optimal, it is important that automatically generated code generators produce code that is competitive with hand-coded generators. Thus naive approaches that oversimplify a machine (for example, by assuming a simple stack or one-register machine) cannot be employed.

- Most machines have *more than one way* to do the same thing. That is, a machine might have a general add instruction, an add immediate instruction, and an increment instruction. A code-generation algorithm that is satisfied with just any code sequence or that is confused by the range of possible instruction choices must be avoided.

- A code generator may need to interface with optimizations that are considered machine-independent. For example, common subexpression analysis, which attempts to eliminate unnecessary recomputations of the same expression, is assumed to be target machine–independent. However, target machine dependencies may complicate matters. For example, it may be cheaper to recompute an expression than to save it, depending on machine details.

- The code generator must be reasonably fast, although some sacrifice of speed for flexibility can be tolerated.

Code generator generators emphasize *description-driven* techniques. These techniques take a formal description of exactly what each instruction of a target machine does and then match it against the operations needed to produce a given computation. Machines differ in the effect their instructions have, but matching the effects of particular instructions against the desired effects is the essence of the code-generation task. An analogy to context-free parsing is apparent—different grammars produce different parsing tables, but the underlying parser driver and parsing model are fixed.

The chief advantage of description-driven approaches is that they completely free an implementor from the chore of deciding what code to generate for a given construct. Rather, the implementor simply states, in a formal manner, exactly what each target instruction does. The code generator then automatically searches the machine description to find the instruction or instructions that produce the desired computation; pattern matching is used to replace interpretation and case analysis.

Instruction patterns may be tree structured or linear. Depending on the choice of the instruction patterns, matching may be performed by heuristic search or by formal parsing techniques.

Heuristic search techniques create subgoals as a search continues and use heuristics to select subgoals and the order in which to try patterns. Parsing techniques use simple LR-like parsing, sometimes augmented with semantic attributes.

To illustrate how description-driven techniques work, consider the following example. Each target machine instruction is defined by the intermediate form subtree that it can compute and the subtree or node that results after the instruction executes. For example, a store instruction that stores a register into an indexed memory location, Store Const(R2),R1, is defined as shown in Figure 15.35.

This rule states that the store instruction computes the subtree pictured and can be replaced by the Null node. The Null node is used to indicate that an entire subtree has been correctly matched. The other instructions are defined as shown in Figure 15.36. #Const is the literal with a value of Const; ↑ is the indirection operator.

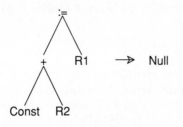

Figure 15.35 Formal Definition of Store Const(R2),R1

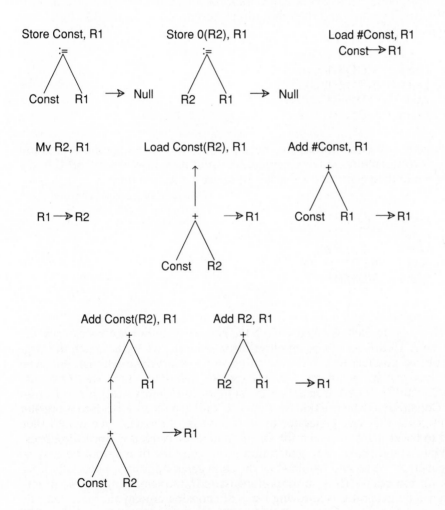

Figure 15.36 Formal Definitions of Machine Instructions

As an example, we generate code for the following Pascal statement:

A := P↑.B + C;   { P is a pointer to a record }

We begin with the expression tree shown in Figure 15.37(a) (D1 is a display register). To generate code, we match subtrees until the Null node is produced. We try to reuse registers within a computation [we prefer Load Const(R1),R1 to Load Const(R1),R2]. However, we do not allow display registers to be overwritten. We load first the address of the record pointed to by P [Figure 15.37(b)] and then the value of field B [Figure 15.37(c)]. (We assume that the pattern matcher knows that + is commutative or that patterns representing both operand orders for + are stored.) P↑.B and C are added [Figure 15.37(d)] and then the sum is stored into A [Figure 15.37(e)]. The code that is produced is

```
Load    P(D1),R1
Load    B(R1),R1
Add     C(D1),R1
Store   A(D1),R1
```

Other code sequences could have been produced by matching the expression tree in a different order. For example, we could have loaded operand C into a register and then generated a register-to-register add, yielding

```
Load    P(D1),R1
Load    B(R1),R1
Load    C(D1),R2
Add     R2,R1
Store   A(D1),R1
```

If our description-driven code generator finds a way to reduce the expression tree to Null, we know we have correct code but not necessarily the best code. Heuristics can be employed (for example, we try to match the largest subtree possible to avoid generating unnecessary instructions), but even this can cause problems. For example, assume that we have an Add Const2(R),Const1 instruction (a memory-to-memory add) instead of an Add Const(R2),R1 instruction; in this case, failing to load P↑.B into a register might cause the code generator to *block* (that is, get stuck). We would then need to backtrack and search for an alternate code sequence. Including backtracking would make code generation more complex (it may not be easy to "ungenerate" code) and would slow the code generator down, especially if we back up too often. Thus, an important issue in implementing a description-driven code generator is knowing ways of choosing among alternate code sequences and avoiding blocking.

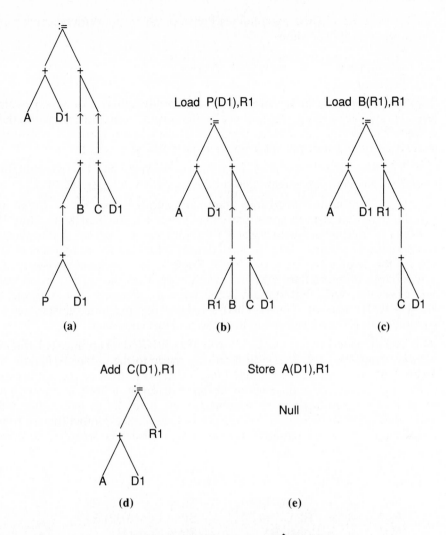

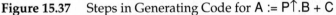

Figure 15.37   Steps in Generating Code for A := P↑.B + C

15.8.1. Grammar-based Code Generators

In Glanville and Graham (1978) it was observed that the problem of matching code templates against an expression tree is very similar to the problem of matching productions against a token sequence during parsing. Glanville and Graham cleverly reformulated the template-matching problem in parsing terms. First, rather than matching directly against a tree, they adopted a linear *code-generation IR* (CGIR), essentially a Polish prefix form. With this approach, our earlier example becomes

$$:= + A D1 + \uparrow + \uparrow + P D1 B \uparrow + C D1$$

This structure can be obtained by a preorder traversal of an expression tree or by expanding tuples, replacing result temporaries with their definitions. Because we wish to exploit available address modes, we explicitly show display registers and stack pointers in the CGIR.

We now recast templates as ordinary productions. For commutative operators, we include both operand orders, as shown in Figure 15.38.

As in ordinary context-free grammars, symbols like R1 or Const are placeholders that denote some particular symbol being matched. Thus R1 does not mean the hardware register 1 but rather some register that is allocated and bound to symbol R1. We shall denote actual hardware registers as D1, D2, ... for display registers and Reg1, Reg2, ... for operand registers. If a symbol appears more than once in a production, then the particular information associated with that symbol is the same in all cases. For example, in R1 → + R2 R1 after the + is matched, whatever real machine register was associated with R1 is considered to hold the sum just computed.

A parsing technique similar to ordinary LR-based techniques (Chapter 6) is used. However, a few modifications are made to the parser to handle the ambiguities in instruction selection. First, if there is a shift-reduce conflict (the parser can recognize a production or keep reading), a shift is always performed. This modification corresponds to the heuristic of generating code only when necessary. Second, if there is a reduce-reduce conflict (two or more productions can be recognized), a set of separate rules is consulted to deter-

Null	→	:= + Const R2 R1	-- Store Const(R2),R1
Null	→	:= + R2 Const R1	-- Store Const(R2),R1
Null	→	:= Const R1	-- Store Const,R1
Null	→	:= R2 R1	-- Store 0(R2),R1
R1	→	Const	-- Load #Const,R1
R1	→	↑ + Const R2	-- Load Const(R2),R1
R2	→	R1	-- Mv R2,R1
R1	→	↑ + R2 Const	-- Load Const(R2),R1
R1	→	+ ↑ + Const R2 R1	-- Add Const (R2),R1
R1	→	+ ↑ + R2 Const R1	-- Add Const (R2),R1
R1	→	+ R1 ↑ + Const R2	-- Add Const (R2),R1
R1	→	+ R1 ↑ + R2 Const	-- Add Const (R2),R1
R1	→	+ Const R1	-- Add #Const,R1
R1	→	+ R1 Const	-- Add #Const,R1
R1	→	+ R2 R1	-- Add R2,R1
R1	→	+ R1 R2	-- Add R2,R1

Figure 15.38   Graham–Glanville Code Templates

mine which instruction sequence is preferable. Also, certain *qualifications* may need to be checked before a production is recognized. Thus, in R1 → +R2 R1 we need to verify that R1 may be changed because it will hold the result of the addition. Qualifications allow us, for example, to guarantee that a display register is not destroyed during a computation.

As an illustration, let us generate code for our previous example. Note that the parser *automatically* tries to match all productions that are feasible, so we know that if an instruction sequence is possible, it will be considered. We first read := + A D1. This must match one of the productions for a store:

```
Null →  := + Const R2 R1     -- Store Const(R2),R1
Null →  := + R2 Const R1     -- Store Const(R2),R1
Null →  :=  Const  R1         -- Store Const,R1
Null →  :=  R2  R1            -- Store 0(R2),R1
```

The first production can be used if the remainder of the expression can be matched by R1. There are other possibilities, however. The second production can be used if we let R2 match the constant A. This possibility is rejected, using the rule that we shift rather than reduce when possible. (This rule allows us to avoid an unnecessary load of A into a register.) Similarly, the fourth production could be used if we allowed R2 to match + A D1. Again this is rejected because we prefer to shift rather than reduce (and again an unnecessary load is avoided).

We now know that the remainder of the expression

$$+ \uparrow + \uparrow + P\ D1\ B \uparrow + C\ D1$$

must be matched by a production with R1 as a left-hand side. The possibilities are

```
R1 → + Const R1            -- Add #Const,R1
R1 → + R1 Const            -- Add #Const,R1
R1 → + ↑ + Const R2 R1     -- Add Const (R2),R1
R1 → + ↑ + R2 Const R1     -- Add Const (R2),R1
R1 → + R1 ↑ + Const R2     -- Add Const (R2),R1
R1 → + R1 ↑ + R2 Const     -- Add Const (R2),R1
R1 → +  R2 R1              -- Add R2,R1
R1 → +  R1 R2              -- Add R2,R1
```

Matching the longest possible prefix, we use the fourth production. This means that the rest of the production, R2 Const R1, must match

$$\uparrow + P\ D1\ B \uparrow + C\ D1$$

We first use R1 → ↑ + Const R2 and generate Load P(D1),Reg1. B matches

Const, and the preceding production is used again to match $\uparrow + C$ D1. We therefore generate Load C(D1),Reg2. Because the add production is fully matched, we generate Add B(Reg1),Reg2. The store production is now fully matched, so we generate Store A(D1),Reg2. The whole code sequence is

```
Load    P(D1),Reg1
Load    C(D1),Reg2
Add     B(Reg1),Reg2
Store   A(D1),Reg2
```

This code sequence isn't quite optimal because two registers were used, where one would have sufficed:

```
Load    P(D1),Reg1
Load    B(Reg1),Reg1
Add     C(D1),Reg1
Store   A(D1),Reg1
```

The problem is that we seek to avoid generating code when possible. Thus we notice that Load B(Reg1),Reg1 can be avoided by making B(Reg1) an operand of the Add instruction. In this case, the strategy does not pay off because we end up having to generate a load of C(D1). Note, however, that if the second operand had already been in a register (for example, because it was an expression rather than a variable), then avoiding the load of B(Reg1) would have been exactly the right thing to do.

In general, on-the-fly code generators must decide how to handle the first operand of an instruction before they even see what the second operand looks like! As a result, they seek to delay necessary operations, especially loads, until absolutely necessary. This sometimes leads to suboptimal code. Improved techniques that examine both operands before generating code are discussed by Christopher, Hatcher, and Kukuk (1984) and Aho, Ganapathi and Tjiang (1989).

A nice aspect of the Graham–Glanville approach is that potential block states can be detected when the code generator is built. In particular, if the parser for the code-generation productions can reach a state in which part of a production is matched but the rest can't be matched by a valid operand or expression, then the code generator may block. For example, assume for some strange reason that we have register-to-storage adds but no register-to-register adds. We might then detect a parser state in which a + and a register had been matched and a storage location remained to be matched. If, however, the second operand were already in a register, we would be stuck. This sort of state represents an error situation in which correct code cannot be produced for all valid expressions.

To fix the problem, we would add new productions to allow the remaining operands to be matched. Thus, in our example, we might add the productions

Value → ↑ Const
Value → R1   –– Store Value(0),R1

These tell the code generator that a value can be obtained by fetching the contents of a storage location. If necessary, a value in a register can be stored in a memory location and then fetched from memory as an operand.

The Graham–Glanville code-generation technique has been tested in a number of experimental compilers and is beginning to appear in production compilers. To increase code-generation speed, often the number of semantic checks is minimized by introducing special symbols and productions. For example, special symbols such as Zero, One, Two, Four, and Eight can represent "magic numbers" that appear in instructions. Similarly, we can use distinct symbols for various attribute values rather than using a single symbol augmented by an attribute (byte, long, real, longreal).

The drawback of using syntax to encode semantic checks is that the number of symbols and productions can become quite large. (For the VAX, a machine description grammar containing 1073 productions, 219 terminals, 148 nonterminals, and 2216 parser states was reported.) Indeed, when machine description grammars are run through LALR(1) generators, often hours of processing time are required to produce code generator tables. However, specially designed table generators can increase throughput rates dramatically (Henry et al. 1984).

Code-generation speed is dominated by the underlying parsing process, mostly in parsing chains of productions, and in unpacking and manipulating parse table entries. Code-generation speeds some 50% slower than production compilers have been reported. With care, generated code is comparable in quality to that produced by ordinary, nonoptimizing compilers.

15.8.2. Using Semantic Attributes in Code Generators

A limitation of the Graham–Glanville approach is that it is purely syntactic. That is, it primarily matches, in a context-free manner, sequences of symbols. Other aspects of the code-generation process are handled informally. For example, symbols have associated semantic values, but exactly what these values are and where they are computed are not shown in the grammar. Similarly, even if a code-generation production matches a sequence of CGIR symbols, it may not be applicable. This is because non-context-free constraints may apply (an address may need to be word aligned, an immediate operand may need to be within a certain range, and so forth). These non-context-free constraints cannot be directly represented in the production and thus must be enforced elsewhere, just as semantic rules are separated from ordinary context-free productions.

In Ganapathi and Fischer (1985) these problems are addressed by using *attributed productions* as code templates. First, explicit *attribute values* are included with grammar symbols. These attributes represent the information associated and stored with the symbol. Along with terminals and nonterminals, two new kinds of symbols, *action symbols* and *predicate symbols* are added to code templates. Action symbols encapsulate the computation of new attribute values and operations that have side effects (particularly code generation). They are prefixed with a #, as were action symbols that invoke semantic routines.

Predicate symbols are similar to action symbols. However, they produce no attribute values. Rather, when invoked, they produce a true or false value. If a predicate is true, matching of the production containing the predicate continues. If a predicate is false, the production is eliminated from consideration. For the sake of clarity, all predicates are suffixed with a ?. Predicates are a convenient mechanism by which to define exactly the circumstances under which a production may be applied. For code-generation purposes this is a major improvement because now a machine description is precisely an attributed production defining the correspondence between intermediate form symbols (with attributes) and machine instructions.

As an example, consider the following:

Long(R) → + Long(A) Long(R) IsOne?(A) Dead?(R) #emit(IncL,R)

This production matches the addition of two long-length operands and produces a long-length result. Before the production can be applied, however, it must be verified that the left operand is the constant 1, and the right operand is dead (and hence may be destroyed). If and only if these conditions are met, an increment long, IncL, instruction may be generated.

The predicates in a production state whether that production may be used. If more than one production is enabled (has true predicates), a disambiguating mechanism must be employed. For code-generation purposes, productions are ordered in two lists. One is in order of increasing instruction size, and the other is in order of decreasing speed. Depending on whether code size or speed is being optimized, we disambiguate by choosing the earliest enabled production on the size or speed list.

For code-generation purposes, attributed productions may be grouped into three classes. The first represents *address mode* productions. These are used to match the intermediate form to target machine address modes. They may or may not generate code. For example

Adr(A) → Index Obj(Offset,Size) Base(Reg) #build_adr(Offset,Size,Reg,A)

matches an indexing operation commonly used to access data in an activation record. If the indexing operation involves a constant offset and a base register, we simply build an address descriptor in attribute A. However, it may happen that the second operand of the index operation is not in a base register. The following production anticipates this:

Adr(A) → Index Obj(Offset,Size) Adr(B) #get_reg(Long,R)
    #emit(MovL,B,R) #build_adr(Offset,Size,R,A)

In this case, we get a register by invoking **get_reg()**, then we generate an instruction to move the contents of the second operand to the register and then build an address involving the offset and newly loaded base register. Note that the ordering of productions is significant because we seek to avoid generating unnecessary code. Further, a second pair of indexing productions is normally created to cover those cases in which the operands of the Index operator are permuted, with the base register or address preceding the offset value.

The second class of attributed productions involves *operand transfers*. These are used to handle conversions, to protect operands when destructive operations are used (as in a two-address add), and to handle nonorthogonality (in which not all operand or address forms may be used with a given operation). These productions are vital to prevent blocking. They may or may not generate code. For example, consider

Long(B) → Adr(B) IsLong?(B)

This production matches a nonterminal representing an address and verifies that it represents an object in long format. If a conversion is required, the following may be used (CvtWL converts a word operand to a long operand):

Long(A) → Adr(B) ConvertLong?(B) #get_temp(Long,A) #emit(CvtWL,B,A)

The third class of attributed productions is used to select instruction sequences to realize various operations. Normally, more than one production appears because different target instructions can be used to implement the same operation. For example, consider the productions shown in Figure 15.39.

The productions are ordered from the most specialized to the most general, with predicates controlling the applicability of various choices. First, the special case of addition of zero is tested. If it applies, no code is generated. Then the special case of addition of one into a dead value is considered. Next, the case in which an operand of the addition is the target of the addition is listed. If one of the operands of the addition is dead, the operand may be overwritten, and this possibility is included. Finally, the most general and costly form of addition—a three-operand add—is considered, either in the

Long(R)   → + Long(A) Long(R) IsZero?(A)

Long(R)   → + Long(A) Long(R) IsOne?(A) Dead?(R) #emit(IncL,R)

Null   → := Long(A) + Long(A) Long(B) #emit(AddL2,B,A)

Long(R)   → + Long(A) Long(R) Dead?(R) #emit(AddL2,A,R)

Null   → := Long(C) + Long(A) Long(B) #emit(AddL3,A,B,C)

Long(R)   → + Long(A) Long(B) #get_temp(Long,R) #emit(AddL3,A,B,R)

Figure 15.39   Attributed Code-Generation Templates

context of an assignment or as a subexpression that produces a long-length result.

To handle commutative operators, such as +, two productions, representing both operand orders, are used. Note that if the last (most general) production for an operation involves no predicates, then blocking cannot occur. Otherwise, we must establish that under all circumstances at least one production for a given operand will be enabled.

As an example of attributed code generation, let us reconsider the example of the previous section: A := P↑.B + C. When translated to an attributed CGIR, we have

:= Index Obj(A,Long) Base(D1) + Index Index Obj(P,Long) Base(D1)
      Obj(B,Long) Index Obj(C,Word) Base(D1)

Attribute values denote operand lengths and offsets and are enclosed in parentheses. We assume that A, P, and B are long-length and that C is word-length. The Index operator is used to access variables allocated in activation records and also to access fields of records. Because addresses and values are made explicit, we do not insert explicit ↑'s (though we could if we wished to force conversion of an address into a value).

First the index operation involving A is recognized, yielding

:= Adr(Long,(A,D1)) + Index Index Obj(P,Long) Base(D1) Obj(B,Long)
      Index Obj(C,Word) Base(D1)

The attributes of Adr show that its operand length is long and its address is (A,D1). Next, operand A is recognized as being in long format:

:= Long(A,D1) + Index Index Obj(P,Long) Base(D1) Obj(B,Long)
      Index Obj(C,Word) Base(D1)

Next P is matched as an Adr:

:= Long(A,D1) + Index Adr(Long,(P,D1)) Obj(B,Long)
      Index Obj(C,Word) Base(D1)

Next the index operation involving P and B is matched. Because this operation involves an Adr rather than a Base, we must allocate a register (R1, say) and load it by generating MovL (P,D1),R1. We now have

:= Long(A,D1) + Adr(Long,(B,R1)) Index Obj(C,Word) Base(D1)

This operand is recognized as a Long operand, and C is recognized as an Adr, whose operand length is Word:

:= Long(A,D1) + Long(B,R1) Adr(Word,(C,D1))

At this point, C is converted into a long-length operand because no mixed-length add operations exist. A temporary, T, is allocated, and C is converted into long-length form by generating CvtWL (C,D1),T. We now have

:= Long(A,D1) + Long(B,R1) Long(T)

This is completely matched, yielding Null, and AddL3 (B,R1),T,(A,D1) is generated. The code sequence generated is

```
MovL    (P,D1),R1
CvtWL   (C,D1),T
AddL3   (B,R1),T,(A,D1)
```

This is a very reasonable translation of A := P↑.B + C given a VAX-like architecture.

One of the real strengths of attributed code generation is that it is easy to enhance the quality of generated code *incrementally* by adding new productions, predicates, or action symbols. Thus if one wishes to use a shift instruction to implement certain multiplications, it is only necessary to add a new production, with predicates defining when it is applicable. Other, more elaborate optimizations are also possible. For example, it is sometimes desirable to delay or suppress an assignment operation. That is, given A := B, we may delay generating assignment code. As long as B is not changed, references to the value of A can be replaced with the value of B (this is called *copy propagation*).

To implement this kind of optimization, we could introduce a new action symbol called delay. delay is analogous to emit except that it delays actually generating an instruction until it is forced to do so. In effect, it acts as a filter does, queuing instructions in a buffer and actually generating them when they are needed. The interesting thing about this approach is that to implement it we need only modify the emit routine to buffer instructions. The basic code-generation mechanism needs no changes at all.

Experimental attribute-based code generators have been produced for a variety of machines, including the PDP-11, VAX, and iAPX-86. On a VAX, creation of a code generator typically requires several minutes. The VAX, which has a very rich instruction set, and the iAPX-86, which has a very nonorthogonal instruction set, each require a grammar of about 600 productions and 1200 parser states. The PDP-11, which is somewhat simpler, requires about 400 productions and 800 parser states. Code-generation speed is several thousand instructions per minute. It is estimated that about one month is needed to bring up a code generator for a new architecture.

The quality of generated code, when compared with native compilers, is very good. It is comparable to that produced by ordinary, nonoptimizing compilers. Attribute-based code generators are especially good at utilizing special instructions, hardware addressing modes, and registers.

15.8.3. **Generation of Peephole Optimizers**

In Fraser and Davidson (1980) ways of automating the creation of peephole optimizers are discussed. The idea is first to define the effect of target machine instructions at the register-transfer level. At this level, instructions are seen to modify primitive hardware locations, including memory (represented as a vector M), registers (represented as a vector R), the PC (program counter), various condition codes, and so on. For example, at the register-transfer level we might have the following (the PC is implicitly incremented as part of instruction execution):

```
R[3]    ← R[3] + 1              -- Add 1 to register 3
M[c]    ← 0                     -- Set memory location c to 0
PC      ← (NZ = 0 ⇒ 140 else PC)   -- If the condition code (NZ) is 0
                                -- then jump to 140
```

A target machine instruction may have more than one effect, and its definition at the register-transfer level may include more than one assignment:

```
Add s,d    d ← d + s;
           NZ ← d + s ? 0    -- ? is the compare operator
```

In this case the add instruction adds its operands, puts its result into the second operand, and sets the condition code according to the sign of the result. These register-transfer effects may be thought of as occurring *concurrently* because they are all part of one instruction.

Operands may utilize various addressing modes, and these too are defined at the register-transfer level and are included with instruction definitions to represent the full effect of an instruction. For example, Add 100(R2),@R3, where @ denotes indirection, is defined as

```
@R3    ← @R3 + 100(R2);
NZ     ← @R3 + 100(R2) ? 0
```

which expands to

```
M[R[3]]    ← M[R[3]] + M[R[2]+100];
NZ         ← M[R[3] + M[R[2]+100] ? 0
```

The peephole optimizer (PO) operates by considering pairs of instructions, expanding them to their register-transfer level definitions, simplifying the combined definitions, and then searching for a *single* instruction that has the same effect as the combined pair. Consider

```
SUB #2,R3    -- Subtract 2 from R3
CLR @R3      -- Clear the location pointed to by R3
```

First, definitions are substituted:

$$R[3] \quad \leftarrow R[3] - 2; \quad NZ \quad \leftarrow R[3] - 2 ? 0$$
$$M[R[3]] \quad \leftarrow 0; \quad\quad NZ \quad \leftarrow 0 ? 0$$

We observe that the first assignment of NZ can be ignored because the second assignment resets NZ before the first value is ever referenced. Also, we can substitute references to R[3] in the second instruction with the expression assigned to R[3] in the first instruction. This yields

$$R[3] \leftarrow R[3] - 2; \ M[R[3]-2] \leftarrow 0 \ ; NZ \leftarrow 0 ? 0$$

This pattern matches that of a clear instruction using autodecrement; hence PO replaces the preceding with CLR −(R3).

To be applicable, an instruction must perform all the register transfers of the combined instructions. It may also do other register transfers as long as these are dead (and therefore have no effect on subsequent computations). Thus an instruction may set a condition code, even if this is not needed, as long as the condition code is not referenced by later instructions.

Instruction pairs that start with a conditional branch get special treatment. In particular, the second instruction is prefixed with a conditional representing the negation of the original condition (the only way the second instruction is executed is if the conditional branch fails). For example, assume we have

```
        BZ    L1
        B     L2
L1:
```

which expands to

$$PC \leftarrow (NZ = 0 \Rightarrow L1 \text{ else } PC)$$
$$PC \leftarrow L2$$
```
L1:
```

We include the negated conditional to obtain

$$PC \leftarrow (NZ = 0 \Rightarrow L1 \text{ else } PC)$$
$$PC \leftarrow (NZ \neq 0 \Rightarrow L2 \text{ else } PC)$$
```
L1:
```

This is then algebraically simplified by the PO to obtain

$$PC \leftarrow (NZ = 0 \Rightarrow L1 \text{ else } L2)$$
L1:

Then we rewrite this to obtain

$$PC \leftarrow (NZ \neq 0 \Rightarrow L2 \text{ else } L1)$$
L1:

Finally, we get

$$PC \leftarrow (NZ \neq 0 \Rightarrow L2 \text{ else } PC)$$
L1:

which is matched by

BNZ L2
L1:

The PO has thus discovered a common optimization—a conditional branch around an unconditional branch can be replaced by a conditional branch with a negated condition.

An unconditional branch is paired with its target instruction. This pairing often allows jump chains (a jump to another jump) to be collapsed. Note, however, that instruction pairs with the second instruction labeled are not optimized. This situation is needed to make jumps to such labels work correctly. However, if all references to a label are removed by the PO, then the label itself is also removed, possibly allowing new optimizations to be discovered.

The analysis and simplification of the instructions just described are not actually done during compilation because this would be too slow. Rather, representative samples of actual programs are analyzed in advance, and the most common peephole optimizations are stored in a table. During compilation, this table is consulted to determine if the instructions currently in the peephole may be optimized.

Davidson and Fraser note that peephole optimization can be used to greatly simplify code generation. The idea is that a code generator need only utilize the most general instruction forms and the most primitive addressing modes of a machine, relying upon peephole optimization to discover special-purpose instructions that might be substituted. In a rather extreme test of this approach, Davidson and Fraser assumed a compiler that generated simple P-code–style instructions. These instructions were expanded in a macro-like fashion to PDP-11 code; then peephole optimization was performed. In most cases the code produced was comparable in size with that produced by a native PDP-11 compiler. The result suggests that this approach of first generating crude code and then using peephole optimization to refine it might be feasible.

15.8.4. Code Generator Generators Based on Tree Rewriting

Cattell has proposed a code generator generator that is tree-based (Cattell 1980). With this approach, first the effect of each instruction is described, using a register-transfer notation. Then a code generator "discovers" appropriate code sequences by matching instructions against IR trees. That is, the code generator discovers ways to decompose an expression tree into combinations of special *primitive* trees.

As noted earlier, there may be more than one way to decompose a tree (that is, more than one code sequence that evaluates it). Further, this decomposition may block if a tree is reached that cannot be further reduced to primitive instructions. Then, backtracking to discover alternate decompositions is needed. However, this kind of code generation might be unacceptably slow. Cattell's approach solves the problem by breaking the creation of a code generator into two parts.

The first, called *select*, creates a finite set of tree patterns that must be expanded into target code. In effect, this set is a catalog of the tree patterns that are implemented. Once the tree patterns are chosen, a second phase, called *search*, is employed. Search looks for possible implementations of each of the selected tree patterns. It is run only once, at code generator creation time. It therefore can carefully examine possible code sequences and select the most appropriate one. This sequence is then stored in a table and substituted, at compile-time, for its corresponding tree. Select is designed to guarantee that all trees that may occur can be decomposed to subtrees whose target code equivalents have been stored in a table (by the search phase).

The performance of Cattell's code generator is quite good. Trees can be mapped to target code at the rate of several thousand instructions per second, though other code-generation components slow the overall speed of code generation. The speed of the code generator generator (the search and select phases) is considerably slower, about ten subtrees per second.

The most interesting aspect of Cattell's approach is the search phase. It has the potential to discover code sequences unknown to the implementor of the code generator (though whether code sequences are subtle enough to require discovery is a matter of dispute). The main drawback of the approach is that code sequences are, in a sense, macroexpanded from fixed subtree templates selected by the select phase. This means that special subtrees not selected by the select phase are not analyzed by search and thus may be expanded into suboptimal code. If a final peephole optimization phase is used, this is not necessarily a problem.

Exercises

1. Assume we are generating code for the BB1 architecture of Section 15.4.3 and have three registers available for use as operand registers. What code would you generate for the following code fragment, assuming all variables are statically allocated integers or arrays of integers?

```
C      := 1;
A      := B–C∗D;
D      := C + B;
X(B)   := C;
X(A)   := X(A) + X(D+1);
```

The successor to the BB1 architecture is the BB2. The BB2 contains all instruction forms of the BB1. It also includes a three-register instruction of the form OP Reg1,Reg2,Reg3, in which Reg3 := Reg2 OP Reg1. What BB2 code would you generate for this code fragment?

2. In some machine architectures, register allocation is complicated by the fact that use of a register R in an instruction implicitly includes another register R'. For example, a multiplication involving R_i may store a double-length product in R_i and R_{i+1}. Alternatively, a three-address instruction, OP Reg_i,Reg_j,Reg_k, can be "squeezed" into two-address form by requiring that k=j+1.

How would you organize a **get_reg()** routine for a machine that includes implicit register references? To make the problem more tangible, assume your **get_reg()** routine will be used with a BB3 architecture. The BB3 is essentially the BB1 machine of Section 15.4.3 except that instructions of the form OP X,Reg_i, in which X is either a register or storage address, store their result in Reg_{i+1} rather than Reg_i.

Illustrate your routine by generating BB3 code for the code fragment of Exercise 1.

3. A code generator for the tuple (+,A,B,C) is shown in Figure 15.1. Generalize the code generator to include the case in which A or B may be zero. Further extend your code generator to include the case in which A, B, and C are not all distinct.

4. In Section 15.4.1 we noted that computations can sometimes be included as part of an address calculation. For example, IBM 360/370 machines include an addressing mode that adds a pair of registers (one a base register, the other an index register) plus a constant displacement to form an address.

Show the tuples that would be generated for A(I), where A and I are local variables accessed via display registers. Outline how a code generator for these tuples might exploit the base-plus-index address mode.

Sometimes addressing modes can be used to efficiently compute ordinary expressions. For example, consider A∗B+C∗D+1. First A∗B and C∗D are computed into (say) R1 and R2. The obvious next steps are to add R2 to R1, then add 1 to R1. A less obvious, but better, code sequence is to generate LA R1,1(R1,R2). This instruction uses the base-plus-index address mode to add R1+R2+1 in one step, storing the result in R1 (LA is a load address instruction). How would you extend a code generator for + to produce this efficient but nonobvious code sequence?

5.   Consider the following code fragment:

```
A(I,J)         := A(I,J)/B(I,J);
B(I+1,J+1)     := B(I,J+1)*A(I,J);
```

The following tuples might be generated for this fragment:

```
(Index,A,I,T1)
(Index,T1,J,T2)
(Index,A,I,T1)
(Index,T1,J,T2)
(Index,B,I,T3)
(Index,T3,J,T4)
(/,T2↑,T4↑,T5)
(:=,T5,T2↑)

(+,I,1,T6)
(Index,B,T6,T7)
(+,J,1,T8)
(Index,T7,T8,T9)
(Index,B,I,T3)
(+,J,1,T8)
(Index,T3,T8,T10)
(Index,A,I,T1)
(Index,T1,J,T2)
(*,T10↑,T2↑,T11)
(:=,T11,T9↑)
```

Use the value-numbering techniques of Section 15.4.2 to identify and re-move redundant tuples in this tuple sequence.

6.   Run-time checks are often required to verify that arrays, pointers, and constrained variables are used properly. If checking code is generated naively, the size and speed of a program can be significantly impaired. For example, assume we have a tuple of the form $(TestRng,I,L,U)$ that tests whether I is in the range L..U. This tuple can be used to check both subscripts and constrained variables. If $L \leq I \leq U$, $(TestRng,I,L,U)$ has no effect; otherwise, a **constraint** exception is raised (probably leading to program termination). A naive code generator will generate a TestRng tuple before each subscript operation. In the example of Exercise 5, as-suming A and B are 10 by 10 arrays, this would produce

```
(TestRng,I,1,10)
(Index,A,I,T1)
(TestRng,J,1,10)
(Index,T1,J,T2)
(TestRng,I,1,10)
(Index,A,I,T1)
(TestRng,J,1,10)
(Index,T1,J,T2)
(TestRng,I,1,10)
(Index,B,I,T3)
(TestRng,J,1,10)
(Index,T3,J,T4)
(/,T2↑,T4↑,T5)
(:=,T5,T2↑)

(+,I,1,T6)
(TestRng,T6,1,10)
(Index,B,T6,T7)
(+,J,1,T8)
(TestRng,T8,1,10)
(Index,T7,T8,T9)
(TestRng,I,1,10)
(Index,B,I,T3)
(+,J,1,T8)
(TestRng,T8,1,10)
(Index,T3,T8,T10)
(TestRng,I,1,10)
(Index,A,I,T1)
(TestRng,J,1,10)
(Index,T1,J,T2)
(*,T10↑,T2↑,T11)
(:=,T11,T9↑)
```

Extend the value-numbering techniques of Section 15.4.2 to identify and remove redundant TestRng tuples. Illustrate your extension on the tuple sequence.

7. Consider the program fragment

```
A    := D/(B*C);
D    := D-(B-C);
A    := A+C;
C    := C+D;
```

for which the following tuples are generated.

(*,B,C,T1)
(/,D,T1,T2)
(:=,T2,A)

(−,B,C,T3)
(−,D,T3,T4)
(:=,T4,D)

(+,A,C,T5)
(:=,T5,A)

(+,C,D,T6)
(:=,T6,C)

Assume a BB1 architecture as defined in Section 15.4.3 with three registers. Using the register-tracking techniques of Section 15.4.3, generate BB1 code for these tuples. Redo the code generation, this time assuming four registers.

8. Redo Exercise 7, this time assuming that a call to subprogram P has been added between the second and third statements. No knowledge of the registers used by P is assumed, so any registers whose contents are to be protected have to be saved before the call and restored after the call. However, if register associations are cleared before the call, unnecessary saves may be avoided.

9. Extend the register-tracking techniques of Section 15.4.3 to include a move-register instruction of the form **Move Reg1,Reg2**. This instruction copies the contents of **Reg1** into **Reg2** and costs 1 unit to generate. Redo Exercise 7 using your extended algorithm.

10. Sometimes the contents of a register are stored into a memory location, and then the value in that location is immediately reloaded into a register. That is, we might see the following instruction sequence:

        Store   L,R1
        Load   L,R2

R1 and R2 need not be the same register. Explain how this instruction pair can be optimized using peephole optimization.

11. In Exercise 4 we saw that the addition of two registers and a constant could sometimes be performed in a single instruction if a base-plus-index address mode is available. Show how we can use peephole optimization to replace explicit register and constant additions with a single instruction that exploits a base-plus-index address mode.

12. Definitions of peephole optimizations often use pattern variables to describe a number of related optimizations in a single rule. Thus

Mult #2,%R ⇒ Add %R,%R

states that the multiplication of any register by 2 can be replaced with an addition of that register to itself. (%R matches any register operand.)

Outline how a peephole optimizer that matches rules containing pattern variables might be implemented.

13. Assume we are translating the following expression:

(A + (B∗C∗D)) / (E–F∗G).

Create the expression tree for this expression (assuming Ada/CS opera-tor precedence), and then use **register_needs()** (Figure 15.11) to la-bel it. Next use **tree_code()** (Figure 15.13) to generate code for the expression, assuming two registers are available. Is the code that is gen-erated improved if **commute()** (Figure 15.14) is used?

14. Show that **register_needs()**, **tree_code()**, and **commute()** each take time proportional to the number of operators in an expression tree to execute.

15. Sometimes the code generated for an expression can be improved if the associative property of certain operators (such as + and ∗) is exploited. For example, if the following expression is translated using **tree_code()**, three registers will be needed:

(A+B) ∗ (C+D) ∗ ((E+F) / (G–H))

Even if **commute()** is used, three registers are still required. However, if the associativity of multiplication is exploited to evaluate multipli-cands from right to left, then only two registers are needed. [First ((E+F) / (G–H)) is evaluated, then (C+D) ∗ ((E+F) / (G–H)), and finally (A+B) ∗ (C+D) ∗ ((E+F) / (G–H)).]

Write a routine **associate()** that reorders the operands of associative operands to improve code quality. (*Hint:* Allow associative operators to have more than two operands.)

16. Consider the following sequence of statements:

A := B+C∗D;
B := A∗(C∗D);
C := (C∗D)∗2;
D := A+C;

Create expression trees for these statements, then use **tree_to_dag()** (Figure 15.19) to transform the expression trees into a dag. Next use **schedule()** (Figure 15.23) and **allocate_v_regs()** (Figure 15.25) to schedule the dag for code generation and to allocate virtual registers.

Finally, map virtual registers to real registers, and generate code to evaluate the dag.

17. Redo Exercise 16, this time assuming B is a formal reference parameter that may alias A.

18. The **schedule()** routine (Figure 15.23) heuristically tries to schedule left operands so they are used after right operands, thus allowing them to be overwritten after their last use. As Figure 15.29 shows, this heuristic can fail. Outline how **schedule()** might be extended to properly handle shared suboperands. Does your extension properly handle both dags in Figure 15.29?

19. Explain how the code-generation algorithms of Section 15.7 might be extended to handle the case in which commutative operators appear in a dag. Your extension should be able to interchange left and right operands of a commutative operator if this leads to better code.

20. Write a program that implements the tree-matching code generator of Section 15.8. Be sure that your program does not block. That is, if part of an expression tree is matched, but the remainder cannot be matched, your program must undo previous matches and try others until the entire expression tree is matched. You may assume that only correct expression trees are processed; hence some correct matching must always exist. Test your program on the example of Figure 15.37.

21. The code generator designed in Exercise 20 guarantees that some correct code sequence will be generated for all correct expression trees. However, it does not guarantee that the code generated is optimal or even acceptably good.

    Assume that each target machine instruction is labeled with a cost (its size or speed). Generalize the code generator of Exercise 20 to match an expression tree with those instruction patterns that lead to the least-cost (smallest or fastest) instruction sequence.

22. The statement A:=B+C+2 is represented as follows in a prefix code-generation IR:

    $$\text{:= + A D1 + + } \uparrow \text{ + B D1 } \uparrow \text{ + C D2 2}$$

    where D1 and D2 are display registers. Match the Graham–Glanville code templates of Figure 15.38 against this sequence, and show the code that is generated. Be sure to show all templates that may be matched and explain, at each step, why a particular template is selected.

23. Extend the Graham–Glanville code templates of Figure 15.38 to include templates that describe the following instructions:

    • An addition of zero to any operand yields that operand without generating any code.

    • Multiplication of a register by 2 can be implemented as an addition of that register with itself.

- A three-address add instruction of the form Add Op1,Op2,Op3. This is defined as Op3 := Op1+Op2. The three operands may all be registers, or any one of the operands may be a direct or indexed address (with the other two operands required to be registers).

24. Assume we are designing a machine that will have two-address instructions. The machine will have N operation codes and A addressing modes. Estimate the number of Graham–Glanville code templates needed to describe this machine.

   Most real machines are not orthogonal. That is, not all combinations of addressing modes can be used with all operation codes. Does the set of Graham–Glanville code templates needed to describe a machine get bigger or smaller when nonorthogonal instructions are introduced? Can you give an upper bound (in terms of N and A) on the number of templates that may be required?

25. Consider the statement A := A+B+C, in which A and C are long-length integers, and B is a word-length integer. In the attributed intermediate form of Section 15.8.2, this statement would be represented as

   := Index Obj(A,Long) Base(D1) + + Index Obj(A,Long) Base(D1)
   Index Obj(B,Word) Base(D2) Index Obj(C,Long) Base(D1)

   Using the techniques and attributed productions presented in Section 15.8.2, show the code that would be generated for this statement.

26. Create attributed code templates, as in Section 15.8.2, that define the following instructions:

   - Multiplication of an operand by a constant that is equal to 2^N, $1 \le N \le Max$, implemented by an arithmetic left shift of N bits

   - Addition of a constant C, $1 \le C \le M$ to any register other than R0, realized as LA C(R),R

   - Multiplications of the form Mult Opnd,R_i that require that i be even-numbered and that R_{i+1} be unused (because the product is formed in R_i and R_{i+1})

27. Using the notation of Section 15.8.3, an unconditional branch instruction is defined as

   B Lab   PC ← Lab

   in which PC is the program counter. Explain how a peephole optimizer can discover, using this definition, that an unconditional branch to another unconditional branch can be collapsed into a single unconditional branch.

   How is this optimization complicated if addresses used in branch instructions are not absolute but rather are relative to the current PC value?

28.   After a peephole optimization is performed, the optimized instruction
      that is substituted for the original instructions is reconsidered and may
      be part of another peephole optimization. Give examples of cases in
      which peephole optimizations may be profitably cascaded.

CHAPTER **16**

Global Optimization

16.1. An Overview—Goals and Limits

Code optimization covers a wide range of algorithms and heuristics that seek to improve the code generated by a compiler. An immense number of optimizations are known. Some optimizations are very simple and are employed in almost all production compilers. Folding of constant expressions and elimination of useless instructions are examples of simple optimizations that are widely employed. *Local optimizations* are applied to individual basic blocks, where instructions are executed sequentially. Because local optimizations ignore flow-of-control considerations, they are comparatively easy to perform and often are integrated with code generation. Local optimizations were discussed in Chapter 15.

Other optimizations are rather complex and are only utilized in special *optimizing compilers*. Assignment of program variables to registers across basic blocks is an example of a rather difficult optimization. There are many program variables and few registers, and minimizing overall load/store overhead involves consideration of an immense number of possible assignments. Optimizations that must deal with the flow of control across basic blocks are termed *global*. Global optimization is the topic of this chapter.

In practice, optimizing compilers rarely generate truly optimal code. There are two reasons for this. First, optimization subsumes problems that are known to be undecidable. Recall that an undecidable problem is one for which no general algorithmic solution is possible. One such problem is that of *reachability*. It is undecidable whether a given piece of code is reachable during program execution (see Exercise 8). Reachability influences optimization because if a piece of code cannot be reached it can be safely deleted. Some compilers exploit especially simple cases of unreachability (for example, when a conditional expression is constant-valued), but, in general, optimization algorithms assume that all the code in a program is potentially reachable during execution.

Even if an optimization problem is solvable, the solution may be prohibitively expensive. For example, in Chapter 15 we noted that generating optimal code from dags required time exponential in the number of shared subdags. Rather than employ optimization algorithms known to be unacceptably expensive, fast heuristics that generally produce good, but not necessarily optimal, code are often substituted.

In adding optimization to a compiler, we actually add methods that usually (or preferably, always) improve the quality of the code that is generated. Optimizations can be judged by two criteria: *safety* and *profitability*. After an optimization is performed, the resulting program may not produce exactly the same results as the original unoptimized program. Optimizations guaranteed to always produce exactly the same results are *safe;* those that may produce different results are *unsafe*. For example, it is common to factor an expression known to be invariant (constant) within a loop to the loop's head. The idea is to evaluate the expression only once and store its value in a temporary. However, the expression may cause an exception when evaluated. Unless we know that the expression must always be evaluated in the original loop, moving the expression from the loop body is unsafe.

A number of optimizations, in certain cases, are unsafe. These include

- Associative reordering of operands
- Movement of expressions and code sequences within a program
- Loop unrolling (expanding a loop into sequential copies of its body, rather than iteratively executing it, may exceed storage limits)

Although a good optimizer should perform only safe optimizations (those that improve performance without affecting results), many valuable optimizations are, in some circumstances, unsafe. Rather than lose potentially valuable optimizations, some compilers allow users to request optimizations that may be unsafe. Warnings or compiler documentation detail the circumstances under which safety may be compromised.

Even if an optimization is known to be safe, it may not always be profitable. The optimization may, in some circumstances, actually degrade performance. The movement of loop-invariant expressions illustrates this concern. Even if we know that evaluation of a loop-invariant expression cannot cause an exception, it may still be the case that in the original loop the expression would not have been evaluated. Hence, factoring the loop-invariant expression and evaluating it in advance is a loss rather than a gain.

Often, optimizations are designed to improve average case performance and may not be profitable in all cases. Loop and procedure call optimizations, for example, usually assume that a loop will iterate at least once and that a procedure will be called at least once. In the rare cases when these assumptions are not met, such optimizations are not profitable.

Aside from safety and profitability concerns, exactly what we seek to optimize can vary, depending on the requirements of the user. Most often we seek to improve program speed or program size. Sometimes program cost (as billed to a user) or system overhead (for example, paging or swapping) is the most critical concern.

Often an optimization satisfies all reasonable optimization criteria. Eliminating an unnecessary instruction, for example, reduces program size, improves speed, and reduces memory traffic. Some optimizations, however, improve one cost measure at the expense of another. For example, inline expansion of a subprogram call improves speed at the expense of code size.

Although we discuss optimizations individually, they cannot be used blindly and cannot always be readily combined. Moreover, the order in which optimizations are employed can be important, as they can interact. For example, constant propagation (in which we identify variables known to hold constant values) can help us identify unreachable code (by folding a conditional expression). Once unreachable code is eliminated, new constant values may be propagated (if conflicting assignments are part of the deleted code).

Because of the wide variety of internal changes optimization can cause, diagnostics issued at run-time for an optimized program can be very confusing. For example, a postmortem dump may not show correct values for a variable if values are sometimes held in registers rather than memory. Similarly, code movement may cause a fault to occur at a location very different from that suggested by a source listing.

Naturally, we would like to optimize only correct programs, but this is often only wishful thinking. Usually the best recourse is to debug from an unoptimized version (this often also helps to identify the all too common case in which the optimizer itself *introduced* the error, perhaps by doing an unsafe optimization). The general problem of debugging optimized code is discussed in Hennessy 1982 and Zellweger 1983.

16.1.1. An Idealized Optimizing Compiler Structure

We model an optimizing compiler as shown in Figure 16.1. This idealization helps us categorize various optimizations:

- **Source language optimizations**
  These are done in semantic routines and are language-specific but essentially target machine independent.

- **Code-generation optimizations**
  These exploit the target machine architecture but are essentially source language–independent.

- **Intermediate representation optimizations**
  Ideally, these depend *solely* on the intermediate representation and can be shared by many compilers for different source languages and/or target machines.

We first review the sorts of optimizations that can be done in each compiler phase.

Source Language Optimizations (in Semantic Routines)

Where possible, semantic routines should generate code that exploits special cases that appear in the construct being translated. These include

- Exploiting constant bounds in loops and arrays.

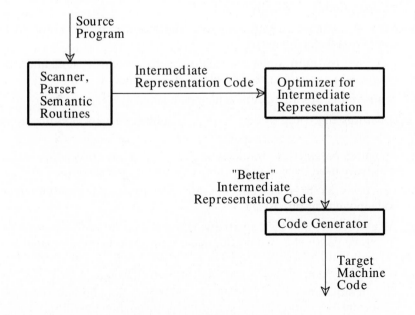

Figure 16.1   An Idealized Optimizing Compiler

- Inhibiting code generation for unreachable code segments.
- *Unrolling* loop bodies into equivalent sequential code:

```
for  I in 1 .. 10 loop              A(1,1) := 2;
    A(I,I) := 2*I;       becomes   A(2,2) := 4;
end loop;                            . . .
```

- Suppressing run-time checks that are redundant. In particular, constant loop bounds allow a loop index to be treated as a constrained subtype, possibly obviating corresponding range or subscript checks.

Later optimizations can also be set up in semantic routines:

- Loop heads and exits can be marked to aid later flow analysis.
- Points where code forks and joins can be marked to aid in identifying immediate predecessors and successors.
- Operands can be put in standardized (canonical) form to aid in the recognition of common subexpressions. (For example, we would generate the same code for A+B+C, A+C+B, and C+B+A.)

Language design has a direct and major impact on the quality of code that can be generated. Well-designed features make it easy to generate good code; poorly designed features lead to poor code. Examples of language constructs that enhance code quality include

- Named constants (variables need not be used as constants).
- Assignment operators (for example, `A[i] += 1` in C). Redundant computations are trivially identified.
- **case** statements, which generate significantly better code than equivalent **if** statements do.
- Protected **for loop** indices, which can be stored in registers and can often be guaranteed to be limited to a fixed range.
- Restricted jumps and **goto**s, which make flow analysis easier.

Language features that produce poor code or inhibit various optimizations include

- By-name parameters, implemented as "invisible" procedure calls, which are used instead of by-value or reference parameters.
- Functions that have side effects, which may make code elimination or code movement impossible.
- Alias creation, in which a variable is referenced through a pointer or reference parameter, which can make redundant expression analysis very difficult.
- Exceptions, which can cause unexpected (and invisible) jumps to handlers that may have side effects. Ada does not allow resumption of normal execution after an exception is raised; however, PL/I does.

Code-generation Optimizations

Code-generation optimizations were discussed in detail in Chapter 15. Recall that optimizations at the code-generation level exploit specific, and often detailed, knowledge of the target machine. Typical optimizations performed by a code generator include

- Careful allocation and use of registers
- Thorough use of instruction sets
- Thorough use of hardware addressing modes
- Exploitation of special hardware considerations (for example, pipelines, caches, and asynchronous functional units)

Intermediate Representation Optimizations

Two levels of intermediate representation (IR) optimization are recognized: *local* and *global*. As described in Chapter 15, a program can be conveniently represented as a graph of sequential code segments called *basic blocks*. Control flow between basic blocks is indicated by directed arcs, and all the basic blocks of a program, linked together to show flow of control, constitute a *data flow graph*.

For example, the code fragment

```
if A = B then
      C := 1;
      D := 2;
else
      E : = 3;
end if;
A := 1;
```

has the data flow graph shown in Figure 16.2.

Optimization within a single basic block is termed *local*. Optimization among basic blocks (which involves flow-of-control analysis) is termed *global*.

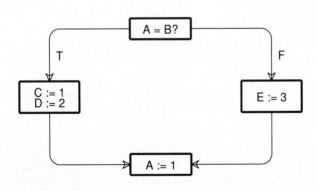

Figure 16.2   A Data Flow Graph

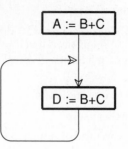

Figure 16.3   A Data Flow Graph Used for Global CSE
Optimization

In

```
A := B+C;
D := B+C;
if A>0 then
    E := B+C;
end if;
```

we find one common subexpression (CSE) using local analysis and a second
CSE using global analysis.

Local optimizations are fairly easy to do (because no flow analysis is
needed) and should probably be considered for most production quality compilers. We included a number of local optimizations in our discussion of code
generation. Integrating local (basic block) analysis with code generation
allows us to improve code quality and better exploit machine-dependent
features, especially registers. In this chapter we focus on global IR optimizations. This focus reflects the fact that what distinguishes optimizing compilers
from ordinary compilers is that the former routinely do flow analysis, to
expose global optimizations, but the latter do not.

Common subexpression analysis across basic blocks is a common global
optimization. For example, given the flow graph shown in Figure 16.3, global
analysis can determine that B+C is a CSE.

CSE optimization, both at the local and global level, is of real value
because array indexing frequently causes common subexpressions to be
created.

Because a great deal of execution time is spent in loop bodies, loops are
especially important as a source of useful global optimizations:

- Expressions invariant in a loop can be moved to loop entry and
  evaluated only once. This can be a very useful optimization but it can
  be unsafe if we are unsure whether the expression will be executed in
  the loop. In

```
while J > I loop
  A(J) := 10/I;
  J := J+2;
end loop;
```

it may happen that I = 0. If 10/I is moved to loop entry, we might get a zero-divide fault due to our "optimization." Even if the operation moved cannot fault, an issue of profitability remains because if a loop executes zero times, no evaluation of expressions in the loop body is needed.

- In a **for loop** an index variable J has successive values J_0, J_0+1, J_0+2, ... This means that expressions of the form $J*b$, where b is a loop-invariant expression, have successive values J_0*b, J_0*b+b, J_0*b+2b, ... That is, they differ, between steps, by a loop constant of b. Because of this, the multiplication can be eliminated in favor of an addition of b at the end of each loop. The multiplication is *reduced in strength* to an addition, which is usually faster.

16.1.2. Putting Optimization in Perspective

Global optimization is complex, expensive, and sometimes unsafe. It is therefore important that global optimization be used in a focused manner. Some optimizers do global analysis and optimization only on loops because that is where the greatest impact can be obtained. In modern languages modularization is encouraged; hence, it is important to make subprogram calls cheap and efficient. It is also important to analyze carefully the effect of calls when performing other optimizations. We emphasize subprogram and loop optimization in this chapter because optimizing these constructs generally yields the greatest return.

Many—indeed most—programs need not be optimized. They will either be used infrequently or will perform adequately without optimization. Critical programs do exist, and these are candidates for optimization. Profiling programs allow us to analyze the run-time behavior of programs and to recognize those subprograms and code sequences (usually loops) that are most frequently executed. This information can allow an optimizer to focus its efforts on key program segments, rather than blindly analyzing everything.

Surprisingly, for those programs that are most critical, optimization may well be insufficient. Optimization can improve the translation of an algorithm, but it cannot replace a poor algorithm with a better one. A good optimizer will improve performance by a constant factor, perhaps reducing program size or execution time by 25–50%. An improved algorithm may change a linear algorithm into a logarithmic one or an n^2 algorithm into an $n \log n$ algorithm. Extensive optimization is no substitute for clever algorithms but rather is a "final polish" after an algorithm has been carefully selected and implemented.

16.2. Optimizing Subprogram Calls

Modern programming languages emphasize modularity. Large main programs are discouraged in favor of a collection of cleanly defined subprograms. Unfortunately, many compilers (and/or machine architectures) make subprogram calls expensive. Calls in block-structured languages involve changes in the referencing environment, allocation of local data, and transmission of parameter values. As a result, modern block-structured languages have acquired an undeserved reputation for inefficiency. In this section we explore ways of optimizing subprogram calls. With care, code comparable in quality with that of unstructured languages is possible.

16.2.1. Inline Expansion of Subprogram Calls

In Chapter 13 we discussed the translation of subprograms into *closed subroutines*. Closed subroutines are distinct code bodies that are *called* and *returned from*. A sometimes attractive alternative to these is to translate a subprogram into an *open subroutine*, whose body is *expanded inline* at the point of call. This is a macro-like view, although simple macroexpansion is not suitable for structured languages like Pascal and Ada because of name scoping rules. Some languages (such as Ada and C++) allow a programmer to suggest or even specify that certain subprograms be expanded inline.

Inline expansion of a subprogram call saves us much of the overhead usually associated with calls (saving registers, manipulating displays, pushing activation records, and so forth). In fact, other optimizations become possible because the actual parameters used in a call become visible in the subprogram body. Especially in the case of actual parameters that are literals, opportunities for folding and deletion of unreachable code can be expected. Ways of estimating in advance the savings realizable by inline expansion have been proposed (Ball 1979).

In discussing inline expansion, we address three issues: how to choose those calls that are most amenable to inline expansion, who (the user or the compiler) does the choosing, and how to do the expansion correctly.

It is evident that inline expansion is largely a space-for-time tradeoff, because the expansion of a call almost always takes more space than a call of a closed subroutine. One notable exception to this rule is the not uncommon case that a subprogram is called only once. In this case, inline expansion reduces both space and time requirements. However, inline expansion of a recursive subprogram may lead to disaster if each embedded call is itself expanded.

To decide whether inline expansion is appropriate, some information is required on how subprograms call each other. This information is conveniently represented in a *call graph*. In a call graph, each node represents a subprogram or the main program. If P calls Q, then an arc is created in the graph from P's node to Q's. For a call of a formal procedure parameter, an arc is created to each subprogram that might be bound to the formal procedure.

Consider the call graph shown in Figure 16.4. The main program contains calls to A, B, and C. From A, C or D may be called. From B, C may be called.

The number of arcs into each node indicates how many different subprograms may call it. Paths through the graph represent possible calling sequences. Recursive subprograms are easily identified—a cyclic path from a recursive routine to itself must exist in the call graph. Similarly, a routine with only one arc to it may be a candidate for immediate inline expansion (if there is only one call of the routine in the sole routine that calls it).

In addition to the call graph, size and frequency of call information can guide the selection of inline expansions. Small subprograms are good candidates for inline expansion, particularly those whose bodies are comparable in size with the code needed to do an ordinary call. The intuition is simple—small subprograms implemented as closed subprograms spend more time being called than in performing their desired function. In fact, simple predefined library subprograms, such as abs or round, are usually implemented as inline expansions precisely because their execution speed would otherwise be swamped by call/return overhead.

If an execution profiler is used, subprograms that are frequently called can be identified. Lacking a profiler, calls that appear in loops can be reasonably assumed to execute frequently. Frequently called subprograms, even if they are not particularly small, are candidates for inline expansion because the time saved by not doing an explicit call and return sequence will be leveraged manyfold.

The preceding criteria can be used to select calls that are candidates for inline expansion. Ada includes a pragma of the form **pragma** Inline(Name, · · ·) that allows users to choose subprograms thought suitable for inline expansion. C++ allows functions to be declared **inline**. The

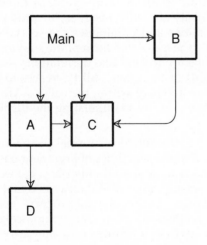

Figure 16.4   A Call Graph

suggestions provided by an Inline pragma or an **inline** keyword may be ignored if they are inappropriate. Hence, recursive subprograms are not normally expanded inline, or if they are, the depth to which they are expanded is limited. [Limited inline expansion of recursive subprograms allows calls like Factorial(5) to be fully expanded, then folded.]

Once a candidate for inline expansion has been identified, we must decide how to implement the inline expansion. At first glance, it might appear that macroexpansion is suitable, but this is not so. The problem is that a call must have the same effect whether it is implemented as an ordinary call of a closed subroutine or as an inline expansion. Macroexpansion does not always have the same semantics as an ordinary call because of scoping rules. Consider

```
declare
    A : Integer;
    procedure P(I : Integer) is
        J : constant Integer := I*2;
    begin
        Write(A,J);
    end P;
begin
    declare
        A : Boolean;
    begin
        P(1);
    end;
end;
```

If the call of P were macroexpanded, a boolean would be written; an ordinary call would write an integer.

Rather than macroexpanding a source representation of a subprogram, we translate the subprogram to an IR form—perhaps tuples or a Diana-like tree. References to nonlocals are fully resolved, to preserve scoping rules; references to local declarations and parameters are specially marked. When an inline expansion occurs, the translated form of the subprogram body is substituted. Local declarations are treated like declarations within a block; they extend the activation record of the caller. All references to locals in the subprogram become references to space within the caller's AR. This means that the overhead of pushing an AR and manipulating the display is avoided for inline calls.

Actual parameters are substituted for formal parameters in the subprogram body in such a way that the semantics of argument passing is respected. In particular, each parameter is evaluated only once, before execution of the subprogram body. Thus an argument of A(J) always denotes the same array element, even if J is changed within the subprogram body. Nonconstant scalar arguments must be copied into a temporary; nonscalar arguments normally passed by reference may be substituted once they are evaluated.

Following these rules, the preceding example would be translated to the following (recall though that the substitution is actually at the IR level):

```
B1: declare
        A : Integer;
    begin
        declare
            A : Boolean;
        begin
            declare
                J : constant Integer := 1*2;
            begin
                Write(B1.A,J); -- Correct A is referenced
            end;
        end;
    end B1;
```

16.2.2. Optimizing Calls of Closed Subroutines

In assembly-language programs, calls to closed subroutines are often realized by a single instruction that saves a return address and jumps to the beginning of the subroutine. In structured languages, calls are usually a good deal more expensive because activation records must be manipulated, displays updated, parameters passed, and registers saved and restored. In this section we explore ways to reduce the cost of calls to closed subroutines in block-structured languages like Ada and Pascal.

An optimization that is often quite valuable follows from the observation that activation records for nonrecursive subprograms can be statically allocated, obviating the need to do any AR or display manipulation when these subprograms are called.

In Section 16.2.1 we introduced the notion of a call graph, which represents possible calling sequences. Any subprogram that appears on a cyclic path in a call graph is potentially recursive and must have its activation record pushed and popped on the run-time stack. The call graph also represents a constraint on the mapping of ARs to memory. If a path exists from subprogram P to subprogram Q, then P could call Q (directly or indirectly) and hence their ARs must be disjoint. However, if there is no path from P to Q (or Q to P), then ARs for the two subprograms can be overlaid.

To assign *static* addresses to activation records, we first identify recursive subprograms and then remove them from the call graph. (Recursive subprograms must have their ARs allocated on the run-time stack.) After recursive subprograms are removed, we *topologically sort* the call graph. A topological sort is simply a listing of the nodes of a graph such that if an arc exists from P to Q, then P precedes Q in the listing. (As long as there are no cycles in a graph, such a listing is always possible.)

Recall the call graph example of Figure 16.4. For this graph, both (Main,A,B,C,D) and (Main,B,A,C,D) are topological sorts. An algorithm for topological sorts can be found in most books on data structures (Knuth 1968). In fact, if a language requires that subprograms be fully declared before they are called, a reverse listing of the order of declaration is a topological sort of the subprograms.

Using a topological sort of the nodes of a call graph, we can formulate a simple rule for allocating activation records. The technique is similar to that used to assign space for blocks within procedure-level ARs.

(1)   Process nodes (that is, subprograms) according to a topological sort so that a subprogram is processed before any of the subprograms it calls.

(2)   Space for a subprogram is allocated immediately after the maximum allocated to its *immediate* predecessors.

For example, using the call graph of Figure 16.4, we would first process Main. Next, the activation records of A and B would be assigned and then the activation records of C and D. The resulting (static) allocation of ARs is shown in Figure 16.5.

It is easy to verify that this allocation is correct. That is, no two subprograms that share space can ever be active at the same time. Also, each subprogram's space is allocated at the smallest possible address, assuming all calling sequences are possible. As was the case for the allocation of space for blocks in procedure-level allocation, our static assignment of space for activation records sometimes uses more space than necessary, because space is preassigned for all possible calling sequences, including those that may never occur.

Dynamic arrays are handled as usual and are assigned space at the top of the run-time stack. It is necessary for each subprogram to store a **stack_top** value so that space for dynamic arrays and recursive subprograms (on the run-time stack) can be correctly allocated and deallocated.

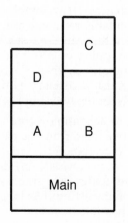

Figure 16.5   Example of Static Allocation of Activation Records

If nonrecursive subprograms have statically allocated activation records, parameter passing is simplified, too. As parameters are evaluated, they can be stored directly into the callee's AR. A subtlety arises, however, when a function appears in the argument list of a call—for example, F(a,b,c,G(x), $\cdots$). We do not want F and G to fully overlap, as execution of G might destroy arguments already evaluated and stored in F's activation record. On the other hand, F and G need not be fully disjoint, because G is done executing before F is even called.

The solution to this problem is to include two nodes in the call graph for each subprogram. One represents that part of the activation record that holds the subprogram's parameters and control information; the other represents that part of the AR that holds the subprogram's local variables. If P calls Q, then we create arcs from both of P's nodes to both of Q's, indicating that allocation of P's space, for both parameters and locals, must precede Q's. For calls such as F(a,b,c,G(x), $\cdots$), arcs are created from F's parameter node to both of G's nodes, forcing F's parameter space to be disjoint from G's space. This approach also works for *partially recursive* calls such as F(a,b,c,F(x,y,z, $\cdots$), $\cdots$). Here F's parameter space may be allocated on the run-time stack, or parameters may be gathered in a distinct area and copied just prior to the call. F's local variable space may be statically allocated because (in this call) there is no real recursion.

Assembly-language programmers often pass parameters in registers rather than storage locations, and this too can be a valuable optimization. It is often a good idea to assign frequently used values to registers, and parameters can be expected to be referenced often. Scalar value parameters and the addresses of reference parameters may be profitably assigned to registers. For these classes of parameters, the caller simply loads actual parameters into the appropriate registers, and transfers control to the callee, who can access them with no further effort. Parameters that cannot be passed in registers (non-scalar value parameters) are passed through the run-time stack or copied directly into the callee's activation record.

But exactly what registers should be used to pass parameters? Often compilers preallocate a few registers for parameter passing. The first few parameters of a call are passed in these assigned registers; additional parameters, if any, are passed through the run-time stack or stored directly into the callee's activation record.

This approach is simple but inflexible. If we assign many registers for parameter use, they will be unavailable for other purposes. If we assign very few registers for parameter use, calls that have many parameters will suffer. Further, there can be subtle clashes in register use as code for calls is generated. Consider

```
procedure P(A,B : Integer) is
begin
   . . .
   Q(1,A);
   . . .
end P;
```

While the call to Q is being initiated, will the parameter registers contain P's arguments or Q's? If we are not careful we may load Q's arguments before all references to P's arguments are completed.

One solution is to save P's parameters before Q's call and reference P's arguments from the save area while Q's arguments are being evaluated (and loaded into registers). This approach works, but it increases the register save/restore overhead associated with the call. An attractive alternative is to assign parameters to registers in such a way that the registers used by the caller and callee are disjoint. This involves the more general problem of minimizing register saves and restores, which we discuss next.

We have considered how to reduce the costs of activation record and display manipulation and parameter passing. Our final consideration is that of saving and restoring registers. In some cases this overhead is unavoidable. In particular, if we have very few registers, or if registers are heavily used, saving and restoring will be inevitable. In these cases all we can do is make saving and restoring as inexpensive as possible. This may involve a block move of registers to a save area. Some RISC architectures automatically allocate and deallocate a register set (or *window*) as part of a subroutine call. In effect, there is an activation record for registers as well as local variables.

If more registers are available than are needed by a typical subprogram, we can reduce register save/restore overhead by careful allocation of registers. The idea is simple. If procedure P can call procedure Q, we try to assign registers so that P's registers and Q's are disjoint. If this can be done, then we need do no saves and restores when Q is called from P.

To reduce save/restore overhead, we label each subprogram and the main program with the number of register temporaries it requires. We do this before actual registers are assigned. As was the case for activation record optimization, we traverse the program's call graph in topological order, determining how register temporaries may be mapped to actual registers. We do this in two steps. First, depending on possible calling paths, we may overlay some register temporaries. If Q cannot call P and P cannot call Q, directly or indirectly, then Q and P can safely share the same register temporaries. This is an exact analogue of how we overlaid activation records earlier.

After we overlay register temporaries, we then map them to actual registers. If there are more temporaries than actual registers, we assign the same register to more than one temporary, forcing save/restore code for *some* calls.

As an example, consider Figure 16.6, which shows our earlier call graph, now with each node marked with the number of register temporaries it requires. The whole program requires 12 register temporaries, but when calling sequences are considered, register needs are reduced to 9. In particular,

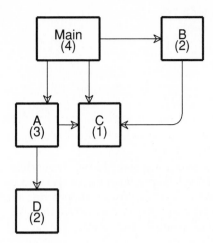

Figure 16.6   A Call Graph Marked with Register Needs

we can allocate registers 1 to 4 to Main; 5 and 6 to B; 5, 6, and 7 to A; 8 to C; and 8 and 9 to D.

If we have 9 registers we are done, and *no* register saves or restores at all are needed. If we have fewer than 9 registers, some saving and restoring will be needed. Assume, for example, that we have 8 assignable registers. Then we reassign register 1 to D. Recall that register saving and restoring can be done by either the caller or the callee. If we have the caller do the saving and restoring, we save and restore only those registers the caller is using that might be used by the callee, directly or indirectly. Thus, in our example, calls to A from Main would save and restore register 1, because A might call D, which uses register 1.

Alternatively, the callee may save and restore registers it will use if those registers may be in use by a caller, directly or indirectly. Under this approach, D would save and restore register 1 because it is used by Main. Code is minimized if we have the callee do saves and restores, because only one save/restore sequence per subprogram is required.

How are recursive subprograms handled? If we have the callee do saves and restores, it does not matter what registers are assigned, because saves and restores cannot be avoided. If the caller does saves and restores, the subprogram may be assigned registers disjoint from the initial caller if the caller is not involved in any cycle in the call graph. Thus saves and restores are done only for recursive calls, when the subprogram calls itself, directly or indirectly.

Assigning parameters and local variables to registers can improve code quality. With care, save/restore overhead can also be minimized. There is, however, a subtle danger. A variable assigned to a register may be accessed nonlocally by another subprogram. For example, we might have

```
procedure P(A : Integer) is
  procedure Q is
  begin
    . . .
    Write(A);
    . . .
  end Q;
  . . .
end P;
```

Assume **A** is assigned to a register. Now, depending on how registers are assigned and how **Q** is called (perhaps indirectly), **A**'s value may not be in a register when it is referenced in **Q**. We can determine whether **A** may have been saved by using the call graph to determine whether **A**'s register may have been reassigned on any path from **P** to **Q**. Assume it has. How do we get **A**'s correct value? One simple solution is to assign a storage location as well as a register to **A**. Within **P**, **A** is accessed from its register; outside **P**, **A** is accessed from its storage location.

Using this approach, whenever a call is made from **P**, **A**'s value must be saved into the corresponding storage location (in case **A** is accessed during the call). Our goal is to reduce call/save overhead, so we can be a bit more clever. We need only save **A** into its storage location if the subprogram we are about to call can ever reference **A**, directly or indirectly. If we can determine that no reference to **A** is possible, **A**'s register value need not be preserved in its memory location. The set of variables that may be read or written during a call can be determined by *interprocedural data flow analysis,* which is the topic of the next section.

16.2.3. **Interprocedural Data Flow Analysis**

During the execution of a subprogram, we know that variables will be read and updated. Unless we have a way of determining what variables will be "touched," we must make worst-case assumptions. We did this in Chapter 15 when we were doing local optimizations in basic blocks. For example, we assumed the values of all variables stored in registers were potentially read or updated during the call. Similarly, we assumed that any variable might be changed during a call, and hence no subexpression values were preserved across the call (all subexpression values were *killed* by the call). As a result, we optimized basic block code between calls but not across them.

We can expect to do better if the effects of a call can be more carefully estimated. The analysis of the effects of a call is generally termed *interprocedural data flow analysis.* In some cases, the exact flow of control within a subprogram must be analyzed, using the techniques of Section 16.4. In other cases, however, we need only analyze possible calling sequences, using the call graph.

Two simple, but very useful, sets associated with a call are Def and Use. Def(P(A,B, $\cdots$)) is the set of all variables that may be defined (that is, assigned to) during a call to P(A,B, $\cdots$). Use(P(A,B, $\cdots$)) is the set of all values

(variables or named constants) that may be used (that is, read) during a call to
P(A,B, $\cdots$).

Def and Use sets allow us to estimate the possible effects of a call. For
example, if none of the variables used in computing a subexpression are in the
Def set of a call, the value of the subexpression will be unchanged after the
call. Similarly, if a variable stored in a register is not in the Use set of a call, it
need not be stored into its corresponding memory location prior to the call
(though it may still need to be saved and restored as part of the call). Furthermore, if a variable stored in a register is in the Def set of a call, the register
value, after the call, will be invalid. Hence the register should be either freed
or reloaded with the updated value after the call. In either case, the register is
not considered in use at the point of call and hence need not be saved or
restored as part of the call.

Def and Use sets are computed in the following way. Assume for simplicity that all object names are distinct (we can create unique internal names if
necessary). We first consider the simple case in which subprograms have no
parameters.

To begin, those variables and named constants that are read from, or
written to, in a particular subprogram are determined. Call these sets
LocalDef(P) and LocalUse(P). These two sets are easy to build as a subprogram is compiled. Whenever a semantic routine generates code to access the
value of a named constant or variable, the object's name is included in
LocalUse of the current procedure. Similarly, generating code to update a
variable causes its inclusion in LocalDef. Because of aliasing, a reference to an
array element is assumed to apply to the whole array. That is, if we see A(i) :=
1; we cannot tell exactly which element has been changed, so we simply
include A in LocalDef.

Now consider the effect of calls made from P. Let Called(P) be the set of
subprograms called directly from P. Called can be trivially obtained from the
call graph. Then

$$\text{Use}(P) = \text{LocalUse}(P) \bigcup_{Q \in \text{Called}(P)} \text{Use}(Q)$$
$$\text{Def}(P) = \text{LocalDef}(P) \bigcup_{Q \in \text{Called}(P)} \text{Def}(Q)$$

These equations are recursive; we seek solutions that are the *smallest sets* consistent with the equations. An iterative approach can be used to obtain such
solutions: First, approximate Use(P) as LocalUse(P) and Def(P) as LocalDef(P)
for all subprograms. Then update Use and Def sets by including sets
corresponding to subprograms in Called. Continue this update process until
no changes in any Def or Use sets occur. This approach is used in
`compute_use_set()`, as defined in Figure 16.7. (A `compute_def_set()`
algorithm would be analogous.) The correctness of this iterative approach is
established in Exercise 15.

```
void compute_use_set(void)
{
    /*
     * Compute Use sets for subprograms
     * including the effects of calls.
     */

    for (S ∈ Subprogram_set)
        Use(S) = local_use(S);

    changes = TRUE;

    while (changes) {
        changes = FALSE;
        for (S ∈ Subprogram_set) {
            for (P ∈ Called(S)) {
                if ( ! (Use(P) ⊆ Use(S)) ) {
                    Use(S) = Use(S) ∪ Use(P);
                    changes = TRUE;
                }
            }
        }
    }
}
```

Figure 16.7   An Algorithm to Compute Use Sets

As an example consider

declare
   A,B,C,D,E : Integer;

   procedure Q **is**
   begin
     Write(A);
   end Q;

   procedure P **is**
   begin
     A := B + C;
     Q;
   end P;
begin
   C := A + B:
   E := C + D;
   P;
   . . .
end;

By inspecting the subprogram bodies we establish that

$$LocalUse(P) = \{B,C\} \quad LocalDef(P) = \{A\}$$
$$LocalUse(Q) = \{A\} \qquad LocalDef(Q) = \varnothing$$

We first approximate Def and Use sets by the corresponding LocalDef and LocalUse sets:

$$Use(P) = \{B,C\} \quad Def(P) = \{A\}$$
$$Use(Q) = \{A\} \qquad Def(Q) = \varnothing$$

Because P calls Q, Q's definitions and uses are included in P's sets:

$$Use(P) = \{A,B,C\} \quad Def(P) = \{A\}$$
$$Use(Q) = \{A\} \qquad\quad Def(Q) = \varnothing$$

No other calls are present, so no further changes to Def or Use sets occur, and our calculation is complete. Using this information we can determine that after the call of P, A+B has been killed but C+D is still valid. Further, if A, B, C, D, and E had been in registers, A, B, and C would have had to be saved before the call because their values are used and A would have had to be reloaded from memory because its value has been changed. Using the flow analysis techniques of Section 16.4, we can do a bit better: Because A is defined *before* it is used, saving A before the call is not really necessary. Note also that other registers might have to be saved if P or Q use them for their own purposes; however, the techniques of Section 16.2.2 allocate registers so as to minimize these extra saves.

We now include parameters. Let F be a formal parameter name. If F is used or defined in a procedure P, we include F in the sets FormalUse(P) or FormalDef(P). We initially include F in a set Formals(F). Formals(F) is the set of all formal parameter names that can represent F. Because a formal parameter of one subprogram can be passed as an actual parameter to another subprogram, we must *close* Formals as follows:

```
if (A ∈ Formals(F) &&
        A appears as an actual parameter in a call
        whose corresponding formal parameter is G) {
    Formals(F)=Formals(F)∪G
}
```

The set Formals(F) is useful because a reference to a formal parameter G, where G ∈ Formals(F), may actually be a reference to F. Such indirect references must be included in the Def and Use sets.

Consider first the three parameter modes used in Ada: **in**, **out**, and **in out**. Let I be a formal **in** parameter. I must be treated as a named constant and can be read but not written. We can check that some name F ∈ Formals(I) appears in the set FormalUse of some subprogram. If it does not, I is incorrectly used, and a suitable diagnostic warning should be issued. In either case, we assume that any variable or named constant passed as an **in** parameter is used during the call, directly or indirectly.

Similarly, let O be an **out** parameter. O may be written to, but not read. We can check that some name F ∈ Formals(O) appears in the set FormalDef of some subprogram. If it does not, O is incorrectly used, and a suitable diagnostic warning should be issued. We assume that any variable passed as an **out** parameter is defined during the call, directly or indirectly.

Let IO be an **in out** parameter. IO may be both read and written to. We can check that some name F ∈ Formals(IO) appears in the set FormalUse of some subprogram and that G ∈ Formals(IO) appears in the set FormalDef of some subprogram. If both a definition and a use of IO are not found, IO either is unused or is being misused as an **in** or **out** parameter. In either event, a diagnostic warning should be issued. We assume that any variable passed as an **in out** parameter is both defined and used during the call, directly or indirectly. Sometimes only assignments to components of a structured data object (an array or record) passed as an **in out** parameter are seen in a subprogram. Because other components are unchanged, an implicit use of the other components (to copy them into the updated structure) is assumed.

The parameter modes found in Pascal, value and reference, are a bit trickier. Value parameters are similar to **in** parameters. A value parameter acts as a local variable, initialized to the value of the corresponding actual parameter. As we did for **in** parameters, we check that for a value parameter, Val, there is some name F ∈ Formals(Val) that appears in the set FormalUse of some subprogram. Writes to names in Formals(Val) are also possible. Using the techniques of Section 16.4, we might want to check that a use of a value *always* precedes any definition of it. This check is useful because experience has shown that Pascal value parameters (the default) are often confused with **var** parameters, and a definition before a use is strong evidence of such confusion. We assume that any variable or named constant passed as a value parameter is used during the call, directly or indirectly.

Pascal **var** parameters may be used as **in** parameters (to avoid the copy implicit for value parameters), as **out** parameters, or as **in out** parameters. If Var is a Pascal **var** parameter, we will characterize it as **in**, **out**, or **in out**, depending on whether any G ∈ Formals(Var) appears in a FormalUse set, a FormalDef set, or both.

As discussed previously, we can classify the parameter modes found in Pascal and Ada as **in**, **out**, or **in out**. Further, assuming that formal parameters are correctly used, **in** parameters will always be used, **out** parameters will always be defined, and **in out** parameters will be both used and defined. We therefore add variables and named constants that are actual parameters to LocalDef or LocalUse sets based on the parameter mode used to pass them.

We can now include parameters in our Def and Use sets:

$Use(P(a_1, \ldots, a_k)) = Use(P) \cup \{a_i |$ name a_i is an **in** or **in out** parameter$\}$
$Def(P(a_1, \ldots, a_k)) = Def(P) \cup \{a_i |$ name a_i is an **out** or **in out** parameter$\}$

Extending our earlier example, consider

```
declare
    A,B,C,D,E : Integer;

    procedure Q(Z : out Integer) is
    begin
        Z := 1;
        Write(A);
    end Q;

    procedure P(I : in Integer; J : in out Integer) is
    begin
        E := I + J;
        A := B + C;
        Q(J);
    end P;
begin
    C := A + B:
    E := C + D;
    P(B,C);
    . . .
end;
```

We first compute the Formals sets:

$Formals(I) = \{I\}$ $Formals(J) = \{J,Z\}$ $Formals(Z) = \{Z\}$

Next we compute FormalDef and FormalUse sets:

$FormalUse(P) = \{I,J\}$ $FormalDef(P) = \varnothing$
$FormalUse(Q) = \varnothing$ $FormalDef(Q) = \{Z\}$

I is an **in** parameter, and because I appears only in FormalUse sets, it is used correctly. Similarly, Z is an **out** parameter, and because Z appears only in FormalDef sets, it is used correctly. Finally, J is an **in out** parameter, and because J appears in FormalUse(P) and $Z \in$ Formals(J) appears in FormalDef(Q), J is used correctly.

LocalDef and LocalUse sets for P and Q are unchanged when we include variables passed as actual parameters; hence, the Use and Def sets are also unchanged:

$$\text{Use}(P) = \{A,B,C\} \quad \text{Def}(P) = \{A,E\}$$
$$\text{Use}(Q) = \{A\} \quad\quad \text{Def}(Q) = \varnothing$$

In P(B,C), B is an **in** parameter and C is an **in out** parameter; hence

$$\text{Use}(P(B,C)) = \{A,B,C\} \quad \text{Def}(P(B,C)) = \{A,C,E\}$$

Using this information, we can determine that after the call of P, both A+B and C+D have been killed. Further, if A, B, C, D, and E had been in registers, A, B, and C would have had to be saved before the call (because their values may be used), and A and C would have had to be reloaded from memory (because their values may have been changed).

Note that Formals, FormalDef, and FormalUse sets are computed only to check that parameters are used "as advertised" by their modes. To simplify matters, we might routinely assume that declared parameter modes accurately describe how actual parameters will be used. Then, to do our analysis we need only initialize LocalDef and LocalUse sets (including actual parameters) and then compute Def and Use sets from them. If formal parameters are not used as their modes indicate, our analysis is still correct but perhaps too conservative. (For example, an **in out** parameter might be used as an **in** parameter, but we would assume that it is defined as well as used.)

16.3. **Loop Optimization**

One of the best known pieces of computer science folklore is the "90/10 rule"—programs spend 90% of their execution time in 10% of their code. The relevance of this insight to optimization is immediate. Rather than trying to optimize everything, it is wiser to identify "hot spots" that will yield the greatest improvements if optimized.

A profiling tool is ideal for locating hot spots whose performance is critical. Lacking actual execution data, loops—especially nested loops—warrant particular attention during optimization. In Chapter 12, we made a special effort to translate loops into efficient code. Moreover, the local optimizations discussed in Chapter 15 are particularly valuable in loop bodies. That is, it is often worthwhile to assign variables to registers, track register contents, and avoid redundant computations. In fact, following the 90/10 rule, it might be reasonable to disable local optimizations except in loop bodies and other heavily used code segments. This action would speed translation without affecting code quality significantly.

In the following sections we discuss optimizations particularly applicable to loops. We focus on techniques that can yield significant optimizations and yet are still comparatively simple to implement.

16.3.1. Factoring Loop-invariant Expressions

A very popular loop optimization involves factoring loop-invariant expressions from the body of a loop to its header. A *loop-invariant expression* is simply an expression that is constant within the loop body. If a loop-invariant expression appears in a loop body, it will be redundantly recomputed during each iteration. An obvious optimization is to factor the loop-invariant expression to the head of the loop, where it is computed only once. As an example, consider the nested loops shown in Figure 16.8. Assuming that arrays are allocated in row-major order, these nested loops are translated as if they had been written as shown in Figure 16.9.

In this example, it is easy to see that I∗J and A(I)(J) are invariant in the inner loop, and hence their calculation may be moved to the intermediate loop. Furthermore, A(I) is invariant in the intermediate loop, and therefore its calculation may be moved to the outermost loop.

To factor loop-invariant expressions, we must first identify expressions that may be moved. Equally important, we must worry about safety and profitability issues. Identifying loop-invariant expressions is not particularly difficult given the techniques developed in earlier sections. Let LoopDef be the set of variables defined (that is, assigned to) within the body of a loop. LoopDef comprises those variables explicitly assigned to within the loop body, those variables potentially changed during calls, and the loop index itself. In the preceding example LoopDef for the innermost loop is {A,K}, LoopDef for the intermediate loop is {A,J,K}, and LoopDef for the outer loop is {A,I,J,K}.

```
for I in 1..100 loop
   for J in 1..100 loop
      for K in 1..100 loop
         A(I,J,K) := I∗J∗K;
      end loop;
   end loop;
end loop;
```

Figure 16.8   Three Nested Loops

```
for I in 1..100 loop
   for J in 1..100 loop
      for K in 1..100 loop
         A(I)(J)(K) := (I∗J)∗K;
      end loop;
   end loop;
end loop;
```

Figure 16.9   Three Nested Loops before Factoring Loop Invariants

The *relevant variables* of an expression are those variables used to compute an expression. An expression is loop-invariant if none of its relevant variables appear in the LoopDef set. For example, A(I)(J) depends on I,J, and the address of A and hence is loop-invariant within the innermost loop. I*J is also loop-invariant, and both may be moved to the head of the loop. Because A(I) is invariant within the intermediate loop, it may be moved again, to the head of the intermediate loop.

The set of expressions that appear in a loop body, as well as in the LoopDef set, can be computed as the loop is translated, when Def sets are computed. Loop-invariant expressions can then be identified and moved before code generation is performed. The routine `mark_invariants()`, defined in Figure 16.10, identifies the set of loop-invariant expressions. The routine `factor_invariants()`, defined in Figure 16.11, factors loop-invariant expressions to the head of a loop.

Because loop-invariant expressions may be factored in more than one level, `factor_invariants()` should be first applied to the innermost nested loop, then the next containing loop, and so forth. Applying `factor_invariants()` to the innermost loop of Figure 16.9, we obtain the code shown in Figure 16.12.

Next, `factor_invariants()` is applied to the intermediate loop to obtain the code shown in Figure 16.13. `factor_invariants()` is finally applied to the outer loop, but no invariants are found, and the program remains unchanged. Although it may not be immediately obvious, factoring loop-invariant expressions in the program of Figure 16.9 yields significantly better performance. The original nested loops will perform three million subscripting operations and two million multiplications. The optimized code of Figure 16.13 will perform 1,010,100 subscripting operations and 1,010,000 multiplications, a significant improvement.

Not all loop-invariant expressions can safely or profitably be factored from the loop body. In particular, what happens if evaluation of a loop-invariant expression at the head of a loop faults? Optimizations should preserve the semantics of a program, and we may need to ignore or delay handling the fault.

```
void mark_invariants(loop L)
{
    /*  Find expressions invariant in loop L. */

    Compute LoopDef for loop L;

    Mark as loop-invariant all expressions whose
      relevant variables are not members of LoopDef;
}
```

Figure 16.10   An Algorithm to Identify Loop Invariants

```
void factor_invariants(loop L)
{
  /*
   * Find expressions invariant in loop L
   * and move their calculation outside the loop body.
   */

  mark_invariants(L);

  for (each expression E marked as loop-invariant) {
      Allocate a new temporary T;
      Replace each occurrence of E in L with T;
      Insert T := E in L's header code immediately after
        the first loop termination test;
      /*
       * If L must iterate at least once
       * T := E may be placed immediately before L.
       */
  }
}
```

Figure 16.11   An Algorithm to Factor Loop Invariants

```
for I in 1..100 loop
   for J in 1..100 loop
      Temp1 := Adr(A(I)(J));
      Temp2 := I*J;
      for K in 1..100 loop
         Temp1(K) := Temp2*K;
      end loop;
   end loop;
end loop;
```

Figure 16.12   Nested Loops with Invariants Moved from Innermost Loop

Ideally, when a factored expression faults, we would like to intercept the fault and have it re-raised when (and if) the expression is used in the loop body. This is rather tricky because we do not want to add extra code to the loop body to test for a pending fault. We might, for example, replace an expression that faulted with an error value that will cause a fault when accessed. Alternatively, we might turn off read access for the location that holds the factored value. If the target machine architecture does not make these approaches feasible, we might replace references to factored values in the loop body with illegal op-codes that will fault when executed. (This

```
for I in 1..100 loop
   Temp3 := Adr(A(I));
   for J in 1..100 loop
      Temp1 := Adr(Temp3(J));
      Temp2 := I*J;
      for K in 1..100 loop
         Temp1(K) := Temp2*K;
      end loop;
   end loop;
end loop;
```

Figure 16.13   Nested Loops with Loop Invariants Factored

involves changing program code during execution and therefore is not suitable for shared or reentrant code.) If nothing else works, we can have two copies of the loop body, one optimized and one not. If evaluation of a factored loop-invariant expression faults, the fault is ignored, and we transfer to the unoptimized body where the invariant will be evaluated in its original location.

Aside from safety, profitability issues must also concern us. A loop may execute zero times, or flow of control within a loop body may not reach a loop-invariant expression. In either case, if we factor the invariant, we will evaluate an expression we do not ever use—hardly an optimization! In some cases we can determine, by merely examining loop bounds, that a loop will execute at least once (this was the case in the preceding example). As was shown in Section 12.2.2, we can generate **for loop** code so that we first test whether a loop body will execute at all and later test whether the loop will execute more than once. If loop-invariant expressions are moved after the initial test, we know they will be evaluated only if the loop executes at least once.

while loops may iterate zero times, and factoring invariants to the head of a **while loop** may be unsafe. Many compilers ignore safety considerations and factor invariants anyway. More careful compilers factor only expressions that cannot fault.

An expression is *very busy* if its value will be used on all possible execution paths (see Section 16.4.2). A loop-invariant expression that is very busy within the loop will always be used if the loop executes at least once, and very busy loop-invariant expressions are excellent candidates for factoring. In our example, the loop body was a single basic block, and therefore all expressions in the body are very busy.

If an expression is not very busy, we may be cautious and not factor it or ambitious and factor it anyway. Probably the best approach is to use data gathered by profiling to estimate how often during loop execution the invariant will be used. If the expected frequency of use is greater than 1, factoring will be, on average, advantageous and should be allowed during compilation. (Very few production compilers actually use profiling data.)

16.3.2. Strength Reduction in Loops

An expensive operation can sometimes be *reduced in strength* by replacing it with a less expensive operation. In loops, multiplications can sometimes be replaced by additions. Because multiplications are typically three to ten times slower than additions, such strength reductions can yield significant speedups.

An *induction variable* (in a loop) is a variable whose value is systematically incremented or decremented by a constant value. Pascal and Ada allow only unit steps; other languages, like FORTRAN, allow larger step sizes. Algorithms to detect induction variables in loops have been proposed (Aho, Sethi, and Ullman 1985, Algorithm 10.9), but we will restrict our attention to the most common variety of induction variable—**for loop** indices.

Define an *induction expression* as an expression of the form $i*c_1+c_2$, in which i is an induction variable and c_1 and c_2 are loop-invariant expressions. We know that the induction variable i will step through the sequence of values: $i_0, i_0+s, i_0+2s, \ldots$, in which i_0 is the initial value for the induction variable, and s is the step size (± 1 in Ada and Pascal). Our induction expression will therefore step through the following sequence of values: $i_0*c_1+c_2$, $i_0*c_1+c_2+s*c_1$, $i_0*c_1+c_2+2s*c_1$, $\ldots$. At each step, the induction expression changes by $s*c_1$.

Each induction expression can be replaced by a temporary that is initialized with the value $i_0*c_1+c_2$ and is incremented at the end of each iteration by the value $s*c_1$. This replacement is profitable because a multiplication (and possibly an addition), performed during each iteration, has been replaced by an addition at the end of each iteration.

To implement strength reduction, we first identify induction expressions. This is easy because such expressions involve loop indices, which are trivial to recognize, and loop-invariant expressions, which can be marked using **mark_invariants()** of Section 16.3.1. A temporary is allocated for each induction expression, and necessary initialization and incrementing code is added at the loop head and loop tail. **strength_reduce()**, an algorithm that performs strength reductions in loops, is defined in Figure 16.14.

As an example, reconsider the program of Figure 16.13, in which loop-invariant expressions have been factored. The expressions $I*J$ and $Temp2*K$ are induction expressions. Applying **strength_reduce()** to each of the three nested loops, we obtain the code shown in Figure 16.15.

Copy propagation (Section 16.4.4) is an optimization that recognizes that after an assignment of the form $A := B$, references to A can be replaced with B if neither A nor B is changed after the assignment. Applying copy propagation to the code in Figure 16.15, we can observe that $Temp2$ must have the value of $Temp4$, and hence all references to $Temp2$ can be replaced with $Temp4$. This gives us the simpler code body shown in Figure 16.16

Another valuable strength reduction is hidden in the subscripting operations. Assume array A is defined as A : **array**(1..100,1..100,1..100) **of** Integer. We know that multiplications are "hidden" in subscripting operations. In particular, $Adr(A(I))$ expands to $A_0+(10000*I)-10000$, where A_0 is A's start address. This complicated-looking expression is an induction expression!

```
void strength_reduce(loop L)
{
  /*
   * Find induction expressions in loop L
   * and strength reduce them.
   */

  mark_invariants(L);

  for (each expression E in L of the form I*C+D
       where I is L's loop index and C and D involve
       only marked loop-invariants) {
    Allocate a new temporary T;
    Replace each occurrence of E in L with T;
    Insert T := I₀* C + D immediately before L
       where I₀ is the initial value of I in L;
    Insert T := T + S * C at the end of L's body
       where S is the step size by which I is incremented;
    /* S is negative if I is decremented. */
  }
}
```

Figure 16.14   An Algorithm to Perform Strength Reduction in Loops

```
for I in 1..100 loop
   Temp3 := Adr(A(I));
   Temp4 := I;  -- Initial value of I*J
   for J in 1..100 loop
      Temp1 := Adr(Temp3(J));
      Temp2 := Temp4;  -- Temp4 holds I*J
      Temp5 := Temp2;  -- Initial value of Temp2*K
      for K in 1..100 loop
         Temp1(K) := Temp5;  -- Temp5 holds Temp2*K = I*J*K
         Temp5 := Temp5 + Temp2;
      end loop;
      Temp4 := Temp4 + I;
   end loop;
end loop;
```

Figure 16.15   Nested Loops after Strength Reduction

Similarly, Adr(Temp3(J)) expands to Temp3+(100*J)−100, which is also an induction expression. Finally, Temp1(K) expands to (Temp1+K−1)↑ where ↑ is the indirection operator. Temp1+K−1 is an induction expression. Substituting these expanded subscript expressions into the code of Figure 16.16, we obtain the code shown in Figure 16.17.

```
for I in 1..100 loop
   Temp3 := Adr(A(I));
   Temp4 := I;  -- Initial value of I*J
   for J in 1..100 loop
      Temp1 := Adr(Temp3(J));
      -- Temp4 holds I*J
      Temp5 := Temp4;  -- Initial value of Temp2*K
      for K in 1..100 loop
         Temp1(K) := Temp5;  -- Temp5 holds Temp2*K = I*J*K
         Temp5 := Temp5 + Temp4;
      end loop;
      Temp4 := Temp4 + I;
   end loop;
end loop;
```

Figure 16.16   Nested Loops after Strength Reduction and Copy Propagation

```
for I in 1..100 loop
   Temp3 := A₀+(10000*I)-10000;
   Temp4 := I;  -- Initial value of I*J
   for J in 1..100 loop
      Temp1 := Temp3+(100*J)-100
      -- Temp4 holds I*J
      Temp5 := Temp4;  -- Initial value of Temp4*K
      for K in 1..100 loop
         (Temp1+K-1)↑ := Temp5;  -- Temp5 holds Temp4*K = I*J*K
         Temp5 := Temp5 + Temp4;
      end loop;
      Temp4 := Temp4 + I;
   end loop;
end loop;
```

Figure 16.17   Nested Loops with Subscripting Code Expanded

Applying `strength_reduce()` to each loop, we obtain the code shown in Figure 16.18. Again, copy propagation cleans things up a bit by removing Temp1 and Temp3, thus yielding the code shown in Figure 16.19.

The resulting code is rather more difficult to read than the original nested loops were, but it is considerably faster—and that is the point of loop optimization. In fact, we can observe that now neither J nor K are even referenced in their loop bodies. It is possible to rewrite loop control in terms of values that *are* referenced (and incremented)—namely, the induction expressions derived from J and K.

```
Temp6 := A₀ -- Initial value of Adr(A(I))
for I in 1..100 loop
   Temp3 := Temp6;
   Temp4 := I;  -- Initial value of I*J
   Temp7 := Temp3 -- Initial value of Adr(A(I)(J))
   for J in 1..100 loop
      Temp1 := Temp7;
      Temp5 := Temp4;  -- Initial value of Temp4*K
      Temp8 := Temp1 -- Initial value of Adr(A(I)(J)(K))
      for K in 1..100 loop
         Temp8↑ := Temp5;  -- Temp5 holds Temp4*K = I*J*K
         Temp5 := Temp5 + Temp4;
         Temp8 := Temp8 + 1;
      end loop;
      Temp4 := Temp4 + I;
      Temp7 := Temp7 + 100;
   end loop;
   Temp6 := Temp6 + 10000;
end loop;
```

Figure 16.18　Nested Loops after Strength Reduction on Subscripting Code

```
Temp6 := A₀ -- Initial value of Adr(A(I))
for I in 1..100 loop
   Temp4 := I;  -- Initial value of I*J
   Temp7 := Temp6 -- Initial value of Adr(A(I)(J))
   for J in 1..100 loop
      Temp5 := Temp4;  -- Initial value of Temp4*K
      Temp8 := Temp7 -- Initial value of Adr(A(I)(J)(K))
      for K in 1..100 loop
         Temp8↑ := Temp5;  -- Temp5 holds Temp4*K = I*J*K
         Temp5 := Temp5 + Temp4;
         Temp8 := Temp8 + 1;
      end loop;
      Temp4 := Temp4 + I;
      Temp7 := Temp7 + 100;
   end loop;
   Temp6 := Temp6 + 10000;
end loop;
```

Figure 16.19　Nested Loops after Strength Reduction on Subscripting Code

Although this section has focused on strength reduction of multiplication, strength reduction of other operators is also possible. For example, the expression length'(A&B) can be strength-reduced to length'(A) + length'(B), which can be a significant optimization because the catenation of strings A and B has been avoided. Strength reduction of complex operations has been studied by Fong and Ullman (1976).

16.4. Global Data Flow Analysis

Global optimizations (those that span more than one basic block) usually depend on an analysis of all possible execution paths in a program. An analysis of how data values are modified across basic blocks is a *global data flow analysis*. In general, it is impossible to know in advance exactly what sequence of basic blocks a program will execute. Therefore, the data flow analyses we perform assumes that all paths through a flow graph are possible. Optimizations based on such analyses are valid no matter what execution path a particular program takes.

16.4.1. Any-Path Flow Analysis

We introduce flow analysis by solving a fairly simple problem involving identification of live variables. Recall that live variables are those whose current value will be used before they are assigned a new value. In the context of global live variable analysis, we consider a variable live if along any path it may be used before it is redefined.

In Chapter 15 we assumed that all variables were live at the end of a basic block. With global live variable analysis we can identify those variables whose current value is not live (that is, whose value is *dead*). The value of dead variables need not be saved at the end of a basic block. Similarly, if we know that the value of a variable is dead upon entrance to a subprogram, we need not save the value of the variable prior to the call *even if* the value of the variable is used within the subprogram.

Let b be the index of a basic block. Define LiveIn(b) as the set of variables that is live upon entrance to basic block b. Similarly, define LiveOut(b) as the set of variables that is live upon exiting basic block b. The LiveIn and LiveOut sets are not independent. Let S(b) be the set of all *successors* of block b in the flow graph. Then it is the case that

$$\text{LiveOut}(b) = \bigcup_{i \in S(b)} \text{LiveIn}(i)$$

That is, a variable is live upon exit from a block exactly when it is live upon entrance to some successor of the block. If a block has no successors, then its LiveOut set is empty.

Let LiveUse(b) be the set of variables in b that are used before they are defined. LiveUse(b) is a *constant set* whose value is determined solely by the statements that appear in block b. It is easy to see that if $v \in$ LiveUse(b), then $v \in$ LiveIn(b); that is, LiveIn(b) $\supseteq$ LiveUse(b).

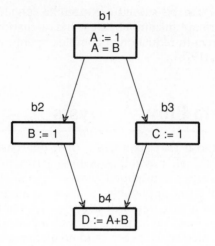

Figure 16.20   A Flow Graph Used for Live Variable Analysis

Let Def(b) be the set of variables that are defined in b. Again, Def(b) is a constant set, determined solely by the statements in b. Def(b) may be computed as basic block b is built.

If a variable is live on exit from b, it is either defined in b or live on entrance to b. That is, LiveIn(b) ⊇ LiveOut(b) – Def(b). Careful consideration establishes that the only way a variable can be live on entrance to a block is either for it to be in the set LiveUse of the block or for it to be live on exit from the block and not redefined within the block. This analysis leads to the following equation:

$$\text{LiveIn}(b) = \text{LiveUse}(b) \cup (\text{LiveOut}(b) - \text{Def}(b))$$

An equation of this form exists for each basic block, relating LiveIn and LiveOut sets for the block. A global live variable analysis must compute LiveIn and LiveOut sets for each block that are consistent with the flow equations of that block.

To make this analysis more concrete, consider the following example:

```
A := 1;
if A=B then
        B := 1;
else
        C := 1;
end if;
D := A+B;
```

The corresponding flow graph is shown in Figure 16.20.

From the basic blocks we first extract Def and LiveUse sets:

Block	Def	LiveUse
b1	{A}	{B}
b2	{B}	∅
b3	{C}	∅
b4	{D}	{A,B}

We can compute a solution by starting with the last basic block and working backward. In fact, in this analysis information flow is from uses of variables back to where they are defined, so live variable detection is sometimes called a *backward-flow* problem. As we shall see, for other data flow problems, information flows in the same direction as flow of control; these are *forward-flow* problems.

Because b4 has no successors, we know LiveOut(b4) = ∅. Therefore

LiveIn(b4) = LiveUse(b4) = {A,B}

Now

LiveOut(b2) = LiveIn(b4) = {A,B}   and
LiveOut(b3) = LiveIn(b4) = {A,B}

There are no live uses in either b2 or b3, so we have

LiveIn(b2) = LiveOut(b2)–Def(b2) = {A,B}–{B} = {A}
LiveIn(b3) = LiveOut(b3)–Def(b3) = {A,B}–{C} = {A,B}
LiveOut(b1) = LiveIn(b2) ∪ LiveIn(b3) = {A} ∪ {A,B} = {A,B}

Finally,

LiveIn(b1) = LiveUse(b1) ∪ (LiveOut(b1)–Def(b1)) = {B} ∪ ({A,B}–{A}) = {B}

Summarizing, we have

Block	LiveIn	LiveOut
b1	{B}	{A,B}
b2	{A}	{A,B}
b3	{A,B}	{A,B}
b4	{A,B}	∅

This example illustrates another use of live variable analysis. If a variable is live at the beginning of the initial basic block, then the variable may be used before it is defined—such use before definition is a common error. In our example, LiveIn(b1) = {B}, and B is in fact used before it is defined.

If we restrict our attention to flow graphs that have a unique starting node (with no predecessors) and one or more ending nodes (with no successors), it is always possible to solve data flow equations. The idea is that we start with values generated in basic blocks (LiveUse sets in our example) and then propagate these values to predecessors, excluding values killed within blocks (Def sets in our example). We iterate until the In and Out sets converge.

It is a bit surprising, but a solution to a data flow problem need not be unique. To see why, consider the flow graph shown in Figure 16.21, which corresponds to a simple loop. In this flow graph no variables are defined, and A is used in block b4. The most obvious solution is to propagate this use backward, concluding that LiveIn = {A} for all four blocks. Unfortunately, less reasonable solutions are also possible. For example, the following solution is valid (in the sense that all the flow equations are satisfied):

Block	LiveIn	LiveOut
b1	{A,B}	{A,B}
b2	{A,B}	{A,B}
b3	{A,B}	{A,B}
b4	{A}	∅

This solution is remarkable in that B is never used in any block! The problem is that blocks b2 and b3 are ancestors of each other, and because B is never defined (all Def sets are empty), once B is included in a LiveIn set it can never be removed.

Our data flow equations can be viewed either pessimistically or optimistically. The pessimistic view assumes that variables are all live unless we see explicit definitions in all successor blocks. The optimistic view assumes variables are live only if we see a live use in some successor block (with no intervening definitions).

The optimistic view is "minimal" in the sense that the (valid) solution that has the smallest possible LiveIn and LiveOut sets is chosen. In Exercise 27, it is established that a minimal solution always exists. For purposes of optimization, a minimal live variable solution is preferred, because live values need to be stored but dead values can be ignored. Phrased differently, a variable is considered live only if a live use of it can actually be seen in a successor block.

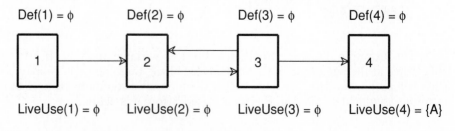

Figure 16.21   Flow Graph for a Simple Loop

We can formulate the problem of detecting variables that are possibly uninitialized as a forward data flow problem. A forward data flow problem traces information flow in the same direction as the flow of control during program execution.

We consider an uninitialized variable to be one that may contain an illegal value. Some compilers—for example, PL/C (Conway 1973)—initialize all variables to a special illegal value and test for that value before the variable is used. In ordinary Pascal or Ada compilers, constrained variables and access variables are often checked for validity before they are used.

Our analysis determines those variables that may be uninitialized at the beginning or end of a basic block. Uninitialized variables are tested before they are used. Those variables not in the uninitialized set *must have* legitimate values and need not be checked prior to use. Let UninitIn(b) be the set of variables that may be uninitialized upon entrance to basic block b. Similarly, let UninitOut(b) be the set of variables that may be uninitialized upon exiting basic block b. A variable is uninitialized upon entrance to block b if it is uninitialized upon exit from a block in P(b), where P(b) is the set of immediate *predecessors* to b in the flow graph. That is

$$\text{UninitIn(b)} = \bigcup_{i \in P(b)} \text{UninitOut(i)}$$

If a block has no predecessors, then its UninitIn set contains all variables. Let Init(b) be the set of variables in b that are known to be initialized at the end of b. This set includes variables assigned a value known to be valid, as well as variables that are tested prior to their use. In the latter case, an illegal value would have caused a fault, and if control reaches the end of the block, the value of the variable must have been valid. From the definition of Init(b), we conclude that UninitOut(b) $\supseteq$ UninitIn(b) – Init(b).

Let Uninit(b) be the set of variables that become uninitialized in b and are not subsequently reassigned or tested in the block. A variable may become uninitialized because of the assignment of an illegal value (for example, **null**), as a side effect of an operation (for example, disposing a heap object), or because the variable has just been created (for example, a locally declared variable in a block). It is easy to see that UninitOut(b) $\supseteq$ Uninit(b).

UninitOut(b) is computed from UninitIn(b) by adding in variables that become uninitialized and removing those known to be initialized:

$$\text{UninitOut(b)} = \text{Uninit(b)} \cup (\text{UninitIn(b)} - \text{Init(b)})$$

Because UninitOut is computed from UninitIn, this is a forward-flow problem; information flows in the same direction as flow of control. Again, solutions need not be unique, so we take the conservative approach and assume that upon entrance to the first basic block all variables are uninitialized. This guarantees that on entrance to a block a variable is considered uninitialized unless it is known to be initialized along all paths to the block.

```
void compute_rel_vars(temporary T)
{
    /*
     * Compute relevant variables for expression
     * corresponding to temporary T.
     */
    RelVar(T) = SET_OF( T );
    while (there exists a temporary T' ∈ RelVar(T))
        Replace T' in RelVar(T) with the variables
            and temporaries used to compute T';
}
```

Figure 16.22   Algorithm to Compute Relevant Variables

16.4.2. All-Paths Flow Analysis

The data flow problems just considered assumed a property to be true if it could be shown to hold along *some* path. Thus a variable was considered live if some path leading to a use existed, and a variable was considered uninitialized if any path lacking proper initialization (or testing) existed. These sorts of data flow problems are called *any-path* problems. A solution to an any-path problem does not guarantee that the desired property must hold, only that it may hold.

Data flow problems can also be cast in an *all-paths* form that states that the desired property holds along all possible paths. In a solution to an all-paths problem, the desired property can be guaranteed to always hold.

An excellent example of an all-paths problem (with forward data flow) is determination of the availability of an expression. An expression is said to be *available* if it has already been computed, and recomputing it would be redundant. Availability information is vital in performing global common subexpression optimization.

Let us first focus on how to determine whether an expression computed in a basic block is available upon exit from the block. At first it might appear that the **last_def** value used in local common subexpression optimization could be used (see Section 15.4.2). Unfortunately, it cannot. The problem is that **last_def** considers only the immediate operands of an expression; assignments to suboperands are ignored. To handle this difficulty, we compute, for a given expression, all the variables needed to determine its value. We do this by defining the set of *relevant variables* to the computation of the expression associated with temporary T. Call this set RelVar(T). We compute RelVar(T) as shown in Figure 16.22.

compute_rel_vars() recursively replaces temporaries with the variables and temporaries used to compute them, until only variables are left.

T is *available on exit* if and only if

$$\forall X \in \text{RelVar}(T) : \text{last\_def}(X) < \text{last\_def}(T)$$

Define AvailOut(b) as the set of temporaries available on exit from block b. Recall that temporary names are uniquely associated with expressions in order to make potentially redundant expressions easy to identify. Define AvailIn(b) as the set of temporaries available on entrance to block b. Because this is a forward-flow problem, we know AvailIn(b) depends on the AvailOut values of b's predecessors. Recall that P(b) is the set of immediate predecessors to b in the flow graph. We now require that a temporary be previously computed along *all* paths, and in all AvailOut sets:

$$\text{AvailIn(b)} = \bigcap_{i \in P(b)} \text{AvailOut(i)}$$

We naturally assume that upon entrance to the first basic block no expressions are available. An expression may become available on exit in one of two ways. First, it may be calculated in a block and not killed after its last calculation. That an expression is calculated and not killed after its last calculation is determined by examining relevant variables. Let Computed(b) be the set of expressions computed, and not subsequently killed, in block b.

Alternatively, the expression may be available on entrance and not killed within the block. That is, none of the expression's relevant variables are assigned to in the block. Let Killed(b) be the set of expressions in block b that are killed due to an assignment to a relevant variable. The equation defining availability on exit is therefore

$$\text{AvailOut(b)} = \text{Computed(b)} \cup (\text{AvailIn(b)} - \text{Killed(b)})$$

All-paths backward data flow problems also exist. A good example is the determination of *very busy expressions.* An expression is very busy if along all paths its value is used before the expression is killed. Very busy expressions are prime candidates for register allocation because we know their value must be used. Very busy analysis can also be used to guide code movement. That is, if, in a loop, a loop-invariant expression is very busy, it will be profitable to factor the expression to the head of the loop (assuming the loop executes at least one iteration).

Let VeryBusyOut(b) be the set of expressions that are very busy at the end of basic block b, and let VeryBusyIn(b) be the set of expressions that are very busy at the start of block b. Then

$$\text{VeryBusyOut(b)} = \bigcap_{i \in S(b)} \text{VeryBusyIn(i)}$$

We assume that upon exit from the last basic block no expression is very busy.

Let Used(b) be the set of all expressions that are used before they are killed in block b, and let Killed(b) be the set of all expressions that are killed before they are used in block b. Then

$$\text{VeryBusyIn(b)} = \text{Used(b)} \cup (\text{VeryBusyOut(b)} - \text{Killed(b)})$$

16.4.3. A Taxonomy of Data Flow Problems

As we have seen, data flow problems admit a very clean taxonomy. For each basic block there is an In set and an Out set. For forward-flow problems, Out sets are computed from In sets within a basic block, and In sets are computed from Out sets across basic blocks. Similarly, for backward-flow problems, In sets are computed from Out sets within a basic block, and Out sets are computed from In sets across basic blocks.

Within a basic block, In and Out sets are related by an equation of the form

$$In(b) = Used(b) \cup (Out(b) - Killed(b)) \quad \text{or}$$
$$Out(b) = Used(b) \cup (In(b) - Killed(b))$$

depending on whether the problem is a backward- or forward-flow problem.

On an any-path problem, a union of predecessor (or successor) values is computed; on an all-paths problem, an intersection of predecessor (or successor) values is computed.

Finally, as a boundary condition, the value of the In set of the initial basic block for forward-flow problems and the value of the Out sets of the final basic blocks for backward-flow problems must be specified. Normally, these boundary condition sets are either empty or contain all possible values, depending on the interpretation of the problem.

In summary, the general pattern is illustrated in the table shown in Figure 16.23.

16.4.4. Other Important Data Flow Problems

We consider briefly a number of other data flow problems. An any-path, forward-flow analysis can be used to compute the set of *reaching definitions*. A definition is any assignment of a value to a variable in a basic block. A definition of a variable, v, *reaches* a use of v if a path from the definition of v to the use of v exists, with no intervening redefinitions of v. Intuitively, if a definition of v reaches a use of v, then that definition might have created the value we are about to use. Reaching definitions are useful for purposes of register targeting. In particular, to minimize register copies, we would like to

	Forward-Flow	Backward-Flow
Any Path	$Out(b) = Gen(b) \cup (In(b) - Killed(b))$ $In(b) = \bigcup_{i \in P(b)} Out(i)$	$In(b) = Gen(b) \cup (Out(b) - Killed(b))$ $Out(b) = \bigcup_{i \in S(b)} In(i)$
All Paths	$Out(b) = Gen(b) \cup (In(b) - Killed(b))$ $In(b) = \bigcap_{i \in P(b)} Out(i)$	$In(b) = Gen(b) \cup (Out(b) - Killed(b))$ $Out(b) = \bigcap_{i \in S(b)} In(i)$

Figure 16.23   Equations Used in Data Flow Analyses

have all definitions of a variable that reach a particular use of that variable assign their values to the same register. Otherwise, we would not have a unique register known to contain the current value of the variable (and hence we would have to load the value from memory).

Reaching definitions are useful in constant propagation. If the only variable definition that can reach a particular use of that variable involves the assignment of a constant, then that use can be replaced by the constant value.

As an example, consider the following code fragment:

```
A := 1;
B := C;
if A=B then
        B := 1;
else  C := 1;
end if;
A := A+B;
```

At the last statement, both A and B are used. Both definitions of B reach this statement, as does the sole definition of A. Because the definition of A involves a constant, we can replace the use of A with the value 1. Similarly, if both definitions of B put their value in the same register, the addition (of 1) can be directly to that register (presuming the value of B in the register is first saved if B is live after this statement).

As is standard for data flow problems, we must formulate the meaning of the In, Out, Gen, and Killed sets. The In and Out sets represent the set of definitions that reach the beginning or end of a basic block. These sets contain the indices (or addresses) of tuples (or trees) that define variables. The In set of the initial basic block is empty. The Gen set of a basic block contains those definitions that appear in the basic block and that reach the end of the block. Normally, if a block contains more than one definition of the same variable, only the last definition reaches the end of a block.

For each variable, v, defined in the basic block, the Killed set contains all those definitions of v other than the one that appears in the Gen set. The Killed set "erases" those definitions superseded by local definitions in the block.

In languages like Pascal and Ada, determining reaching definitions is complicated by the effect of subprogram calls and aliasing. In particular, if we call a subprogram, or assign to an aliased object (an array or heap object), a variable may or may not be defined. We call these definitions *ambiguous* because it is unclear whether they will actually occur. Explicit definitions to a variable in a block are *unambiguous*. Ambiguous definitions in a block are included in the Gen set, but they do not kill other definitions and hence have no effect on the Killed set. In effect, they add possible new definitions but never remove definitions as unambiguous definitions do.

Reaching definitions are sometimes encoded in a data structure called an *ud-chain* (use-definition chain). Its name notwithstanding, an ud-chain is the set of reaching definitions associated with each use of a variable. This information is gathered prior to optimization and used during optimization and code generation.

A cognate of the ud-chain is the *du-chain* (definition-use chain). A du-chain is the set of uses of a variable associated with each definition of a variable. That is, a du-chain allows us to find all the tuples (or trees) that might use the value assigned a variable at a particular point in a basic block. Du-chains can be used for a variety of purposes, including register targeting.

Du-chains are computed using an any-path, backward-flow analysis, similar to that used to compute live variables. In and Out sets represent those tuples (or trees) that might use the current value of a variable. The Out set for final basic blocks is empty. Gen(b) is the set of tuples that use a variable in b before that variable is defined. Killed(b) is the set of tuples that use variables defined in b.

A flow analysis can be used to determine the feasibility of *copy propagation*. It is sometimes possible to eliminate a copy statement of the form A := B by replacing references to A with B. (We did this in our register assignment algorithm of Section 15.4.3.) If, at a point at which A is used, we determine that A := B is a common subexpression (that is, is redundant), then a reference to A can be replaced with B. If all uses of A are replaced with B, then A becomes dead and the assignment can be suppressed.

A use of A can be replaced with a use of B if A := B is the only definition of A that reaches the use of A (ud-chains can be used to check this) *and* if no assignments to B can have occurred after the copy statement was executed. The latter condition is checked by an all-paths, forward-flow analysis. Let In(b) be the set of copy statements that we know have been executed without subsequently reassigning either the left- or right-hand variables. Copy statements in In(b) are candidates for copy propagation. Out(b) is similarly defined. The In set for the initial basic block is empty.

Gen(b) is the set of copy statements in b that do not later reassign the left- or right-hand variable. Killed(b) is the set of copy statements *not* in b whose left- or right-hand variables are assigned in b.

As an example, consider

```
A := D;
if A=B then
        B := 1;
else
        C := 1;
end if;
A := A+B;
```

A := D reaches both the comparison, A=B, and the addition, A+B. Because neither A nor D is reassigned prior to either use, copy propagation is feasible. Further, by consulting the du-chain of A := D, we see that A is used in only two places, both of which we are about to replace with D. This change reduces the number of uses of A to zero, making the assignment unnecessary. We therefore obtain

```
if D=B then
      B := 1;
else   C := 1;
end if;
A := D+B;
```

16.4.5. Global Optimizations Using Data Flow Information

In this section we briefly consider how information gathered by data flow analysis can be used to actually implement various global optimizations. We do not discuss all possible optimizations that might be performed—there are far too many. Rather, we show how the data provided by data flow analysis is used to control code movement or elimination.

In the table shown in Figure 16.24, the data flow analyses we have studied are categorized by their flow direction, path form (all or any), and initial conditions. Initial conditions for forward-flow problems define the In set of the first basic block; initial conditions for backward-flow problems define the Out sets of the final basic blocks. Normally, initial values for sets are the empty set($\emptyset$) or the universal set (which contains all possible values).

Using this information, each of these data flow analyses can be performed as needed. The issue then is when to perform the analyses and how to use the data that is gathered. In the following subsections, we address these concerns for each of the data flow problems we have studied.

Very Busy Expressions

As noted in Section 16.3.1, loop-invariant expressions that are very busy are excellent candidates for movement from a loop body. Loop-invariant expressions can safely be removed from a loop body. Very busy loop-invariant expressions are always used in a loop body, and hence their evaluation at the head of a loop is also profitable. The **factor_invariants()** routine of Section 16.3.1 can be recast as shown in Figure 16.25. Now the detection of very busy loop-invariant expressions is required, making the routine more complex. However, the invariants that are factored are now exactly those whose movement is guaranteed to be profitable.

	Forward-Flow		Backward-Flow	
	Problem	Initial Value	Problem	Initial Value
Any Path	Reaching Definitions (Ud-chains)	$\emptyset$	Live Variables	$\emptyset$
	Uninitialized variables	All variables	Du-chains	$\emptyset$
All Paths	Available Expressions	$\emptyset$	Very Busy Expressions	$\emptyset$
	Copy Propagation	$\emptyset$		

Figure 16.24   Global Optimizations and Corresponding Data Flow Analyses

Code that is computed in more than one basic block can sometimes be moved to a common ancestor. This optimization is called *code hoisting;* it saves space by computing an expression once in an ancestor block rather than many times in different successor blocks. For example, in

```
if I = 1 then
       A(I) := 0;
else
       A(I) := 1/(I-1);
end if;
```

computation of A(I) can be hoisted to the **if** header.

Only very busy expressions should be hoisted; otherwise, expressions might be unnecessarily evaluated. But how do we locate those basic blocks that are good targets for code hoisting? In general, a basic block b is said to *dominate* a set of blocks S if all paths to blocks in S must pass through b. Because b is a necessary predecessor for blocks in S, it is a good target for code that might be hoisted from S. Algorithms to compute dominators for arbitrary flow graphs are known (see Exercise 24), but structured languages like Pascal and Ada provide conditional execution constructs (**if** and **case** statements) that are very well suited for code hoisting. In particular, **if** and **case** headers dominate all the statements in their bodies. The

```
void factor_very_busy_invariants(loop L)
{
    /*
     * Find very busy expressions invariant in loop L
     * and move their calculation outside the loop body.
     */

    mark_invariants(L);
    Compute VeryBusyInvariants, the set of marked
     expressions that are very busy at L's header.

    for (each expression E in VeryBusyInvariants) {
        Allocate a new temporary T;
        Replace each occurrence of E in L with T;
        Insert T := E in L's header code immediately
           after the first loop termination test;
        /*
         * If L must iterate at least once
         * T := E may be placed immediately before L.
         */
    }
}
```

Figure 16.25   An Algorithm to Factor Very Busy Loop Invariants

code_hoist() routine of Figure 16.26 exploits the structure of conditional statements to identify and hoist expressions. Because **if** and **case** statements may nest, **code_hoist()** should be applied in an inside-out manner, allowing code to be hoisted from nested constructs to containing ones.

Global Common Subexpression Elimination

In Section 15.4.2 we studied the problem of local common subexpression (CSE) elimination. In particular, we saw that if an expression E is computed more than once in basic block b, redundant computations can be identified and eliminated. When only local optimization is performed, the first computation of any expression in a basic block is never redundant. However, when global CSE optimization is performed, the first computation of an expression may be redundant if it has been computed by predecessor blocks. The algorithm **remove_global_cses()** in Figure 16.27 identifies and removes redundant first calculations of expressions in basic blocks. We assume later redundant calculations have been removed by local CSE optimization. Each expression identified as a global CSE has a temporary assigned to it to hold its value across basic blocks (in most cases this will be a storage temporary).

Live Variable Analysis

The values of live variables must be saved at the end of basic blocks; the values of dead variables need not be stored. Similarly, if global CSE elimination is performed, CSE values between blocks must sometimes be preserved. In particular, if the locations that hold the CSE values are treated as variables, CSE values must be saved when their locations are live.

```
void code_hoist(conditional_statement C)
{
    /*
     * Find very busy expressions in C
     * and hoist them to the header of C.
     */

    Compute VeryBusy, the set of expressions in C's body
       that are very busy at C's header.

    for (each expression E in VeryBusy) {
        Allocate a new temporary T;
        Replace each occurrence of E in C with T;
        Insert T := E immediately before C;
    }
}
```

Figure 16.26   An Algorithm to Hoist Very Busy Expressions in Conditional Statements

```
void remove_global_cses(void)
{
    /*
     * Find redundant initial calculations
     * of CSEs in basic blocks and remove them.
     */

    Compute GlobalCSEs, the set of expressions that
          are computed in more than one basic block;
      /*
       * Recall each expression is hashed to a unique
       * result temp, so potential CSEs are easy to
       * identify.
       */

    for (each expression E in GlobalCSEs) {
        Do an available expression data flow
            analysis for E;
        Assign a temporary location, temp_loc(E), to E;
    }

    for (each basic block B) {
        for (each expression E in GlobalCSEs) {
            if (E is computed in B
                    && E is available on entrance to B) {
                Remove the first calculation of E in B
                    and replace it with a reference
                    to temp_loc(E);
            }
        }
    }
}
```

Figure 16.27   Program to Remove Redundant Initial Computations of CSEs

remove_dead_stores(), as defined in Figure 16.28, locates instructions that store dead variables and removes them.

Uninitialized Variable Analysis

In diagnostic compilers, it is very useful to identify potential uninitialized variables. Once identified, a warning may be issued, or run-time checks that detect illegal references to uninitialed variables may be generated. The procedure **find_uninitialized_vars()**, defined in Figure 16.29, finds possible uses of uninitialized variables and either issues compile-time warnings or generates code to detect illegal references to uninitialized variables.

```
void remove_dead_stores(void)
{
    /*
     * Find unnecessary stores of dead variables
     * and global CSEs in basic blocks and remove them.
     */

    for (each basic block B) {
        for (each V that is a variable or
                 global CSE location) {
            if (a store into V follows all references
                 to V in B) {
                Perform a live variable analysis for V;
                if (V is not live on exit from B) {
                    Remove the store of V from B;
                }
            }
        }
    }
}
```

Figure 16.28   Algorithm to Remove Stores of Dead Variables

```
void find_uninitialized_vars(void)
{
    /* Find possible uses of uninitialized variables. */

    Perform an uninitialized variable data flow analysis
    for (each basic block B) {
        for (each use of a variable V in B) {
            if ( (this is the first use of V in B
                     && V is uninitialized on entrance to B)
                 || instructions since the last use of V may
                     have made V uninitialized) {
                Issue a warning that V may be uninitialized
                  or generate code to check that V is
                  properly initialized
            }
        }
    }
}
```

Figure 16.29   Algorithm to Find Uses of Possibly Uninitialized Variables

Constant Propagation and Copy Propagation

It is often useful for a compiler to know that at a given point in a program a variable must have a particular value. This allows the known value of the variable to be substituted for it, effectively treating the variable as if it were a named constant. This optimization is called *constant propagation* and is especially useful in languages, like FORTRAN, that do not have named constants. However, even in languages that do include named constants, constant propagation can improve code quality in those cases in which a variable is referenced immediately after it is assigned a constant value (for example, A := 100; B := B + A;).

As noted in Section 16.3.2, copy propagation exploits the fact that in some cases, after an assignment of the form X := Y, references to X may be replaced with references to Y. This change may allow the assignment to be deleted and may even allow X to be removed entirely. It is clear that constant propagation is a special case of copy propagation.

The algorithm **propagate()** of Figure 16.30 identifies cases in which constant and copy propagation may be performed. If possible, expressions should be simplified so that new opportunities for optimization can be recognized.

16.4.6. Solving Data Flow Equations

We now address the problem of solving the data flow equations formulated in the previous sections. Various approaches have been studied. We consider two in detail. The first is an iterative approach that computes approximate solutions until convergence is obtained. The second approach exploits the fact that flow graphs are structured for modern languages because such graphs are derived from structured constructs (conditional statements and loops). Starting with flow equations for basic blocks, equations for structured constructs are built recursively until a single equation for the whole program or subprogram is built. Then initial conditions are applied to obtain a solution.

Iterative Solutions

Our data flow problems have been formulated in terms of sets, and our first problem is to find compact and efficient implementations for sets and the set operations (union, intersections, difference) that appear in the data flow equations.

A good representation for sets is a bit vector. The vector contains one bit for each possible object in the set. A 1 bit indicates that the object is present, and a 0 indicates that the object is absent. In fact, this representation is very commonly used to represent sets in Pascal.

Set operations correspond nicely to boolean operations on bit vectors. Union and intersection correspond to bitwise "or" (the | operator in C) and bitwise "and" (the & operator). The set difference, A–B, corresponds to **(Va & (˜ Vb))**, where **Va** and **Vb** are the bit vectors that represent A and B.

```
void propagate(void)
{
  /*
   * Propagate constant and variable assignments and
   * simplify resulting expressions.
   */

  Perform a reaching definition data flow analysis;
  Perform a du-chain data flow analysis;
  Perform a copy propagation data flow analysis;

  Mark all uses of variables in the program;

  for (each marked use of a variable V) {
     Unmark this use of V;
     if (the only definition of V that reaches this use
           of V is V := C, where C is a constant) {
        Replace this use of V with C and
           try to simplify the resulting expression;
        if (this substitution and simplification
           creates a constant assignment X := K) {
           Replace the original assignment with X := K;
           Mark all uses of X that this
             assignment reaches;
        }
        Remove this use of V from the du-chain of V := C;
     } else if (the copy propagation analysis shows that
              the only definition of V that reaches this
              use of V is V := X, where X is a variable) {
        Replace this use of V with X;
        Remove this use of V from the du-chain of V := X;
     }
  }

  for (each definition of a variable V)
     if (all uses of this definition have been removed by
            constant or copy propagation)
        Remove this definition from the program;

  for (each variable V)
     if (all uses of this variable have been removed)
        Remove this variable from the program;
}
```

Figure 16.30   Algorithm to Perform Constant Propagation and Copy Propagation

The basic data flow equation linking In and Out sets for the same block is always of the form

$$In(b) = Gen(b) \cup (Out(b) - Killed(b)) \quad \text{or}$$
$$Out(b) = Gen(b) \cup (In(b) - Killed(b))$$

depending on whether we have a backward- or forward-flow problem. Because Gen(b) and Killed(b) are constants, determined by the statements in basic block b, we can rewrite these equations as

$$In(b) = F_b(Out(b)) \quad \text{or} \quad Out(b) = F_b(In(b))$$

where F_b is a function corresponding to basic block b that maps Out sets to In sets (or In sets to Out sets).

For each In(b) or Out(b) set, let $In_i(b)$ and $Out_i(b)$ be the ith approximation to the desired set. Our algorithm iterates until we converge—that is, until we reach an i for which $In_i(b) = In(b)$ and $Out_i(b) = Out(b)$ for each block b.

Let us focus on forward-flow problems; backward-flow problems are symmetric. We first define the values of the In_0 sets. For the first basic block (call it block 0), this set is provided in advance. It is the case that $In_i(0) = In(0)$ for all i [that is, we start with the correct value for In(0)].

For any-path problems, other In_0 sets are initialized to $\emptyset$. The reason for this is that for any-path problems we use the union operator to combine predecessor values, and $\emptyset$ is the identity value for set union ($S \cup \emptyset = S$ for all S). By starting with $\emptyset$ values, we ensure that no unexpected (and unwanted) values are introduced during iteration.

For all-path problems, In_0 sets (other than $In_0(0)$) are initialized to **U**, the *universal set* containing all possible values. For all-path problems, we use the intersection operator to combine predecessor values, and **U** is the identity value for set intersection ($S \cap U = S$ for all S). By starting with **U** values, we ensure that no correct values are lost during iteration. After In_0 values are defined, we simply iterate until convergence, as shown in Figure 16.31.

As an example, consider the program fragment shown in Figure 16.32, which reads and sums a sequence of numbers. The corresponding flow graph is shown in Figure 16.33.

We will do an uninitialized variable analysis. In and Out sets represent possibly uninitialized variables. Killed sets represent uninitialized variables that are killed by giving them a value. Gen sets are variables that are made uninitialed. In our example, this occurs only after the end of the **for loop**, when the index becomes uninitialized (and in Ada also inaccessible). For each of the basic blocks we have

	b0	b1	b2	b3	b4	b5	b6
Gen	$\emptyset$	$\emptyset$	$\emptyset$	$\emptyset$	$\emptyset$	$\emptyset$	{I}
Killed	{Limit,I}	$\emptyset$	{J}	{Sum}	{Sum}	{I}	$\emptyset$

```
Initialize all In₀ sets;
i = 0;

do {
    for (each basic block b)
        Outᵢ(b) = Fᵦ(Inᵢ(b))

    for (each basic block b) {
        if (this is an any-path problem)
            Inᵢ₊₁(b) =  ⋃  Outᵢ(j)
                      j∈P(b)
        else   /* Must be an all paths problem. */
            Inᵢ₊₁(b) =  ⋂  Outᵢ(j)
                      j∈P(b)
    }
    i += 1;
} while (there is at least one block b
         for which  Inᵢ(b) ≠ Inᵢ₋₁(b));
```

Figure 16.31   Algorithm to Iteratively Compute In Sets

```
Read(Limit);
for I in 1..Limit loop
   Read(J);
   if I=1 then
       Sum := J;
   else
       Sum := Sum + J;
   end if;
end loop;
Write(Sum);
```

Figure 16.32   Program to Read and Sum Numbers

On the initial iteration, $In_0(b0)$ = {Limit,I,J,Sum}, and all other In sets are empty (this is an any-path problem). We next compute Out sets from In sets using the rule Out=(In–Killed)⋃Gen. This gives us

	b0	b1	b2	b3	b4	b5	b6
In₀	{Limit,I,J,Sum}	∅	∅	∅	∅	∅	∅
Out₀	{J,Sum}	∅	∅	∅	∅	∅	{I}

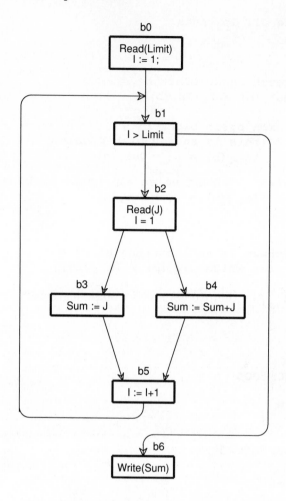

Figure 16.33   Flow Graph for the Program of Figure 16.32

The next approximation to In values, In_1, is computed by taking the union of Out_0 values for predecessor blocks. Then Out_1 is computed from In_1:

	b0	b1	b2	b3	b4	b5	b6
In_1	{Limit,I,J,Sum}	{J,Sum}	$\varnothing$	$\varnothing$	$\varnothing$	$\varnothing$	$\varnothing$
Out_1	{J,Sum}	{J,Sum}	$\varnothing$	$\varnothing$	$\varnothing$	$\varnothing$	{I}

We continue to iterate:

	b0	b1	b2	b3	b4	b5	b6
In_2	{Limit,I,J,Sum}	{J,Sum}	{J,Sum}	∅	∅	∅	{J,Sum}
Out_2	{J,Sum}	{J,Sum}	{Sum}	∅	∅	∅	{J,Sum,I}

	b0	b1	b2	b3	b4	b5	b6
In_3	{Limit,I,J,Sum}	{J,Sum}	{J,Sum}	{Sum}	{Sum}	∅	{J,Sum}
Out_3	{J,Sum}	{J,Sum}	{Sum}	∅	∅	∅	{J,Sum,I}

	b0	b1	b2	b3	b4	b5	b6
In_4	{Limit,I,J,Sum}	{J,Sum}	{J,Sum}	{Sum}	{Sum}	∅	{J,Sum}
Out_4	{J,Sum}	{J,Sum}	{Sum}	∅	∅	∅	{J,Sum,I}

After the fourth iteration, all sets have converged.

The value of this flow analysis now becomes apparent—we have uncovered a bug in what appears to be a correct program. Normally, we expect all values to be defined before they are used. However, $Sum \in In(b6)$ and Sum is used in b6. The program was probably written under the assumption that the loop would iterate at least once, thus guaranteeing that Sum would be defined before it is written. However, in Pascal and Ada a loop may iterate zero times, which, as our analysis discovered, would lead to an attempt to write a Sum value that is undefined.

Our analysis also warns us that Sum is potentially uninitialized upon entrance to b4. However, this is a "false alarm" induced by the fact that the flow analysis has no way of recognizing that b4 will be entered only after b3 has been executed (on a previous iteration), which guarantees that Sum will be properly initialized.

It is not difficult to see that if our iterative algorithm terminates, it will produce a proper solution. This result follows from the fact that upon termination all data flow equations are satisfied. What is less clear is whether the algorithm must always terminate. And even if it does, might convergence be unacceptably slow?

Fortunately, both of these fears are unfounded. Our iterative algorithm always produces a solution and in a reasonable amount of time. Consider first termination. Recall that the F_b functions that compute Out values are of the form $F_b = (In(b) - Killed(b)) \cup Gen(b)$. Because Killed(b) and Gen(b) are constant, it is easy to see that the F_b functions are *monotonic*. That is, if $s_1 \subseteq s_2$, then $F_b(s_1) \subseteq F_b(s_2)$.

For any-path problems, $In_{i+1}(b) = \bigcup_{j \in P(b)} Out_i(j) = \bigcup_{j \in P(b)} F_j(In_i(j))$. We know that the F functions are monotonic, and the union operator is also monotonic. Let In_i be the vector of $In_i(b)$ values for all blocks b. We say that $In_i \subseteq In_j$ if $In_i(b) \subseteq In_j(b)$ for all blocks b. This means that one vector of sets is contained in another vector of sets if each of the component sets in one vector is a subset of the corresponding set in the other vector.

We now rewrite our previous equation as $In_{i+1}(b) = G_b(In_i)$, where $G_b = \bigcup_{j \in P(b)} F_j(In_i(j))$. F functions and union are monotonic, and so are the G functions. This means that if $In_i \subseteq In_{i+1}$, then $G_b(In_i) \subseteq G_b(In_{i+1})$ for any block b. This is the key point; the rest falls neatly into place.

Recall from our initialization rule that $In_0(b0)$ is provided in advance and $In_0(b)=\emptyset$ for other blocks. Because $In_0(b0) = In(b0)$, it is easy to see that $In_0 \subseteq In_1$. This means that after the first iteration we may have added values to In sets, but we certainly have not removed any. Now we exploit the monotonic nature of the G_b functions. For any block b, $In_1(b) = G_b(In_0)$ and $In_2(b) = G_b(In_1)$. Because $In_0 \subseteq In_1$, we conclude that $In_1(b) \subseteq In_2(b)$. This relation holds for all blocks; hence, $In_1 \subseteq In_2$. After the second iteration we may have again added values to sets, but again, we have not removed any values. Proceeding inductively, we conclude that $In_0 \subseteq In_1 \subseteq In_2 \dots$.

At each iteration we add values but never remove them. However, the size of In sets is finite, so we cannot add values indefinitely. Eventually, we must reach a point where $In_i=In_{i+1}$, and at this point we terminate with a solution. In fact, it is shown in Exercise 27 that the solution we obtain is a *minimal solution*. This means that if two distinct solutions exist (where In is computed by our algorithm and In' is any other valid solution), then $In \subseteq In'$. For data flow purposes, the minimal solution is preferred, for it contains only values derived from the initial In set and from the Gen and Killed sets of the various basic blocks.

For all-paths problems, our algorithm again exhibits a monotonic property. We now start with $In_0(b0) = In(b0)$ provided in advance, and $In_0(b) = \textbf{U}$ for other blocks. Now we monotonically remove set values as we iterate, but we never restore an element after it is deleted. This means our sequence of approximations to the In sets obeys the relation $In_0 \supseteq In_1 \supseteq In_2 \dots$. Again, because the In sets are finite, we must eventually terminate with a solution that is *maximal*. A maximal solution contains (componentwise) any other solution. For all-paths problems, maximal solutions are preferred because we start with all possible values and remove those that do not appear along all paths. We want to retain those values consistent with all paths—that is, those values that satisfy a maximal solution.

Let us estimate how long a data flow analysis takes for a program or subprogram with B basic blocks and In and Out sets containing as many as V values. During each iteration, we compute an Out set from an In set (or vice versa) for each basic block. Each block manipulates bit vectors of length V, taking O(V) time. For all B blocks, the time is O(B×V). We must also propagate In or Out sets to predecessors or successors. The time to do this depends on the number of predecessors or successors. This number can vary, but *on average* it will be a small constant. Therefore, the time to propagate values is proportional to V, and for B blocks this again is O(B×V).

To estimate the number of iterations needed for convergence, it is important to observe that distinct values in In and Out sets are *independent*. That is, if we are manipulating sets with V values, we are really doing V different data flow analyses *in parallel*. If we did a flow analysis for a single value (perhaps a live variable or available expression), the monotonic property we established would require no more than B iterations because at least one value must change during each iteration. Because values are independent, considering V>1 values does not change the bound on the number of iterations. The total analysis should take no more than $O(B^2 \times V)$.

In practice, B would probably be no more than 1000, and probably less (recall that subprograms are analyzed independently). V is perhaps 100 or so. The overhead constant should be small because we are doing mostly bit-level operations, and these operations are done word by word (therefore handling 16 or 32 values per operation; $1000^2 \times 100 = 10^8$). Assuming perhaps 10 microseconds per value (recall that we handle 16 or 32 values in parallel), the analysis can be bounded at 1000 seconds, a nontrivial but acceptable amount of time. Our estimate of B iterations is probably far too high (it assumes that each block affects every other block), so a few hundred seconds is a sounder upper bound.

Another way of solving flow problems (Cocke 1970) is to break a big flow graph into a number of subgraphs called *intervals* (these usually correspond to loops in the program). These subgraphs are analyzed individually, and then, after processing, the entire subgraph can be treated as a single node in the graph that contains it. In effect, inner loops are processed first, then containing loops, and so on. The computational advantage comes from the fact that it is cheaper to apply a nonlinear algorithm to many small problems than to one big problem. Using our estimate of $O(B^2 \times V)$, even dividing the graph into two halves of size B/2 would reduce the cost of each subproblem by a factor of 4 and reduce the total time by a factor of 2. Dividing the graph into many still smaller pieces would lead to still greater savings. In the next section we consider a structured data flow analysis technique that exploits the fact that in modern languages such as Ada and Pascal, the structured control constructs of the language lead to a natural factoring of the corresponding flow graph.

Structured Solutions

For modern languages such as Ada and Pascal, data flow graphs are derived, for the most part, from structured control constructs. Structured control constructs exhibit a single entry/single exit property. This means that no matter how complex the flow of control is within the construct, it has a well-defined entrance point and exit point. Constructs with a single entrance and exit can be used wherever a single statement is allowed, thus creating uniformity and clean nesting. Not all structures must be single entry/single exit. In particular, if we may jump into or out of a construct, the single entry/single exit property will be lost.

For purposes of data flow analysis, structured control constructs can be solved independently. We combine the Gen and Killed sets of components of the structure into composite Gen and Killed sets for the whole structure. The structure can then be treated as a single unit, mapping an In set into an Out set or vice versa. Starting with basic blocks, we solve data flow equations for progressively larger structures until the entire program or subprogram is solved or until only unstructured constructs remain. In the latter case, the techniques of the previous section can be used to obtain a solution (again treating structured constructs as a single unit).

After a solution is obtained for the whole program, it can be propagated into structured constructs, yielding solutions for nested constructs and finally individual basic blocks.

We focus our attention here on the fundamental control mechanisms: sequential execution, conditional execution, and iterative execution.

The simplest of these constructs is, of course, sequential execution. Assume we have two structures, S1 and S2. These structures may be basic blocks or control structures that we have already analyzed. Each of the structures is characterized by its own data flow equation in the standard form: $\text{Out} = (\text{In}-\text{Killed}) \cup \text{Gen}$.

The diagram shown in Figure 16.34 summarizes the flow of data through the two structures. Now $\text{In} = \text{In}_1$, $\text{Out}_1 = \text{In}_2$, and $\text{Out}_2 = \text{Out}$. Further, $\text{Out}_1=(\text{In}_1-\text{Killed}_1)\cup\text{Gen}_1$ and $\text{Out}_2=(\text{In}_2-\text{Killed}_2)\cup\text{Gen}_2$. Combining these, we get

$$\text{Out} = (((\text{In}-\text{Killed}_1)\cup\text{Gen}_1)-\text{Killed}_2)\cup\text{Gen}_2 =$$
$$((\text{In}-(\text{Killed}_1\cup\text{Killed}_2))\cup((\text{Gen}_1-\text{Killed}_2)\cup\text{Gen}_2)$$

For the combined structure we have

$$\text{Killed} = (\text{Killed}_1\cup\text{Killed}_2) \text{ and } \text{Gen} = (\text{Gen}_1-\text{Killed}_2)\cup\text{Gen}_2)$$

That is, values may be generated or killed in either structure, and values generated in the first structure may be killed in the second structure.

We model conditional execution as shown in Figure 16.35. Normally, a predicate is evaluated and tested prior to conditional execution of S1 or S2. This can be modeled by using the sequential construct to catenate predicate evaluation to the conditional execution structure. The data flow rules for the conditional execution structure are $\text{In} = \text{In}_1 = \text{In}_2$. For an any-path problem, $\text{Out} = \text{Out}_1\cup\text{Out}_2$. For an all-path problem, $\text{Out} = \text{Out}_1\cap\text{Out}_2$.

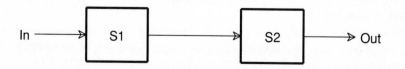

Figure 16.34   Sequential Execution of S1 and S2

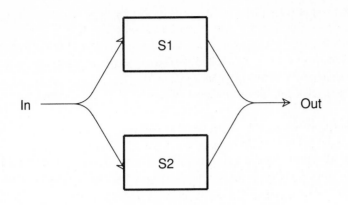

Figure 16.35   Conditional Execution of S1 or S2

Consider the any-path case first. Using the equations for S1 and S2, we have

$$Out = ((In-Killed_1) \cup Gen_1) \cup ((In-Killed_2) \cup Gen_2)$$
$$= (In-Killed_1) \cup (In-Killed_2) \cup Gen_1 \cup Gen_2$$
$$= (In-(Killed_1 \cap Killed_2)) \cup (Gen_1 \cup Gen_2)$$

For the any-path case, we have

$$Killed = (Killed_1 \cap Killed_2) \text{ and } Gen = (Gen_1 \cup Gen_2)$$

This says that a value is killed if it is killed on both paths of the conditional, and a value is generated if it is generated on either path of the conditional.

For the all-paths case

$$Out = ((In-Killed_1) \cup Gen_1) \cap ((In-Killed_2) \cup Gen_2)$$
$$= ((In-Killed_1) \cap (In-Killed_2)) \cup$$
$$((In-Killed_1) \cap Gen_2) \cup ((In-Killed_2) \cap Gen_1) \cup (Gen_1 \cap Gen_2)$$

We can simplify this equation by observing that we can always assume that a Killed set and its corresponding Gen set are disjoint. That is, if we kill a value and then (in the same block or construct) regenerate it, the kill really makes no difference. Given that corresponding Killed and Gen sets are disjoint, it can be established that

$$((In-Killed_1) \cap Gen_2) \subseteq ((In-Killed_1) \cap (In-Killed_2))$$
$$((In-Killed_2) \cap Gen_1) \subseteq ((In-Killed_1) \cap (In-Killed_2))$$

These inequalities allow us to simplify things:

$$\text{Out} = ((\text{In}-\text{Killed}_1)\cap(\text{In}-\text{Killed}_2))\cup$$
$$((\text{In}-\text{Killed}_1)\cap\text{Gen}_2)\cup((\text{In}-\text{Killed}_2)\cap\text{Gen}_1)\cup(\text{Gen}_1\cap\text{Gen}_2)$$
$$= ((\text{In}-\text{Killed}_1)\cap(\text{In}-\text{Killed}_2))\cup(\text{Gen}_1\cap\text{Gen}_2)$$
$$= (\text{In}-\text{Killed}_1-\text{Killed}_2)\cup(\text{Gen}_1\cap\text{Gen}_2)$$

$$\text{Killed} = (\text{Killed}_1\cup\text{Killed}_2) \quad \text{and} \quad \text{Gen} = (\text{Gen}_1\cap\text{Gen}_2)$$

In the all-paths case, a value is killed if it is killed on either path of the conditional, and a value is generated if it is generated on both paths of the conditional.

Finally, we consider iterative structures. There are many forms of loops, as shown in Figure 16.36. We concentrate on the most common form—**while loop**s. This form also represents **for loop**s, if initialization code is catenated to it using the sequential constructor.

S1 represents the loop termination test; S2 represents the body of the loop. To understand the possible paths in the loop, we can "unwind" it. If the loop executes zero times, S1 is executed. If the loop executes one time, the sequence S1;S2;S1 is executed. If the loop executes two times, the sequence S1;S2;S1;S2;S1 is executed, and so forth. This all looks forbiddingly complex because the loop can iterate indefinitely. Fortunately, a nice simplification is

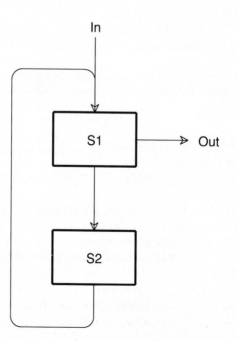

Figure 16.36   Iterative Execution of S1 and S2

possible. Let F1 represent the function that maps In sets to Out sets for structure S1. Let G represent the function that maps In sets to Out sets for sequence S1;S2. From our rule for sequential execution we know that G can be written in the standard form $((In–Killed) \cup Gen)$. The Out set corresponding to executing zero times is F1(In). The Out set corresponding to executing one time is F1(G(In)). The Out set corresponding to executing two times is F1(G(G(In))), and so forth.

Now consider G(G(I)). Because G is in standard form, we can write this as

$$(((I–Killed) \cup Gen)–Killed) \cup Gen$$
$$= (I–Killed) \cup (Gen–Killed) \cup Gen$$
$$= (I–Killed) \cup Gen = G(I).$$

The fact that G(G(I)) = G(I) means that executing the loop body more than once does not change the Out set that is computed. In fact, the loop reduces to two cases: The loop is executed zero times and the loop is executed one or more times.

The data flow equations for the loop are very similar to those for conditional execution. For the any-path case:

$$In_1 = In \cup Out_2 \quad Out = Out_1 \quad In_2 = Out_1$$

$$Out_2 = G(In) \cup G(G(In)) \cup G(G(G(In))) \cup \cdots = G(In)$$

G is the function corresponding to the sequential execution of S1;S2; as derived above, it is

$$Out_2 = (In–(Killed_1 \cup Killed_2)) \cup ((Gen_1–Killed_2) \cup Gen_2)$$

$$In_1 = In \cup Out_2 = In \cup (Gen_1–Killed_2) \cup Gen_2$$

$$Out = Out_1 = (In_1–Killed_1) \cup Gen_1$$
$$= ((In \cup (Gen_1–Killed_2) \cup Gen_2)–Killed_1) \cup Gen_1$$
$$= (In–Killed_1) \cup (Gen_2–Killed_1) \cup Gen_1$$

$$Killed = Killed_1 \quad \text{and} \quad Gen = (Gen_2–Killed_1) \cup Gen_1$$

This equation states that for any-path analyses for a loop, the Out set is the In set less what is killed in S1 plus what is generated in S1 plus what is generated in S2 and not killed in S1.

For the all-paths case, we observe that In_1 corresponds to either executing nothing or executing the sequence S1;S2 one or more times. We can use the all-paths solution we obtained for conditional execution, with one path being the null statement (Killed=Gen=∅) and the other path being S1;S2 (the G function represents this sequence). We therefore have

$$In_1 = (In-(Killed_G-\varnothing))\cup(Gen_G\cap\varnothing)$$
$$= (In-(Killed_G)) = (In-(Killed_1\cup Killed_2))$$

To obtain the Out set, we apply the data flow equation for S1:

$$Out = (In_1-Killed_1)\cup Gen_1$$
$$= ((In-(Killed_1\cup Killed_2))-Killed_1)\cup Gen_1$$
$$= (In-(Killed_1\cup Killed_2))\cup Gen_1$$

$$Killed = (Killed_1\cup Killed_2) \text{ and } Gen = Gen_1$$

The all-paths solution kills those values that can be killed on any path through the loop (that is, only those values preserved on all paths are retained). The Gen set includes only Gen_1 because only S_1 is always executed.

To illustrate the structured approach we have developed, let us reconsider the example illustrated in Figure 16.33. The Gen and Killed sets for the individual basic blocks are

	b0	b1	b2	b3	b4	b5	b6
Gen	$\varnothing$	$\varnothing$	$\varnothing$	$\varnothing$	$\varnothing$	$\varnothing$	{I}
Killed	{Limit,I}	$\varnothing$	{J}	{Sum}	{Sum}	{I}	$\varnothing$

We process the flow graph from inside out, combining individual basic blocks into composite structures:

Step	Structure	Combining Rule	Killed	Gen
1	b3,b4	Conditional	{Sum}	$\varnothing$
2	b2,b3,b4	Sequential	{J,Sum}	$\varnothing$
3	b2,b3,b4,b5	Sequential	{J,Sum,I}	$\varnothing$
4	b1,b2,b3,b4,b5	Iterative	$\varnothing$	$\varnothing$
5	b0,b1,b2,b3,b4,b5	Sequential	{Lim,I}	$\varnothing$
6	b0,b1,b2,b3,b4,b5,b6	Sequential	{Lim,I}	{I}

In and Out sets are propagated in an outside-in manner, first solving the equation for the whole program and then solving equations for nested structures.

Step	Block	In Set	Out Set
1	b0	{Limit,I,J,Sum}	{J,Sum}
2	b1	{J,Sum}	{J,Sum}
3	b6	{J,Sum}	{I,J,Sum}
4	b2	{J,Sum}	{Sum}
5	b3	{Sum}	∅
6	b4	{Sum}	∅
7	b5	∅	∅

The greatest advantage of our structured data flow approach is that it is linear. Blocks are first combined. After each combining step, the total number of blocks and structures is reduced by one, and so we need only B steps, where B is the number of basic blocks. Each step takes $O(V)$ time, where V is the size of the Gen and Killed sets (usually represented as bit vectors). After the combining phase is completed, we can visit individual blocks, using known set values, and equations for blocks and combined structures, to determine individual In and Out sets. This again is proportional to $O(B \times V)$, which leads to an overall $O(B \times V)$ algorithm, a distinct improvement over the $O(B^2 \times V)$ worst case of the iterative approach.

16.5. Putting It All Together

We have discussed a wide variety of optimizations in the last two chapters. We now deal briefly with the issue of integrating various optimizations into the compilation process. Most optimizing compilers allow users to select the level of optimization desired. In many cases no optimization is required, and in other cases moderate or extensive optimization is appropriate.

Code optimization is an investment in which added compile-time complexity is used to buy run-time performance improvements. Optimization costs take many forms. Optimizing compilers are bigger, slower, and more costly to develop than ordinary production-quality compilers. Moreover, not all optimizations are safe, and hence an optimized program is often less robust than its nonoptimized counterpart.

While programs are being developed and debugged, optimization of any sort is unnecessary. It is not until after a program has reached the stage at which it is used for production work that local optimizations, integrated with careful code generation, are appropriate. For most production programs, local optimization is all that will ever be needed. In heavily used or critical programs, further optimization may be required. At this stage, it is unnecessary and unwise to simply "shoot the works" and enable all possible optimizations. Instead, it is preferable to use profiling tools to examine a program for hot spots that are performance bottlenecks. In general, subprograms and code segments, especially loops, will be identified as critical components.

Global optimization of components known to be critical to program performance is the next step. For loops this may involve factoring invariants or strength reduction. For subprograms, inline expansion, call optimization, or interprocedural analysis may prove useful.

After critical components have been optimized, profiling again is needed to see if new hot spots have been created or if critical components, even after optimization, are still bottlenecks. In the latter case, code segments or subprograms will need to be reprogrammed. It is exactly because optimization alone is no panacea for performance problems that profiling is so valuable a tool. Poorly chosen algorithms, even if extensively optimized, are no substitute for clever algorithms tailored to the problem at hand. If algorithms are judiciously chosen, they may not even need to be optimized. In other cases, careful optimization of key routines is a valuable final polish.

When global optimization is performed, either for individual subprograms or for an entire program, the order in which individual optimizations are performed is significant. In general, optimizations that can expose other optimizations are performed first, and local optimizations, integrated with code generation, are performed last. In particular, the following sequence of steps is suggested.

- As program constructs are analyzed and synthesized into IR code, optimizations that expand program structures are performed (typically, loop unrolling and inline expansion). This allows further analysis and simplification of expanded constructs. For example, actual parameters of subprograms expanded inline replace formal parameters and may expose opportunities for folding.

- As IR code is synthesized, basic blocks are built. Parameters used in data flow analyses that characterize basic blocks (**Def** and **Killed** sets) are also computed.

- After basic blocks are built, the flow graph for a program or subprogram can be built. In data flow analyses, the effect of calls that appear in basic blocks must be considered. If the main program and each subprogram are analyzed in isolation, then worst-case assumptions may be made in basic blocks whenever a call is seen. That is, it may be assumed that all expressions are killed, all variables are referenced and updated, and so forth.

  Alternatively, the text of a subprogram may be examined without considering flow of control, to obtain a better estimate of the subprogram's effects. Thus, during a call, if a use of v appears anywhere in a subprogram's body, we assume v is used during the call.

  Still more-precise information can be obtained if the flow graph of a subprogram is analyzed for each call in order to determine possible effects of the call. That is, the flow graph of a subprogram is substituted for the call, and the expanded flow graph is analyzed. This is *interprocedural* flow analysis. Because of recursion, flow graphs cannot actually be substituted. Rather, an iterative approach is used in which successive approximations to the actual effects of a call are computed (see Exercise 22).

- Data flow optimizations that can expose other optimizations are performed next. In particular, constant and copy propagation make it possible to recognize that certain basic blocks are unreachable and hence may be deleted as dead code. Thus, in

    if A = 1 **then**
      B := 1;
    end if;

    propagating a constant value to A may show that the assignment to B is unreachable. In turn, deleting the assignment to B may expose other opportunities for constant and copy propagation, so these optimizations are performed iteratively until no further changes in the flow graph occur.

- Next, optimizations that expose redundant code are performed. These include CSE analysis and dead variable identification. Deletion of redundant code does not change the structure of a flow graph, and hence these analyses only need be performed once.

- Basic blocks are next translated to target code by the code generator. As code is generated, local optimizations within the basic blocks are performed. These optimizations are integrated with code generation because they interact closely with register assignment and code selection. In machines that have long- and short-form branch instructions, such as the PDP-11 and VAX, the form of branch instructions that link basic blocks is selected after basic blocks are translated to target code. Basic blocks may be reordered in memory to replace long branches with short branches. More often, basic blocks are simply mapped to memory as they are translated to target code, and long branches are replaced with short branches wherever possible.

- Finally, a peephole optimization phase may be employed to screen the code that has been generated and to make any final improvements.

In organizing these optimization steps, it is wise to make each phase (except code generation) optional. This eases development and debugging and also makes it easy to disable unwanted optimizations.

Exercises

1. Of the following optimizations, which are always safe? Which are always profitable?

    - Code hoisting (Section 16.4.5)

    - Constant propagation (Section 16.4.5)

    - Loading scalar variables into unused registers

- Partially unrolling loops of the form

```
for I in 1 .. 2*N loop
{loop body}
end loop;
```

into

```
for J in 1 .. N loop
   {loop body with I replaced by 2*J−1}
   {loop body with I replaced by 2*J}
end loop;
```

2.   In most compilers, the decision to optimize all or part of a program is made by a user, usually by setting an option or flag. An alternative is to automate the decision, so that optimization is automatically triggered when certain criteria are met.

   What criteria should be used to trigger optimization? How is the optimization process changed when the decision to optimize occurs after a program is in production use?

3.   Consider the following subprogram:

```
type MarkedVocabulary is array(Vocabulary) of Boolean;

function MarkLambda(G : Grammar) return MarkedVocabulary is
   -- Mark those vocabulary symbols found to derive λ (directly or indirectly)
DerivesLambda : MarkedVocabulary;
Changes : Boolean := True;        -- Any changes during last iteration?
RHS_Derives_Lambda : Boolean := False;   -- Does the RHS derive λ?
NumProds : Integer := 100;   -- Number of Productions in Grammar
RHSLen : Integer;    -- Length of Current RHS
begin
   for V in Vocabulary loop
      DerivesLambda(V) := False; -- Initially, nothing is marked
   end loop;
   while Changes loop
      Changes := False;
      for P in 1 .. NumProds loop
         RHS_Derives_Lambda := True;
         RHSLen := RHS_Length(P);
         for I in 1 .. RHSLen loop
            RHS_Derives_Lambda :=
               RHS_Derives_Lambda and DerivesLambda(RHS(P)(I));
         end loop;
         if RHS_Derives_Lambda and not DerivesLambda(LHS(P)) then
            Changes := True;
            DerivesLambda(LHS(P)) := True;
         end if;
```

          end loop;
       end loop;
    end MarkLambda;

Identify the local and global optimizations that might be performed. Which are the most profitable? Which are the most difficult to perform?

4.   Show the call graph corresponding to the following program skeleton:

```
program Main is

    procedure A is
        D;
        . . .
        B;
    end A;

    procedure B is
        C;
    end B;

    procedure C is
        . . .
    end C;

    procedure D is
        C;
        . . .
        E;
    end D;

    procedure E is
        . . .
    end E;

begin
    A;
    . . .
    B;
end Main;
```

5.   Can the activation records of the subprograms of Exercise 4 be statically allocated? If so, show an allocation that uses the minimum possible space.

6.   Show that the static activation record allocation technique of Section 16.2.2 always uses the minimum possible space, assuming that all calling sequences shown in a call graph are possible.

7.   Consider the program of Exercise 4. Assume that the program has been translated but registers have not yet been allocated. The following table shows the number of registers needed by each routine:

Routine	Registers Needed
Main	3
A	1
B	2
C	1
D	3
E	2

Assume eight hardware registers are available for allocation. How would you allocate these eight registers to the main program and the subprograms to minimize register saves and restores across calls?

8.   It is well known that the problem of deciding whether an arbitrary program that does no I/O ever halts is undecidable. That is, no algorithm that correctly decides program termination in all cases can ever be created. Show that the halting problem can be reduced to the reachability problem. If it could always be determined whether a given statement in a program was reachable during execution, then the halting problem could be defined in terms of reachability and be solved. Because we know the halting problem cannot be solved, we may therefore conclude that the reachability problem must also be undecidable.

9.   Explain how inline expansion of the following procedure call would be performed. What optimizations are made possible by the inline expansion?

```
A : Real := 2;
B : Real := 21;

procedure P(Flag : in Boolean; S : in out Real) is
begin
   if Flag then
        S := S *2;
   else
        S := S/A;
   end if;
end P;

P(False,B);
Write(B);
```

10.   Explain how constant propagation can be used to optimize references to value parameters when inline expansion is performed. Explain how copy propagation can be used to optimize references to scalar **in out** parameters when inline expansion is performed.

11.   Inline expansion of Ada/CS subprograms must correctly resolve references to parameters and nonlocal variables. A subprogram Q defined within a package P may access variables local to P that normally are inaccessible outside the package. Is it possible outside of P to expand inline a call to Q, given that some of the variables accessible to Q are

inaccessible at the point of call? If it is possible, how are references to normally inaccessible variables handled?

12. We noted that recursive calls can cause problems if they appear within a subprogram that is expanded inline. It is clear that in some cases such recursive calls can be tolerated. For example, if Fact is a factorial function, implemented in the usual recursive manner, a call Fact(5) can readily be expanded inline, and the expansion may be optimized to a single constant value.

    Can recursive calls whose arguments are constants always be safely expanded inline? If not, what further restrictions are needed to control inline expansions that involve recursion?

13. Compute Def(P(B,C)) and Use(P(B,C)) for the following code fragment. Using this Def and Use information, are A+B and D+F killed by the call of P(B,C)?

```
declare
    A,B,C,D,E,F,G : Integer;

    procedure Q(Z : out Integer; X : in Integer) is
    begin
        Z := X + F;
        Write(A);
    end Q;

    procedure P(I : in Integer; J : in out Integer) is
    begin
        E := I + J;
        A := B + C;
        Q(J,G);
        if E > F then
            P(J,E);
        end if;
    end P;
begin
    C := A + B:
    G := D + F;
    P(B,C);
    . . .
end;
```

14. Calls to a function are easier to optimize if it is known that the function has no side effects. Ada and Ada/CS allow only **in** parameters, so actual parameters cannot be changed during a function call. However, variables may be changed during a call, and this sometimes leads to side effects. Assume the Def set of a call to a function is computed. Explain how this set may be used to decide if the call causes side effects.

15. Show that the `compute_use_set()` algorithm of Figure 16.7 always terminates. Next show that the Use sets it computes are exact. That is, if a variable v is used during a call to P, then v∈ Use(P), and if v∈ Use(P), then v actually may be used during a call to P.

16. Consider the following program fragment:

```
for I in 1 .. N loop
   for J in 1 .. N loop
      if M(J)(I) then
         for K in 1 .. N loop
            M(J)(K) := M(J)(K) or M(I)(K);
         end loop;
      end if;
   end loop;
end loop;
```

Use `factor_invariants()` (Figure 16.11) to factor loop-invariant expressions.

Now rewrite the indexing expressions to expose the calculations needed to perform indexing. Assume M is an N by N array of booleans. Use `factor_invariants()` to factor invariant expressions contained in the indexing code. Use `strength_reduce()` to strength-reduce multiplications contained in the indexing code.

17. In Section 16.3.1 we noted that factoring loop-invariant expressions from **while loop**s is unsafe, even if the expressions are very busy. The reason for this is that **while loop**s may iterate zero times, and in general it is impossible to predict in advance whether the boolean expression that controls the loop will initially be true. On the other hand, Pascal's **repeat-until** loop allows loop-invariant very busy expressions to be safely factored, because it must iterate at least once.

Show that a **while loop** can be rewritten into a **repeat-until** loop entered through an **if** statement. Explain how this transform can be used to safely factor loop-invariant very busy expressions in **while loop**s. Under what circumstances is this transformation undesirable?

18. Create the data flow graph for the following subprogram:

```
type ArrayArg is array(Integer range <>) of Integer;

procedure Sort(A : in out ArrayArg) is
   Temp : Integer := 0;
begin
   for I in reverse A'First .. A'Last-1 loop
      for J in A'First .. I loop
         if A(J) > A(J+1) then
            Temp := A(J+1);
            A(J+1) := A(J);
            A(J) := Temp;
```

```
            end if;
          end loop;
        end loop;
      end Sort;
```

19. List the expressions that are computed in Sort, as defined in Exercise 18. For each basic block, b, in Sort's data flow graph, determine Computed(b), the set of expressions computed and not subsequently killed in b. Determine also Killed(b), the set of expressions killed in b.

    Using Sort's data flow graph and the Computed and Killed values, do an available expression analysis for Sort, determining AvailIn and AvailOut sets for each basic block. Do this data flow analysis two ways, first using the iterative technique and then the structured approach (both in Section 16.4.6). Naturally, both techniques should yield the same solution.

    Finally, use the available expression information just computed to do CSE optimization in Sort.

20. Reconsider Sort as defined in Exercise 18. This time do a live variable analysis. Again, do the data flow analysis two ways, first using the iterative technique and then the structured approach (Section 16.4.6). Verify that both techniques yield the same solution. Can any assignments in Sort be removed because the variable assigned to is dead?

21. In Pascal, value and reference parameter modes are often confused. In particular, because value mode is the default, value parameters are sometimes used in a manner that suggests reference mode was intended. A sign of this confusion is an assignment to a value parameter before its value is used. Show how data flow analysis can be used to identify value parameters that are defined before they are used.

22. Assume we wish to create a program `live_s_vars(P)` that identifies variables that are live upon entrance to subprogram P. When compiling a call to P, `live_s_vars(P)` could be used to determine what variables must be saved prior to P's execution. We have already studied live variable analysis, but `live_s_vars(P)` suggests an additional concern—how to handle subprogram calls that appear in P. Because of possible recursion, insertion of a subprogram's data flow graph at the point of call is infeasible.

    As an alternative, use an iterative approach. Let `live_s_vars(P,1)` be a first approximation to `live_s_vars(P)` that assumes all variables are live on entrance to P. To compute `live_s_vars(P,2)` use `live_s_vars(Q,1)` to characterize the effect of a call to Q in P. Similarly, to compute `live_s_vars(P,i)` use `live_s_vars(Q,i-1)` to characterize the effect of a call to Q in P. Continue until `live_s_vars(P,i) = live_s_vars(P,i+1)`.

Show that this iterative approach terminates and that at termination

$$\texttt{live\_s\_vars(P,i)} = \texttt{live\_s\_vars(P)}.$$

23. *Sinking* is an optimization that complements the hoisting optimization of Section 16.4.5. Hoisting computes a value in a common predecessor, making recomputation in a number of successor blocks redundant. Analogously, sinking moves an assignment to a common successor, making a number of identical assignments in predecessors redundant. For example, in

> **if** A = B **then**
>   C := A + B;
>   B := 0;
> **else**   C := A − B;
>   B := 0;
> **end if**;

the assignment of zero to B can be moved to just after the **if** statement. This makes the two assignments to B in the **if** statement unnecessary assignments to dead variables.

For sinking to be feasible, it is necessary that the assignment be moved to a block that is a necessary successor to all the original assignments. Moreover, along all paths from an original assignment to the new assignment, it is necessary that the value of the right-hand side of the assignment not be changed and that the value of the left-hand side of the assignment not be referenced.

Formulate a data flow problem that determines whether an assignment that appears in one or more predecessor blocks may be moved to a given basic block. Use the results of this analysis in a routine **code_sink()** that is an analogue of the **code_hoist()** routine of Figure 16.26.

24. Recall that a dominator of a basic block b is any basic block d such that all paths to b must pass through d. One crude way to compute Dom(b), the dominator set of b, is to list all acyclic paths from the initial block b_0 to b. The set Dom(b) is exactly the set of nodes that appear in all the acyclic paths listed.

A neater approach, however, is the following. By definition, $\text{Dom}(b_0) = \{b_0\}$. Approximate Dom(b), $b \neq b_0$, as B, the set of all basic blocks. This approximation is clearly an overestimate. Now observe that for any basic block b, $\text{Dom}(b) = \{b\} \cup \bigcap_{i \in P(b)} \text{Dom}(i)$. That is, b always dominates itself. Moreover, if c dominates b, it must also dominate all of b's immediate predecessors.

Create an iterative algorithm that computes dominator sets for all basic blocks using the approach outlined earlier. Show that the dominator sets that are computed are correct.

25. Assume that dominators are computed as outlined in Exercise 24. Show that for each dominator set $Dom(b)-b$ there is a unique member $i \in Dom(b)-b$ that is an *immediate dominator* of b. That is, for all $j \in Dom(b)-b$, $j \in Dom(i)$. If block i is the immediate dominator of block b, then i is the "closest" dominator to b and hence the most reasonable place to move code factored from b.

26. In some programming languages, the types of variables are not declared. Rather, variable types are inferred from how they are used. For example, in $A := B+1.0$, if addition involving a real must always yield a real, then A's value must be real. Assume that we can determine the types of all literals, that there are no automatic type conversions, and that the result types of all expressions are determined by the types of their operands. Show how to determine the types of variables using data flow techniques. Initially, all variables should be assumed to be of any type. At the end of a program, the data flow analysis tells us exactly what type a variable must have, or it tells us that no type is consistent with how the variable is used, or it tells us that a unique determination of a variable's type was not possible (owing to insufficient context).

27. Show that for any-path problems the algorithm of Figure 16.31 computes a minimal solution. That is, if $\overline{In}$ is any valid solution to the data flow equations, and In is the solution computed by the algorithm of Figure 16.31, then $In \subseteq \overline{In}$. (*Hint:* Initially $In_0 \subseteq \overline{In}$.)

28. We have generally assumed that it is wise to keep frequently used variables in registers if sufficient unused registers are available. Thus loop indices and procedure parameters are often assigned to registers under the assumption that these objects will be frequently accessed within loops or subprograms.

Rather than resort to generalities that may or may not be true, it is possible to estimate how often each variable will be referenced. If this is done, the most frequently referenced variables can be assigned to registers, until all free registers are assigned. The best way to estimate frequency of reference is to profile a program. If profiling data is not available, a frequency analysis, similar in form to a data flow analysis, can be performed.

This analysis can be done by a structured analysis of a program's data flow graph. The main program is executed once. If a statement is estimated to execute N times, then its sequential successor will also execute N times. If a conditional statement executes M times, then the sum of the execution estimates for all the alternatives must be M. Often in an **if**, an estimate of $M/2$ for the **then** and **else** parts is assumed. If a loop is executed L times, then the loop body will be executed $L \times P$ times, where P is the estimated number of iterations for the loop. P can be determined exactly for **for loop** with constant loop bounds; for other loops, an estimate may be used (ten iterations per loop may be assumed).

Once the expected frequency of execution for each statement is determined, the expected number of references to each variable can be computed easily, with the most frequently referenced variables assigned to registers. Assuming loops iterate ten times, and that **then** and **else** parts are equally likely, estimate how often each statement in the subprogram of Exercise 18 will be executed. Assuming we have three registers available for allocation, which variables does our analysis suggest be assigned to these registers?

29.   The analysis performed in Exercise 28 assumes a particular variable is assigned to a particular register throughout a program or subprogram. This is somewhat wasteful in that in certain regions of a program, a variable may be inaccessible or dead and need not be allocated to a register while in those regions. Suggest how to use live/dead information to improve the register allocation scheme outlined in Exercise 28.

CHAPTER 17

Parsing in the Real World

In Chapters 3, 5, and 6 we studied in some detail the problems involved in building scanners and parsers for modern programming languages. In this chapter we consider two issues that are of vital importance in parsing in the "real world"—table compaction and error repair.

The tables produced by automatic scanner and parser generators are both large and sparse. With care, tables can be effectively compressed with little degradation of access time to table elements. A survey and analysis of various table compaction techniques is the subject of Section 17.1.

The parsing theory we have developed addresses the problem of efficiently parsing correct inputs. In practice, some way of handling erroneous inputs is required. This is a complex issue, and no one best solution exists. In Section 17.2, we survey a variety of practical approaches. *Automatically generated* error handlers are especially easy to use, and they will receive special attention.

17.1. Compacting Tables

The most obvious way to store the tables produced by tools such as Scangen, LLGen, and LALRGen is in ordinary one- or two-dimensional arrays. This representation can be costly for two-dimensional tables in terms of space, particularly when the table is *sparse*. In a sparse table most entries are set to a special *default* value. For example, an LL(1) grammar for Ada/CS contains 70 terminals and 138 nonterminals. The LL(1) parser action table, stored as an array, would require about 10,000 entries (138×70). Because these tables, as a rule of thumb, tend to contain only about 10% nonerror entries, significant space savings can be obtained by using something other than an ordinary array.

We consider a number of alternate representations for a two-dimensional (N by M) table, T. Assume that E entries are nondefault, where $E \ll N \times M$. Our goal is to represent the table so that space proportional to E rather than $N \times M$ is used, while fast access to $T[i][j]$ is maintained.

The representations we initially consider are similar to those often used in symbol tables. A significant difference between ordinary symbol tables and a compacted table is that the entries in a table, T, are known in advance, but symbol table entries are created and destroyed, on the fly, during compilation.

We use the 5×5 table that appears in Figure 17.1 as an example in the discussions that follow. Default entries are blank; others are represented as single letters.

Binary Search

A table can be created ordered by the indices of nondefault entries. The table requires $3 \times E$ entries (for the indices i and j, and the value of the entry). Lookup is by binary search on the indices of the desired entry and requires $O(\log(E))$ time. For the array of Figure 17.1, we might create the binary search table shown in Figure 17.2.

We gain in space use if $3 \times E < N \times M$, assuming each entry takes one unit of memory. Lookup time is proportional to $\log(E)$. As E becomes large, lookup time may become unacceptably slow.

L			P	
	Q			R
		U		
W	X			
	Y		Z	

Figure 17.1   A Sparse Array

1	1	L
1	4	P
2	2	Q
2	5	R
3	3	U
4	1	W
4	2	X
5	2	Y
5	4	Z

Figure 17.2   A Sparse Array Represented as a Binary Search Table

Hash Table

The indices **i** and **j** can be hashed to a position **k** in a hash table, using the rule that if position **k** is filled, we try **k + 1 % S**, then **k + 2 % S**, and so on. (Remember, **%** represents the modulus operation in C.)   **S** is the size of the table, and this method of handling collisions in the table is called *linear resolution*. Each position in the hash table requires three entries **{i, j, T[i][j]}**, and we require **S > E** (one vacant position in the table is required to avoid an infinite loop while searching for an entry not in the hash table).

Using the example of Figure 17.1, we create the hash table shown in Figure 17.3, with **S = E + 1**. The hash function used is **h(i, j) = i * j % S**.

This hash table requires an average of ≈ 1.89 lookups in order to find a nondefault entry and an average of ≈ 4.5 lookups to find a default entry.

In general, a hash table saves space if **3 × S < N × M**. The lookup time is sensitive to the size of the table, the hash function, and the number of unused entries (the difference between **S** and **E**). If we try to set **S** too close to **E**, lookup time may be degraded because of frequent collisions. However, because all the entries in **T** are known in advance, **S** and the hash function can be adjusted to reduce the average number of lookups in the hash table needed to find an entry. In fact, using the perfect hashing techniques of Section 3.5, one probe into the table will suffice to locate any nondefault entry.

Compressed Rows

A two-dimensional array can be viewed as a vector of pointers to individual rows. That is, **T[i][j]** can be mapped to **V[row[i] + j]**, where **V** is a vector that contains individual rows, placed end to end.   **row[i]** gives the starting position of the **i**th row in **V**. This sort of mapping is, in fact, routinely used in finding the position of a given array element in memory, using the rule **row[i] = (i − 1) * M**.

2	5	R
1	1	L
5	2	Y
5	4	Z
1	4	P
2	2	Q
4	1	W
4	2	X
3	3	U

Figure 17.3   A Sparse Array Represented as a Hash Table

To save space, we can eliminate default entries in a row and store the value and column index of each nondefault entry. A vector called **row[i]** must also be stored, giving the offset in **V** of the **i**th row after default entries have been squeezed out. Entries from **V[row[i]]** to **V[row[i + 1]] − 1** are searched to find an index value **j**. If it is found, the next value is **T[i][j]**; otherwise, **T[i][j]** must have the default value.

For our 5 × 5 example, we would have the tables shown in Figure 17.4. This representation requires **2 × E** entries, rather than **3 × E** entries, plus

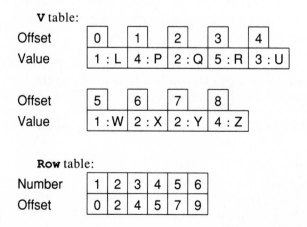

V table:

Offset	0	1	2	3	4
Value	1 : L	4 : P	2 : Q	5 : R	3 : U

Offset	5	6	7	8
Value	1 : W	2 : X	2 : Y	4 : Z

Row table:

Number	1	2	3	4	5	6
Offset	0	2	4	5	7	9

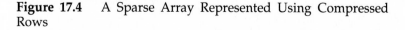

Figure 17.4   A Sparse Array Represented Using Compressed Rows

$N + 1$ entries in the **row** vector. If sequential search is used, lookup time for **T[i][j]** is, on average, **ND(i) / 2**, where **ND(i) = row[i+1] − row[i]** is the number of nondefault entries in row **i** of **T**. If binary search is used, lookup time is $\log(\mathbf{ND(i)})$.

Double-Offset Indexing

If some rows of **T** have a significant number of nondefault entries, lookup time may be a problem when using the compressed rows approach. The double-offset indexing method seeks to guarantee fast lookup at the expense of a modest increase in the space needed. The idea is a clever one: Individual rows of **T** are overlaid at an offset relative to each other so that nondefault entries in one row always overlay default entries in other rows. This guarantees that only one nondefault entry is placed in a given position. Row numbers are stored with entries to identify which row nondefault entries are associated with. We can represent our example array using the tables of Figure 17.5.

To get **T[i][j]**, we look at **V[row[i] + j]**. If the entry is blank, we return the default entry. If the first component of **V[row[i] + j]** is **i**, then we return the second component as the value of **T[i][j]**; otherwise, we return the default entry. In all cases we examine exactly one entry in the **V** table, so lookup is very fast. The best-case space requirement is almost exactly that used by the compressed rows approach, $2 \times \mathbf{E} + \mathbf{N}$ entries. This best-case space requirement is usually not realized, but empirical results suggest that the space required in practice is reasonably close to the best case.

As an experiment, the double-offset representation was investigated for an LL(1) parse table for Ada/CS. The uncompacted table size was 9660 entries

V table:

Offset	1	2	3	4	5
Value	1 : L	2 : Q	3 : U	1 : P	2 : R

V table (continued):

Offset	6	7	8	9	10
Value	4:W	4: X	5: Y		5: Z

Row table:

Number	1	2	3	4	5
Offset	0	0	0	5	6

Figure 17.5   A Sparse Array Represented Using Double-Offset Indexing

(70 terminals by 138 nonterminals).   **E**, the number of nondefault entries, was 629, which represented 6.51% of all entries. When rows of length 70 were compacted (each row representing the predictions for one particular nonterminal), 660 entries were required in the **V** table (4.9% over the best possible). When rows and columns of the parse matrix were transposed and rows of length 138 (each corresponding to predictions for a given terminal lookahead symbol) were compacted, 879 entries were required in the **V** table (39.7% over the best possible). The difference in sizes of the **V** table in the two cases is because longer rows (138 versus 70) are harder to mesh into the table.

The order in which rows are overlaid in the **V** table can affect the final size of the table. Thus, if in our earlier example we had overlaid rows in the order 1,5,2,4,3 we would have obtained the *optimal* layout shown in Figure 17.6.

In general, the problem of overlaying rows in an optimal manner is NP-complete (Garey and Johnson 1979). This means that the best-known algorithms require time exponential in the number of rows to be overlaid and thus are no better than trying all permutations.

A good heuristic for overlaying rows is called *best-fit decreasing*. Rows are overlaid in order of decreasing density of nondefault entries, and each overlay is chosen to minimize the size of the **V** table. The key point is to overlay rows with many nondefault entries first (they will have the most conflicts with other nondefault entries), leaving the easiest rows (those with few nondefault entries) for last (to fill in holes in the **V** table). An array compaction utility that uses the best-fit decreasing approach to create a double-offset array representation is discussed in Appendix F. Double-offset indexing is discussed further by Tarjan and Yao (1979).

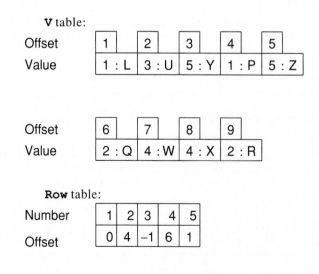

Figure 17.6   An Optimal Representation of a Sparse Array Using Double-Offset Indexing

17.1.1. Compacting LL(1) Parse Tables

Special properties of the LL(1) parse table can be exploited to further reduce space requirements with little effect on lookup speed. Recall that in storing a compacted table one or both indices had to be stored with an entry to identify it. Thus for a table with **E** nondefault entries, we require either $2 \times$ **E** or $3 \times$ **E** entries. In the LL(1) parse table, indices are a nonterminal, which is to be expanded, and a terminal, which is the lookahead symbol. Default table entries represent parsing errors; nondefault entries are the names of productions. But if **T[A][a]** is the name of a production (coded typically as an integer), then **A** must be the left-hand side of that production. This means **A** need not be explicitly stored with **T[A][a]** in a compacted table. Rather, we can create a vector **LHS** that maps productions into their corresponding left-hand sides. If **T[A][a]** is not an error entry, then **LHS[T[A][a]]** = **A**. If the number of productions is less than the number of nondefault entries in the table (this usually is the case), we obtain a further reduction in space by storing an **LHS** vector, rather than an index, with each entry.

This improvement can be realized in the compressed rows technique, when rows correspond to a given terminal lookahead symbol, and in the double-offset technique, when rows correspond to a given nonterminal symbol. In the compressed rows approach, we examine entries from **V[row[a]]** to **V[row[a+1] − 1]**. Each entry is a production index. If **LHS[V[i]]** = **A** (for **row[a]** ≤ **i** ≤ **row[a+1] − 1**), then **V[i]** = **T[A][a]**; otherwise, we consider **V[i+1]**.

Similarly, for the double-offset technique, we examine **V[row[A] + a]**. If **LHS[V[row[A] + a]]** = **A**, then **T[A][a]** = **V[row[A] + a]**, else **T[A][a]** = **error**. To gauge the value of this modification, let us return to our LL(1) table for Ada/CS. If we explicitly store an index along with its corresponding entry and use shorter rows (because they overlay better), we require 660 entries $\times$ 2 + a **row** vector (of size 138) = 1458 entries. If we use an **LHS** vector to avoid storing any indices, we now require 660 entries $\times$ 1 + a **row** vector (of size 138) + an **LHS** vector (of size 252) = 1050 entries, a reduction of 28%.

17.2. Syntactic Error Recovery and Repair

When a compiler detects a syntax error, it is usually desirable to attempt to continue with the parsing (or the entire compilation) process to detect additional errors. This involves doing either *error recovery* or *error repair*.

Error Recovery

With error recovery, we try to reset the parser so that the remaining input can be parsed. This process may involve modifying the parse stack or the remaining input. Depending on how well the recovery process is done, subsequent syntax errors may be real, or they may be cascaded from a previous syntax error. For example, in · · · A:=B C+D; · · · a recovery algorithm might try to restart parsing by predicting a statement at token C. This would induce a false syntax error at the +.

The primary measure of quality in an error-recovery routine is how few false or cascaded errors it induces; that is, how accurately it resynchronizes the parser with the remaining input. Normally, semantic and code-generation routines are disabled after error recovery is done because there is no intention of executing the output of the compiler.

The simplest form of error recovery is called *panic mode*. In panic mode, a parser attempts to "bail out" of a construct, looking for a safe symbol (such as a delimiter or statement header) at which to restart parsing. Panic mode is usually unsatisfactory when used alone, but it is often a fall-back when all else fails.

Error Repair

With error repair, we try to repair the user's input into a valid program. This process can involve modifying that part of the input already parsed or, more commonly, modifying the remaining input. After compilation is restarted, subsequent errors may be detected. Again, these may be real user errors or they may be false errors induced by an earlier repair action. Thus, in · · · A:=B C+D; · · · a repair algorithm might insert a ; after the B, which would induce a false, or cascaded, syntax error at the +. Alternately, if a repair algorithm inserted an **or** after the B, a false semantic error would probably be induced.

The accuracy of an error-repair algorithm can be measured by how few false errors its repairs induce. A repair algorithm actually tries to repair an erroneous input, and semantic processing and code generation are continued after a repair is done. Normally, the output of an error-repairing compiler can be executed, although semantic errors may generate run-time calls to a termination routine or debugger.

Error repair is sometimes called error correction, but this is a misnomer. Correction suggests that we can provide what the user actually meant. This cannot be done. Rather, the most we can hope to do is to repair an illegal construct into something reasonable. Hence, "error repair" is more descriptive of what actually happens than "error correction" is.

In general, an error-repair algorithm is a good deal more complex than an error-recovery algorithm because it must actually try to repair an erroneous input while maintaining the semantic information needed to continue translation. A recovery routine only needs to be able to restart parsing and can grossly alter (or discard) both the parse stack and remaining input.

However, an error-repair algorithm can always be used for error recovery, because if we can repair an input we can certainly continue parsing it.

In designing error-recovery and error-repair algorithms, we exploit the fact that all parsing techniques of interest, including SLR(1), LALR(1), LR(1), and LL(1), have the *correct prefix property*. That is, if we are in an input configuration yTz, in which input string y has been read, terminal T is found to be syntactically illegal, and string z is the remaining input, then we know that y is a prefix of some legal program [y $\cdots \in L(G)$] but yT is not [yT $\cdots \notin L(G)$]. In this context three distinct types of repair operations are possible:

(1) Modification of y

(2) Insertion of a string v between y and T so that yvT $\cdots \in L(G)$

(3) Deletion of T so that yz is considered for processing [(1), (2), or (3) may then be applied to this modified input string.]

These three kinds of repair operations are not all equally attractive. In particular, (1) is decidedly inferior. Usually y is not directly available because it has already been processed. Further, if error repair is to be performed, modification of y in general requires that semantic and code-generation operations be undone in a one-pass compiler—this is difficult or impossible to do simply and efficiently.

Recovery algorithms sometimes modify y (by popping a parse stack), but this is considered a drastic step because y has already been accepted and verified as syntactically valid. Indeed, when y is known to be valid, we need never modify it. All repair operations can be limited to classes (2) and (3). As a result, most repair algorithms choose never to modify y (to avoid semantic changes), and recovery algorithms modify y only as a last resort.

Note, however, that ruling out modifications to y may rule out some desirable repairs. The canonical example is the "missing **if**" in, for example

   $\cdots$; B **then** C:=0; **end if**; $\cdots$

Here B would normally be reduced to a left-hand side before any error is detected. At this point, insertion of an **if** would, in effect, be a modification to y, the accepted input prefix. This error seems to be rare in practice, and many repair algorithms simply ignore it. An attractive alternative might be to use an *error production* to anticipate this possibility. An error production is a production specially added to a grammar in anticipation of a particular error. In effect, it extends the syntax of a language to cover the expected error. When an error production is recognized, a special error message is issued describing the repair that the error production represents. For a missing **if** header we might use

   <if> → **if** <b expr>
   <if> → <b expr>

in which the latter production covers a missing **if** header. Adding error productions must be done with care, as it is possible to introduce parsing conflicts that must subsequently be resolved.

Now compare the utility of inserting tokens to the left of an error token with deleting the error token. Normally, insertion is preferable to deletion: It is generally safer to build a correct program around a user's input than to delete possibly large portions of that input. In fact, for certain languages, termed *insert-correctable*, it is always possible to repair any sequence of tokens using only insertions. Ada/CS is insert-correctable because an Ada/CS program is a sequence of packages. That is, in Ada/CS any terminal symbol (except the end marker) can be generated as part of a package. When a syntax error occurs, it is always possible to complete the current package and generate the error symbol as part of the next package. Thus, any syntax error can be repaired by a suitable insertion of tokens.

Insert-correctability is of special interest in recovery algorithms, in which the simplicity obtained by insertion operations is of real value. That is, a simple, cheap, and compact recovery algorithm that always works, and usually works well, is ideal. The additional complexity introduced by repair operations other than insertions is not necessarily cost-effective in recovery algorithms. Error-repair algorithms, on the other hand, usually must allow deletions (although in practice, insertions are more common than deletions).

17.2.1. **Immediate Error Detection**

To maintain the widest latitude in repair operations, it is necessary to guarantee that a parser will detect an error at the earliest possible opportunity. Ideally, we would like to discover a syntax error the first time an error token appears in the lookahead. Parsers that detect an illegal token when it is first seen are said to have the *immediate error-detection property*. Unfortunately, ordinary SLR(1), LALR(1), and LL(1) parsers may detect an error a bit later—when an attempt to shift the illegal token is made. This slight delay in error detection can have a surprisingly large impact on the range of error-repair operations that can be employed.

Consider grammar G_1, shown in Figure 17.7. Assume we parse ID) $\cdots$ $ using an LL(1) parser. The sequence of stack moves that occurs is

$$S' \Rightarrow E\$ \Rightarrow TE'\$ \Rightarrow ID\ E'\$ \Rightarrow E'\$ \Rightarrow \$$$

and the error is detected. The last move occurs because) $\in$ Follow(E'). Now, because only $ is left on the stack, the only repair operation possible is to delete *all* the remaining input up to the endmarker. This is a rather extreme action, especially when the language being generated is insert-correctable.

As discussed in Section 5.11, the LL(1) parsers used in practice are actually Strong LL(1) parsers. Strong LL(1) parsers predict a production $A \rightarrow \lambda$,

$$
\begin{aligned}
S' &\rightarrow E\$ \\
E &\rightarrow TE' \\
E' &\rightarrow +TE' \\
E' &\rightarrow \lambda \\
T &\rightarrow ID \\
T &\rightarrow (E)
\end{aligned}
$$

Figure 17.7   Grammar G_1

with a lookahead symbol a if a ∈ Follow(A). Whether a is actually valid is determined after the prediction. In contrast, full LL(1) parsers do not make any prediction unless the lookahead symbol is known to be valid. Strong LL(1) parsers require significantly smaller parse tables than full LL(1) parsers, but they lack the immediate error-detection property of LL(1) parsers. Similarly, SLR(1), LALR(1), and optimized LR(1) parsers lack the immediate error detection property of full LR(1) parsers.

Although the immediate error detection property is valuable, we avoid using full LL(1) or LR(1) parsers because of the excessive table sizes they entail. As an alternative, we can *buffer* the parse moves and semantic routine calls induced by a lookahead symbol. If the symbol is eventually shifted, we know it is legal. We can then clear the buffered parse moves and perform the buffered semantic routine calls. If we cannot shift the lookahead, we use the buffered parse moves to *restore* the parse stack to the configuration that existed when the illegal lookahead was first used.

In general, for LL(1) parsers we buffer on a stack predictions that are made until a successful shift occurs, at which point the buffer stack can be cleared. To undo predictions, right-hand sides on the parse stack are replaced by the left-hand side from which they were predicted. Thus, in the preceding example we buffer the move predict $E' \to \lambda$. When we discover that) is illegal, we use this buffer to undo the prediction, replacing $ with E'$.

Similarly, for SLR(1), LALR(1), and optimized LR(1) parsers, we stack productions that are reduced. To undo a reduction, we pop one state from the parse stack, then push successor states for each symbol on the right-hand side of the production. For example, if we had a parse stack of $s_1 \cdots s_n$, with s_n at the top, and wished to undo the reduction $A \to abc$, we would first pop one state, exposing s_{n-1}. We would then push $\hat{s}_n, \hat{s}_{n+1}, \hat{s}_{n+2}$, where $go\_to[s_{n-1}][a] = \hat{s}_n$, $go\_to[\hat{s}_n][b] = \hat{s}_{n+1}$, and $go\_to[\hat{s}_{n+1}][c] = \hat{s}_{n+2}$.

If only error recovery is to be performed, buffering is not usually needed (though performance may be degraded). If error repair is to be attempted, buffering (to undo improper predictions or reductions) is recommended. (An attractive alternative to buffering for Strong LL(1) parsers is discussed by Mauney and Fischer [1981]).

17.2.2. Error Recovery in Recursive Descent Parsers

A simple and uniform approach to error recovery in recursive descent parsers is discussed by Wirth (1976, section 5.9). Each parsing procedure is designed to match a terminal string generated by some nonterminal. For error-recovery purposes, each parsing procedure is provided with a set of symbols that can be matched after the procedure returns. This set, **follow_set**, can be used to resynchronize the input if an error is detected. If necessary, the parsing procedure can skip input tokens until a symbol in **follow_set** is found. At this point it is safe to return, as we know that the next input symbol will be matched by the calling procedure.

In most languages there are header symbols, such as **begin** and **if**, that are too important to skip. **follow_set** is augmented with a **header_set** to guarantee that header symbols are preserved, to be later matched by some subsequent parsing procedure. For example, consider the following Ada program fragment:

> · · · **if** B **then** A := 1 **else** · · ·

Statements in Ada must end in a semicolon, but we would not want to skip past the **else** in search of one. Inclusion of **else** in `header_set` guarantees that the separation of the **then** part and **else** part is not lost.

Finally, because of possible input errors, a parsing procedure cannot be sure that it can match the current input. A `valid_set`, which represents all expected legal inputs, is used to screen the current input. Normally, `valid_set` contains members of First(A), where A is the nonterminal the parsing procedure matches. If A can generate λ, `valid_set` also contains members of Follow(A). Wirth suggests that the routine shown in Figure 17.8 be called upon entry to each parsing procedure.

After `check_input()` has been called, we know that either `next_token()` is valid or that it will be processed by the calling procedure. In either case, error recovery has been conveniently factored into a single routine.

The only other major change to our recursive descent parser involves syntax errors discovered by calls to the `match()` procedure. Recall that a call of `match(T)` unconditionally attempts to match `next_token()` as **T**. If the match fails, we have discovered a syntax error. To recover from a syntax error discovered by `match()`, we call `syntax_error()` to mark the error and then return. `next_token()` is unchanged and will be reconsidered and either matched or skipped upon return. In effect, because `match(T)` knows the next token must be **T**, we insert it if we cannot match it. As a special case, `match(SCANEOF)` skips all remaining input, if any is left. It does this because

```
void check_input(terminal_set valid_set,
                 terminal_set follow_set,
                 terminal_set header_set)
{
   if (next_token() ∈ valid_set)
      return;     /* Input looks valid */
   else {
      syntax_error();    /* Mark next token as illegal */
      while (! (next_token() ∈
             (valid_set ∪ follow_set ∪ header_set)))
         skip_token();
         /* Skip this token;
             call scanner() to get next token. */
   }
}
```

Figure 17.8   An Algorithm to Skip Illegal Tokens

prior to matching the end-of-file symbol, all input must be processed and consumed.

syntax_error() marks tokens thought to be illegal. Usually a number of consecutive tokens are so marked. A syntax error message is generated for the first marked token but not for the remainder. We do not really know that the remainder are illegal, only that they have been skipped. Sometimes, a message ("parsing resumed") is generated for the first unmarked token, emphasizing the fact that intervening symbols have been ignored by the parser.

As an example, consider Figure 17.9 which shows a parsing procedure from Chapter 2 that has been augmented to perform error recovery.

Upon entry to **statement_list()**, we use **check_input()** to screen the current input. The **valid_set** is First(<statement list>). The **follow_set** is received as a parameter, although an examination of the Micro grammar shows that it must always be the singleton set (**end**). In richer languages, the **follow_set** depends on the context in which a parsing procedure is called. Thus in Ada, **follow_set** contains **else** if the <statement list> being matched is the **then** part of an **if** statement.

header_set contains the Eof symbol because we do not wish to ever skip past the end of the input. The **header_set** could also contain statement headers like **ID** and **READ**, but this would be redundant as they already appear in the **valid_set** and certainly would not be skipped. Calls to **statement()** in the body of **statement_list()** are given the **follow_set** parameter, because the statement being matched may be last in the list. Actually, the **follow_set** could be augmented with

```
void statement_list(terminal_set follow_set)
{
    check_input(SET_OF( ID, READ, WRITE ),
                follow_set,
                SET_OF( SCANEOF ));
    statement(follow_set);
    while (TRUE) {
        switch (next_token()) {
        case ID:
        case READ:
        case WRITE:
            statement(follow_set);
            break;
        default:
            return;
        }
    }
}
```

Figure 17.9   A Parsing Procedure with Error Recovery

First(<statement>), but this is unnecessary, as symbols in First(<statement>) will be matched immediately by **statement()**.

This approach has been used in practice and performs adequately. Like all panic mode techniques, its main drawback is that it skips input rather freely, attempting to resynchronize the current input with an appropriate parsing procedure. Skipping does not work particularly well for nested structures, which is why the set of header symbols is added heuristically.

Recursive descent error repair is rarely, if ever, done. The problem is that the parsing state is implicitly stored in the call stack of the parsing procedures, and it is not easy to determine what repairs might be accepted as valid. Further, parsing procedures bundle parsing and semantic processing in one unit, and it is not easy to test potential repairs when more than one appears plausible.

17.2.3. Error Recovery in LL(1) Parsers

The recovery ideas developed for recursive descent parsers can be readily adapted to LL(1) parsers. The routine shown in Figure 17.10, called when a syntax error is discovered by the LL(1) parser driver, skips input symbols and pops stack symbols until the parse can be restarted.

ll_recovery() must reset the parser so that parsing may resume. It may do so by skipping input symbols or popping parse stack entries. If the top of the parse stack is a terminal that does not match the current lookahead, we pop the parse stack, effectively inserting the required terminal. If the top of the parse stack is a nonterminal, we may either pop it or we may delete the current lookahead.

If parsing can be resumed after popping the parse stack, we do so. This situation is analogous to that of a parsing procedure returning so that its caller can resume parsing. If popping the parse stack does not allow parsing to resume, we delete the current lookahead if it is not a protected header symbol. Protected symbols are not deleted; rather, the parse stack is popped so that protected symbols can be matched by some deeper stack symbol.

This recovery algorithm is fairly heuristic. Sometimes it pops the parse stack, forcing a match; sometimes it skips, hoping to match the next token. The **header_set** is needed to prevent skipping important tokens, but it is not precisely defined. In Section 17.2.4, we present a more formal approach to LL(1) recovery and repair. In particular, we do a more careful analysis to determine when to delete or insert symbols and introduce a notion of best choice when more than one repair is possible.

17.2.4. The FMQ LL(1) Error-Repair Algorithm

We now consider the FMQ error-repair algorithm proposed by Fischer, Milton, and Quiring (1980). This is an *automatically generable* error-repair algorithm designed to work with insert-correctable LL(1) grammars. An extension that can operate with arbitrary LL(1) grammars is presented in Section 17.2.5.

```
/*
 * Will this combination of stack_top
 * and token cause a syntax error?
 */

static boolean parse_error(symbol stack_top,
                           terminal current_token)
{
    if (stack_top∈Vₙ)
        return T[stack_top][current_token] == ERROR;
    else
        /* stack_top∈Vₜ */
        return stack_top != current_token;
}

void ll_recovery(void)
{
    /* Let S be the parse stack;
       let a be the current input token. */
    while (parse_error(top(S), a)) {
        if (top(S)∈Vₙ) {
            /* top1() "peeks" at top(pop(S)) */
            if (parse_error(top1(S), a)
                  && ! (a ∈ header_set))
                scanner(a);   /* Skip current token */

            else      /* Remove top stack symbol */
                pop(S);

        } else {      /* top(S)∈Vₜ */

            if (top(S) == SCANEOF)
                scanner(& a);
                /* Never skip past endmarker */
            else
                pop(S);
                /* Match expected terminal; */
                /* then try again */
        }
    }
}
```

Figure 17.10   Simple Error-Recovery Routine for LL Parsers

Because this algorithm operates on insert-correctable languages, it can limit its repair actions to insertion of terminal strings. This is in contrast to previous techniques, which were biased toward deletion of input symbols.

One advantage of an insertion-only approach is that it builds repairs around existing tokens, obviating the need to define a protected set of header tokens.

If a language is insert-correctable, then for any syntax error $(S \Rightarrow^+ x \cdots$ and $S \not\Rightarrow^+ xa \cdots$, $x \in V_t^*$, $a \in V_t$), we can always select a terminal string $y \in V_t^+$ that can be used to effect a repair $(S \Rightarrow^+ xya \cdots)$. As suggested earlier, typical programming languages are very close to being insert-correctable.

In what follows, we assume that we detect a syntax error as soon as possible (that is, when the erroneous symbol is first used as a lookahead). Because we are using an ordinary LL(1) parser, we also assume that some technique described earlier, such as buffering, is used to restore the parse stack to the configuration that existed when the error symbol first appeared in the lookahead.

Unlike many repair and recovery techniques, the FMQ algorithm can be proved to have the following desirable properties:

- It can repair any input.

- Its repair actions are tunable via insertion costs.

- It is entirely table-driven and can thus be automatically generated.

- It is linear in its time and space requirements.

- The repair actions it chooses are always locally optimal.

To control the choice of insertions the repair algorithm makes, we specify a vector of integer repair costs. That is, $\forall a \in V_t$, a value $C[a] \geq 0$ is provided. $C[a]$ is the cost of inserting a. The higher $C[a]$ is, the less likely it is that a will be inserted (if there is a choice).

Insertion of λ is equivalent to inserting nothing, and hence $C[\lambda] = 0$. Similarly, the endmarker is always the last token parsed and never needs to be inserted. Thus $C[\$] = \infty$. Finally, we introduce a new symbol $? \notin V_t$, for which $C[?] = \infty$. For a string $X_1 \cdots X_n$ $(n \geq 0)$, $C[X_1 \cdots X_n] = C[X_1] + \cdots + C[X_n]$. [In our algorithms, we will use a function $c(a)$ that returns the value of $C[A]$ for any string of terminals.]

To drive the repair algorithm, we compute and store, in advance, the following two tables:

(1) $S: V \rightarrow V_t^*$

$S[A]$ = the *lowest cost* $z \in V_t^*$ such that $A \Rightarrow^+ z$

Also, for $a \in V_t$, $S[a] = a$.

(2) $E: V \times V_t \rightarrow V_t^* \cup \{?\}$

For $A \in V_n$: $E[A][a] = ?$ if $A \not\Rightarrow^+ \cdots a \cdots$

Otherwise, $E[A][a]$ = the lowest cost $w \in V_t^*$ such that $A \Rightarrow^+ wa \cdots$.

For $a \in V_t$: $E[a][b] = ?$ if $a \neq b$ $E[a][a] = \lambda$

Informally, S[X] gives the lowest cost string derivable from X, and E[X][a] gives the lowest cost prefix that allows a to be derived from X.

These two tables can easily be computed and kept in memory or in a file until needed by the error-repair algorithm. Using these two tables, a rather simple error-repair algorithm, shown in Figure 17.11, can be defined.

The algorithms presented in the rest of this chapter are in a higher-level pseudo-code than we have previously used. The following new features are added: Simple string assignment via = and string comparison via ==, the @ operator to perform string concatenation, and the ability to specify slices of an array by specifying the lower and upper bounds of the slice.

find_insert() simply searches down the LL(1) parse stack, looking for the cheapest way to derive the error symbol a. Because the grammar is insert-correctable, we know that some stack symbol must be able to derive a.

As an example, let us reconsider G_1 (Figure 17.7), a grammar that generates simple expressions. First we must determine insertion costs. There is no firm rule on how to choose costs. In general, terminal symbols whose insertion is undesirable are given a higher cost than those symbols whose insertion is innocuous. In G_1 insertion of an ID is undesirable because identifiers have semantic content. Similarly, insertion of a (is unattractive because a matching) may have to be inserted later. However, insertion of) or + is less troublesome. This analysis leads to the insertion costs shown in Figure 17.12.

```
terminal_string find_insert(stack_of_symbol parse_stack,
                             terminal a)
{
    /* a is the error symbol */
    terminal_string insert, least_cost;

    insert = "?";
    least_cost = λ;
    for (i = 0; i <= depth(parse_stack) - 1; i++) {
        if (C(least_cost) >= C(insert))
            break;
            /* No lower cost insertion can be found */

        if (C(least_cost @ E[parse_stack[top-i)]][a])
                < C(insert)) {
            /* A better insertion has been found */
            insert = least_cost @ E[parse_stack[top-i]][a];
        }
        least_cost = least_cost @ S[parse_stack[top-i]];
    }
    return insert;
}
```

Figure 17.11   An Algorithm That Computes LL(1) Least-Cost Insertions

Symbol	Cost
(	2
)	1
+	1
ID	2

Figure 17.12   Insertion Costs for G_1

Symbol	Least-Cost Insertion
S'	ID $
E	ID
E'	λ
T	ID

Figure 17.13   S Table for G_1

Nonterminals	Terminals				
	ID	(	)	+	$
S'	λ	λ	(ID	ID	ID
E	λ	λ	(ID	ID	?
E'	+	+	+ (ID	λ	?
T	λ	λ	(ID	(ID	?

Figure 17.14   E Table for G_1

Once insertion costs are chosen, the S and E tables can be computed, as shown in Figures 17.13 and 17.14. Now assume we are parsing ID +) + ID $. A syntax error is detected when the) is encountered. At this point, the LL(1) parse stack contains T E' $.   **find_insert ()** is now invoked, with) as the error symbol. G_1 is insert-correctable, so) must be derivable from one of the stack symbols. First, the top symbol, T, is considered. E[T][')'] = (ID; this insertion has a cost of 4. Next, E' is considered. S[T] = ID and E[E'][')'] = + (ID. Hence ID + (ID is a possible insertion, but it costs 7 and is rejected as too expensive. Finally, $ is considered, but it cannot derive the error symbol. Thus the least-cost insertion returned is (ID.

In spite of the remarkable simplicity of the **find_insert ()** algorithm, we can easily establish the properties listed earlier:

- It can repair any input because each invocation of **find_insert ()** allows at least one more input symbol to be accepted.

- Its repair actions can be adjusted by merely changing the values of the cost vector and recomputing the S and E tables.

- It is driven entirely by the S and E tables, which are automatically generable.

- It can be guaranteed to be linear in execution time. Real parsers usually use a *bounded-depth* parse stack (that is, a stack whose maximum depth is some implementation constant). For bounded-depth parse stacks, one invocation of **find_insert()** takes at most bounded time, and $O(|x|)$ invocations need only $O(|x|)$ time. Even in the general case, where a parse stack depth of $O(|x|)$ is allowed, we can create a version of **find_insert()** that needs only $O(|x|)$ time for all invocations (see Exercise 16).

- The insertions chosen by the S and E tables are *locally optimal* in the sense that no lower cost insertion can exist that allows the error symbol to be accepted by the parser.

It should also be obvious that the simplicity of the algorithm allows for very efficient implementations. In addition, if the S and E tables are kept in files, correct programs pay almost nothing for the error-repair capability built into the compiler.

The question of how good the repair operations effected by **find_insert()** are naturally arises. Based on test cases the answer is: reasonably good but not always excellent. A summary of **find_insert()**'s merit seems to be

- It is an excellent recovery technique because of its good performance and extreme simplicity.

- It is a decent, but by no means excellent, repair algorithm. Note however that as we shall see, simple extensions to **find_insert()** can greatly enhance the quality of its repairs without too great an increase in cost or complexity.

If necessary, the S table can be stored in a more compact form than has been suggested in our discussion so far. That is, rather than indexing into a table of terminal strings, we can store with each nonterminal the production that begins a least-cost derivation from it. A least-cost derivation from A is performed whenever S[A] is needed. Generation of S[A] is fast, and only a nonterminal to production map needs to be stored. Moreover, the E table entries can be computed, as needed, from S table entries and the productions of the grammar (see Exercise 7b). This computation is fast, requiring only a fraction of a second to build E[X][a], where a is a particular error symbol.

17.2.5. Adding Deletions to the FMQ Repair Algorithm

A high-quality error-repair algorithm must, at times, do deletions to obtain the best possible repairs. Further, if deletions are allowed, we can use FMQ with any LL(1) grammar and not just insert-correctable LL(1) grammars.

We now investigate how to add deletions to FMQ. As we did for insertions, we assume an integer vector D, where for $a \in V_t$, D[a] is the cost of *deleting* a. Naturally, $D[\$] = \infty$ and $D[X_1 \cdots X_n] = D[X_1] + \cdots + D[X_n]$. Similarly, **D(a)** returns the value of D[a] for any string of terminals. Assume that the remaining input symbols are $b_1 \cdots b_m$, where b_1 is the error symbol. In order to have $b_1 \cdots b_m$ available, it may be necessary to scan the remaining input and store the resulting tokens in a queue. Recall that a repair is determined by two parameters: **delete**, the number of input symbols to be deleted, and **insert**, the string to be inserted *after* deletion. The algorithm shown in Figure 17.15 can be used to obtain least-cost values for **delete** and **insert**. That is, the algorithm minimizes the following:

$$\underset{0 \leq i \leq m}{\text{Min}} \quad \underset{y \in V_t^*}{\text{Min}} \{ D(b_1 \cdots b_i) + C(y) \mid xyb_{i+1} \cdots \in L(G) \}$$

where the input $= xb_1 \cdots b_m$, insert $= y$, and delete $= i$.

As an example, let us reconsider the example used in Section 17.2.4. We must now define deletion costs as well as insertion costs, as shown in Figure 17.16. For simplicity, we use the same costs for insertion and deletion; in more complex grammars, insertion and deletion costs for a particular symbol usually are not the same.

```
void ll_repair(terminal_string *ins, int *d)
{
   /*
    * Remaining input = b₁ · · · bₘ.
    * Optimal repair is to delete d tokens,
    * then insert string ins.
    */

   *ins = "?";
   *d = 0;
   for (i = 1; i <= length(b); i++) {
      if (D(b[1 .. i-1]) >= C(*ins) + D(b[1 .. *d]))
          break;
          /*  No lower cost repair is possible */

      if (C(find_insert(parse_stack,b[i]))
                 + D(b[1 .. i-1])
         < C(*ins) + D(b[1 .. *d])) {
         /* Better repair found */
         *ins = find_insert(parse_stack,b[i]);
         *d = i-1;
      }
   }
}
```

Figure 17.15   An Algorithm That Computes LL(1) Least-Cost Repairs

While parsing ID +) + ID $ using an LL(1) parser, we detect a syntax error when) is encountered. At that point, **11_repair()** is invoked. We consider first deletion of zero symbols, then one symbol, then two, and so forth until we are sure that a least-cost repair has been found. If zero symbols are deleted, we have an insertion-only repair. As we learned in the last section, the least-cost insertion that repairs this error is (ID, which costs 4. The) may be deleted at a cost of 1. Now + is considered the error symbol, and **find_insert()** suggests insertion of ID, at a cost of 2. The total cost of this repair is the deletion cost plus insertion cost, which is 3. This cost is an improvement over the insertion-only repair cost. Next, deletion of) + is considered. This costs 2. The error symbol is now ID, and **find_insert()** reports that the least-cost insertion is λ. (Inserting λ is equivalent to doing no insertion at all.) The total cost of this repair is 2, another improvement. Deletion of) + ID is considered next, but this deletion costs 4 and cannot lead to a cheaper repair. **11_repair()** therefore chooses deletion of) + and insertion of λ as the best repair.

11_repair() is a fairly straightforward algorithm, but it can have an $O(|x|^2)$ worst-case time bound. Here, assuming that the stack is bounded-depth does not work; we can repeatedly reprocess the remaining input for each of $O(|x|)$ errors, and we may need to look at all of the remaining input. However, for cases of practical interest we can show that an $O(|x|^2)$ execution time cannot happen. In particular, assume again a bounded-depth parse stack and $\forall a \in V_t$, $D[a] > 0$ (in the general case $D[a] = 0$ is possible but not very useful—it makes deletion too easy). It can be established that a given input symbol, over successive calls to **11_repair()**, can be considered for deletion at most a constant number of times, and from this, linearity is immediate. By using a more complex version of **11_repair()**, linearity for the general case $[O(|x|)$ stack depth, $D[a] = 0$ allowed] can be established (Fischer, Mauney, and Milton 1979).

In practice, we certainly would not scan and queue all the remaining input when **11_repair()** was invoked. Rather, as input symbols needed to be considered, we would incrementally scan and queue tokens. That is, either a token would be deleted immediately (because no insertion can make it legal) or just a few input tokens would need to be examined and saved beyond the point where parsing is restarted (to verify that no lower cost repair is possible).

When deletions are allowed, the quality of FMQ repair operations becomes quite good. The real beauty of the method, however, is its ease of

Symbol	Cost
(	2
)	1
+	1
ID	2

Figure 17.16   Deletion Costs for G_1

use. A compiler writer need only specify a vector of insertion and deletion costs—the rest is automatic. Certainly simplicity and efficiency of LL(1) error repair and recovery are other factors favoring the use of LL(1) in actual real-world compilers.

17.2.6. Extensions to the FMQ Algorithm

Error-repair algorithms are often evaluated by dividing repairs into three classes: *excellent*, *good*, and *poor*. Excellent repairs are those that are exactly what a human would do. Good repairs are those that are not what a human would do but nonetheless are reasonable. Poor repairs are manifestly inferior to what a human would do; they often lead to later spurious errors.

The FMQ algorithm, tested using a standard suite of error tests (Ripley and Druseikis 1978), yields about 28% poor repairs. A reduction in this category is clearly desirable. (The distinction between good and excellent repairs is highly subjective, but tuning of costs can be helpful in making good repairs better.)

A number of researchers (Graham, Haley, Joy 1979; Burke and Fisher 1982) have concluded that *validation* of repairs is extremely useful in filtering out poor repairs. To validate a repair, the parser is restarted (with semantics disabled). If the parser is able to accept some minimum number of tokens without any syntax errors, the repair is validated and used to actually repair the input. If a proposed repair fails validation, it is rejected, and other repairs are considered.

Mauney (1982) generalized the locally least-cost concept to *regionally* least-cost repairs. In a regionally least-cost repair, cost is minimized within a fixed-size region of a program. A region may include the repair of one error with right context included to validate the repair. A region may also contain repairs for two or more adjacent errors. Using a region size of five tokens, Mauney found that the percentage of poor repairs could be reduced to less than 9% in the Ripley–Druseikis test suite. The algorithm proposed by Mauney is probably too expensive to be used in ordinary compilers, but it does suggest the level of improvement that validation can contribute.

Including a validation component in the FMQ repair algorithm is not too difficult. The LL parse stack and a prefix of a trial repair can be fed to a skeletal parser, which accepts or rejects the repair. The routine shown in Figure 17.17, based on our **ll_driver()**, can be used to validate repairs.

ll_repair(), of Section 17.2.5, can be generalized to **validated_ll_repair()**, as shown in Figure 17.18. The two routines are identical except that **validated_ll_repair()** requires v+1 symbols of validation before a repair is accepted.

validated_ll_repair() requires that an insertion be validated before it is included in a repair. A routine **find_validated_insert()**, shown in Figure 17.19, computes a least-cost insertion that allows a string of symbols, **validation_prefix**, to be accepted after parsing is restarted. The problem to be solved in the design of **find_validated_insert()** is what to do if a least-cost insertion is rejected by the validation check. With

```
boolean ll_validate(stack_of_symbol parse_stack,
                    terminal_string prefix)
{
    /* If all of prefix can be parsed,
       it is considered validated. */

    i = 0; /* Initial position in prefix string */
    while (i < length(prefix) && depth(parse_stack) > 0) {
        if (top(parse_stack)∈Vₙ) {
            if (T[top(parse_stack)][prefix[i]] ==
                            X → Y₁ · · · Yₘ)
                /* Expand nonterminal */
                Replace top(parse_stack) with Y₁...Yₘ;
            else
                return FALSE;
                /* Validation attempt has failed. */

        } else {   /*  top(parse_stack)∈Vₜ */
            if (top(parse_stack) == prefix[i]) {
                pop(parse_stack); /* Match worked. */
                i++;
            } else
                return FALSE;
                /* Validation attempt has failed. */
        }
    }

    /* The whole prefix was correctly parsed. */
    return TRUE;
}
```

Figure 17.17   An Algorithm That Validates LL Repairs

validation, a series of increasingly more expensive insertions may need to be considered before a suitable repair is found.

Let us generalize the E table to include a third parameter (index), an integer i. Informally, $E[A][a][i]$ is the ith cheapest prefix that allows a to be derived from A. That is

$$E: V \times V_t \times N \rightarrow V_t^* \cup \{?\}$$

For $A \in V_n$: $E[A][a][i]$ = the ith lowest cost $w \in V_t^*$ such that $A \Rightarrow^+ wa \cdots$

Otherwise, $E[A][a][i]$ = ?

For $a \in V_t$: $E[a][b][i]$ =? if $a \neq b$ or $i > 0$ $E[a][a][0] = \lambda$

```
void validated_ll_repair(terminal_string *ins,
                         int *d, int v)
{
    /*
     * Remaining input = b₁  · · ·  bₘ.
     * Optimal repair is to delete d tokens, then insert
     * string ins.  v is a validation count: we must
     * validate the repair on b_{d+1}  · · ·  b_{d+1+v}.
     */

    *ins = "?";
    *d = 0;
    for (i = 1; i <= length(b); i++) {
        if (D(b[1 .. i-1]) >= C(*ins) + D(b[1 .. *d]))
            break;
            /* No lower cost repair is possible */

        len = min(i+v, length(b));
        if (C(find_validated_insert(parse_stack,b[i .. len]))
            + D(b[1 .. i-1]) < C(*ins) + D(b[1 .. *d])) {
            /* Better repair found */
            *ins = find_validated_insert(parse_stack,
                                         b[i .. len]);

            *d = i-1;
        }
    }
}
```

Figure 17.18   An Algorithm That Computes Validated LL Repairs

Note that $E[A][a][0]$ values are identical to $E[A][a]$ values, using our original definition.

We still want the cheapest possible insertion, now subject to the requirement that the next input symbol plus v validation symbols be parsable. Let $X_1 \cdots X_i$ be the topmost i symbols of the parse stack, y the input symbols already parsed, and $b_1 b_2 \cdots$ the remaining input symbols. We must somehow solve the following:

$$\min_{1 \le i \le n} \min_{0 \le j} \{ C(S[X_1]) + \cdots + C(S[X_{i-1}]) + C(E[X_i][b_1][j]) \mid$$
$$y\, S[X_1] \cdots S[X_{i-1}] E[X_i][b_1][j] b_1 \cdots b_{v+1} \cdots \in L(G) \}$$

This minimization looks daunting, but it really says that we must now get the lowest cost insertion subject to v-symbol validation. If $E[X_i][b_1][0]$ does not work, we may need to consider $E[X_i][b_1][1]$, $E[X_i][b_1][2]$, ... **find_validated_insert()** solves this minimization. It finds the cheapest insertion and then attempts to validate it. If validation fails, it tries the next

```
terminal_string
find_validated_insert(stack_of_symbol parse_stack,
                      terminal_string validation_prefix)
{
  /*
   * Find a least-cost insertion that allows
   * the validation_prefix to be accepted.
   */
  terminal_string insert, least_cost, t;
  terminal a = validation_prefix[0];
  auto int last_soln[depth(parse_stack)] = {/* all 0s */};
  int soln_i;   /* i value used in least-cost solution */

  /* Loop until a validated insertion is found. */
  while (TRUE) {
     insert = "?";
     least_cost = λ;
     for (i = 0; i <= depth(parse_stack) - 1; i++) {
        if (C(least_cost) >= C(insert))
            break;
            /* No lower cost insertion can be found */

        t = least_cost @
            E[parse_stack[top-i]][a][last_soln[i]];
        if (C(t) < C(insert)) {
            /* A better insertion has been found */
            insert = t;
            soln_i = i;
        }
        least_cost = least_cost @ S[parse_stack[top-i]];
     }

     /* Now try to validate insert */
     if (insert == "?")
         return insert;
         /* Failure return; */
         /* no validated insertion found */
     else if (ll_validate(parse_stack,
                          insert @ validation_prefix))
         return insert;
     else
         last_soln[soln_i]++;
         /* Record rejected solution and try again */
  }
}
```

Figure 17.19   An Algorithm That Computes Validated LL Insertions

cheapest, then the next, and so on until a validated insertion is found, or until no finite cost insertions remain.

In the minimization formula, insertions are characterized by two parameters: i, the parse stack position at which the E function is used, and j, the index selecting the jth cheapest value. Our algorithm knows that $j = 0$ gives the cheapest possible E-table value, so it initially considers each stack position using $j = 0$ and finds the position (call it i) that gives the cheapest overall insertion. This process is identical to that of the **find_insert()** we defined earlier. If validation fails, we look for the next cheapest, remembering not to retry our earlier insertion. This is done by using a j-value of 1 when stack position i is reconsidered. In general, we use a vector **last_soln**, indexed by stack position, that records the j-value last used in a solution. This approach guarantees that we try insertions in least-cost order and yet never retry an insertion that failed validation.

We must still find an efficient representation for the E table. It is obviously impossible to precompute all possible values of E[B][b][i]. To make simple repairs especially fast, we might precompute E[B][b][0] values. If space is a concern, even these values can be computed on demand.

In **find_validated_insert()**, all references to the E table have the same second component, which is the first symbol of the **validation_prefix** parameter. Initially, we need only E[X][a][0], where a = validation_prefix[0]. This is a vector indexed by X, a nonterminal. The vector may be extracted from E[B][b][0] if this has been precomputed. Alternatively, E[X][a][0] may be computed from S table values and the productions of the grammar (see Exercise 7b). This computation is fast, requiring only a fraction of a second. If necessary, E[X][a][1], E[X][a][2], and so on may be computed as needed until a validated insertion is found (see Exercise 19).

There is an alternative to computing complete E[X][a][i] vectors. As insertions become more expensive, they become less desirable, and whether a repair is least-cost becomes less important. We therefore consider a routine **compute_E()** that produces the original E-table value, stored in **E_table**, followed—in order of cost—by one-symbol prefixes. Because E function values of length 1 are computed as needed, we may replace them in the original E table with ?. Entries of length 1 are fairly common (20% of the total in a Pascal grammar), so this is a nontrivial savings. Assume that globally we have defined

```
const terminal sorted_terminals[NUMBER_OF_TERMINALS];
```

and initialized it to the set of terminal symbols, sorted by insertion cost.

We now have the routine shown in Figure 17.20. Using this routine to compute E values, and using only one or two symbols of validation beyond the error symbol, experimenters reduced poor repairs in the Pascal test suite to under 11%. Interestingly enough, increasing the validation window from one to two symbols does not make much of a difference (less than a 1% change in errors rated poor). Two-symbol validation does sometimes select a better repair, but this is counterbalanced by cases in which a second error appears

```
terminal_string compute_E(symbol A, terminal a, int i)
{
  /*
   * Find E[A][a][i], restricting
   * values for i > 0 to one symbol.
   */

  /* Index of last valid prefix found */
  int num_found = -1;
  terminal_string prefix = "?";

  if (E_table[A][a] != "?") {
     prefix = E_table[A][a];
     num_found = 0;
  }

  for (j = 0; j < NUMBER_OF_TERMINALS; j++) {
     if (i == num_found)
        return prefix;

     if (ll_validate(SET_OF( A ),
                     sorted_terminals[j] @ a)) {
        /*
         * sorted_terminals[j] is a legal prefix if
         * it and a can be parsed with A as stacktop.
         */
        prefix = sorted_terminals[j];
        num_found++;
     }
  }
  /* All possibilities examined;  */
  /* could not find E[A][a][i]    */
  return "?";
}
```

Figure 17.20   An Algorithm to Compute E Table Values

near the original error. In such cases, a larger window can misconstrue the second error as an indication that the trial repair under consideration is inappropriate.

In summary, the extensions to the FMQ algorithm produce a very significant improvement in repair quality. Naturally some penalties are incurred. Because searching and validation, rather than simple table lookup, are employed, error repair is slower. However, speed does not appear to be a significant factor. A straightforward implementation will average less than a second per repair. A more careful implementation will certainly increase repair rates, which in any event are adequate for both interactive and batch applications. The most obvious improvement is to have **compute_E()** cache state information so that a call of E[A][a][i+1] starts calculation where E[A][a][i] left off rather than starting from scratch.

17.2.7. Error Repair Using LLGen

One of the reasons that we have discussed FMQ error-repair algorithms in detail is that our LLGen parser generator is also an error-repair generator. If the option **errortables** is used, a file containing insertion and deletion costs, as well as the S and E tables, is created. The E table may or may not be needed, depending on the version of FMQ that is used.

Insertion and deletion costs are provided as input to LLGen. In the ***terminals** section, each token definition line may contain an integer insertion cost and an integer deletion cost of the form:

token_name   insertion_cost   deletion_cost

Figure 17.21 illustrates the definition of Micro's tokens, with insertion and deletion costs included.

If no costs are provided, default costs of 1 are assumed. This means that least-cost repairs default to shortest length repairs.

The choice of repair costs is subjective but usually not critical. Recall that only repairs known to be correct (and possibly validated) are selected by the algorithms. Repair cost is primarily used to choose among acceptable alternatives. Often, a cost is updated to tune an algorithm to force a particular repair. As a rule of thumb, delimiters with little semantic content are cheap to insert or delete; keywords and important delimiters [like (] are made more costly. Because it is usually better to build around an input rather than to delete it, deletion is usually made more costly than insertion. Sometimes a

```
*terminals
ID              8     15
INTLITERAL      8     15
:=              4     8
,               2     4
;               2     4
+               2     4
−               2     4
(               10    20
)               4     8
begin           7     12
end             7     12
read            7     12
write           7     12
```

Figure 17.21   Insertion and Deletion Costs for Micro

symbol, such as **if**, appears in more than one context (for example, in Ada as a header and closer symbol). If significantly different insertion costs are appropriate, distinct symbols can be created for use in cost analysis, and a single terminal is retained for parsing and repair purposes.

Experience has shown that any reasonable set of costs, with a modest validation window (one to five symbols), produces generally high-quality repairs.

17.2.8. LR Error Recovery

Error-recovery techniques for LR parsers are usually variants of the panic mode approach. These techniques can be used in isolation, or as a fall-back in more ambitious error-repair algorithms.

In the simplest version of panic mode recovery, we first define a set of *safe symbols* (;, **end**, $, and so on). When a syntax error is detected, we skip forward in the input to the first occurrence of a safe symbol. The parse stack is then popped until we reach a state in which the safe symbol can be read. Then parsing is restarted.

The intended effect is to bail out of an erroneous construct and resume parsing at the beginning of the next (presumably correct) construct. This process works best in unstructured languages like FORTRAN or BASIC in which it is easy to find the start of the next statement.

To limit the amount of input that is skipped while searching for a safe symbol, we can define a set of header symbols that mark the beginning of a statement or statement list (perhaps, **begin**, **then**, and **else**). If we are skipping forward looking for a safe symbol and encounter a header symbol, we stop at the header symbol and mark it. Parsing is restarted (to process the statements expected). The forward skip is restarted when a marked header is reduced by the parser.

A somewhat nicer version of panic mode appears in James (1972). This method automatically searches for safe symbols to skip to.

When an error is detected the algorithm does the following steps:

(1)   Pop 0 or more states until a state that can read at least one nonterminal is reached. Call that state s.

(2)   Consider the possible successors to s, obtained by reading various nonterminals. Assume this set of states is $\{s_1, s_2, \ldots, s_n\}$.

(3)   Skip forward 0 or more symbols to reach a symbol T that one of $\{s_1, s_2, \ldots, s_n\}$ can read. Then push any state in $\{s_1, s_2, \ldots, s_n\}$ that can read T and restart parsing.

(4)   If no such symbol T can be found, pop off 1 stack state and retry step 1.

The basic idea of the algorithm is to complete the recognition of some nonterminal by pushing the successor state to it. Parsing is then restarted with a terminal symbol that can follow the nonterminal. In effect, we bail out of a phrase and restart parsing immediately after that phrase. This scheme is clearly more general (and automatic) than panic mode. It can recover from any syntax error (at worst, it pops to the start state, takes the successor under the start symbol, and reads forward to the $ at the end of the input). The greatest liability of the algorithm is that the choice of which phrase to complete (that is, which successor state to push) is arbitrary. An inappropriate choice can lead to cascaded errors.

17.2.9. Error Recovery in Yacc

When a syntax error is discovered by a Yacc-generated parser (Section 6.6.12), a subprogram **yyerror()** is called, and parsing is terminated. (**yyerror()** is responsible for printing a syntax-error message.)

Yacc does provide for a measure of user-controlled error recovery. When an LALR(1) grammar specification is given to Yacc, a special symbol, **error**, may be placed in the right-hand sides of productions.   **error** marks where error recovery (after a syntax error) is desired. For example, the production

```
statement : error ';' ;
```

indicates that after a syntax error, parsing may resume by matching a semicolon, thus completing recognition of a statement. The remainder of the current (erroneous) statement will be skipped.

When a syntax error occurs, a Yacc parser enters an error phase. It pops its parse stack until a state that can shift **error** is found. (Parsing is terminated if no such state can be found.)   **error** is then shifted, and parsing is resumed with the current token (which caused the syntax error). If three consecutive tokens can be parsed, the parser leaves the error phase, and normal parsing resumes. Otherwise, tokens are deleted until three tokens can be parsed.

For example, assume we are parsing A := B C; and a syntax error is discovered at token C. Using the error-recovery production just shown, we would pop the parse stack back to the state that existed when A was first seen. **error** would then be shifted, reaching a state requiring a semicolon. C would then be deleted, which would allow the semicolon following it to be shifted. Assuming that a valid statement follows, parsing will be correctly resumed. Productions that include **error** markers may also include semantic routines, allowing user intervention after error recovery, perhaps to reset semantic processing or to issue a special error message.

error markers give the user control over where parsing is to be resumed—typically, after a major construct such as a statement, expression, or declaration. For example, given the Micro specification of Figure 6.32, the two productions

```
statement : error ';' ;
expression : error ;
```

would allow recovery at the end of a statement or expression context.

Yacc's approach to recovery is simple to use and is automatically included in all Yacc-generated parsers. It can be used alone or as a fall-back if more elaborate repair or recovery techniques fail.

17.2.10. Automatically Generated LR Repair Techniques

A least-cost repair technique for LR-based parsers was developed by Dion (1982). The technique is analogous to the FMQ algorithm used with LL(1) parsers. That is, the least-cost insertion and deletion sequence needed to resume parsing is determined. Unfortunately, Dion's technique is rather more complex than the FMQ approach. The problem is that whereas the LL(1) parse stack directly encodes what remains to be matched, equivalent information is much harder to obtain for LR techniques. In particular, individual items in parse states must be analyzed and linked to their predecessors in various states. The net effect is to trace all possible ways of resuming the parse, so that the cheapest possible repair is chosen.

The tables needed to implement Dion's technique are extensive, often requiring hundreds of thousands of bytes for typical programming languages. The least-cost repairs produced by Dion's technique are quite satisfactory, especially when validation is performed. However, to be practical, smaller tables are needed, and we therefore focus on cost-based repair techniques that are as effective as Dion's but that require far less space.

Continuation-based LR Error Repair

We now consider an LR error repair algorithm that uses continuations to determine possible repairs. A *continuation*, as introduced by Roehrich (1980), is a terminal string that if inserted when a syntax error occurs, will allow a parser to be restarted without further errors. At worst, a continuation can be substituted for the remaining input to effect a repair; more often, a prefix is inserted to allow some suffix of the remaining input to be parsed. As an example, consider G_2, a grammar that generates simple expressions:

$$S \rightarrow E\$$$
$$E \rightarrow T \mid E+T$$
$$T \rightarrow ID \mid (E)$$

While parsing (ID + (ID ID)) $, a syntax error is discovered when the third ID is reached. Any sequence of terminals that may be inserted after the program prefix we have already accepted, (ID + (ID, to form a valid program is a continuation. LALR(1) parsers only accept valid program prefixes, and a valid continuation must always exist. In fact, for a given program prefix, an infinite number of distinct continuations may exist. Thus in our example,)) $ is a valid continuation, as is)) + ID $, and)) + ID + ID $, and infinitely many more. When given a choice of continuations, the shortest or least-cost continuation is most desirable.

Error repair using only continuations would be inadequate because we rarely want to delete all the remaining input when a syntax error occurs.

However, a prefix of a least-cost continuation can often be used as an insertion in a repair. After such an insertion, we delete zero or more input symbols and then try to restart parsing. As was the case for LL error repair, we use a cost criterion to choose the best combination of insertions and deletions, and we validate a repair before we accept it. Let

```
boolean lr_validate(stack_of_state parse_stack,
                    terminal_string prefix);
```

be a validation routine that determines whether **prefix** can be parsed in the context represented by **parse_stack**.

choose_validated_insert(), defined in Figure 17.22, calls a subprogram **get_continuation(parse_stack)** to obtain the least-cost continuation that corresponds to the symbols in **parse_stack**. **choose_validated_insert()** examines continuation prefixes, attempting to find the cheapest insertion that allows **validation_prefix** to be accepted.

Continuations are normally least-cost, which means that optional constructs in a program are ignored. In our earlier example, (ID + (ID ID)) $, the least-cost continuation corresponding to (ID + (ID is))$. An obvious repair is to insert a + after the second ID, but + does not appear anywhere in))$.

Roehrich observed this problem and suggested including a special list of *separator symbols* that may be inserted immediately before an error symbol. LeBlanc and Mongiovi (1983) improved upon this idea by considering all syntactically legal terminal symbols as insertion candidates. Therefore, **choose_validated_insert()** first checks whether it is possible to parse **validation_prefix** without any insertion. Next it tries single-symbol insertions, from cheapest to most expensive. Finally, it tries prefixes of the continuation string.

validated_lr_repair(), defined in Figure 17.23, considers possible deletions of input symbols, using **choose_validated_insert()** to compute corresponding insertions until a least-cost validated repair is found. Some validated repair always can be found, for in the worst case it is possible to insert all of the continuation and delete all of the remaining input.

As an example, let us return to the problem of repairing (ID + (ID ID)) $. For simplicity, assume all insertion and deletion costs are 1 and that we require three-symbol validation. First, **validated_lr_repair()** considers deleting zero symbols. It calls **choose_validated_insert()** with the parse stack corresponding to (ID + (ID and a **validation_prefix** of ID)). As outlined earlier, an insertion of +, costing 1, is found. Next, **validated_lr_repair()** considers deleting the third ID. This costs 1 and hence cannot lead to a cheaper repair. Neither can deletions of more than one symbol, so **validated_lr_repair()** inserts + to repair the error.

In practice, **validated_lr_repair()** performs quite well. Using the Ripley and Druseikis test suite, more than 75% of the repairs were rated excellent. With careful tuning of repair costs, and a validation mechanism that

```
terminal_string
choose_validated_insert(stack_of_state parse_stack,
                         terminal_string validation_prefix)
{
  /*
   * Find a least-cost terminal or continuation prefix
   * for the validation_prefix.  Assume that globally
   * we have defined an array of terminals sorted by cost:
   */
  extern const terminal sorted_terminals[NUMBER_OF_TERMINALS];

  terminal_string continuation = get_continuation(parse_stack);
  terminal_string insert = "?";

  if (lr_validate(parse_stack, validation_prefix))
     return ""; /* Best insertion is no insertion */

  for (j = 0; j < NUMBER_OF_TERMINALS; j++)
     if (lr_validate(parse_stack,
              sorted_terminals[j] @ validation_prefix)) {
        insert = sorted_terminals[j];
        break;
     }

  /* Check prefixes of length >=2 */
  for (i = 2; i <= length(continuation); i++) {
     if (C(continuation[1 .. i]) >= C(insert))
        return insert;

     if (lr_validate(parse_stack,
            continuation[1 .. i] @ validation_prefix))
        return continuation[1 .. i];
  }

     return insert;
}
```

Figure 17.22   An Algorithm to Compute Validated LALR Insertions

accommodates two adjacent errors, the fraction of repairs rated excellent increases to 81%, with only 4% judged poor.

Equally important, this repair technique is inexpensive. Beyond the parse table, only the continuation action table, used to compute continuations, and the cost vectors need to be stored. Repairs can be computed at a rate of about ten per second, which is suitable for both interactive and batch processors.

```
void validated_lr_repair(terminal_string *ins,
                              int *d, int v)
{
  /*
   * Remaining input = b₁ · · · bₘ
   * Optimal repair is to delete d tokens, then insert
   * string ins.  v is a validation count:  we must
   * validate the  repair on b_{d+1} · · · b_{d+1+v}.
   */
  terminal_string val_ins;

  *ins = "?";
  *d = 0;
  for (i = 1; i <= length(b); i++) {
     if (D(b[1 .. i-1]) >= C(*ins) + D(b[1 .. *d]))
         break;
         /* No lower cost repair is possible */

     len = min(i+v, length(b));
     val_ins = choose_validated_insert(parse_stack,
                              b[i .. len]);
     if (C(val_ins) + D(b[1 .. i-1])
              < C(*ins) + D(b[1 .. *d])) {
        /* Better repair found */
        *ins = val_ins;
        *d = i-1;
     }
  }
}
```

Figure 17.23   An Algorithm to Compute Validated LALR Repairs

Computing Continuations

In this section we discuss how to compute continuations from the parse stack that exists when a syntax error occurs. Roehrich's original formulation did not use costs. We therefore use an extension proposed by LeBlanc and Mongiovi (1983). To compute a continuation, we examine each state in the parse stack to determine the terminals it is expecting. Superficially, this is simple; however, there can be pitfalls.

Consider a parse state with the following basis items:

$$A \to \alpha \cdot \beta$$
$$B \to \delta \cdot \gamma$$
$$\cdots$$
$$Z \to \zeta \cdot \omega$$

The basis items show productions that have been partially matched. To complete the parse, one of them must be completed. An obvious approach is to insert a terminal string (presumably least-cost) that matches β, or γ, . . . , or ω.

Selection of which terminal string to insert must be done with care. Assume we have the basis items

$$A \rightarrow E \, . \, \textbf{end}$$
$$E \rightarrow E \, . + ID$$

where the cost of inserting **end** is higher than that of inserting + ID. It would seem that insertion of + ID would be appropriate, but this would lead to an infinite insertion loop. In particular, if + ID is inserted, after we reduce $E \rightarrow E + ID$ and shift E, we return to exactly the same state, which then forces insertion of + ID again. A correct continuation algorithm must realize that insertion of **end** is appropriate, even though it is more costly than + ID.

To determine continuations, we examine LR parse states. We pay special attention to the order of items in a state, treating a state more as a list of items than as a set of items. If lists are properly ordered, items at the head of a list can always be used to determine a continuation.

Assume we start with some grammar, G. As was the case in Section 17.2.4, let C(a) be the cost of inserting a terminal a and S[γ] be the lowest cost terminal string derivable from γ.

Productions in G that share a common left-hand side are reordered by the cost of their right-hand sides. That is, if we have $A \rightarrow \alpha$ and $A \rightarrow \beta$, and $C(S[\alpha]) < C(S[\beta])$, then $A \rightarrow \alpha$ precedes $A \rightarrow \beta$. This is done so that the cheapest productions are considered first.

The LR shift and closure algorithms are updated to preserve the correct ordering among items, as shown in Figure 17.24.

As an example, reconsider G_2, ordered using unit insertion costs:

$$S \rightarrow E\$$$
$$E \rightarrow T \mid E+T$$
$$T \rightarrow ID \mid (E)$$

list_closure([S → . E$]) = [S → . E$,
                                 E → . T,
                                 T → . ID,
                                 T → . (E),
                                 E → . E+T]

Unlike the usual LR(0) closure algorithm, **list_closure()** performs a *depth-first* rather than *breadth-first* search in adding new items. This is done so that items added by prediction are ordered by cost and grouped with the item that first caused their introduction.

```
configuration_list list_closure(configuration_list L)
{
    configuration_list L' = L;

    do {
        if (B →δ . Aρ ∈ L' for A∈Vₙ) {
            /* Predict productions with A
               as the left-hand side. */
            Add, in order of definition, all
               configurations of the form A → . γ
               immediately after B →δ . Aρ
        }
        if (Some configurations appear more than once)
            Remove all but its first (earliest) occurrence

    } while (more new configurations can be added);

    return L';
}
```

Figure 17.24   LR Parse State Closure Using Lists

To create the initial configuration list, L_0, we predict the augmenting production and close it: $L_0 =$ **list_closure**($[S → .α\$]$).

Given a configuration list L, we compute its *successor*, L', under a symbol X using the **list_go_to()** function of Figure 17.25.   **list_go_to()** computes successor items in the usual manner, preserving the correct ordering among items on the list.

Item lists, as defined, are equivalent to item sets for parsing purposes. The ordering is imposed to make it easy to extract continuations (discussed later). As detailed by Roehrich (1980), we must occasionally create two or more distinct item lists that are the same when viewed as a set. This has the effect of slightly increasing the size of the corresponding CFSM but does not otherwise affect parsing. In the following discussion, we denote the set of LR(0) item lists for a particular grammar as L_0.

Define CV, the set of continuation values, as $CV = P \cup V_t \cup \{Accept\}$. A production, p, in CV denotes that production p is to be reduced; a terminal value, t, denotes that t is to be appended as the next symbol in the continuation. Accept denotes a completed continuation.

We map configuration lists to continuation actions using the function CA (continuation action):

$$CA: L_0 → CV$$

CA is defined as follows. Let $L \in L_0$ be a configuration list. Let I be the first item in L of the form $A→α.aβ$ or $A→γ.$ —that is, the first item that predicts a terminal or completes a production.

if l = A→α . aβ **then** CA(L) = a;
elsif l = S→δ$. **then** CA(L) = Accept;
elsif l = A→γ . **then** CA(L) = p, where production p is A→γ; **end if**;

As an example, the CFSM for G_1, using item lists rather than item sets, is shown in Figure 17.26. The corresponding continuation action table is shown in Figure 17.27.

We can now define in Figure 17.28 the routine **get_continuation()** used earlier by **choose_validated_insert()**. **get_continuation()** takes an LR parse stack and uses the continuation action table, **CA**, and the **go_to** table to compute a continuation. It operates by following the **CA** table, shifting terminals and reducing productions until an accept action is reached.

As an example, assume we are parsing (ID + (ID ID))$ using G_2. When the syntax error is discovered, the parse stack is 0 6 7 3 6 7. The **get_continuation()** routine performs the steps shown in Figure 17.29 in computing a continuation.

The value computed,))$ is clearly a valid continuation and in fact is also least-cost. It is not too difficult to show that **get_continuation()** always produces valid continuations. Normally the continuations generated are also least-cost, although this cannot be guaranteed (see Exercise 13).

Validity is easy to establish because the **get_continuation()** routine simply emulates a parser, shifting continuation symbols and performing reductions until an accept action is reached. The only thing that might go wrong is that **get_continuation()** might not terminate. The secret to showing termination lies in the ordering of items in parse lists. During closure, a predicted item follows the item that first caused it to be added. This means that after an item is completed and reduced and its left-hand side

```
configuration_list list_go_to(configuration_list l,
                              symbol x)
{
   /* Compute a basis list, L_b: */
   configuration_list L_b = L;

   for (I in L_b) {
       /* Advance the . past the symbol X (if possible) */
       if (I is of the form A →β . Xγ)
               Replace I with A →βX . γ
       else
               Remove I from L;
   }

   return list_closure(L_b);
   /* Add new predictions to L_b via closure operation */
}
```

Figure 17.25   go_to Calculation for LR Parse Lists

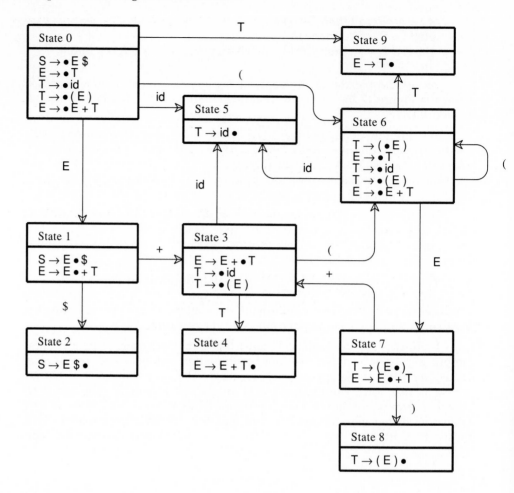

Figure 17.26   CFSM for G_1 Using Item Lists

State:	0	1	2	3	4	5	6	7	8	9
Continuation Action:	ID	$	Accept	ID	p5	p3	ID	)	p4	p2

Figure 17.27   Continuation Action Table for G_1

shifted its initial predictor will head the parse list and thus will be completed next. In effect we work backwards, first completing an item and then its initial predictor. This process avoids cycles and hence guarantees termination.

```
terminal_string get_continuation(stack_of_state parse_stack)
{
    terminal_string continuation;
    production p;

    continuation = λ;
    while (TRUE) {
      if (CA[top(parse_stack)] == ACCEPT)
          return continuation;
      else if (CA[top(parse_stack)]∈Vt) {
          /* Add to continuation */
          continuation = continuation @ CA[top(parse_stack)];
          push(parse_stack,
              go_to[top(parse_stack)][CA[top(parse_stack)]]);
      } else {
          /* Reduce a production */
          p = CA[top(parse_stack)];
          pop(parse_stack, length(p.rhs));
          push(parse_stack,
              go_to[top(parse_stack)][p.lhs]);
      }
    }
}
```

Figure 17.28   An Algorithm to Compute Continuations

Stack	Action	Continuation
0 6 7 3 6 7	Shift)	)
0 6 7 3 6 7 8	Reduce T → (E)	)
0 6 7 3 4	Reduce E → E + T	)
0 6 7	Shift)	))
0 6 7 8	Reduce T → (E)	))
0 9	Reduce E → T	))
0 1	Shift $	))$
0 1 2	Accept	))$.

Figure 17.29   A Trace of **get_continuation()**

17.2.11. Error Repair Using LALRGen

One of the reasons that we have discussed LM error-repair algorithms in detail is that our LALRGen parser generator is also an error-repair generator. If the option **errortables** is used, a file containing insertion and deletion costs, as well as the continuation action table, is created.

Insertion and deletion costs are presented to LALRGen in the same format used in LLGen (see Section 17.2.7). In the *terminals section, each token definition line may contain an integer insertion cost and an integer deletion cost of the form

   token_name   insertion_cost   deletion_cost

If no costs are provided, default values of 1 are assumed.

17.2.12. Other LR Error-Repair Techniques

A number of other LR error-repair techniques have been proposed, including those of Druseikis and Ripley (1976), Mickunas and Modry (1978), and Pennello and DeRemer (1978). We focus on a few of the most recent approaches that have been demonstrated to be effective and efficient.

A technique of Graham, Haley, and Joy (1979) is used in the Berkeley Pascal system. It utilizes parse tables produced by Yacc, adding to them a powerful error-repair component. The GHJ technique first tries simple error repair involving the insertion, deletion, or replacement of a single token. Each repair that is considered is validated, using a window of five tokens. Validation includes a semantic component, as a variety of type checks are enabled during validation. Either a syntactic or semantic error may disqualify a repair.

Each repair is assigned a cost, and repairs that can be validated over only a portion of the validation window receive a penalty. If the last parser action was a shift, the terminal shifted may be unshifted, and repairs involving a single insertion, deletion, or replacement are again evaluated.

After all single-symbol repairs of the current token (and possibly the previous token) are evaluated, the cheapest is chosen if its cost is below a threshold. If it is not, a special check is made to see if only a single terminal may be shifted in the current state. If so, this terminal is inserted, even though another error will probably be detected soon (or else validation would have rated this repair as acceptable). Care is needed to avoid an insertion loop, so consecutive single-shift insertions are forbidden.

If a single-shift insertion is inappropriate, a second-level error recovery occurs. This is essentially the standard Yacc recovery mechanism (that uses error markers), with the inclusion of Wirth's header symbols (Section 17.2.2) to bar excess deletion of input symbols. Special care is made to distinguish between declaration sections and statement sections. If necessary, a **begin** may be inserted to open a statement section, or states may be popped to reopen a declaration section.

The GHJ technique also utilizes error productions to handle situations beyond the scope of ordinary error repair. For example, in Pascal, declaration sections (labels, constants, types, variables, and subprograms) must be correctly ordered. Incorrect ordering is a common error; error productions accept declarations that appear in the wrong section.

In practice, the GHJ technique has been found to be fast, compact, and effective. Parse tables are increased by only about 10% to include error marker entries. Repair speed is a small fraction of a second per repair, and repair quality is very good, with more than 80% of the repairs in the Pascal test suite rated good or excellent.

The main drawback of this approach is that it involves a number of heuristics used in combination for a particular language. The repair component was built by hand rather than automatically, and transporting it to a new language might not be easy. Nonetheless, the GHJ approach shows that efficient and effective error repair in production compilers is achievable. It sets a standard for more automatic techniques to match or exceed.

Another noteworthy repair technique, designed for Ada, is described by Burke and Fisher (1982). As was the case for the GHJ technique, two repair levels are used, with validation screening possible repairs. Most full Ada compilers are not one-pass; rather, an intermediate form Diana tree is first created and analyzed, then code is later generated (see Chapter 14). As a result, the BF technique is not constrained to keep an already accepted input prefix, and a *backward move* over already parsed input is included.

In the *primary* phase, a *simple repair* is attempted, initially at the current (illegal) token. A simple repair is a *token merge*, a single insertion, a token replacement, a *scope recovery*, or a single deletion. A token merge is the catenation of the previous and current token, or current and next token, into a single token (for example, : and = into :=). Replacement is limited to probable misspellings (for example, begim to **begin**). Scope recovery is the insertion of a *scope closer* such as) or **end if**. Each possible repair is evaluated by checking how far validation can proceed, up to a maximum of 25 tokens. The repair that validates the farthest is selected, as long as a minimum distance (typically three tokens) is achieved.

If no satisfactory repair is found, the algorithm removes a state from the parse stack and catenates the state's entry symbol to the input. In effect, the algorithm moves left one symbol (either terminal or nonterminal) by removing a state corresponding to an already accepted symbol. Simple repairs are again attempted (excluding token merger) and evaluated. This process is repeated until an acceptable repair is found or until the algorithm attempts to back up past a scope opener (such as **begin** or **package**). At this point, a *secondary* phase is invoked.

To begin the secondary phase, the parse stack is reset to the configuration that existed when the syntax error was first discovered. The parse stack is popped, looking for a state that can shift the current input token (possibly prefixed with necessary scope closers). If validation accepts at least five tokens, parsing is resumed. Otherwise, the current input token is deleted, and we again pop states until an input prefix can be satisfactorily validated. Deletion continues until a validated recovery is discovered or until the end of file is reached. In the latter case, recovery is forced as a special case.

The BF technique has been found to give an excellent performance, with better than 90% of its repairs in the Pascal test suite rated good or excellent. Its speed is about one repair per second, which is quite acceptable.

Exercises

1. Consider the following sparse array:

	A				B
C					
	D	E		F	
			G		
				H	I
	J		K		

    Show how this array would be represented using the compressed rows technique and the double-offset technique.

2. The array compaction utility discussed in Appendix F uses a best-fit decreasing approach to build a double-offset array representation. That is, rows are meshed together in order of decreasing density. Moreover, when a row is meshed into the V table, the row is placed so that the V table is extended as little as possible.

    Suggest an alternative to best-fit decreasing in selecting the order in which rows are meshed to form a double-offset array representation. Under what circumstances will your alternative be superior to best-fit decreasing?

3. In some cases an array contains two or more rows that are identical. Explain how the table compaction techniques of Section 17.1 can be extended to exploit identical rows in a sparse array.

4. **if-then** and **if-then-else** statements in Pascal are typically generated by productions of the following form:

    >   <stmt list> → <stmt>
    >   <stmt list> → <stmt list> ; <stmt>
    >   <stmt>   → **if** <expr> **then** <stmt>
    >   <stmt>   → **if** <expr> **then** <stmt> else <stmt>

    A common syntax error in Pascal is the "; **else**" problem—a ";" is immediately followed by an **else**. This error is surprisingly difficult to repair. The obvious solution is to ignore a ";" if it is immediately followed by an **else**. However, in a one-pass Pascal compiler, parsing a ";" after a **then** part will cause recognition of an **if-then** statement, with the **else** appearing to be the beginning of a new statement.

    Add error productions to this grammar so that a ; **else** sequence is treated as equivalent to an **else**. Be sure that the updated grammar is still LALR(1).

5. Add **check_input()** calls to the Micro parsing procedures of Section 2.4. Show how the following syntax errors would be handled:

    (a) **begin** ID := 1 **end** $

    (b) **begin** ID := **end** $

    (c) **begin end** $

    (d) $

6. Assume we are using the LL(1) table of Figure 5.5 to parse Micro programs and that the **ll_recovery()** routine of Section 17.2.3 is used to handle syntax errors. Show how the following syntax errors would be handled:

    (a) **begin** ID := 1 ; ; **end** $

    (b) **begin** ID := 1 **end** $

    (c) **begin** ID := **end** $

    (d) **begin end** $

    (e) $

7. a. Give an algorithm that uses a CFG and a vector of insertion costs to compute the S table of Section 17.2.4. (*Hint:* Use an iterative algorithm that examines the right-hand side of each production.)

    b. Generalize the algorithm you defined in part (a) to compute E table values.

8. Consider the following grammar:

<program>	→ <statement list>
<statement list>	→ <statement> <statement tail>
<statement tail>	→ <statement list>
<statement tail>	→ λ
<statement>	→ ID := <expression> ;
<statement>	→ **if** <expression> **then** <statement list> **fi** ;
<statement>	→ **null** ;
<expression>	→ ID <expression tail>
<expression tail>	→ + ID <expression tail>
<expression tail>	→ λ

    Suggest insertion and deletion costs for each terminal of this grammar. Using these costs and the algorithms you defined in Exercise 7, compute the S and E tables for this grammar.

9. Using the grammar and error-repair tables of Exercise 8, show the repairs that would be computed for each of the following using the **find_insert()** routine of Figure 17.11:

   (a) ID := ID ID := ID ;

   (b) ID := ID ID + ID ;

   (c) ID := **fi** ;

   (d) ID **then null**; **fi** ;

   (e) **if** ;

   (f) **then** ;

   (g) **fi** ;

   What repairs would you obtain if you allowed deletions, using the **ll_repair()** routine of Figure 17.15?

   Which of the repairs computed using **ll_repair()** would be rejected if five-symbol validation were required?

10. Put the following grammar into the form required by Yacc, and add **error** tokens to specify error recovery:

<program>	→ <statement list>
<statement list>	→ <statement list> <statement>
<statement list>	→ <statement>
<statement>	→ ID := <expression> ;
<statement>	→ **if** <expression> **then** <statement list> **fi** ;
<statement>	→ **null** ;
<expression>	→ <expression> + ID
<expression>	→ ID

    How well are the error programs of Exercise 9 handled?

11. Using the techniques of Section 17.2.10, create a CFSM and continuation action table for the grammar of Exercise 10. What continuations would be computed by **get_continuation()** for each of the error programs of Exercise 9?

12. Suggest insertion and deletion costs for each terminal of the grammar of Exercise 10. Using the CFSM and continuation action table computed in Exercise 11, and assuming three-symbol validation, what repairs would the **validated_lr_repair()** routine of Figure 17.23 compute for each of the error programs of Exercise 9?

13. Show that the continuations computed by **get_continuation()** of Figure 17.28 are not always least-cost.

14. Validation of error repairs can be improved if semantic as well as syntactic validity is checked. Outline how semantic routines can be designed so they can either screen error repairs or do full semantic processing.

15. The LL(1) buffering technique of Section 17.2.1 is designed to handle any LL(1) grammar. Often LL(1) grammars have the property that nonterminals that derive λ do so directly. That is, if $A \Rightarrow^* \lambda$, then $A \rightarrow \lambda$. Outline a simpler way of undoing parser actions for illegal lookaheads if all λ derivation is direct.

16. Assume we are parsing an input x. Design a version of **find_insert()** (Figure 17.11) for which $O(|x|)$ invocations need only $O(|x|)$ time, even when the parse stack depth reaches $O(|x|)$.

17. Prove that the **ll_repair()** algorithm of Figure 17.15 computes locally optimal error repairs—that is, that the insertion string y and the deletion count i that it computes satisfies

$$\underset{0 \le i \le m}{\text{Min}} \quad \underset{y \in V_t^*}{\text{Min}} \{D(b_1 \cdots b_i) + C(y) \mid xyb_{i+1} \cdots \in L(G)\}$$

where the input $= xb_1 \cdots b_m$.

18. When a syntax error is discovered, we normally do not undo parsing actions because semantic actions are difficult or impossible to undo. Because semantic actions are initiated by action symbols, undoing parsing actions up to the last action symbol processed should be feasible. This would allow a wider range of repair actions without requiring that semantic actions be undone. Outline how the standard LL(1) driver of Figure 5.11 can be revised so that when a syntax error is discovered, parsing is undone up to the last action symbol processed.

19. Let a be some particular error symbol. Assume that we wish to use the **find_validated_insert()** routine of Figure 17.19 and that we have already computed the vectors $E[X][a][0]$, $E[X][a][1], \ldots,$ $E[X][a][i]$. Explain how to compute $E[X][a][i+1]$ using these vectors, the S table, and the grammar being parsed.

20. One way to measure the effectiveness of an error-repair algorithm is to take a valid program and systematically "mutate" it into a series of syntactically illegal programs. For example, if a program contains n tokens, n mutants could be created by deleting one token. Similarly, n more mutants could be created by inserting a random token to the immediate left of each token. A few of the mutants will be syntactically legal and can be ignored. All the rest are syntactically illegal but can be repaired by insertion or deletion of a single token.

    An error-repair algorithm can be evaluated by how many mutant programs are repaired to the original program. Use this mutation analysis approach to automatically evaluate your favorite error-repair algorithm.

APPENDIX A

Definition of Ada/CS

A.1 Introduction

Ada/CS is a Computer Science subset of Ada, chosen to illustrate concepts in the design and implementation of programming languages and their compilers. This appendix is meant to serve two purposes. The first is that it provides the definition of a language that may be used effectively for a compiler implementation project in a course taught using this book. Secondly, it can serve as a tutorial on the language features that are discussed in detail in Chapters 10-13 and that form the basis of the pseudocode we use in the programming examples throughout the book.

A.2 Lexical Considerations

The standard character set is implementation-dependent but must contain all the special symbols needed to form Ada/CS tokens. Comments are delimited by –– (double minus) and end-of-line. Comments may appear anywhere an end-of-line may appear; they are ignored by the scanner. Upper- and lower-case letters are considered equivalent in all tokens except strings. White space (spaces, tabs, and ends-of-line) serves to separate tokens; otherwise it is ignored. White space may not appear in any token except a string constant (see below). End-of-line may not appear in any token. The maximum allowed line length is implementation-defined.

A.3 Tokens

Let letter = 'A'..'Z','a'..'z'; digit = '0'..'9';

(1)   The following are keywords. They are all reserved.

abs	access	all	and	array	begin
body	case	constant	declare	else	elsif
end	exception	exit	for	function	if
in	is	loop	mod	not	null
of	or	others	out	package	pragma
private	procedure	raise	range	record	return
reverse	subtype	then	type	use	when
while					

(2)   Literals are integer, float, or string.

Integer literals contain only digits and underscores and start with a digit. An underscore may appear between any pair of digits; it is used to group digits to enhance readability. It does not affect the actual value represented. For example, one million can be written as 1_000_000 or 1000000 or even 1_0_0_0_0_0_0.

by the letter E or e. At least one digit must both precede and follow the decimal point. Underscores are allowed in float literals. The following are all valid float literals:

        1.0   1.0E–5   1_000_000e4

String literals begin and end with a double quote (") and contain any sequence of *printable characters*. Nonprinting characters must be created by the Char attribute (see below). If a double quote appears inside a string constant, it must be repeated (for example, """Help!"" he cried").

The allowable range of integer values and the range and precision of Float values are implementation-defined.

(3)   Using a regular expression notation in which ',' represents set union, '.' represents set product (catenation), '*' represents Kleene closure, λ represents the null string, Not represents set complement, – represents set difference, literals are delimited by quotes ("), and parentheses are used for grouping, the above definitions may be made more precise:

        Literal = IntLiteral , FloatLiteral , StrLiteral

        IntLiteral = digit . (digit , '_')*

        FloatLiteral =
          IntLiteral . '.' . IntLiteral ,
          IntLiteral . ('E','e') . (λ, '+', '–') . IntLiteral ,
          IntLiteral . '.' . IntLiteral . ('E','e') . (λ, '+', '–') . IntLiteral

        StrLiteral = "" . (Not("") , "" . "")* . ""

(4)   Identifiers are strings of letters, digits, and underscores starting with a letter.

$$\text{Identifier} = (\text{letter} \cdot (\text{letter} , \text{digit} , \text{'\_'})*) - \text{Reserved}$$

There is no limit on the length of an identifier (except that it must fit on one line).

(5)   The following classes of operators are provided:

MultOps   *, /, **mod**

UnaryOps   **abs, not**

PlusOps   +, −

RelOps   =, /=, <, <=, >, >=

LogicalOps   **and, or, and then, or else**

(6)   The following are the remaining operators and delimiters ($ represents end-of-file):

$$\text{Delim} = \text{''} , \text{'..'} , \text{':'} , \text{';'} , \text{','} , \text{'.'} , \text{'|'} , \text{'\&'} , \text{'('} , \text{')'} , \text{'**'} , \text{':='} , \text{'<>'} , \text{'=>'} , \text{'\$'}$$

Adjacent identifiers, reserved words, and numeric literals must be separated by white space (or comments). This rule prevents ambiguity in the way tokens are scanned (that is, begina is one identifier, not **begin** followed by a).

A.4 **Pragmas**

A *pragma* of the form **pragma** ID; may appear between packages, as well as anywhere a declaration or statement may appear. A pragma is a compiler directive. The effect of a pragma and the set of legal command IDs are implementation dependent. Typical pragma commands include ListOn, Optimize, Pack, and Inline.

A.5 **Types**

Ada/CS contains four types predefined in the Standard package (the Standard contains all declarations needed to create a standard environment):

Boolean: As in Pascal and Ada

Float: Like Real in Pascal

Integer: As in Pascal and Ada

String: A character string of variable length (as in Snobol IV). The maximum possible string length is in general determined by implementation considerations (but in principle is unlimited). Small string length limits (such as 256 or 1024) should be avoided. This definition of string is more general than that found in most Ada implementations.

These type names are *not* reserved and may be redefined in a local name scope.

Ada/CS contains four *type generators* that create new types:

(1) Enumerations (as in Pascal) of the form

> **type** ID **is** (ID, ID, . . .);

This generator creates a *new* enumeration type with the ID's defined as constants of this type. The order of the ID's in the definition list determines a total ordering on the values, with the least value first in the list and the greatest value last. The types Integer and Boolean are considered to be enumeration types (**type** Boolean **is** (False, True);). Float is *not* an enumeration. Float and enumerations are called *scalar* types. Integer and Float, but not enumerations, are *arithmetic* types, to which predefined arithmetic operators (like '+' and '*') may be applied.

(2) Arrays defined as

> **type** ID **is array**(<bounds list>) **of** <component type name>;

In the <bounds list>, individual bounds (separated by ','s) are of the form <expr> .. <expr> or <type name>. Range expressions may contain variables. <type name> must be the name of an enumeration type (possibly constrained). If any array bound contains a variable, the array is *dynamic*. Bounds are evaluated (and fixed) when the scopes containing the appropriate array, enumeration, and subtype definitions are entered. The component type of an array may be any type including **array**.

The elements of the <bounds list> may also have the form <type name> **range** <>, defining an *unconstrained array type*, for which the index bounds are unspecified. Such types are particularly useful for specifying the types of arrays passed as parameters to subprograms. (See the section on subprograms for further discussion of unconstrained array types.)

For example

> **type** Arr1 **is array** (1..9) **of** Integer;
> **type** Arr2 **is array** (Boolean) **of** Arr1;
> **type** Matrix **is array** (Integer **range** <>, Integer **range** <>) **of** Float;

(3) Records of the form

```
type ID is
record
    <component list>
end record;
```

and with variants

```
type ID is
record
    <component list>
    <variant part>
end record;
```

For example

```
type R1 is
record
    I, J : Float;
    C  : Integer;
end record;

type R2 is
record
    C : String;
    E : Integer;
    F : R1;
end record;

type R3 is
record
    K : Integer;
    case T : Integer is
        when 1 => A : Integer;
        when 2 => B : Float;
        when 3 => C : Integer;
                  D : Float;
    end case;
end record;
```

A component declaration in a record is syntactically identical to a variable declaration (see below). All arrays in a record must have constant bounds. The field names within a record are local to that record and must be unique in that record only.

Variant records allow the specification of alternative components within a single record type. Each variant describes the components of the record corresponding to a specific value (or values) of a discriminant (Ada) or tag field (Pascal and Ada/CS). To simplify our presentation of the techniques used to compile variant records, the variant record feature of Ada/CS is somewhat simpler than that of Ada. As noted, it is based on use of a tag field, like in Pascal. In addition, each variant may have only a single label (rather than a list of labels).

A record with no fields (useful only as a placeholder) is declared as follows:

```
type R3 is
    record
        null;
    end record;
```

(4) Access types of the form

```
type ID is access <object type name> ;
```

Dynamically allocated objects in Ada/CS are referenced by *access* types, which are equivalent to pointer or reference types in other languages. In Ada/CS, references to entire dynamic objects are expressed using a **. all** suffix after an access object name (e.g., **A.all**). However, references to components of referenced objects require no special syntactic designation. Therefore, A.D may mean a reference to field D of record A, or it may be a reference to field D of the record pointed to by the access object A.

Incomplete type declarations are included in Ada/CS (as in Ada) to handle forward references in access type declarations, such as in defining a recursive type. For example

```
type Cell;                  — incomplete type declaration
type Link is access Cell;   — Cell must already be declared

type Cell is
    record
        Value : Integer;
        Succ : Link;
        Pred : Link;
    end record;
```

A.6 Subtypes

Subtypes are defined as

```
subtype ID is <type name> <constraint>
```

One form of <constraint> is **range** Lower .. Upper, which is called a range constraint. Unlike in Pascal, Lower and Upper can be expressions (yielding the same enumeration type). These expressions may contain variables and so may not be evaluated at compile-time. The <constraint> is optional; if it is omitted, the subtype is simply a renaming of the original type. The <type name> is also optional; if it is omitted, it is the type of the Lower and Upper bounds.

A subtype is the original (or *base*) type restricted to the constraints imposed in the range constraint. As a result, only values within the Lower and Upper bounds of the constraint may be assigned to an object of such a subtype. A subtype of a subtype may be declared, as long as constraint ranges are *proper* (i.e., a subtype can't include any values not allowed in its parent type).

A second form of constraint is an index constraint: (<range list>). An index constraint can only be applied to an unconstrained array type. As with bounds in array type definitions, the range expressions in a range constraint may contain variables. Variables may not be declared with an unconstrained array type as their type. Either a constrained type or an array subtype must be used so that the size of the variable is defined by the applicable declarations.

It is important to understand that a subtype does not create a new type. A subtype name denotes the combination of a constraint and a type, with the constraint defining further restrictions on which values of the type can be assigned to variables declared to be of the subtype.

A.7 Variable Declarations

Variables are introduced by declarations of the form

> ID, ID, . . ., ID : <type> := <expr>;

The := <expr> is an optional initialization.

For example

> **subtype** Week **is** Integer **range** 1 .. 7;
> A, B : Week := 1;

A.8 Variable Denotations

Fields of a record are designated by appending qualifications to a record identifier. For example, if we use the above definition of record R2 to obtain

> A,B : **array**(1 .. 10) **of** R2,

all of the following are legal names

> A(1).C, A(1).F.C, B(I).F

but the following are illegal

> B(1).I, A.E, A.E(1), F.J.C

Multidimensional arrays cannot be partially indexed. For example, given

type AR **is array**(Boolean,1..10) **of** Float; C : AR;

C(True, 3) is legal, but C(True)(3) and C(False) are illegal.

Unlike Pascal, multi-dimensional arrays *are not* arrays of arrays (but arrays of arrays are allowed). Also, functions may return arrays and records, and these may be qualified. Thus F(1).A and G(2)(1,2) are legal expressions if F and G are functions.

A.9 Named Constants

An identifier may be given an initial value and declared constant. The syntax is very close to that used for variables:

ID, ID, . . ., ID : **constant** <type> := <expr>;

If <expr> involves only literals, manifest constants, and predefined operators and functions, the constant is *manifest* and may be evaluated at compile time. Otherwise, the constant is (in effect) a read-only object whose value is determined at run time but that cannot be altered after initialization. After definition, a manifest constant may be used anywhere a literal (of the same type) may appear.

A.10 Operators and Expressions

The operators, in decreasing order of precedence, are

(1)   Field qualification ('.') and subscripting ('(' and ')')

(2)   Exponentiation and unary operators: **, **abs**, **not**

(3)   Multiplying operators: *, /, **mod**

(4)   Unary plus and minus: +, −

(5)   Adding operators: +, −, &

(6)   Relational operators: =, /=, <, <=, >, >=

(7)   Logical operators: **and**, **or**, **and then**, **or else**

Operators at the same precedence level are evaluated from left to right. All operators are left-associative except ** and the relational operators, which are not associative at all. Thus X ** Y ** 2 is illegal (although both (X ** Y) ** 2 and X ** (Y ** 2) are legal).

A.11 **Operator Descriptions**

(2)   Exponentiation and Unary Operators.
A ∗∗ B is defined if A is an integer or a real and B is a nonnegative integer. In particular, A ∗∗ 0 is equal to 1 or 1.0 (depending on whether A is integer or real). For B > 0, A ∗∗ B is equal to A∗A∗. . .∗A (B copies).

abs is the absolute value operator; **not** is Boolean negation.

(3)   Multiplying operators.
The operator ∗ is multiplication; the operator / is division. Both operands must be float or integer; the result type is the same as the operand type. (Recall that constrained subtypes of integer are of type integer.)

The **mod** operator applies only to integers. The identity

$$A = (A/B)*B + (A \textbf{ mod } B)$$

always holds. (A **mod** B) has the same sign as B, and its absolute value is less than B's absolute value.

(4)   Unary plus and minus.
These are defined on all arithmetic types, and always return the type of the operand. + is the identity operator; − is the complement operator.

(5)   Adding operators.
The operator + is addition; the operator − is subtraction. Both operands must be float or integer; the result type is the same as the operand type. The & operator is string catenation.

(6)   Relational operators.
For the operators <, <=, >, >=, =, /=, both operands must be of the same type; the result is Boolean. Equality and inequality (= and /=) are defined for all types. The others are defined for scalar types and strings. For strings, comparisons are lexicographic.

(7)   Logical operators.
and is Boolean and; **or** is Boolean or. The operands must be Boolean. Both operands are always evaluated, and **and** and **or** are commutative.

The operator **and then** is Boolean conditional and. The operator **or else** is Boolean conditional or. Operands must be Boolean. For both operators, the left operand is evaluated first. The right operand is evaluated only if necessary. Neither is commutative.

A.12 **Assignment Compatibility**

A value may be assigned to an object only if both have the same base type. If the target type is a constrained subtype, any value assigned to it must satisfy its constraint. Otherwise, subtypes are assignment compatible with their base type and other subtypes of the same base type. Two distinct type definitions, even if structurally identical, are considered different. This rule is called *name equivalence* of types.

For example

    type T1 **is array**(1..10) **of** Float;
    type T2 **is array**(1..10) **of** Float;
    A, B: T1; C, D: T2;

A:=B and C:=D are legal, but A:=C is not legal.

A.13 Null Statements

Null statements are represented as **null**;

A.14 Assignment Statements

Assignments are as in Algol 60 or Pascal, given that the left and right sides of the assignment are compatible (as defined above). Compatible objects of any type may be assigned. The order of evaluation is implementation-defined.

A.15 Blocks

Block structure, name scoping (for variables, named constants, types, and subprograms) and dynamic allocations are the same as in Algol 60. A block has the form

    declare
        Type, variable, constant and subprogram declarations
    begin
        Statement list
    exception
        Exception handler declarations
    end;

If there are no declarations, the keyword **declare** may be omitted. If there are no exception handlers, the keyword **exception** may be omitted. A block may appear wherever a statement may appear (as in Algol 60). A block may be prefixed with a block identifier of the form "ID:"; the same identifier must follow the closing **end**.

For example

```
B1:   begin
         . . .
      end B1;
```

A.16 if Statements

The **if** statement has the form

```
if boolean expression then
   sequence of statements
elsif boolean expression then
   sequence of statements
      . . .
elsif boolean expression then
   sequence of statements
else
   sequence of statements
end if
```

The **else** clause and the **elsif** clauses may be omitted. The conditions are evaluated in sequence until one of them is true (treating **else** like **elsif** True **then**). Then the corresponding sequence of statements is executed. If none of the conditions evaluate to True, none of the sequences of statements are executed.

A.17 loop Statements

The **loop** statement comes in three forms. The first has the form

```
loop
   sequence of statements
end loop;
```

This is a "loop forever," but **exit** can be used to terminate iteration (see below).

The second loop form is a conventional **while loop**:

```
while <boolean expr> loop
   sequence of statements
end loop;
```

The third form is essentially a Pascal-like **for loop**:

```
for ID in <range> loop
    sequence of statements
end loop;

for ID in reverse <range> loop
    sequence of statements
end loop;
```

<range> is either an explicit range pair (that is, Lower .. Upper) or the name of an enumeration type or subtype. In the latter case, Lower and Upper are extracted from the limits or constraints of the type or subtype. ID is *implicitly declared* in the loop body and thus is unavailable outside the loop body. ID's type is determined by the <range> expression.

In the first form, iteration begins with ID set to Lower (if any iterations occur) and terminates after ID = Upper. The <range> expression is evaluated only once, at loop entrance. Zero iterations are possible (if initially ID > Upper). At the end of each iteration, ID receives the next value in the <range> sequence.

In the second form, iteration begins with ID set to Upper (if any iterations occur) and terminates after ID = Lower. Zero iterations are possible (if initially ID < Lower). At the end of each iteration, ID receives the next value in the <range> sequence, traversed in *reverse* order.

It is required that the **for** ID be treated as read-only. It may not be assigned to, used as an **out** parameter, etc. As with blocks, a loop (in any form) may be labeled, with the same label following the loop end.

A.18 The **exit** Statement

Ada/CS has no **goto** statement. Rather, an **exit** statement of the form

```
exit;
```

   or

```
exit ID;
```

acts as a restricted form of **goto**. An **exit** is used to leave a loop. An unlabeled **exit** leaves the innermost loop structure containing the **exit**. A labeled **exit** leaves the loop labeled with the corresponding identifier. In both cases, the loop exited must be in the same subprogram or package that contains the **exit** statement. An **exit** *may not* imply a return from a subprogram.

A conditional **exit** is implied by a **when** clause, which is of the form

```
exit ID when <bool expr>;
```

The **exit** is performed only if the boolean expression evaluates to True. (An **if** statement could be used, but the **exit-when** syntax is considered more readable.)

A.19 **case** Statements

The **case** statement has the form

```
case <expr> is
    when <choice> | . . . | <choice> =>  sequence of statements;
    when <choice> | . . . | <choice> =>  sequence of statements;
        . . .
    end case;
```

The expreesion is evaluated and the sequence of statements corresponding to the choice that matches expression's value is executed. Each choice is either a constant expression or a <range> specifier as defined for **for loops**, except that the bounds of all ranges used in **case** statements must be determinable at compile time. The last **when** clause may use the keyword **others** as its sole choice. This represents all values not covered by other choice clauses. All possible values of <expr> must be covered by exactly one choice. Any enumeration type or subtype may be used in a **case**, and, of course, the types of the expression and **when** choices must match.

A.20 Read

In programming language design, a recurring problem is whether to treat Read and Write as statement types or as predefined procedures. There are problems with both approaches. Considering Read and Write to be predefined procedures (as Ada does) isn't really satisfactory because, unlike ordinary procedures, we'd like them to take an indefinite number of arguments and perhaps allow nonstandard parameter syntax (such as Pascal's width specifications). On the other hand, reserving Read and Write seems to obviate the chance of allowing users to extend these statements to handle new data types.

In Ada/CS, we'll essentially treat Read and Write as predefined procedures that are *overloaded*. To allow lists of input or output items (which Ada doesn't really support), we'll introduce a notational extension to procedure call syntax. If you wish, you can envision a *preprocessor* that translates our extension into standard syntax. (C takes this approach in handling **#include**s, **#define**s, etc.) Arguments in Ada are separated by commas. We'll allow *parameter groups* separated by semicolons. Each parameter group is extracted by the preprocessor and inserted into a *separate call* of the procedure. Thus Write("Date ="; month; day;year); would expand into

Write("Date ="); Write(month); Write(day); Write(year);

This extension can be used by *all* procedures, not just Read and Write.

In Ada/CS, only scalars and strings may be read. That is, the standard package contains definitions for Read that accept Integer, Float, Boolean, and String values. When an enumeration type is defined, Read is automatically overloaded to handle the new type. Read *is not* predefined to handle arrays or records, though user-defined routines for such types can be written.

Read can handle components of structured types, as long as the components are strings or scalars. Input is read free format, and string values are quoted. Our preprocessor forces Reads to handle items one by one, so, e.g., Read (I;A[I]); is legal.

The identifier Next (part of a predefined enumeration type) may appear in a read list. This causes an immediate skip to the start of the *next* input line.

A.21 Write

All scalar values (and expressions) as well as strings are handled by predefined Write procedures. Each scalar type has a default output width (implementation determined) that is sufficient to print any value of that type without truncation. The default output width of a string is its length.

Any variable or expression in a write list may be followed by a second integer parameter representing an *explicit* output width.

- For scalars, if a width value i is sufficient to print the output value without truncation, the value is printed using i columns with blank padding on the left (if necessary). If the width is insufficient to print the scalar value without truncation, it may be overridden with the smallest value that allows the value to be printed.

- For strings, if the width value i ≥ the string length, the string is padded on the left with blanks and printed using i columns. If i < the string length, the leftmost i characters of the string are printed. If i < 0, no symbols are printed.

- For floats, the format used (exponential, fixed decimal, and so on) is implementation-dependent, as is the definition of when an output width causes truncation.

The predefined identifier Next may appear in an output list. Next causes an immediate skip to the *next* output line. If an output line is too long to be printed on one physical line, it may be broken without an explicit Next appearing.

Width expressions may be (optionally) included in parameter groups:

Write("Date = "; month,2; day,3; year,5);

thus expands into

Write("Date ="); Write(month,2); Write(day,3); Write(year,5);

A.22 **Subprograms**

Just as in Pascal, subprograms are used as either procedures or functions. A call of a procedure is P(Arg,Arg2,. . .); and a call of a procedure with no arguments is P; (an empty argument list isn't needed).

Function calls occur in expressions; for example A + F(3,A). Functions of no arguments are denoted as F (and look exactly like variables). Both varieties of subprograms may be recursive. A function may return any type (including records and arrays—even dynamic arrays).

At the beginning of every subprogram is a list of its formal parameters. For each parameter, its position, name, type, and mode (**in**, **out**, or **in out**) is specified (the default is **in**). If the subprogram is a function, the header is terminated by **return** <type name>; which defines the type computed by the function.

For example, consider

procedure P(X : Float; Y,Z : **in out** Integer);

Three formal parameters (X,Y,Z) are declared. All formal parameters are considered to be local to the body of the subprogram. The types of all formal parameters as well as the type of the return value (if a function) must be specified with a type name. An explicit type generator or range specification may not be used.

Ada/CS subprograms follow the same scope rules as Pascal: Every variable is automatically visible in any function, procedure, or block contained within the block of definition, except when an inner scope contains another declaration of the same variable. Ada/CS allows no forward references, so the scope of a declaration actually extends from the point of its definition to the end of its containing scope.

A procedure, like a block, can also declare local constants, variables, types, and subprograms. The general structure of a subprogram body definition is similar to that of a block:

```
procedure ID ( <formals list>) is
    Type, variable, constant and subprogram declarations
begin
    Statement list
exception
    Exception handler declarations
end;
```

Both the (<formals list>) and the **exception** part are optional.

It is often useful to allow a subprogram to accept as a parameter not a single array type (whose bounds are fixed) but rather a whole class of array types that differ only in the number of array components allocated. In Ada/CS we allow the definition of *unconstrained arrays* in which the index bounds are unspecified. An example of an unconstrained array is

```
type Matrix is array(Integer range <>, Integer range <>) of Float;
```

Unconstrained arrays can be used in subprograms to represent a class of legal actual parameters, all having the same index and component types but differing in their actual bounds. Thus

```
procedure Invert (M_In: in Matrix; M_Out: out Matrix);
```

can accept two-dimensional matrices of any consistent sizes.

If a type name denoting an ordinary array rather than an unconstrained array is used in an argument definition, then only arrays of exactly that type may be passed. Thus an argument can be limited to a particular array type, or a whole class of arrays having common structure may be allowed.

Functions are declared as follows:

```
function <name> ( <formals list>) return <type name> is
    Type, variable, constant and subprogram declarations
begin
    Statement list
exception
    Exception handler declarations
end;
```

Any type can be returned. Only **in** parameters are allowed, reflecting the view that functions ought not to have side effects (though they can change nonlocal variables). A function must return by executing

```
return <expr>;
```

where <expr> is assignable to the function's type; the value of the expression is returned as the value of the function call. Procedures return by executing a **"return;"**. There is an implicit **return** at the end of each subprogram.

The name of a function can (of course) be an identifier. It can also be any of the following operator symbols, enclosed in quotes (like a string literal): **, *, /, **mod**, +, –, **abs**, **not**, &, =, <, <=, >, >=, **and**, **or**. Functions with operator names must take one or two arguments, depending on whether the operator is unary or binary (or both). The '=' operator must return a **boolean**. Whenever '=' is defined, '/=' is *automatically* defined as its negation.

A.23 Parameter modes

When a procedure is called, actual parameters are matched with corresponding formal parameters.

- Parameters of mode **in** are local constants initialized at the time of call to the corresponding actual parameter. The type of the actual parameter must be *assignable* to that of the formal parameter, and any range qualifications on the formal parameter are checked (if necessary) at the point of call. If the formal parameter is an unconstrained array, then the actual parameter must be of a constrained subtype of the formal type. An actual parameter passed as an **in** parameter may be any expression of the proper type. **In** parameters are the safest kind, because they cannot be altered. That's why they are the default.

- Parameters of mode **out** are uninitialized local variables that may be assigned to but not read. Upon return, their values are assigned to the corresponding actual parameters. The type of the formal parameter must be *assignable* to that of the actual parameter, and any range qualifications on the actual parameter are checked (if necessary) at the point of return. If the formal parameter is an unconstrained array, then the actual parameter must be of a constrained subtype of the formal type. An actual parameter passed as an **out** parameter must be a variable name (possibly qualified) because it will be the target of an assignment.

- Parameters of mode **in out** are local variables, initialized at the point of call to the value of the value of the actual parameter. At the point of return, the local variable's value is assigned back to the corresponding actual parameter. The types of the formal and actual parameters must be mutually assignable. Further, range qualifications on the formal and actual parameters are checked (if necessary) at the points of call and of return. If the formal parameter is an unconstrained array, then the actual parameter must be of a constrained subtype of the formal type. An actual parameter passed as an **in out** parameter must be a variable name (possibly qualified) because it will be the target of an assignment.

in, **out**, and **in out** parameters can obviously be implemented by performing copy operations. In fact, this is required for scalar parameters. For records, arrays, and strings, copy operations may be expensive. Ada/CS therefore allows such parameters to be implemented by passing an *address* rather than doing an actual copy. Programs that depend on how nonscalar parameters are implemented (copy or address) are illegal.

A.24 **Forward References**

In Ada/CS, no forward references are allowed. If a constant, variable, type, or subprogram is to be used, it must already have been defined. It may happen that a subprogram must be called before it has been defined (for example, if A calls B and B calls A). For this reason the declaration of a subprogram may be separated from its actual definition. To declare a subprogram, we just provide its header that specifies its name, its parameters, and its result type (if any). Later in the same name scope, we must provide a complete subprogram definition (including the header).

A.25 **Predefined Functions and Language Attributes**

Ada/CS includes ordinary predefined functions (like Substr) that are included in the standard environment. Ada/CS also includes the concept of a *language attribute* that provides some property of an object or type. Attribute expressions are of the form Name'Attribute. Name is the name of an object or type; Attribute is the particular attribute we wish. Thus T'First gives the first of the range of values allowed by the type or subtype named T.

(1) A'Len
     Defined if A is a string expression. It returns an integer result denoting the number of characters in the string.

(2) Substr(A,S,L)
     A must be a string expression, S a positive integer, and L a non-negative integer. It returns the substring of A beginning at position S that is L characters long. It is an error if this substring does not exist. The left-most character of A is position 1.

(3) T'Succ(A)
     A must be a value of an enumeration type T. The result is its immediate successor, if one exists. Otherwise a Constraint_Error is raised.

(4) T'Pred(A)
     A must be a value of an enumeration type T. The result is A's immediate predecessor, if one exists. Otherwise a Constraint_Error is raised.

(5) I'Char
     I must be an integer. The result is a 1 character string corresponding (in the character sequence) to the integer; if no such character exists, a Constraint_Error is raised.

(6) T'Val(A)
     A is a value of any enumeration type, and T is the name of any enumeration type or subtype. A is converted to the corresponding value in the enumeration type as follows:

All enumerations have an ordinal value determined by the order of enumeration of the type's values. For enumerations other than integers, this starts at 0. For integers, a value i is its own ordinal value. Two values correspond if and only if they have the same ordinal value. Thus, given **type** Boolean **is** (False,True) and **type** Color **is** (Red,Blue,Yellow,Green) we have

> Integer'Val(False) = 0
> Boolean'Val(Blue) = True

If no value in the enumeration type corresponds to A, a Constraint_Error is raised. (Both Boolean'Val(−1) and Boolean'Val(Green) raise an error).

(7)   T'First
      If T is an enumeration type or a subtype, T'First is the first value in the range allowed by T. If T is an array type or object, T'First gives the lower bound of the first index; T'First(J) gives the lower bound of the Jth index.

(8)   T'Last
      If T is an enumeration type or a subtype, T'Last is the last value in the range allowed by T. If T is an array type or object, T'Last gives the upper bound of the first index; T'Last(J) gives the upper bound of the Jth index.

(9)   T(E)
      If T is an arithmetic type or subtype and E is an arithmetic expression, then E is converted to type T.

(10) T'E
      T must be a type name; E is any expression. E must be evaluated to produce a value of type T. This form of type designation is useful for resolving overloading conflicts.

A.26 Overloading

As described below, packages are designed to make it easy for users to define new types and operations. Unless overloading is allowed, the newly defined types can't use existing operator and subprogram names, leading to non-uniform and awkward programs.

In Ada/CS, operators and subprogram names can be overloaded. Two definitions can share (that is, overload) an operator or subprogram name if they differ in the number or type of their arguments or in their result type. We will decide from context which of the coexisting definitions to use. If a unique choice can't be made, the program has an error. Such errors can often be resolved by qualifying an identifier or operator with the block, subprogram, or package in which it is defined (for example, Sqrt.Min(X) rather than Min(X)). Operators or subprograms that have exactly the same number and type of arguments and the same result type can never coexist. If one definition is in a different scope from the other, normal scoping rules apply, and the inner definition *hides* the other. If both are defined in the same scope, the program has a multiple-definition error.

In all cases of hiding (including variable, type, and constant names), explicit qualification can be used to reference an otherwise hidden name (that's why blocks are allowed names). Only operators and subprogram names can be overloaded. All other names must have a unique definition determined by scoping rules.

A.27 Packages

Real-world programming languages require a mechanism to modularize programs. Modularization is necessary to structure large programs into manageable units, to allow libraries of program fragments, and to allow separate compilation of program units. In Ada/CS, the unit of modularization is the *package*. An Ada/CS program is simply a sequence of one or more packages. A package is of the form

```
package ID is
    Type, variable, constant and subprogram headers
private
    Type declarations
body
    Type, variable, constant and subprogram declarations
begin
    Statement list
exception
    Exception handler declarations
end;
```

The **private** and **exception** parts may be omitted if there are no private types or exception handlers; the statement list part and the preceeding **begin** are also optional.

In Ada, a package must be divided in separate declaration and body parts, as illustrated below. In Ada/CS this division is allowed but not required.

```
package ID is
    Type, variable, constant and subprogram headers
private
    Type declarations
end;
```

```
package body ID is
    Type, variable, constant and subprogram declarations
begin
    Statement list
exception
    Exception handler declarations
end;
```

This separation serves two purposes. If two packages must reference each other, we can avoid forward references by first listing the package declarations and then their bodies, much as was done for subprograms. More importantly, the package declaration section contains all the information needed to compile references to package components. This means that package's bodies can be precompiled and linked to form an executable object program.

The type, variable, constant, and subprogram headers that appear in the package declaration section can be made visible to other packages. This is therefore called the *visible part* of the package. Objects can be referenced by qualifying the object's name with the name of the package in which it appears. Thus P.A would name object A in package P. An alternate way to access objects in a package declaration is to use a **use** statement, as discussed below.

We wish to use packages to implement abstract data types, but this use leads to a problem. If we place the definition of a type in the visible part of a package, its implementation is visible outside the package. This visibility is undesirable, as we wish to characterize an abstract data type by its operations, not its implementation. Declarations placed in the body of a package are never visible outside the package, so the definition of an abstract data type can't be placed there. The **private** part of a package declaration exists to address this problem. In the visible part of the package, the type is declared to be **private**. The implementation of the type is hidden in the **private** part. Thus in the declaration

```
package Set_Stuff is
type Set is private;
private
    type Set is array(1 .. Max_Set) of Boolean;
end Set_Stuff;
```

The type name Set is made visible, but not the fact that it is implemented as an array. If the full declaration were in the visible part, its implementation would be visible. By making types private, we can guarantee that they are manipulated only by operations defined in the package itself, plus the assignment and equality operators automatically provided for private types. All declarations in the package body are completely hidden outside the package. Declarations in the specification part are visible in the body, which is responsible for implementing the subprograms declared in the specification part. Subprograms declared in the declaration must be defined in the package body. If no subprograms are declared, the package body isn't needed. For example

```
package Set_Stuff is
type Set is private;
function In (I:Integer; S:Set) return Boolean;
private
   type Set is array(1 .. Max_Set) of Boolean;
body
   function In (I:Integer; S:Set) return Boolean;
   begin
      return S(I);
   end;
end Set_Stuff;
```

The statements (if any) in the package body following the declarations are executed when the package body is executed. Package bodies are executed in the order in which package bodies are sequenced to form the main program. If a package is separately compiled, we insert the stub

package body ID **is separate**;

to mark where the separately compiled body is to be inserted. Usually all but the last package body contains only initialization code. The last package body is effectively the main program, and hence this package most likely *will* have statements following the declarations.

All variables and constants declared in packages (but not variables and constants declared in subprograms within packages) are *static*. That is, they are created when the package is executed and continue to exist after the package body is executed. This design is necessary because later packages may reference objects in such packages.

A.28 The **use** Clause

A **use** clause (which optionally heads a declaration section) can name one or more packages whose visible parts are to be made accessible. The declaration

use p1, p2,. . ., pn;

(where p1, p2,. . ., pn name packages) causes all the visible definitions of the packages to be made accessible (as if they had all been locally defined). However, special rules govern name clashes:

- If a name can be found using the usual scoping rules (and excluding the names provided by the packages), then it always applies. (Names from packages are allowed only if they don't hide any existing name).

- If the same name is provided by more than one package on the **use** list, then *none* of the clashing package definitions are included. (This rule makes sure that the order in which packages are named in the **use** list is irrelevant).

use clauses may introduce overloading, as long as no definitions are hidden and no clashing definitions are introduced. For example, assume

function "+" (X,Y : Matrix) **return** Matrix;

is in the visible part of some package named in a **use** clause. This definition of "+" will be allowed to overload existing definitions as long as no definition of "+" on two Matrix objects already exists or appears in the other packages named in the **use** clause.

A.29 Exceptions

Programs must sometimes handle unexpected or error conditions. Ada/CS provides exceptions for this purpose. Exceptions are declared in the declaration section of a block, subprogram, or package. For example

Illegal_Data, Symbol_Table_Full : **exception**;

Ada/CS provides a number of predefined exceptions:

- Constraint_Error
  Raised if an array index is out of range, or if a range constraint is violated
- Numeric_Error
  Raised on overflow, underflow, zero divide, and illegal exponentiation
- Storage_Error
  Raised if a storage request can't be satisfied
- Time_Limit
  Raised if an execution time limit is reached
- Eof_Error
  Raised by an attempt to read past end of file
- Invalid_Input
  Raised by an attempt to read an invalid input item

Predefined exceptions can be automatically raised during execution as a result of run-time errors. All exceptions can be explicitly raised by the **raise** statement, as in this example:

raise Invalid_Input;

When an exception is raised during execution of a statement, execution is suspended, and the exception part of the immediately containing block, subprogram, or package is examined for an *exception handler*. The exception part looks exactly like a **case** statement except that choices are labeled with exception names:

exception
    when exception | . . . | exception => sequence of statements;
    when exception | . . . | exception => sequence of statements;

    . . .

As was the case for the **case** statement, the last **when** may use the choice **others** to cover all exceptions not explicitly named.

    If a handler is found, the corresponding statements are executed, and the block, subprogram, or package is then exited. The statements executed obey the same scope rules as other statements in the block, subprogram, or package. Execution at the point where the exception was raised is *not* resumed.

    If a handler is not found, the exception is *propagated*. An exception is propagated from a block by examining the exception part of the block, subprogram, or package that immediately contains the block. An exception is propagated from a subprogram by returning to the point of call and examining the exception part of the block, subprogram, or package that immediately contains the call. An exception is propagated from a package by terminating execution with a message naming the exception that was raised.

    Exceptions raised during execution of declarations or exception handlers are handled by propagating the exception from the block, subprogram, or package that immediately contains the offending declarations or exception handlers.

A.30 Ada/CS Grammar

Listed below is an extended BNF grammar for Ada/CS. Non-terminal symbols are enclosed in '<' and '>'. Reserved words are in **bold**, token classes are undelimited words, and all other symbols (except [,], {, and }) represent themselves. The symbol → separates the left- and right-hand sides of a production. If no left-hand side is shown, the left-hand side of the preceding production is assumed.

<compilation>	→ <pragma list> <compilation unit> { <pragma list> <compilation unit> }
<pragma list>	→ { <pragma> }
<pragma>	→ **pragma** id ;
<compilation unit>	→ <package declaration>
<package declaration>	→ **package** <package spec or body> ;
<package spec or body>	→ <id> **is** { <spec declaration> } [<private part>] <body option> **end** <id option> ;

	→ **body** \<id> **is** { \<body declaration> } [**begin** { \<statement> }] [\<exception part>] **end** \<id option> ;
\<body option>	→ [**body** { \<body declaration> } [**begin** { \<statement> }] [\<exception part>]]
\<id option>	→ [\<id>]
\<spec declaration>	→ \<private type declaration> → \<declaration>
\<private type declaration>	→ **type** \<id> **is private** ;
\<private part>	→ **private** \<private item> { \<private item> }
\<private item>	→ **subtype** \<id> **is** \<subtype definition> ; → **type** \<id> **is** \<type definition> ;
\<body declaration>	→ \<subprogram body decl> → \<declaration>
\<declaration>	→ \<object declaration> → \<type declaration> → \<subtype declaration> → \<pragma> → \<subprogram declaration> → **use** \<name list> ; → \<id list> **exception** ;
\<object declaration>	→ \<id list> : \<constant option> \<type or subtype> \<initialization option> ;
\<id list>	→ \<id> { , \<id> }
\<id>	→ Identifier
\<constant option>	→ [**constant**]
\<type or subtype>	→ \<type> → \<subtype definition>
\<initialization option>	→ [:= \<expression>]
\<type declaration>	→ **type** \<id> **is** \<type definition> ; → \<incomplete type decl>
\<type>	→ \<type name> → \<type definition>
\<type name>	→ \<id>
\<type definition>	→ \<record type definition> → \<array type definition> → \<enumeration type def> → **access** \<subtype>
\<incomplete type decl>	→ **type** \<id> ;
\<record type definition>	→ **record** \<component list> **end record**

<component list>	→ <component declaration> { <component declaration> }
	→ { <component declaration> } <variant part>
	→ **null** ;
<component declaration>	→ <id list> : <type or subtype> <initialization option> ;
<variant part>	→ **case** <id> : <type name> **is** <variant>
	{ <variant> } **end case** ;
<variant>	→ **when** <v choice> => <component list>
<v choice>	→ <simple expression>
<array type definition>	→ <unconstrained array def>
	→ <constrained array def>
<unconstrained array def>	→ **array** <unconstrained index list> **of** <element type>
<unconstrained index list>	→ (<index subtype def> {, <index subtype def>})
<index subtype def>	→ <type name> **range** <>
<constrained array def>	→ **array** <constrained index list> **of** <element type>
<constrained index list>	→ (<discrete range> {, <discrete range>})
<element type>	→ <type or subtype>
<enumeration type def>	→ (<enumeration id list>)
<enumeration id list>	→ <id> { , <id> }
<subtype declaration>	→ **subtype** <id> **is** <subtype definition> ;
<subtype>	→ <type name>
	→ <subtype definition>
<subtype definition>	→ [<type name>] <range constraint>
	→ <type name> <index constraint>
<range constraint>	→ **range** <range>
<range>	→ <simple expression> .. <simple expression>
<index constraint>	→ (<discrete range> {, <discrete range>})
<discrete range>	→ <subtype>
	→ <range>
<subprogram declaration>	→ <subprogram specification> ;
<subprogram body decl>	→ <subprogram specification> **is** { <body declaration> }
	begin { <statement> } [<exception part>]
	end <id option> ;
<subprogram specification>	→ **procedure** <id> <formal part opt>
	→ **function** <designator> <formal part opt>
<designator>	→ <id>
	→ <operator symbol>
<operator symbol>	→ StrLiteral

<formal part>	→ (<parameter declaration list>)
<formal part opt>	→ [<formal part>]
<parameter declaration list>	→ <parameter decl> { ; <parameter decl> }
<parameter decl>	→ <id list> : [<mode>] <type or subtype>
<mode>	→ **in** [**out**]
	→ **out**
<exception part>	→ **exception** { <exception handler> }
<exception handler>	→ **when** <exception when tail>
<exception when tail>	→ **others** => { <statement> }
	→ <name> {	<name> } => { <statement> }
<statement>	→ <pragma>
	→ <null statement>
	→ <assignment statement>
	→ <call statement>
	→ <block>
	→ <loop statement>
	→ <if statement>
	→ <exit statement>
	→ <return statement>
	→ <case statement>
	→ <raise statement>
<null statement>	→ **null** ;
<assignment statement>	→ <name> := <expression> ;
<call statement>	→ <name> ;
<block>	→ [<id> :] [<decl part>] **begin** { <statement> } [<exception part>] **end** [<id>] ;
<decl part>	→ **declare** { <body declaration> }
<return statement>	→ **return** [<expression>] ;
<raise statement>	→ **raise** <name option> ;
<if statement>	→ **if** <b expr> **then** { <statement> } { **elsif** <b expr> **then** { <statement> } } [<else part>] **end if** ;
<else part>	→ **else** { <statement> }
<loop statement>	→ [<id> :] [<iteration clause>] <basic loop> ;
<basic loop>	→ **loop** { <statement> } **end loop**
<iteration clause>	→ **while** <b expr>
	→ **for** <id> **in** [**reverse**] <discrete range>
<exit statement>	→ **exit** [<name>] [**when** <b expr>] ;
<case statement>	→ **case** <expr> **is** <when list> <others option> **end case**;

<when list>	→ { **when** <choice list> => { <statement> } }
<others option>	→ [**when others** => { <statement> }]
<choice list>	→ <choice> { | <choice> }
<choice>	→ <expr>
	→ <expr> .. <expr>
<expression>	→ <relation> { <logical op> <relation> }
	→ <relation> { **and then** <relation> }
	→ <relation> { **or else** <relation> }
<relation>	→ <simple expression>
	[<relational op> <simple expression>]
<simple expression>	→ [<unary adding op>] <term> { <adding op> <term> }
<term>	→ <factor> { <multiplying op> <factor> }
<factor>	→ <primary> [** <primary>]
	→ **not** <primary>
	→ **abs** <primary>
<primary>	→ <literal>
	→ <name>
	→ (<expression>)
	→ aggregate
<literal>	→ IntLiteral
	→ FloatLiteral
	→ StrLiteral
<logical op>	→ **and**
	→ **or**
<relational op>	→ =
	→ /=
	→ <
	→ <=
	→ >
	→ >=
<adding op>	→ +
	→ –
	→ &
<unary adding op>	→ +
	→ –
<multiplying op>	→ *
	→ /
	→ **mod**
<name>	→ <simple name> { <name suffix> } [. **all**]
<simple name>	→ <id>
<name suffix>	→ . <selected suffix>
	→ (<expression> { , <expression> })
	→ ' <id>

<selected suffix>	→ <id>
	→ <operator symbol>
<aggregate>	→ <name> ′ (<component> { , <component> })
<component>	→ [<agg choice list> =>] <expression>
<agg choice list>	→ <agg choice> { | <agg choice> }
<agg choice>	→ <simple name>
	→ <simple expression>
	→ <discrete range>
	→ **others**
<name list>	→ <name> { , <name> }

Scangen

ScanGen was written by Gary Sevitsky and subsequently enhanced by Robert Gray. Later changes were made by Charles Fischer. ScanGen accepts descriptions of tokens written as regular expressions and produces tables that may be used to drive a lexical analyzer.

B.1 Input Specifications

The input format will be introduced by means of annotated examples, starting with Figure B.1.

Specifications to ScanGen contain three parts: options selected, class definitions, and regular expression definitions.

The options section is optional. If it appears, it is headed by the reserved word **Options**, followed by one or more option names (which are not reserved). The option names may appear in any order, separated by blanks or commas. A complete list of options appears in section B.3.

```
Options
    tables,list
Class
    letter        = 'A'..'Z', 'a'..'z';
    digit         = '0'..'9';
    blank         = ' ';
Definition
    Token emptyspace {0}    = blank+;
    Token identifier {1}    = letter.(letter, digit)*;
    Token number {2}        = digit+;
```

Figure B.1 A Simple ScanGen Specification

Class definitions specify the character classes that make up the alphabet used by the regular expressions. The character classes are sets of characters, which are defined, as in Figure B.1, by using single characters within quotes or by using ranges of characters. To specify the quote character, use *""*. An unprintable character is specified by using its decimal equivalent. For example, the line-feed character can be specified by **linefeed = 10;** (or whatever it is in your character set).

If a character is not mentioned in the class definitions, it will not create any scanner actions in the output table: it will be ignored. The generator puts unmentioned characters into the character class **Epsilon**. Each character may be assigned to at most one character class.

The regular-expression definitions, which specify the tokens, are built using the character classes and the following operations (listed in order of decreasing precedence): positive closure (+) and Kleene closure (∗), catenation (.), and union (,). Precedences can be overridden by use of parentheses. Each token name is followed by a token number. Token numbers appear in the output table so that the scanner can return a token number upon recognition of a token.

Figure B.2 illustrates more-sophisticated ways in which regular expressions may be defined. The second definition, which defines **Letter**, does not define a token; it defines an auxiliary regular expression that can be used in later definitions. Tokens may also be used in later definitions; for example, **IntLit** is used in the definition of **RealLit**.

Another feature of the specification language is the *exception list*, which is used above in the definition of **Identifier**. The exception list is made up of strings, which are called *reserved words*, and are of length 12 or less, followed by token numbers. The exception list will not affect the output table; it is stored separately so that the scanner can access it.

In the definitions of **IntLit**, **RealLit**, and **StrLit**, there are two token numbers following the token name: the *major token number* and the *minor token number*. The major token number can be used to define a token class, with the minor token number used to specify the member of that class. If the minor token number is not specified, the generator will supply the default value 50. Token numbers must be nonnegative integers. The same token number may be used for different tokens. By convention, tokens that are to be deleted (comments, spaces, tabs) are assigned a major token number of 0.

In the definition of **RealLit**, the character class **Epsilon** is used so that the output table will recognize numbers without exponents and numbers with unsigned exponents.

The **Not** operation is used in the definitions of **StrLit** and **RunOnString**. This operation may only be used to complement a union of character classes. The complement is taken relative to the classes specified in the class definitions. In other words, character class **Epsilon** stays out of complements.

The **Toss** feature appears in the definitions of **StrLit** and **RunOnString**. This feature is used to tell the scanner whether or not to ap-

```
Options
    List, tables
Class
    E               = 'E', 'e';
    OtherLetter     = 'A'..'D','F'..'Z','a'..'d','f'..'z';
    Digit           = '0'..'9';
    Blank           = ' ';
    Dot             = '.';
    Plus            = '+';
    Minus           = '_';
    Quote           = '"';
    Linefeed        = 10;
Definition
Token EmptySpace {0}    = (Blank, Linefeed)+;
Letter                  = E, OtherLetter;
Token Identifier {1}    = Letter.(Letter,Digit)*
                            Except
                                'begin' {4},
                                'end' {5};
Token IntLit {2,1}      = Digit+;
Token RealLit {2,2}     = IntLit.Dot.IntLit.
                          (Epsilon, E.(Epsilon, Plus, Minus).IntLit);
Token StrLit {2,3}      = Quote{Toss}.
                          (Not(Quote, Linefeed),Quote{Toss}.Quote)*
                          . Quote{Toss};
Token RunOnString {3}   = Quote{Toss}.
                          (Not(Quote, Linefeed), Quote{Toss}.Quote)*
                          . Linefeed{Toss};
```

Figure B.2 A More-Sophisticated ScanGen Specification

pend a character to the token string it is building. If a character is not to be appended, put a **Toss** after the name of its character class in the token definition. A **Toss** may only appear after the name of a character class or after **Not(···)**. Careless use of the **Toss** feature can lead to a toss/save conflict. For example, a toss/save conflict would occur if **StrLit** were defined by

```
Quote{Toss} . (Not(Quote, Linefeed), Quote.Quote{Toss})*
    . Quote{Toss}
```

This conflict can be seen by comparing scanner actions on the strings 'a' and 'a"b'. In the first case, the scanner is told to toss the quote character following the **a**, but in the second case this character is saved. When a toss/save conflict arises, the generator will print an error message.

The input specifications may be written free-format with up to 132 characters in a line. Illegal symbols are ignored, and a warning message is printed. Identifiers may be any length, but only the first 12 are examined. Case in identifiers is ignored (that is, **ABC** and **abc** are the same identifier). Case is also ignored in the reserved words **Class**, **Definition**, **Epsilon**, **Except**, **Not**, **Token**, **Option**, and **Toss**. When a syntax error is encountered, the generator will print an error message and terminate.

B.2 The Output

When the **tables** option is used, the external file **tables** will be produced. This file consists of the following five sections:

Section 1: Parameters for the Scanner

A list of five integers separated by spaces

NumStates
>Number of states of the minimal dfa

StartState
>Initial state of the minimal dfa

NumClasses
>Number of character classes defined by the user (does not include **Epsilon**)

NumResWords
>Total number of reserved words defined in **Except** clauses

NumLists
>Number of token names that have exception lists

Section 2: Character Class Mapping

A list of N integers separated by spaces that specify the character class that each character has been assigned to. N is determined by the character set that that ScanGen is configured for (N=128 for ASCII; N=256 for EBCDIC). The ith element of the list is the class number assigned to the character whose value (ord) is i. The character class **Epsilon** is numbered 0, so characters not explicitly assigned to any class will be given a class number of 0.

Section 3: Reserved Word to Token Mapping

Contains NumLists records, each of the form

Major Minor FirstRSW LastRSW

Major and Minor are the numbers of the the token class for which the reserved words FirstRSW through LastRSW are exceptions. FirstRSW and LastRSW are indices into the table of reserved words that comprises section 4 of this output file. Reserved word numbering starts at 1. The information in this section is important only when more than one token definition has an exception list.

Section 4: Reserved Word List

Contains NumResWords records, each of the form

Word (columns 1-12) Major Minor

Major and Minor are the token numbers of the reserved word and are separated by spaces.

Section 5: Transition Table of the Minimal Deterministic Finite Automaton.

The transition table is written as an array of NumStates × NumClasses entries. Numbering of states and classes starts at 1. The array is written in row-major order, which means that classes vary more rapidly.

The first integer of each entry indicates the type of transition: Error, MoveAppend, MoveNoAppend, HaltAppend, HaltNoAppend, and HaltReuse. Following this integer are from 0 to 2 integers, depending on the transition type, that give more information about the transition.

The transitions are of the following forms:

0		— Error
1	NextState	— MoveAppend:	Move to NextState and append the current character to the token being assembled
2	NextState	— MoveNoAppend:	Move to NextState and consume the current character, but do not append it to the token
3	Major Minor	— HaltAppend:	Halt, return token number Major and Minor, and append the current character to the token
4	Major Minor	— HaltNoAppend:	Halt, return token number Major and Minor, and consume the current character, but do not append it to the token
5	Major Minor	— HaltReuse:	Halt, return token number Major and Minor, save current character for reuse in the next token, and do not append it to the token

B.3 **Miscellaneous**

This scanner generator produces tables that use only one character lookahead. The tables cannot directly handle the ".." problem of Pascal and Ada/CS or the ".EQ." problem of FORTRAN. However, multicharacter lookahead problems can be handled by saving the sequence of states visited while scanning a token and backing up to the last final state.

The tables always recognize the longest possible token string. An entire token class may fail to be recognized if every occurrence of this class is a prefix of a member of another class.

If a state is the final state for more than one token class, the first token class defined in the input file is the one accepted. This convention can be significant if one token class subsumes another. For example, in the definitions used for Ada/CS (see below) the definition of **RealLit** includes integer constants. However, because the definition of **IntLit** precedes that of **RealLit**, sequences of digits are correctly scanned as integer rather than real constants.

Depending on the size and complexity of the regular expressions to be processed, the value of the constant **MaxSubsets** in the ScanGen source can be altered (its initial setting is 75000). Decreasing **MaxSubsets** can significantly reduce program size; increasing it will allow larger and more-complex definitions to be handled.

ScanGen Options

List:	List input specifications on the standard output file.
Dfa:	Print the minimal dfa that the scanner generator constructed.
Report:	Print a report consisting of

    1) Correspondence of character class names to character class numbers

    2) Mapping of characters to character class numbers

    3) List of reserved words and the token class numbers to which they are assigned

Test:	Test the dfa using a file **testfile** as a sample input to the scanner. The scanner will list actions upon scanning each symbol and will terminate when end of file is reached. It is suggested that testfile be kept short. Also, it is good to have the output of option **Dfa** around.
Tables:	Produce file **tables** containing the character class mapping, reserved word lists, and the transition table.

Optimize: Optimize tables created by ScanGen. This option should *always* be used in producing tables to be used in scanning. It need not be used for debugging runs.

Other options, used for debugging ScanGen itself, are documented in the source of ScanGen.

B.5   ScanGen Definitions for Ada/CS

The following definition represents an ASCII version of Ada/CS; an EBCDIC version would differ in the assignment of particular character codes.

```
Options
  tables,optimize
Class

E               = 'E','e';
OtherLetter     = 'A'..'D','F'..'Z','a'..'d','f'..'z';
Digit           = '0'..'9';
Linefeed        = 10;
Blank           = ' ';
Amper           = '&';
Quote           = '"';
SingleQuote     = '''';
LParenChar      = '(';
RParenChar      = ')';
Star            = '*';
PlusChar        = '+';
MinusChar       = '-';
DotChar         = '.';
Slash           = '/';
ColonChar       = ':';
Semi            = ';';
Less            = '<';
Equal           = '=';
Greater         = '>';
BarChar         = '|';
CommaChar       = ',';
UnderScore      = '_';
Tab             = 9;
Unprintable     = 0..8,11..31,127;
Illegal         = '!','#','$','%','?','@','\','^','`', '{','}', '[', ']','~';

Definition

Letter                  = E,OtherLetter;
Token  Ampersand{6}     = Amper{Toss};
Token  Bar{5}           = BarChar{Toss};
Token  Box{23}          = Less{Toss} . Greater{Toss};
Token  Becomes{8}       = ColonChar{Toss}.Equal{Toss};
Token  Choose{24}       = Equal{Toss}. Greater{Toss};
```

```
Token   Colon{19}        = ColonChar{Toss};
Token   Comma{15}        = CommaChar{Toss};
Token   Dot{16}          = DotChar{Toss};
Token   DotDot{17}       = DotChar{Toss}.DotChar{Toss};
Token   LParen{26}       = LParenChar{Toss};
Token   Minus{21}        = MinusChar{Toss};
Token   MultOp{22}       = Star{Toss};
Token   DivOp{25}        = Slash{Toss};
Token   Plus{20}         = PlusChar{Toss};
Token   LT{9}            = Less{Toss};
Token   LE{11}           = Less{Toss}.Equal{Toss};
Token   EQ{7}            = Equal{Toss};
Token   NotEQ{13}        = Slash{Toss}.Equal{Toss};
Token   GE{12}           = Greater{Toss}.Equal{Toss};
Token   GT{10}           = Greater{Toss};
Token   RParen{27}       = RParenChar{Toss};
Token   Semicolon{18}    = Semi{Toss};
Token   Tic{4}           = SingleQuote{Toss};
Token   ToThe{14}        = Star{Toss}.Star{Toss};
Token   IntLit{2,1}      = Digit.(Digit,UnderScore{Toss})*;
Token   RealLit{2,2}     = IntLit.(Epsilon,DotChar.IntLit).
                           (Epsilon,(E.(Epsilon,PlusChar,MinusChar)
                           .IntLit));
Token   StringLit{3}     = Quote{Toss}.
                           (Not(Quote,Linefeed,Tab,Unprintable),
                           Quote{Toss}. Quote)*.Quote{Toss};
Token   EmptySpace{0}    = (Blank{Toss},Linefeed{Toss},Tab{Toss})+;
Token   Comment{0}       = MinusChar{Toss}.MinusChar{Toss}.
                           (Not Linefeed{Toss})*.
                           Linefeed{Toss};
Token   Identifier{1}    = Letter.(Letter,Digit,UnderScore)*
                              Except
                              'abs' {28},
                              'and' {29},
                              'array' {30},
                              'begin' {31},
                              'body' {32},
                              'case' {33},
                              'constant' {34},
                              'declare' {35},
                              'else' {36},
                              'elsif' {37},
                              'end' {38},
                              'exception' {39},
                              'exit' {40},
                              'for' {41},
                              'function' {42},
                              'if' {43},
                              'in' {44},
                              'is' {45},
                              'loop' {46},
                              'mod' {47},
                              'not' {48},
                              'null' {49},
                              'of' {50},
```

```
'or' {51},
'others' {52},
'out' {53},
'package' {54},
'pragma' {55},
'private' {56},
'procedure' {57},
'raise' {58},
'range' {59},
'record' {60},
'return' {61},
'reverse' {62},
'access' {63},
'subtype' {64},
'then' {65},
'type' {66},
'use' {67},
'when' {68},
'while' {69},
'all' {70};
```

LLGen User Manual

LLGen accepts a context-free grammar specification and produces tables for parsing the language so specified. It will produce tables for any LL(1) grammar and provides a simple conflict resolution mechanism for grammars that are not LL(1). LLGen is a subset of FMQ, an LL(1) parser/error-corrector generator. FMQ was written by Jon Mauney.

This report describes a tool for language translation—specifically, for parsing context-free languages. LLGen is a table generator. It accepts an LL(1) grammar specified in the format described below and produces tables that can be used for parsing. LLGen also provides an interface to user-supplied semantic actions through semantic action numbers. These numbers are specified in the input to LLGen and appear in the resulting tables.

A typical session with LLGen might go as follows:

(1) Create a file specifying the desired grammar.

(2) Run LLGen, directing the grammar file to standard input. LLGen will send optional output and error messages, if any, to the terminal (or whatever the standard output is) and create a file, **ptableout** or **ptablebin** (see the following section on output).

(3) If the grammar is not acceptable to LLGen, repeat 1 and 2.

(4) Use **ptableout** or **ptablebin** in an LL(1) parser driver.

C.1 Input to LLGen

The input to LLGen has three main sections: options desired for the run, terminal symbols of the grammar, and production rules of the grammar. The general form of the input is

```
        <comments>
*fmq
        <options>
*define
        <constant definitions>
*terminals
        <terminal specifications>
*productions
        <production specifications>
*end
        <comments>
```

An example appears in Figure C.2.

In the following, *symbol* will refer to a symbol in the grammar for which tables are to be generated, and *token* will refer to an entity in the input to LLGen.

The input to LLGen is divided into tokens by three simple rules:

- All tokens must be separated by one or more blanks, tabs, or ends of line.
- Tokens may not contain blanks or tabs, unless the token is surrounded by angle brackets, **<** and **>**. Tokens may not run across line boundaries.
- If a token begins with **<**, then it must end with **>**.

That is, everything in the input—option names, reserved words, grammar symbols—must be surrounded by white space. Angle brackets may be used when a symbol contains white space, but they are special if and only if the first character is **<**. Angle brackets appearing in any other circumstances are legal but not special (a warning will be issued in such cases). The only other character endowed with special properties is **#**, which begins all *action symbols*. Action symbols consist of **#** followed immediately by an unsigned integer or a defined constant (as described below).

Upper- and lower-case letters are considered distinct; however, the reserved tokens and the options are recognized in either case or a mixture. The examples shown in Figure C.1 illustrate the above rules.

The following tokens are reserved:

```
*fmq     *define    *terminals    *productions    *end
::=      ...         <Goal>        $$$
```

End of line is required as a terminator for specifications of terminals, productions, and constant definitions as described below. The input to LLGen is otherwise free-format.

Anything before *fmq or after *end will be considered a comment and will be ignored. However, comments must not contain any of the above reserved tokens. Following *fmq is a list of zero or more options, separated, as always, by blanks, tabs, or ends of line. All options have the form of switches and are enabled by including the name in the option list. An enabled

token	comments
ABC	OK
abc	OK, different from **ABC**
123	OK
< Expr >	OK
<id list>	OK
<>	OK
&:=	OK
"<"	Legal, gets a warning
—>	Legal, gets a warning
<not<>equal>	Legal, gets a warning
much<<lessthan	Legal, gets a warning
<LHS>::=<RHS>	Legal, gets a warning. This is one token, not three.
2<two tokens>	Legal, two tokens, two warnings
	(< is special only if it appears first)
∗fmq	Reserved
∗FMQ	Reserved, same as **∗fmq**
∗Fmq	Reserved, same as **∗fmq**
#13	Legal, action symbol for routine 13
#add	Legal, add should have been defined
	in the ∗**define** section
∗fmq∗terminals	legal, one token, no warning
<=	Illegal, no closing bracket
<	Illegal, no closing bracket
<bad>token	Ditto, (**>** must be followed by space)

Figure C.1   Examples of LLgen Tokens

option may be disabled by placing **no** before the name, without a space; thus, to prevent construction of parse tables, use **noparsetable**. All options are initially disabled, except for **checkreduce** and **text**. Options are recognized in upper or lower case. The available options are

(1)   **bnf**
Print the grammar rules.

(2)   **first**
Print the **First** sets for all nonterminals.

(3)   **follow**
Print the **Follow** sets of all nonterminals.

(4)   **parsetable**
Print the parse action table in tabular form. A number in the table indicates prediction of that production; blank entries indicate error. This table can be quite large.

(5)   **checkreduce**
Check whether the grammar is reduced; report all symbols that cannot

produce a terminal string and those that are not reachable from the start symbol. If the grammar is not reduced, and checkreduce is enabled, tables will not be produced. **Checkreduce** is normally enabled.

(6) **resolve**
If the grammar given is not LL(1), generate the parse tables anyway, and resolve parse conflicts pairwise in favor of the production that appeared earlier in the input. This option should be used with caution; see discussion under "Error Handling within LLGen." If **resolve** is not enabled, computation of parse tables will be suppressed in the presence of parse conflicts.

(7) **shortline, longline**
Control the length of printed lines in human-oriented output (**vocab**, **parsetable**, etc.) **Shortline** causes lines to be less than 80 characters (suitable for a screen), and **longline** is 132 (for a printer). **Shortline** is synonymous with **nolongline**, and vice versa. The default is **shortline**.

(8) **statistics**
Print assorted statistics on the grammar.

(9) **vocab**
Print the symbols of the language.

(10) **text, binary**
The tables created by LLGen can be written as text (file of characters), as binary (file of integers), or both. Text output is written on the file **ptableout**; binary is written on **ptablebin**. Binary files tend to be larger, at least on a 32-bit machine (about 30% larger on the VAX under UNIX[tm]), but are usually faster to read. The default is **text** and **nobinary**.

The constant definition section is optional. If present, it begins with the reserved token *define and consists of a list of definitions, each on a separate line. Each definition has the form

<const name> <integer value>

in which <const name> is a token as described above, and <integer value> is an unsigned integer (i.e., a token containing only digits). This constant can then be used whenever an integer constant is called for: in subsequent constant definitions and for semantic routine numbers. Note that this feature is not as nice as it seems at first, because the output listing of LLGen will use the numeric value, not the constant name.

The reserved token *terminals begins the list of terminal symbols. The terminal specification section consists of a list of such specifications, each on a separate line. All terminals *must* appear in this list.

The token *productions separates the terminals from the productions. The productions are specified by a list of rules, each on a separate line.

Specification of one production has the form

    <lhs> ::= <rhs>

Either <lhs> or <rhs> may be absent. <lhs> is one token representing a non-terminal symbol. If it is absent, the <lhs> of the preceding production is used. <rhs> is a string of tokens, containing the grammar symbols of the production and action symbols indicating semantic routines to be called when the appropriate point in the production is reached. An action symbol consists of a # followed by an unsigned integer or defined constant, without intervening blanks. If <rhs> is absent or contains only action symbols, then <lhs> derives the null string. <rhs> may be continued on subsequent lines by beginning those lines with the reserved token "″ . . .″" (only productions may be so continued).

The productions are terminated by *end. After all of the productions have been processed, the augmenting production is added. Two symbols, **<Goal>** and **$$$**, and one production

    <Goal> ::= <S> **$$$**

are added to the grammar, where <S> is the left-hand side of the first production specified, **<Goal>** is the start symbol, and **$$$** the end-marker.

C.2 Output from LLGen

The output controlled by the above options is written to the standard Pascal file **output**. In addition, files containing tables are created. The tables for parsing are written to **ptableout** (text) or **ptablebin** (binary). These files may be assigned or redirected, depending on the operating system.

The formats of the output files are the same, whether they are created as **text** or **binary** files. In **binary** files, character values are written as **ord** of the character.

The files **ptableout** and **ptablebin** contain the following tables: the right-hand sides of all productions, the parser action table, a list of symbols that can derive the null string, and symbolic representations of all symbols in the grammar.

The format of the file is

header line:
The first line gives the sizes of the various tables. It contains the number of terminals in the language (numterms), the number of symbols in the grammar (numsymbols), the number of productions in the grammar (numprods), the size of the character string for the symbol images (stringsize), and a flag indicating whether error-repair tables were produced. The value of the flag is a character **T** if the repair tables were produced, and **F** if not.

productions:
The right-hand sides of all the productions are given; all right-hand sides are *reversed* and can be pushed onto the parse stack in the order given. Each production consists of a length, followed by the corresponding number of symbols. Action symbols are included in the right-hand sides, encoded as the negative of the number given in the grammar.

parse table:
The LL(1) predictions for each nonterminal symbol are given by the parse table. The predictions for each nonterminal are stored in a list of pairs of integers. The first pair in a list is a zero followed by the number of the nonterminal symbol. The subsequent pairs have the form

    terminal prediction

in which prediction is the production predicted when terminal appears in the lookahead. The list is terminated by the start of the next list. The table is terminated by 0 0.

lambda productions:
Lambda productions are those that have no symbols (except action symbols) on the right-hand side. The list consists of a length, n, followed by n integers representing the production numbers. (This table isn't needed for ordinary LL(1) parsing, but it is useful in avoiding unnecessary parser moves when error repair is done.)

string table:
The symbol table information is in two parts. First is an index, consisting of numsymbols pairs of integers. The first integer of each pair is the starting point of the symbol in the character string, and the second is the length of the symbol. Following the index are stringsize characters, 132 per line.

C.3 Error Handling within LLGen

Syntax errors in the input to LLGen will be handled by an error recovery routine. Table generation will be suppressed if errors are present in the input.

An attempt to use the symbols `<Goal>` and `$$$` (the start symbol and the end-marker) will be treated as a syntax error.

All terminals must be listed in the `*terminals` section. If any terminal is not listed or if a nonterminal does not appear on the left of any production, the symbol will be flagged, and no tables will be generated. Similarly, a symbol declared as a terminal may not appear on the left of a production.

If the grammar specified is not LL(1), all conflicts will be reported. If the option `resolve` is enabled, productions will be given precedence in the order of appearance (the first production specified has highest precedence). Thus the dangling **else** of Pascal and other languages can be parsed by

```
<if stmt>      ::= if <expr> then <stmt> <else part>
<else part>    ::= else <stmt>
               ::=
```

The conflict will be resolved in favor of the first form of the statement, matching the **else** with the most recent **if**.

This resolution mechanism should be used with caution. Conflicts must be carefully examined to ensure that the parse action taken is the action desired. For example, reversing the order of the above **<else part>** productions would be perfectly acceptable to LLGen but would have a disastrous effect. When **else** appears in the lookahead, the parse action taken would be always to predict **<else part>** deriving the null string; the **else** would never be accepted.

If the grammar specified proves too large for the limits of LLGen, the program will print a message describing the limit that was exceeded and will terminate. LLGen must then be recompiled with increased limits. Normally, exceeding one limit suggests that others will also be exceeded, and increasing them all at once will save on recompilations. Notice though that LLGen processes in order terminals, productions, and parse table. Therefore, if the number of productions in the grammar is exceeded, the number of terminals must be within limits, as they have been completely processed already. Some of the dimensions of a particular grammar are easy to discover; others must be tackled by rule of thumb and trial. Easily determined are the number of terminals, number of symbols (terminals+nonterminals) and number of productions. Less simple, but still easy to estimate, are the total number of symbols in the productions and the total number of characters in all the distinct symbols.

C.4 Using LLGen

The grammar specification is read from the standard input file, and human-oriented output is written to standard output. Parse tables produced are written to **ptableout** or **ptablebin**. The above names are the internal names as declared in the program header and may be modified by the system environment in which the program is run.

Figure C.2 illustrates a sample LLGen input specification; Figure C.3 illustrates the ptableout file that would be produced.

```
Grammar for DCL, a desk calculator language

(the action symbols here don't mean anything,
 they just illustrate how they might be used)

*fmq
statistics
checkreduce
```

```
vocab bnf
text   binary
*terminals
    id
    constant
    end
    ;
    :=
    (
    )
    +
    –
    *
    /
    write
    read
    ,


*productions

<prog>            ::= <st list> end
<st list>         ::= <st> #1 <st list tail>
<st list tail>    ::= ; <st list>
                  ::=
<st>              ::= id #2 := <expr> #5
                  ::= read  #3 ( <id list> #6 #14 )
                  ::= write  #4 ( <expr list> #6 )
<expr>            ::= <term> <e tail>
<e tail>          ::= + <term> #20 <e tail>
<e tail>          ::= – <term> #20 <e tail>
                  ::=
<term>            ::= <primary> <t tail>
<t tail>          ::= * <primary> #21 <t tail>
<t tail>          ::= / <primary> #21 <t tail>
                  ::=
<primary>         ::= – <primary> #7
<primary>         ::= ( <expr> )
                  ::= id #8
                  ::= constant #9
<expr list>       ::= <expr> #30 <e list tail>
<e list tail>     ::= , <expr list>
                  ::=
<id list>         ::= id #15 <id list tail>
<id list tail>    ::= , <id list>
                  ::=

*end
```

Figure C.2   Sample LLGen Input

```
 15 29 26 243 F
2 3 17 3 19 -1 18 2 17 4 0 5 -5 20 5 -2 1 7 7
-14 -6 21 6 -3 13 6 7 -6 22 6 -4 12 2 24
23 4 24 -20 23 8 4 24 -20 23 9 0 2 26
25 4 26 -21 25 10 4 26 -21 25 11 0 3 -7 25 9 3
7 20 6 2 -8 1 2 -9 2
3 27 -30 20 2 22 14 0 3 28 -15 1 2 21 14 0 2 15 16
0 16 13 1 12 1 1 1 0 17 13 2 12 2 1 2 0 18 12 7 13 6 1 5
0 19 3 4 4 3 0 20 9
8 6 8 2 8 1 8 0 21 1 23 0 22 9 20 6 20 2 20 1 20 0 23 9
12 6 12 2 12 1 12 0 24 14 11 7 11 4 11 3 11 9 10 8 9 0 25
2 19 1 18 6 17 9 16 0 26 14 15 9 15 8 15 7 15 4 15 3 15 11
14 10 13 0 27 7 22 14 21 0 28 7 25 14 24 0 29 13 26 12 26
1 26 0 0 5 4 11 15 22 25 95 2 97 8 105 3 108 1 109 2 111 1
112 1 113 1 114 1 115 1 116 1 117 5 122 4 126
1 7 3 127 6 133 9 142 4 146 14 160 6 166 9 175 11 186 6 192
8 200 9 209 8 217 13 230 14 1 6
<Goal>$$$ grammarforDCL(theactionsymbolsheredon'tmeananything,
theyjustillustratehowtheymightbeidconstantend;:=()+-*/wr
iteread,<prog><st list><st ><st list tail>< expr><id list><exp
r list><term><e tail><primary><t tail><e list tail><id list tail>
```

Figure C.3 `ptableout` Produced by LLGen Given the Input File of Figure C.2

APPENDIX D

LALRGen User Manual

LALRGen accepts a context-free grammar specification and produces tables for parsing the specified language. It will produce tables for any LALR(1) grammar and provides a simple conflict resolution mechanism for grammars that are not LALR(1). LALRGen is a subset of ECP, an LALR(1) parser/error-corrector generator. ECP was written by Jon Mauney.

This report describes a tool for language translation—specifically, for parsing context-free languages. LALRGen is a table generator. It accepts an LALR(1) grammar specified in the format described below and produces tables that can be used for parsing. LALRGen also provides an interface to user-supplied semantic actions through semantic action numbers. These numbers are specified in the input to LALRGen and appear in the resulting tables.

A typical session with LALRGen might go as follows:

(1) Create a file specifying the desired grammar.

(2) Run LALRGen, directing the grammar file to standard input. LALRGen will send optional output and error messages, if any, to the terminal (or whatever the standard output is) and create a file, **ptableout** or **ptablebin** (see the following section on output).

(3) If the grammar is not acceptable to LALRGen, repeat steps 1 and 2.

(4) Use **ptableout** or **ptablebin** in an LALR(1) parser driver.

D.1 Input to LALRGen

The input to LALRGen has three main sections: options desired for the run, terminal symbols of the grammar, and production rules of the grammar. The general form of the input is

```
    <comments>
*ecp
    <options>
*define
    <constant definitions>
*terminals
    <terminal specifications>
*productions
    <production specifications>
*end
    <comments>
```

An example appears in Figure D.2.

In the following, *symbol* will refer to a symbol in the grammar for which tables are to be generated, and *token* will refer to an entity in the input to LALRGen.

The input to LALRGen is divided into tokens by three simple rules:

- All tokens must be separated by one or more blanks, tabs, or ends of line.
- Tokens may not contain blanks or tabs, unless the token is surrounded by angle brackets, **<** and **>**. Tokens may not run across line boundaries.
- If a token begins with **<**, then it must end with **>**.

That is, everything in the input—option names, reserved words, grammar symbols—must be surrounded by white space. Angle brackets may be used when a symbol contains white space, but they are special if and only if the first character is **<**. Angle brackets appearing in any other circumstances are legal but not special (a warning will be issued in such cases).

Upper- and lower-case letters are considered distinct; however, the reserved tokens and the options are recognized in either case or as a mixture. The examples shown in Figure D.1 illustrate the above rules.

The following tokens are reserved:

```
*ecp    *define    *terminals    *productions    *end    ##
::=     ...        --            <Goal>          $$$
```

End of line is required as a terminator for specifications of terminals, productions, and constant definitions as described below. The input to LALRGen is otherwise free-format.

Anything before ***ecp** or after ***end** will be considered a comment and will be ignored. However, comments must not contain any of the above reserved tokens. Comments may also be placed at the end of any line; all text between the token — and the end of the line will be ignored.

Following ***ecp** is a list of zero or more options, separated by blanks, tabs, or ends of line. All options have the form of switches and are enabled by including the name in the option list. An enabled option may be disabled by

token	comments
ABC	OK
abc	OK, different from **ABC**
123	OK
< Expr >	OK
<id list>	OK
<>	OK
&:=	OK
"<"	Legal, gets a warning
—>	Legal, gets a warning
<not<>equal>	Legal, gets a warning
much<<lessthan	Legal, gets a warning
<LHS>::=<RHS>	Legal, gets a warning. This is one token, not three.
2<two tokens>	Legal, two tokens, two warnings
	(< is special only if it appears first)
*ecp	Reserved
*ECP	Reserved, same as ***ecp**
*Ecp	Reserved, same as ***ecp**
<=	Illegal, no closing bracket
<	Illegal, no closing bracket
<bad>token	Ditto (> must be followed by space)

Figure D.1   Examples of LALRGen Tokens

placing **no** before the name, without a space; thus, to prevent construction of parse tables, use **noparsetable**. All options are initially disabled, except for **checkreduce** and **text**. Be warned that most of the output options will create a large amount of output for a grammar the size of a real programming language. The figures in parentheses after each output option give the order of magnitude of the lines printed and the actual number of lines for a Pascal grammar that has 69 terminals, 258 productions, and 226 states. Options are recognized in upper or lower case. The available options are

(1) **bnf**
Print the grammar rules. (Number of productions, Pascal = 258)

(2) **cfsm**
Print the characteristic finite-state machine for the grammar, with LALR(1) lookahead sets. (Number of configurations, Pascal = 2893)

(3) **links**
If **links** and **cfsm** are both enabled, then for each item of a state, list the successor items. (Number of configurations, Pascal = 5809 + size of cfsm)

(4) **first**
Print the First sets for all nonterminals. (Number of nonterminals, Pascal = 175)

(5)   **parsetable**

Print the parse action table in tabular form. In the parse table, an unmarked entry signifies a transition to the given state. An entry marked **L** denotes a lookahead reduction by the production number given, and **R** donotes a simple reduction. A blank indicates error. (Number of states times number of terminals, Pascal = 1855)

(6)   **checkreduce**

Check whether the grammar is reduced; report all symbols that cannot produce a terminal string and those that are not reachable from the start symbol. If the grammar is not reduced and **checkreduce** is enabled, tables will not be produced. **Checkreduce** is normally enabled.

(7)   **resolve**

If the grammar given is not LALR(1), generate the parse tables anyway, and resolve parse conflicts pairwise in favor of the production that appeared earlier in the input. This option should be used with caution; see discussion under "Error Handling within LALRGen." If **resolve** is not enabled, computation of parse tables will be suppressed in the presence of parse conflicts.

(8)   **shortline, longline**

Control the length of printed lines in human-oriented output (vocab, cfsm, **parsetable**, etc.). **Shortline** causes lines to be less than 80 characters (suitable for a screen), and **longline** is 132 (for a printer). **Shortline** is synonymous with **nolongline**, and vice versa. The default is **shortline**.

(9)   **statistics**

Print assorted statistics on the grammar. For all runs the number of productions, symbols, and states are reported. If **statistics** is enabled, additional information such as average number of basis items, length of paths through the closure graph, and execution times will also be printed. (Constant, 25)

(10)   **vocab**

Print the symbols of the language. (Number of symbols, Pascal = 124)

(11)   **text, binary**

The tables created by LALRGen can be written as text (file of characters) or as binary (file of integers), or both. Text output is written on the file **ptableout**; binary is written on **ptablebin**. Binary files tend to be larger, at least on a 32-bit machine (about 30% larger on the VAX under UNIX[tm]), but are usually faster to read. The default is **text** and **nobinary**.

The constant definition section is optional. If present, it begins with the reserved token *define and consists of a list of definitions, each on a separate line. Each definition has the form

    <const name> <integer value>

in which <const name> is a token as described above, and <integer value> is an unsigned integer (i.e., a token containing only digits). This constant can then be used whenever an integer constant is called for: in subsequent constant definitions and for semantic routine numbers. Note that this feature is not as nice as it seems at first because the output listing of LALRGen will use the numeric value, not the constant name.

The reserved token *terminals begins the list of terminal symbols. The terminal specification section consists of a list of such specifications, each on a separate line. All terminals *must* appear in this list.

The token *productions separates the terminals from the productions. The productions are specified by a list of rules, each on a separate line. Specification of one production has the form

<lhs> ::= <rhs> <semantic routine #>

Any of <lhs>, <rhs>, and <semantic routine #> may be absent. <lhs> is one token representing a nonterminal symbol. If it is absent, the <lhs> of the preceding production is used. <rhs> is a string of tokens, representing grammar symbols, separated by blanks. If <rhs> is absent, then <lhs> derives the null string. <rhs> may be continued on subsequent lines by beginning those lines with the reserved token "..." (only productions may be so continued). <semantic routine #> has the form

<number>

and specifies the semantic routine to be called when the production is recognized. <number> is either an unsigned integer or a defined constant. If absent, zero will be used.

The productions are terminated by *end. After all of the productions have been processed, the augmenting production is added. Two symbols, <Goal> and $$$, and one production

<Goal> ::= <S> $$$

are added to the grammar, in which <S> is the left-hand side of the first production specified, <Goal> is the start symbol, and $$$ the end-marker.

D.2 Output from LALRGen

The output controlled by the above options is written to the standard Pascal file **output**. In addition, files containing tables are created. The tables for parsing are written to **ptableout** (text) or **ptablebin** (binary). These files may be assigned or redirected, depending on the operating system.

The formats of the output files are the same, whether they are created as **text** or **binary** files. In **binary** files, character values are written as **ord** of the character.

The files **ptableout** and **ptablebin** contain the following tables: the encoded parse action table, the lengths of the right-hand sides of the productions, the left-hand side symbols of the productions, the semantic routine numbers associated with the productions, a symbol table giving the character representations of the symbols of the grammar, and the entry symbol for each state of the cfsm. The symbols of the grammar are encoded as integers. The terminals are numbered, starting with one, in the order they are listed in the terminal specification section. The end-marker, **$$$**, is the highest numbered terminal. The nonterminals are assigned numbers in the order in which they are encountered in the grammar, beginning one higher than the end-marker. The goal symbol, **<Goal>**, is the highest numbered nonterminal. The format of the file is

header line:

The first line gives the sizes of the various tables. It contains number of states of the CFSM (numstates), number of symbols in the grammar (numsymbols), number of productions (numprods), size of the character string for the symbol table (stringsize), number of nonerror parse table entries, and a flag (errortables) indicating whether error-correction tables were created for this grammar. The flag is one character, a **T** if correction tables were created and **F** if not.

parse actions:

Parse actions are given as lists of symbol/action pairs for each state. Each list is headed by a pair zero/state-number; the action table is terminated by a pair of zeroes. If a symbol does not appear in the list for some state, then the parse action for that state and symbol is error. The actions are encoded as follows:

> n > 2000:
> Lookahead reduction by production p = n–2000. Pop rhslength(p) states from the stack but do not consume the current input symbol.

> 2000 > n > 1000:
> Simple reduction by production p = n–1000. The current symbol completes production p. Pop rhslength(p)–1 states and consume the symbol.

> 1000 > n > 0:
> Transition to state n. Push n onto the stack. Consume the symbol.

rhs lengths:

Following the action matrix are numprods integers, indicating the number of symbols on the right-hand side of the corresponding productions.

lhs:

Next are numprods integers giving the symbols on the left-hand side of each production.

semantic numbers:

Numprods integers give the semantic routine numbers associated with each production.

string table:

The symbol table information is in two parts. First is an index, consisting of numsymbols pairs of integers. The first integer of each pair is the starting point of the symbol in the character string, and the second is the length of the symbol. Following the index are stringsize characters, 80 per line. In the binary format, the characters are written one per word, using ord.

entry symbols:
Finally, there are numstates integers, giving the symbol that is shifted on entry to each state.

D.3 Error Handling within LALRGen

Syntax errors in the input to LALRGen will be handled by an error recovery routine. Table generation will be suppressed if errors are present in the input.

An attempt to use the symbols **<Goal>** and **$$$** (the start symbol and the end-marker) will be treated as a syntax error.

All terminals must be listed in the **terminals* section. If any terminal is not listed, or if a nonterminal does not appear on the left of any production, the symbol will be flagged, and no tables will be generated. Similarly, a symbol declared as a terminal may not appear on the left of a production.

If the grammar specified is not LALR(1), all conflicts will be reported. If the option **resolve** is enabled, productions will be given precedence in the order of appearance (the first production specified has highest precedence). Thus the dangling **else** of Pascal and other languages can be parsed by

```
<if stmt>   ::= if <expr> then <stmt> else <stmt>
            ::= if <expr> then <stmt>
```

The conflict will be resolved in favor of the first form of the statement, matching the **else** with the most recent **if**. A conflict between two configurations with the same underlying production will be resolved in favor of the reduction. The following ambiguous grammar can be used to parse expressions involving + and **id**, with left association properly enforced because reduction will always be chosen over shifting.

```
E   ::= E + E
    ::= id
```

This resolution mechanism should be used with caution. Conflicts must be carefully examined to ensure that the parse action taken is the action desired. In the above **if** statement grammar, for example, interchanging the two productions would be acceptable to the generator, causing a preference of reduction over shifting. This would have a disastrous effect on parsing, as the **else** would never be accepted.

If the grammar specified proves too large for the limits of LALRGen, the program will print a message describing the limit that was exceeded and will terminate. LALRGen must then be recompiled with increased limits. Normally, exceeding one limit suggests that others will also be exceeded, and increasing them all at once will save on recompilations. Notice though that LALRGen processes in order: terminals, productions, parse table. Therefore, if the number of states in the CFSM is exceeded, the number of terminals and productions must be within limits, as they have been completely processed already. Some of the dimensions of a particular grammar are easy to discover; others must be tackled by rule of thumb and trial. Easily determined are the number of terminals, number of symbols (terminals+nonterminals), and number of productions. Less simple, but still easy to estimate, are the total number of symbols in the productions, the number of paths through the closure graph, and the total number of characters in all the distinct symbols. Rules of thumb are number of states $\approx$ number of productions; number of items, for Pascal, $\approx$ 12 times number of states ($\approx$ 2500); number of links, for Pascal, $\approx$ 2 times number of items ($\approx$ 5000).

D.4 Using LALRGen

The grammar specification is read from the standard input file, and human-oriented output is written to standard output. Parse tables produced are written to **ptableout** or **ptablebin**. The above names are the internal names as declared in the program header and may be modified by the system environment in which the program is run.

Figure D.2 illustrates a sample LALRGen input specification; Figure D.3 illustrates the **ptableout** file that would be produced.

```
Grammar for DCL, a desk calculator language


*ecp
      vocab bnf
      nobinary text    — only generate text files
*define
      <do assn> 2 — semantic actions
      add 5
      subtract 6
*terminals
    id
    constant
    end
    ;
    :=
    (
    )
    +
```

```
        –
        *
        /
        write
        read
        ,

*productions
<prog>          ::= <st list> end
<st list>       ::= <st list> ; <st>
                ::= <st>
<st>            ::= id := <expr> ## <do assn>
                ::= <read> ( <id list> ) ## 3
                ::= <write> ( <expr list> ) ## 4
                ::=
<expr>          ::= <expr> + <term> ## add
                ::= <expr> – <term>
                       ... ## subtract
                ::= <term> ## 7
<term>          ::= <term> * <primary> ## 8
                ::= <term> / <primary> ## 9
                ::= <primary> ## 10
<primary>       ::= – <primary> ## 11
                ::= ( <expr> )
                ::= id ## 1
                ::= constant ## 12
<write>         ::= write ## 20
<read>          ::= read ## 21
<id list>       ::= <id list> , id ## 23
                ::= id ## 24
<expr list>     ::= <expr list>
                       ... , <expr>
                ::= <expr>

*end
```

Figure D.2   Sample LALRGen Input

```
27 26 24 180 126 F
0 1 13 1019 12 1018 1 6 20 5 22 4 4 2007 3 2007 18 1003 17 3
16 2 0 2 15 1024 0 3 4 27 3 1001 0 4 6 22 0 5 6 19
0 6 5 7 0 7 9 11 6 10 1 1016 2 1017 25 1013 24 9 19 8 0 8 8
14 9 13 4 2004 3
\2004 0 9 10 17 11 16 14 2010 9 2010
8 2010 7 2010 4 2010 3 2010 0 10 9 11 6 10 1 1016 2 1017 25
1013 24 9 19 12 0 11 9 11 6 10 1 1016 2 1017 25 1014 0 12 8 14
9 13 7 1015 0 13 9 11 6 10 1 1016 2 1017 25 1013 24 18 0 14 9
11 6 10 1 1016 2 1017 25 1013 24 15 0 15 10 17 11 16 14 2008
9 2008 8 2008 7 2008 4 2008 3 2008 0 16 9 11 6 10 1 1016 2
```

```
1017 25 1012 0 17 9 11 6 10 1 1016 2 1017 25 1011 0 18 10 17 11 16
14 2009 9 2009 8 2009 7 2009 4 2009 3 2009 0 19 1 1021 21 20 0
20 14 21 7 1005 0 21 1 1020 0 22 9 11 6 10 1 1016 2 1017 25 1013
24 9 19 24 23 23 0 23 14 25 7 1006 0 24 8 14 9 13 14 2023 7 2023
0 25 9 11 6 10 1 1016 2 1017 25 1013 24 9 19 26 0 26
8 14 9 13 14 2022 7 2022 0 27 13 1019 12 1018 1 6 20 5 22 4 4 2007
3 2007 18 1002
0 0 2 3 1 3 4 4 0 3 3 1 3 3
1 2 3 1 1 1 3 1 3 1 2 16 17 17 18 18 18 18 19 19 19 24 24 24 25
25 25 25 22 20 21 21 23 23 26 0 0 0 2
3 4 0 5 6 7 8 9 10 11 0 1 12 20 21 23 24 0 0 -1 76 2 78 8 86 3
89 1 90 2 92 1 93 1 94 1 95 1 96 1
97 1 98 5 103 4 107 1 7 3 108 6 114 9 123 4 127 6 133 6 139 9 148
7 155 11 166 6 172 9 1 6
<Goal>$$$grammarforDCL,DeskCalculatorone1two2three3<do assn>2add5
subtract6idcon stantend;:=()+-*/writeread,<prog><st list><s
t><expr><read><id list><write><expr list><term><primary>
15 16 17 22 20 1 5 19
24 6 9 19 9 8 24 11 10 24 6 21 14 6 23 19 14 19 4
```

Figure D.3 `ptableout` Produced by LALRGen Given the Input File of Figure D.2

Error Repair Features of LLGen and LALRGen

LLGen and LALRGen can generate error-repair tables as well as parse tables. This document describes only the error-repair features. All parsing options and tables are the same as those described in Appendices C and D.

The actions encoded in error-repair tables are determined by the context-free grammar that is specified and a list of repair costs. You must choose the repair costs; otherwise default values of one apply. There is no algorithm for selecting the best set of costs. However, here are some useful heuristics: Symbols that begin a construct, such as **if** or **begin**, should have relatively high costs, because inserting or deleting such a symbol could cause many more subsequent errors. Symbols that close constructs, such as **end** or), may have lower costs. Very low costs may be given to symbols that appear only in limited contexts, for example, '..' in Pascal. A table of Ada/CS repair costs, in the form required by LLGen and LALRGen, appears in Figure E.1.

The reserved token `*terminals` begins the list of terminal symbols and their corresponding insert and delete costs. The specification for each terminal symbol has the form

<terminal symbol> <insert cost> <delete cost>

in which <terminal symbol> is a token, and <insert cost> and <delete cost> are unsigned integers or defined constants. Repair costs are user-supplied values used for controlling and fine-tuning the actions of a repair algorithm. The terminal specification section consists of a list of such specifications, each on a separate line. All terminals must appear in this list.

```
*terminals
<id>                     4    2
<numeric literal>        2    2
```

`<character string>`	5	2
`'`	1	3
`|`	1	3
`&`	3	1
`=`	1	2
`:=`	2	2
`<less than>`	2	2
`>`	2	2
`<less than or equal>`	2	2
`>=`	2	2
`/=`	2	2
`**`	3	1
`,`	1	2
`.`	3	2
`..`	3	2
`;`	2	4
`:`	2	3
`+`	1	1
`−`	1	1
`*`	2	1
`<>`	1	3
`=>`	1	3
`/`	3	1
`(`	8	4
`)`	4	6
`abs`	3	1
`access`	5	3
`all`	5	2
`and`	3	1
`array`	8	2
`begin`	8	4
`body`	6	4
`case`	8	2
`constant`	6	4
`declare`	8	4
`else`	5	4
`elsif`	5	4
`end`	4	5
`exception`	6	4
`exit`	5	2
`for`	8	2
`function`	4	6
`if`	8	2
`in`	6	4
`is`	1	3
`loop`	5	4
`mod`	3	1
`not`	3	1
`null`	5	3
`of`	5	4

or	3	1
others	6	4
out	6	4
package	4	6
pragma	6	2
private	5	3
procedure	4	6
raise	5	2
range	4	2
record	8	2
return	4	2
reverse	5	4
subtype	6	4
then	5	4
type	6	4
use	6	2
when	8	2
while	8	2

Figure E.1   Sample Repair Costs for Ada/CS

E.1   Options and Output Formats for LL(1) Error Repair

LLGen generates tables that can be used with FMQ-style LL(1) repair algorithms (Sections 17.2.4—17.2.7). The following options are available:

errortables: Create the tables needed for FMQ-style least-cost error repair. This option is normally disabled. Error-repair tables are written to **etableout** if the **text** option is enabled and to **etablebin** if the **binary** option is enabled. (The default is **text, nobinary**.) These files may be assigned or redirected, depending on the operating system.

If errortables are computed, they may be printed using the options described below. Individual tables may be printed only if they have been computed, so the following options require that **errortables** be enabled.

s: Print the least-cost string derivable from each nonterminal (the S table).

e: Print the least-cost prefix to derive terminal from nonterminal (the E table). This table is usually rather large.

All FMQ-style repair algorithms require the S table. This table is small enough that it can be easily stored in main memory. Some FMQ-style repair algorithms also require the E table. This table can be fairly large (about 40K bytes for Pascal). Because only a portion of it is needed for any one repair, you may wish to leave it in a file and read only the portion immediately required.

The files **etableout** and **etablebin**, if created, have the following form:

Header: One line containing 3 integers: the number of terminals in the language, the number of symbols (terminals + nonterminals), and the maximum repair cost

Costs: The insertion and deletion costs of all terminal symbols

S table: The least-cost string derivable from each nonterminal (the S table)

E table: The least-cost prefix needed to derive each terminal from each nonterminal (the E table). Prefix values = ? are not included in this table

The format of the error table file is summarized in the following chart. In the chart, a name corresponds to an integer in the file. (string)*<name> means that the contents of (string) are repeated <name> times. (string)* means that string is repeated an unknown number of times (the list is terminated by −1). "name:" labels a logical division of the file and does not appear physically in the file. Comments to the chart (which don't appear in the file) are enclosed by { and }.

Header: NumberOfTerminals NumberOfSymbols Infinity

Costs: (InsertCost   DeleteCost)*NumberOfTerminals

S table: (Cost   Length   (InsertSymbol)*Length
            or −1 {if same as previous; this optimization is not guaranteed}
)*NumberOfNonterminals
            { where NumberOfNonterminals
              = NumberOfSymbols − NumberOfTerminals }

E table: 0 TerminalSymbol 0
            (NonterminalSymbol Cost Length (InsertSymbol)*Length)*
                { where the above repetition is ended by the next
                  0 TerminalSymbol 0 sequence or by
                  the final sequence 0 0 0}
)*NumberOfTerminals
            0 0 0

E.2 Options and Output Formats for LALR(1) Error Repair

LALRGen generates tables that can be used with continuation-based LALR(1) repair algorithms (Sections 17.2.10—17.2.11). The following options are available:

errortables: Create the tables needed for continuation-based error repair. This option is normally disabled. Error-repair tables are written to **etableout** if the **text** option is enabled and to

etablebin if the **binary** option is enable. (The default is **text, nobinary**). These files may be assigned or redirected, depending on the operating system.

If errortables are computed, they may be printed using the option described below. Repair tables may be printed only if they have been computed, so the following option requires that errortables be enabled.

ca: Print the continuation action table.

The files **etableout** and **etablebin**, if created, have the following form:

Header: One line containing 3 integers: the number of terminals in the language, the number of CFSM states, and the maximum repair cost

Costs: The insertion and deletion costs of all terminal symbols

Ca table: The continuation actions corresponding to each state

The format of the error table file is summarized in the following chart. The notation m ∗ [n] means a list of items of type m containing n items.

Header: NumberOfTerminals   NumberOfStates   Infinity

Costs: (InsertCost   DeleteCost) ∗ [NumberOfTerminals]

Ca table: ContinuationAction ∗ [NumberOfStates]

Entries in the continuation action table are coded as follows. Let ca = catable(state). If ca is

1 .. NumberOfTerminals	— Insert the terminal symbol whose index is ca
1000 < CA < 2000	— Simple reduction by production ca − 1000
> 2000	— Lookahead reduction by production ca − 2000

Compiler Development Utilities

A number of utility programs, coded in Pascal, are available to aid compiler development and debugging. Included are a double offset compaction routine and an object machine interpreter. Also available are routines to perform arithmetic operations while trapping errors (such as overflow), to transfer bit strings between integer and real variables circumventing strong type checking, and to pack and unpack Ada/CS machine instructions and character strings.

F.1 Array Compaction Utility

ArrayComp is a utility program that reads a sparse matrix and compresses it for access using double offset indexing (Section 17.1). It can be used to compact scanning and parse tables after they are produced by ScanGen, LLGen, and LALRGen.

Input is read from the standard input file. Data read are

N M Default
InArray (with elements in row major order)

N and M are the bounds of the array to be compressed. That is, InArray is an **array**(1..N; 1..M) **of** Integer. Default is the element that will be assumed as a default in the compressed representation. For this compression to be effective, most elements of InArray must be the default value.

InArray, in compressed form, is written onto file outtable. Data written are

N M Default CompressedLen
Row   (containing N values)
OutArray (containing CompressedLen entries)

The compressed table is accessed as follows:

To access InArray(i,j):
   if OutArray(Row(i)+2∗i) = j
   then InArray(i,j) = OutArray(Row(i)+2∗i+1)
   else InArray(i,j) = Default

Statistics describing data structure sizes and the degree of compression achieved are written to the standard output file.

F.2   The Ada/CS Object Machine

The Ada/CS object machine has a simple register-oriented architecture similar to that of the IBM 360/370 series. Generating code for this machine simplifies compiler development because an interpreter with debugging options is provided. Moreover, the details of the actual machine and operating system used for compiler development are hidden, making it easy to utilize any available machine.

The Ada/CS object machine has some number of words of storage (depending on the model purchased) numbered consecutively from 0 up to MaxAdr. Each word contains 32 bits. (The Ada/CS machine differs from the VAX, PDP-11, and IBM machines, which address each *byte* separately.)

There are 64 registers, which overlap the first 64 words of main memory (0-63): Register i is stored in Memory[i]. Instructions are 32 bits long and have the format

OP Code	Register	Base	Displacement
6 bits	6 bits	6 bits	14 bits

The *effective address* (EAdr) of an instruction is defined as follows:

EAdr =
   if Base = 0 **then**
      Displacement
   else
      Displacement + Memory[Base]
   end

Displacement and Base are the contents of the corresponding fields of the instruction. We follow the IBM 360 convention that Base = 0 means no base register rather than base register 0, so only registers 1-63 can be used as base registers. Displacement is treated as a signed 14-bit quantity extended to a full-word quantity by duplicating the left-most bit. It is then added (in two's-complement arithmetic) to the contents of the specified base register (if any). Negative Displacements are legal and can be quite useful.

We will let R denote Memory[Reg], the contents of the register selected by the Reg field of the instruction, and let M denote Memory[EAdr]. The rightmost bits of a memory cell are the least significant; the left-most ones are the most significant.

The following data formats are used:

Integers: 32 bits, two's complement.

Reals: The same format as 32-bit reals on the machine used to run Ada/CS object machine interpreter.

Booleans: Stored in the low (right-most) bit of a word.

Characters: A single character, represented using the character set of the machine used to run Ada/CS object machine interpreter, stored in the least significant (right-most) part of a word.

Strings: One word (32 bits) that stores the length, followed by the characters, packed four to a word, from left to right (within the word). If the number of characters is not a multiple of four, the last word is right-filled with zeros.

The following machine operations are available

Op Code	Mnemonic	Definition
1	FIX	Convert real to integer: R := Integer(R)
2	NEGI	R := –R (integer)
7	NEGR	R := –R (real)
3	FLOAT	Convert integer to real: R := Float(R) (limited precision)
4	NOTL	**if** EAdr ≥ 0 **then**
		one's complement the rightmost EAdr bits of R
		else
		one's complement the leftmost Abs(EAdr) bits of R
		end if
6	B	PC := EAdr (Jump to EAdr)
8	BZ	**if** R = 0 **then** PC := EAdr **end if**
10	BNZ	**if** R ≠ 0 **then** PC := EAdr **end if**
12	BGZI	**if** R > 0 (integer) **then** PC := EAdr **end if**
13	BGZR	**if** R > 0 (real) **then** PC := EAdr **end if**
14	BNGZI	**if** R ≤ 0 (integer) **then** PC := EAdr **end if**
15	BNGZR	**if** R ≤ 0 (real) **then** PC := EAdr **end if**
16	BLZI	**if** R < 0 (integer) **then** PC := EAdr **end if**
17	BLZR	**if** R < 0 (real) **then** PC := EAdr **end if**
18	BNLZI	**if** R ≥ 0 (integer) **then** PC := EAdr **end if**
19	BNLZR	**if** R ≥ 0 (real) **then** PC := EAdr **end if**
20	BAL	Branch and link: R := PC; PC := EAdr
21	BKT	Block transfer:
		R = source address
		EAdr = destination address
		Memory[Reg + 1] = number of words to transfer
		Operands are processed left to right
		One word is moved at a time

22	SVC	Supervisor call: The interpreter returns with Result = EAdr. EAdr = 0 means halt.
23	TRNG	Test range, interrupt unless Memory[EAdr] $\leq$ R $\leq$ Memory[EAdr+1]
24	SHL	R := R shifted left EAdr bits (zero fill)
26	SHR	R := R shifted right EAdr bits (zero fill)
28	LDA	R := EAdr
30	ST	M := R
31	STPC	M := PC
32	LD	R := M
34	ADDI	R := R + M (integer)
35	ADDR	R := R + M (real)
36	SUBI	R := R − M (integer)
33	SUBU	R := R − M (integer)
		Subtraction is unchecked and cannot cause an overflow exception. In all cases the *sign* of the result is correct, although the result will be incorrect if SUBI would have signaled an overflow.
37	SUBR	R := R − M (real)
38	MULI	R := R * M (integer)
39	MULR	R := R * M (real)
40	DIVI	R := R / M (integer)
41	DIVR	R := R / M (real)
42	EXP	R := R ** M (integer)
43	EXPRE	R := R ** M (real ** int)
44	ANDL	R := R **and** M (bitwise)
46	ORL	R := R **or** M (bitwise)
48	BXOR	R := R **xor** M (bitwise)

Input is free-format. There may be more than one data item per line. Invalid items will generate an exception. The following input operations are available:

47	RDLN	Skip to the start of the next input line
49	RDCH	Read one character into M (rest of word is cleared)
50	RDL	**if** the next five input characters are FALSE (case ignored) **then** clear the rightmost bit of M; **elsif** the next four input characters are TRUE (case ignored) **then** set the rightmost bit of M to 1 **else** signal an invalid input exception **end if**
51	RDR	Read a real into M
52	RDI	Read an integer into M
53	RSTR	Read a string into M. The string may appear anywhere on the input line. It must be surrounded by quotes (').

The following output operations are available:

54	WL	**if** rightmost bit of M = 1

> **then** print TRUE
> **else** print FALSE
> **end if**

55	WR	Print M as a real
56	WI	Print M as an integer
57	WRCH	Print M as a character
5	WBITS	Print M as a string of bits
58	WSTR	Print M as a string

> if necessary, line breaks may be inserted.

60	SKP	**if** EAdr ≤ 0 **then**

> writeln
> **elsif** 0 < EAdr ≤ 57 **then**
> skip EAdr lines
> **elsif** 57 < EAdr **then**
> go to a new page
> **end if**

Notes:

(1) WL, WR,WI, and WRCH:

If Reg = 0, then use the default output format; otherwise use R as the minimum width of the output field (padding with blanks on the left if necessary).

(2) WL, WR, WI, WRCH, WBITS:

If the output item will not fit entirely on the current line, skip to a new line.

(3) WSTR:

if Reg = 0 **then** L := len(str) **else** L := R **end if**. Print max(0, L − len(str)) blanks followed by the leftmost min(L,len(str)) characters of the string.

The following string operations are provided:

59	CAT	M := Catenation of S1 and S2,

> where Memory[Reg] points to S1 and
> Memory[Reg+1] points to S2

61	BSUBSTR	M := a copy of the substring of S starting at

> position P of length L.
> The address of S is in R, and P and L
> are in Memory[Reg+1] and Memory[Reg+2].

62	STEQ	S1 is at Memory[R].

> **if** S1 = M (as strings)
> **then** PC := PC + 1; (skip the next instr).
> **end if**

63	STLSS	As above, but skip if S1 < M (in lexicographic order).

The following hardware exceptions will cause the Ada/CS machine interpreter to return to the calling program with the indicated negative values in the Result parameter.

−1	Invalid instruction (0, 9, 11, 25, 27, 29, or 45)
−2	Address out of range
−3	Overflow (real or integer)
−4	Timer interrupt
−5	End of file on input
−6	Divide by zero (real or integer)
−8	Real underflow
−9	TRNG instruction failed
−10	Invalid input item
−11	EXP with negative second operand

The ADA/CS machine interpreter simulates a virtual computer whose memory is an array of MaxAdr+1 words denoted Memory(0..MaxAdr). To run the interpreter, allocate an array of integers to act as the simulated memory for the machine, initialize it appropriately and call the external procedure

procedure interp(Store : **in out** Memory; LastAdr : **in** integer;
                InFile : **in out** text; PC, Time : **in out** integer;
                ReturnCode : **out** integer; Trace : **in** Boolean);

where

Memory : **array** (0..MaxAdr) **of** integer;

Memory: The simulated memory.

LastAdr: The last address in Memory that may be accessed without causing an illegal address fault. It must be that LastAdr ≤ MaxAdr.

InFile: An open file from which the Ada/CS machine will get its input (for RDLN, RDCH, and similar instructions).

PC: The initial program counter (address of the first instruction in Memory to be executed). If an exception or supervisor call (SVC) instruction occurs, PC will point to the offending instruction.

Time: The time limit. Each time an instruction is executed, Time is decreased by 1. When Time = 0, a timer interrupt occurs (and PC points to the next instruction to be executed).

Result: The return code: If Result ≥ 0, then Result is the EAdr of an SVC instruction. Otherwise, Result is an interrupt code.

Trace: Specifies that an instruction trace should be produced.

F.3   Other Utilities

Arithmetic routines:

procedure integerop(Op : **oper**; A,B : integer; C : **out** integer; Flag : **out** status);

procedure realop(Op : oper; A,B : real; C : **out** real; Flag : **out** status);

where
oper = (AddOper, SubOper, MulOper, DivOper);
status = (OK, Overflow, Underflow, ZeroDivide);

If Flag = OK, then C = A Op B.
Otherwise, C's value is unpredictable.

Packing and Unpacking routines:

function packinst(OpCode, Reg, Base, Offset : integer) **return** integer;

procedure unpackin(Inst : integer; OpCode, Reg, Base, Offset : **out** integer);

For packing, all arguments are truncated to the appropriate length. For unpacking, Offset is sign-extended, and all other arguments are zero-extended.

function packchar(C1,C2,C3,C4 : char) **return** integer;

procedure unpackch(n : integer; C1,C2,C3,C4 : **out** char);

C1 goes at the high-order (left-most) end of the word, and C4 goes at the low-order (right-most) end. (This is the order the Ada/CS machine expects.)

Routines for bypassing strong type checking:

function intcast(R : shortreal) **return** integer;

function realcast(I : integer) **return** shortreal;

Bibliography

Aho, Alfred V.; Ganapathi, M.; and Tjiang, S. 1989. "Code generation using tree matching and dynamic programming." *ACM Transactions on Programming Languages and Systems* 11(4): 491–516.

Aho, Alfred V.; Johnson, S. C.; and Ullman, Jeffrey D. 1975. "Deterministic parsing of ambiguous grammars." *Communications of the ACM* 18(8): 441–52.

———. 1977. "Code generation for expressions with common subexpressions." *Journal of the ACM* 24(1): 146–60.

Aho, Alfred V.; Sethi, Ravi; and Ullman, Jeffrey D. 1985. *Compilers: Principles, Techniques, and Tools.* Reading, Mass.: Addison-Wesley.

Aho, Alfred V., and Ullman, Jeffrey D. 1972. *The Theory of Parsing, Translation and Compiling, Vol. 1.* Englewood Cliffs, N.J.: Prentice-Hall.

———. 1977. *Principles of Compiler Design.* Reading, Mass.: Addison-Wesley.

Aigrain, P.; Graham, Susan L.; Henry, R. R.; McKusick, K.; and Pelegri-Liopart, E. 1984. "Experience with a Graham-Glanville style code generator." *SIGPLAN Notices* 19(6): 13–24.

ANSI. 1989. *Standard for the programming language C.* New York, New York: American National Standards Institute.

Appel, Andrew W. 1985. "Semantics-directed code generation." In *Twelfth Annual ACM Symposium on Principles of Programming Languages* 315–24.

Aretz, F.E.J. 1989. "A new approach to Earley's parsing algorithm." *Science of Computer Programming* 12: 105–21.

Archer, James, and Conway, Richard. 1981. "COPE: a cooperative programming environment." TR 81-459. Ithaca, N.Y.: Cornell University.

Baker, T. 1982. "A one-pass algorithm for overload resolution in Ada." *ACM Transactions on Programming Languages and Systems* 4(4): 601–14.

Ball, J. 1979. "Predicting the effects of optimization on a procedure body." *SIGPLAN Notices* 14(8): 214–20.

Bell, J. R. 1973. "Threaded code." *Communications of the ACM* 16(6): 370–72.

Bjorner, D., and Jones, C. 1978. "The Vienna Development Method: the metalanguage." In *Lecture Notes in Computer Science, #61.* New York: Springer-Verlag.

Bochmann, G. V. 1976. "Semantic evaluation from left to right." *Communications of the ACM* 19(2): 55–62.

Brodie, L. 1981. *Starting FORTH.* Englewood Cliffs, N.J.: Prentice-Hall.

Burke, Michael, and Fisher, Gerald A. 1982. "A practical method for syntactic error diagnosis and repair." *SIGPLAN Notices* 17(6): 67–78.

Cattell, R.G.G. 1980. "Automatic derivation of code generators from machine descriptions." *ACM Transactions on Programming Languages and Systems* 2(2): 173–90.

Chaitin, G. J. 1982. "Register allocation and spilling via graph coloring." *SIGPLAN Notices* 17(6): 98–105.

Christopher, T. W.; Hatcher, P. J.; and Kukuk, R. C. 1984. "Using dynamic programming to generate optimized code in a Graham-Glanville style code generator." In *Proceedings of the SIGPLAN '84 Symposium on Compiler Construction* 25–36.

Cichelli, R. J. 1980. "Minimal perfect hash functions made simple." *Communications of the ACM* 23(1): 17–19.

Cocke, J. 1970. "Global common subexpression elimination." *SIGPLAN Notices* 5(7): 20–24.

Cocke, J., and Schwartz, J. T. 1970. *Programming Languages and Their Compilers: Preliminary Notes, Second Revised Version.* New York: Courant Institute of Mathematical Science.

Conway, R. W. 1972. *The ASAP Systems Reference Manual.* Ithaca, N.Y.: Compuvisor, Inc.

Conway, R. W., and Wilcox, T. R. 1973. "Design and implementation of a diagnostic compiler for PL/I." *Communications of the ACM* 16: 169–79.

Cormack, G. V. 1981. "An algorithm for the selection of overloaded functions in Ada." *SIGPLAN Notices* 16(2): 48–52.

Davidson, J. W., and Fraser, C. W. 1982. "Eliminating redundant object code." *In Ninth Annual ACM Symposium on Principles of Programming Languages* 128–32.

———. 1984. "Automatic generation of peephole optimizations." *SIGPLAN Notices* 19(6): 111–16.

DeRemer, Frank L. 1969. "Practical translators for LR(k) languages." Ph.D. dissertation, M.I.T.

———. 1971. "Simple LR(k) grammars." *Communications of the ACM* 14: 453–60.

DeRemer, Frank L., and Pennello, T. 1982. "Efficient computation of LALR(1) look-ahead sets." *ACM Transactions on Programming Languages and Systems* 4(4): 615–49.

Dion, Bernard A. 1982. *Locally Least-cost Error Correctors for Context-free and Context-sensitive Parsers.* Ann Arbor: UMI Research Press.

Druseikis, Frederick C., and Ripley, G. David. 1976. "Extended SLR(k) parsers for error recovery and repair." In *Proceedings of the ACM Annual Conference* 396–400.

Earley, J. 1970. "An efficient context-free parsing algorithm." *Communications of the ACM* 13(2): 94–102.

Farrow, R. 1982. "Linguist-86: yet another translator writing system based on attribute grammars." *SIGPLAN Notices* 17(6): 160–71.

Fischer, C. N.; Johnson, G. F.; Mauney, J.; Pal, A.; and Stock, D. L. 1984. "The POE language-based editor project." In *ACM SIGSOFT/SIGPLAN Symposium on Practical Software Development Environments*

Fischer, Charles N., and LeBlanc, Richard J. 1977. *UW-Pascal Reference Manual.* Madison, Wis.: Madison Academic Computer Center.

———. 1980. "The implementation of run-time diagnostics in Pascal." *IEEE Transactions on Software Engineering* SE-6(4): 313–19.

Fischer, Charles N.; Mauney, Jon; and Milton, Donn R. 1979. "A locally least-cost LL(1) error corrector." Technical Report #371. Madison, Wis.: University of Wisconsin.

Fischer, Charles N.; Milton, Donn R.; and Quiring, Sam B. 1980. "Efficient LL(1) error correction and recovery using only insertions." *Acta Informatica* 13(2): 141–54.

Fleck, A. C. 1976. "On the impossibility of content exchange through the by-name parameter transmission mechanism." *SIGPLAN Notices* 11(11): 38–41.

Fong, A. C., and Ullman, Jeffrey D. 1976. "Induction variables in very high-level languages." In *Third Annual ACM Symposium on Principles of Programming Languages* 104–12.

Fraser, C. W., and Davidson, J. W. 1980. "The design and application of a retargetable peephole optimizer." *ACM Transactions on Programming Languages and Systems* 2(2): 191–202.

Ganapathi, M., and Fischer, Charles N. 1985. "Affix grammar-driven code generation." *ACM Transactions on Programming Languages and Systems* 4(7): 560–99.

Ganzinger, H.; Giegerich, R.; Moncke, U.; and Wilhelm, R. 1982. "A truly generative semantics-directed compiler generator." *SIGPLAN Notices* 17(6): 172–84.

Garey, M. R., and Johnson, D. S. 1979. *Computers and Intractability: A Guide to the Theory of NP-Completeness.* San Francisco: W.H. Freeman.

Glanville, R. S., and Graham, Susan L. 1978. "A new method for compiler code generation." In *Fifth Annual ACM Symposium on Principles of Programming Languages*

Goos, G., and Wulf, W. A. 1981. "Diana Reference Manual." CMU-CS-81-101. Pittsburgh: Department of Computer Science, Carnegie-Mellon University.

Graham, Susan L.; Haley, Charles B.; and Joy, William N. 1979. "Practical LR error recovery." *SIGPLAN Notices* 14(8): 168–75.

Graham, Susan L.; Harrison, Michael A.; and Ruzzo, Walter L. 1980. "An improved context-free recognizer." *ACM Transactions on Programming Languages and Systems* 2(3): 415–62.

Graham, Susan L.; Joy, William; and Roubine, Olivier. 1979. "Hashed symbol tables for languages with explicit scope control." *SIGPLAN Notices* 14(8): 50–57.

Gray, Robert W. 1988. "γ-GLA: A generator for lexical analyzers that programmers can use." In *Proceedings of the Summer Usenix Conference.*

Gries, David. 1981. *The Science of Programming.* New York: Springer-Verlag.

Hennessy, J. 1982. "Symbolic debugging of optimized code." *ACM Transactions on Programming Languages and Systems* 4(3): 323–44.

Hopcroft, John E., and Ullman, J. D. 1969. *Formal Languages and Their Relation to Automata.* Reading, Mass.: Addison-Wesley.

———. 1979. *Introduction to Automata Theory, Languages, and Computation.* Reading, Mass.: Addison-Wesley.

Horwitz, L. P.; Karp, R. M.; Miller, R. E.; and Winograd, S. 1966. "Index register allocation." *Journal of the ACM* 13(1): 43–61.

Hsu, Wei-Chung. 1987. "Register allocation and code scheduling for load/store architectures." Ph.D. dissertation, University of Wisconsin, Madison.

James, L. R. 1972. "A syntax-directed error recovery method." Technical Report CSRG-13. Toronto: Computer Systems Research Group, University of Toronto.

Jacobsen, Van. 1987. "Tuning UNIX Lex, or, it's not true what they say about Lex." In *Proceedings of the Winter Usenix Conference* 163–64.

Jazayeri, M.; Ogden, W. F.; and Rounds, W. C. 1975. "The intrinsic exponential complexity of the circularity problem for attribute grammars." *Communications of the ACM* 18(12): 697–706.

Jazayeri, M., and Walter, K. G. 1975. "Alternating semantic evaluator." In *Proceedings of the ACM Annual Conference* 230–34.

Johnson, S. C. 1975. "Yacc—yet another compiler compiler." C.S. Technical Report #32. Murray Hill, N.J.: Bell Telephone Laboratories.

———. 1978. "A portable compiler: theory and practice." In *Fifth Annual ACM Symposium on Principles of Programming Languages* 97–104.

Johnsson, R. K. 1975. "An approach to global register allocation." Ph.D. dissertation, Carnegie-Mellon University.

Kernighan, Brian W., and Ritchie, Dennis M. 1978. *The C Programming Language.* Englewood Cliffs, N.J.: Prentice-Hall.

———. 1988. *The C Programming Language,* 2d ed. Englewood Cliffs, N.J.: Prentice-Hall.

Kim, J. 1978. "Spill placement optimization in register allocation for compilers." IBM Research report RC 7251.

Knuth, Donald E. 1965. "On the translation of languages from left to right." *Information and Control* 8(6): 607–39.

———. 1968. "Semantics of context-free languages." *Mathematical Systems Theory* 2(2): 127–45.

———. 1973. *The Art of Computer Programming,* 2d ed. Vol. 1. Reading, Mass.: Addison-Wesley.

LeBlanc, Richard J., and Mongiovi, Roy J. 1983. "A practical method for automated LR error repair." Technical Report GIT-ICS-83/18. Atlanta: School of Information and Computer Science, Georgia Institute of Technology.

Lesk, M. E., and Schmidt, E. 1975. "Lex—a lexical analyzer generator." In *UNIX Programmer's Manual 2.* Murray Hill, N.J.: AT&T Bell Laboratories.

Lewis, P. M.; Rosenkrantz, D. J.; and Stearns, R. E. 1976. *Compiler Design Theory.* Reading, Mass.: Addison-Wesley.

Logothetis, George, and Mishra, Prateek. 1981. "Compiling short-circuit boolean expressions in one pass." *Software-Practice and Experience* 11: 1197–1241.

Magnusson, K. 1982. "Identifier references in Simula 67 programs." *Simula Newsletter* 10(2):

Mauney, Jon. 1982. "Least-cost error repair using extended right context." Technical Report 495. Madison, Wis.: University of Wisconsin.

Mauney, Jon, and Fischer, Charles N. 1981. "An improvement to immediate error detection in Strong LL(1) parsers." *Information Processing Letters* 12(5): 211–12.

McCarthy, John. 1965. *Lisp 1.5 Programmer's Manual.* Cambridge, Mass.: MIT Press.

McKeeman, W. M. 1965. "Peephole optimization." *Communications of the ACM* 8(7): 443–44.

Mickunas, M. D., and Modry, J. A. 1978. "Automatic error recovery for LR parsers." *Communications of the ACM* 21: 459–65.

Nestor, J. R.; Wulf, W. A.; and Lamb, D. A. 1981. "IDL—interface description language: formal description." Technical Report CMU-CS-81-139. Pittsburgh: Department of Computer Science, Carnegie-Mellon University.

Notkin, D. 1985. "The Gandalf project." *Journal Systems Software* 5: 91–106.

Pager, D. 1977. "A practical general method for constructing LR(k) parsers." *Acta Informatica* 7: 249–68.

Patterson, D. 1985. "Reduced instruction set computers." *Communications of the ACM* 28(1): 8–21.

Paxson, Vern. 1990. "Flex users manual." Ithaca, N.Y.: Cornell University.

Pennello, Thomas J., and DeRemer, Frank L. 1978. "A forward move algorithm for LR error recovery." In *Fifth Annual ACM Symposium on Principles of Programming Languages* 241–54.

Perkins, D. R., and Sites, R. L. 1979. "Machine independent Pascal code optimization." *SIGPLAN Notices* 14(8): 201–7.

Pratt, T. W. 1975. *Programming Languages: Design and Implementation.* Englewood Cliffs, N.J.: Prentice-Hall.

Ripley, G. David, and Druseikis, Frederick C. 1978. "A statistical analysis of syntax errors." *Computer Languages* 3: 227–40.

Roehrich, Johannes. 1980. "Methods for the automatic construction of error-correcting parsers." *Acta Informatica* 13(2): 115–39.

Rowland, Bruce R. 1977. "Combining parsing and the evaluation of attributed grammars." Ph.D. dissertation, University of Wisconsin.

Sethi, Ravi. 1983. "Control flow aspects of semantics-directed compiling." *ACM Transactions on Programming Languages and Systems* 5(4): 554–95.

Sethi, Ravi, and Ullman, Jeffrey D. 1970. "The generation of optimal code for arithmetic expressions." *Journal of the ACM* 17(4): 715–28.

Soisalon-Soininen, E. 1982. "Inessential error entries and their use in LR parser optimization." *ACM Transactions on Programming Languages and Systems* 4(2): 179–95.

Stallman, Richard M. 1989. "Using and porting GNU CC." Free Software Foundation, Inc.

Steel, T. B., Jr. 1961. "A first version of UNCOL." *Proceedings of the WJCC* 19: 371–78.

Stroustrup, Bjarne. 1986. *The C++ Programming Language.* Reading, Mass.: Addison-Wesley.

Sussman, G. 1981. "Scheme-79, Lisp on a chip." *IEEE Computer* 14(7): 10–21.

Szymanski, T. G. 1978. "Assembling code for machines with span-dependent instructions." *Communications of the ACM* 21(4): 300–8.

Tanenbaum, A. S.; van Straveren, H.; and Stevenson, J. W. 1982. "Using peephole optimization on intermediate code." *ACM Transactions on Programming Languages and Systems* 4(1): 21–36.

Tanenbaum, A. S. 1974. "Implications of structured programming for machine architecture." *Communications of the ACM* 21(3): 237–42.

Tarjan, R. E., and Yao, A. C. 1979. "Storing a sparse table." *Communications of the ACM* 22(11): 606–11.

Teitelbaum, T., and Reps, Thomas. 1981. "The Cornell program synthesizer: a syntax-directed programming environment." *Communications of the ACM* 24(9): 563–73.

Valiant, L. 1975. "General context-free recognition in less than cubic time." *Journal Computer and Systems Sciences* 10(2): 308–15.

Wand, M. 1982. "Deriving target code as a representation of continuation semantics." *ACM Transactions on Programming Languages and Systems* 4(3): 496–517.

WATFIV. 1981. *WATFIV Users Guide.* Waterloo, Ontario: University of Waterloo.

Watt, David A. 1977. "The parsing problem for affix grammars." *Acta Informatica* 8: 1–20.

Wetherell, Charles, and Shannon, A. 1981. "LR—automatic parser generator and LR(1) parser." *IEEE Transactions on Software Engineering* SE-7(3): 274–78.

Wilcox, T. R. 1971. "Generating machine code for high-level programming languages." Technical Report 71-103. Ithaca, N.Y.: Cornell University.

Wirth, Niklaus. 1976. *Algorithms + Data Structures = Programs.* Englewood Cliffs, N.J.: Prentice-Hall.

Wirth, Niklaus, and Weber, H. 1966. "Euler: a generalization of Algol and its formal definition: Part 1." *Communications of the ACM* 9(1): 13–23.

Wulf, W. 1981. "Compilers and computer architecture." *IEEE Computer* 14(7): 41–7.

Zellweger, Polle. 1983. "An interactive high-level debugger for control-flow optimized programs." *SIGPLAN Notices* 18(8): 159–71.